Single Adults Want
to Be the Church,
Too

Single Adults Want to Be the Church, Too

Britton Wood

Broadman Press
Nashville, Tennessee

Dewey Decimal Classification: 259
Subject Headings: CHURCH WORK WITH SINGLE ADULTS // SINGLE ADULTS

Library of Congress Catalog Card Number: 77-78471
Printed in the United States of America

Dedication

This book is dedicated
to the many single adults at Park Cities Baptist Church
who have helped me learn more about ministering.

Foreword

Britton Wood in 1970 became the first full-time minister to single adults in the Southern Baptist Convention and perhaps in any denomination. He began with a small group of single adults in Park Cities Baptist Church, Dallas, Texas. The church, in hiring Britton, had expressed its commitment to the need and potential for single adult ministry.

Most persons in a new vocation seek out books and resources about their work and talk with other persons in the field. Britton found few of the former and none of the latter. Society in general and churches in particular were either trying to minister with single adults through their traditional family orientation or were ignoring them altogether.

Britton Wood began a ministry that from its inception has been characterized by two things. First, single adults have been involved in the processes of identifying what they want their ministry to be and in assuming major responsibility and leadership in all its facets. Second, innovation in organization, in programming, and in leading singles to minister has been at the heart of the Park Cities ministry.

Beginning with no data, Britton has grown a ministry that works effectively in one church. He also has developed a philosophy which can be applied in any church. And as it is applied, a ministry can be shaped which meets the needs of single adults in that community.

Single Adults Want to Be the Church, Too represents a statement of a philosophy of ministry and one illustration of that philosophy at work. Because Britton has willingly shared himself and his vocational pilgrimage with others, his concept is at work in different ways in many churches. Therefore, while the concept can be applied in any church, the illustration of the ministry at Park Cities cannot be interpreted as *the* way to do single adult ministry. To try and duplicate all the programs and activities being implemented at Park Cities would be a violation of the philosophy behind those programs and activities. Leading single adults to be the church means tuning in to the interests and needs of the singles in your congregation and, with them, building a ministry that best meets their needs and provides opportunities for growth and reaching out to others.

Using This Book

You can make best use of this book by continually relating the concept discussed to your own church and the single adults with whom you minister. Identify where you are and where you want to be. With your single adults and the leadership of your church, identify actions for achieving your goals. Some ideas from the Park Cities ministry may be helpful here. Also, find out what other churches are doing. Use these ideas along with those you generate as possibilities for working with your single adults. By doing so, you can build a ministry which enables single adults to work with one another and the total community of the church in the mission of being the church.

About Britton Wood

Britton Wood is uniquely qualified to lead others to be the church. He provides both leadership ability and a positive model of a Christian at work in the world. He uses well his gifts of gentleness and strength in helping persons who hurt, supporting single adults in building their ministry, and being a friend to those with whom he ministers. Through his life and the positive impact of his ministry, people can see Christ.

LINDA LAWSON, *Single Adult Specialist*

Baptist Sunday School Board
Nashville, Tennessee

Introduction

For ten years, I was a campus minister. Then, as far as I know, I became the first single adult minister in both title and scope of responsibility in my denomination. No work, in my estimation, could have provided better preparation for working with singles through a local congregation than ten years as a campus minister.

The campuses I related to (a small Baptist school for four years and a large state university for six years) were composed of students who (1) had been turned off by the local church; (2) had been turned on through the local church; (3) had not been involved in local churches for four to six years; (4) had been married, were now single, and did not feel comfortable in local congregations; (5) had not been involved in churches at all; (6) had neither a positive nor a negative attitude toward local congregations; or (7) became active Christians through our campus ministry.

Since the campus world is where most of these students live, in attitude if not in location, my involvement with them provided relationship, awareness of need, and confrontations on most subjects of importance. It was impossible for me to issue "pious" or naive statements without genuine questioning. The persons I encountered on campus encouraged me to be honest with the students and with myself about the Christian faith and my personal beliefs. Everything I thought or had been taught was probed and given full examination. This inquisitive climate caused me to ask questions that were valid and not to be satisfied with inadequate answers.

I was relating generally to single persons who were called college students, although I was not aware of the significance of this ministry at the time. On the state campus where I ministered, the average age of the students increased to age twenty-four for women and twenty-five for men as the campus became more of a graduate school. Questions came up on a regular basis regarding suicide, abortion, drugs, alcohol, mixed racial marriage, students' living together (coed), divorce, disillusionment with the establishment (church and government), disintegration of family life, the problem of good and evil, the validity of various religions, and hypocrisy, plus numerous other issues. It has become obvious that the questions or concerns of single adults are not much different now, but their hurt is often deeper. Hopefully, my reactions or responses are more mature.

Other factors that directly related to my responsiveness to the local congregation ministry were: (1) Few churches had healthy ministries for recent college graduates in 1970. I had encouraged several friends who were pastors to provide such ministries, but those men were generally overworked and underpaid and needed to concentrate on other programs or ministries. (2) The opportunity came to consider working with single persons in and beyond college through Park Cities Baptist Church in Dallas. At this point I began to think that God had helped me see the need for churches to be involved in a good ministry with young singles. I had encouraged my pastor-friends to do what I now was being asked to do. I felt I needed to respond to this possibility or refrain from laying the responsibility off on my friends. I found myself saying, "OK, Britton, you have been telling church leaders that they needed to have this kind of ministry—now put up or shut up!" (3) The church presenting this new challenge to me had unlimited potential in facilities, finances, resource persons, and availability of single adults. I am challenged with situations that are yet to be explored. I like hammering out new ideas, concepts, and ministries. (4) This new ministry was close enough to North Texas State University for the students there to come to at least one church that was styling itself for ministry to former college students. I still felt such a closeness with the students at NTSU that I wanted to be in a church they would want to come to. That attitude was short term because, as I became aware of the needs and concerns of my new friends in the Park Cities church, I saw many new aspects of ministry.

Factors that have surfaced since I became part of the single adult community, at least on the ministry-friend level, are: (1) my own extended family involvement regarding divorce and remarriage. While I was still a campus minister, different relatives requested that I perform their marriage ceremonies—which raised the question of my own involvement in a remarriage situation; (2) my own relatives becoming involved in divorce and my openness in accepting them as they were rather than the way I preferred them to be; (3) my involvement on the college campus during the sixties, which forced me to accept persons as they revealed themselves to be rather than to prejudge them on the basis of dress, hairstyle, or speech; (4) my parents' openness when I was growing up. Very seldom did I receive an emphatic *no* from them; they allowed me many privileges and freedoms, and they shared the same opinions in matters of social mores but put the responsibility upon my shoulders. My mother also encouraged me to accept all kinds of persons and not to ever feel I was better than anyone else.

All of these factors influence me both directly and indirectly in my present ministry. God continues to teach me through persons, and he has blessed me with many teachers. My wife, Bobbye, and my three wonderful daughters have taught me much and are very supportive with their love and patience.

Why write a book such as this? The single adult area of ministry is so new that any added insight can be helpful to leaders in churches who work with singles or to the single adults who participate in their church. This book is not really intended to be the last word in ministry with singles. My goal is to share the insights gleaned from ministry with one group of singles in one congregation: Park Cities Baptist Church.

One of my assumptions is that being single is a valid life-style option. My hope is that more single adults will deem life important *now* rather than living for the day when they may get married. Singles ministries in churches can contribute greatly to this new attitude by encouraging singles not to feel that they must be living in an in-between period of life.

The requests for information about our ministry with singles have become numerous, and this book is partly an attempt to adequately respond to as many requests as possible in the briefest time span.

My prayer is that the verbal explanations of this ministry will provide the springboard for many churches to surpass anything God has helped us at Park Cities accomplish through our single adult ministry.

BRITTON WOOD

Acknowledgments

I am most thankful for what I believe to be God's leadership in providing me the opportunity to minister with singles at Park Cities Baptist Church. I'm thankful to the members of this wonderful church for allowing me the freedom and flexibility to minister.

To my capable and tireless secretary, Mrs. Lewis (Ruth) Layton, I am most grateful. She has made this singles ministry more than a job; to her it is a real ministry. She has been invaluable in much detail work through the years and has gone the second mile on several occasions.

I am blessed with a loving wife who is also candid about what I say and write. Bobbye risks being honest with me and gives me wise counsel regarding many situations.

I am also thankful to my three daughters, Carol, Stacy, and Leigh Ann, for their encouragement and their healthy maturing that has enhanced our dialogue and our closeness to one another during these days of writing.

A special thanks to Davye Dawn Carter and Mrs. Neil (Wyoma) Fussell for their willingness to type my handwritten manuscript. There are numerous other persons who have made an impact on my life in ways that have helped to shape my sharing in this volume.

BRITTON WOOD

Contents

1.
Society in Transition

It was a brief article in an obscure section of the newspaper. Yet there were over fifty phone calls within one hour asking for more information about the single adult conference that was to begin that evening at our church.

Why is there such a hunger for a gathering of single persons, regardless of their reason for single status? The answer is multifaceted and will be dealt with as thoroughly as possible, but the fact is our society is in a state of transition.

Changing Attitudes Toward Marriage

In the last few years our society has awakened to the fact that almost everything we do is styled to meet the needs of the family. The family-oriented approach was sufficient until recently, but the growing number of singles in our midst necessitates our reassessment of terminology and programming in the church and society. This book attempts to speak to society in transition only as it relates to the church.

New statistics have come out regarding breakup in marriages. Over one million marriages dissolved in America in 1976. One out of three adults is single—or, to put it another way, in America there are approximately 43,000,000 single persons. Some estimates run as high as 46,000,000. To focus on a real setting, Dallas has approximately 350,000 single adults. It is also estimated that there are nearly 12,000,000 widows and widowers—who must be considered single—in the United States.

It is my feeling that the disenchantment with "establishment," widely publicized in the sixties, has finally hit the family. Couples who have been married for fifteen, twenty-three, thirty years are calling it quits—they can take it no longer (for a variety of reasons). Episodes we formerly read about in movie magazines now touch our own neighborhoods (communities) and even our own families.

17

Early in my ministry divorced relatives of mine caused me to examine seriously what the Bible has to say regarding divorce and remarriage. Since then divorce has touched my closest relatives. Many persons have been very close to the uncomfortableness of divorce; some know the trauma personally.

Most divorced persons do not believe in divorce, but certain circumstances in their lives have caused them to face the reality of their situation and to choose divorce as an alternative to an unhealthy marriage.

Trust Level Problems

In the midst of our own life dilemmas, we tend to find a degree of pharisaical comfort in the opinion that what we do is really nothing compared to what takes place in high places. We seem to find some comfort from our own turmoil by reading about Nixon's final days or seeing the movie *All the President's Men.* The credibility gap is really big "out there" in the political scene, the athletic arena, and the corporate organizations.

Our day is salted and peppered with some "in here" crumbling trust level problems, too. It seems that the new interpretation of the brass rule (the tarnished golden rule) is to "do unto others before they do unto you." Even the brass rule is being redefined—"Do unto others and split."

Who *can* you trust anymore? So often the people you work with or under can't be trusted or depended on—they cut you down. Often they are so busy protecting themselves that they step on you and others. On a more personal basis—people you call "friends" let you down.

Not only are we reexamining our trust level with institutions and persons; we who are in or related to the single adult world are well aware that society takes a second-class-citizen view of singles.

The Double Standard and Singleness (*Society*)

In our family-oriented society, it is assumed by many that young adults should be married or engaged by age twenty-two and that anyone who is not married is incomplete, undeveloped, immature, or, at worst, as one psychologist has put it, thought of as a failure because he is not capable of family life.

During income tax season many single adults become aware of the governmental inequities that generally favor the two-adult family. If opportunity would permit, we could hear singles testify about loans, credit opportunities, employment, advancement (you know how those singles are—they may decide to leave tomorrow).

Let me say here, just in case you haven't grasped it, that I am painting a picture of how singles generally seem rather than how I view single adults. With that in mind, let us continue.

Many single adults are a threat to married adults. The single adult may be wanting to take one's husband or wife. Many married men think that single men are all swingers and really have the good life. It is often assumed that the nine million unmarried women between ages twenty and thirty-four are either promiscuous or frigid.

In conversation with a single woman, I naively asked, "Wouldn't it be nice to have a married man to relate to?" Without hesitation she answered, "Married men I can get—it's the single men who are hard to find." Quite a commentary on our society.

There is so much pressure in our society to get married or to have a couple front that it even affects the person who is single by choice. My wife, Bobbye, and I were invited to have supper with a single woman, and she asked which one of three single men we would rather visit with around the supper table. When I asked why she wanted us to choose one, she replied, "I thought you would feel more comfortable if a man were present whom you enjoy talking with." I responded by saying, "We are coming to visit you, and if you want to invite someone as your guest—go ahead—but we are more interested in visiting with you." She said, "You mean you would want to visit with *just* me?" My reply was "Yes!" She didn't invite a fourth person.

Many persons who "didn't make it to marriage" by age twenty-two may be embarrassing their parents because they are still single. Many parents of singles married early, perhaps by age nineteen. So it is understandable for a mother and father to suggest that a single son or daughter attend church so he/she can meet some nice young person to marry. What parents don't say is—*so I can relax and feel that I have not been a failure as a parent after all.*

The Double Standard and Singleness (*Church*)

Even within the church, we have seen similar reflections of our society in the way we have, without being aware of it, treated the single person.

Generally, the local congregation is composed of two-adult family units, and the program of the church is styled to meet their needs.

Many churches are just now becoming aware of the need to have a single adult class or department.

Attitudes regarding the single person are often not even given a second thought. In most churches there is usually the Adult Division and the Single Adult Division rather than married/single adults. I once heard a minister pray from his pulpit, "How blessed we are to *be married.*" I wondered how single adults would regard that prayer—would they think of themselves as "unclaimed *blessings*"? It would have been healthier to indicate, "How blessed we are to *be,* whether married or single." In my estimation this statement was very subjective and did not take into consideration the diversity of the congregation.

A minister who was working with our singles on a special project asked, "What do you call your people? The terms I've always used with groups of persons do not fit this group. They are not kids; they are not young people; they are not old people; they are not all divorced persons; and they are not all widowed persons. When I get ready to talk about them, I find I'm not accustomed to calling them by any particular group name." This conversation was gratifying because, after getting to know our single adults, here was a minister who wanted to use adequate and fair terminology to describe them.

At the present time, the term *single adult* seems to be the term that is the most inclusive and the least offensive used to describe persons who are single either by choice or lack of choice (never married), who are single without choice (widow/widower), who are single because of the choice of one or both partners (divorced), or who are in the process of becoming single (separated).

In several churches attitudes toward singles have improved, as evidenced by revisions in terminology regarding single adults. Some churches, however, still need to listen to the ways they categorize their single adults. Many still use the term *college and career.* As one of our single men, who has been active for several years, has stated, "We may be single, but we don't plan to make a *career* of it." By way of contrast, many married adults have careers, but they are not so designated. Some interesting terms have been used that have depicted unfortunate attitudes toward singles, such as the Warm Class (*W*omen *a*nd *R*eluctant *M*en), The Misfits, or SCOUP (*S*ingle *C*areer and *Ob*viously *U*nattached *P*ersons).

At Park Cities, our choice has been to relate to singles as single adults rather than to place an emphasis on reason for single status.

We now have a Married Adult Division and a Single Adult Division instead of an Adult Division and a *Single* Adult Division. Many organizations for singles operate from a negative point of view, although they do some worthwhile things. For example, Parents *Without* Partners, a national organization, continually reminds its members through its title that they are *without* spouse.

Aims of a Single Adult Ministry

Attitudes of married adults toward singles are awkward at times, such as when the word to an attractive twenty-seven-year-old single (or never married) is "Why hasn't a fine person like you gotten married?" or when a parent says, "Honey, you get yourself involved in Park Cities Baptist Church and you'll meet some fine young man there." Many do, but our ministry needs to reach out to persons who are single rather than to be known as a marriage bureau. Just recently, a man in our church told me that I had done "a great job" with his daughter, who had met a fine young man whom she married through our singles ministry. It was as if my task were to get all the singles married. I see my task as ministering to the needs of persons who are single to help them become free to honor and respond to God. If marriage is part of that response to God, well and good; but if it is not, I'm just as anxious for them to grow in their "favor with God and men."

We encourage our single adults to assume they will never get married so they can get busy in living their lives rather than waiting until they get married to live or to have a home. By assuming that the single status will continue, one is surprised if marriage occurs rather than disappointed if it doesn't happen. If a person is not happy as a single, marriage won't bring happiness. Happy and healthy single adults tend to make happy and healthy married adults.

Most singles have similar needs of identity, goals for living, acceptance, Christian growth, finances, vocational guidance, and family. These needs are real, even though the singles come to this point in their lives from various trails.

Ministering to Formerly Married Persons

In several ways, because of the church's attitude toward single adults—particularly toward the formerly married persons—ministry will be difficult and slow. A few reasons are:

1. The formerly married will tend to blame God for their present

marital status. This shifting of responsibility generally grows out of an inaccurate understanding of prayer and God's will and a lack of willingness to accept responsibility for all that occurs in one's life.

2. The divorced adult feels guilty because the official word from the church regarding divorce is "Thou shalt not." Not long after we came to our present church situation a lady in our church said to Bobbye, "I'm Mrs. So and So; you've probably heard of me. I'm the divorced one." She felt as if she had been described, pointed out, and stereotyped as divorced. Bobbye said, "No, I was not aware that you were divorced, but I am glad to meet you."

3. The formerly married usually feel out of place in most churches because adequate programming has not yet been developed to meet their needs. For example, the director of a department composed mainly of married persons may announce a social and express that each person should bring his spouse. If widowed or divorced adults are in that department, they are ignored.

4. The formerly married resent the attitude of the married adults that reflects a superior-inferior kind of relating. Introductions such as "This is Mary Brown; you know her husband passed away two years ago" rather than "I want you to meet one of my friends, Mary Brown" reveal much about a person's attitude. Another unfortunate method of introduction is "This is one of our recently divorced persons, Jim Smith."

5. Some church leaders are uncomfortable about being given the responsibility of styling a program that meets the needs of single adults. This difficulty is often compounded by the fact that churches often are already too understaffed to carry on the programs and ministries they are presently engaged in.[1]

Understanding the Needs of Singles

There are some ethical concerns involved in an authentic ministry with single adults, such as a biblical understanding regarding divorce and remarriage and a healthy understanding regarding sexuality. We must love persons in the midst of various life-styles (single persons living together, single pregnant women, singles who choose abortion or homosexuality). Ministry must be approached from a particular stance, and there is no need to apologize for that stance. However, it is also biblical to love persons wherever they happen to be rather than *if* they move to the spot we have designated for them.

Needs of singles who are over thirty-five years of age tend to shift somewhat as some persons peel off more of their hope and idealism and become resentful of persons who have something good happen in their lives. In some singles groups, a female visitor who happens to be attractive is not easily accepted by the single women in the group. After all, who needs *more* competition? If someone in the group gets engaged, some have difficulty rejoicing with that person because they are too busy wondering why they are not getting married instead.

The growing prevalence of single adult ministries in churches is not only an attempt to respond to needs, but it is revealing where the local church has fallen short in caring for persons.

Marriage Education

The whole idea of marriage in our society needs help. It has been assumed that when a person reaches a certain age he gets married, and no marriage education is necessary. Churches need to begin and upgrade premarital education. Beginning with junior high students, a progressive program should include insights regarding interpersonal relationships, communication skills, and ability to develop close friendships. An educational ministry such as this one will do much to assist single adult ministries, which often inherit the results of poor premarital education.

My own high-school-age daughter has scheduled me into her home and family living class to talk about preparation for marriage and the need for premarital counseling. She feels this is a real need for her peer group. Churches need to lead in this field, not follow.

Our church leaders need to encourage our churches to take seriously the Christian meaning of marriage. We must stop being the dispenser of religious weddings that are no more than ceremony. At each wedding, every marriage covenant needs to provide a challenge of renewal or reaffirmation of vows. Each marriage covenant needs to provide through the church a program of marital nourishment for the couple getting married.

As one minister suggested, we need to have the same freedom in the church to say "How is it with your marriage?" as we ask someone how he is feeling. When we have more honesty among our married Christians, we will see more realistic marriages and fewer false expectations concerning marriage on the part of singles.

Unlimited Potential for Ministry with Singles

There is a great need for interchurch communication regarding singles ministries throughout our nation. In 1975, the most mobile group in our country was the twenty-five to thirty-four age group. Let's help mobile America get some roots and a relationship with the Christian community!

Churches need to provide ministries that encourage divorced persons to be whole persons again. As one Christian counselor has said, "When have we taken a casserole to a recent divorcee?" Divorce adjustment seminars are being held with excellent response because needs are being met.

Let our churches accept reaching single adults as a ministry of great need and unlimited potential and as the avenue for an honest, growing, contagious, exciting spirit that can break loose in our entire family of God. Only God knows what kind of power he will be able to unleash in the church through the single adults.

2.
Stretch the Vision of the Church to Include Singles

"This is the first time I've felt accepted in the church in the four and a half years since my divorce." At first glance, this comment can be considered complimentary because the spirit and attitude of our single adult community (church group) made this statement possible. However, this was more of a commentary of what had happened in the past to an active church member in a church that was probably trying to do its best, even though this single adult had been relieved of the Sunday School class she was teaching and her leadership position in the women's missionary organization.

Some ministry attitudes that churches have in working with single adults have taken shape for me as I have talked with pastors, religious educators, involved lay persons (both single and married), and disenchanted single adults. Attitudes generally fall into the patterns indicated in the following pages.

Patterns of Ministry Attitudes

1. *The triangular-rectangular frustration.*—Probably more churches fit into this pattern than into any other. They approach whatever ministry they have to singles by trying to fit the singles (as represented by the triangle) into the married adult program (as represented by the rectangle). I started to call this the round-square pattern, but *square* has emotional connotations; and some married adults could resent being called square. I might add that some singles are still equipped with some rough edges and that not all are well rounded. Thus the triangle-rectangle approach.

Basically, this approach to ministry works on the theory that "whatever organization we now have in our church is adequate"—any new person can fit into what we have or move on to another church, since this person may not be "our kind" of person anyway. If he or she were our kind, he/she would fit in better. Method for ministry seems to be locked into a "sacred" state, and change does not occur easily or often.

In this ministry method, vision is often blurred to the point that triangles and rectangles look about the same; and individual differences are not factors in approach to ministry. Another aspect of this method is that at one point in this church's history a group of people *did* help give birth to the present method, but the method has not kept up with changes in family structure or congregational makeup.

My wife and I visited a church of another denomination one Sunday evening to hear a certain minister. That evening he was leading a discussion on worship (although there was no worship service). It happened to be the night that the subcommittees reported their recommendations for the new order of worship. The people were excited that they had worked through several ideas and had come up with the worship expression their church needed. The feeling I got from the meeting was that the old order of worship was not adequate or expressive enough and that the new one would be all that would ever be needed. My thought was that it was very possible that, several years prior to this event, another group of people from this same congregation were very excited about their new order of worship. They had probably been sure that their method would always be adequate for their church community—the same method that was being discarded by the group we were visiting.

Even though some vision is evident in this situation, it remains blurred because they put too much weight on the method by giving it such lofty sanction.

2. *The second-class church citizen relegation.*—Churches that approach ministry to singles with a recognition of the double standard have a better vision in that they recognize something *ought* to be done. Unfortunately, the motives for this approach are not always healthy. Some see the singles as a way for the church to show an appreciable increase numerically and monetarily. Some feel that divorced singles tend to contaminate the married classes and that "we need a separate place for them." Others just perpetuate the method they have used with other nonmarried adult areas of church life. For example, most churches have someone to serve as the youth director and some married couples to be leaders of the high-school group. Generally, all programs are planned by the youth leaders (directors *for* the youth). This allows

all control of activities to remain in the hands of the leaders, and the youth are in fact second-class church citizens.

A pastor of a large, prominent church in another city said to me, "Britton, we've tried everything with our single adults, and nothing seems to work. We've paid their way on retreats, provided banquets, suppers, and socials for them, and numerous other events have been planned *for* them." I was about to share some insight singles had taught me when he said, "I don't think there is a thing you can tell us about working with single adults because we've done everything." I remained silent and thought, *You are so right; there is nothing I can tell you as long as you perpetuate the second-class-citizen approach by having activities* for *single adults instead of* with *them.* I felt he didn't have ears to hear. (As I write this, I am compelled to communicate my feelings with this pastor-friend.)

3. *The awareness-acceptance learning process.*—Just as is the case with all groups of persons (youth, college students, senior citizens, etc.) who are not in the married adult category, the single persons who come to your church need to be accepted as they come rather than the way the congregation may want them to come.

In most churches, if a married couple presented themselves for membership in a congregation, the response of the church would be that of immediate welcome. It could be possible for that same couple to be recently married. The man may be his wife's fourth husband, and two of her former husbands may have died suddenly of some mysterious cause; but nothing was ever proven against her. He may be in his fifth marriage and could have had some very unhealthy situations in his life. However, because the couple is married (and therefore like most persons in the church, who are also married), there is little or no question regarding their coming. I am aware, however, that many churches do carefully screen new members.

When a single adult is presented for membership, the questions begin to fly in some churches. Is he divorced? I wonder why he is not married. Do you think he is homosexual? I wonder if he is a swinging single.

My point is simple. The lack of questions in receiving the married adults and the numerous questions members may have when receiving some single adults are not fair. Actually, neither situation is fair. Each person who presents himself for membership in a congregation should be accepted as he comes, and a growing awareness of that person's unique needs for Christian growth should be a part of the learning process or dialogue.

The church needs to be aware that different life circumstances tend to affect the specific needs of an individual. The church that sees all persons as individuals—and is not only aware of their particular needs but also accepts them as they come—will have a growing, learning ministry.

The Church's Composition

One of the most important concepts to catch in the single adult ministry is the idea that the church is composed of both two-adult family units (married adults or nonsingles) *and* one-adult family units (single adults). Too often, by default, it is assumed that the church *is* the married adults and that when the singles get married and have homes, then they, too, can be the church. We need to stretch our vision of the church to include the single adult.

In a meeting with a group of singles from another church, a single stated, "They don't care about us singles." "Who doesn't care?" I said. "The church doesn't care," was the reply. "Who do you mean 'the church'?" I asked. "Them," came the answer. "Who do you mean when you say 'them'?" I asked. "The leaders!"

Again I asked, "Who do you mean when you say 'leaders'? Your pastor? Your minister of education?" "No, I mean the leaders—you know—the married folks." Then I understood. This person saw the church as the married adults only. At a singles conference in the Chicago area, I talked with a single who wanted to be active in the church; but she assumed that only married persons could serve God. In the minds of many single adults and certainly in the minds of most married adults, the church is composed of married adults. "They" run the programs. The perpetuation of this attitude is always unfortunate.

I must say that it is not surprising that married adults have the attitude that the church is composed of married adults. Most churches until recently *were* composed almost entirely of married adults and their children. One pastor told his college student group that "you should either be married by the time you graduate from college or have plans to be married, with some specific person in mind." He was in one way stating the assumption that all persons need to be married and then can be a full part of the church.

Single adults want to be the church, too. They say: "Hey, church that is made up of married persons with families, we are here, too;

don't overlook us! We have lives to give to God, too. Give us a hearing. We want you to accept us as we are."

A Family Illustration

My own children have helped me understand this feeling of useless-ness, of not being seen, heard, or depended on. I share a most touching event in our family life.

When our third daughter, Leigh Ann, was brought home, a most interesting situation took place. Our oldest daughter, Carol, was five and, we thought, old enough to hold her new sister (with assistance from Dad). We felt, however, that our three-year-old, Stacy, was not quite old enough to put her baby sister in her lap (she didn't really have a lap). What resulted from this was "Carol, you're OK; Stacy, you're not OK." As Carol was holding Leigh Ann and all eyes were on Carol and Leigh Ann, Stacy ran full speed into the living room wall. We asked her not to do that because she would hurt herself. Our eyes went back to the baby and the eldest daughter.

Then Stacy ran to the middle of the room, jumped high in the air, and hit the floor with a thud. Just watching her hurt me. "Stacy, stop!" Stacy got up and ran into the wall again. Finally, it dawned on Bobbye and me what was happening. We realized that Stacy had been ignored. By our actions we had said, "You are not ready to be responsible for the care and feeding of the young in our family. When you mature, you can be given responsibility like your older sister."

Isn't this the way many single adults feel? Churches tend to call only married ministers to serve as pastors. Single adulthood is often thought of by the married church as an in-between period—a time between home or college and marriage. Singles have been considered "not permanent" in their work and have, at times, been overlooked for promotions.

In the words of a well-known song, "The times, they are a-changing." I am delighted with our single adults and their ways of wanting to be the church.

The Role of the Single Adult Minister

Many of the single adults I talk with have been introduced to me by mutual friends who cared enough about them to bring them to church, ask them to call me, or arrange a lunchtime for us to talk. What I do in conversations with these single persons is very simple.

1. I do not *expect* the single adult to have certain attitudes regarding the church, God, or goals in life. This person, as far as I'm concerned, does not have to be a certain way for us to communicate. I'm convinced that persons down on the church, God, and the people in the church have met with a distortion of the gospel and have rejected that falseness rather than the genuine Christian faith. This person really cares about quality of life, or he would not take time to express anger when he sees a lack of quality of life. The attitudes of apathy or indifference that indicate a lack of hope for change disturb me. Very few persons actually feel *all* is hopeless. Thank God for the hope they do have.

2. I express concern about his concerns. I cannot assist a person who will not express personal needs and concerns. I assume that there is a point of need. Time and communication will eventually reveal the point of ministry for this person's life.

3. I encourage initial participation with our single adults. The sooner I can get our singles involved with caring for this person, the sooner that person will feel accepted. I may have the ability to encourage a person to visit us, but it is the single adults themselves who encourage this person to plant his life among us.

4. I explore with this person any spiritual or physical needs he has while referring him to our single adults for ministry. If he is not a Christian, I will continue our conversations along this line. For example, one of our single adults had suggested that a friend at work talk to me about the concerns of her life (not to get her into our church, but to assist her at the point of her need). She called, and we set up an evening meeting at our church. In between the time we set the conference itself, one of our single adult leaders needed to be taken to another city to a hospital. I offered to do the transporting.

The result was that I returned to our church about thirty or forty minutes late. My appointment had come, waited two or three minutes, and then left. I had stopped en route to Dallas and called the church to inform my appointment I would be late. She had already come and gone. When I arrived at the church, I realized I had only her work phone number. Fortunately, I was able to secure her home phone number from the directory. I called her to apologize for my lateness and to reschedule our appointment. Our schedules would not cooperate with each other for the next two or three weeks, so I finally said, "I don't know if you would want to come back to the church or not;

but I am here now, and we could visit now rather than waiting two or three weeks." She came to visit that evening.

We talked about her family, her work, and her dating situation. Finally I indicated that I was hearing a longing for something meaningful for her life. We talked about trying to please parents, employer, and boy friend—and none of these efforts seemed to bring the meaning that she wanted in her life. I told her what God wanted to be in her life and that only his lordship is adequate and fulfilling in our lives. Anyone or anything less in our lives is incomplete. I encouraged her to ask that Christ come into her life. She was most eager to respond to God and became a Christian that very evening. She was baptized and became an active member of our church, and she later married a fine young Christian man who was actively seeking God's will for his life. I shared in the privilege of sealing their marital covenant.

Whether the concern of a person is lack of employment, a place to live, ability to relate with other persons, or even to be suddenly single due to divorce or death of spouse, it is most important to move to that person's point of need. Until his point of concern is dealt with, he is too preoccupied to respond to God.

The only way my wife and I could express to our daughter that she really was OK was to include her in our family, to allow her to have the freedom to be a full member of our family with all the rights, privileges, and responsibilities of family life. This is, in parallel fashion, what the church as a whole needs to do with single adults.

The Role of the Single Adult Members

If the single adults are going to *be* the church, then the ministry of the church is *with* singles and not *for* singles. Only married adults can be the church that the married adults need to be. For the same reason, only single adults can be the church the singles need to be.

My contention is that the responsibility for the needs and ministries for the one-adult family units (single adults) rests entirely with the single adults. It is good to be reminded that if the two-adult family units assume responsibility for planning, programming, and preparing for the one-adult family units, the single adults are relegated to a second-class church citizen level or an adolescent level (as with high-school students). Single adults need to and must become the church; but they cannot become the church until the responsibility for being the church is given to them freely and in a spirit of understanding.

The Role of Other Church Members

There are certain beginning steps the church can take that will assist the single adults in becoming the church or the people of God who happen to be single.

First, accept the group of singles who already are members of your church. Many times ministers or lay leaders have implied to me that they could really have some great singles ministries if they had as many single adults as our church has or even had some of our single adults. In other words, they seemed to be saying (1) it must be wonderful to work with the singles *you* work with and (2) we don't have any singles like yours. Both statements are true because it is wonderful to work with the persons who are single in our church. On the other side of the picture, we do not have any of the singles in their church; and we have yet to see what kind of a unique ministry they can have if they feel loved, accepted, and encouraged to be the church.

Second, trust your singles to *be* the church. It takes time for the singles to feel trusted and to begin to assume responsibility for their own ministry. If given time, *they will respond.*

I do feel that growth of a group comes more naturally as we provide opportunity for growth to occur. For example, when we felt the need for an under-twenty-five-year-old group of singles, we chose to provide (1) a place for such a group to meet, (2) a teaching leader who was able to listen and relate to singles, (3) good content in the Bible study on Sunday morning, and (4) a director of the department who would be a friend and who would encourage the singles to believe that whatever they chose to do to be the church could be done.

For this particular group of singles, we provided everything but the ministries or activities that occupied their time and interests outside our scheduled services and Sunday School. In essence, we gave a potential base from which the singles could go in ministry.

The trust level also must express patience because a single adult group is generally slow to take responsibility for themselves. This factor may result in a group that limps along for a few months, slowly getting frustrated that "we meet on Sunday mornings, but we never do anything else." I consider frustration because of desires for more to happen within a group a good sign rather than a problem. A few singles get so frustrated that they say that if no one else is going to do anything, they are going to have to see that it gets done That is what we want our singles to do. We want to entrust them with the ministry that only they can do. Single adults are generally very peer-group oriented; therefore, they respond best to the ideas and events they deem important.

Third, encourage your single adults to develop a *koinonia* spirit. The kind of fellowship that is caring, sharing, laughing, crying, hurting, and responding is contagious.

Developing a Koinonia Spirit

One exceptional example of this kind of fellowship or spirit within a singles group is what happened in our twenty-five-and-under department about the time I came to Park Cities. This group began as a result of two single adults who felt a group was needed for their age. On the first Sunday these two members met with twenty others (church visitors from recent Sundays and church members not in Sunday School) who had been contacted to help initiate the group. (Any church can begin with at least *two* members, regardless of the size of the church.) The group met from April to July with no activities other than Sunday School. Attendance was quite inconsistent, from fifteen to twenty-five, with six to eight visitors each Sunday, many of whom chose not to come back. (Regardless of what kind of program a church has with singles, there are persons who visit who do not come back.)

In July I planned the first and last event that I initiated. I suggested we go to a lake resort for the weekend and stay at two large lake homes owned by our church members. It really seemed to be a good idea because we could swim, water ski, sail, play tennis or golf, and relax at a beautiful lake. Thirteen persons indicated they wanted to go, but only three were singles. The singles who signed up felt they should go because they were the appointed leaders in the singles group. The rest of us were the nonsingles leaders. The result was that we postponed the event.

By September the six singles who were leaders (by that time we had three areas of leadership—program, fellowship, and membership) suggested that the group have a retreat. This was the first suggestion made by the single adults themselves since April. So I became immediately available to pursue this idea by asking them when would they like to have the retreat, where would be a good place, and how many singles we could anticipate to go on the retreat. The "how many" question received a realistic response from the singles. One said, "I don't see why we should expect anyone to go because we don't know each other well enough."

A new question was posed. "What could we do to get to know each other better?" One suggested a party or get-together. Another said the party could be at her parents' home. A young man who had not offered to do anything said that he would be glad to cook hamburgers. Little did he know that it would rain that evening and he would be standing in a smoke-filled garage over the charcoal grill. We had this event in November with twenty-two present. Everyone thoroughly enjoyed fellowshiping together and seemed a little surprised that everything went so well.

The party was good for several reasons. First, the single adults wanted to have the event. It was important to them. Second, they wanted to work on making it a good event. The program cochairmen were responsible for the games and activities. The fellowship cochairmen were in charge of decorations and food. The membership cochairmen were responsible for calling all the singles. Just involving these leaders in doing the tasks they did because they wanted to was assuring success. Their attitude was good and positive and their motivation healthy, regardless of the number of singles who would participate. Third, it was a manageable event. Every group needs a success under their belts. If the event is something *they* feel they *can do,* then they are comfortable enough to attempt it. If the challenge is too great, it may well fail because singles don't need any more failures. They are in need of some successes.

In February, we finally had our retreat with twenty-five persons in attendance. Our retreat theme was worship. The retreat schedule was worked out at the retreat site, and the singles helped to determine our procedure. Our retreat leaders suggested some options, and the singles chose the ones most helpful to them. On Sunday morning (we began the retreat on Friday evening with supper) the singles planned their own worship experience, which was meaningful to everyone because all had a part in the planning; and all were actively contributing to the worship experience in spirit and content.

There was an air of anticipation that something important was about to happen. It did! The *koinonia* of this group that was not a group at all prior to the retreat overflowed into many other lives. This single adult group has grown so much that within four months after the retreat the department was running 50 to 60 in Sunday School and eventually grew to 80 to 95 in attendance.

Due to the limited space where this group could meet and in order to provide more personal ministry to more of these individuals, we decided to regroup our singles who were 28 years of age and younger into two groups (23 and under; 24 to 28). This helped us for about two and one-half years. By April of 1976, we had 190 enrolled in the 24 to 28 group; and many of these persons were between the ages of 28 and 32. For various reasons, we regrouped our entire single adult Sunday school to form five groups (22 and under; 23 to 26; 27 to 34; 35 to 45; and 46 and up).

Singles Must Work to Become the Church

Let your leadership and organizational style emerge through the lives and needs of your single adults. I cannot stress too much the importance of letting the singles feel the responsibility for what takes place in their singles group.

Soon after I came to the Park Cities church, one of our singles departments was selecting officers for the next six months; and the nominating committee was having a problem getting anyone to accept the position of president. Finally, we did get someone who was very capable; but six months later we had five persons who were willing to accept the position of president, all of whom were capable. The leaders had begun to emerge as they were given encouragement to be the church. The organizational needs in a single adult group are quite different from those of the married adults. It is important to style the organization according to needs rather than trying to fit the singles into an organization set up and styled for married adults.

One example of letting the singles be trusted with the ministry and of letting the organizational style emerge can be seen in what happened at one of our officers' meetings.

A little background is needed here. I had initiated a challenge my first summer at the church for the singles to go to either the single adult conference at Glorieta or to Corpus Christi and roof a mission as a "labor of love" during the Labor Day weekend. I told them that all expenses would be theirs, that we would sleep on cots and in sleeping bags, and that we would cook our own meals and help the people in a Mexican mission whose worship center had been badly damaged by a hurricane. The labor of love was truly that, as twenty-five singles went on a mission and *really* worked. As one schoolteacher said to a local television interviewer, "You couldn't pay me to do this, but I'm paying my own way to be a part of this exciting experience." So I had tried to help our singles see the need for ministry to others and had continued to encourage the idea with individual singles.

I was most pleased when, over a year after we had our "labor of love" project, a single spoke up in this particular officers' meeting. He began by saying, "You know, I feel selfish. I have been enjoying what has been going on here for over a year now. Everything we do here is with us. We aren't doing anything for anybody outside this group." (The group was really growing and reaching several people per week.) "I need to do something for someone else for a change." I responded by saying, "What do you think we need?" He answered, "We need to get involved some way in our community." "How would you suggest we get 'involved in our community'?" I asked. He said, "Let's have a community missions committee."

That night we organized such a committee. This group led our singles to work with a Mexican mission in West Dallas in painting the building inside and outside and the furniture in the children's Sunday School rooms. We also put a new ceiling, new paneling, and new pews in their worship center, plus a new sign in front of the church. We said when we began this work that it would be on a side-by-side basis with the members of the mission rather than *for* them. Each Saturday the ladies of the mission prepared the best Mexican food we had ever tasted.

At another point we took about thirty-five singles to Monterrey, Mexico, and worked in an orphanage for a week. Utilizing the professional skills of our singles, we had a medical team that categorized and labeled all the donated drugs so they could be dispensed by the leaders of the orphanage. We repaired tile roofs. We installed windowpanes, built partitions in the dining hall, painted, dug a ditch for a sewage pipe, repaired all the automobiles and buses, repaired the shortwave radio, bought some permanent playground equipment, played soccer and gave them a new soccer ball, sized and categorized a room full of donated clothing, and let some Mexican children weave their lives into our own lives.

Also, we began a basic adult education program at another mission in West Dallas. This project was quite challenging and continued for one school year. Many who had limited educations or who needed to learn English as a second language came to our night classes.

Other projects have resulted from this one realization by one single adult. There have been clothing drives, food drives, and special projects with needy families that the singles would read about in the newspaper and organize help for.

When the single adults choose to respond to God in service, their labors will be successful. When the singles are given the freedom and the opportunity to serve as the people of God who happen to be single, great things happen. Stretch your vision—it's worth the effort!

3.
Single by Choice
(Always Single)

By far the largest group (more than 50 percent) of single adults is made up of persons who have always been single. These persons are generally categorized as never married. Unfortunately, most terms for singles are indicated from marriage as the assumed norm. The term *always single* is better than *never married*, but my preference in terms is *single by choice*. Persons who remain single are doing so by choice. They have either not chosen the persons who have asked to marry them or have chosen not to encourage relationships that seemed to be moving toward marriage.

The "Having It Made" Myth

While social stigma has been related to divorce, there has been a societal pressure related to the always single person. The American dream has helped set up this societal pressure. Part of being successful in life has been the idea that to really have it made is to become successful in business (or marry someone successful in business) and acquire a healthy mate. When a person has success in business, success in marriage, and success in having kids (preferably a boy and girl), he really has it made.

The "having it made" myth has been evangelized by parents who have lived through the Depression. The people who look at life with a dollar value rather than with a meaning or integrity value tend to put too much weight on the material aspects of life. The mothers of America have contributed greatly to this myth of having marriage as a definite goal in life when they tell their daughters what the daughters want to be when they grow up. A mother might say, "My dear, we know what you want to be when you grow up—to be a good wife to your husband and a good mother to your children."

While young men have been encouraged to think of achievement outside the home—in business—young women have been encouraged to be successful inside the home. It is not surprising that compatibility often proves difficult because young men and young women are not developing similar goals in life. Only in recent years has the goal for many young adults (men and women) become "achieving a healthy personhood."

Premarital Counseling

Since I work with so many singles, it's not surprising that marriages occur within our singles ministry. Often in premarital counseling sessions the conversation with a couple will lead me to ask, "What do you want to be in this marriage?" Many young women have responded, "I want to be a good wife to my husband (turn to fiancé and squeeze his hand) and a good mother to our children." (This statement is followed by a smile indicating *Boy, I really was ready for that question.*) I usually counter with "That won't be adequate for your marriage."

As I pause for this new thought to sink in, some of the women will begin to cry. They say, "What do you mean, it won't be adequate?" My answer is: "A man can't love a 'wife'—he loves the *person* who happens to be his wife. He doesn't love the mother of his children; he loves the *person* who is the mother of his children. God created us to be persons, and anything short of that is inadequate."

The process in counseling would be to begin to understand personhood and the vast difference in being an authentic self and trying to fulfill all the role expectations of parents, friends, spouse, and self.

Marriage as a Goal

With the multifaceted opportunities in business today, it is often difficult to know what one should choose to do vocationally. Also, many fields require a graduate degree for advancement possibilities. It is not unusual for a young man to postpone marriage for a few years after college. As young men postpone getting married, automatically the number of young women who remain single increases.

When marriage is a goal in life, not to achieve the goal leaves one incomplete, unfinished, or not yet fulfilled. With marriage as a goal or an anticipated goal, anything less is "second best." Many coeds in college have stated to me, "I really don't want to work professionally in the field of my academic training. I really want to get married, but this preparation gives me something to fall back on." The "fall back on" syndrome is one more illustration of the lack of awareness or of concern for personhood.

More women are prepared physically and cosmetically to meet a man than are prepared to be a woman. Generally a man is looking for a woman who is a person; but since he sees excellently groomed objects most of the time, he may not realize that what he really wants and *needs* is a woman who is a person.

Marriage needs to be a fortunate outgrowth of a healthy interpersonal relationship rather than a goal. My goal in life is to be the person God wants me to be and to become the person God wants me to become. I imperfectly learn who I am to be as a person and become the person I need to be through Christ, God's Son, as revealed in the Holy Spirit. So, even though I am married, my goal in life is no different now than it was when I was a single by choice.

Paul's Opinion of Marriage

In 1 Corinthians 7:1 and following Paul expressed his opinion about choosing to remain single. In Paul's way of looking at life, "A man does well not to marry" (1 Cor. 7:1, TEV). In the same chapter, verse 8, Paul stressed again that "I say this to the unmarried [single by choice] and to the widows [single without choice]: it would be better for you to continue to live alone [as a single adult], as I do."

Paul continued his discourse on the single-by-choice person in verse 25, "Now, the matter about the unmarried: I do not have a command from the Lord, but I give my opinion as one who by the Lord's mercy is worthy of trust.

"Considering the present distress, I think it is better for a man to stay as he is. Do you have a wife? Then don't try to get rid of her. Are you [single] unmarried? Then don't look for a wife." Paul went on to indicate that there is little time left, so we should get on with following Jesus and telling of his return.

His purpose in encouraging singles not to marry is simple. Verse 32 states, "I would like you to be free from worry. An unmarried man concerns himself with the Lord's work, because he is trying to please the Lord." In verse 34 we read, "An unmarried woman or a virgin concerns herself with the Lord's work, because she wants to be dedicated both in body and spirit." In essence Paul was saying that a married person is not as free to follow God, since "a married [person] man concerns himself with worldly matters, because he wants to please his wife" (vv. 33-34).

Many single adults have emphasized the disadvantages of being single and have missed the blessing of their singleness. Emphasis for singles needs to encourage the development of the advantages of being single. Let me pick up on one statement Paul made. In verse 27 he asked the question "Are you unmarried [single]? Then don't look for a wife." I find this excellent advice. Single adults need to get on with living purposeful lives *now*. Too many persons long to be married so they can start living.

Unfortunately, many persons live unhappily because they did not fulfill a goal that they felt was important for them but, in reality, was unrealistic. In my own life, for example, I had dreamed of being a professional baseball player when I grew up. At age thirteen, I was as good as any person my age in fielding, hitting (I was very consistent as a hitter and usually got on base), and pitching. When I was sixteen I had improved somewhat, but I lacked height. All of my friends had outgrown me and, since I was not extremely fast in running, I had no special "salable" item.

I began to see my future as a baseball player diminish realistically. I have continued to play on intramural teams in college and on church teams since then. But I have never felt deprived because that "dream" was not fulfilled. To follow a dream that may not be mine (or what God hopes for me to do) is to postpone my openness to God's will now.

Preoccupation with Marriage

I believe that always-single people continually renew goals for themselves. Let's assume a young lady considers marriage a desired goal by age twenty-five. If it doesn't occur then, she reprograms her marriage chart to age twenty-seven. If it doesn't occur then, she reschedules matrimony for age twenty-nine because she would like to be married before age thirty.

Now she is thirty-two and still single. Many pressures have come upon her from family and friends. They all tell her that some guy is really missing a fine person, which accentuates her dilemma. So the young lady talks with herself once again and says, "Look, babe, you're not going to get married no matter how great a person you are or how great your family thinks you are. You are going to be single all your life, so do you want to lay down and die or to get quality living *now?* It's up to you, baby!" So a young, thirtyish, healthy woman decides to get on with living without the unrealistic goal setting and enjoys life.

I am convinced that if all a person wants to do is to get married, he can get married. One single man came to me at a meeting with our singles and asked, "Britton, how do I go about getting a wife?" He married soon after that, and the marriage lasted less than two months.

Needless to say, this marriage preoccupation is no small concern. However, I do like the unusual turn given by Linda Lawson in her book *Life as a Single Adult*. She says, "One of my goals is to be married someday. But, whether for now or forever, I am committed to the belief that a person can be happy and single, be growing and single, be loving and loved and single." [1]

Many of the concerns of singles by choice are similar to those of other human beings. In fact, it is often amazingly simple to meet the needs of these single persons. When a single adult is responded to and listened to as a person of worth rather than as one who has several hurdles to jump before being a success (with marriage as one hurdle yet to get past), that single-by-choice person is so aware of the difference that he feels genuine gratefulness. The fact that *some* people do care in a genuine way for the person who happens to be single gets a positive response from the single adult.

Attitude Toward Family

One concern of the single-by-choice person is his attitude toward his own family. Many singles are not free from their parents regardless of age, whether in their twenties or their forties. Too often singles make an effort to please their parents, and seldom can one please his parents by *trying* to please them. In a larger sense, no one can please another by trying to please him. The only way, I feel, that I can please another is to do that which is most pleasing to me. I am more authentic, whether another likes my authentic self or not, when I am pleasing my best self. It is important to note here that what is most pleasing to God will please my best self.

This concept is valid in relation to one's parents. I recall a situation in which a single adult had spent time preparing herself for teaching by acquiring experience and a graduate degree. Two schools wanted her to teach for them in the areas of her interest. One school (school A) was over a thousand miles from where her parents lived and the other (school B) less than one hundred miles away. She wanted the position which happened to be farther from home, but her parents told her that they were getting old and would like to see her more often. Besides, they didn't have the money to fly to visit her; but they could drive to see her if she were not too far away. She rejected school A and accepted school B.

It was at this point that we began to converse. She was feeling that she had made the wrong decision. I asked her which school she would teach in if she could make the decision at that very moment while we were talking. She said, "It's too late; I have already sent the contracts in." I asked, "When did you send them?" Her reply was that she had mailed them that morning.

I pointed out that the contracts had not actually arrived at their destination. Since we were talking on a Friday, it was unlikely that anything would be done at either school before Monday. I suggested she choose again. "Which school would you choose now, A or B?" She said, "I would choose school A because I really want to teach there. I accepted school B just to please my parents."

I further suggested that her parents, in the long run, would want her to do what was most pleasing to her and that it was not too late to change her mind. She asked, "How?" I suggested that she could call school A and verbally agree to the contract, asking them to send another contract for her to sign and to tear up the one in the mail. She could then call school B and verbally communicate that she had already accepted another position and that they should tear up the contract coming through the mail to them now. She chose to follow up on this plan. We prayed about her parents' attitude.

On Monday she came into my office and was obviously very excited. She read me a portion of a letter she had just received from her parents. They said that they had reconsidered their encouraging her to teach at school B; if she really did not want to, then they would not want her to either. What they really wanted her to do was what she wanted to do. She went to school A and was very happy about her choice.

What if she had lived her life just to please her parents? Probably she would have resented them and respected herself and them less.

On the other hand, some singles are doing everything they can *not* to please parents. It is important for a person to recognize that doing something out of spite or out of false independence ("I'll show you I'm free to do just as I please") is an adolescent way of handling conflict.

To do, out of rebellion, acts opposite to those a parent demands or requests is to be controlled by those parents. To respond to life from a reactionary position is to not be free to respond as an adult but to maintain a rebellious child stance with parents.

Further study into actions that shape attitudes on the part of parents and child can be most helpful. Some insight from transactional analysis and other psychological methodology could provide practical awareness of reasons for the kinds of relationships a person has with parents.

Some single adults feel responsible for a parent or a brother or sister. Many family members will allow a single person "who doesn't have any responsibility, anyway" to take care of them. Seeing a good counselor would be a realistic avenue toward making a decision. All decisions need to reflect the self-dignity every individual should have. Some guilt feelings that people have are not valid.

Attitude Toward Self

A second concern, which is interrelated to family, is a single person's attitude toward self. I have known singles by choice with almost every kind of self-identity, from the low self-esteem to the gregarious caring for other kinds of persons. Much needs to be done within singles groups to help singles learn to like and love themselves. In Luke 10:27, we are reminded that we are also to love ourselves. One psychologist has said that he who can love only others cannot love at all. Christ loved us so much that he died for us "while we were still sinners" (Rom. 5:8).

It is most important, to me if not to anyone else, that I clarify my attitude toward singles and singles groups. I do not feel negatively toward singles, and I see much potential in most singles. I do not try to put them in categories of either winner or loser. I see them as persons who are in the process of learning about the unique identities that God wants them to become. If a person has some particular need regarding his attitude about himself, a single adult ministry can help him discover that he is OK just as he is and that God's love and mercy are sufficient for each person.

Attitude Toward Others

Some of the healthiest persons I have ever known are single, a fact which brings me to a third consideration. A common concern of singles is interpersonal relationships. Most singles desire to have some healthy friendships with other singles who are working on the same life concerns they are and who desire to approach life with the Christian faith as the foundation for life.

Recently my family and I had Sunday lunch at a restaurant near our church, and we saw about twenty-five single adults from our church. I was so pleased to know them; but more than that, I was pleased to know about their concern for each other, their genuine friendships with each other, their desire to please God, and their honesty about their own needs and concerns. Most of these persons are single by choice and love living. Their warm spirit is contagious.

Not all single adults feel at ease in relating to other singles. In fact, some singles who seem unfriendly and tend to be aloof are probably shy individuals. I feel the church can minister to such persons.

The director of counseling on a college campus where I once worked felt that one of the major concerns of college students was peer-group relationships. In a radio interview, the interviewer asked him what resources he had available to him to help meet the needs of these young adults. He said that his best resource was the campus ministry center (the Baptist Student Center). The radio announcer questioned him further: "Oh, you mean that the students have a religious problem?" The counseling director said the problem was that the students needed to relate to their peer group and didn't know how to begin.

He added that the students in our center were trained, in a natural way, to care for persons who came to the center and to help them discover their own interests so they could become involved in at least one of the numerous activities available through the center. Our student leaders and I were not aware that students were being sent to the counseling center for fifteen-minute intervals three times per week. The director indicated that he was responsible for sending troubled students over to our center and that our students took care of everything else. The fact was that our students related to the newcomers at the point of their need, after learning of these needs through casual conversation.

It is important to note that there is quite a difference in one's desire to communicate and one's skill in communicating. There is also a difference in one's awareness of what is important in communicating and one's ability to actually communicate.

The need to communicate is so basic to healthy lives. The single Christian community is a great avenue for seeing lives blossom and bear fruit in ways that honor God.

Overcoming a Negative Attitude Toward Church

After several visits to our various singles activities, one young lady of another denomination talked to me about her participation in our church. She said that Park Cities was really fortunate to have the kind of ministry that we had. While in college, she had said that she would never attend a Baptist church again. As I recall, she had seen some unhealthy models and understandably could not style her life by theirs. She eventually chose to become a member of our church and has grown spiritually.

Many singles, especially men, are not presently involved in the church because they made a decision against the church or the Christian "religion" when they were in their middle teens (ages fourteen to sixteen). As adolescents, they may have made their decisions on the basis of misconceptions or distortions about religion rather than on the basis of genuine Christian faith.

I once traveled by air to Austin to visit the college singles from our church who were attending classes at the University of Texas. On the plane trip, I sat by a twenty-six-year-old attorney. This young man was most impressive. He was friendly, enjoyed good humor, and was eager to talk. After we had talked about him for a while, he asked what kind of work I did. When I told him I was a minister to single adults, he said, "I'm single, but I don't want to talk about religion. I'm through with that."

After talking about other topics for a while, I asked him what about religion had turned him off. Everything he described was a distortion of the faith rather than the faith itself. He talked about some early disappointments he had experienced in adults he had admired when he was growing up. He mentioned having thought, *If that's Christianity, I don't want to have anything to do with it.* Then he added, "I said I didn't want to talk about religion."

My response was that I would not be interested in talking about religion either if what he described was all there was to it. But I *was* interested in talking about a God who dislikes hypocrisy more than my fellow passenger did. I told him that this same God loves us, just as we are, so much that he sent his Son to die for our sins. Because of Jesus Christ's sacrifice, we do not have to be separated from God any longer. Religion that majors on the ritual, the righteousness of some men, instead of on the change that takes place inside a person, keeps one from God. But the Christian faith helps persons become very close to God through Christ.

My new friend responded by saying, "You've given me something to think about; perhaps we can talk again." We parted after we deplaned and have not visited again. I hope we can someday. I trust that God will build on what did occur.

Physically Handicapped Singles

Among the single-by-choice persons are many who have some particular limitation which is often termed a *handicap*. Specifically, these are persons who are deaf or blind or who have cerebral palsy or some other physical or intellectual limitations due to accident or birth defect. These persons are in need of the single adult ministry through the church.

I have known some wonderful persons who fit into the category of the physically handicapped. Despite their handicaps, they have all excelled in some other way and have become my teacher in one way or another.

Some of the insights handicapped adults have taught me are:

Handicapped Singles Need Respect

First, handicapped persons have every need any other single has, such as acceptance, consideration, respect, avenues for caring, sense of worthwhileness, a way to cope with sexual needs, and spiritual concerns. As one of our handicapped adults stated in talking with our singles on "Relating to Handicapped Persons," someone has to help bridge the gap. She indicated that handicapped adults are reaching out and that someone needs to get in touch with them—or close the gap that postpones communication.

I recall walking on a slight slope with a young man at a retreat. He walked too fast and fell, face forward, on the ground. My immediate inclination was to reach down and help him up; instead, I asked if he needed any help. He said, "No, but thank you." I learned that I needed to respect his right to help himself. However, we cannot assume that all handicapped persons can help themselves in all situations. There are times when they need physical help to move a chair, to get across a busy street, and so forth.

One of my blind friends (physically blind) admonished me for petting his seeing-eye dog. He helped me realize that if the dog became interested in seeing new friends, he would not be as disciplined in being the eyes for his master. One dog almost caused my friend to walk off a high platform once because of his lack of concentration. Naturally, the dog was replaced. Many persons who have eyes do not understand that petting a seeing-eye dog can be harmful.

Handicapped Singles Need Honest Friends

Second, handicapped persons need friends who are honest in their relationships. There are times that a handicapped person cannot see what he or she is doing to a relationship. One young woman who was blind was so hungry for acceptance that she fell in love with all the young men who dated her. She smothered every relationship to the point that some guys intentionally avoided being around her. Telling her so was difficult, but it seemed best.

Another blind person often wore clothes that didn't match too well. The combinations didn't bother him because he didn't have to look at them, but they bothered me because of the reactions of some unkind persons. I told him about his appearance and made some suggestions for the present. I also made some purchase suggestions for the future. He appreciated my honesty; and when he had made a purchase, he immediately came by to see me and show me what he had bought.

In essence, some handicapped adults need social and psychological help. It is important that they ask for it or that you ask them if they would like the suggestions.

Handicapped Singles Need the Church

Third, handicapped adults can relate to the mainstream of the single adult ministry in the church. A separate program is not necessary or advisable. Simple methods can be used for handicapped singles to be involved, such as: (1) invite them to the activities because they tend to feel left out too often; (2) encourage them to participate by going by to get them for a particular event; (3) plan something that they can enjoy and participate in with the other singles; (4) even if you fear relating to them because you don't know how, relax and enjoy your relationship with them. As one person said, "As a rule, we don't bite."

Handicapped Singles Need to Date

Fourth, dating is probably the most difficult area of need. Most handicapped persons consider themselves to be normal; and they are in almost all ways. Persons who choose to date handicapped adults need to recognize the tendency for the handicapped person to overreact, to respond in an out-of-balance way with the level of the relationship. Persons who date a handicapped individual need to be honest in their feelings and to never lead the other person to assume a deeper relationship than really exists.

Handicapped Singles Need Acceptance

Fifth, if the handicapped person feels resentment for "the way I am," spiritual growth and following God's will can become difficult. This attitude can develop easily because many handicapped persons fantasize or analyze themselves often. The more persons become close and understanding friends with the handicapped, the more handicapped individuals communicate their feelings and have more realistic self-concepts.

Young Singles

The group of single-by-choice persons who really need the help of the church—and who really need to be the church—is the eighteen-to-thirty crowd. The young single is shaping his or her life-style within the first few years of adulthood. Choices made during these years often determine what takes place in later single years.

I like May and June. The beginning of summer is certainly a time for change, adjustments, and new beginnings. It is a time when a graduate from an out-of-town university comes by to tell me in an exciting way that she has been accepted by a graduate school in our area, will get an apartment (rather than live at her parents' home), and will be able to participate in our multifaceted single adult ministry. Her college roommate may be involved at our church, too. It is also a time when a graduating high-school senior says to me, "Britton, when do you get me?" (I get high-school graduates in June, following their graduation, as they move into our college singles community.)

These attitudes are quite different from the "When I get out of high school, they will never see me again at that church" we heard a few years ago.

What has brought about this changed attitude among our own young people who move into the single adult life on a chronological basis? An interesting process has occurred out of simple ministry needs.

Ministry to Campus Singles

I arrived on our church scene on June 15, 1970. I soon learned that most of our 250-plus students would be in colleges and universities outside our city. The most recent high-school graduates were already out of high school when I arrived, and the returning college students were already in summer jobs; so I found it most difficult to become acquainted with many of these students during my first summer there. Many left for the fall semester about August 15.

I could not imagine my waiting another nine months to get to know these students. So I decided to go visit our students wherever possible and get to know them in their own environment—the campus. This type of visitation would also provide me with a continuing update of what is happening on the college campus and would help me remain aware of students' needs—much more than if I stayed at my office and attempted to minister to students.

My initial encounters with students were sluggish on both their part and mine. A typical approach to the campus visit fell into this pattern: I asked laypersons to call the parents of all college students on our church roll and write down the name of the student, college, college mailing address, college phone, classification, home address and phone, major, and anticipated graduation date. The parents would also be asked if the student in their home would like to receive the *Student* magazine, our state Baptist paper, our church paper, and the *Home Missions* magazine (juniors or older). We would then have an address stencil made for each student at the college address and the home address (college-away file and at-home file).

From our college-away file we would pull the names of the students from one campus, such as Baylor (fifty-five students), and send each a letter from me indicating when I would be there to visit with them. I usually would set a time and location for our getting together and let them know where I would be staying.

My first year of campus visitation was really interesting. At one campus I met with a dozen students. One said, "Did you come here for a speaking engagement?" I said, "No, I just came to visit you." She asked, "You are on your way to some other meeting and just stopped by to say hello?" I said, "No, I just came to see you." She asked, "Did someone, like our parents, ask you to come to see us?" I said, "No, I just came to get acquainted with you and our other students here." She had been standing as she asked the previous questions but sat down as she said, "No one ever treated me this way before." (I read her statement as "No one ever cared for me that way before.")

Now I am asked each August, "Britton, when will you be coming to my campus?" I answer, "Fall or spring." The students say, "Do you want me to save pizza coupons or contact anyone?" Some say, "I'll be glad to fix supper at my apartment for all of us."

When I get to the campus, some students know that we will have thirty-to-forty-five-minute conversational times on a one-to-one basis. One student said, "I have six questions. How can I witness to a friend who is having an affair and still be his friend? How can I start a Bible study in our Greek organization when some Christians in my fraternity will think I'm hypocritical because I take a social drink now and then? How can I relate better to my parents? How can I get them to understand my vocational choice? I am having trouble with priorities. I have a hard time praying." So in forty-five minutes we talked about these heavy items.

I visit twelve to fifteen campuses per academic year and see about 150 students. I call other students at some campuses I can't visit because of distance, in states such as California or Virginia or in schools such as West Point.

After more than six years of ministry with our college singles, many of the ones I visited during their college days are the ones who choose to be active as young single adults who are in the business world.

Reorientation Sessions with Campus Singles

Just this year, I have begun a new phase of this campus visitation—a reorientation session with college seniors. For a senior to leave the sheltered environment of the college campus for the cold, impersonal, unsheltered adult business world can be a cultural shock.

By the time a university student is a senior in college, the campus is a very familiar place. The senior knows who to talk with regarding any administrative decision and probably shows little hesitancy in initiating conversations with deans if necessary. The boundaries on the campus are well marked so that a student has little difficulty knowing where to park his car, what courses to take for a particular degree, what campus events are available for entertainment, when to register, when to take exams, when to come to school, and when to leave the campus. In essence, a student gets much help for scheduling from the paternal campus.

Things really change for the ex-college student when he is in the beginning stages of the working world. The anticipation of these young single adults is high for an exciting beginning and for good things to happen in their lives.

Yet in the midst of excitement there is some inner turmoil. This inner conflict is wrapped up in unproven abilities in a carry-your-own-weight working situation, uncertainty in living quarters location, and an unsettling shift of identity because of friends, campus, and home left behind.

The college graduate has an identity crisis upon leaving the comfortable security of the campus. It is for this reason that some students continue to go to graduate school rather than leave the sheltered niche that the campus offers them.

Other identity crises occur when the young single ventures into the city to determine what kind of job to get or what kind of job is actually available, where to live, who to live with, and how and where to cultivate new friends. Add to this dilemma the concern for making good at the new job, relating to parents in a different role (nonstudent), and trying to maintain friendships with college friends who are in a variety of places. There are also some tremendous money demands all at once, before the first paycheck comes in.

The result of these pressures for many young single adults is an overwhelming sense of responsibility toward doing well in the new work situation. A single with this tendency pours many hours into the work situation because of the unrelenting drive to be successful. Often this person takes little time for fun activities such as dating, parties, weekend trips, or movies. The thought regarding fun is, "When I get better established in my work, I can enjoy more things and have more fun." It has not yet occurred to this person that social and interpersonal development can grow in parallel fashion with the work responsibilities.

Practical Suggestions for Young Singles

Some of the relocation suggestions I give at the college senior reorientation sessions on campuses are quite practical and, hopefully, will be helpful to other workers with single adults. These suggestions were first listed in an article I wrote for *College* entitled "After Graduation."

My advice to singles included:

1. Choose your living quarters on the basis of convenience and space rather than on image and fantasy. It is important to have a home base that you want to come to, but it need not be chosen to please or impress friends and family. Your initial apartment need. not be what you have always dreamed of. It is possible to overtax your budget too soon and to have to move to less expensive housing in a few months, when unexpected bills occur.

2. If you choose to have charge. accounts, charge no more in any given month than you can pay for that month. Many persons allow financial charges to consume too large a portion of their monthly income. Use charge accounts for sale items, but pay cash for as much as possible.

3. If you need to establish credit, make a small loan of one hundred to five hundred dollars at your bank to provide a local credit reference soon after your move. Schedule your payments on a lower scale than you can handle, and pay out the loan early. This looks good on your credit rating. It also leaves you with a little rather than a lot of pressure.

4. One of your best sources of advice for personal services is the church. Seek out recommendations from your campus minister or pastor for a church to visit and participate in. Not only will the church be helpful in giving you balance in life, but there you can receive good advice about a doctor, dentist, auto mechanic, and other personal services.

5. Develop your ability to relate to persons by identifying with a single adult group in a church in your new location. Too often Christian single adults postpone involvement with a church group and then wonder why things don't go well. Many church "floaters" move from church to church, depending on the dating possibilities or where the best show is for that particular time. Deep relationships that cultivate lifelong friendships or marriage cannot occur unless the investment of time and sharing of self is given to individuals in a group situation.

6. Realize that your personal morality will be tested by persons who are intellectually capable of confusing you. The single adult "swinger" option is not only available; this option has evangelists in every apartment complex in the city. The Christian single adult has some real adjusting to do if attempts at relationships continue even though lifestyles differ. The pressures to conform are very real and often very subtle.

7. Learn how to enjoy being alone. It is often difficult for single adults to make constructive (self-enhancing) use of the time they have to themselves. Many persons burn up an entire day without an enriching alone time. This can be a devotional time or useful in just thinking about who you are in relation to what you have done that day. It can be an "instant replay" of situations in your daily flight pattern.

8. Be a person of integrity. Seek to be your full self with all persons. This policy eliminates the extra baggage of taking masks with you, and it also keeps you from being caught somewhere with your mask down. It is difficult to maintain integrity if you try to be one type of person at work, another at the apartment, and another with your church crowd. If your friends don't like you as you really are, it would be wise to invest your time with persons who can accept you as you are.

9. Weigh the advice you receive, and sift it to meet the needs of the unique self you are. Some advice will be helpful; much will be beneficial only at the point of telling you more about the person giving the advice. No one can relate to or perform tasks in your work just as you can.

10. You cannot please other persons by seeking to please them. The way to be the most pleasing person to others is to be the most pleasing person to yourself. Much energy is expended in trying to determine what your parents want you to do. In fact, many college students major in pleasing their parents. This same desire to please carries over into your world of work. Seek to please yourself; selfishness is not the attitude intended. The desire is for your best interest and your best self to be considered.

11. Stay tuned to God's will for your life. As adults we need to continue to determine, as best we can, how we can glorify God through our lives.

You may want to pass some or all of these suggestions on to the singles you reach. The potential of the church that happens to be single is just now getting ready to rear its head. When this tremendous potential is tapped, the church will be in one of its most fulfilling times, in spirit and in growth, up to this point in history.

4.
Single After Marriage—Without Choice
(Widowed)

Recently I was involved as minister in two funerals. Both deaths occurred suddenly in what seemed to be fairly healthy marriages. Now, in two separate households, two persons had become single without having a choice in the matter.

When one is single without choice, one needs time to become a single adult. Even though one is single in status, it does not mean one is single in attitude. In fact, the widowed is probably the most reluctant of all single persons to accept singularity as a style of life.

This attitude is certainly understandable because widowed persons had an identity (married) that they enjoyed and a relationship that was probably growing or at least fairly good. About two weeks after the death of the husband of a well-known family in a church, another single adult (who was also widowed) asked the new widow if she would begin coming to the singles class. I happened to be in the church soon after this had occurred. The new widow said to me, "I just wasn't prepared to be a single adult, but I suppose in the long run I need to know that I am single now rather than married."

Attitude of the Church Toward the Widowed

The widow has had a privileged place in the church throughout history. The first deacons were given the specific task of caring for the widows and the orphans. In our society, the widow is readily accepted in many areas of life. She is excused from responsible action for a season and is allowed to mourn.

The church is generally kind to the widowed person. Probably the most meaningful group to someone who has lost a spouse by death is his/her Sunday school class. These friends tend to stay in touch by having lunch with the widowed person, coming by to visit, helping to determine what to do with the spouse's clothes and other items, preparing food that can be eaten later, and so forth.

Facing Separation by Death

It is good, in a way, that the widowed person has much to do both legally and domestically. It seems to force one to face the reality of the separation by death.

In the book *On Death and Dying,* Dr. Elisabeth Kübler-Ross gives five steps or stages of the grief process. These steps are valuable in ministering to widowed persons and are also valid for the dying person when there is a time span involved from awareness of impending death until death itself. The stages as summarized in Dr. Elisabeth Kübler-Ross' book *Death, The Final Stage of Growth* are:

1. *Denial.*—"No, not me." This is a typical reaction when a patient learns that he or she is terminally ill. Denial, says Dr. Kübler-Ross, is important and necessary. It helps cushion the impact of the patient's awareness that death is inevitable.

2. *Rage and anger.*—"Why me?" The patient resents the fact that others will remain healthy and alive while he or she must die. God is a special target for anger, since he is regarded as imposing, arbitrarily, the death sentence. To those who are shocked at her claim that such anger is not only permissible but inevitable, Dr. Kübler-Ross replies succinctly, "God can take it."

3. *Bargaining.*—"Yes, me, but . . ." Patients accept the fact of death but strike bargains for more time. Mostly they bargain with God—"even people who never talked with God before."

They promise to be good or to do something in exchange for another week or month or year of life. Notes Dr. Kübler-Ross: "What they promise is totally irrelevant because they don't keep their promises anyway."

4. *Depression.*—"Yes, me." First the person mourns past losses, things not done, wrongs committed. But then he or she enters a state of "preparatory grief," getting ready for the arrival of death. The patient grows quiet and doesn't want visitors. "When a dying patient doesn't want to see you anymore," says Dr. Kübler-Ross, "this is a sign he has finished his unfinished business with you, and it is a blessing. He can now let go peacefully."

5. *Acceptance.*—"My time is very close now, and it's all right." Dr. Kübler-Ross describes this final stage as "not a happy stage, but neither

is it unhappy. It's devoid of feelings, but it's not resignation; it's really a victory." [1]

These stages provide a very useful guide to understanding the different phases that dying patients may go through. They are not absolute; not everyone goes through every stage, in this exact sequence, at a predictable pace. But this paradigm can, if used in a flexible, insight-producing way, be a valuable tool in understanding why a patient may be behaving as he does.

I think it is appropriate to note at this point that this grief process is also valid for persons who are going through the process of divorce (death of a relationship). More will be said on this subject later.

Although my experience with widowed persons is somewhat limited, I have observed that generally widows handle the grief process better than the widowers do. If a widower has had a good marriage, he seems to be eager to get back into a marriage. It is also possible that the widower's spouse catered to him and that he misses the pampering and the good care given him by his deceased wife.

The relationship the widowed person has with God makes a great difference in his/her ability to cope.

Resentment May Be a Dominant Attitude

1. A dominant attitude may be resentment for God's taking the spouse away. In many situations, the strong decision-maker dies; and the seemingly weaker follower is left to live alone. Some husbands with children resent their wives' leaving them with the domestic duties and the breadwinning responsibilities as well.

Resentment is the kind of attitude that asks, "Why did this have to happen to me? Look at all the murderers, dope peddlers, and skid row people who aren't amounting to much in their lives. Why couldn't it have been one of them? It is just *not* fair." The "Why me?" attitude can only be answered *in time.* It is important to ask with equal impact, "Why not *me?*" If one question is valid, so is the other one. But to ask both questions does not answer either.

The only partial answer I feel I can give to the bereaved individual is that we cannot fully understand how God works in our lives at a time such as this; but we need to trust him to be faithful to us (he is), not to leave us comfortless (he will not), and to trust that "all things work together for good to them that love God, to them who are the called according to his purpose" (Rom. 8:28). Also, it is my firm belief that God is concerned with how we live and how we react or respond to all of life's situations, realizing that nothing can separate us from the love of God through Christ Jesus—not death, not life, not *anything*. God is more concerned about our continued obedience to him than why this or why that. God allows many things in life to take place rather than causing events to happen. Whatever takes place in our lives God will and can use "for good." Our attitudes toward God are of the utmost importance.

In a symposium on death and the process of dying recently, Dr. John Claypool indicated that gratitude was the best way to cope with loss. He encouraged the young ministers to "give to your people the hope that he who gave the good things which we have lost still can be depended on to give us the good things we need." [2]

Guilt Feelings Must Be Overcome

2. Many widowed persons are overcome with a great sense of guilt. Either they feel responsible for their spouse's death because of something they did, or they feel that they didn't do something they should have done, had they known to do it. This feeling of guilt is quite a heavy burden. Unfortunately, guilt is a judgmental attitude and can only be removed by the person who places the judgment of guilt on the widow/widower. Generally the guilt is self-inflicted. It is important to note here that no judgment of guilt can be accepted by an individual unless he/she chooses to accept it. The attitude of "I chose to accept guilt for my wife's/husband's death" is a choice of the individual.

The good news of Christ comes to us at this point and encourages us to ask for forgiveness for any wrong done and to trust God to work in our lives. The psalmist said, "Cast your burden upon the Lord, and he will sustain you" (Ps. 55:22, RSV). Only God is able to take our guilt upon himself. He is acquainted with grief and understands our sorrow. But Christ's concern is for more than a physical death. He redeems us all from a spiritual death.

A Tendency Toward Self-Pity May Develop

3. Some widowed persons get bogged down in a "poor little ole me" rut. If one has a tendency to do this, it is easy to get caught up in telling what a tragic situation *I'm* in. This *is* a rut because people

who choose to tell "poor me" stories seem to become stuck right there. Each time they are greeted with a cordial "How are you?" they respond with their story, which may begin like this: "Oh (sigh), it is so bad with him/her gone . . . ."

Do not misunderstand the intent of this writing. The grief process is most important, and each person must go through it after the death of the one he/she loved so dearly. But it is also important to *get on with living!* A new chapter in one's life now needs to be written. Reciting the story of death does not change the fact of that death. What it does do is to postpone expending energy in living today. This is not to say that one doesn't still have painful moments; but most persons alive have painful moments *and* "poor me" stories.

When I speak to a group of singles and have a talk-back time, if we seem to be getting into the "poor me" sharing, I request a moratorium on the "poor me" stories and say, "Let's assume we all have a 'poor me' story. Let's see where we can move with our lives because we have this starting point." Sometimes a ripple of applause bursts from some of the singles because they want to get on with living.

A pertinent passage in Catherine Marshall's book *To Live Again* is worth recalling at this point. "What then is the solution? It must lie somewhere in the realm of relationship. As solitaries we wither and die. We long to be needed; we yearn to be included; we thirst to know that we belong to someone. The question is . . . how can we achieve that sense of belonging?

"There is a price to be paid. The first tribute exacted is a modicum of honesty with ourselves. Do we so want to be rid of self-pity that we will allow ourselves no more wallowing in loneliness? How badly do we want to make connection with other people? Do we really want to find happiness again?

"In the light of honest answers to questions like those, suddenly we find that we do not ever need to be lonely, unless we choose to be. For there are always others eager to receive our friendship if only we will take the first step out of our solitary shell." [3]

A word of caution is necessary here for those who have moved past the "poor me" stories. Patience is of the utmost importance. Maintain respect for the "poor me" person. Do not lose sight of the fact that each person has to choose to work through this point. It is much better to love a person through it than to demand that he get past it.

God's Strength Must Be Relied On

4. The persons who excite and challenge me are the ones who recognize that God's strength is adequate for the moment. None of us can bear all the tensions, problems, dilemmas, or burdens at once. A mature comment from a widowed person might be: "This first Christmas is hard for us (the family that is still together). Some moments have really been rough, like when we were putting up the decorations, but I'm doing all right. We will make it, but we need your prayers. Keep praying that God will help us moment by moment."

One reason for the community of believers to work out a means of continuous caring for the widowed is that neither they nor the members of the congregation know when the low moments will be. When a natural contact is maintained, communication with caring persons is readily available.

Quality of Marriage Affects Adjustment

The kind of marriage the widowed had will make a difference in relational developments. For instance:

1. If the widowed person was free to be busy with hobbies or community activities, more than likely this tendency will increase. This is probably one of the most important rehabilitating aspects of the widowed situation. For example, my wife's mother is very good at needlepoint and sewing. Since her husband's death, she has made many beautiful items; and she is needed as a seamstress for our three daughters and my wife. She feels she is contributing to persons she cares about with a talent she has. She has an exceptional talent in making clothes that look great and are excellently tailored. Her hobbies caused her to get acquainted with persons in the area where she lives. She has begun to travel on her own. She feels free to go when and where she chooses.

2. If the widow/widower was already gainfully employed before the death of the spouse, this situation is most fortunate. The continuing level of responsibility can help the widowed person face persons and situations soon after the spouse's death so as to keep life in a more realistic perspective. The work situation provides an avenue of purpose and a livelihood that will probably be needed.

3. If the marriage had taken on a change due to a long illness of the spouse who died, there may be a sense of relief on the part of the widowed. Relief is not a bad feeling because the suffering is now

completed for the one who has died. There is also the relief from the physical strain of the widowed person. Many times the surviving spouse is near exhaustion and tends to get sick soon after the funeral.

In time this relief will show itself with some positive signs of life in the form of a new hairstyle, new clothes, some redecorating in the home, and perhaps some travel.

The Church Can Help with Emotional Struggles

What can the local congregation do to assist the widowed person?

The people of God in the local congregation can help these bereaved persons understand that every situation in life can make one *better* or *bitter*. The role of the single adult worker is crucial at this point. Hopefully, they will choose to go the *better* way. Bitterness repels people, but the betterness attitude tends to attract persons. Some insights of the *better* way, as I have learned them from widowed persons, are:

1. Trust God with who you are and all you have. God can help us change our attitudes about any dilemma in life.

2. Be thankful to God for everything. Thank God for this day in which to live. Christ never will allow us to be completely alone, for "Lo, I am with you alway" (Matt. 28:20).

3. Time alone is important. There is a great difference in being alone and lonely. When one is lonely there is too much time; but when one is creatively alone, time passes too fast.

4. Plan your schedule creatively. *Choose* to do what you do. Give yourself some alternatives to enhance your choices. Some persons, unfortunately, just wait to die.

5. Let flexibility be a part of your life pattern. Don't let life's circumstances control you; let your response to God control you and help you in the circumstances.

6. Continue to be the individual you are. "Don't let the world squeeze you into its mold," reads Romans 12:2 in the Phillips translation. Many people give advice as to how one *ought to* or *should* live. It is important that one seek to be who he or she is. So the widow/widower is "discovering self" at this point in life.

7. Continue to be a learner. There is nothing like the death of the spouse to jolt one into becoming aware once again that we are finite and that we have much to learn. It is interesting to note here that *disciple* means learner.

8. Happiness comes from within one's life rather than from out there

somewhere or with someone out there. Happiness is not intended to be a goal, anyway; it is to be a by-product. Waiting is not always a happy process; but if one waits for what he wants, happiness occurs.

9. Respond to God with your life. Any other approach to living will mess us up. God is the only adequate one who is worthy of our response. We need to respond to God so we won't spend our lives reacting to persons and circumstances around us.

The Church Can Help with Practical Struggles

The people of God in the local congregation can provide healthy, practical nurturing avenues. Any practical assistance given the widowed is part of caring. Some of the practical ideas now in progress through the church where I serve are:

1. Make available any legal aid or financial adviser as deemed necessary. The legal details that follow a death are quite extensive, and usually assistance is most appreciated. Some financial advice is also helpful.

2. If possible, encourage the widowed person to remain in the same living quarters for a period of time not less than three months and preferably more than one year. This advice helps the widowed person face the environment where his/her spouse was and deal with some emotional needs more quickly. It is also possible for one to move out early without thinking through the situation and later regret the move. It is better to stay a little too long than to leave too early.

3. Assume a long life ahead, and postpone parceling out material possessions to one's family. There seems to be a numbness of feeling soon after the funeral, and at times an "I don't care" attitude takes over. If not given good advice, the widowed person may act hastily and give everything away, then regret doing so later on.

4. Provide some healthy avenues of service through the church so the widowed person's need to give love is channeled in a good way.

5. Maintain a channel of communication to encourage participation with the single adult activities when widowed persons feel inclined to participate. Allow them the freedom of not participating, but maintain interest in their coming to the first event.

6. Give back the responsibility of caring to the deacons in the congregation. Help them shepherd this often-neglected group. Churches are very good at being responsive at the point of death and for the next four to six weeks. But the maintenance for this ministry needs to continue for a year or a year and a half.

Attitudes Show Up in Introductions

A singles ministry with widowed persons should help them at the point of their need, but they need to be treated as persons who happen to be widowed rather than always seen as widow or widower. We generally introduce married individuals as John and Mary Jones; but when it comes to Jack Smith we add, "You know, he lost his wife last year." It is possible that Mary Jones has remarried after the death of her first husband, but we seldom say, "This is John and Mary Jones. You know, she lost her husband three years ago."

It is good to relax in the presence of single persons and to know that introductions need only consist of their names.

5.
Single After Marriage—By Choice (Divorced)

Divorce is one of the most difficult issues the institutional church faces in ministering with single adults today. A question often asked in leadership conferences is, *What do you do with those who are divorced?*

At the outset of this discussion, it is imperative to review some attitudes that churches presently have toward divorce. I contend that churches minister to the divorced person in direct parallel with the *real* attitude (as contrasted with a *stated* attitude) of that particular congregation or denomination regarding remarriage.

It is my understanding that ministers generally view remarriage for a divorced person in one of four ways:

A No Answer to a Remarriage Request

First, some ministers opt for a simple no when informed that one or both potential marital partners has been divorced. This attitude was common among ministers until the 1960s. Since then many ministers have chosen to rethink their reasoning for such answers. A question remains, however: What kind of help is given to the divorced persons seeking guidance for marriage?

To say no is to eliminate, more than likely, any opportunity for ministry with those particular individuals. The end result for persons who have been divorced, whether remarried or not, is to seek spiritual nutriment elsewhere. In essence, the real attitude of the church shows up in the simple no of the minister; and the already limited ministry to persons who are divorced is then avoided. If the divorced person chooses to remain in a such a church, a second-class church citizen role is likely. One divorced mother, when married, was an active leader in the Woman's Missionary Union and a Sunday School teacher. This same person was asked to resign from her positions of leadership upon becoming divorced.

A Yes Answer to a Remarriage Request

Second, some ministers who do not want to be labeled closed-minded yield to an equally extreme position by opting for a simple yes when told that at least one of the engaged persons is divorced. This position or attitude tends to carry with it a compromise that says, "If I don't marry them, someone else will." This type of minister builds up a "marrying Sam" reputation. Marriage is too important to give so little respect to such a personal and holy covenant.

This lack of respect for marriage was apparently behind a conversation I had with a man who wanted me to perform his wedding within a week. I asked him why he had waited so long to get in touch with a minister. Had he just decided to get married? He said that he and his fiancée had been considering marriage for three or four months; but since the home they wanted became available at this time, they decided to go ahead and get married.

I told him that I required three premarital conferences with the couple (which I do not feel is enough). I would have to say no on the basis of the time element, but I would have been glad to visit with them if given more time. I later learned that this couple did get married, but the marriage lasted only three or four months. At other times, I have suggested that a couple go to a justice of the peace if they just want someone to make their marriage legal.

I do not totally blame couples who have these attitudes. I place much of the responsibility on ministers who have encouraged little or no dialogue with couples considering marriage. One of the most disheartening sights I have ever seen is the wedding chapel row at places such as Las Vegas. These places could not be in business if people didn't frequent them or if ministers would not be willing to perform marriages on such short notice. If we think so little of the marriage covenant, we should not be surprised at the alarming increase in divorces today.

Only as ministers lead churches to a more healthful approach to marriage can we see a turnaround in the current divorce trend.

An Individual Answer to a Remarriage Request

Third, some ministers are choosing to explore the attitudes and intentions of each couple who request marriage so as to give a yes or no response on an individual couple basis. Granted, the minister is limited in his own ability to discern the real intentions and the genuine honesty of the prospective bride and groom. It is certainly possible to be misled and to be misinformed.

If a person who desires to marry chooses to be dishonest with the one he/she is to marry, it is impossible to know of this dishonesty through counseling or relationship unless much time is given to both before the marriage. Some persons are very adept at getting what they think they want (for the wrong reasons) and, in the process, aid in destroying a relationship that could be much better if honesty were part of the courtship. Engaged persons run the risk of a lack of integrity on the part of their mate-to-be. Most marriages begin with trust and honesty and openness, but a few lack these ingredients and never really have a chance to make it.

Unless both persons *want* a quality relationship in the marriage, and unless both persons put forth the effort to see the quality come through, it is impossible for one of the two marriage partners to hold the marriage together indefinitely. Within some marriages, staying together means the emotional destruction of one or both persons. Divorce may be the only means to mentally healthy life again. This approach does not make divorce right—it may just be the better choice of the two.

One Solution: Premarital Counseling Sessions

It has been my practice to listen to a couple in three premarital sessions (each approximately one hour); and if I have had any clues as to problem areas, we have dealt with them. Some couples choose to break off the relationship after one or two sessions, and some wait until we are in the midst of the third session before deciding not to marry at the designated time. One couple was looking at the marriage ceremony with me in the third session when the man said, "We have decided to postpone our marriage for a year." His fiancée's astonishment was evident as she said, "We *what?*"

Needless to say, I, too, was surprised. Once again, however, I felt the importance of expressing a willingness to talk with couples with the understanding that if I, at any time, felt it unwise for me to be the minister in their marriage, I would tell them so. I thought that if I had said no, this couple might have been married by someone else; and the marriage might have lasted only for a season. Or if I had said yes and not required the three sessions, they would have married without seriously looking at some of the real issues in their relationship.

Hopefully, the congregation who encourages a serious look into marriage for every couple contemplating such a step will not take lightly any two persons' request for marriage—whether they are divorced or not.

The result of seeing marriage as for the mature only is a more realistic attitude toward all persons—including divorced individuals.

Is Divorce the Unpardonable Sin?

Divorce is a symptom of our sinful nature, which is the result of being disobedient rather than obedient to our Lord and Savior Jesus Christ. Divorce is wrong because it falls below God's ideal for marriage—for one man to be married to one woman for life. However, anything that falls short of glorifying God is sinful and wrong.

A faith stance is that God forgives sin for those who believe in his saving power to forgive and redeem them to walk in a new kind of life. Who are we, as God's children, to judge another man's servant? Responsible to his own master, he stands or falls (Rom. 14:4).

In Dwight H. Small's book *The Right to Remarry*, this statement is made in reference to divorce and remarriage: "This relationship in life is precisely like any other that is subject to failure; whatever falls short of the ethical ideal is subject to redemptive grace which holds the good of the individuals as its end." [1]

It is truly good news that the God who redeems can redeem a life caught in the unfortunate snare of divorce. Life for the divorcée is *not* over. Divorce is *not* the unpardonable sin. God can redeem lives for fruitful ministry. Why would it be more difficult for God to forgive and work through a divorced person than any other individual (an alcoholic, an embezzler, a drug addict, etc.)? Be certain that the divorced person likes divorce less than anyone else. I have yet to meet a divorced person who *believes* in divorce.

The Scars of Divorce Remain

A distinction needs to be made between God's forgiveness and the human seeds that have been sown in one's life. For God to forgive does not uproot the seeds already sown. The scars of divorce remain. The difference is in God's forgiveness and God's ability to sustain a life in the midst of all kinds of adversity. "Whatever a man sows, that will he also reap" (Gal. 6:7) is still valid. God doesn't eliminate the circumstances, but his grace is sufficient in the midst of the circumstances—no matter how difficult they may be.

As Dr. Small further indicates, "The justification for remarriage in God's sight must arise from the reality of grace. Remarriage is always related to the renewing grace of God, which meets a person in his or her failure and grants another chance. This is not only true of the 'innocent party,' but the 'guilty party' as well. For grace to be grace means that there is no intrinsic justification at all, no 'right' which enters the picture to guide our evaluation and action. It is not a matter of personal right, but of God's grace in Christ . . . the right to remarry is neither a personal nor an absolute right at all; it is granted, not by the creation orders, nor by the law of the Kingdom (of God), but only by the grace of a forgiving Lord. It is neither *granted* for any cause nor *not granted* for any cause; it is not related to cause at all. It is related only to grace." [2]

A Denominational Answer to a Remarriage Request

Fourth, some ministers choose to refrain from performing marriages involving divorced persons because of their denominational or institutional church position rather than on the basis of their own belief. In so doing, these pastors are saying yes but no. In pastors' meetings on this subject, several have said that they usually have a list of pastors who will perform such weddings. They may express the thought that after the couple is married, perhaps that couple will want to come back to the church that could not seal their marital vows.

It is time for ministers to take bold action regarding a church's theology on divorce and to begin to be more consistent with the New Testament concept of forgiveness in our practical ways of relating to persons.

Factors in Ministering to the Divorced

The growing numbers of church ministries with singles express the church's attempt to care for persons who are divorced. Therefore, some helpful insights to keep in mind when ministering to persons who are single due to divorce are:

Loss of Identity

1. Recognize that divorced persons often feel a sense of loss of personal identity. This attitude comes from several aspects of the traumatic upheaval divorce causes in one's life. (A) The divorced person already *had* an identity in his life that was assumed to be an identity

for the rest of his life. All of a sudden that identity, marriage, is gone. A new identity will have to emerge before health can return to the divorced individual. (B) The ego deflation that usually takes place in divorce can be devastating. To move from the "girl of my dreams" to rejection or "I don't love you anymore" is difficult to accept or cope with.

Low Self-Esteem

2. Realize that divorced persons often lack a feeling of self-worth or have low self-esteem. In counseling with divorced persons, I have found that one of the most important gifts I can give individuals is the gift of worth. To honor them or respect them as persons of worth when the person closest to them (the ex-spouse) has rejected them, I attempt to remind them that (A) all of *us* have sinned (in different ways) and fallen short of God's glory (Rom. 3:23); (B) no one is righteous, whether he has been involved in divorce or not (Rom. 3:10); (C) while we were yet sinners (whether through divorce or some other act of disobedience) Christ deemed us worthy; he died for us (Rom. 5:8); (D) for us to feel we have no worth (even to the point of contemplating suicide) is to deny God's gift of grace or, in essence, to say that Christ's death was not for me (Eph. 2:8-10).

Also, I feel that it is important to counsel with divorced persons to help them see that (A) their life is not over; (B) it is OK for them to dislike everything about divorce—so what are they going to do with their lives *now;* (C) any feeling they have is OK, but the important thing is what they do with the feelings they have. God created us as feeling persons, so feelings and temptations are not sin. The sin occurs in unacceptable responses to feelings and/or temptations. It is not a sin to be angry, for example, but we are not to let the devil take charge of our anger and use it for his purpose (Eph. 4:26-27).

Loss of Sexual Activity

3. Recognize that divorced persons have had a life-style (marriage) that included an acceptable sexual activity. This awareness should help leaders relate to divorced persons with more understanding and forgiveness. More understanding is needed in that sexual activity for the newly single person is not only still a need but has been a practice prior to separation and divorce. It is important for the leaders of singles to encourage a sexual abstinence or celibacy through choice. Often

individuals who are newly divorced become vulnerable to a soft shoulder or a sympathetic date.

To be emotionally empathetic does not mean that a date must be followed by a sexual involvement. Generally, the "I'll show you" or "I'm going to catch up with your playing around" adolescent attitudes do more harm to the individual who plays the games than to the ex-spouse, the aim of the revenge. The more broken relationships I become aware of, the more I see that sexual intercourse outside of marriage does not enhance a relationship. It does, in fact, tend to dull one's objectivity and limits one's freedom as a single person.

Many divorced women (actually, this statement would apply to any single woman, regardless of reason for single status) become emotionally and psychologically married to their lovers. These women are generally quite faithful, as if they were married. This situation can be explained in that many single women want to be married; and if they choose to respond to a man they respect enough to marry, they can easily become faithful to him emotionally and sexually before marriage.

It is important to add at this point that this insight comes from women who have suddenly realized that their relationship was not going in the direction they had hoped it would go. They also realized that they were emotionally married to the man they had been dating.

Forgiveness is needed because some divorced persons will disappoint themselves more than once. Leaders do not have to like what a person chooses to do with his life-style, but to ever look down on persons for doing anything that is contrary to God's will is to become self-righteous and be guilty of the same thing—sin. A leader is not the judge of another person. Both persons are subject to God's judgment, and both are recipients of Christ's forgiveness.

Rules and legal restrictions such as a simple *Don't* may keep some singles from sexual activity for a season; but love, acceptance, and forgiveness are much stronger means of encouraging divorced adults to postpone the physical and emotional involvement of sexual activity.

I might add here that sexual abstinence is not a popular approach with singles, even with some Christian singles; but it can, in the long run, prove to be the healthier approach. I know some Christian singles who have not chosen the abstinence route. And they are, in many ways, where they were spiritually a few years ago. They choose to save their lives from any needs now, and they can very easily lose their lives. On the other hand, I know some singles who are choosing to lose their lives for Christ's sake and the gospel's, and they are growing immeasurably (Matt. 16:24-26). Be certain that what eats on us will soon eat us up—unless we change.

Loneliness

4. Anticipate that divorced persons will sometimes be lonely. Loneliness is understandable in a man who had a dutiful wife. She may have been boring because she was so predictable, but she did everything a wife *should* do—cook his meals, care for the house, and wash his shirts, socks, and underwear. He misses her. He begins to think that she wasn't *that* bad after all. Also, loneliness is understandable for a woman who had a husband who took care of the income tax, car repairs, maintenance on the house, mowing the lawn, and who generally made most of the decisions as to where and when to take vacations and where to eat out.

It is also important to note here that many divorced persons get divorced too soon—but some not soon enough. Divorce is never right, but the lonely feelings that a person has for an ex-mate might have been avoided if some pride had been swallowed by one or both and if some efforts had been made by both persons toward constructive conversation. One couple felt that they communicated better during the process of divorce than during the marriage because they *talked* for a change.

Lonely people need more than the comfort of God's presence. They need the warm caring of concerned friends. And God's love helps friends care. One single said recently that her faith had been encouraged because some people took time to care for her in a practical way. She didn't feel *all alone.* Someone *did* care.

Need for Christian Companionship

5. Provide avenues for companionship. A married adult made an announcement in one of our single adult communities (departments) and noticed the warm hugs and gentle greetings given by the singles to their friends. He said, "You can really tell this is a single adult group." I said, "How can you tell?" His answer spoke volumes. He said, "You never see married adults greeting each other so warmly."

Single adults who are divorced need healthy companionship. They need to know that they have friends of both sexes who really care—people they can talk with. Companionship can provide some good physical touching that is not offensive, but therapeutic. Good companionship cares for the single person's need for community and family.

Decrease in Monetary Income

6. Recognize that divorce is costly in many ways but specifically in regard to money. The divorcée has recently been labeled "the new poor." The lack of money is no small matter with most divorced people. The erratic arrivals of child-support checks can put a household in a quandary. Some women discover as they enter the job market that the lack of employable capabilities limits their earning power.

Some couples on the verge of marital collapse do some adolescent things in relation to their financial situation. I spoke to one young couple who were making a last-ditch effort to remain together. A most recent flare-up in their stormy marriage was that the husband, being fully aware of the family needs (clothes for children and wife, settling overdue utilities bills) decided to spend six to seven hundred dollars on camera equipment. When asked why he had done this, knowing his family needs, he said he had always wanted a good camera and decided to get one. One could get the feeling from this situation that the husband felt tied down or not free; and rather than work through numerous relational problems, he demonstrated his attitude by spending money irrationally.

Another aspect of financial problems that accompany divorce is the fact that one of the persons in the divorce may have such low self-esteem that the other divorcing member tends to take advantage in financial and property settlement. The result is that one of the parties is debilitated in devastating ways.

Emotional Scars

It is difficult to help a couple who, over a period of time, have allowed their communication gap to widen beyond repair. There is usually much resentment, pride, lack of trust, genuine hurt, bad words, disappointment, hate, lack of hope for reconciliation, feeling of being wronged, and little or no mutual or individual effort to allow God to work in each life.

The fact is that the good news of Christ includes the divorced person, too. If a person is injured in an auto accident and has some deep flesh wounds, the wounded individual does not need a lecture on what should have been done to avoid the accident. The needs are more basic than that. The wounds need attention. Wounds take time to heal; and when a protective scab has formed, one can live in the illusion of being healed.

Yet when the scab is knocked or pulled off, the tenderness is revealed. A new scab will form to protect the tender area. As healing occurs, the scab will not be needed any longer, but will fall off when its usefulness is completed. The scar that remains from the wound is a reminder that the accident did occur. To remember the accident again and again is also to remember the pain; but as health returns, the pain lessens.

Any situation in life—divorce included—that inflicts an emotional or psychological wound on a person requires the process of time to heal the wound. There is a glimmer of hope that the churches are slowly responding to these healing needs and will become more skilled in caring for divorced persons in the next few years.

6.
Single But Not Single
(Separated)

Probably one of the most difficult groups of single persons to minister to is the single but *not* single group—commonly termed *separated.* Separated generally means that a couple is attempting to learn something about their relationship by living apart from each other. Usually this is a time for one or both of them to "get their heads together" or to sort out mixed feelings, disappointments, or changes in personal direction.

Persons who are separated are not all moving toward divorce. In fact, the concern that the church has for the separated individual needs to be broadened. There are several ways an individual can become a single, but *not* a single in today's world.

Separation that Leads to Divorce

The most common kind of separation is one that results in the dissolution of marriage. This separation generally occurs after the priority of the marriage relationship has been subordinated to some other priority. The communication has broken down because of the lack of effort exercised by one or both persons. Erosion of the marital relationship is allowed to increase the unity gap. In most cases a seemingly insurmountable wall is built, little by little, until both partners feel separated or isolated from each other.

In one writer's opinion, there are stages of divorce.[1] It seems that emotional divorce takes place while the couple remains in the same household. Following the emotional stage is the physical stage. During this second phase of divorce, the couple actually has a physical separation—one of them moves out. During the trial separation at least one of the parties may find it hard to believe that this is really happening to him/her. After a while it becomes more evident that reconciliation looks hopeless, and the couple enters into a legal separation. The legal separation has different legal ramifications according to the state one lives in or where any legal steps were taken.

For example, in some states a couple may set up a legal separation which would include visiting privileges and child support (if children are involved) and/or alimony; but neither partner is free to marry again until divorce papers have been filed and a proper waiting period has taken place. A person who has no intention or inclination to remarry may find the legal separation a convenient approach.

The final stage of separation, which is optional, is the legal divorce itself. From this point on the individual is a divorced person rather than merely separated from his spouse.

The Work-oriented Separation

One type of separation is the work-oriented separation. Some of the most common situations in this type are:

1. *Military status.*—Because of the assignment given the person in military service, the family is separated. For all practical purposes, the individual is single. He has the same concerns that single people have as to loneliness, child care without two parents around, sexual tensions, daily advice on the running of the household, an available escort for social gatherings, and numerous other needs within a one-parent family.

2. *Traveling businessman status.*—This type is more of a short-term separation, generally lasting no longer than three weeks. The absence could extend into months if the person is in construction or some overseas business endeavor. The danger of this kind of separation is that, at times, the conflicts that occur in most marriages (including healthy ones) may be heightened. For example, the businessman may use his schedule as an escape; his wife may be resentful of having to stay home.

3. *Sports, art, or media-related status.*—Some persons who are involved in a public-oriented business wind up with an imbalance of priorities due to the schedule of their particular trade. It is difficult for a superstar in pro football to remain at home on the West Coast if he plays for a team on the East Coast. It is certainly more advantageous for a family to remain in one place, to put down some roots, and to establish a semblance of normalcy—especially if children are involved. Often the growing public image of one of the married partners and the lack of fame of the other has an unhealthy effect on the marriage.

4. *Lack of work status.*—Loss of employment is, for some persons, devastating. Often one's pride takes over and a separation occurs even with persons living in the same household. A withdrawal from society can occur if one does not want to swallow his pride and risk "losing face." This situation may occur with a minister, a politician, a coach, a corporate officer, or a blue-collar worker.

5. *Involvement in potentially incarcerating work status.*—Unfortunately, some married persons choose types of work that are either hazardous to one's health or are dead-end streets for a continued livelihood. Specifically, persons who attempt to make quick money by embezzlement, fraud, robbery, narcotic sales, or involvement in any other type of illegal business are in effect planning separations from their spouses; they will likely receive prison sentences. Many of these persons are not involved in the church, but they do represent a portion of the separated individuals in our society.

The Health-oriented Separation

Another type of separation is *health oriented.* A person may be single but not single because of a sick spouse. The spouse may be physically confined because of a stroke which has left him incoherent and/or paralyzed; he may be the victim of some debilitating disease which is long term (ten to twenty years). He may be experiencing a slow deterioration of the body (as with cancer or some other physically sapping disease). Or one may be emotionally confined because of an inability to deal realistically with life. This confinement may take place at home or in a hospital. When one spouse is disoriented from life, the other partner usually finds it difficult to maintain the relationship. Suspicion and persecution become a part of the daily diet; and a healthy marriage is almost impossible to have without two healthy individuals.

The Background-oriented Separation

Still another kind of separation is caused by an extreme *lack of common backgrounds.* One example is the *language or cultural* difference. Marriages suffering from this type of strain were probably begun because of an out-of-wedlock pregnancy, loneliness in a foreign country, or an attempt to prove lack of prejudice with someone of another race or culture. Even though initially the marriage was OK for both partners, many differences may not have been resolved.

Another is the *religious difference.* Many persons feel that when they marry, the differences they have do not seem very big. They are sure that they can combat any problem. They are too naive, too idealistic, or both. If a couple will not seek guidance before they get married and repress or deny differences in their relationship, they are probably in for some rough sledding in their marriage.

Helping Separated Persons Within the Church

What can the church do to assist the single but not single person?

First, recognize that separated persons exist within your church. The tendency for most churches, in dealing with such persons, is to assist with the problem in the marriage—but to forget that the separated person has needs too. Also, many times a church tends to assist only one of the marriage partners in a separated situation. Both persons need help.

Second, relate to the situation individually to meet specific needs. No two situations are alike, even though similar in description. At one point in our single adult ministry I became aware of about ten situations involving separated persons. I wrote these persons notes saying that I wanted them to meet each other because they were at similar points in their lives. I set a 12:00 noon until 2:00 P.M. meeting on Friday. Many persons can make arrangements with their employers to extend their lunch period for certain kinds of appointments. I encouraged them to tell their employers that they were having a conference with their minister.

Six to eight persons came the first time and were amazed to find that they were not alone in their feelings. At first, the one man who came received the brunt of all the hostility the women felt from their own situations; and the women received a little of the hostility the man felt. My role became that of a referee or of one who attempted to remind each person that no one in the room had been the cause of the feelings he was having. Everyone had had those feelings before coming to the group.

After the second week of our being together, the man suggested that we meet in each other's homes and share a common meal. He volunteered to be the first host. He prepared a terrific meal, and the walls came tumbling down. We met only about five times because the group didn't seem to be needed anymore.

Most of these individuals have married again (not their former mates) and are having healthy relationships in their marriages. They seemed to have found something precious within the group: A person could be accepted as he was in his single state and was allowed to feel any way or think anything he chose—then he was free to be a person again. Everyone needs personal affirmation in order to be personally healthy.

Third, expect changes to occur in the separated person's life. Do not assume that the person will remain at one particular attitudinal level. Too often a tendency in relationship is to label an individual one way, such as insecure or ego deflated, and to assume that he will remain there. It is difficult to assist a person who is in a state of transition if we place a permanent label on him. Trust that God's Spirit can and will change persons.

Fourth, maximize the sources of help already present in the church. Recognize that the Sunday School class where the individual is already involved is probably the greatest avenue for assistance the church can have—especially if the single but not single person has been involved in the class for some time.

Helping Separated Persons Outside the Church

If, however, the separated individual has not been a part of the church or a class in the church, some special considerations may be employed.

1. If the separated individual is moving toward divorce, all attempts to provide counseling for both persons should be made. Friends need to be persons of courage and speak up so as to help at the point of need rather than remaining silent until divorce occurs.

If I become aware that any of my friends are encountering marital difficulties, I will initiate conversations with them on my own. I recall one incident with a friend who lived in a neighboring city. I learned from a student that my friend was having marital problems and was about to get a divorce. I couldn't believe it, but was so concerned about it that I called him. He was shocked that I thought divorce could happen to him and that such a rumor had gotten to me. He said that possibly someone at his place of business was having marital difficulties and that the rumor about him could have been confused. After a while he was able to thank me for coming directly to him. We tried to anticipate where the rumor would next travel and to squelch it immediately. I was relieved at the outcome; it had been hard to initiate this kind of conversation with a good friend.

In another situation, I called a friend and told him that I had heard of some marital problems he and his wife were having. I said I didn't want to know any details but wanted to offer my friendship. If it would help for Bobbye and me to come see them (they lived over one hundred miles away), we would come at our own expense; or if either or both of them wanted to come and stay with us for a few days, we would welcome them. We wanted to respond to their situation in a helpful way. The husband expressed genuine gratitude for our caring enough to call, and he said he would let us know if he felt there was anything we could do. After concluding the conversation, I felt that my attempt to help had been one sided; so I called his wife and expressed the same desire to help. My concern was for both persons.

2. If low self-esteem is evident, the single but not single person needs to develop some new friendships with persons who have experienced the same feelings and have worked through them. One of our best sources of help to the separated person comes from our single adults themselves. I ask the separated individual's permission for another single adult (who usually has been separated from his spouse) to call him. After getting an OK, I ask one of our single adults (of the same sex as the troubled person) to get to know this person. Usually this step is well received by both persons because the single adult recognizes how far he has come in accepting his own self-worth; and the separated individual is suddenly aware that others have lived through this kind of traumatic situation.

Ground Rules for Fellowship

If the separated person desires fellowship with single people before his divorce, some specific ground rules are in order.

When one is not free to marry, one is not free to date. It is unhealthy for either person in a dating relationship to not yet be single. I have seen unfortunate situations in which one of the two persons was not free to marry, but felt strongly for the person he was dating. The single person wanted to get married and was just living for the day when the divorce would be final.

Generally, when the divorce became final for the separated adult, his new freedom became important to him. Getting right back into marriage seldom became the most feasible alternative. The result usually was a breakup, and an emotional or psychological divorce took place in the life of the single adult in the twosome. I have seen this happen over and over again. Dating should be reserved for persons both of whom are free to get married. If one is not free to marry, the other person cannot trust his words, even though the person is as sincere as he knows how to be. This statement cannot be stressed too much. Anyone can confuse "I love you" with "I need somebody to love me and to let me know I am worth loving."

When one is not free to marry, he should inform others of his separated status. This is not a popular stance to take, but it is a healthy stance. When a person is frequenting a single adult group, the other members assume that he is single. It is unfair to the person requesting the date to assume that the separated individual is single, only to learn later that he is not yet single. It is much better for the separated individual to thank the person asking for a date and say that he plans to begin dating after December 1 (or whatever date the divorce is final).

When one is not free to marry, he is probably vulnerable to attention from persons of the opposite sex. When a separated individual has been unable to have sex relations with his spouse for a long time, he tends to have a bottled-up sexual need. Unfortunately, some single adults are aware of this need and make it their practice to help relieve these tensions. I have cautioned persons about this tendency; and within a brief span of time they have called me and have been overwhelmed with how quickly these cautions moved from academic speculation to aggressive reality. What often surprises the separated individual is that he could so easily become interested in another person. My observation is that the separated individual feels the need to love, to be loved, and to be accepted by another human being; and he often mistakes those feelings for a love for another human being.

When one is not free to marry, all heterosexual encounters and conversations need to be in group settings and never in one-to-one settings. It is always OK to develop friendships, but friendships should be maintained in group situations. Generally it is best to postpone offers of transportation in a one-to-one situation until one is free to marry. Also, requesting that one's friends be present so the separated person can be with the single person (as if on a date) is unfair. One should not use friendships in such a manner.

Rewards of Ministering to Separated Persons

I assume that some of this information is surprising to some and repulsive to others. Some can probably respond with a resounding amen. The intention of such matter-of-factness is to guide our churches into a more realistic ministry with all persons who are single but not single.

One separated single adult sent me a quote and said, "You have been this kind of pastor to me. Thank you" The quote read:

> Do not talk to me of sin when I have sinned; talk to me of hope when I confess. Do not shame my shame-filled mind, and thrust me deeper into loneliness; show me the way and give me strength, to stand again and walk with confidence. When I am angry let me vent my hate, to free my burdened feelings from the barbs that penetrate my soul, my heart, my hope and joy. When I am lonely and feel sorry for myself, when the devils of my lesser self arise, do not rebuke but wait patiently, and do not think me only a coward; a stronger self will soon arise, the heated moments soon will pass, and pass more quickly then by far, because you wait in trust and listen through the gloom. You hope, you smile, you nod; you suffer, too, with me. Surely then your waiting and your patience is of God; no mortal man can know these things alone, no mortal touch alone can heal.[2]

7.
Considerations for Beginning a Single Adult Ministry in the Local Church

On a Sunday evening recently, two single adults from a small church in a nearby city visited our Sunday-evening single adult discussion. The next day one of these ladies called me and inquired about the single adult activities for her age group in our church. I shared several possibilities that might be interesting to these two persons. She indicated that they (she and her friend) would visit the next Sunday.

She mentioned to me that her church didn't sponsor any activities for singles. It seemed to her that the singles in her church were fifth wheels, in the way, or not really wanted. She and her friend had attempted to get the singles together, but they didn't feel good about what they had done. I asked her to tell me about it. She said that she and her friend contacted eleven persons. Only two out of the eleven showed up, and the small number really disappointed her. I asked, "You mean you and your friend got two more to join you?" The answer was yes.

I commented that four may be a good response and that it represented a 100 percent increase, which very few groups could accomplish. It certainly was not too large a number to get acquainted with, either. I could tell, however, that her feelings of failure could not be removed by my choosing to look for optimistic aspects of her leadership attempts.

On the basis of this illustration, let's see what advice would be helpful to this lady if she chose to stay where she is and begin a single adult ministry in her church.

Becoming Aware of Single Adult Members

One of the first suggestions I would give any church desiring to begin a singles ministry is to become aware of *all* potential church members who are single (regardless of reason for single status). If there are eleven persons to begin with, as many of them as possible can look through the entire church roll for other singles. Generally, 20 percent to 30 percent of the adult membership in most churches will be single.

In one of our older married adult departments (Sunday School) 80 percent of the members are single. Most of these persons are well pleased with their location in our Sunday School because they have established friendships; but some have said that if we had a singles group for their age, they would like to be a part of our ministry. At this point we have not begun a sixty-five-and-older single adult group. We do have groups up to age sixty.

Close examination of the church records will reveal a number of single persons already interested in the programs of that church. Some of the persons who are eligible for the singles ministry may be former college students who have moved back into the community, persons who are listed on married-adult rolls but who are divorced or widowed, or persons whose children are on the church's rolls but who do not attend the church. Once this list has been completed, the efforts to begin a ministry with singles has begun.

Determining the Organization of the Group

Another consideration is to determine the need for a singles group or groups, according to the age variance of the available single persons. For example, if the ages tend to fit into an under thirty (age) crowd and an over forty-five (age) crowd, perhaps it would be appropriate to start two classes. It is also possible to begin both classes in one department. If only four or five persons from each group come, that would be an excellent beginning. Remember, reaching all available persons is not necessary to succeed. If I went fishing and caught only eight to ten fish out of a school of forty to sixty fish, I would not feel I had failed. Too often certain imposed expectations tend to slow the progress of a group. It is easier to get to a deeper level of fellowship with a smaller group, anyway.

Discussing the Expectations of the Group

Still another suggestion is to get these single persons together for a discussion about the possibilities for a single adult ministry. I have found that one workable idea is to invite all single persons to an informal discussion built around a meal (at a restaurant or a covered-dish supper in a home). By bringing dishes for the meal, they become involved.

Find out what these single adults feel they need from a single adult group in the church. Your question might be, "What does a single adult ministry need to have in it for it to include *me?* " Basically, the request is to get to the heart of individual needs and hopes of the singles present at the discussion.

Here is a good example of a group desiring to begin a single adult group in their small city. The single adults from the First Baptist Church announced through their local newspaper that any single adult who was interested in fellowship with other single adults was welcome to come to the local steak house at the corner of Main and First Streets for a meeting. The meeting was open to all persons, regardless of their church affiliation or their reason for single status. Persons interested were instructed to go through the serving line and to gather in the room reserved for the single adult meeting. The article indicated that Britton Wood, Single Adult Minister, would share ideas about beginning a single adult group.

The room was set up to take care of about thirty-five persons. By the time I got up to speak, there were some sixty persons packed into the room. There was an air of expectancy and much conversation about the feelings each one had before coming. I shared briefly my philosophy of ministry with singles and some of the needs I felt singles had in common. The remainder of the meeting included ideas that the singles shared in and plans for the second meeting the next month.

The singles who initiated this meeting on faith and with prayer rejoiced over the response and the attitudes of the persons who came. This group demonstrated the real need in communities everywhere, of any size, for single adult groups.

Some of the responses singles have given when asked what the organization should include are fellowship with other singles; a chance to develop friendships that do not include the dating pressures; some good, practical Bible study that relates to life; something to do; opportunity to grow as Christians; a group to bowl with, travel with, eat with, go to the theater with; and numerous other concerns. Most requests could be included under the broad headings of Christian fellowship, Christian growth, and activities with Christian friends.

A Practical Example of Analyzing Expectations

At a single adult leadership workshop, I was asked to lead a conference entitled "Utilizing Single Adults in the Church." I was delighted that a workshop had been scheduled. It was one more expression of the growing openness of church leaders in that particular locality.

As I began my conference I asked the participants, who were single adult leaders from the various churches in the area, to share with me what the title of our conference meant to them. They responded by saying that it meant to channel the talents of the singles; to motivate singles to be involved in the church; to show that singles are normal, average members (not freaks) like everybody else (married); and to help the singles in their churches to build a growing singles community.

I found their reactions to the topic very hopeful and kind. In responding to the topic, I assumed an attitude many churches have taken with singles. I chose to assume that the word *utilizing* meant using—which I feel too many churches have done through the years with the few willing singles who have been active in the church. To use single adults to the point of taking them for granted ("You can always count on ole Jim; he's always there") is to not respect or to adequately care for the singles.

I interpreted the words *single adults* in the topic as being the untapped financial and numerical resources of the church. The idea is almost as if the single adults are the new market for the church. How can we increase our offerings and our attendance? Just start a single adult program. My genuine hope is that single adult ministries are begun out of a need for God within the singles themselves. To be sure, ministering to singles will yield a return; but may it be a plus factor rather than the justifying reason for the ministry.

The last three words of the topic, *in the church*, seemed to me to relate to the way churches usually feel about themselves. Most churches assume that the church is composed of families, with little regard for the fact that singles do not generally relate to that concept because they understand the church to mean "four-cornered families" (a husband, a wife, a son, a daughter).

Once again I feel it is important to state that I see the church as composed of one-adult family units (singles) and two-adult family units (married persons). Both have equal access to God through Christ, and both have equal responsibility for being the people of God—whether they happen to be single or married.

Some Basic Needs of Singles

Single adults come to a particular church out of specific needs. It is important to review some of the basic needs a single adult has even before he gets involved in a singles group through the church.

First, single adults desire *acceptance.* The information given out about singles in apartment complexes and townhouses would cause one to assume that singles are all swingers. Many singles choose not to fit in to the single's bar, complex mixers, or poolside meat market approach to life, in which one finds a partner for the evening. It is very possible that what this type of person really wants is acceptance; but he is consistently disillusioned because the hunger for acceptance remains unquenched with the advertised "good life" approach.

Acceptance can never come from other persons unless there is an inward acceptance of self. The Christian faith is in the "business" of introducing persons to the Adequate One, who accepts us fully and forgives us for *all* we have done that keeps us from meriting his acceptance. We are accepted by God any way we are. He will take us where we are and help us move to our best level of personhood.

Second, self-worth is an important ingredient in a healthy personhood. Failure in a marital relationship tends to cause a person to feel insecure about all of life and himself. The loss of the feeling of self-worth usually develops. Sometimes a person who has been secure in a college environment or in living at home feels a lack of self-worth as he ventures into the working world.

Too often persons seek to gain self-worth through material possessions, success in business, or an active personal engagement schedule, and miss the fact that only God through Christ gives us worth.

Third, combating loneliness is a real need of single adults. Many singles feel they have a corner on the market of loneliness; but it is a concern for almost every human being, whether married or single. However, loneliness often consumes the alone time of many singles. The result is that many singles seek to eliminate loneliness through some unwise methods.

A single adult ministry cannot eliminate loneliness, but it can help singles communicate in an accepting fellowship that they are, at times, lonely. Just getting this bottled-up feeling out can help some. Of course, the fear is "What will they think of me now that I've revealed my feelings?" More than likely the response is "You feel that way, too? I thought I was the only one who felt that way."

Fourth is the need of relationship or *companionship.* Every person needs good friends who accept him and feel he is a person of worth.

Unfortunately, some single adults are so hungry for companionship that they do desperate things to attempt to be in touch with another human being. One very attractive single in her late twenties was so much in need of companionship that she paid several hundred dollars just to join a club where she could meet people. Even though she was more than adequately attractive, she felt she needed showy cosmetics and unusual clothing to make her more attractive. I sensed in her a lack of self-worth and a fear of venturing into a singles group for fear of rejection. The result was that she bought her way in, like all the other members of that club. She remained disappointed.

The nonthreatening fellowship of a single adult ministry can be good for many individuals who have this need for companionship. It can be one of the most exciting aspects of a single adult ministry. I have known shy persons, who very much needed the fellowship of a group, slowly relax and become some of the most outgoing, dynamic leaders I have ever seen.

Fifth, contrary to the public image of singles, *money* is a real need of singles. Young singles getting started in their jobs usually have an enormous outgo of money compared to a limited income. Sometimes idealistic planning, as opposed to realistic budget planning, causes some difficult times in honoring obligations. Generally, a person does not plan for the unexpected emergencies such as major car repairs (is there such a thing as minor car repairs today?), lengthy illness, loss of job, or a poor investment or loan to an acquaintance.

The single adult ministry can lead some discussions on how to budget and can encourage the singles community to become realistic about money. Leaders can also assist singles in valid ways such as buying groceries, helping a single move to a less expensive place to live, or aiding with specific expenses such as hospital bills, rent, utilities, or some other real need. It is important to care for these needs in such a way as to enhance rather than diminish the dignity of the person(s) assisted.

Sixth, since many single adults are parents, *assistance with children* represents a real need. Some parents have shared with me that, at times, they resent their children very much and wish they didn't have any in their home. These same single parents can also talk of the beautiful things their children do that make the trouble and effort worthwhile.

Some of the most beautiful meetings I have been in have involved single parents. We have had family camping trips with our single families; Christmas programs in which the children performed their talents; picnics; and ice-skating, roller-skating, and swimming parties. The nonparent singles enjoyed these events because they were able to see that they could respond to children and that children would respond to them. They were able to give some healthy love expressions to some children who needed some healthy love expressions.

Not long ago I was sitting in the snack-bar area of our church, and two daughters of two of our single parents walked by. As the eight-year-old came by me, I spanked her (not hard) and said, "Thank you; I feel so much better now that I've spanked someone today. Come here and let me spank you again so I can feel even better." She came close to me, and I spanked her with the same hardness (or lack thereof). I said, "Oh, that is so much better." Then her little friend came over close to me, and I spanked her. I said, "Thank you" and they went on to get their candy.

I went back to my conversation with the persons I was sitting with, but I could not take my mind off the fact that such a simple exchange with those girls could mean that someone cared enough to notice them. I, in my way, affirmed their presence. They had not sought affirmation, but they got it anyway. I will add that I had related to both of them before that moment. My behavior was not out of character with my relationship to them.

I have had children of singles ask me, in front of their mothers, if I could be their daddy. My answer has been, "I already am a daddy to three girls. I would like to be your friend. Could we be friends?" They say, "OK."

Seventh, what a single adult chooses to do regarding *physical sex relations* is certainly a concern. For a single adult ministry to ignore this issue is to play ostrich and not to face a real issue. The emphasis need not major on "to have sex relations or not to have sex relations," but should emphasize the fundamental truth that all persons are created in God's image; all are created as sexual beings; all have a choice to respond to God or respond to self; and all are created as persons of unity in that what we do in part affects our whole person.

A single adult minister needs to move from the "sex and the single adult" approach to the idea of "being a healthy sexual person." This goal cannot be reached if one speaks with closed-minded judgment or a condoning spirit. It can only happen when we realize that we need to work toward the ideal of sexual purity in the midst of imperfect living. Love the persons who choose to live differently from the ideal without approving of the practice that differs with the biblical teachings.

Eighth, single adults want to learn of *God's will* for their lives. Many may have thought several times that they had discovered God's will. Too often any shaking of our securities, whether it be our marriage, our vocation, our friends, or our health, causes us to reject doing or desiring to do God's will. We need to learn that God works in the midst of our circumstances, whatever they happen to be, rather than making the bad things happen to us. We can learn a lesson in some tragic or near-tragic event, but we learn because we are open to learn. This truth does not mean that God causes hardship to teach us a lesson. We need to come to the place where the psalmist was when he said, "I delight to do thy will, O my God" (40:8). Only then can we enjoy the will of God.

Organizing a Ministry to Meet Singles' Needs

Another consideration closely follows the point of determining the needs of the singles. Organize your singles group in a simple way so as to meet their desired and stated needs. Probably this is one of the most important insights to catch. Sometimes groups come up with some stated needs and seek to build too fast. Going too fast is like going to the cafeteria and getting everything you want, only to learn that your stomach won't hold all that your eyes found appealing.

It is important that a new singles group have some mild successes. Each time a planned event goes well, the group is encouraged. Projects can backfire, however. Sometimes one strong leader in the group pushes through an idea to the point of becoming chairperson for that event. The group lets the leader go with it; and only when the event comes about does the leader learn that the group didn't want the event. The leader gets upset because so much effort has been put into the event and usually sees the lack of response as a vote against him. Instead, all the group did was say by lack of response, "This is not an event we want right now." Unfortunately, a lack of assertiveness on the part of several members allowed the event to take place. The group might have said to the leader, "You may want us to have this event, but we really don't want it. Could we use your idea at a later date?"

Let the group of singles, as a group, lead out in all that is done. In essence, trust the single adults to be the church that happens to be single and to take responsibility for what they feel is important to help them be the church. I have found that the more I trust our singles to be the church, the more responsibility they assume because they are enjoying being the church.

Styling Your Ministry According to Your Singles

One consideration for beginning a single adult ministry is to style your ministry around the unique needs and abilities of the singles you have. The singles in your church may not have interests in the areas some church leaders feel they should. It is important to give the singles time to grow. Don't demand certain results from them. They don't need someone else's standard of success because they don't need another failure or a feeling from the two-adult-family church that singles are unequal. Allow singles to move at their own pace (much slower, at times, than you want them to move); and in time they will outrun or run equally with the leadership. Once the single adults genuinely feel that what happens is *really* up to them, they will respond in a grand way to God and to the responsibility of being the church.

Changing Traditional Patterns When Necessary

Singles need a different organizational approach from the type that works with married adults. In many churches, the feeling is that the same organizational structure works with all adults. Some married adults might say, "It meets our needs; why isn't it good enough for the singles?"

One difference is that single adults seem to prefer the six-month officer time span, whereas many married adults think little about a year's responsibility. In our single communities (departments), the term of office is six months. Seldom do I hear any complaints about the length of one's term of office. In fact, the most complaints I've ever heard occurred at the point of allowing a person to repeat for a second term in the same office. The change is good for everybody. It gives new life to the office and encourages the person who has led for six months to be open to other possibilities. Much more will be said regarding leaders in chapter 10.

The Program-to-People Approach

Religious educators generally use two basic approaches in working with single adults. One method is the *program-to-people* approach, which is most commonly chosen. Using this approach, an educator can plan a full program *for* singles in a relatively short time. A program planned *for* singles usually has to draw from resource persons outside the singles group. Speakers or entertainers are scheduled by the educator to draw a satisfactory number of singles to the meetings. The hope in this approach is that the singles will eventually take over more of the responsibility for the events.

One of the reservations I have with this approach is that the early events bring in more singles than the existing nucleus can handle. Suppose there is a core group of five to twenty-five singles. If, after the first two meetings, there are thirty to one hundred singles, then the spirit of the original group is lost in the overnight growth pattern. On the other hand, if there had been a negative attitude in the original group, then the new community may be better for the church.

Another reservation is that the singles available to minister with the new singles have limited time for growth opportunities. Two drawbacks to this approach are the physical limitations and endurance of the educator himself. One such educator, who has been quite successful in this approach, asked me how I ever found time for my family. I responded by saying that I never planned anything *for* our singles; we only did what they *really* wanted to do. If the singles wanted to see the activity work, then they made it work because it was theirs from the beginning.

The People-to-Program Approach

The second approach is the *people-to-program* style. Instead of centering on planning programs first, this method encourages time with the single people. After we learn from the singles what their needs are, planning discussions are held. The singles feel they can say anything about any idea. If they don't feel that a certain event is practical or needed, we move to another idea to determine if it fits into the thinking of the group. I continually remind our singles that we need to respond to God in our choice of ministry ideas. If we don't *need* to do something, let's not do it.

The people-to-program method is much slower in developing than the program-to-people method. However, it is a steady growth approach; and it is handleable in the sense that there is an adequate number of caring single persons for new persons coming into the program.

The intent of our singles ministry has been to let the unique spirit or caring fellowship develop within each of our single adult communities. Also, we have encouraged whatever leadership needs the community of singles had to be allowed to emerge as the group changed and new needs came into their awareness.

Keeping in Touch with the Singles

It would be unfair to my style of ministry to omit one important factor. My greatest resource for knowing what directions we need to take in our ministry with singles is continual conversation with the singles themselves.

In my first meeting with about twenty singles at our church at least four months before I came to our church, I listened to their needs before I made any response. After listening to each of these single adults, I said, "I know nothing about working with single adults . . . at Park Cities Baptist Church because I do not know any of you. I do not bring a program with me. I come with some insight and some understanding of persons who are single, but I have no program for you. I come only to get to know you. And after getting to know you, I want to work with you in ministering in this place."

This kind of statement was for me a freeing word. I was free to be me in relation to each of these single adults. The ministry God would want us to have would occur. I was also free from having to be a man with all the answers. I came to help shoulder the needs and concerns. And God has blessed our singles ministry. Most of our singles feel that our ministry has been a godsend in their lives; and many of them see that we have a long way to go. We all regret the fact that we have not ministered to some singles who needed a ministry.

8.
A Growing Single Adult Ministry Thrives on Flexibility

A growing single adult ministry is always changing. Flexibility is an imperative for a developing ministry. Unfortunately, some persons feel that to set up a certain format and to keep it that way brings security or establishes the program.

Exercising Flexibility in Singles Groups
In one of our single adult communities, which had taken about a year and a half to gain some health in organization and spirit, fifteen persons married within a two- to three-month period. Seven of these couples had met in the group, and one single was marrying someone who was not in the community. Most of the persons getting married were leaders of the group. The spirit of the group changed upon their departure, and no wonder! The group remaining was in a state of shock. They anticipated some change, but they didn't realize how much had been accomplished by those who had gone to married adult classes.

Efforts were made to continue some of the same activities and programs already begun, but the response was not as good. I began to hear statements such as these: "Our group is just not the same." "What's wrong with our group?" "Nobody wants to do anything." "No one comes to anything anymore." "Something's missing."

Most of their concerns about the group were valid. It *was* different. The spirit *had* changed. Trying to carry on with a group that really wasn't the same was difficult work. What we needed was some time to heal without losing a spirit of "all things are possible." When a group becomes vulnerable as this group was, opportunists can come along and destroy what was already there. We needed for several of those who had been followers to become leaders. What did happen was that some new members who were strong willed and vocal came in; and the followers allowed them to become leaders, at least in a vocal way. A period of disruption followed, and some members chose not to return to the group.

The group almost died. In working with them, we tried several combinations of events, leaders, and teachers. Persons in the group wanted it to grow, but seemed to be upset with their good friends who had married and left them. The singles who remained were the logical leaders; but no one who should have led the group, on the basis of insight and rapport, would assume the responsibility.

I knew of only one solution . . . patience. In time, the strong but critical leadership would tire of its unsuccessful attempts to "whip" the group into shape. Eventually, the followers would realize the importance of this community or fellowship in their lives and would begin to do something about what was *not* happening. Both occurred.

The group dwindled drastically in number, but that should have been expected on the basis of what was taking place on Sunday mornings. The leaders tired of a group that wasn't going to do anything. The followers began meeting for lunch, going to social events together, having covered-dish suppers together, sharing life concerns, and praying together. The basic difference was that this fellowship was outside any organized group. Eventually, it dawned on some of the persons within that fellowship that they were all members of the Sunday School group that "wasn't doing anything." Why didn't they (who up to now had been followers) bring this good spirit and simple organization into their Sunday School group?

They did; and fresh leaders (two of the fifteen who had married from the group) were secured. The group is now at an all-time high in health of spirit and concern and is open to growth. Guests come to visit, and they come back. Several have joined the group. A group that was pessimistic and small is now cheerful and composed of persons who are exciting to know.

This story illustrates what I mean by flexibility. Allowing a group to hammer out what it needs to do is most important. God has never called me to be the church *for* the singles, but to assist them in being and becoming the church. They must have the freedom to fail and to still be loved and accepted. When a community of singles is free to be who they really are—warts and all—there is a warmth of spirit that is contagious.

Flexibility in General Group Situations

Personally, I experienced this full acceptance in a healthy community at different points in my life with different kinds of groups. One experience I remember in particular occurred with my campus minister colleagues. We were at a beautiful retreat setting. Our group sessions had been stimulating and informative.

We had moved past conversations related to our personal financial limitations, health problems, and considerations of possible vocational changes. We were duly challenged in our sessions to be complete campus ministers, those who excel in relationships with students, faculty, university administration, pastors and members of churches in the campus community, and leaders in our state denominational office. All of these insights had given us a kind of unity of concern. We all recognized our need for one another.

On the third day of the retreat we had some free time in the afternoon. Several of us (ten or twelve) decided to go on a hike in the rugged hill country of Texas. We laughed and told jokes for the first twenty to thirty minutes. At that point we stopped to visit with another friend who lived on the property. When we left him after a brief visit, we seemed to be sharing more of our honest feelings. When one would share a deep concern, the other group members strove to hear him well, to respond to him, or to allow another to respond. Our camaraderie grew, and we walked around for at least two hours.

Finally, we were near our rooms. We just stood together, talking and laughing and not wanting to leave the presence of the group. However, our biological necessities were trying to communicate to us, too. One person said, "Time! We all need to go to our rooms, but none of us wants to leave this terrific fellowship. Let's have a silence pact and meet here in ten minutes." All of us were back within the time frame, and we moved spontaneously into smaller groupings of three to five men per group. We continued to talk until time for our next session.

Keys to Group Flexibility

I learned much from that afternoon walk which could relate to groups of singles within the institutional church.

First, we wanted to be together. Each one of us wanted to be where we were at that moment. We chose that situation to be our first priority for that period of time. Since it wasn't planned ahead, we could have very easily missed this experience. Before a community of singles can grow, they have to *want* to be together. We learned we wanted to be together by sharing common concerns that did not involve too much personal risk. Unfortunately, some persons predetermine how things will be in a group before getting with that group. In essence, they decide prior to being with certain persons that they are not going to like them or that the people will not like them. So they don't go.

Second, we had a common identity. In our case, we were all campus ministers. We were all imperfectly following God's will in our lives. Our sharing had brought our awareness level of each other to a point of vulnerability. We hurt in similar ways, but we were able to laugh *and* cry. In a singles group, each person has an identity that is similar to that of all other singles—regardless of the reason for single status.

Third, we continued to have a hilarious time together. A sense of humor, in my opinion, is basic to personal health. Often people take themselves so seriously that they are not free to see the humor in a given situation. In my marriage with Bobbye, we have been able to laugh with each other from the beginning of our relationship. We still see much humor in our lives together. In fact, Bobbye gets more mileage out of anything funny or humorous than anyone I know. At times Bobbye laughs so long that our daughters and I get tickled at her laughing. Laughter is contagious and much better therapy than any attitude that does not encourage laughter.

It is important to remember that our laughter needs to be *with* persons and not *at* them. Christ died for all of us, and no one of us should seek to be funny at the expense of another person.

Fourth, we left our masks in our rooms. Often persons who want to be accepted attempt to be someone else who seems to be more acceptable. During our walk together that afternoon, we said what we thought; and we were accepted.

Some single adults want so much to be accepted in a group that they sit silently and brood about what response they could have made to this statement or that statement. They mentally kick themselves because they ended up being silent. Then they leave frustrated, and others wonder why that person didn't like them. Being yourself in a group is generally worth the risk. A person is usually awkward the first time he ventures into new territory or attempts to be himself in new ways.

The *fifth* insight is the most difficult to accept. After the retreat I thought to myself, *Never again can this experience happen.* It is history and never to be re-created. Many persons seek a certain feeling. They are always disappointed because it is never available. I have known people who went on retreats because the last one was so great or who are disappointed in a revival or some other religious gathering because "I just don't *feel* the same as last time."

We can never *bank* on the return of a feeling we once had. We don't need *that* feeling now. We did need that spiritual experience when we had it. However, we can *build* on every experience. Our *new* experiences would not be possible without our previous ones.

Consider a bricklayer building a home. The first day he works, he is able to place five levels of bricks on the foundation. Suppose he comes to work on the second day and says, "My, what a nice house I have built!" We would consider him mistaken because the house is not finished until all the bricks have been laid. Each brick laid follows the pattern of the previously laid bricks. When the home is completed, one sees the completed structure rather than the individual bricks. Because each brick forms a progressive structure, each is necessary to make the parts a whole.

Flexibility in Group Relations

If we concentrate on the relationships in our organization, we continue to meet the needs of singles. If we allow the organization to become sacred rather than a tool or a method used in relating to these persons, we miss the mark.

In my relationship with our single adults I attempt to do two basic things in order to remain flexible.

I choose to allow persons to disappoint me. I work hard at only being disappointed in persons who say one thing and do another. I build on the premise that I, too, have disappointed persons throughout my life. I am aware that I have disappointed some people, while others, I am sure, never let me know their feelings. Since I desire that the persons whom I disappoint forgive me, I must, in like manner, forgive others.

One single man helped me see this point quite clearly. Our singles wanted to do a musical drama, and we needed some more men to try out. One young man I asked to try out told me that he would be starting a new job on the very day of our tryouts. He said that he really had no concept of what his time schedule would be that day, but if he could come he would. He requested only one thing from me: "If I don't come, don't be disappointed in me." He may have thought that he would be marked off my list if he didn't come. Or he may have wanted our friendship to remain open and have chosen not to have anything preventable hinder it. Whatever his reason was, I told him that my request hinged on whether he chose to respond. I had not already cast him in a part, so I would not be disappointed if he couldn't come. Not only was I *not* disappointed; I was most thankful for his honesty and for that important interchange.

Almost never in my relationships with literally thousands of persons have I been discouraged by a person. I seek never to be discouraged by another person. To me, feeling discouraged about someone is like saying there is no hope for that particular individual. Less than five persons come to my mind when I think about this possibility. I have been deeply hurt by some individuals who either used me or who seemed to do little to care for their own lives (in my limited understanding). I seek *not* to have plans for any person's life because no one answers to me. Each of us answers to God.

I cannot accept the fact that God is through with some of these persons. I hurt for them. I desire God's goodness to permeate their lives, but the limited data I have regarding them tends to discourage me.

It is OK for persons to disappoint me. I will not say that hurt doesn't matter to me because it does. I just seek to allow any person the freedom to disappoint me without my feeling that he doesn't like me or he wouldn't have done this to me, that he is not *really* interested in this project or assignment, or that he is just not dependable. None of these reasons may apply to why he was unable to carry through with what he said he would do. I remind myself, *Have I ever failed to call someone, write someone, meet someone, or respond to someone in the way I said I would do?*

One of my most embarrassing disappointments occurred when I was a campus minister. I called a breakfast meeting with a bank president and two other businessmen to discuss the formation of a student organization we were all interested in. I failed to get up early. I got up at my usual time, ate breakfast, and went to work. About 11:00 A.M. that day I remembered what I had not done. I called each one and apologized. They were most forgiving.

One even told me, "We had a great breakfast together, and I got to know two men I hardly knew." Now I know why that man was a bank president. He had a healthy attitude toward people. The fact that I was owning up to my failure and that this president was so gracious brought us together for several discussions about life, God, family, and Christian growth. We would, at times, visit in his office for over an hour. I assumed he would indicate that our conversation time was up if he needed to. He had not written me off.

I seek to never predetermine how a person is, will react, or feels before I gain the information from him. Often individuals in groups label a person. They decide, for instance, that a person who chooses not to respond warmly to conversation is stuck up or aloof. In reality the person may have been deeply hurt emotionally and may feel too tied up in knots to be free to communicate. It is also possible that the individual is shy and fears rejection if he reveals himself even slightly in conversation.

It is also important to learn the meaning of a person's statement rather than to impose my own interpretation to a comment. When my youngest daughter was in the fourth grade, she said simply, "Dad, is it all right to 'make out' in sixth grade?" I said calmly, "Why do you ask?" She answered that "Stacy (sister who is three years older) said you 'made out' when you were in sixth grade." I said calmly, "What do you mean by 'making out'?" She said (in a tone that said *Everybody knows that*), "Kissing."

I said, "Oh! Well, I did play some kissing games at parties in the seventh grade, but I didn't date anyone." End of conversation. What if I had imposed my advanced interpretation upon the situation? I would have become very upset with my daughter over my interpretation rather than being flexible or open enough to hear hers.

It takes much effort to be flexible in the now. But doing so is the only way to stay alive. When we live on the answers to the questions we have already asked, we are dying.

Variables Necessitate Flexibility

There are many variables that require flexibility in a ministry with singles. The singles community is constantly changing.

1. *Location.*—Singles move from your city to another because of a new job offer or some family concern or to run from the place they are which may be uncomfortable. Others move within the city, from one apartment to another, from one job to another, or from one set of values or experiments to another. All of these changes tend to bring about new friends and different time sequences for the person.

2. *Attitude change.*—Persons change in their attitude toward them-

selves. They like themselves better or not as much. They are embarrassed by what they have done: "I cannot face them or him again." Our friends will see our failures in a different light, and we can be wrong—if we are flexible enough to risk it.

Some persons have put too much trust or faith in another person and have become disillusioned. They feel that they will never trust another person again. Anyone who puts more trust in an individual than he does in God can expect to take a tumble. No one can accept another person's worshiping him.

Much anger that is aimed at God is not valid. Often a person prays selfishly and is mad at God for not answering his prayer. God is not like a spare tire. He is not to be called on if needed and to stay in the trunk at all other times. God is actively beaming his love toward us at all times.

Not all changes in attitudes toward self, others, and God are negative. Each day I see more positive discoveries taking place within the people who live where I do.

3. *Leadership change.*—A church staff can move well (or not well) with individuals. Changes such as a staff member or leader's moving elsewhere can be good if the people in that place rally around their needs. Much growth can come about. If the leadership has not been too healthy, some healing time is necessary; but the singles who really want to be the church will eventually come through because "God is able to make [them] stand" (Rom. 14:4).

Some laypersons get the feeling that nothing can change in their church because of the attitudes of some of the church leaders. This feeling may be true in a few churches; but if a group of single adults and their leaders seek to love their way into the hearts of these leaders, the changes that can occur may prove to be surprising. Most leaders I know resist any group who seeks to force its way in. However, to love others is the pattern Jesus wants us to follow, if we maintain our love for God as well.

At times, some lay leaders feel a burden for the single adult ministry and put their creative energies to work. The results are often very good. When a group of singles has a new leader who shows that he cares, some changes can occur in the singles themselves.

In our groups we believe in changing leadership fairly often. Many of our Bible teachers are secured for one- or two-month intervals. This change provides some continuity, but does not build the group around the teacher.

Among the single adult officers there are changes every six months. This six-month term of office allows time enough to plan some major emphases but not too long a time to get burned out on the responsibility of the leadership. This plan not only helps to develop numerous leaders, but also gives the group a different style every six months.

Movements Necessitate Flexibility

One of the most difficult kinds of letters for me to answer is a request for me to send someone a packet of materials about our single adult program. Since our program is constantly changing, we have yet to prepare a brochure about our ever-enlarging ministry. As a result, I seek not to include in a printed publicity piece a full description of what we do. It's possible that as soon as we print a description, we will change our plans. I really don't mind the letters coming our way, and several hundred have come; but I would prefer to have persons visit us for a little while and walk with us. This writing is one attempt to answer the letters.

Most good ideas in ministry start as a movement. The single adult ministry in our churches is still in the movement phase. In time, it will become institutionalized. As a movement, it can go in many directions. Most institutional leaders wait until the movement seems to be going in a healthy direction before they risk jumping on the bandwagon. This waiting period is probably necessary.

Evaluate: Is Change Necessary for Change's Sake?

One way to help the church's single adult ministry stay in the movement stage is to make certain that the programming needs reflect the current needs of the singles.

An excellent example of this point is the debate among our singles regarding our programming for Sunday evening. For more than seven years, there has been a Sunday-night single adult discussion at 7:15. The discussion follows the 6:00 church worship hour. At 8:30 on Sunday evenings, the singles go to someone's home (a single adult member's apartment) for a supper fellowship. This plan has become "the Sunday night program."

Recently some of the single parents have been questioning this format. Is it practical? Since several parents put their children to bed early, they need a baby-sitter from 6:00 until 10:30 P.M. That cost is financially impractical for many of our single parents. If they brought the children to the church and used the nursery facilities, the children would not get home until very late.

The debate goes on because some say, "We have always had a discussion and a fellowship on Sunday night." We already have an institutionalized event. My position is that I want what is best for all concerned. One alternate plan is to have the discussion on Wednesday evening and the fellowship on Sunday evening.

Some singles will not like this statement, but here goes. Singles often talk about their freedom to change; and they do change when doing so is convenient to their needs. They change their dating partners, jobs, residences, and churches. However, if you try to change a single adult group from something they are personally locked into, you will see that many singles are quite traditional. Many go to the same barber (or beauty) shop, the same laundry, the same stores, the same service station they have gone to for years. They have a Sunday schedule that is usually the same unless they are out of town. Monday night may be their bowling night. Many of our singles have blocked out Tuesday night for Single Adult Choir and game night. Some are more faithful to game night (volleyball, pool, ping-pong, etc.) than they are on Sunday mornings.

My point is simple. If the singles like their routine, why change it? The change needs to come only if the change will be for the better. Change is not necessary just so change can occur. The change must have a valid purpose that equally—or more than equally—ministers to the needs of the singles.

A Park Cities Example of Flexibility

In January of 1976 our singles met to discuss possible changes in our number of groups, our format for Bible study, and some of our organizational styles. These considerations for change were brought about by (1) an exciting experiment going on in one of our singles groups, (2) the lack of substantial growth in other groups, and (3) the need for more correlation of the different single adult groups in our church in a common ministry.

The exciting thing happening in one of our singles groups was their shift from the large-group teaching situation to having a choice of three or four activities. This change brought about a growth because more individual needs were being met. For example, a preregistration was held two weeks before a new Bible study series began. More persons had preregistered by the day we began the Bible study than had been present the Sunday prior to the beginning of the new series.

The other groups of singles seemed to gain new members, but the attendance remained the same as the enrollment grew. The groups were losing some of their holding power. Also, the age groupings that were set up were not accomplishing their purpose.

Our January meeting was a significant one. About 125 singles attended this open meeting. I was delighted to see that so many of our singles were interested in participating in a meeting that could shape our future singles program.

Background of Park Cities' Growth Pattern

A little background explanation is appropriate here. In June of 1970, when I began ministry with the singles at Park Cities, there was one brand-new group for singles twenty-five and under and one established group of singles for persons twenty-six and up. These groups were designated Single Adult 1 and Single Adult 2. About 1972 (or late 1971) a new group was begun for persons who were thirty-nine or above. This group, Single Adult 3, was affectionately called our thirty-nine and holding crowd.

The group showing the most growth by 1974 was our twenty-five and under group (which began with two members). It was divided into Single Adult 1–A (twenty-three and under) and Single Adult 1–B (twenty-four to twenty-eight). This change caused our Single Adult 2 to be composed of the twenty-nine to thirty-eight age group.

By October, 1975, the Single Adult 1–B group had grown again to 193 members strong. They had decided to have multiple Bible studies for their members in order to meet more needs of more people. I had received many concerned statements from the members that something needed to be done about the size of their group. There were so many new persons every Sunday that they didn't know who the members were or who the visitors were.

It soon became obvious that many new members in the 1–B group were twenty-two to twenty-six and that most of the leaders (officers) were between twenty-eight and thirty-two. Through much conversation by November, 1975, it became apparent that a new group was needed for the twenty-three to twenty-six group. If we were to make that change, the 1–B group would be divided into two groups again (twenty-three to twenty-six and twenty-seven to thirty-two). However, Single Adult 2 was to minister to persons twenty-nine to thirty-eight. In order to meet some needs of our singles who were thirty-two and under, we needed to get the advice of our thirty-two and above persons.

Conclusions of Park Cities Singles

So, against that backdrop, the January 1976, meeting was held. At that meeting the following information was presented. (A portion of the information presented that evening dealt with Bible study and will be included in a later discussion.)

SINGLE ADULT MINISTRY 1976

PARK CITIES BAPTIST CHURCH

Dallas, Texas

OUR MISSION:

To relate the good news of Christ to single adults who have various needs. Our intent is to help single persons become the persons God wants them to be, through a great variety of activities and ministries which will assist them in their spiritual maturity.

OUR COMMUNITY:

To be the people of God on the congregational level in 1976 is to provide healthy communities where individuals feel needed, wanted, and accepted, and have an opportunity for personal Christian growth. These communities need to continue to dialogue with the world as a whole and yet continue to look to God, in the midst of these communities, for inner strength. The organization of these communities needs to be healthy so that the maximum number of persons can be touched with valid personal relationships. The suggestions for this organization are as follows:

1. *Age Groupings.*—The following age groupings accurately fit their present departmental groupings except for the new Single Adult 3 group.

The new Single Adult 3 group will be composed of persons from Single Adult 1–B and the present Single Adult 2. The majority of the current Single Adult 2 membership will be in the Single Adult 4 group. Keep in mind that our age groupings provide basic organizational units; therefore, each person is encouraged to be in the unit closest to his age. Our concern is for persons and that the group they are a part of has meaning for them.

Single Adult 1	(Since 1954)	Age 18 to 22
Single Adult 2	(1950 to 1953)	Age 23 to 26
Single Adult 3	(1942 to 1949)	Age 27 to 34
Single Adult 4	(1932 to 1941)	Age 35 to 45
Single Adult 5	(1922 to 1931)	Age 46 to 55
Single Adult 6	(1911 to 1921)	Age 56 to 65
Single Adult 7	(Before 1911)	Age 65 and above (not to be organized now)

2. *Single Adult Council.*—For better coordination of all single adult activities that will involve single adults within one particular department (age groupings) or all single adults, a single adult council is suggested. This council will be made up of representatives from the various departments for the purpose of coordinating Bible study, missions and outreach opportunities, worship experiences, general promotion and the newspaper, single adult conferences/retreats, community projects, choral and dramatic presentations, and any other activity or ministry deemed important for the Park Cities Baptist Church program. In each department there will be elected leadership for the specific needs of each department, such as fellowships, programs, socials, outreach, and spiritual growth needs.

3. *Format.*—Each Sunday morning the schedule will be as follows:

9:00—9:30 A.M.   Informal fellowship; coffee and doughnuts.

9:30—9:50 A.M.   Gathering by departments for fellowship, announcements, recognition of visitors and new members, and singing.

9:50—10:40 A.M.   Bible Study. The Bible study will

be on an elective basis, with eight to ten options each Sunday morning. These Bible studies will not be handled through departments. Any age person can go to any Bible study on the basis of interest. The only restriction in these Bible studies will be the available space where that Bible study is being taught. Popular studies will be repeated from time to time. The Bible study curriculum will be determined by the program committee of the Single Adult Council (SAC). The intent of this "college" approach is to meet more personal needs concerning Bible study for a larger number of single adults.

10:55—12:00 A.M.	Worship with the entire Park Cities Baptist Church family.
6:00 P.M.	Sunday evening worship.
7:15—8:15 P.M.	Sunday-evening single adult discussion. These discussions will be determined by the program committee of the SAC. There may be one discussion or more, depending on the need and interest level of the single adult ministries.
8:30 P.M.	Fellowship by departments.

BIBLICAL CONTENT AND LEADERSHIP:

Details to be given later.

AVENUES FOR PARTICIPATION:

This is a limitless area of concern because of our multitalented membership and a great variety of interests on the part of our single adults.

We need to channel singles into fuller ministry opportunities within our church and into a greater variety of outlets in our Dallas area.

What Singles Liked About Our Community

Before this information was presented, I asked persons who had been in our single adult program to share what they liked about the program. Statements such as the following were shared by persons of various ages: "In addition to the fellowship I have found here, I was accepted in spite of some differences (in belief and church background). I felt really pleased to be around here, more so than any other church I had attended. It is really neat."

Another said, "I found that no matter what I wanted to do, I could easily find someone to join me—for worship, for watching football on TV, or for playing volleyball—because here there are friendly, caring people."

Another single said, "I have been in the group for seventeen years; and the unique thing about our church is that the people here are concerned with the spiritual as well as with other concerns, and they want to share with each other."

Someone else responded by saying, "The community provides an entrée to other areas of the church. By being in our single adult groups, we are able to participate in the various church committees; and people know the single adults exist. Otherwise, I could attend church every Sunday and no one would know I was there. This way I can get involved in the church as a whole."

A woman stated, "I became a Christian here three years ago. I was away most of that time attending college, but it was nice to be kept informed by receiving newsletters and literature sent by my church. I knew that the people in my church were praying for me and that I had someone to come home to. The fellowship here was and is great."

Still another single said, "My priorities have changed for the better as a result of the single adult groups here. Everyone accepts you whether you are a Baptist or not. I think it is great that many denominations attend here and feel relaxed and comfortable . . . this acceptance you don't find in all churches. This quality is important at this point in our lives."

A divorced person stated, "Because of the attitudes of the people in this group, I feel relaxed and comfortable in any area of the church."

One other said, "Coming to this church as a single, I found comfort in the Bible study group. I really appreciate this group."

Evaluation by Questionnaires

After we listened to the expressions of good feelings, the ministry sheets were distributed. I gave time for each person to scan the information; then I said, "Please keep in mind that *you* are the church, the community of believers. I feel that I can assist you to be the church more completely than we have been in the past by having smaller and more groups. We do not need to continue to do the same things we did in 1970 or 1971. There are changes in our group every day.

"We don't even have the same persons we had in 1971. You who have been here for a while either had to change with your group or be left behind. Change is an important part of living. I do not say this to indicate that we definitely need a change. There are suggestions for possible changes on this ministry sheet; and if we are to be the church (that is single), we are the ones who must make the changes."

Several valid questions were asked. One person asked, "How does the number of persons enrolled now and those active compare with the proposed new groups? Will each group be too fragmented when divided into so many groups? A nucleus of active people would need to be in each group."

This question proved to be a crucial one. As the discussion developed that night, it became increasingly evident that we had a younger bunch who wanted to change. However, the older bunch (thirty-two and up) were not convinced a change for them was appropriate if it meant breaking up the good fellowship and community that was already present in the existing groups.

Discussion of Need for Change

One suggestion made was that the younger singles be allowed to make the changes they felt necessary, for they were younger and more flexible. The person who made this suggestion added, "Our group is older and more hesitant."

Another person stated that he thought the younger groups were in a growing process; therefore, they needed and *wanted* changes. He felt that the older groups tended to stay at a more constant level for a longer period of time.

Almost immediately another older single (the singles themselves used the terms *younger* and *older*) stated, "The change from high school to college and just beyond college is great, but associating with persons between thirty and fifty gives you a chance to help those who come in and need help. We are able to minister to people either younger or older than we are. Our people want to be with all ages. When people come in suffering from a hurt experience, perhaps they fit into our group better at first. When they get over the hurt and are ready to get back into the stream of life, they can go to their own age groups."

My response was, "It is so exciting to me to witness the deep concern all of you have for our ministry here. Just a few minutes ago we were talking basically about age groups. Now you have automatically moved to the deeper level of ministry, which we hope will be enhanced by these new groupings. Understand that ages are only guidelines. We want to minister to all persons; and if smaller groups can be a partial way to do this (and some feel they are), then we want to make these changes."

At this point in our discussion, a person who identified himself as a visitor (but who talked like a member) said, "I support change; but in the midst of change, let us never lose sight of our mission—that of relating the good news of Christ and of helping single persons become the persons God wants them to be, through a great variety of activities and Bible study."

The meeting was concluded after an hour and a half of honest discussion. It was a beautiful meeting. Several people understood other groups' feelings better, and a total single adult community began to form.

Much happened in the next few months. Some persons left our older groups because they heard secondhand (or thirdhand) that they would be assigned to groups according to their age rather than according to their preference. Others returned to the community and became involved again in a new group.

The Meaning of Flexibility in Age Grouping

Generally, age grouping is fairly healthy because of a more or less common level of maturity, interests, experience in work or social relationships, economic freedom (most older singles groups like to eat out at dinner theaters or nice restaurants and *can* do so), and personal marital history. A church could use other methods to group people, such as favorite colors (blues, greens, browns, etc.) or interests (sports, sewing, cooking, car repairing, etc.). Unless there is to be one *big* group, age grading is probably the best method for division.

Flexibility in age grouping is important. When a person is allowed to go to an older or younger community that he feels comfortable with, flexibility is being exercised. For example, a twenty-one-year-old college graduate already using his professionally trained skill does not feel at home with college students, even though he is their age. Flexibility would permit him to go to the group who would have more in common with him, despite the fact that that group is slightly older than he is.

Another example of flexibility according to meaning is a twenty-four-year-old mother who has a good deal in common with the twenty-seven to thirty-four age group. Two reasons may be her life experiences and the fact that there are more mothers with children the ages of hers in that group than in the twenty-three to twenty-six age group.

A man who is thirty-five may have more in common with the twenty-seven to thirty-four-year-old group than with the thirty-five to forty-five age group. If so, meaning for his life takes precedence over correct age grouping.

There are times when it is best for a person to stay with his own age group. Suppose a forty-five-year-old man, fairly successful in his profession, would rather be with the group that is twenty-seven to thirty-four. The men might be somewhat intimidated by his presence, and some of the women would probably prefer to date persons closer to their age group. In situations such as this I have attempted to talk with the individual on a practical basis, stating that he could stifle some leadership among the men in that group and might not be personally challenged in a professional way by some of the same men. Besides, there would be numerous opportunities to get to know some of the persons in the younger group. The result usually is that a person stays in the group closest to his age in order to help him and, in the long run, both groups.

Flexibility within age grouping is not generally a problem. When the new groups are set up, options are given to the presently enrolled persons to participate in either their age group or their original group. All persons who are enrolled after the new groups are formed are taken to their age groups. Very few choose to change later, but some do. It is nice to have options available.

A Park Cities Example of Change in Age Grading

In April of 1976 we officially changed our age groupings. We followed the basic format described at our January meeting, with multiple Bible studies available to all persons. The age groupings remained the same through Single Adult 4, but we only organized a total of five communities. Our community 5 is for persons forty-six and up.

We had an awkward beginning in April for several reasons. Changing the age groupings meant change enough; but to couple with it a change in Bible-study format almost overwhelmed us. We also had a lame-duck officer group for April through June. We saw growth in leadership in some groups and not much in others during this time.

When we moved into our new leadership period from July to December, 1976, we began to see some progress. Our Single Adult 5 group selected the slogan "Come Alive with Community 5." They have really come alive, too.

The various aspects of the new format had been shaped by experiments within the single adult community. Although some groups were reluctant to enter into the new format, all are moving into some new activities that are signs of health.

A drama group has been started. Their first presentation was the musical drama *Beginnings*, by Buryl Red, at the Glorieta Single Adult Conference in September, 1976. *Beginnings* was also the first major production of our new Single Adult Choir, which has about seventy-five members.

During this same span of time, a smaller group of musically inclined singles formed the singing group *Alive* and have refined their abilities and presentation through weekly rehearsals and various singing opportunities. Keeping ministry through music as a basic purpose has been helpful in this group's growth process.

Flexibility in Ministry

In November, 1976, the singles seemed to be anxious to move on to some new challenges; and I did something I rarely do. I chose to relate some dreams I had for our singles ministry, and the singles picked up on two of the dreams (I shared at least twenty ideas).

The two projects selected by our singles were (1) an outreach ministry to apartment complexes where our singles live and (2) a child-care program for single parents.

The idea for a third project came from the singles upon the retirement of our senior minister. They suggested that our church have a day of prayer. The singles would organize it, host each hour, send information about the day to each family unit (both one-adult and two-adult family units), and inform the entire Sunday School of the emphasis. The entire congregation responded to the day (as best they could, since driving was hazardous due to snow and ice on the streets).

When a single adult ministry enjoys some growing pains, many opinions are given as to what should take place next. Not all of these opinions will be practical for the church to follow. The result is having to make decisions in favor of or against these differing opinions and at great risk. It is a risk to choose one idea over another. What if the idea chosen is wrong? What if the idea not chosen proves to be costly in the loss of some very fine persons?

It is difficult to choose a direction that is in opposition to the wishes of some of the people and still maintain what I call the people-to-program approach to ministry. (See chap. 7 for more information.)

It is always important to anyone's ministry to learn from other ministries, and I certainly have; but I do not have time to learn what other churches are doing that might work at our church. We have more needs and more ideas than we have person power or time to accomplish.

I am constantly amazed at the creativity of our singles and at their tremendous sense of responsibility to see ideas accomplished in a worthy manner. I truly believe our singles sense a basic freedom to be the church and to do the work of the church that happens to be single.

In the past, singles would say, "Britton, why can't we do . . . ?" I would stop them before they finished and say, "We *can do* anything that honors God and edifies his people. Now, what was it you wanted to ask me?" They would say, "Why can't we . . . ?" I would interrupt again and say, "We can." They would say, "OK, Britton, let's do . . ." They would then share an idea, which would get a full hearing, and some suggestions for a next step to test the idea out with others.

Ministry Ideas from Park Cities Singles

Some of our single parents who are also interested in drama wanted to have a children's theater for the children of singles. After some of these parents talked to me for a couple of months, they finally got me to help them call a meeting (not that they couldn't call one by themselves). The meeting went very well, but the outcome was different from what we had expected. Instead of a children's theater, the group came up with a children's drama workshop that would be free and open to any school-age child. Every week the children would do some activity related to being creative, aesthetic, and relational, and having some moral teaching to it. Some eager performers would then be asked to take part in a children's theater production with the approval of parent(s), who would share some of the cost of the production.

I have been interested in another project for a long time, but following the people-to-program approach has delayed my carrying out this idea. The idea is to have a four-or five-week emphasis with divorced persons that would attempt to meet their needs concerning their new identity. This idea is being carried out with ample skill and good insight at other churches, but I wanted our singles to want the project. So we have waited until now to begin. A committee of singles has been appointed because some felt very strongly that we needed such a program.

The result of the planning thus far has been to work out a seminar lasting for four or five weeks, but meeting only once a week. This seminar would cost a nominal fee per person and would include on our resource team persons who are single due to divorce. The event needs to be held on a night when the nursery and activities building (for school-age children) can be available, so the parent would have no reason (except work or illness) to miss. We want to make it easy, not hard, for the divorced persons to attend. Also, we have been working with the divorce courts in informing all persons getting divorces that this service is available. Hopefully, some judges could assign some persons to this seminar.

Now the participants in the divorce seminar are able to relate to many of our active singles because this program (from its inception) belongs to the singles.

Ministry Ideas Must Come from the Singles

Instead of my pressuring the people into a ministry, it seems wiser in the long run to let the people choose to care for the whole idea. To develop a singles ministry at the pace of the singles takes longer; but it also will last longer because whatever ministry is chosen belongs to the singles. The singles truly are the people of God who happen to be single.

9.
A Growing Single Adult Ministry
Responds to Good Biblical Content

A question often asked in single adult leadership conferences is, "How do you obtain names of singles not active in any church in order to enlarge your program?" This common concern majors on getting different persons involved rather than on caring for the persons already involved.

Value the Singles You Have as Members

The emphasis of caring for the singles already attending Bible study (Sunday School) is basic to growth. If the biblical content is meeting their needs, they tend to share with their friends that "I'm finding some help for my life here." Somehow the word gets around to different singles that "help is available at this place." Another way of expressing this feeling is, "Here is a 'good news' place."

If a singles ministry is committed to the concept that growth comes as people's needs are met, then patience will be part of the process. Growth is slow at the beginning, but occurs steadily. Also, the emphasis in all aspects of the ministry is to meet the needs of the persons who are active. It is important to go with the singles who choose to participate rather than attempting to build a program around the singles who do not desire to be a part of the ministry. The result of the latter situation is that some of the persons the leaders thought would respond do not; and persons the leaders had not thought about at all are the ones who respond. Rather than being disappointed in the persons who do not participate, the leaders need to be thankful for those who do participate.

After a meeting in our area, five or six singles approached me and shared the concerns of their group. They were concerned that their church didn't care for them and felt that they were leaderless. I suggested that they ask their church to allow the singles to do what they deemed

119

important and to see what might happen. The singles responded by saying, "We already have the church's permission to do what we can." Then I suggested that they try to organize their group into some basic leadership areas and do what the group wanted to do in activities and Bible studies. They responded by saying, "Oh, we have officers; and we have good attendance at our activities and Bible study."

It seemed to me that this group was trying to minister to their real needs; they had over twenty persons involved. I commended them and encouraged them to relax, continuing to love and care for the people God had given them. In time he would give them some more people to care for and relate to, and they would be ready for them. Also, the church family would soon catch the spirit of the singles, and God's Spirit would open the doors that needed to open: whether those doors were marked more leadership, a larger facility, more church recognition, or a need in another area.

Care for the Singles' Personal Needs

It is possible to get singles to come to Sunday School without good biblical content, but it is difficult to get them to come back unless their needs are being met. Not only should the Bible study meet the single person's needs, but the people should care who he is. Basically the question is, Does this Bible study carry over into a caring relationship with *him?*

Some churches seem to have little problem in getting singles to initially become involved. Some of these same churches do not have a good stickability record. How many singles participate is not as important as what happens to the lives of these singles who do participate.

The mood of a singles group changes often, and the individual persons within a singles group change. Their needs also change; therefore, there should be a continual emphasis on evaluating the selection of Bible study curriculum.

Care for the Singles' Spiritual Needs

Although the quality of Bible study varies in our church, we try to always have helpful Bible studies. The quality of the Bible studies needs to be coupled with a caring membership (the singles) who show evidence of the love and forgiveness emphasized in the Bible studies. The numerical growth rises as the biblical themes are translated into caring action. In most of our single adult communities (departments), we have an ample number of singles to contact. So the way to get the names that most churches want is to meet the needs of the names (people) you have, and the people will come. Good content and genuine care are prerequisites for reaching out to persons not involved.

A question singles may ask is, "Where does all this Bible study take us, anyway?" Hopefully, Bible study helps us grow into the persons God wants us to become "in favor with God and man" (Luke 2:52).

Not all singles are alike in personality, reason for single status, or individual Bible study needs. It is imperative that a growing singles ministry learn that one particular diet of Bible study will not meet every person's needs. Single adults respond to Bible study best when the curriculum centers around their personal needs and focuses on how the Bible speaks to those needs.

Single adults have helped me understand that they have at least three basic needs as persons. Discovering what these needs are aids greatly in providing quality Bible study.

The Need for a Healthy Self-esteem

First, some singles have a low self-esteem or a low estimation of themselves. They don't like themselves because of the way they look, walk, talk, don't talk; because of their hair or lack of hair, their constant failures, their deep hurts that cause them to feel bad about themselves; or because of not fulfilling expectations at home or at work or with friends, of not having any friends, and many other reasons.

Persons in this category are generally so preoccupied with their problems that they don't have ears to hear. It becomes important to have Bible studies that *affirm* the person. Topics on love, acceptance, forgiveness, reconciliation, salvation, patience, and the weakness-strength tensions are most appropriate in assisting the person who has a poor self-image.

The Need for an Understanding of Self

Second, some singles have a healthy self-esteem. These persons are eager to better understand themselves. They are not interested so much in caring for others as they are in caring for who they are now and who they want to become. Areas of Bible study that would appeal to this group are an emphasis on Christian liberation, Christian ethics, biographical studies of Old and New Testament personalities, the creation story, some of the psalms—any kind of biblical survey that helps the individual understand the Bible better and emphasizes self-identity, personhood, and the Christian growth process.

The Need for an Understanding of Others

Third, some singles have a healthy concern for others. These persons are anxious to know how to better relate to persons (both believers and nonbelievers), desire avenues of service within both the church and the community, feel a need to communicate better, and want to see other persons included in projects, activities, and helpful events. Some of the Bible studies that appeal to them include any emphasis on missions, personal witnessing, group interaction study, the Christian and politics, the Christian and moral responsibility, and studies concerning how Jesus related and responded to persons and situations.

Park Cities' Approach to Bible Study

In attempting to touch these various need levels in our Sunday-morning Bible studies, we have moved to offer electives or options (as an alternative approach to traditional Bible study curricula). Instead of having *a* teacher for *a* class, we have chosen a variety of themes. The teachers are selected on the basis of the theme, or the theme is chosen because the teacher was interested in that topic. The result is that leaders teach one particular topic (or study theme) for four to eight weeks. The Bible study is built around the needs of the group rather than around the personality of the teacher. We recognize that this is only one approach to Bible study, but the approach is working in our situation.

Another plus for this style of teaching is that persons who are exceptionally good Bible teachers are often available for a four- to eight-week period but, because of other commitments, would not be available for a full year's commitment.

One other benefit of this approach is that the singles become more flexible in their growth pattern and can learn from several teachers instead of just from a few favorites.

This type of curriculum format places the responsibility for the spirit of acceptance and caring on the group itself rather than on the teacher. So the group is committed to a growth process without having to wait on any particular teacher or leader. One of our singles who helps plan the curriculum for his community stated recently, "We just have Bible studies that meet our needs. We know what we need, and we just go after it. Our Bible studies have been terrific."

. To meet all the spiritual needs of a growing singles group that is quite diverse is practically impossible. However, to recognize that all persons are at a slightly different place in their attitudes toward self, others, and God is a good place to begin to meet these various needs.

In our organizational approach (which, again, is only one approach), we have officers in each of our communities. The president and single adult council representative of each community (department) compose our single adult council. These persons are responsible (in counsel with the single adult minister) for choosing all the biblical content for our Sunday school.

Four Series of Bible-Study Sessions

We have chosen to have biblical studies each Sunday from each of four series or categories. *Series A* is *advanced* Bible study. This study attempts to follow a curriculum set forth with commentary notes from one of the Southern Baptist Sunday School Series. It can also include any in-depth study that enhances the Bible students' understanding of the Scriptures in a "dig-in" sort of study.

In *Series B*, we study any facet of *Bible survey*. The subject may be an overview of the Old and New Testaments, or it may be a survey of themes from the various sections of the Bible. This series is intended to help the new Christian understand the Bible better, as well as to help the Christian who has just become serious about being a learner.

Series C is wide open to any *Christian life concerns*. Helping the Christian live with a full awareness of what it means to be a Christian, relate as a Christian, cope as a Christian, share as a Christian, and care as a Christian are all parts of this important series.

In *Series D* the emphasis is on the *dialogical* (conversational). So often persons who want to relate their faith more clearly need to have a sounding board to help them express what they believe. This series is styled for small groups. In the small groups the opportunity to share and talk about the chosen topic is more readily available. This series generally enhances the *koinonia* (Christian fellowship) of the group and helps the participants to feel more accepted by God and the group.

An example of a particular Sunday Bible study offering for singles who attend Sunday School is:

Single Adult Bible Study

Our Bible study groups are formed by personal interest in selected topics or themes instead of being formed by age grouping. Please select the study you feel will be most beneficial to your life. Be sure to register in the room where your Bible study will be held, even if you preregistered for one of these studies. All studies will be continuing through this month. We prefer that you stay in one study, if at all possible, for the duration of the course.

SERIES A—Advanced Bible Study

What Is Christian Freedom? This is a study of the book of Galatians. The free theme in Galatians is not that of political freedom; it speaks of that freedom in Christ which is the spiritual basis for all true freedom. Among the key themes in Galatians are the gospel of grace, the basis for Christian fellowship, justification through faith, the meaning of Christian freedom, the fruit of the Holy Spirit, and the practice of Christian love.

Parenthood—Privilege and Responsibility. Parenthood is definitely an important responsibility. It is therefore important to have a healthy foundation in the way we approach our responsibility as parents. Single parents have a unique kind of responsibility. This Bible study is designed to be helpful to single parents and to potential parents.

SERIES B—Bible Survey

An Introduction to the Bible. This study examines what kind of book the Bible is, how it came together, what its unifying themes are, and what it says to persons today. Fuller understanding of the Bible as the Word of God can be a help to genuine faith.

SERIES C—Christian Life Concerns

Biblical Understanding of Self-Identity. Loving God and other human beings is contingent upon a proper regard for love for self. This study will focus on the understanding of self and the meaning of personhood, which the Christian faith expresses as valid *and* important.

The Christian Faith and Current Moral Dilemmas. This study will explore several current moral dilemmas and their implications upon

Christian principles. Biblical insight and ethical teachings will be the emphasis of this study. Flexibility of the issues studied will depend on the participants and any new crisis that occurs during the process of this study.

Giving My Christian Faith Away—Naturally. This emphasis will give biblical insight regarding an authentic Christian witness. One's best witness occurs in the context of his daily walk. Certain understandings helpful to a genuine sharing of one's faith will be discussed.

SERIES D—Dialogue

Breaking Free. What does one's personal Christian liberty consist of? This dialogical study will explore, through selected biblical passages, the freedom to reminisce, relax, be content, share, ask, and go.

Some of the other Bible study ideas that have come from our curriculum study on the basis of need are:

What Did Jesus Say? This study will be an examination of some of the conversations Jesus had and what these conversations have to say to us about how we are to relate to Christ, how we relate to others, and how we relate to ourselves. This is a "dig-in" study. (Dictionaries, commentaries, and concordances are made available in this small-group research study.)

Hanging in There with Faith. Paul's charge to Timothy to keep the faith is a challenge to Christians of all times. It is imperative that we each understand what Paul's calling really means. This study will be concerned with Timothy and its relevance to today.

Faith in Action. "Faith without works is dead" is a familiar emphasis. We actually live our faith. What we choose to do or what we choose *not* to do depends on our faith. This Bible study will draw from the letter of James some "faithing" insights for our lives.

How to Be a Christian Without Being Religious. Are you religious? Do you sometimes feel you have been trapped into playing a game called "church"? This study speaks to religious hypocrisy; it shows why "religion" has failed and points to true Christianity and a faith that is valid for life. The studies are from Romans. (One resource is the book *How to Be a Christian Without Being Religious* by Fritz Ridenour.)

Old Testament Personalities: Their Faith and Their Lives. This Old

Testament biographical study series will investigate the lives of Joseph, David, Solomon, and Esther. The intent of this study will be to better understand their faith and the motivation for living the kind of lives they lived, with applications to our lives today.

Sharing Christ in a Secular World. This study is a part of our Life and Work curriculum and will be dealing with such themes as "Marketplace Religion," "God's Expendables," "Why Go to Church?" and "Belonging to One Another."

Following Christ's Example—Interpersonal Relationships. This biblical study will center around the encounters Jesus had with both men and women, how he dealt with them, the results of these conversations in the lives of these people, and what we can learn from these situations about our own relationships with other persons today.

There Is Life After Birth—Now What? In this biblical study, effort will be made to examine the growth process of Christians from spiritual infancy to Christian maturity. The emphasis will basically be on how one can have a victorious Christian life in the midst of problems, conflicts, doubts, and disappointments.

What Do You Mean, I'm a New Creation? This biblical study will examine the beginnings of a new life in Christ and what it really means to become a new creation as a growing Christian.

Personal Friends of Jesus. This biblical study will center on persons whom Jesus knew and the concerns of their lives, including being faithful in the midst of life's perplexities, being a believer who doubts, being a believer who gets angry, being a believer who makes good decisions in life, and being a believer who knows the meaning of forgiveness. This study is part of our Life and Work Curriculum.

Three Stages of Salvation. A study of Romans 1—8. This is a concentrated study of the meaning of salvation and its freeing aspects. An excellent resource for Christians who want to dig deeper in the understanding of this most basic doctrine in the Christian faith.

How Can I Love My Neighbor Better—Or At All? This study will explore some of the reasons and possibilities for one's inability to "love your neighbor." Many times the "as you love yourself" portion of the Christian commandment (Luke 10:27) gives clues to our ability to "love our neighbor" better.

Prayer—Practicing the Presence of God. A biblical understanding of healthy praying. This series will explore the meaning of prayer, attitudes of praying, the question of answered and unanswered prayer, how we are to pray, developing a private prayer life, and resources for devotional readings. The leaders for this series are bringing their own understanding and discoveries regarding prayer as one Christian pilgrim to another. A different leader will be in charge each Sunday.

Determining Priorities for Life. A topical biblical study—how often is it in our lives that the "things we ought to do we don't do and the things we ought not to do we do"? This emphasis can give insight from varied life-style perspectives as to how some Christian individuals are personally working through choices and their own decision-making process.

Making It to Adulthood. This study will explore the shift in life that occurs from a dependence upon others to a joint responsibility with others. This Sunday the topic will be "Becoming the Adult Leader I Can Be." Recent high-school graduates are encouraged to attend this special emphasis.

The Living God and His People. This study is most appropriate for the beginning of the third century of our nation's life. We will study at least three major crises in the history of Old Testament Israel. Included in this series is "The Birth of a Nation" and "Covenant Faith Versus Pagan Culture." This study is part of the Life and Work Curriculum and can be most helpful for the person who desires to understand our Christian faith heritage better.

The Witness Within You. This will be an in-depth Bible study on God's Spirit within us. Much discussion in churches today deals with this topic. The approach of this study will be to examine closely what the Bible does say about how God works through us as Christians in areas such as: "Know the Holy Spirit," "Understand the Holy Spirit and Conversion," "Understand the Holy Spirit and Life's Greatest Venture," "Be Victorious Through the Spirit," "Allowing the Spirit to Be in Control," "Be Filled with the Holy Spirit," and "Continuing in Communion with the Spirit."

Moving Toward a Genuine Intimacy. This is more than a marital preparation study. One of the greatest needs that persons have in relationship with others is to develop an ability for closeness. The intent of this study is to explore openness and healthy closeness at this point of life—so that *if* marriage occurs, we will not be distant persons in the midst of such a relationship.

In-depth Bible Study. This is a free-lance Bible study with some definite direction. This in-depth material is for singles who want to "dig in" on some pertinent biblical topics. "Study to shew thyself approved unto God, a workman that needeth not to be ashamed, rightly dividing the word of truth" (2 Tim. 2:15).

Do You REALLY Know Christ? A study of 1 John, with an emphasis on three tests that help us *know* we are followers of Christ. The tests are moral, social, and spiritual.

Studies in James: Lessons in Daily Living. This study will explore problems of trials in life, the demand of a true religion, responsibilities of teachers of the faith, problems in interpersonal relationships, problems of presumption, problems of affluence, the coming of the Lord, the importance of work, and the power of the church at prayer.

Applying the Gospel. Most Christians need a more complete understanding of how to apply the gospel in a way consistent with daily living. This study will include three emphases: (1) "Applying the Gospel: Its Relevance," (2) "Applying the Gospel: Its Biblical Base," and (3) "Applying the Gospel: Its Social Implications."

Facing the Future with Hope. This topic is the last portion of a study of the living God and his people in the Life and Work Series. The emphasis of these Old Testament studies will be on "What if the Worst Comes?," "Coping with Change," "Keeping the Faith," and "Sustained by Hope."

What the Bible Has to Say About Marriage, Divorce, and Remarriage. This study explores the meaning behind these sayings: (1) "They lived happily ever after," (2) "Divorce is the unpardonable sin," and (3) "A divorced person who remarries commits adultery." The subject then turns to what the Bible says about these three topics.

The Christian Single and the Current Political Scene. How can we, with good insight, face these election days with more than a political bias? This Bible study will examine the Christian's responsibility to authority, the attitudes of leaders, and some actions Christians might take. This study will have different leaders each Sunday, each of whom is capable in this field.

When Christians Pray. This Bible study is designed to challenge single adults to give more attention to prayer responsibilities through consideration of the meaning, nature, and purpose of prayer.

The Christian's Responsibility Regarding Money. Money management is part of our stewardship of life, and this Bible study is intended to give added insight to one item—money—which causes many of us much anxiety. Our attitude regarding money can make quite a difference in our daily decision making.

Telling Others About Christ. Witnessing is more than preaching and teaching, and it is a vital theme for today's Christians. The Bible and the needs of society make witnessing a priority task; yet, for one reason or another, many professing Christians make no serious effort to witness for Christ. This study will give a better understanding of biblical teachings about the role of Christians and churches in today's world. (A Life and Work study.)

Living and Sharing in Christian Joy as God's People. As God's people, we place great value in studying the Bible effectively and evaluating our prayer life in the light of New Testament models. This Bible study series is intended to help us share more completely in the joy of Christ's coming and to encourage joy in daily living. This study is part of the Life and Work Series.

Jesus and His People. This study will correlate the Old Testament prophecy as it relates to Christ's earthly mission, the effect Jesus had upon the people (his disciples) around him, the effect Christ's Spirit had on other New Testament people, and the effect of Jesus on us today.

Digging In with Some Scripture Heavies. This study will give opportunity for the participants to share in some familiar but profound Scripture passages. The selections for this four-week study are specifically geared to self-examination as to "how I'm cutting it in my Christian life." There will be some participant research tied in with this study. The four topics are: (1) "How Is Your Love Life?" (2) "Back to Basics," (3) "How Is Your Equipment?" (4) "Making the Tough Decisions." (A Serendipity series.)

God's Intent for Us—Christian Living and Giving. This study will involve God's original intention for his created order and man as the climax of this creation. This emphasis will also deal with how sin marred God's original purpose for creation and for man. The climax of the study will help us learn how God in his divine redemption seeks to restore the created order and man to his original purpose for them.

Meeting the Need for Personal Growth Through Bible Study

A good indication that the Bible study is meeting needs is the request for more intensive studies. More singles are wanting to gain biblical insight, and some are embarrassed that they have been coming to church most of their lives and are now learning things about the Bible and the Christian faith that they never knew or heard before. One person commented, "I could have stayed there [his class] another hour."

One of the helps I seek to give our singles has to do with diet. Encouragement is made to vary our Bible teachers so that more nourishment is given to a greater number of persons. The examples of some of the Bible study themes are indications of variety. Much more variety is now possible because of the genuine hunger of the single adults.

A tension that accompanies the singles' opening themselves to God's Spirit and beginning to feed on God's message to them in the Bible is a feeling of dissatisfaction. A dissatisfaction with self is a part of this attitude. For the first time in many singles' lives, God is very personal; and they are getting a taste of the joy of following Christ. The question "Why didn't someone help me see this before?" rises. It is possible that several persons (pastors, parents, teachers, friends) had attempted to help this person see certain aspects of the Christian faith; but only now is the person willing—in fact, eager—to learn (to be a disciple).

Another dissatisfaction a person may feel is that many persons around him are not as serious about the Christian life and studying the Bible as he is. It is interesting to see a person become hungry; he sometimes thinks all other persons *should* be equally anxious to learn. Most persons are prone to feel that what is happening to them *ought* to happen to everyone else *now*, and in almost the same way. Patience is, once again, the Christian fruit that needs developing here. If other persons who were growing spiritually before this individual got "turned on" had been as critical of him as he is of others, he might never have had his eyes and ears opened to God's Spirit.

The Christian Single: a Learner and a Minister

The more one learns about Christ and the Christian pilgrimage, the more he sees that there is to learn. Part of being a disciple is to be a learner. There is always a need for more spiritual understanding and growth. In a sense, the stance of the Christian needs to be that of one who is somewhat frustrated about what is yet to be learned. Full satisfaction that allows one to rest on what has already been learned misses the mark of the Christian.

Good biblical content and a caring spirit will come with the growing desire of the single adults to minister verbally or to take action in mission service. Bible study that does not bear fruit in a relational way misses its intent. Consider trying to fill a sponge with water and not squeezing the water out of it before using it. Sponges are helpful when an emptying effect takes place first. Christians are vessels that need to spill over into the lives of others.

The style of teaching the Bible to singles is important. Some singles want an authority to tell them how to live their lives. Others do not want anyone telling them how to live. What is of prime importance here is for the teacher not to yield to either position, but to yield to the Holy Spirit as authority.

Importance of Space Facilities

The facilities available to a singles group can make a difference in the approach taken in the Bible study period. Generally, singles prefer to be in a large coeducational grouping rather than in small classes. This arrangement provides some anonymity for some who are uncomfortable reading the Bible aloud or praying aloud in a group. If the department or class is not too large, the members will feel more at ease in sharing personal concerns related to the Bible studies.

If a facility could be ordered for a singles group and placed at Park Cities Baptist Church, I would want a large, open, carpeted room that would have round tables for discussions or informal fellowship time and also have adequate space for large-group settings. It would have a piano and numerous bulletin boards and chalkboards; the walls would reflect a cheerful attitude. There would be a magazine resource section, containing a few soft chairs that would provide an adequate setting for semiprivate counseling, committee meetings, or casual reading. It would also be helpful to have a sink deep enough for washing and filling a coffeepot and a refrigerator for some food and soft drinks or juice.

One important consideration regarding any new singles group in a church is to keep the group located in the main educational area if at all possible rather than placing them in a house or similar facility away from the main area. Many churches relegate a singles group to "the little house" across the street and go right on with the ministry they were doing before the singles needed a place. When the singles are placed in the mainstream of the life of the church, they become a part of the whole church earlier; and this arrangement also eliminates the attitude of some singles that "the church has put us over here out of the way."

When a singles ministry has a healthy identity among its members, moving to a house or a new facility especially designed for the singles would not be harmful.

The facilities and the location of the facilities that a congregation provides the singles ministry say much about the church's attitude and vision. Churches need to carefully plan with the singles in mind rather than protecting the favorite spots in the church for the nonsingles.

The facility does not make the biblical content great, but it does affect the attitude of the persons who come for the Bible study. The care given to a facility that singles use can be but one expression from the whole congregation that says, "You have worth; we care for you." (For more information, see chap. 8 of *Working with Single Adults in Sunday School,* available from Convention Press, Nashville, Tennessee, available in early 1978. Further bibliographical data is given at the end of this book.)

10.
A Growing Single Adult Ministry
Respects a Caring Leadership

I disagree with the statements some people make about single adults: "Single adults are irresponsible." "You can't depend on them." "All they do is gripe about the way things are." I have found singles to be quite different. In fact, singles will respond in healthy ways to a caring leadership.

Insights into Working with Singles

In working with single adults, I have gained several insights into their feelings about leadership. First, single adults are most capable of speaking for themselves and should be given opportunity for shaping the single adult program in a church. When I speak to singles on some subject relating to "how singles feel," I mention a disclaimer like "It is presumptuous of me to assume I can speak *for* singles." I would rather state, "I'm speaking to you about what singles have taught me."

Another insight is that single adults will generally respond to concerns valid to them. In a meeting with single parents, one mother stated that she wished there were someone she could call about the joys and the problems she has with her son. She felt that just to share an idea she had with a friend would be very helpful. Immediately three people expressed their willingness for her to call them. The meeting stopped until she wrote down the phone numbers offered her.

A third insight is that single adults are basically honest with life and with themselves. Some of the most honest sharing sessions I have ever been in have included singles. It is true that many are reluctant to open up because they have either been burned in a relationship or have attempted to open up with persons who were not sensitive. At times healthy sharing needs to be encouraged rather than the leader's allowing some potentially harmful conversation to continue. When singles feel an accepting and caring spirit in a group, however, their honesty comes to the surface. I predict that this honesty will soon permeate the whole body of Christ in such a way that the married adults will become more candid about their life struggles. It seems that some singles can teach some married adults about pitfalls to avoid in marriage.

A fourth insight is that many singles are open to learn, but some come with a reactionary spirit. Due to some preconceived notions about the church, Christians, and how it is going to be with a singles group—or simply because a personal rejection has recently occurred—some singles are prone to take extreme points of view. Statements like "You can't trust anybody anymore" or "You don't *really* care what happens to me" or "God can't really love me" reveal a small window into the hurt portion of a person's life. However, to assume that all singles have deep hurt and come to the singles group while still in the process of healing is incorrect. Many singles come as healthy persons who choose to be part of a healthy group.

Often I receive thank-you notes or phone calls from grateful singles because of something good that took place in a Bible study or a discussion. One young man stopped me just to say thank you for all the wonderful experiences he had had in the various activities with our singles. He said that he was learning more, meeting more wonderful people, and having more good experiences than he ever had before.

One other insight is that singles have little time for the meaningless. Singles are jealous of their time and money. If they get poor service or poor food at a restaurant, they probably will not go back. If a single feels that he is not getting a quality return on his time, he will often cut out.

However, the single must be the one to interpret what is or is not meaningful. To be critical of a single's life-style and to say that what he is doing is not meaningful causes him to be defensive. Early in our ministry with singles, some persons would come to a retreat late, judge whether it was going to be good, and cut out early if it didn't meet their preconceived expectations.

One should be aware of these insights in order to adequately lead singles. It is good to know where some of the singles are coming from.

Functions of the Ministers

Let's examine the levels of leadership within the church. The pastor or senior minister is an important leader in both a direct and an indirect way. In my situation, our senior minister was directly interested in our church's calling a person to work exclusively with single adults. Indirectly, the pastor oversees the ministry with singles. In a direct way, the pastor has an influence on the congregation's attitude toward the single and various aspects of singles' concerns, such as divorce and remarriage. The staff member who has the assignment of leading the singles communities serves directly as a liaison between the singles and the rest of the church.

Functions of the Group Directors

The director of the singles group is a direct-relationship leader, too. In our church, we seek to find directors who do not feel they need to take over. We are interested in a director's serving for more than one year and working with different single adult officers each six months. The director needs to let the group know about any churchwide conflict in schedule regarding a certain event the singles are planning. The director also can make observations related to Bible study themes, speakers, locations for social events, or any need the group has.

Most important to the singles group is the fact that the director is willing to be a good friend. Singles appreciate a director's calling to say that they have been missed and encouraging them to come back. One director asked me what approach I wanted him to take with absentees. I said, "Be a caring person with these singles. Nothing you can do is more important than that. For some of these singles, you represent our entire church. Let them get to know you. We want to love them rather than impose on them the 'oughtness' of their faithfulness."

Functions of the Officers and Committee Members

The officers and committee members of a singles group or community are directly in charge of all single adult activities that take place within that particular group. In our present situation, the officers elected by a group provide the leadership within that group or community. Any activity that encompasses more than one group is to be planned by the Single Adult Council.

The Single Adult Council is composed of the single adult minister, the presidents of each group, and the single adult council representatives from each community. Officers in each group compose the vertical leadership within each community of singles; the Single Adult Council

(SAC) provides the horizontal leadership for coordinating the plans for the entire singles program. The present listing of officers and their responsibilities is as follows:

1. *Community leadership.*—Each single adult community is requested to establish leadership positions necessary for the best possible overall programs with the members and visitors of the different groups. The following leadership suggestions are basic for each age group. Each individual community may desire officers other than these to meet the special needs of that department. Term of office is from January—June or July—December.

2. *President.*—Responsible for presiding at all activities of community, leading other officers in planning all community activities, and serving as a public relations person for all events of community, single adult ministry, and PCBC (Park Cities Baptist Church). It is assumed that this person is a member of PCBC. Serves on the Single Adult Council along with a SAC representative.

3. *Program.*—Responsible for all community and intercommunity programming. Makes suggestions to SAC regarding total single adult programming ideas. Programming should be designed to enhance the lives of the single adults (three to five on a committee).

4. *Membership.*—Responsible for encouraging visitors to become involved in our program and for encouraging members to be active participants in activities that help them grow as Christians. It is assumed that this officer is a member of PCBC. Coordinates the PCBC singles directory (four to six on a committee).

5. *Fellowship.*—Responsible for healthy fellowship and warm spirit within the community. This may include regular Sunday-evening fellowships and family fellowship groupings within the community (four to six on a committee).

6. *Social.*—Responsible for at least one social event per month and the Sunday-morning coffee/doughnut refreshments of the community. Plans events far enough in advance for maximum participation. Plans events that will have maximum participation. Clears dates of events with single adult calendar before final announcement of event is made (three to five on a committee).

7. *Music.*—Provides all music needed for any community events. Is responsible for enlisting persons who can ably assist with music. Serves

on single adult choral committee for planning music for the single adult choir (three to five on a committee).

8. *Publicity-reporter.*—Responsible for getting all news about community activities to members and visitors. Serves on single adult newspaper staff (three to five on a committee).

9. *SAC representative.*—Responsible for being the community representative on the Single Adult Council. Serves on the biblical studies committee to determine and enroll persons in Sunday-morning Bible studies. Is responsible for development of single adult ministries that are needed. Needs to be a member of PCBC and should be active in Sunday School.

. 10. *Ministries concern.*—Responsible for providing ministry outlets for single adults. Provides avenues of assistance to persons within the community (blood donors, visitation of ill members, flowers, food, employment, etc.) and to persons not related to PCBC. Plans special projects with the SAC (three to five on a committee).

11. *Secretary/treasurer.*—Responsible for all record keeping of members and visitors. Responsible for accurate reception and disbursement of all monies needed and available to the community. Serves as a participant and member of the membership committee (two to four on a committee).

In some of the communities the program chairman is also the vice-president. In others, the SAC representative serves in the dual capacity of vice-president.

Advantages of Family Groupings

In some of the communities much care is given to family or care groupings of singles. These families are to provide an avenue of acceptance for every member of the community. The families are usually organized by our listing all active participants and dividing them equally into groups of five to eight per family. A second grouping would be the persons who attend sporadically, who are to be equally divided into the active families. A third group would be composed of those who never attend. In like manner, we place them with the active family groupings on an equal-number basis. Assuming that a community had fifteen active members, twenty sporadic attenders, and seventeen who never came, the family groupings would be divided as indicated below.

	Family #1	#2	#3	Total
Active members	5	5	5	15
Sporadic attenders	7	7	6	20
Those who never come	6	6	5	17

The result of dividing the membership roll into these three categories is that a family of fifteen to twenty persons is provided. Active members get to know persons who attend infrequently and keep them informed about the group's activities.

One family group chose to have a covered-dish supper at a member's apartment. The active members invited each inactive member, hoping to get acquainted with some new friends. One young man who had never come to our church came with six or eight others. He decided to visit Sunday School after that. He eventually became active; then he became a leader.

About a year and a half later he came to me and said, "I've been on the receiving end long enough. Is there something I can do to give back what I've received?" He became a high school boys' Sunday School teacher. Our high school minister has commented several times about his quality of teaching and relating with those boys. He became their friend. He had time for them. He enjoyed being with them. I have seen several of these guys visiting with him at different times, although some had moved to another class (he taught them only one year each).

The family or care group has several functions. *First,* it serves as a group for every person to belong to. Everyone needs "a place to be," as Paul Tournier states in a book by that title. *Second,* the family is encouraged to get together at least once a month for some activity: to have lunch together some Sunday, to have a covered-dish supper, to go to a movie, to go bowling, or to get together to share concerns. *Third,* the family members are given a list of the others' names, addresses, and phone numbers. Each one is told that any family member may call any other family member at any time about anything. The phone list also helps in communicating news about any community event. *Fourth,* new members are assigned to families on a rotation basis so that all members can be cared for. *Fifth,* if any family member needs assistance from the director of the community or the single adult minister, someone who has that information can notify the proper person.

The singles came up with the family idea; and it is a good one, but it works only if the singles want it to function. Some age groups do not want a family (they just left one), while others even want to adopt a grandparent.

Attitudes Vital to a Caring Leadership

Basic to a caring leadership are the attitudes the leaders have. Both verbal and nonverbal expressions reveal the attitudes of leaders. Singles can generally recognize a phony or a nonauthentic leader. They have sensitive "radar equipment." Of course, it is also possible for singles to misread an individual leader.

The first attitude a leader needs is *humility*. A leader needs to be able to state, "Hey, I'm in need of help, too." Leaders who seem to have everything worked out and who are not vulnerable at all cannot identify with most people—whether married or single. A humble leader is one who recognizes his fallibility and his need of God. He is a good witness to those he leads who also need God.

A second attitude needed by leaders of singles is *a forgiving spirit*. Why do we not forgive others when Christ has already forgiven us? If God can forgive us, who are we not to be forgiving or merciful to others? Another facet of showing forgiveness is being nonjudgmental. This attitude is usually difficult to achieve because leaders anticipate that the single persons they work with will respond to God and will have certain values.

Jesus was compassionate to persons who were living contrary to God's plan unless they were hypocrites, as he indicated the Pharisees were. Our attitude needs to be one of love and not one of judgment for each other. For a leader to love a person enough to attempt to communicate with that person as a worthy individual, even though there is a vast difference in conviction or life-style, is quite Christian. We do not have to like what a person says or does to love him in the Christian love (agape) sense.

Several singles have begun a conversation with me by saying, "You are not going to like me when I tell you what has happened." I usually respond by saying, "Our friendship is not based on what you do or do not do." When persons let me into their lives enough to tell me about something that deeply concerns them, I like them better. I appreciate their willingness to share. Also, I appreciate their risking openness over rejection in our relationship. I ask myself, *Would I be that brave in a similar situation? Who would I trust?*

Leaders need to *maintain a level-ground spirit.* It is not unusual for married adults to feel that singles "finally arrive" when they get married. This attitude is subtle, but it conveys a superior-inferior outlook on others. Singles know when a leader feels superior to them. This attitude shows up sometimes when leaders seem helpful and seem to indicate interest in the singles, but they reveal that they feel a notch better than the singles. An example is a married adult's saying to a single, "We ought to be able to find a nice young man (woman) for you." Many married adults feel that they need to be matchmakers. One such lady said, "Britton, could you introduce Susie to Sam? I think she might like him."

Another way of expressing the superior-inferior attitude is the statement, "The adult leadership will meet in room 4, and the *single* adult leadership will meet in room 6." All are adults—some single and some married.

Leaders should *accept singles as they are* rather than expecting them to fit into the mold the leaders have for them. No two singles are alike; all singles are individuals and need to be treated as individuals. By accepting the singles as they are, the leader is free to relate to the best in each person. This accepting stance does not require that the leader approve of the things the single does but that the single is accepted as he is.

In my own relation with singles, I find that if I concentrate on being the person God wants me to be while I am with them, I have enough to think about. Too often our attitudes are determined by the persons around us instead of by our continually responding to God.

Single adults can identify with persons who have struggles and questions. It is not as important that the leaders be able to answer every question as it is that they cause important questions to be asked. For many persons, the first step in discovering a solution to a problem or concern is to frame right questions.

Bobbye and I were leading a Bible study on intimacy. After a few Sundays spent discussing this emphasis, which included some sharing of our life as married adults, one of our singles said, "When I came in here I was ready to get married. Now I am beginning to see that there is a lot more to marriage than I had realized." Our sharing had caused the right questions to formulate in his mind. His marriage fantasy bubble was popped, but a healthy discovery replaced it. At least in him, our purpose for the study was accomplished because he recognized that he needed to change some attitudes toward marriage and to be more realistic about life.

Another attitude that is vital to a growing single adult fellowship is the *ability to listen*. Single adults want to talk. I asked a single to bring me home after a meeting one evening. In group meetings he would respond only to questions asked directly to him. On the way home he began to talk, and he talked continuously for over thirty minutes after we got to my home. I thoroughly enjoyed conversing with him; and he helped me realize that singles want to talk when someone is willing to listen.

Singles come to church out of a need and a desire to learn. They may not even know what their own needs are, but they are to be commended for coming. Most singles are willing to learn, and some have beautiful spirits that are pliable and hungry to learn. Working with these singles is most exciting. If most of our church attenders came with the same eagerness and anticipation as do many singles I know, churches would be filled to overflowing; and changes would occur in whatever direction the church beamed its light.

An Example of Effective Organization

Good singles leaders will fight to allow the singles to be the church, too. When the singles feel that the weight of being the church—that is single—is on their shoulders, they will either run from the involvement or respond in some phenomenal ways.

In April of 1976 our ministry shifted, and new single adult communities were initiated. One of the new groups formed (the twenty-three to twenty-six group) had an unknown quality in their leaders (officers). They were challenged by the new opportunity. They were eager to do well. One officer in particular came alive in her position of membership chairperson. She and her committee typed and made copies of the procedure they came up with so the committee members would know exactly what to do. For the next few minutes, assume that you are on Susan's committee.

On the first Sunday you would receive this printed form.

Single Adult 2
Procedures for Members and Visitors

FOR VISITORS:

1. Have them fill out slips.
   A. Check visitor box on slip.
   B. Write "SA 2" (Single Adult Dept. 2) on it.
2. Assign a member to introduce a visitor in department meeting.
   A. Write *member's* name on visitor's slip.
   B. Tell member to make sure visitor wants to be introduced.
3. Make them name tags.
   A. Write a "2" for SA 2 in the right-hand corner.
   B. Use a PCBC stick-on tag and a green pen.
   C. Help visitor choose a class and go to that class or help find someone to go with him/her.

FOR NEW MEMBERS:

1. Have them fill out slips.
   A. Check new member box on slip.
   B. Write "SA 2" on it.
2. Make them permanent name tags.
   A. Use yellow paper and a green pen.
   B. Put in plastic holders.
   C. Tell them to turn tags in *before* they leave the Activities Building and to put them on the board.
3. Tell them they will be introduced as new members in department.

FOR PRESENT MEMBERS:

1. Have them sign envelopes at Karon's desk in clubroom.
2. Find their name tags on board.
3. Return name tags to board *before* leaving Activities Building.

You would also receive a list of potential members for Single Adult 2 with the following information: name of potential member, your name or the person on the committee who suggested the potential member's name, address, zip, home phone number, and work phone number. You would be requested to contact them and to encourage them to become involved members.

On the second Sunday you would receive a new printout of the procedures because new information is needed. So you read this:

ATTENTION: Please add *all* information to printout for all new members and transferrals.

FOR VISITORS:

1. Have them fill out slips.

    A. Check visitor box on slip.
    B. Write "SA 2" on it.
  2. Assign a member to introduce a visitor in department meeting.
    A. Write member's name on visitor's slip.
    B. Tell member to make sure visitor does not object to being introduced.
    C. Help visitor choose a Bible study class and go to that class with him/her or help find someone to go with him/her.
  3. Make them name tags.
    A. Write a "2" for SA 2 in the left-hand corner.
    B. Use a PCBC stick-on tag and a green pen.

FOR NEW MEMBERS:

  1. Have them fill out slips.
    A. Check new member box on slip.
    B. Write "SA 2" on it.
  2. Make them permanent name tags.
    A. Use yellow paper and a green pen.
    B. Put in plastic holders.
    C. Tell them to return name tags to board *before* leaving the Activities Building. They should wear name tags to Bible study classes. The tags on the board should be in alphabetical order.
  3. Tell them that they will be introduced as new members in department meeting.

FOR PRESENT MEMBERS:

  1. Have them sign envelopes at Karon's desk in clubroom.
  2. Find their name tags on board (alphabetical order).
  3. Return name tags to board *before* leaving Activities Building. Do wear name tags to Bible study classes.

FOR MEMBERS WHO MAY CHANGE DEPARTMENTS:

  1. Have them fill in visitor's forms from SA 2 (see above).
  2. Let them wear name tags from their own departments.
  3. Fill in a transferral form—pink form—if they desire to change membership from department, and make them permanent name tags.

FOR MEMBERS WHO ARE INCORRECTLY LISTED ON THE PRINTOUT AND NEED TO MAKE CHANGES AND FOR MEMBERS OF ANOTHER DEPARTMENT BUT ON SINGLE ADULT 2 PRINTOUT:

  1. Have them fill out transfer forms, noting changes.

You also receive the information sheet that informs the leaders of the age groupings for and locations of each group:

Ages for and Locations of Single Adult Departments

Department	Age	Location
SA 1	18-22	Lower floor (turn left at bottom of stairs)
SA 2	23-26	Clubroom (across from pool tables)
SA 3	27-34	Gym (back of Activities Building)
SA 4	35-45	Activities parlor (door at top of stairs)
SA 5	46-	Small parlor (first door on left at top of stairs)

Name Tags

Department	Color/Name Tag	Color/Pen
SA 1	White	Black
SA 2	Yellow	Green
SA 3	Light blue	Dark blue
SA 4	Orange	Black
SA 5	Light green	Black

Department	Membership Officers	Secretary/Treasurers
SA 1	Greg	Laura
SA 2	Susan	Karon
SA 3	Doris	Carolyn
SA 4	Nancy	Anne
SA 5	Jean	Mildred

On the back of this page was an activities schedule so the membership committee could be as informed as possible when they contacted visitors or inactive members.

SUNDAY

9:00— 9:30 A.M.	Informal fellowship; coffee and doughnuts
9:30— 9:50 A.M.	Departments meet for welcome and activities information
9:55—10:45 A.M.	Elective Bible studies
10:55—12:00 A.M.	Morning worship
6:00— 7:00 P.M.	Evening worship
7:15— 8:15 P.M.	Single Adult Discussion and Fellowship

TUESDAY

6:30— 7:30 P.M.	Single Adult Choir
7:00— 9:30 P.M.	Single Adult Game Night—Activities Building
9:30 until . . .	Informal get-together—Clubroom, Activities Building, or local restaurant

WEDNESDAY

5:15— 6:25 P.M.	Family Night supper
7:00— 7:30 P.M.	Prayer service
7:45— 9:15 P.M.	Single Adult PraiShare

FRIDAY/SATURDAY
  —Monthly Socials
  —Retreats
  —Community Mission Projects

By the second month of Susan's leadership, she *really* got organized. The membership committee received the following information:

MEMBERSHIP COMMITTEE

Name	Assignment
1. Cheryl	Adams through Bryan
2. Richard	Bumpas through Cox
3. Martha C.	Creel through Freise (Do not call Donna)
4. Eileen	Garner through Helweg (Do not call Diane)
5. Donna	Hodges through Kutner
6. Diane	Lantz through McNeill
7. Larry	Moore through Quillen
8. Patty	Rippletoe through Stites (Do not call Susan)
9. Farley	Stone through Walker
10. Martha W.	Wall through Young

I will call Cheryl, and she will call Richard, and he will call Martha C., and she will call Eileen, and she will call Donna, and she will call Diane, and she will call Larry, and he will call Patty, and she will call Farley, and he will call Martha W.

COMPARE YOUR PRINTOUT TO THE ABOVE LIST. IT IS CORRECT AS OF APRIL 28, 1976!

PROCEDURES

1. THE *FIRST* TIME YOU CALL A PERSON

  A. Find out if all information on the printout is correct. If it is not, correct it.
  B. Add the following information to the printout:
      Name, name of business firm, C, M, B-phone,
      ext., H-phone, address, city, zip code.
    1) Make sure that the name is correct. Underline the name that the person would like to be called.
    2) Ask the women if they want to be Mrs., Miss, or Ms.
    3) You do not need to find the address of the business firm.
    4) The C stands for children. Put the number of children, if any.
    5) The M stands for member of Park Cities Baptist Church. Put a Y for yes and an N for no. If no, find out what church he belongs to, if any. Write under name.
    6) The B stands for business. Also, the *ext.* stands for extension

of his business phone number. Ask if you can call him at work.
   7) The *H* is for home.
C. Is he receiving mail from the Single Adult department? If not, call
   the records secretary at church and find out why.
D. Mark *A* for active and *I* for inactive for members who are on your
   list, according to your knowledge or records in church office.
E. When you have contacted all your group and have all information
   listed above on each of them (by Sunday, May 2, or as soon as possible),
   call the records secretary and give her the new information. Also,
   send the change forms (pink forms in your packet) to her or leave
   them in church office. Tell me what you have done.

2. WEEKLY PROCEDURES AND INFORMATION FOR CALLING

A. The membership will get together immediately after the department
   meeting for 2 *minutes* to make sure that we all tell our groups the
   same thing about special events, announcements, or special business.
B. General information:
   1) Tell them the times for all regular Single Adult events (see back
      of page on SA ages for and locations of departments).
   2) Tell them the location of the Sunday night fellowship for that
      week. Find out if they want to eat supper. Get a definite answer.
      Have them call you back by Friday if they change their minds.
   3) Tell them the topics and a summary of the Bible study classes.
C. Special events:
   1) Socials.
   2) Special announcements made that morning.
   3) Any mission project happening soon.
   4) Any other news.
D. If they were absent the Sunday before:
   1) Find out why.
   2) Send them cards. (Enclosed in your packet—extras in single
      adult closet in Activities Building by pool tables. Ten stamps
      also enclosed.)
   3) Call Mary C. to add them to her list of Ministries Concerns.
E. If they are continually absent (2 weeks) or they express little interest.
   the first time you call, call me for list of people who will call them;
   or ask another committee member or officer to call them.
   1) If they still do not come to any events, ask them if they want
      to remain on the Sunday School roll. If not, call records secretary
      and me and give us the information. Fill out a pink slip.
   2) If you call someone who causes problems (for instance, if a boy
      calls a girl and has trouble because she wants to date and he
      does not), call me and we will move that person's name to
      someone else's list. (In this case, to a girl committee member!)
F. Keep a list of your expenses for this SA 2 committee for such things
   as stamps, and turn in a list to Karon each week.

3. OTHER INFORMATION YOU SHOULD KNOW

  A. The following assignments are to start this week. These people should be at the table in the Activities Building at 9:00 A.M. on Sunday morning to help register visitors and new members.
  First Sunday of each month—Cheryl and Richard
  Second Sunday of each month—Martha C. and Eileen
  Third Sunday of each month—Donna and Diane
  Fourth Sunday of each month—Larry and Patty
  Fifth Sunday of each month—Farley and Martha W.
  For fifth Sunday people—Martha and Farley should also check the suggestion box *each* Sunday and pass out the suggestions to the appropriate officers or to Britton. Box is in clubroom. FEEL FREE TO TRADE PLACES. JUST LET ME KNOW!
  B. Packets will be available beginning May 9 for our new members. They should be in the clubroom or in the Single Adult closet. Make sure each new member gets a packet as soon as you register him at the visitors' table.
  C. Remind all members to wear name tags and sign an envelope each week.

SPECIAL EVENTS FOR THIS WEEK, BEGINNING MONDAY, APRIL 26:

  1. BIKE-A-THON
  1:30 Sunday, May 2, at Caruth Park
  You may leave your bike at my house, 3556 Colgate, if you live too far from the church to go home and eat lunch, too.
  2. Single Adult Retreat May 21-23—Methodist Camp on Lake Palestine—Cost is about $25. More facts about this on Sunday. Keep the times open and plan to go.
  3. Class on Christian witnessing has ended. Other choices will be announced at community meeting.

Now if anyone can still feel that singles are irresponsible or not dependable and always gripe, then this unusual example just hasn't gotten through.

Let me say that within three months Susan and her committee, along with the other officers, had turned around a group of singles that was not even a group or community before that three-month period. I watched as all of this happened and was consulted on several points, but the singles chose to lead and truly became the church, too. They just wanted to care in a quality way for the persons in their Christian community.

Today this vibrant group has nearly tripled its attendance and is still growing. The group is more honest today in its relationships. It is diverse in its membership, and it is coming up with all kinds of good ideas for activities. For instance, a recent Sunday-evening fellowship was a "roots" covered-dish supper. Each person was to bring a dish that reflected his or her heritage (Spanish, Scotch-Irish, German, Swedish, etc.). Some who claimed to be just American brought a good ole hamburger. After the food was eaten, they had an exciting discussion about needs for the group. The single adult officers are fully in charge of their ministry. They want everything they plan to glorify God.

The Single Adult Minister's Part in Growth

How do I get them to do all of this? Just by letting them see that they truly are the church that happens to be single. In the body of Christ, if the singles are the left arm, then no one but the singles can be that left arm. As their minister, I cannot be the left arm because I'm not single. I can be a facilitator and keep the supplies available and keep opening the doors they choose to walk through. But nothing takes place unless they want it to happen.

This approach includes the idea that we never fail in our single adult ministry. We may have some learning experiences we will not attempt again, but we will not fail. We learn from everything we do. We are hammering out a ministry. We are writing our own book on how it's done. So we do not fail. Besides, God has promised that his Word will not return void. God uses all we do, and he can help us see the good in everything.

Our concern is not so much what can we do to get our group going as it is how we are going to get all the things done that we need to do.

Some people think that by our trusting the church that is single to the single adults, the singles would not want to associate with the whole congregation. Singles often ask me how they can become involved in some all-church relationships. I suggest that they pray that God will give them discernment to respond to the right requests. I then recommend them in two or more directions, according to their interests and abilities. Out of some thirty-five church committees, singles are on at least thirty of them. They are involved in the children's missionary organizations, are coaches of teams, participate in the church stewardship program—and the list keeps on growing.

Singles Sharing with Married Persons

Our twenty-seven to thirty-four group wanted to dialogue with more of the married adults, so they approached persons in a married adult department who would be near their parents' age. In fact, several were parents of active members of this group. At a Sunday-night fellowship, the singles provided the meat dishes; and the married adults provided the vegetables, salads, and desserts. The get-together was held in the home of one of the members. The single adult minister was in charge of the activities.

We grouped all persons into fours (two singles and two marrieds) and asked them to share their names, vocations, hometowns, and one thing that each person liked about himself. An immediate roar of conversation took place. When we finally (after ten minutes of conversation) got them quiet enough to pray, we instructed them to get their food and stay with their same group. After they ate, they were to share a personal concern they had and to conclude with a prayer time.

The evening moved rapidly, and everyone seemed to thoroughly enjoy meeting each other. The young people enjoyed meeting the wonderful persons who were older, and the "older" people were pleased that the "younger" people wanted to get to know them. Good friendships have developed, and more singles feel a part of the whole church now. The most often-heard comment at the conclusion of the evening was "When can we do this again?"

Single Adults Are Powerful Witnesses

Being the church in the midst of our singles is actually fun. I find that I need to continually challenge them to have programs, Bible studies, and social events *only* if the singles feel that the activities are pertinent. As one single adult leader said recently, "We know what we need; we just need to do that instead of sitting back and waiting for someone to spoon-feed us. We are adults. We can follow Christ, too."

One Christian psychologist stated that if he were going to point people to a group who were closest to the first-century Christians, he would point them to the single adults. That's a pretty powerful statement; but the singles I know come very close to being worthy of his statement. It is exciting to see their contagious spirit and to be caught by it.

11.
Insights and Ideas for Programming Effectively with Single Adults

"We tried *that* idea at our church, and it didn't work at all." I've heard this statement from several single adult leaders.

Using Borrowed Ideas

One of the risks in sharing ideas for programming is that some leaders would rather borrow ideas than to hammer out the programming actually needed in their church.

Ideas are like the main thought in the parable of the talents in the New Testament. If one attempts to hang on to an idea, he will eventually lose it. Good ideas that honor God and help persons grow in the Christian faith do not belong to anyone but God. New ideas come in direct proportion to our giving them away and using them *only* if they meet needs.

It is important to note that a good idea for one church is not automatically a good idea for another church. Some leaders transplant ideas without cultivating the soil.

Reworking a Borrowed Idea

An example of this point is that for some time we have needed a child-care program, such as other churches have, that our singles would take responsibility for. Finally our singles decided we needed such a program, so they prepared a questionnaire to present to all the singles at Sunday School. The questionnaire was a result of the singles' meeting together and styling it according to their needs. The following survey is the result of their efforts.

Interest Survey

Single Adult Child-Care Cooperative

Some interest has been generated in the possibility of creating a

151

child-care cooperative run by singles, not only for our single department members but as a ministry to any single with a child-care problem.

Please express your interest by completing this questionnaire and providing any comments and ideas you may have. Please return to your community secretary or president.

1. Do you have children who might possibly participate in a child-care co-op? If so, how many?

2. Would you utilize the service of the child-care co-op? Approximately how many times per month?

3. Would you be willing to help with child care in exchange for the use of the co-op?

4. If you are not a parent or do not have your children, would you utilize the co-op for the children of friends? How often?

5. What day or days of the week do you feel the greatest need for the child-care co-op?

6. What hours of the day do you feel the greatest need for the child-care co-op?

7. Comments, suggestions, and ideas:

The survey suggested that a meeting with single parents would be helpful in caring for the children's needs. The next step was to invite the single parents to a meeting. A group of singles put together the following letter.

Dear Single Parents:

Are you ever faced with dilemmas or problems you wish you could share with some caring individuals? If so, you may want to be with us on Wednesday night, February 16, 7:25 P.M. in the parlor of the Activities Building for an important discussion of "How to Better Help the Single Parent."

Many of us who are single parents have learned from experience that discussing or sharing our concerns with others is helpful in working through certain issues in our lives.

We hope that as an outgrowth of this meeting, we will minister more completely to the parent and the child in the one-adult family unit. One point of discussion will be the feasibility of a child-care co-op program for single parents. Another consideration will be programming that will assist the single parent in parenting and in healthy personhood.

We have chosen the 7:25 P.M. Wednesday time because church facilities for children are available. The nursery will be open for pre-schoolers. The Activities Building will be open for skating (25¢), television watching, pool, ping-pong, table games, and study.

Come and encourage any friends who are single parents to come with you.

Sincerely,

Single Adult Committee on Single Parents

At the first meeting we asked that each parent indicate on paper five concerns he had as a single parent. Afterward the group shared their concerns. A secretary was appointed, and their sharing revealed the following concerns.

1. The need of a friend—someone with whom to share the good as well as the bad. (Call-a-friend list; meet with a friend often; group activities.)

2. What to do with free time? How to fight loneliness.

3. Child care for sick children, during school holidays, when parent must be out of town, twenty-four-hour situation, on short notice. (Adopt a grandparent; baby-sitter list—among ourselves and with married couples having children the age of our own.)

4. Coping with the other divorced parent. Being able to talk with and see ex-spouse; being able to conduct the relationship in a way that is not hurtful to the child or to yourself.

5. Social readjustment—environment. Schedule of activities (with or without children, working out sitting arrangements among ourselves. Include interested singles who do not have children). How to handle dating. How to help your child accept your dating. How to handle sexuality. How to handle the feeling of left-outedness. How to maintain a good self-image.

6. How to help children cope with living in a one-parent environment in a two-parent world.

7. Help children to accept themselves, good or bad, and help ourselves to accept the role of the only parent.

8. Be stable, but be yourself. Be a friend, but be honest; be firm;

maintain a good discipline; love each other no matter what happens; share your life with your child; and always be an adult. How to cope with children's power plays (one against the other).

9. How to cope with disillusionment in children.

10. How to cope with the child who has lost a mother or father image.

11. Be a friend to a child who needs someone other than his parents.

12. How to cope with child development stages. (Arrange for speakers: TA for Tots; family guidance counselors.)

13. Learn to control negative feelings.

14. Learn to listen to your child; learn to play with your child.

15. Help child and self to develop emotionally, spiritually, and physically.

16. Spend quality time with your child. *Don't just be there.*

The meeting lasted a brief hour and a half. Parents from about age twenty to over age forty-five were there. Several parents opened up and shared some problems they were having with their children or with their own attitudes. The tone of the meeting was very hopeful.

Because this single parent group is meeting a need and because the singles have been in charge from the beginning, momentum is not a problem. It is moving well. My task is to guide the group in healthy ways and to not let the "tail wag the dog."

We really don't need another organization operating separately from and in competition with our existing singles structure. The leaders in this single parent group came to me on the Sunday following the first meeting and said that three weeks was too long to wait for another meeting. (They had set the time for the second meeting themselves.) They wanted it a week earlier. Adequate time to communicate the change was limited, however; so we decided to continue with the regularly scheduled meeting in three weeks, but to meet in two weeks to plan the later meeting.

The result of the meeting two weeks after the first one was a mail-out item informing the parents of a Saturday-night get-together for all interested one-parent families (including children). There was no reason to stay at home and eat alone (or just with your children) when good fellowship and food was available.

Having the Saturday-evening meal meant that this group was enlarging its calendar from just a meeting night to a fellowship night as well. Since our officers in each community plan all activities for the singles, I asked them if the supper conflicted with any other plans. Since it didn't, I suggested that they inform the presidents of the various communities of this event and ask the presidents to consider a new officer in each community who would be in charge of single parent activities in the future.

In none of this process have we looked to other places to gather ideas. We have been too busy trying to do what *we* need to do to minister to our single parents.

At present, our plan is to have special meetings of single parents but not to isolate single parents from the communities of which they are now a part. Also, it is the intention of the parent group to invite any interested single to events that include the children. Some singles who are not parents want to be around children and would enjoy such an event.

Effective programming keeps the needs of the people in mind; and all plans should reflect a sensitivity and care toward all aspects of the program.

Large-scale Single Adult Conferences

One of the best examples of effective programming on a multichurch scale has been the single adult conferences, which, from beginning to completion, have reflected the needs and concerns of the singles in different churches. The themes of these conferences reflect a growth process on the part of the single adult and the single adult programs in the churches.

The theme of our local conference in 1972 was "Putting It All Together." The emphasis was on relating to the fragmented concerns that singles have and channeling the problems to a healthy solution level. Probably the two most helpful lessons learned in that conference were (1) the conference was long overdue, and (2) the next conference will not include everything done in this conference. Some three hundred singles attended the conference, which lasted from Friday evening through Sunday morning. The main concern seemed to be "sex and the single adult."

The next conference was held in 1974. It was the first statewide singles conference, and the theme was "The Single Adventure—a Christian Alternative." Over one thousand singles shared in an emphasis on the adventure of life as a single rather than on the problems of life as a single. The main concern of this group of participants was self-identity.

Held in 1975, the third conference regionally limited to the North Texas area. By design, it was not going to be as large as the state conference. However, over seven hundred singles attended. The theme was "Christian Community: What a Way to Grow!" The main concern of the singles was spiritual growth.

The second statewide singles conference was in March, 1977, and the theme reflected a new attitude among singles—"Bold Direction: a Single Consideration." Singles and single adult programs in churches are growing and healthy. Christian singles are becoming bolder about their faith. The emphasis of this conference was on telling the good news of Christ to a world full of persons (particularly single adults) who are searching for meaning in life. This conference did not dwell on the problems or the personal concerns of singles, but on insights singles need in order to mature in their Christian faith. Response for this event has been great.

Just to indicate the quality of programming in the seminars, the topics alone made this conference a worthwhile experience. The topics were intended to challenge singles workers to move in bold direction. The topics were: World Hunger; What You Can Do About Politics—Right Now; Interpersonal Communication; Creative Single Parenting; Growing Through Divorce; Developing a Personal Theology; My "Response-Ability" to Difficulty; Single Adults and Their Parents: Letting Go; Personal Discoveries After Divorce and Before Remarriage; After My Mate's Death . . . A New Beginning; Being a Healthy Sexual Person; Discovering Personal Values; Growing Through Personal Bible Study; Sharing My Faith Authentically; Spiritual Growth: A Personal Process; The Art of Being Friends; Marriage: Before or After You Get Serious; Being a Christian Man in Today's World; Being a Christian Woman in Today's World; Over 40 . . . the Realities of Singleness; Balancing the Tension: Being Single; Open to Marriage; Single Avenues for Mission Involvement; The Christian and the Arts; Helping the Grieving Person; Ministering with Singles Through the Church; Teaching Singles the Bible; Working with Single Adults in Sunday School; Being a Single Adult in Your Home Church; Ministering to Exceptional Singles; and Pastoring Singles.

Each of the state conferences has included a miniconcerns packet. The miniconcerns committee predetermined some concerns of singles that were important but that they felt did not merit a full seminar period. They made available to all participants the following information about concerns of singles; why not share it with your singles?

A Single Miniconcern Is Selecting a Living Place

A consistently basic concern for single adults is the selection of a place to live. But it is a concern that is often dealt with on an almost thoughtless basis. Here are a few tips on what to think about and do in selecting a living place—which the average single adult does once every eleven months.

1. *Economic cost.*—Price of lease or cost of buying; utility costs; maintenance costs; furnishings costs; if buying—interest rates, taxes, insurance. Ask yourself what percentage of your salary is the monthly cost of your living place. Does the cost require a roommate to share expenses?

2. *Location.*—Proximity to job, public transportation, grocery store, laundromat, shopping areas, parks, schools, church, etc. The energy crisis has made proximity a matter of good economics. Do you like the neighborhood?

3. *Environment and facilities.*—Is what you get really worth what you pay? Will you really use all those facilities you are paying for? Could a cheaper place be fixed up? Do you fit in with the general life-style in the apartment complex or neighborhood?

The key "do" in selecting a living place is to think about it; don't just rush out and do it. Plan ahead enough to spend a few weeks looking around. The effort of planning is worth avoiding dissatisfaction with a place you bought or have leased for twelve months. Use the newspaper as your primary source of finding new living places, but don't overlook scouting around neighborhoods you like for vacant places or checking in neighborhood stores, schools, or churches for rental notices or asking friends. Depending on the amount of free time you have, an apartment selector service may be appropriate—but be clear on what you are getting into before you go this route.

To roommate or not? The only clear answer here is that the potential for problems in your at-home life increases with roommates. If there are clearly compensating values in living with others who you think are compatible, and if you are ready to deal with the drawbacks, then go to it. But start with and maintain a frank, open dialogue about likes and dislikes. Remember, the most uncomfortable situation of all is to have a place that costs enough for two but no roomie—so be sure of compatibility and availability of roommates before you obligate yourself.

Don't sign leases without understanding them; and if you don't understand yours, take it to someone who does understand lease talk. The key provisions to look for are the length of the lease, requirements for notice of moving out, acceptable reasons for breaking the lease (there should always be some—new job, etc.), and the how and when of getting your deposits back. When you are shopping around for apartments you like, compare the leases as well as the decors. Get a copy of the lease at each place you look. If they won't let you take one, then you don't want to live there.

Renting or buying? Renting gives you freedom. Buying gives you responsibility. Which are you ready for? Buying is generally better economics if you are ready for keeping up with maintenance, property taxes, insurance, yards, and the hassle of selling it someday. If you aren't really attracted by all this or are a mobile person, then renting is your best bet.

A Single Miniconcern Is Personal Finance

1. Budgeting

Your personal budget should be kept simple and should be flexible enough to allow for minor surprises. Some basic rules for setting up a budget are:

A. For two or three months, keep *close* records on how much you spend. The best way to do this is to get receipts for all your expenses (grocery tapes, credit card slips, etc.).

B. Prepare a list of one-time-a-year expenses, such as license plates, insurance policies (auto, life, health, etc.), and property taxes.

C. Divide the items in letter B above by twelve to see what the approximate monthly expense would be.

D. Prepare a list of all the loans you have and the monthly payment for each loan.

The sum of numbers 1, 3, and 4 above will give you a good idea of how much of your check is being spent on regular monthly bills. The remainder of your take-home pay can be used for surprises, savings, or anything that would be unusual for your personal budget.

Note: Be sure to remember that a budget is only a guideline to spending and is only as good as you make it. *No* system is going to prevent overspending and mismanagement unless you have the desire to control those tendencies.

2: Installment Buying

Installment purchases are an extremely vulnerable area for anyone. Don't be swayed by the "low monthly payment." There are two basic questions you should ask about any loan.

A. *What is the interest rate?* Lenders are required by law to show you the interest rate *in writing.* They may mention different types of rates (add-on, percentage of the unpaid balance per month, or simple), but they will be required to disclose the *simple* rate on the form you sign. (Simple interest is the method the banks use to calculate interest on a business loan.)

B. *What is the total number of payments?* By multiplying the number of payments by the amount of one payment and subtracting from that the purchase price of the product, you can determine how much interest you are paying for the product. (This must also be disclosed on the loan form.)

The most important thing to remember about installment purchases is that they will be with you for some time. If you overextend yourself in this area, you could surely damage your credit rating, which will be discussed in the next section.

3. Credit Rating

A person's credit rating is his most important financial asset. It can help in business investments and large purchases that must be financed (cars, homes, etc.) and is a source of funds in case of a financial emergency. Here are some guidelines for establishing and maintaining a good credit rating.

A. Set up your own personal budget, using the outline previously described, and *stick to it.*

B. Take out loans only when doing so is absolutely necessary, and set up a reminder system so that you don't forget to make the payments on time. (Good intentions don't make good credit ratings.)

C. About once every two years, have a credit check made on yourself. The cost is minimal and is well worth it. If any false or misleading information is listed, then you have the right to make a formal complaint to have it corrected.

4. Insurance

Insurance needs will vary from individual to individual, depending upon income and property; however, each individual should carry some basic coverage (some policies may be provided by your employer).

A. *Life insurance.*—$10,000 to $20,000. This could be either cash value or term. Cash value will be a form of savings and also will guarantee a constant monthly charge as long as you hold the policy. Term insurance will eventually expire and possibly could be canceled if your health is not good. (Term is less expensive than cash value.)

B. *Major medical health insurance.*—$20,000 to $30,000. Types and limits of coverage vary greatly. This is usually provided by your employer. If so, contact him for the specifics of his policy. If you have no coverage of this variety, contact your insurance agent and try to secure a group rate. He will be able to explain in detail the coverage you are buying.

C. *Auto insurance.*—A minimum liability is required by Texas law. If you drive a newer car, the lending agency will probably require some collision coverage for the life of the loan. If your lender will agree, you might consider having a larger deductible ($250 instead of $100). This plan will lower your premiums without your incurring a substantial loss in coverage.

The above are necessary; however, other policies and increased coverage on the above should be considered. You should consult your personal insurance agent for your particular needs. He will have a better understanding of your individual situation.

5. Income Tax Matters

Income tax returns can be fairly simple or extremely complicated, depending upon your financial transactions. A person simply working for one or two withholding employers with little or no outside income can, with some basic instructions, file his own return. If you have several investments of a complicated nature or are self-employed, a local CPA can probably handle your return better unless you are somewhat acquainted with the matter.

Things to remember when filing your own income tax return:

A. If you intend to itemize your deductions, keep all receipts for tax-deductible items. Page __ of your 19__ tax-return booklet outlines these items very explicitly.

B. Calculate your tax both ways—using the standard deduction and itemizing your deductions, to see which way would cost you less. You are allowed to switch from standard deductions to itemizing deductions from one year to the next.

C. Recalculate your tax return to make sure there are no mathematical errors. Any error could cost you penalties and interest for not paying all of your taxes on time. It will definitely slow down your receiving a refund.

D. To avoid a delay in receiving your refund, file *before* January 31. The IRS will try to get the refund back to you within four to six weeks.

E. If you have questions on your return, don't hesitate to call the Internal Revenue Office. They have people on their staff who do nothing but answer your questions. Their numbers are:

Local area: _____

Outside local area: _____ (toll free)

6. *Investments*

It would be impossible to discuss all investment opportunities adequately in this guide. Therefore, the avenues mentioned will be those with which most individuals are associated.

A. LAND
1. Land should only be used for long-term investments.
2. Be acquainted with the person selling the land.
3. Ask for specific information concerning zoning (commercial or residential), accessibility to major highways, and future growth plans for that area.
4. Remember that the value of the land is what someone offers to pay for it, not what a salesman quotes.
5. Be sure to look at the land you are buying.
6. There have been many sorry investors who did not take the time necessary to analyze their land purchase adequately before buying. There is money to be made in land investment; however, to do so will take some time and knowledge.

B. SAVINGS
This is the safest investment an individual can make. Although

the gains are lower than other investments, there is virtually no risk. Everyone should have some form of savings set aside for emergencies. Be sure the bank or savings and loan company you use is insured by an agency of the government (FDIC for banks and FSLIC for savings and loans). This guarantees that if anything happens to that bank or savings and loan company, the government will return all of your savings up to $20,000.

C. CERTIFICATES OF DEPOSIT

These are distinguished from savings accounts in that they cannot be withdrawn before the date mentioned on the certificate (from ninety days to four years) without your paying a penalty and losing interest. These do have a fair rate of return and are the safest of any long-term investments. One thing to remember: Certificates are automatically renewed unless you instruct the bank to do otherwise. Be sure to keep track of due dates so that you can determine whether or not you wish to continue this type of investment or use the cash for some other purpose.

D. STOCK MARKET

Needless to say, fortunes have been made and lost here. The best advice anyone can offer you is to consult with a stockbroker (referred to you by a friend) who uses the stock market as a source of investment. A broker will charge for his services by taking a commission off of what stock you buy and sell. If he is a successful broker with quite a few successful clients, he is well worth the small fee.

A Single Miniconcern Is Car Buying and Maintenance

A frequent question of single women is, "How do I buy a car and keep it in good running shape without getting cheated?" The truth is that this complaint is universal—but single men often just don't voice it.

The first hurdle is to decide that you *are* going to learn something about cars. The second hurdle is doing it. The public library is full of books and magazine articles on buying and keeping up cars; many schools or community organizations offer short courses in auto repairs. Talk to knowledgeable friends.

1. Car Buying

Cost is usually the first thought here, but maybe it shouldn't be.

Think about what you really minimally need, the length of time you want to keep the car, and the sort of travel you will be using it for most of the time. Also, shop around for car sellers with good reputations or deal with ones you have personal confidence in.

Inspect any car you buy—look around it and pull and tug on things (if they come loose or sound funny, you should be concerned); and if you are worried, take the car to an independent garage and pay a mechanic to look it over while you are standing there. Buying a car from an individual owner may be a savings, but individual owners rarely guarantee the condition of the car.

It is usually best to arrange your own financing. Use a bank. They like car loans. They may even give you some tips on price.

Remember, cost is a matter of several things—not just purchase price but also upkeep, car life, *gas mileage,* and resale value.

Several consumer magazines, such as *Changing Times* and *Consumer Reports,* give reports on how different makes of cars compare. A few hours of reading time spent in a library may mean money in your pocket.

2. Car Maintenance and Repair

1. Inspect tires for wear and air pressure twice a month. If tires wear uneven or spotty, have them rotated and the alignment checked.

2. Have front-end alignment checked twice a year or after hitting a severe bump.

3. Have a tune-up—that is, new spark plugs, points, condenser (and sometimes new rotor or distributor caps) every 12,000—15,000 miles. Cost runs $25—$40. It is worth it in car durability and *gas* savings.

4. Check battery water level and battery posts for acid buildup *often*—any time your car doesn't start check battery connections for tightness and posts for acid buildup (any carbonated liquid will clean posts). Battery life is about two and one-half years.

5. Find and replace cracking hoses and worn belts before they break through.

6. Keep car maintained at proper intervals—see car manual (comes with car or may be available in library or at car dealer).

7. Brakes—if you hear a dragging sound, get linings replaced immediately.

3. Finding Mechanics

When in doubt, go to a big car dealership for repair work. Shade-tree and independent mechanics may be less expensive, but their work is very often sloppy or inexpert. A small measure of self-protection is to check the auto repair business' reputation through the Better Business Bureau before taking your car in. Bells should ring and warnings should flash if work is not accomplished within the time first promised. This is the common prelude to a series of broken promises. Get your car out and to another mechanic immediately.

A Single Miniconcern Is Use of Professional Services

As society becomes larger and more complex, the specialization of services grows. The question for the single adult is when to utilize the specialized service to advantage.

Laymen frequently find just the decision to seek professional help and the picking of a good doctor, lawyer, dentist, and so on perplexing.

There is little doubt, however, that the use of a competent professional service will enhance and simplify the single adult life. If nothing else, the self-assurance that an important problem—health, taxes, auto accident—is being attended to properly is worth a lot.

1. Medical and Related

Developing the habit of periodic general physical checkups is a hedge against future serious physical problems. A really detailed physical exam with electrocardiograms and other tests of specific body conditions runs in the range of $90—$150. Have one of these every few years, or as recommended by a doctor, plus simple, yearly checkups which cost less and are really inexpensive when considered on a per annum or lifetime basis. There is also the added advantage of being generally familiar with medical procedures and knowing a doctor in whom you have confidence.

Periodic checkups with dentists and opthalmologists provide similar benefits.

Remember that any specific physical problem is likely to get worse if not attended to, and the cost of getting healthier gets higher.

2. Legal

Outside of estate planning, which even single adults probably need if they have significant life insurance proceeds, there are few general life conditions that need the regular attention of a lawyer. But there are many specific problems single adults encounter that would be advantageous to the single adult if brought to a lawyer—warranty and repair problems with autos and appliances, on-the-job injuries, personal injuries, employment contracts and terminations, traffic tickets that would affect insurance rates, small business investments, deposit problems with apartment leases, and home-buying contracts. There is a tendency to regard these sorts of problems as of little worth. Often this is not true. Benefits that are available by law are often lost by one's listening to what may be the one-sided advice of insurance adjusters, real-estate agents, and others. The key advice here is that if you get good legal advice, it will include a frank answer as to whether your problem really needs the attention of a lawyer.

3. Financial

Financial advice is often available from many sources. The problem is sorting the good from the bad. One test is whether your adviser is going to benefit directly from your expenditure. If so, then it is appropriate to be cautious about getting your question fully answered to your satisfaction. And if you can't get full answers, forego the advice or seek the independent advice of a CPA, a banker, or a lawyer.

In summation, the keys to advantageously using professional services are:

1. Don't put off finding out if your problem needs professional attention.

2. Find and stick with professionals you like and trust—there's no point in dealing with a professional whose competence you question.

A Miniconcern Is Single Parenting

1. Keep the lines of communication open. Listen as well as advise. If parents do not take time to listen, children quit trying to talk; and the problems grow larger and larger.

Develop these attitudes about listening:

A. You must want to hear what the child has to say.
B. You must genuinely want to be helpful to him.
C. You must be able to accept his feelings.
D. You must trust the child's capacity to handle his feelings and to find solutions to his problems.

    E. You must appreciate that feelings are transitory, not permanent.

    F. You must be able to see your child as someone separate from yourself, an individual.

2. Give their problems the importance they deserve . . . from their point of view. When they come with a small problem and parents discount it as such, they are reluctant to bring big problems to us.

    Be an *active* listener! An active listener will:

    A. Give feedback on what he actually heard the child say.

    B. Give feedback on what he thinks the child means . . . "Do you mean . . . ?"

By using the skill of active listening, we:

    A. Help the child express negative feelings so he can get rid of them.

    B. Help the child become less afraid of negative feelings.

    C. Promote a feeling of warmth between parent and child.

    D. Influence the child to be more willing to listen to the parent's thoughts and ideas.

    E. Facilitate problem solving by the child.

    F. Help him think for himself and develop his own constructive solutions.

3. Spend some time each week with each child *alone.* This practice seems to make them feel that they are as special as they really are and gives us time to build the close relationship we enjoy.

4. Have family meetings where any problems are discussed or special times are planned. This seems to be a favorite time for everyone. Many ideas are exchanged, and personal experiences are shared. This also contributes to bringing us closer together as a family.

5. Be happy where we are now! Most single parents don't have plans for being single always, but let's not wait until someday to be happy. Philippians 4:11 says, "For I have learned, in whatsoever state I am, therewith to be content." Our children get their zest for living from us; and if we start and end our days with the weight of the world on our shoulders, our children may never want to become adults.

6. We need to set examples for our children, and the most important one is to show them that we trust the Lord to work out the problems and provide for our needs. Philippians 4:19 says, "But my God shall

supply all your need according to his riches in glory by Christ Jesus." This means all our needs, not just material things!

7. Start each day by asking God for direction, guidance, and wisdom. He never fails to give us what we ask if we ask and believe.

A Final Word

Some singles programs cross denominational lines. It is important to recognize that many groups change and that programming will not remain the same. Some groups leave their original intent and may have already outlived their usefulness as an organization.

It is not a tragic thing when an organization dies because it is not presently meeting needs. Why continue to attempt to sustain life when life has already departed? A good idea may be seasonal (like friendships), yet some ideas may be good for all seasons (like a few friendships).

Just in case this emphasis on effective programming has offended the person who looks for ideas everywhere and uses the ones that seem feasible, I have no quarrel with a person who is always wanting to learn. My regret is for the singles in a church who are given ideas from various sources and who are encouraged to respond to an idea because it works somewhere else. I support any group of singles doing *anything* that is working for them, regardless of where the idea comes from. Needs of singles are similar (but not the same) in almost every church. Allow singles the freedom to help style their program and ministries, and both will bear fruit.

Notes

Chapter 1

1. Britton Wood, chapter 5, *It's O.K. to Be Single,* Gary R. Collins, ed. (Waco: Word Books, 1976).

Chapter 3

1. Linda Lawson, *Life as a Single Adult* (Nashville: Convention Press, 1975), p. 5.

Chapter 4

1. Elisabeth Kübler-Ross, ed., *Death, The Final Stage of Growth* (Englewood Cliffs: Prentice-Hall, Inc., 1975).
2. John Claypool, *Southwestern News,* November 1976.
3. Catherine Marshall, *To Live Again* (New York: McGraw-Hill Book Company, 1957), pp. 107-108.

Chapter 5

1. Dwight H. Small, *The Right to Remarry* (Old Tappan: Fleming H. Revell Company, 1975), p. 163.
2. Ibid., p. 183.

Chapter 6

1. Esther Oshiver Fisher, *Divorce, The New Freedom* (New York: Harper and Row, 1974), p. 27.
2. Russell Dicks, *Faith at Work* (March 1975), p. 31.

Bibliography

The following bibliography is the work of the Resource Committee for the State Single Adult Conference. This example of good effort on the part of the singles in a multichurch conference is intended to be helpful rather than exhaustive.

I. NEVER-MARRIED SINGLES

Anders, Sarah Frances. *Woman Alone: Confident and Creative.* Nashville: Broadman Press, 1976. Written especially for today's breed of single women who face life by looking ahead instead of back.

Bontrager, Frances M. *The Church and the Single Adult.* Scottsdale: Herald Press, 1968. Gives a good definition of what happiness for a single, fulfilled person should be. Also, has very practical suggestions on how the church's ministry can aid a single woman to feel fulfilled.

Buytendijk, F. J. J. *Woman—a Contemporary View.* New York: Associated Press, 1968. An in-depth study dedicated to helping a woman understand herself better in a twentieth-century context.

Collins, Gary R., ed. *It's O.K. to Be Single.* Waco: Word Books, 1976. This is a challenge to singles to adopt full and meaningful life-styles and to become whole persons, determined to follow Christ.

Evening, Margaret. *Who Walk Alone—a Consideration of the Single Life.* London: Hodder and Stoughton, 1974. Thought-provoking, with good, practical answers to many questions which singles have. Written from a celibate viewpoint.

Gilder, George. *Naked Nomads: Unmarried Men in America.* New York: Quadrangle, 1974. Focus on the single man. Contrasts the world view of the single man with that of the real single man.

Hugen, Walter D. *The Church's Ministry to the Older Unmarried.* Grand Rapids: William B. Eerdmans, 1960. Outlines the major problems and needs of the older unmarried. A very significant contribution to aid the church in reassessing its attitudes toward this group.

Hunt, Gladys. *MS. Means Myself.* Grand Rapids: Zondervan Publishing House, 1972. Deals with the issues of helping women become whole persons, discover the meaning and beauty of life, maximize their potential, and

171

learn that godliness with contentment is gain.

Jepson, Sarah. *Devotions for the Single Set.* Carol Stream, Illinois: Creation House, 1972. A series of daily devotions for the singles dealing with subjects such as creativity, fear, identity, jealousy, loneliness, and so forth.

Jepson, Sarah. *For the Love of Singles.* Carol Stream: Creation House, 1970. Using real-life situations and character studies from the Bible, Jepson gives a positive look at the single life as a wholesome life in Christ.

Kosten, Andrew. *How You Can Conquer Loneliness.* New York: Twayne Publishers, 1961. A constructive, applicable help to conquer man's basic problem, loneliness. A practical, systematic approach that can be applied to one's own personal life.

McGinnis, Marilyn. *Single.* Old Tappan: Fleming H. Revell Company, 1974. The author talks to single women about how to handle finances, roommates, loneliness, parents, and other problems facing them.

Moore, Allen J. *The Young Adult Generation.* Nashville: Abingdon Press, 1969. An interpretative research that uses clinical observations. Written from a theological perspective based on social and psychological data on contemporary man and his culture.

Mumaw, Evelyn. *Woman Alone.* Scottsdale: Herald Press, 1970. A subjective look at various phases of life situations of the single woman. Directed toward Christian single women seeking the lordship of Christ.

Narramore, Clyde. *This Way to Happiness.* Grand Rapids: Zondervan Press, 1972. Drawing from numerous case histories and experiences as a consulting psychologist, Narramore discusses a positive outlook on life and the need of its basic ingredient, happiness, regardless of the marital status.

Towns, Elmer L. *Ministering to the Young Single Adult.* Grand Rapids: Baker Book House, 1974. Deals with pertinent issues and trends today and how/why the church should be concerned about single adults now more than ever before. Seeks to provide a better understanding of the single adult as a person.

Andrews, Gini. *Sons of Freedom.* Grand Rapids: Zondervan, 1975. Written for single men, this book deals with the conflicts and problems faced by the single man.

Lawson, Linda. *Life as a Single Adult.* Nashville: Convention Press, 1975. Part of the Family Enrichment Series. Emphasis on acceptance of yourself and the role of the single.

II. CAMPUS SINGLES

Becker, Howard S. *Campus Power Struggle.* Aldine Publishing Company, 1970. A brief series of observations by authorities from campuses around the world. Deals with the causes of campus strife as well as some viable solutions.

Bell, Daniel, and Kristol, Irvine, eds. *Confrontation: the Student Rebellion and the University.* New York: Basic Books, Inc., 1968. Insightful research into the troubles of American college students. An in-depth look into:

1) the rise of mass higher education; 2) the burgeoning of research; 3) the multiplication of scholarly fields and differentiation of subjects into newer and smaller specializations; 4) the "national" university system.

Blaine, Graham B., Jr. *Emotional Problems of the Student.* New York: Appleton-Century-Crofts, 1961. A collection of articles describing the psychiatric problems of students and the manner in which they are dealt with. Covers subjects such as faculty counseling, student neuroses, study problems, character disorders, homosexuality, depression, suicide, and therapy as related to the university student.

Brickman, William W., and Lehrer, Stanley, eds. *Conflict and Change on the Campus.* New York: School and Society Books, 1970. Timely group of statements by nationally known leaders. A look at what is happening on the American college scene from inside the university structure and without. Some of the contributors include: Art Buchwald, Margaret Mead, Richard Nixon, Edward Kennedy, Shirley Chisholm, and John Mitchell.

Brown, Michael. *The Politics and Anti-Politics of the Young.* Beverly Hills, California: Glencoe Press, 1969. A short but stimulating look at the turmoil of the sixties. It includes the origin of youth militancy, demands for student and black "power," an analysis of "anti-politics," and a chapter containing statements by many leading radicals from campuses across the nation.

Cole, Luella, and Hall, Irma Nelson. *Psychology of Adolescence.* New York: Holt, Rinehart and Winston, 1970. A thorough book dealing with youth psychology. Helpful to parents, counselors, teachers, and friends of youth. The sections of the book cover the physical, emotional, social, moral, and intellectual development of young people.

Dennis, Lawrence E., and Kaullman, Joseph F. *The College and the Student.* Washington, D.C.: American Council on Education, 1966. A handbook for the college student, especially the mature single student. Many contributors from a wide field of study make it worthwhile. Covers such areas as the perspective of higher education, the campus environment, freedom and the law, stress, and the moral revolution.

Freedman, Mervin B. *The College Experience.* San Francisco: Jossey-Bass Inc., 1967. A psychologist (and professor) gives his views on life in the university environment. He discusses the college and society, the personality development of the student, sexuality on campus, and the woman's future in education. The final chapters deal with significant campus issues.

Gottlieb, David, and Ramsey, Charles E. *The American Adolescent.* Homewood, Illinois: The Dorsey Press, 1964. An extensive look at the adolescent. Written by a parent in easy-to-understand terms. Valuable to the parent and the young person. The book answers many questions raised by adults concerning the reasons behind their children's behavior.

Handlin, Oscar, and Handlin, Mary F. *The American College and American Culture.* New York: McGraw-Hill, 1970. A scholarly look at the history of higher education and what it can tell the reader about the future. Of special interest to those who work with college students. The book is actually an essay that was delivered to the Carnegie Commission on Higher Education.

Katz, Joseph. *No Time for Youth*. San Francisco: Jossey-Bass Inc., 1968. This
book is based upon an impressive study of college students over a four-year
period. Over two hundred students were interviewed twice a year from
an original sample of several thousand students. The book is a reaction
to the way that these students felt. Subjects include: 1) how students
change; 2) from curriculum to career; and 3) student life and its problems.

Lloyd-Jones, Esther, and Estrin, Herman A., eds. *The American Student and
His College*. Boston: Houghton Mifflin, 1967. One of the most complete
books about the American student. Much time is given to the practical
side of student life and issues. The new breed of college students, the
American college campus, student culture, pressures and tensions, morals
and sex mores, student activities, and students' rights and responsibilities
are covered at length.

Martin, David, ed. *Anarchy and Culture: the Problem of the Contemporary
University*. Ypsilanti, Michigan: Eastern Michigan University Press, 1970.
An English professor looks at the worldwide student scene. He probes
the effect that students have upon the press and society. He also explains
why unrest is common to the university culture of today.

Minneman, Charles E., ed. *Students, Religion, and the Contemporary University*. Ypsilanti, Michigan: Eastern Michigan University Press, 1970. A
relevant insight into the realms of the university and religion, written
by the director of religious affairs of a large state university. The book
deals with the isolation of the university from the rest of the world. It
handles the area of conflicting values between churches and schools and
also provides some ways for a reconciliation between the two.

III. WIDOWED SINGLES

Anders, Sarah Frances. *Woman Alone: Confident and Creative*. Nashville:
Broadman Press, 1976. Written especially for today's breed of single
women who face life by looking ahead instead of back.

Decker, Bea, as told to Gladys Kooiman. *After the Flowers Are Gone*. Michigan:
Zondervan, 1973. This is a story of Bea Decker, the founder of They
Help Each Other Spiritually (THEOS), an organization of widowed
men and women helping each other face common problems.

Hunt, Morton M. *The World of the Formerly Married*. New York: McGraw-Hill,
1966. This book follows the formerly married through the process of
marital dissolution, separation, divorce, death, and the various phases
of self-discovery and readjustment.

Jackson, Edgar N. *Understanding Grief*. New York: Abingdon, 1957. A Methodist minister who has studied psychotherapy has written this integrated
study of the psychology, therapy, and philosophical aspects of bereavement.

Langer, Marian. *Learning to Live as a Widow*. New York: Julian Messner,
1957. This book is a discussion of bereavement and the feelings involved.
Also covers the areas of finances, careers, social life, effect on children,

adjustment to dating and to remarriage.

Lewis, Alfred Allan. *Three Out of Four Wives.* New York: Macmillan Publishing Co., 1975. The author gives valuable information about the realities and possibilities of life alone.

Newman, Joseph, ed. *Teach Your Wife to Be a Widow.* Washington, D.C.: U.S. News and World Report, Inc., 1973. This book is intended to help both men and women face up to the realities of death.

Oates, Wayne E. *Anxiety in Christian Experience.* Philadelphia: The Westminster Press, 1955. Presents a basic issue in any adequate psychology of religious experience. The needs of anxious persons focus the message of biblical and psychological truth, on the one hand, with the theory and practice of pastoral counseling, on the other hand.

Parkes, Colin Murray. *Bereavement.* New York: International Universities Press, 1972. This book describes the nature of the principal components of the reaction to bereavement, the effects of bereavement upon physical and mental health, and the nonspecific reaction to stress in general.

Scott, Nathan A., Jr. *The Modern Vision of Death.* Richmond, Virginia: John Knox Press, 1967. The book leads directly into central issues of human experience, especially as it is felt along the pulse of the people of our own time. It is a diverse collection that gathers everything from an analysis of the vision of death to one man's account of his own father's death and its meaning to him.

Walker, Harold B. *To Conquer Loneliness.* New York: Harper and Row, 1966. This is for those who feel they are walking alone in a fellowless world, haunted by days and nights of isolation from friendship and love.

Wiebe, Katie F. *Alone.* Illinois: Tyndale, 1976. This is a story of how a widow found strength to survive loneliness and loss of identity and how she moved from widowhood into a new life. It offers practical encouragement.

Young, Richard K., and Meiburg, Albert L., eds. *Spiritual Therapy.* New York: Harper and Row, 1960. The book goes into the spiritual therapy and the healing process of the sick.

Zalk, Louis. *How to Be a Successful Widow.* New York: Fleet Publishing, 1967.

IV. DIVORCED SINGLES

Berson, Barbara, and Bova, Ben. *Survival Guide for the Suddenly Single.* New York: St. Martin's Press, 1974. A personal account of two people. Gives many practical suggestions of meeting people freely, living in a house or apartment, and working out financial problems.

Cardwell, Albert L. *Life Alone: The World of the Formerly Married.* Nashville: Convention Press, 1976. A short booklet that discusses practical aspects of divorce and many of the problems that will face the divorced individual. The stages of grief and process of adjustment for a new widow are explored. Brings Christian insight into life alone.

Crook, Roger. *An Open Book to the Christian Divorcee.* Nashville: Broadman

Press, 1974. A candid, sensitive look at the controversy surrounding the
Christian who is divorced.

Epstein, Joseph. *Divorced in America.* New York: E. P. Dutton and Co., 1974.
The author touches upon factors causing divorce and the mental and
emotional grief it causes to both partners.

Hope, Karol, and Young, Nancy, eds. *Momma: the Source Book for Single
Mothers.* New York: Plumb Books, 1976. A book of readings by the two
organizers of the MOMMA organization. It is a hard-hitting story of the
emotions of today's single mothers. A source book of ideas, feelings, and
emotions.

Hudson, R. Lofton. *'Til Divorce Do Us Part—a Christian Looks at Divorce.*
Nashville: Thomas Nelson, 1973. The book is a help for the agony of
one who is burying a marriage dead through divorce. Useful for Christians
seeking help in this area.

Krantzler, Mel. *Creative Divorce.* New York: Signet Books, 1974. A personal
account. Deals with emotional anguish; building new relationships with
children, friends, and the world; and the struggle to discover one's true
self.

Peppler, Alice Stolper. *Divorced and Christian.* St. Louis: Concordia, 1974.
Deals with Christian divorce—not the causes, the church's position, or
the righteousness or wrongness of the parties involved. For people who
have tried to save their marriages and failed.

Sheresky, Norman, and Mannes, Maya. *Uncoupling: the Art of Coming Apart.*
New York: The Viking Press, 1972. A discussion of the social and legal
principles operative in divorce proceedings. Advocates less emotionalism
and greater objectivity on the part of the parents. The act of divorce
could be accomplished with minimum difficulty and maximum compatibility.

Smoke, Jim. *Growing Through Divorce.* Irvine, California: Harvest House, 1976.
A practical guide for persons who have become single because of one
person's choice. This book helps the individual move to a point of growth
instead of remaining in a attitude problem situation.

Towner, Jason. *Warm Reflections.* Nashville: Broadman Press, 1977. One man's
struggle to overcome the bitterness he feels after his divorce and to
recreate in himself the stirrings of hope and zest for life.

Wheeler, Michael. *No-Fault Divorce.* Boston: Beacon Press, 1974. Since traditional divorce laws do not often reflect the realities of contemporary
marriage, new approaches are recommended to make family dissolution
more truthful and humane.

V. SINGLE PARENTS

Bel Geddes, Joan. *How to Parent Alone—a Guide for Single Parents.* New
York: Seabury Press, 1974. Written from a practical knowledge and
research view. Deals with working out problems within oneself before

dealing with the problems of the children.

Despert, J. Louise. *Children of Divorce*. Garden City: Doubleday, 1953. Contemporary in style, this book discusses the emotional problems faced by parents after a divorce.

Goldstein, Joseph; Freud, Anna; and Solnit, Albert J. *Beyond the Best Interests of the Child*. New York: Free Press, 1973. A provocative application of psychoanalytic insight to child custody laws, psychiatry, and child study.

Grollman, Earl A. *Talking About Divorce—a Dialogue Between Parent and Child*. Boston: Beacon Press, 1975. Includes drawings by children and their views of divorce. The parent is to sit down with the child and use the book to talk to the child about the divorce. It also contains twelve pages of resources.

Hallet, Kathryn. *A Guide for Single Parents*. Millbrae, California: Celestial Arts, 1974. A useful and effective approach (using transactional analysis) to help children of divorced and single parents.

McFadden, Michael. *Bachelor Fatherhood—How to Raise and Enjoy Your Children as a Single Parent*. New York: Ace Books, 1974. Gives men a viewpoint not often seen in print on how to work with your children. The author has interviewed over fifty men in his research. While humorous in places, it deals mainly on a serious level.

Schlesinger, Benjamin. *The One-Parent Family*. Canada: University of Toronto Press, 1969. A social-work consultant discusses the different aspects of parenting alone.

Steinzor, Bernard. *When Parents Divorce*. New York: Pantheon Books, 1969. Practical information is offered on dealing with children and their divided loyalties.

Stuart, Irving R., and Abt, Lawrence E. *Children of Separation and Divorce*. New York: Grossman Publishers, 1972. A collection of articles written by specialists-psychologists, lawyers, clergy, and social workers. Examines the problems the children face in a divorce situation.

VI. SINGLE ADULTS IN SUNDAY SCHOOL

Lawson, Linda, editor/compiler. *Working with Single Adults in Sunday School*. Nashville: Convention Press, 1978. Written by a variety of qualified persons, this book lends insight into the why and how of planning effective Sunday School sessions with single adults. It is broad in scope, dealing with related areas such as physical space needs of singles groups.

Final Revision Checklist

ORGANIZATION

DEVELOPMENT

PARAGRAPHS

SENTENCES

WORDS

VOICE

MECHANICS

The Writing Commitment

SECOND EDITION

Michael E. Adelstein

UNIVERSITY OF KENTUCKY

Jean G. Pival

UNIVERSITY OF KENTUCKY

The
Writing Commitment

SECOND EDITION

Harcourt Brace Jovanovich, Inc.

NEW YORK   SAN DIEGO   CHICAGO   SAN FRANCISCO   ATLANTA
LONDON   SYDNEY   TORONTO

The Writing Commitment, Second Edition
Michael E. Adelstein   Jean G. Pival

Copyright © 1980, 1976 by Harcourt Brace Jovanovich, Inc.

ISBN: 0-15-597851-9
Library of Congress Catalog Number: 79-90526
Printed in the United States of America

Copyrights and Acknowledgments

The authors wish to thank the following publishers and copyright holders for permission to reprint material used in this book:

BRITISH LEYLAND MOTORS, INC., Leonia, N.J. and BOZELL & JACOBS ADVERTISING for the Jaguar E-type ad, reprinted from *Playboy,* June 1974.

CHANGE MAGAZINE for "Self-Knowledge for Students" by Harriet C. Selgisohn, reprinted from *Change,* Vol. 10, No. 6, June-July 1978. Copyright © 1978 Council on Learning, NBW Tower, New Rochelle, N.Y. 10801.

COWLES COMMUNICATIONS, INC., for "Motherhood: Who Needs It?" by Betty Rollin, reprinted from *Look,* September 1970. Copyright © Cowles Communications, Inc.

FIELD NEWSPAPER SYNDICATE for "There's No Pleasing a Lawn Freak" by Erma Bombeck, from her column *At Wit's End,* and for "Illogical Thinking in Gun Law Debate" by Sydney J. Harris, from his column *Strictly Personal.* Both articles © Field Enterprises, Inc.

HARCOURT BRACE JOVANOVICH, INC. and SECKER & WARBURG LTD. for the excerpt from "Some Thoughts on the Common Toad" by George Orwell, from *Shooting an Elephant and Other Essays.* Copyright 1945, 1946, 1949, 1950 by Sonia Brownell Orwell; renewed 1973, 1974, 1977 by Sonia Orwell; renewed 1978 by Sonia Pitt-Rivers.

THE LEXINGTON (KY.) HERALD LEADER for excerpts from an editorial on the ERA and a response to it, April 27, 1975 and May 3, 1975.

THE LOS ANGELES TIMES for "Nuclear Power: Death Trip?" by Paul R. Ehrlich.

THE LOUISVILLE COURIER-JOURNAL for the editorial "Use of Leaded Fuel Imperils Effort to Clear Worsening Air," from the Opinion Page. Copyright © 1978 *The Courier-Journal.*

McGRAW-HILL BOOK COMPANY for the excerpt from *Themes, Theories, and Therapy* by Albert R. Fitzhaber. Copyright © 1963 McGraw-Hill, Inc.

NATIONAL COUNCIL OF TEACHERS OF ENGLISH for the American dialect map, adapted from *Discovering American Dialects* by Roger W. Shuy. Copyright © 1967 National Council of Teachers of English.

THE NEW YORK TIMES COMPANY for "Vive La France" by Ted Morgan, from *New York Times Magazine,* May 12, 1974. © 1975 The New York Times Company.

UNIVERSITY OF KENTUCKY for "Ricky" by Roger Fain. © 1976 JAR, journal published by the Honors Program at the University of Kentucky.

THE WALL STREET JOURNAL for the editorial "Junk Food Ads." © 1975 Dow Jones & Company, Inc. All rights reserved.

THE WASHINGTON STAR SYNDICATE, INC. for "Government Meddling Can Be Hazardous to Freedoms" by James J. Kilpatrick. © The Washington Star Syndicate, Inc.

WOMAN'S DAY MAGAZINE for "How to Read a Road Map" by Julie Candler. Copyright © 1965 CBS Publications, Inc.

ZIFF-DAVIS PUBLISHING COMPANY for the excerpt from "Communal Sex and Communal Survival" by Laurence Veysey, reprinted from *Psychology Today.* Copyright © 1974 Ziff-Davis Publishing Company.

Preface

What's done is done. People usually have to live with their errors, omissions, and misjudgments. But not writers fortunate enough to revise their work for a second edition. Thus we have had the chance to improve *The Writing Commitment*.

This time around, we have added the experience of others to our own combined teaching experience of thirty-five years and our ten years of administering Freshman English at the University of Kentucky. We have incorporated suggestions from our colleagues at the University of Kentucky and at hundreds of other colleges and universities throughout the country. The second edition, even more than the first, therefore, has benefited from testing in a wide variety of classes, and from being used by a broad cross-section of instructors—composition specialists, literature specialists teaching one section of composition, linguists, and graduate assistants beginning their teaching careers.

As a result, we are confident that our second brainchild is far superior to the first—not merely a clone, but a fraternal twin; like its predecessor in many respects, but different. Besides making minor changes throughout, we have updated the examples, improved the exercises, clarified the instructions, and condensed and simplified the theoretical explanations. Specifically, the following major changes appear in this edition. We have:

● added a reference guide to provide a brief, clear discussion of grammar, usage, punctuation, spelling, mechanics, and the business letter, with many cross-references to items treated more fully in the text.
● strengthened the instruction in pre-writing by adding pre-writing approaches for description, exposition, and argument in chapters 12, 17, and 21.

- reduced the introductory sections and consolidated other material, resulting in nine fewer chapters. The text was shortened by tightening the prose, not by omitting any topics or changing the conversational tone. Indeed, the treatment of exposition has been expanded.
- organized the assignments into three sections—For Discussion, For Practice (short writing exercises suitable for homework), and For Writing (theme assignments).
- furnished summaries for all chapters except those that deal with special topics.
- added instruction on writing essay exams in chapter 16.
- simplified and clarified the treatment of argumentation and persuasion, and added a discussion of the problem-solution argument to the more traditional, deductive organization of persuasive writing.
- used a different short story in Part 5, and condensed the discussion of critical writing.
- emphasized the use of endnotes in the research paper, and updated documentation practices to conform with the *MLA Handbook;* a new student paper on the Amish exemplifies the discussion.

What remains unchanged is the organization of the first edition, a rhetorical approach that takes students from writer-oriented personal journal and autobiographical narrative to reader-oriented exposition and argument. As in the first edition, students can begin to write with relative freedom for an intimate, friendly audience and move sequentially on to the tighter restraints of form, language, usage, and sentence structure required in writing for a more distant, critical audience. We have also retained the spiral, integrated approach that proved so popular in the first edition. As before, instead of having separate chapters on sentences, diction, paragraphs, pre-writing, organization, revision, and so forth, we have presented these topics throughout the book, relating them to the mode being discussed, and circling back in later sections to pick up and assimilate skills taught earlier. But, as in the first edition, we have kept the sequence flexible, so that instructors can adapt the material to their own needs.

The format of the instructor's manual, *The Teaching Commitment,* also remains unchanged. In addition to answers to the exercises and suggestions for writing assignments, the manual includes suggestions for teaching and evaluating writing skills, background in the current state of the profession, and a bibliography of recent works relating to the teaching of composition. In 1978 Harcourt Brace Jovanovich published our second book, *The Reading Commitment,* a collection of short but complete readings planned to accompany *The Writing Commitment.* We designed this anthology to help students improve their reading as well as their writing, and to provide them with essays that would interest and challenge them. The new manual includes a group of syllabuses for one- and two-semester courses, both with and without the parallel use of *The Reading Commitment.*

Finally, our second edition retains the philosophy that no language usage is "wrong" or "incorrect" in itself, but may be undesirable when it is inappropriate to its context, audience, and purpose. We have tried to motivate students to consider the rhetorical situation and to adopt a stance designed for it. Our aim, as before, reflects our own philosophy of teaching —that a course in composition should open up the language horizons of students; that it should introduce them to the many voices available in written English; and that it should make them aware of their commitment to themselves and to their readers.

For their comprehensive reviews and for their invaluable advice, we are grateful to Lynn Z. Bloom, College of William and Mary; Wilsonia E. D. Cherry, The Florida State University; Connie C. Eble, The University of North Carolina at Chapel Hill; Stephen H. Goldman, The University of Kansas; Eleanor M. Hoffman, The University of Minnesota at Duluth; Gerald Levin, University of Akron; and Clemewell Young, Manchester Community College, Connecticut.

We are particularly indebted to four colleagues at the University of Kentucky: Kenneth W. Davis, for his continuous critical help and judicious arbitration of coauthor disagreements; Thomas Olshewsky, for his sage counsel on logic and persuasion; Alexander Gilchrist, for his thorough review of the library reference material; and William Magretta, for his common-sense help about linguistic matters.

We also appreciate the comments of the many instructors who helped us benefit from their classroom experience with the first edition. Among them are John Baker, Marshall University, West Virginia; Harry E. Batty, Western Wyoming College; Suzanne Berger, Western Illinois University; Judith L. Brown, Western Illinois University; Ruth M. Brown, San Diego State University; Julie Carson, University of Minnesota, Twin Cities; Sandra Clark, Anderson College, Indiana; Lillian Collingwood, University of Texas at El Paso; Daniel Colvin, Western Illinois University; Martha Day, Richard Bland College, Virginia; Peter DeBlois, Syracuse University; Brian J. Delaney, Blue Ridge Community College, Virginia; Robert Denham, Emory & Henry College, Virginia; R. Stanley Dicks, Wheeling College, Virginia; Beverly B. Dunklee, Rappahannock Community College, Virginia; Joyce Erickson, Seattle Pacific University; Paul Escholz, University of Vermont; Frank L. Fennell, Loyola University, Illinois; Joyce Flamm, Eastern Arizona College; Richard Fulkerson, East Texas State University; Shearle Furnish, University of Kentucky; Sr. M. Ruth Gehres, Brescia College, Kentucky; B. J. Gooch, University of Kentucky; Marion E. Hawkins, University of Wisconsin, River Falls; Odis G. Hill, University of Kentucky; Lee Hillenmeyer, University of Kentucky; John Howell, University of Kentucky; Henry Hutchings, III, Lamar University, Texas; Hugh J. Ingrasci, De Paul University, Illinois; David James, Oakland University, Michigan; Patricia Mavis Jenkins, Fairfield University, Connecticut; D. G. Kehl, Arizona State University; Norman V. L. Lanquist, Eastern Arizona College;

Dougald McMillan, University of North Carolina, Chapel Hill; Peter L. McNamara, University of North Carolina, Chapel Hill; Neil Nakadate, Iowa State University; Henry R. Norton, Huntington College, Indiana; Gerald R. O'Donnell, Niagara University, New York; Darwin Patnode, University of Wisconsin, River Falls; William M. Ramsey, University of North Carolina, Chapel Hill; Larus Reed, Virginia State University; Richard Regan, Fairfield University, Connecticut; Kay W. Rickard, University of Kentucky; Kenneth Risdon, University of Minnesota, Duluth; Al Rosa, University of Vermont; Joan Rosen, Oakland University, Michigan; Dale H. Ross, Iowa State University; Margaret Rouse, North Kentucky University; Edward Ruch, Catonsville Community College, Maryland; Sarah J. Schwartz, University of Wisconsin, River Falls; Barbara M. Smith, Western Wyoming College; Richard Veit, University of North Carolina, Wilmington; Sylvia S. Waggonheim, University of Maryland; Margaret Watson, Quinsigamond Community College, Massachusetts; Arlene Wesswick, Western Wyoming Community College; and David E. Williams, De Anza College, California.

At Harcourt Brace Jovanovich, we appreciate the personal interest and meticulous work of our manuscript editor, Natalie Bowen, and the special concern of our copy editor, Jean T. Davis, particularly for her laudatory work on the Index. And to the godfather of both editions, Eben W. Ludlow, we owe a lifetime of gratitude for his faith and guidance.

In addition, we wish to thank Deborah Combs, our unusually accurate and cooperative typist, who met every deadline, no matter how impossible.

Nor can we ever forget to thank our spouses, Carol and Joe, whose patience, understanding, and support have made life and work less trying during our labors.

MICHAEL E. ADELSTEIN

JEAN G. PIVAL

Contents

part four   The Argumentative Voice: Persuasive Writing

part five   The Critical Voice: Writing about Literature

part six   **The Authoritative Voice: The Research Paper**

Reference Guide

Introduction:
In Praise of
Writing Well

As a student in a writing course, you deserve answers to certain questions—the ones we hear in our classes:

Why learn to write?
Can I learn to write? How?
What is good writing?

As a reader of this textbook, you are entitled to the answers to other questions as well:

What is this book about?
How can I best use this book?
What does the title mean?

First questions first.

WHY LEARN TO WRITE?

Some teachers of composition may assume that students are naturally eager to learn how to write. We don't. We are aware that writing can be one of the most upsetting, frustrating, and exasperating of all human activities. Seldom do the words pour out; seldom do they sound or look the way we want them to. And seldom do we or our students—or most people, for that matter—want to write. Then why learn to do so?

True, some people do find writing a release, an act of creation, a means of self-expression comparable to painting, sculpting, or composing. For other people, writing can provide emotional relief or ego satisfaction by allowing them to sound off, to state their ideas in articles and books or their gripes in letters to college or community newspapers. But you may have neither artistic urges to satisfy nor strong opinions to air. If so, what's the point of learning to write?

The honest answer is that occasionally you will *have* to write even though you won't be eager to do so—just as you have to write in freshman English. What's more, the subjects may be even less appealing. Look, for example, at the writing you've done in the past. Let's start with that thank-you letter you struggled over to an aunt, uncle, or other relative for a graduation or birthday gift. If you're like most people, you probably put it off as long as possible, always finding something else that had to be done, telling yourself that you would get to it . . . soon. Finally, nagged by your parents or tormented by your conscience, you dragged yourself to face the torture of scratching out a few sentences of gratitude. Because you wanted to? Or because—for social or other reasons—you were compelled to?

Then there was that application letter for a summer job. Or the biographical sketch for a high school or college form. Or your letter of inquiry about a scholarship, loan, or dorm room, or about camping facilities, group travel rates, baseball tickets. Or the speech you prepared for a contest, debate, class election, graduation. Weren't you required to write in these situations?

And what of the road ahead? Largely on the basis of your writing skills, you will be evaluated by college professors who will determine what you have learned and understood in their courses from written examinations and papers. As you progress from introductory courses to more advanced ones, more writing will be required. And then there are various organizations, scholarships, or honors competitions that require you to furnish written information: applications, biographical material, project plans.

And after the undergraduate years? Admission to graduate, law, medical, and other professional schools often hinges on written applications and the verbal ability you can demonstrate in entrance examinations. Graduate and professional schools require research papers, comprehensive examinations, master's and doctor's theses. And your career may be chock-full of writing assignments. If you plan to enter business, government, or one of the professions, you should heed the words of Peter Drucker, a nationally recognized management consultant: "As soon as you move one step up from the bottom, your effectiveness depends on your ability to reach others through the spoken or written word."

Which brings us back to where you are: at the bottom, in a sense—looking ahead to two or four years of college, perhaps graduate school, and a career. For many important purposes in that future, you will be represented by your writing. You will be known, evaluated, admitted, given a job, promoted—achieve success or not—on the basis of your writing. Professors, registrars, deans, award and admissions committees, personnel managers, executives, and others ordinarily cannot take the time to listen to you at length. You must state your case in effective writing. Your message is you.

There is another reason for learning to write—less practical, perhaps, but more meaningful. Writing is a form of discovery about who you are and what you think. Learning about yourself may not guarantee that you will attain better grades in college or a rewarding job later on, but it can help lead you to self-realization. Writing, then, can be a process of self-discovery. How?

Usually you don't know exactly what you think until you've expressed it in either speech or writing. In speech, you talk with an instantaneous rush of words, taking little time for deliberation or reflection, organization or arrangement, refinement or revision. Also, in speech you can generally get by with flip remarks; in writing, you are forced to express your ideas more carefully. Suppose you were called upon in another class to express your views on abortion, the death penalty, homosexuality, or women's rights. Even though you may not have thought much about the subject, you probably would provide an answer. But if you were asked instead to write a paper on that topic, you would consider the issue at some length, weighing the arguments for and against, taking the time to reflect on your ideas, deliberate about particular words, consider the implications of some sentences, change, shift, eliminate, revise, edit. Speaking is easier, less demanding, but writing is more likely to bring out the best in us, producing our clearest and most comprehensive statement on any subject. In the process of writing, we give full shape to our thoughts, our feelings, even our values. Thus, the writing process involves discovery of self.

Finally, although writing is hard work, we believe it brings its own rewards. There is something very satisfying and fulfilling about completing a paper that expresses your feelings or opinions about a subject. It may be compared to other creative acts: cooking a gourmet meal, taking photographs, designing a house, making pottery—all contain your flavor, your signature, your touch.

Even if you concede that practicality, self-discovery, and creative fulfillment are admirable reasons for learning to write, the second question may still plague you: Can I learn to write?

CAN I LEARN TO WRITE? HOW?

Of course you can. Every college freshman can learn to write. But we are not talking about writing stories, poems, or plays. Imaginative literature requires creative gifts—unusual powers of imagination, perception, sensitivity, and intelligence. Not every college student can write literature or probably even learn to write gracefully and fluently. But every college student can learn to write the clear, concise, appropriate prose required in college and the working world. Writing may come more slowly to some than to others, but with interest and effort, come it will.

Learning to write, like learning practically any other skill, involves three components: instruction, practice, and criticism. Let's apply them to learning how to play a sport—say, tennis. Instruction is provided by a book or a coach, telling and showing you how to hold a racquet, how to stand, how to swing, and the like. Then come hours of practice, hitting a ball against a backboard, volleying with friends, entering tournaments. And during this time, your coach or a relative or friend often provides criticism, pointing out that you're not throwing the ball up properly on your serve or not getting your racquet back far enough on your backhand. So you practice throwing the ball up properly or getting your racquet back. Instruction, practice, criticism. That's also how you learned to swim, read, or fish; or play the piano, chess, or hearts; or drive a car, truck, or tractor.

How will you learn to write? You guessed it. This textbook and your professor will provide the instruction. And you will write papers—to some extent, the more the better. You can learn to write and improve your writing only by writing. There is no other way. And just as college football players spend hundreds of hours in practice—blocking, running, tackling, passing, catching, punting—so you will spend many hours in practice—planning, organizing, writing, revising, and proofreading papers. It would be delightful if you could merely read this book or listen to your instructor or pop answers into workbook exercise slots, but unfortunately none of these can replace practice in writing. And your instructor will criticize your efforts, acting like a coach to praise what you are doing well, point out what you are doing poorly, and show you how to improve.

That's how the semester will pass—instruction, practice, criticism— and that's how you will learn to write.

We assume, of course, that you are willing to learn to write and to work hard at it. It will not come easily or quickly; nothing complex and demanding and significant ever does. At times you may doubt that you are making progress, but we assure you that at the end of the term, by comparing your first papers with your later ones, you will be able to see that your writing has improved a great deal.

WHAT IS GOOD WRITING?

Since "good writing" is one of those ideal abstractions that are seldom pinned down—held in high esteem, but rarely defined—let's list some of its characteristics.

● Good writing reflects the writer's ability to use the appropriate voice. Even though all good writing conveys the sound of someone talking to someone else, the voice heard through the writing must also suit the purpose and audience of the writing occasion. Just as you change speaking styles when moving from highly informal to formal situations, so too your writing voice should vary to create your desired relationship with your readers. A good writer is adaptable: capable of shaping language usage, writing form, and methods of handling the material to the purpose of the writing and to the needs of the intended readers.

- Good writing reflects the writer's ability to organize the material into a coherent whole so that it moves logically from a central, dominant idea to the supporting points and finally to a consistent ending, conveying to the reader a sense of a well-thought-out plan.

- Good writing reflects the writer's ability to write clearly and unambiguously—to utilize sentence structure, language, and examples so that the only possible meaning is the writer's intended one. Readers should not have to strain or struggle to understand what is written.

- Good writing reflects the writer's ability to write convincingly—to interest readers in the subject and to demonstrate a thorough and sound understanding of it. Important, too, in developing a tone of conviction is economy: all unnecessary words and repetitive phrases are eliminated, and every word contributes to meaning.

- Good writing reflects the writer's ability to criticize the first draft and revise it. All the previously discussed characteristics are rarely achieved at a first writing. You must learn early that thorough revision—painful though it can be—is the key to effective writing.

- Good writing reflects the writer's pride in the manuscript—the willingness to spell and punctuate accurately, to check word meanings and grammatical relationships within the sentences before submitting the finished product to the scrutiny of an audience. A good writer realizes that such surface defects can ruin the overall effect of the written material.

We assure you that none of these characteristics is beyond your capacity to master. As you work your way through the textbook and the course, you will be given instruction, practice, and criticism at each step. If you are willing to experiment, start over, and revise until you achieve the effect you want, then you will be on your way to writing well. Remember, writing is a complicated, ongoing skill: you cannot hope to master it in a one- or two-semester course. We can point you down the right road, but you must do the traveling toward good writing yourself. We hope that you find this book a useful road map.

WHAT IS THIS BOOK ABOUT?

The Writing Commitment uses a rhetorical approach, which means that it provides instruction in the art of discovering the most effective way to express ideas. Rhetoric is practical, involving a search for the form of writing that will succeed in achieving a particular purpose with a particular audience in a particular context. Thus rhetoric is primarily concerned with effectiveness, with what works best.

Underlying a rhetorical approach such as this is a key concept: not all writing is the same. Everything you write—a letter home for money, a newsy note to a friend, an application for a work-study grant—is written for a particular purpose to a particular audience in a particular context. The purpose of the letter home is to persuade, the audience is friendly, the context is serious. The newsy note aims to inform and entertain, its audience is friendly, its context is informal. The application tries to persuade, the audience is unknown, the context is formal.

The rhetorical approach to writing can help in these and all other writing situations by preparing you for the different problems in each and by making you aware of the different ways to cope with them. In a manner of speaking, rhetoric provides you with numerous game plans to use in various circumstances instead of giving you one set pattern to use in all situations. Consequently, mastering rhetorical principles requires reason rather than memory and necessitates an analysis of purpose, audience, and context. These principles, indeed, are more difficult to learn than a set of rules. But they are more interesting, practical, and valuable because they prepare you for the various writing assignments you will receive in college and in your career.

HOW CAN I BEST USE THIS BOOK?

To make this book more useful to you, we have organized it according to types of writing, moving from what is usually the simplest form—personal narrative—to the most difficult—the formal research paper.

In personal narrative you write about a subject you know well—yourself and your experiences—to an intimate audience—yourself, friends, and members of your family. The familiar subject and sympathetic readers in this kind of writing place few restraints on you. Next we move to descriptive writing, in which the subject—an object, scene, or person—is familiar, but the audience is often unknown to you and likely to expect more careful observance of writing conventions. Then on to expository writing: papers of classification, definition, analysis, and opinion. These kinds of subjects generally are more difficult to select and organize than are those in personal narrative and descriptive writing. Also, there may be special problems with readers because they are likely to be larger in number and more diverse in background. In the fourth kind of writing we discuss, persuasion and argumentation, the subject must be thoroughly understood, its logical structure analyzed, its surface and underlying assumptions tested. And the material must be shaped according to the backgrounds and attitudes of readers, who may favor, oppose, or be neutral toward the subject.

Finally, we discuss two special writing assignments: literary and research papers. Writing critical papers about literature requires some understanding of character, plot, setting, time, theme, and technique. And writing research papers demands a knowledge of the library, research techniques, and such formal conventions as endnotes and bibliography.

Within each unit of this six-part sequence about various kinds of writing is a consideration of certain rhetorical principles. Instead of going along with the traditional textbook treatment of these matters by providing separate chapters on sentences, language, paragraphs, organization, and the like, we discuss each of them as it pertains to a particular writing problem. The result is an integrated, spiral structure in which we take up each major rhetorical principle in relation to each kind of writing. Language use, for example, is considered in relation to its desired effect: in narrative and descriptive writing, language is selected for its richness of meaning; in expository writing, for its clarity; in persuasion, for its logical impact. Similarly, organization is not treated in one chapter but in several. In the discussion of personal writing, the emphasis is on chronological organization; in descriptive writing, on spatial arrangment; in expository writing, on logical, cause-and-effect patterns. To offer you a single chapter that advocates one organizational plan for all kinds of writing would be to create a rhetorical torture rack, one that would force you to stretch all writing problems onto a single monstrous form.

We believe that our approach is not only more functional, presenting material when you need it most, but also more realistic. Instead of seeing a paper as a composite of separate parts gleaned from individual chapters on language, sentence structure, the paragraph, and so forth, you can see in this book how each of these aspects contributes to a particular writing assignment to make your paper an organic whole.

Because no aspect of the writing process is exclusively the property of any one kind of writing, we must circle back now and then to refer to what we discussed previously. For example, in a consideration of descriptive writing, we discuss sentence combining by insertion because this technique is particularly helpful in papers of description. But because this technique may also be valuable in other kinds of papers, we remind you of it later. To give you easier access to all the references in the various parts of the book to sentences, punctuation, usage, and other writing concerns, we have provided a reference section in the back of this book, and a reference chart and aids for revision on the inside covers. The index will also help you to locate quickly all the references in the book to a particular aspect of writing.

WHAT DOES THE TITLE MEAN?

We selected *The Writing Commitment* as our title to impress upon you the fact that every time you write, you commit some portion of yourself to paper, and you also enter into a commitment with readers. When you turn in a well-organized, logically reasoned, adequately developed, and carefully written paper, it reflects advantageously on you as an individual, conveying

The Intimate Voice: Personal Writing

Personal writing is the form that perhaps provides the most delightful opportunity for exploration of self. It is a statement of your ideas, feelings, emotions, and impressions about your own experiences, written either for your own pleasure or for the interest and enjoyment of family and friends. It may take the form of a diary, journal, autobiographical narrative, friendly letter, or poem. It is a self-portrait, a picture of your personal life.

Reading what you have written about a past experience is much like looking at a snapshot of the event, but it is also different: a photograph may stir memories by reminding you of how everything and everyone *looked,* but your memory of the occasion may be dulled by time or sweetened by nostalgia. Only a written personal account can recapture exactly how you *felt.* For example, you may have memories of your high-school graduation, your first day on a job, a musical recital, a friend's wedding, a thrilling basketball game, or an automobile accident, but unless you have written about the experience, you will not be able to retain a permanent, vivid, complete, and accurate memory of it.

Apart from this usefulness of a written account, the very act of writing is itself valuable. Anne Morrow Lindbergh discloses the reason when she explains why she wrote such voluminous letters and diaries:

I must write it all out, at any cost. Writing is thinking. It is more than living, for it is being conscious of living.

—*Locked Rooms and Open Doors*

Writing is "being conscious of living," because when we put our thoughts about life into words, we become more aware of life itself. In your first weeks of college, for instance, you encounter many new experiences. Writing letters about these experiences to your family or friends causes you to become more fully conscious of them by making you recall and reflect upon their nature and significance.

Personal writing may also be therapeutic, a means for self-analysis that allows you to understand yourself better. Eldridge Cleaver, in *Soul on Ice,* was referring to this benefit when he stated that he started to write in prison "to save myself":

I realized that no one could save me but myself. The prison authorities were both uninterested and unable to help me. I had to seek out the truth and unravel the snarled web of my motivations. I had to find out who I am and what I want to be, what type of man I should be, and what I could do to become the best of which I was capable.

Writing forced Cleaver to evaluate himself. In this process, he realized how he had failed as a civilized human being and what he must do to redeem himself. Personal writing may also allow you to realize your failures as well as your successes, your weaknesses as well as your strengths, your disillusionments as well as your dreams. In this process of discovering and exploring your inner self, you may learn more about who you are and why you act, think, and feel as you do.

Personal writing also prepares you for more difficult writing assignments. It enables you to practice with a subject that you can organize easily in a simple chronological time sequence from past to present and with a subject that you know well—yourself. And this subject has great appeal to readers. Everyone is curious about what others say and do, fascinated by their motives, amused at their eccentricities, absorbed by their problems and predicaments. Personal writing provides you with an appealing, built-in subject.

Finally, personal writing is more fun than most other kinds of writing. Because you are naturally concerned with yourself, you should find pleasure and fulfillment reflecting and reminiscing about your experiences.

This section on personal writing is devoted to three forms—the journal, the autobiographical narrative, and the personal essay. In discussing each, we will point out its particular purpose, its characteristics, and its special writing problems. We will also try to help you deal with these problems in your own work by providing student and professional examples to emulate and instructions to heed.

By understanding the purpose, characteristics, and problems involved in the journal, autobiographical narrative, and personal essay, you will realize the nature of the commitment you must make in writing each. And by following the specific instructions, you should be able to fulfill not only the commitment to yourself but the commitment to your readers.

The Forms of Personal Writing

THE JOURNAL

Perhaps you can best find your natural unique voice in a diary. But because of their intimate nature, diaries are usually locked away from the eyes of others. Keeping a diary, then, might be an excellent way for you to practice writing in a free, sincere voice, but you would probably be reluctant to show these personal thoughts to others, such as a classmate or teacher, for advice about writing. Keeping a journal, however, is an excellent alternative that provides the same advantages.

In both a diary and a journal, you and your experiences form the basic subject matter. In both a diary and a journal, you primarily write to and about yourself. But there is a difference in approach. In writing a journal, you are also prepared for a friend to share your experience, emotions, and thoughts and thus learn something about you. This dual purpose of writing to yourself and to a sympathetic second party has made the journal an especially effective tool in learning to write. It helps you to deal with the most acute problem in writing: developing a method of expression satisfying to yourself as writer but interesting and acceptable to others as readers.

Why Keep a Journal?

Unless required to do so in school, why would anyone want to keep a journal? Some novelists, poets, and journalists keep journals to improve their writing and to preserve their experiences and impressions. Sometimes their entries serve as the basis for books or articles; sometimes the journal itself appears in print. One of the most prolific journal keepers of all time, James Boswell, the biographer of Samuel Johnson, vividly portrayed eighteenth-century London and gave readers an acquaintance with great historical figures that more objective reports could not provide. Many writers, following Boswell's example, have used journals to record their experiences with famous people or their close contact with great historical events. Others have kept a journal to preserve the memory of a journey or a cherished vacation.

Journals often satisfy several purposes. The journals of Leonardo da Vinci record observations about birds and flight dynamics as well as important events in his life. Those of Lewis and Clark were begun to keep a careful record of the previously unexplored Northwest, but they also created a vivid historical document of an exciting expedition. In writing to record the experience of hiding from the Nazis during the Second World War, a Jewish teenager, Anne Frank, used the journal to "support and comfort" her through her frightening, dehumanizing exile.

Keeping a journal, then, can be more than an assignment in a composition class to give you writing practice. You may be inspired to keep a journal for the rest of your life, thus acquiring an extremely valuable personal history that will help you record, assimilate, and enrich your experience in a way that photographs, tape recordings, films, and souvenirs cannot.

In fact, good journal writing should combine all the possibilities of these three devices for recording experience: a journal entry can create as graphically descriptive a picture as a photograph; it can capture the essence of a moment as effectively as a tape recording; and it has the ability of a souvenir to trigger a memory. But the journal entry can do even more. It can capture you, your personality, your thoughts, and your emotional reactions to the experience. According to Anne Morrow Lindbergh, a journal is kept "not to preserve the experience but to savor it, to make it more real, more visible and palpable, than in actual life."

The Characteristics of Journal Writing

This passage from a student journal illustrates how a writer can capture a photographic image in words and at the same time embellish it with information that a picture cannot always provide.

To walk up Park Avenue in New York City is a delightful experience. In midtown the fashionable little shops, ornate hotels, and glittering limousines serving their occupants. As one moves on uptown the sidewalks are full of doormen walking diamond-stud-collared poodles and other breeds, all as elegantly groomed as their owners always are. But on arrival at Park and 96th Street, there is a sudden departure from the extravagant to the deprived. No doormen—instead, garbage cans with rats and flies, ill-kept and ragged children playing hopscotch on the sidewalks. Alley cats and mongrels scrounging and pulling over garbage cans. Smothering odors of garlic cooking from rooms occupied by ten or twelve people. In summer, recreation consists of children turning on a fire hydrant for thirty minutes or so—a kind policeman, black or white, turns his back and lets them flood the street. Then with all the "authority vested in me," he indignantly makes an appearance, when the basements look ready to flood. The children scatter. He turns it off. The children, wet and sticky, sit on their stoops with the flies and the rats and the cats and the dogs. Sing, clap hands, and think up some other scheme.

Note that the freshman writer not only captures an impression of a place, she also instills a touch of personal philosophy. But she does not sermonize on the contrast between wealth and poverty, using instead words and details to accent the difference. However, the example does not force the writer's reaction upon the reader. Instead, readers are involved in the experience itself but can reject the inherent philosophy, substituting their own interpretations or reactions.

A good example of how journal writing can re-create a situation is illustrated in this excerpt from one kept by thirteen-year-old Anne Frank. Note that she not only re-creates the experience for herself but permits other readers to share in it as if they were there—as if they, too, were hiding in a warehouse attic, in constant fear of detection and capture by the Nazis.

Continuation of the "Secret Annexe" daily timetable. As the clock strikes half past eight in the morning, Margot and Mummy are jittery: "Ssh . . . Daddy, quiet, Otto, ssh . . . Pim." "It is half past eight, come back here, you can't run any more water; walk quietly!" These are the various cries to Daddy in the bathroom. As the clock strikes half past eight, he has to be in the living room. Not a drop of water, no lavatory, no walking about, everything is quiet. As long as none of the office staff are there, everything can be heard in the warehouse. The door is opened upstairs at twenty minutes past eight and shortly after there are three taps on the floor! Anne's porridge. I climb upstairs and fetch my "puppy-dog" plate. Down in my room again, everything goes at terrific speed; do my hair, put away my noisy tin pottie, bed in place. Hush, the clock strikes! Upstairs Mrs. Van Daan has changed her shoes and is shuffling about in bedroom slippers, Mr. Van Daan, too; all is quiet.

—*Diary of a Young Girl*

Re-creating an experience requires putting down on paper its specific details. When this is done effectively, the writing becomes vivid, alive, colorful, and authentic. Anne Frank's details about the restrictions of movement and time—"not a drop of water, no lavatory . . . noisy tin pottie . . . shuffling about in bedroom slippers . . . the clock strikes . . ."—give her readers the opportunity to become involved in the experience, not simply read about it. Suppose Anne Frank had described the experience in this way:

We were always anxious about the time and whether our daily activities would be detected.

You can see that without the specific details most of the urgency of her situation would be lost.

Hints for Writing a Journal

In keeping your journal, try to follow these suggestions:

- Try to write something every day, even if only a few sentences. The entries can be about any subject: something you experienced that day or some memory triggered by an experience. It helps to carry your journal with you so that you can make an entry when you have a free moment and while the incident is fresh.
- Restrict each journal entry to an account of only one major or unusual subject. A running discussion of the day's activities will have no more interest or vividness than a bus schedule.
- Be more concerned with capturing every significant detail of the experience than with the mechanics of writing. Keep the words flowing; write on and on and on, not stopping to look up words or revise. Don't worry about incomplete sentences. Just try to re-create the experience.
- Tell it in your own language. Slang and idiomatic expressions are discouraged in most other forms of writing because they may be too informal for the situation and may not be understood by readers, but they are appropriate in journal writing because you are trying to write as if you were talking naturally to a friend.
- Occasionally read your entries a day or two later. Check the ones you think were most successful in re-creating the experience. Try to discover why these entries succeeded.

THE AUTOBIOGRAPHICAL NARRATIVE

Although each of the personal writing forms suggested in this chapter is a satisfying writing experience in itself, each is also designed to develop skill that can apply to future writing assignments. The assignments in this chapter could be compared to learning the fundamentals of swimming. Journal writing is like jumping into the water in order to become less fearful of the experience and to accustom yourself to it. You can practice "stroke" and "breathing" techniques without restraint—strike out with a poem, a brief story, a comment on life, a description of something that interested you. But autobiographical narrative—a story about a personal experience—requires more of a commitment to a plan. The writer can't flounder from one episode to the next: the narrative must move along in time from one event to another. Details should be selected with care. And because writers rarely tell stories to themselves, they must make sure that their readers will understand how one event is related logically to another.

Even though these pre-planning and organizational considerations may change in purpose, they are essential ingredients of all writing.

Planning an Autobiographical Narrative

To be effective, a short autobiographical narrative should not only be interesting, but should have a central action, a time framework, believable characters, and a setting. Of course, if you have a good story in mind, all these aspects of narrative may fall naturally into place as you write. Like most endeavors in life, success in writing rarely results from lucky accidents, but depends on intelligent planning. Setting up a list of questions for yourself is often an invaluable aid in any pre-writing process. For narrative writing, the list should include at least the following concerns:

● How do I choose an incident that will be interesting to others?

Obviously, you can't question all your potential readers to find a definite answer. However, if you choose an event in your life that had great significance to you, one that you still think of often, one that you feel you know and understand, the chances are excellent others will also find it interesting. Like many writers, you may feel that "Nothing has ever happened to me; I don't have anything to write about." If this is one of your concerns, take heart. Your narrative need not involve a world-shaking event; everyday happenings common to everyone's experience often make the most interesting stories. The following student narrative illustrates how a single small event can have significance and interest.

I was spending the weekend at Grandma's, as I had done many, many times before. I woke up early in the morning, about five o'clock. All the lights were on and Grandpa was sitting in his big chair across the room waiting for Grandma to cook breakfast. I rolled off the sofa where I had spent the night. I picked my pillow off the floor and walked into the smell of bacon and eggs. In the kitchen Grandma turned and smiled a wide wrinkled smile, her shaggy gray hair in tufts like chicken down. "What do you want for breakfast, Michael?" "Bacon and eggs and coffee," I said, running back into the living room to tell Grandpa his breakfast was ready. He was asleep in the big chair. Then I shook him. Startled, he snorted. "Hey there, big boy." As I followed him into the kitchen, he shouted back over his shoulder, "Let's go eat some breakfast." Grandma laughed as she told Grandpa, "He says he wants coffee for breakfast."

Grandpa chuckled. "He's gettin' to be a big boy now, Mom, I think he can handle it."

I sat up straight in my chair and stretched my neck to make myself tall. Grandma brought me a big white glass coffee mug—just like Grandpa's. She set the steaming bacon and eggs down in front of me, but I didn't immediately dig in. With both hands, I eagerly extended the cup. Grandma poured.

● How can I restrict the narrative to a single, unifying action?

An important consideration in planning and writing a narrative is to decide on which details to include and which to exclude. Only those that contribute to the action and that move the action along should be included. In the student example, for instance, the trip back into the living room to get Grandpa could have been distracting to the action, but the grandfather's greeting of "big boy" and his leading the child to the table enhance the human relationships and contribute to the message in the story. Remember that everything in the narrative should be closely related and should somehow contribute to the purpose for telling the story. A good rule of thumb is to permit no digression; instead, follow the action through in as straight a line as possible.

● How should I handle time?

Narratives, like events in real life, move chronologically. That is, the action begins at some moment and moves forward to a future time. Although fiction writers often use flashback and other time devices, writers of autobiographical narrative usually prefer handling time in the most natural way possible—the sequence in which events occur in real life.

Here, too, the student narrative offers a good example. Even though the event actually took place in the student's past, the narrative time moves forward from five o'clock in the morning to breakfast as if it were currently happening. Besides contributing realism to a story, natural chronological sequence creates immediacy, suspense, and moves the narrative along at a rapid pace.

● How can I make my characters seem real?

First, remember that your characters do not require extensive physical description, only those features important in establishing personality or the character's link to the situation. Characters are best developed through what they say and do, and by how they interact with others in the story. Note that in the student example, readers know little of what the characters look like: Grandma's "shaggy, gray hair in tufts like chicken down" and Grandpa's falling asleep in the big chair help to establish them as old. But it is the interaction of the grandparents with each other and with the child that portrays them as warm, loving personalities. This is exemplified in their ability to suppress their amusement over the child's "grown-up" request for coffee and to respect him as a person. If characters think, talk, act, and seem like human beings, and if the included details are vivid and significant, readers will supply the rest.

● How should I handle the setting?

In autobiographical narrative, setting is usually realistic and factual. But again you need only include those descriptive details necessary to establish the place of the action or to indicate the importance of the setting. For example, in writing of an embarrassing event in a high-school classroom, you need not provide a detailed description of the room—only enough to give your readers a sense of the place. However, if the location of the teacher's desk or the door to the hall contributed to the situation, then obviously you would need to discuss the spatial arrangement of the room at greater length. But remember, unnecessary details slow down the action and create digression. Concentrate, rather, on wording your descriptions so that they create vivid pictures that contribute to the action. Avoid description for the sake of description.

Techniques of Autobiographical Narration

Dramatic and Descriptive Approaches Narrative writers can approach their subjects in two major ways: a dramatic approach, relying heavily on dialogue; and a descriptive approach, relying primarily on description of the action and conversation. In the dramatic approach, the action moves forward and characters are developed through direct discourse. The characters are made to speak as they might in a real conversation.

Dramatic Approach—Direct Discourse:

"I intend to get to the bottom of this crime if it takes the rest of my life!" snarled the detective.

Descriptive Approach—Indirect Discourse:

The detective jumped to his feet and began shouting to the people assembled in the room. Purple with rage, he made it clear that he would solve the crime if it took the rest of his life.

Each approach has its advantages and writers may use one exclusively throughout a narrative; in longer works, they may combine the two. The two student examples that follow illustrate both methods, the first relying heavily on the dramatic approach.

RICKY

Roger Fain

One of the things I dislike most about November is having to strip tobacco on Saturdays. Even though the work isn't hard, and the stripping room is always warm compared to the rest of the barn, it gets boring. You spend most of the day standing in the same place, pulling leaves off the same part of each stalk, and tying them into "hands" about the same size. The only things that break the monotony are listening to the radio and talking, so one day seems pretty much like another. One of the few Saturdays that sticks out in my mind is when Ricky, an eleven-year-old from up the road, came down to help my Uncle Buford and me for the first time.

About two-thirty that afternoon Buford reached in his hip pocket and got out his pouch of chewing tobacco. I had noticed that Ricky loved to watch Buford playing with his chew, and this time Ricky stopped work completely to watch Buford. Ricky stood quietly as Buford reached in his pouch and got a wad of tobacco between his thumb and two fingers, leaned his head back, dropped the chew in his mouth, and brushed the crumbs from his moustache.

Buford started chewing slowly, to get the tobacco mashed together, and got ready to slip the pouch back into his pocket. Before he got the pouch settled in, Ricky said, "Hey, Buford, how 'bout givin' me a chew?"

Buford looked around, with his eyebrows arched higher than a cat's back. When he had chewed his tobacco down to a manageable size, he spit and said, "You ever chewed before?"

"Nope. But you look like you like it, so I figger I'd like to try it."

I turned to Buford and said in a very serious voice, "C'mon, Unk, give the man a chew. It's just Red Man, so it can't hurt him. That stuff's mild as a mother's love." Buford knew why I'd said that. He'd given me some Red Man when I was about Ricky's age, and told me it was mild as a mother's love. I'd spent what seemed like half a Sunday afternoon vomiting up my mother's love and her Sunday dinner.

Buford pushed his cap back and scratched his shiny head. He handed me the pouch to pass to Ricky and said, "Here ya go, Ricky."

When I watched Ricky I felt like I was watching a little Buford. He went through the same motions as Buford, except he didn't get as big a chew, and he dropped some of the tobacco before it got to his mouth. After he'd spit once he passed the pouch back to Buford. "Thanks," he said, nodding solemnly.

Nobody spoke for a long time. I was watching Buford and Ricky. Buford was nervous because he was doing this to a stranger, although it hadn't bothered him when he did it to me. I was watching Ricky, to see how long it would take him to get sick. Buford was watching Ricky, hoping he wouldn't get sick. Ricky was trying to pretend he wasn't watching anybody or anything but his work. He chewed and spit a lot faster than Buford, and his spit was a lot lighter colored. After about ten minutes he slowed down some, and I hoped he was beginning to be sick. When I looked at him, though, he seemed to be enjoying himself.

After about thirty minutes I decided Ricky wasn't going to get sick, and Buford had relaxed. He and Ricky were both holding their chews in their jaws, stopping work every now and then to spit. When Buford threw his chew in the stove, Ricky threw his in too.

At four-thirty Buford got himself another chew, and Ricky asked for one. Buford smiled proudly and threw Ricky the pouch. "Help yourself." Ricky got his chew and threw the pouch back. I almost asked for some too, so I wouldn't feel left out, but I knew it would make me sick.

When five o'clock came, Buford and I were helping Ricky get caught up for the last time. When we finished we carried the stalks out and cleared the presses. We covered all the tobacco up with a tarpaulin to keep the leaves moist. Buford and Ricky were still chewing, with Ricky spitting every time Buford did, like a little echo.

The three of us went back in the stripping room and stood around the stove, warming our hands before we left for the night. I decided to play a trick on Ricky I'd seen Larkin Reynolds pull on a man around the store once. I reached down and touched the palm of Ricky's hand, making him think he'd backed into the stove. I'd meant to make Ricky scream, like the man at the store had, but I got something better. Ricky swallowed his chew.

Ricky clapped his hand over his mouth, then ran out the door. Buford started to say something, but I held up my hand and shushed him. We listened as Ricky ran through the barn and swung open the back door. When I heard him gagging like a dog chewing on a weed, I burst out laughing.

"What happened?" asked Buford.

"I touched his hand to make him think he'd backed into the stove, and he swallowed his chew," I said, laughing.

"Why that was mean, boy!"

"Well, it woulda been funnier if you'd done it to me, I reckon, but you never thought of it when I was young."

Buford laughed and said, "No, but I wish I had. That was mean to do it to Ricky, though. He was doin' alright. You weren't man enough to chew when you was young."

"I know, but it's still funny."

In a few minutes Ricky came back and stood in the door. When I saw his pale complexion and his trembling chin, I almost got sick myself. He looked the same way I must have that Sunday afternoon in the orchard, and seeing him brought back the sickness I'd felt then.

"How ya feel?" asked Buford.

"All right," Ricky answered in a voice that was just above a whisper.

"Ready to go home?" Buford's voice was even calmer than usual.

"Yeah, I guess so."

"C'mon out an' I'll take ya in the pick-up."

I noticed Ricky's cap had been lost, so I went and hunted for it. After I found it out in the barn I pulled the switch to turn out the barn lights and closed the doors. I heard Ricky and Buford talking as they walked over to the truck.

"You gonna tell Mr. Stinnett what happened?" Ricky asked.

"Yep," Buford said. "Gonna tell 'im you got sick to your stomach right at quittin' time, and I broughtcha home."

They got in the truck and I ran over and opened Ricky's door. "Ya lost somethin'," I said, putting the cap on his head.

"Thanks."

I looked over at Buford, then said, "Listen Ricky, you gonna be back to help next Saturday?"

12

"I don't know. You'll probably find somebody by then."

I looked at Buford again, and he said, "We probly won't, but even if we do, we can still use ya."

I slapped Ricky on the knee and told him, "If we ain't strippin' tobacco, you come by with that dog and the three of us 'll go huntin'." Then I shut the door and Buford started the truck. After I watched them go up the road, I went and climbed the gate and headed home.

The student writer uses direct discourse wisely. The dialogue with its features of relaxed pronunciation and its occasional use of dialect lends an air of authenticity and realism to the story. Also, it allows the writer to reveal the narrator's guilt and sympathy in a more subtle way than would have been possible in a descriptive explanation of how he felt.

In contrast, the next student example benefits from the use of indirect discourse with heavy emphasis on description in the opening and closing paragraphs.

THE CARNIVAL

Brett Johnson

It was unusually cold for an autumn night. A delicate blanket of frost had silently formed on the tent tops. But the gay calliope music from the merry-go-round and the whirling masses of multicolored lights and the laughter of happy people and the tempting smell of hot dogs, cotton candy, and popcorn made me feel warm inside. I didn't even notice the cold. I stuffed my hands in my coat pockets and casually made my way through the milling crowd. Overhead, the Ferris Wheel was revolving like a giant neon top in an ocean of black. To my right I noticed a pack of people, thick, like a swarm of bees. The center of interest was a shriveled old man with a thin moustache. "Step right up folks. See the headless woman. Eighth wonder of the world!" As I silently chuckled at the old man, I blindly collided into a squat, roly-poly lady. She was violently attacking a huge mound of cotton candy and the sudden jolt set her plump face squarely into the sticky mass. I mumbled a sick "Excuse me" and promptly disappeared into the crowd.

As I rounded the Bingo stand, I noticed a small tent by the penny arcade, one I had not seen before. I sauntered over to where several men were engrossed in a boisterous game of chance. Behind the counter was a tawdry, gypsy-looking woman arrayed in layers of cheap costume jewelry. As I turned to leave, my eye caught an unobtrusive, sandy-haired little girl of about eight or nine. She was clad in a scanty cotton dress and her frail body trembled like a tiny leaf in a windstorm. She stood in her bare feet beside one of the burly men. Her dirty face looked up at me and her sad, pale blue eyes met mine.

Presently the little girl gave a tug at the man's weatherworn coat. "Daddy, Daddy, I'm cold," she whispered. As she spoke, gray puffs of steam rose into the crisp night air and then melted. With a curse her father brusquely pushed her aside and resumed his game. The gypsy lady gave a sensuous shriek of laughter as she raked a pile of money into her apron.

Disgusted, I turned and walked away. The tin-like calliope music droned monotonously above the harsh sounds of moving machinery. My nostrils were filled with the pungent odor of stale food. An icy draft of wind swept down my collar and I sank deeper into my coat. I leaned against a huge post and closed my eyes. The swirling masses of bright lights made me ill. "Step right up folks. See the headless lady. Eighth wonder of the world!"

As you can see, the descriptive approach was an effective vehicle for the author of "The Carnival" to paint two different versions of the scene. The setting is the same, but the words to describe it reveal the writer's mood and his impressionistic reactions—not easily achieved with exclusive use of the dramatic approach.

Creating Suspense These two student examples illustrate another aspect of narrative writing. Frequently, narrative builds suspense by creating a conflict or obstacle to be overcome. In "Ricky," the real conflict is between the narrator and Uncle Buford; Ricky is the innocent pawn in a "revenge" aimed at the uncle for an earlier trick with the chewing tobacco. The uncle obviously enjoyed the trick when he played it on the nephew, but suspense is created when a stranger is involved. The tobacco chewing becomes an initiation rite, creating tension between the narrator and the boy, who initially proves to be more of a "man." In "The Carnival," however, the writer internalizes the conflict. He is angered and disgusted, unable to resolve the problem, and it temporarily colors his outlook on the world. Because the conflict and reaction in both stories are common to us all, we are able to identify with them; thus the writer, through the narration of one personal experience, can make a subtle comment on a larger problem.

Maintaining Consistency Both student narratives maintain a consistency of character, particularly in the portrayal of the narrator. Each narrator's reaction at the end is "true to character"—that is, it is consistent with the character's personality and development up to that point. For instance, the narrator's offer of a hunting trip at the end of "Ricky" had been prepared for by his empathy with Ricky's nausea and his search for the boy's hat.

The resolution of the action must also be consistent. If a writer does not fulfill the expectations previously established, readers feel betrayed and angry. Even surprise endings should permit your readers to recall hints and clues, however subtle, that in some way foreshadow what happens.

The setting, too, should be consistent: historically accurate and suitable to the purpose. For instance, if you were to write about an experience you had in 1970, your narrative would be inconsistent if the setting were the Winter Olympics of 1980. Your characters of the late sixties might be listening to records of the Beach Boys, but not those of Shawn Cassidy or Debbie Boone.

Finally, the language you use should be consistent with the time of the narrative. Avoid using current slang if your autobiographical narrative is set in your early childhood.

Hints for Writing an Autobiographical Narrative

Many of these techniques will evolve naturally as you write about personal experiences. But if you want to learn to write effective autobiographical narrative, you might keep the following in mind as you write or as you map out your pre-writing strategy.

- Try to limit your paper to a single action—that is, to one incident or situation that includes several closely related events. Try to develop your characters through their dialogue and action.
- Before you start to write, choose whatever narrative technique will best suit your purposes: the dramatic approach of "Ricky," the descriptive approach of "The Carnival," or a combination of both.
- Keep characters, setting, and action consistent throughout the narrative. If there are to be surprises, make certain that they are not only possible but probable and foreshadowed.
- Choose details and events carefully. Use only those that will contribute to the characterization, the setting, or the action. Whenever you write about your own experiences, there will be a strong temptation to include everything, down to the smallest and least relevant details. A good way to avoid this is to call to mind the most tedious storytellers you know and analyze why they bore you. Chances are it is because they include meaningless details and meander off on long digressions. Avoid these pitfalls by sticking to the main story line, being selective, and striving always to be interesting.
- Try to add interest and suspense by including some kind of conflict in your narrative: a struggle between yourself and another person or other people; or a conflict within yourself that involves moral values.

THE PERSONAL ESSAY

Less intimate and more public than journal writing and autobiographical narrative is the personal essay. True, the writer of this form of essay deals with personal experience and expresses a personal attitude toward the subject, but the emphasis changes. Instead of re-creating an experience, the writer explains the effect it has. Thus, the personal essay demands different organizational skills of the writer. Instead of presenting a story arranged step by step in time, the writer focuses on some generalization or conclusion. In this respect, the personal essay is similar to writing forms you will be expected to handle later.

Still, the contemporary personal essay is closely related to narrative because short narratives or anecdotes are often included, but to exemplify, not to re-create the experience. Unlike the autobiographical narrative that builds on some conflict, step by step as it happens, the personal essay focuses on a central idea or theme observed in a series of incidents or as some emotional response to a particular incident. These opening paragraphs from a personal essay express a frustration developed over a long period of time, resulting from numerous occasions when the writer has been asked to identify strangers.

"Don't you remember me?" I always hear the question with an uncontrollable sinking of heart. I cannot put aside the feeling of panic. I do not remember the person and the person knows perfectly well that I do not. I am desperately trying to find some adequate answer, although I know there is none, and the person is trying, with more or less success, usually less, not to show his pique.

One of my latest experiences was in Asbury Park. I was lecturing on a warm night. There was a large audience in a low-ceilinged room—a kind of audience who listened a long time, not simply to what I said, but to what many others said. It was late before I was released, and I was tired. I came out on the darkened street. A man was standing in the shadow. I saw his bulk but I had not yet seen his face clearly. He was very dark and reticent.

"Don't you remember me?" he said. I wanted to say, "I have not seen your face yet," but tried to be pleasant. "I am afraid—" I began gropingly.
—W. E. B. DuBois, "Don't You Remember Me!" *W. E. B. DuBois: A Reader*

The first paragraph introduces the central idea or *theme* of the essay: DuBois's panic at being asked to identify someone. The next two paragraphs sketch an encounter, similar to many others that collectively have been responsible for his reaction to this one. Together, these incidents form a recurring pattern in his life. And as his opening paragraph indicates, he is more concerned with the frustration resulting from the encounter than with the incident itself. His purpose is to *talk about,* not *re-create* the experience.

All of us have had recurrent experiences such as the one in the example. They can involve our relationships with other people or everyday misadventures with the products of our machine age—encountering vending machines, starting the car on cold mornings, catching the bus or commuter train daily, fighting the red tape of computer billing systems. Out of these recurring events, we begin to formulate attitudes, to generalize about them, as DuBois does: "I always hear the question with an uncontrollable sinking of heart." A series of such personal experiences might be prefaced by a generalization such as: "There's a little gremlin who sits on my choke every morning"; "That vending machine in the lobby is a con artist"; or "Why is it that the bus on my line is the only one that doesn't run on schedule?" Even comparatively minor irritations—always being warned to be careful when you take out the family car, for example—can make an interesting essay.

As these examples show, the subject matter of personal essays can range across the whole spectrum of human experience. But they dwell especially on the ordinary situations that are common to all of us and take up so much of our time and thoughts. Their universal appeal is exemplified by the popularity of such columnists as Art Buchwald and Erma Bombeck, whose essays deal with the frustrations and incongruities of such widely diverse subjects as family relationships, suburban living, physical fitness programs, and political absurdities.

But, although their subject matter is virtually unrestricted, most contemporary essays do display similarities in form and style. Characterized by first-person pronouns (*I, we*) and a tone that is usually relaxed, informal, genial, somewhat amused, conversational, they reflect the writer's personality. Especially in newspapers and magazines, the essay is mildly satirical, poking gentle fun at the subject matter.

Not as flexible in form as the autobiographical narrative, the personal essay focuses on an opening generalization or conclusion about the subject. Usually this focusing statement appears in the first or second sentence of the opening paragraph. Not only does it introduce the theme, but it establishes the tone of the essay and indicates the writer's attitude toward the subject. Note how the following opening statements achieve these ends.

Surely nothing in the astonishing scheme of life can have nonplussed Nature so much as the fact that none of the females of any of the species she created really cared very much for the male as such.

—James Thurber

In this beginning statement, Thurber introduces his subject and theme, the universal indifference of females toward males. In addition, this sentence establishes the tongue-in-cheek tone that is sustained throughout the essay. The words "astonishing" and "nonplussed" contribute to this end, as does the ironic suggestion that this indifference is not what Nature intended.

There is a book out called *Dog Training Made Easy* and it was sent to me the other day by the publisher, who rightly guessed that it would catch my eye. I like to read books on dog training.

—E. B. White

Here again, in his opening statement the writer introduces his subject and establishes his sympathetic point of view toward it. Note, too, how the first-person pronouns and the commonplace vocabulary help to establish a conversational, familiar tone.

I'm wild about walking. . . .

—Leo Rosten

In this succinct statement, Rosten introduces his subject, walking, and establishes his enthusiasm for it by using the word *wild*. To make yourself aware of how one word can make a difference in tone and point of view, try substituting different adjectives for *wild*. "I'm *fond* of walking," for instance, has a markedly different tone.

From these examples, we can see that the opening statement acts as a direction pointer and a barometer: it sets the personal essay off in a particular direction and indicates its climate or the writer's attitude toward the subject—sympathetic, sardonic, hostile, or amused. Sustained throughout the paper, this attitude supplies the second characteristic necessary to the personal essay: focus, or unity. In the following personal essay, the opening statement focuses the subject—living with a husband obsessed with his lawn—and the essay retains its coherence or unity, its sense of direction, from the writer's amused attitude toward the situation.

THERE'S NO PLEASING A LAWN FREAK

Erma Bombeck

I just figured out if my husband paid just half the attention to me as he does the lawn, my 70-year-old mailman would never have started to look like Robert Redford.

If ever there were a valid suit for alienation of affection, it's that lousy lawn.

There is something about the ability of a man to grow a few blades of grass that contributes to his masculinity. He is either a grass grower or he is not a grass grower. I have seen virile men move into the neighborhood with tattoos on their lips, but if they have fungus on their dwarf tiff, forget it. They're just not one of the boys.

A lawn enthusiast has two moods: irritable and irritable. These are interchangeable depending on whether the grass is growing or whether the grass is not growing.

When the grass is not growing, my husband goes to the library to see what could be missing, has his soil analyzed, waters, soaks, fertilizes, and has the nurseryman who sold him the seed make a house call.

When the grass is growing, he runs the mower back to the store to make sure the blade is cutting, trims, rakes, rolls and makes an obscene phone call to the dog next door who over-fertilized it in the first place.

There is no pleasing a lawn freak.

Some say it is normal for a man to want a pretty lawn. I don't know what is normal anymore. I sent the kids to Mother's, blew an entire food budget on steaks and wine, put a dab of garlic on the lightbulb and slipped into something that had not been paid for. "What are you thinking?" I teased, turning off the TV set.

"Did you turn the hose off?" he asked.

Is it normal for a man to call the police and report a flock of birds that are eating our grass seed! Is it normal for a grown man to mourn a brown spot for three years!

I was all set to tell the mailman about my infatuation with him when he said, "I see your husband uses a chemical fertilizer of nitrogen, phosphorus, and potash. Tell him if he invested in a little sheep dip, he'd do away with that crabgrass. Is there something you wanted?"

"I thought you looked like someone I knew," I said. "But I was mistaken. You all look alike."

Bombeck sustains the breezy, humorous tone established in her first sentence by using several rhetorical devices: hyperbole (exaggeration), rhetorical question (one that requires no answer), and direct discourse. Exaggeration for effect is a primary ingredient of Bombeck's style. For example, she writes that her mailman is seventy years old (past the usual retirement age); men whose grass is invaded by a fungus cannot be virile; her husband's mood depends entirely on whether the grass is growing, and when it is, he makes obscene phone calls to the dog next door. Even her rhetorical questions employ hyperbole: "Is it normal for a grown man to mourn a brown spot for three years?" The use of direct discourse for the crucial conversations heightens the breeziness of tone and continues the fast pace sustained throughout. Note that she ends the essay with a surprise twist, a technique common in the humorous personal essay. This contributes to the final focusing on the subject: it closes the circle by linking the ending with the beginning; it ties the knot, leaving the reader satisfied.

Not all personal essays are as openly humorous as Bombeck's, but most are light in tone and subject matter. They deal with the minor, petty joys and discomforts of human existence; weighty problems deserve a more formal and serious treatment. Writing a personal essay should be fun; you need not worry about explaining difficult concepts or relationships. Just keep in mind that two ingredients are essential: an opening, focusing statement and brief narrative examples.

Hints for Writing a Personal Essay

The personal essay, although widely varied in subject matter and fairly loose in form, demands more attention to structure than journal entries and autobiographical narratives.

- In the opening statement or paragraph, introduce your theme—a generalization about your subject that also reveals your attitude toward it.
- Provide focus by expressing this attitude throughout the paper.

- Include briefly sketched narratives or anecdotes to add life and interest. Be sure that they relate to the focusing attitude in the essay.
- Remember that the personal essay often ends with a humorous twist or sardonic observation that reinforces the content and tone of the opening statement, and sometimes serves as a link to the introduction.

SUMMARY

In this chapter, we have introduced you to some forms that personal writing can take: journal writing, the autobiographical narrative, and the personal essay. Each can make a contribution to your writing skills. In keeping a journal and making writing a daily habit, you gain fluency and confidence. Retelling an experience strengthens your ability to add colorful details and helps you find your writing voice. Learning the fairly simple organizational skills of the personal essay will aid you in making the transition to the more complex structure of expository and persuasive writing. But perhaps most importantly, the chapter introduces you to the gratifying act of writing to yourself about your individual experience, thus making you more "conscious of living."

Assignments

For Discussion

1   What is the advantage of writing about some incident instead of entrusting it to memory? Can you provide an example from your own life of how you cannot remember an event vividly or how your memory has distorted some episode in your life?
2   Do you agree with Anne Morrow Lindbergh's statement on page 2 that writing "is being conscious of living"? Explain.
3   Why is personal writing likely to be easier and more pleasant than other forms of writing?
4   Define personal writing and explain how a personal account of a wedding, accident, or death would differ from a fictional narrative account.
5   The following are opening statements from student papers. Discuss whether each is effective in identifying the subject and establishing the paper's tone and purpose. Suggest some types of anecdotes that might be used in a paper written on each subject.

   a   Mother's school days were not *my* school days.
   b   Let's face it. I'm a hypochondriac. I know because I immediately develop the symptoms of any new disease that I hear about.
   c   Why am I the only one who doesn't understand football?
   d   Hiking in the woods is a healthy activity?

    e It isn't only the three-year-olds who can't open the child-proof packages.

    f After a day of shopping, I look in the mirror to see if I'm really there. The clerks obviously think of me as the Invisible Person.

For Practice

1 List chronologically all the incidents that occurred on your pre-registration day at college, your first day on campus, or your first day of classes. If you were writing a narrative about the frustration you felt on one of those days, which incidents would you delete?

2 Jot down two possible journal subjects based on experiences that have occurred within the past twenty-four hours. In addition, list five significant details about each that would make the entries vivid.

3 Following the six hints provided for writing an autobiographical narrative, select two possible subjects and decide on the techniques to use. Prepare to discuss your ideas with your classmates to see which subject they would prefer reading about and how they respond to the way you plan to write about it.

4 Write two opening statements or short paragraphs for two possible personal essays. Prepare to discuss them in class to determine which one would be more effective.

5 Read this personal essay and write brief answers to the questions that follow.

IF I COULD CHANGE MY NAME

We are living in an age when a person must be able to prove at any time that a particular name belongs to him or her. Nearly everyone carries some kind of identification. Driver's licenses, Social Security cards, and military registration cards are samples of acceptable proof that your name is what you say it is.

    Most people are happy with their name and love the sound and sight of it. However, I am not a member of this fortunate group. Since my sister, in a word study class, traced the origin of our last name and found it was derived from a word meaning ignorant, I have been a little dissatisfied. But as I have hope of changing it in the future, this is a minor problem.

    Mary Jo, on the other hand, I seem to be stuck with. Mary, pronounced from Murry to Merry, is a nice, conventional, feminine name, but I think my mother was a little confused when she added the Jo. Relatives who don't visit us very often are usually surprised that I am a girl because mother always refers to me as "Jo."

    When I answer the phone with "Jo Ingram speaking," the person on the other end of the phone quite often calls me son or Mr. Ingram. I do believe if I could change my name to some nice, definitely feminine name, it could clear up the confusion of my identity.

However, when I think of the fact that all of my brothers were named after some "beloved" relatives, I review the list of family names mine could have been chosen from. Juletia, Axie, Mahalia, Hannah, Biddy, Obedience, Polly, and Willy are some of the possibilities. Maybe Mary Jo isn't so bad, after all.

a Does this personal essay have a focusing statement? What is it?
b Does the first paragraph catch the reader's interest? Could it be better related to the second paragraph?
c Does the opening paragraph or the focusing statement adequately establish the tone of the essay?
d What improvements would you suggest to the writer?

For Writing

Journal Entry
1 Write about the subject decided on in 4 above.
2 Describe a recent college experience in order to preserve your feelings and sensations so that you can relive it months or years from now.
3 Write a journal entry about one or both of your parents, describing how embarrassed, proud, hurt, grateful, annoyed, or happy you felt on some recent occasion involving them.
4 Friendships formed at college often last for a lifetime. With that in mind, try to preserve your thoughts and feelings about a person you have met recently so that perhaps you both can reread and relive the experience months or years from now.

Autobiographical Narrative
1 Write about some event that time or your memory has probably distorted. Then it may have caused you embarrassment, anguish, despair, or fear, but now you can laugh about it. Or you may have thought highly of yourself on some past occasion but now can view your achievement in proper perspective.
2 Reminisce about some fascinating, unusual, significant, or memorable incident in your life. You might begin with the sentence, "It all comes back to me now."
3 Write about the tension between you and your parents that was caused by an episode involving your attempt to assert your independence.
4 Write an action-focused narrative about some personal experience that had a lasting significance to you:

a An episode that contributed to better understanding of someone in your family.
b An incident or series of related incidents that changed your outlook on human nature, your school, parental authority, or whatever.

   c An incident that helped you decide on a different course of action—for example, a change in career plans, college or summer plans, marriage plans.

5 "The Carnival" has several levels of meaning. It depicts a personal experience and at the same time makes a social comment on an aspect of our society. Write a narrative about a personal experience you have had that implicitly contained a universal situation. Be careful to avoid moralizing. Permit the action, the dialogue, and the expository description to convey the "message" to your readers.

6 Write a narrative including several related events that rely on a unifying perspective. The central theme could be your developing a tolerance for someone different from you in race, religion, or age; or it could be a series of events that contributed to your perfecting a skill, developing an awareness and appreciation of the opposite sex, or learning the give and take of dormitory life.

7 Write a short narrative from your own experiences that might be used in the introduction to a paper on one of these subjects:

Fly-fishing	Band or orchestra experience
Drag racing	Birthday parties
Christmas shopping	Dating practices
Acting	Registering for classes
Camping	Overcoming shyness

8 Relate an incident from your past that you would like to live over to change your actions or behavior.

Personal Essay

1 Write the personal essay decided on with the class in Discussion Exercise 5.

2 Write a personal essay on coping with some fairly insignificant, everyday, recurrent activity that has an absurd aspect. The following suggestions may be helpful:

    Dialing wrong numbers
    Commuting
    Church experiences
    Trying to make a good impression
    Applying for a job
    Finding a campsite or motel
    Getting the family car
    College meals
    Opening plastic and cardboard packages
    Receiving junk mail
    Finding a parking space

Language
in Personal
Writing

"Watch your language!"

You may have heard this warning from your parents when you were a child. Here it is again, this time referring not only to rude, vulgar, or offensive language but to the importance of selecting all words thoughtfully and carefully. In personal writing, word choice is particularly important because writers reveal much about themselves through the words they use. For example, they can disclose their real attitudes about eighteen-year-olds not only by what they say about them but by how they refer to them: *kids, teenagers, adolescents, juveniles, youngsters, young men and women*—terms that reflect disdain, tolerance, or respect.

Consequently, you must watch your language to determine that it is saying what you want it to say and revealing what you want it to reveal. Realize that language is distinctive and personal. Often you can characterize your friends by their pet expressions or favorite words. You can recognize them on the phone by their speaking voice, but you can also tell who they are by their use of language. Likewise, language is an important part of your writing voice, distinguishing your papers from those of others in the class. But your writing voice reflects your unique personality only when you express yourself naturally, choosing your own words and phrases, not those sounding like someone else.

In addition, you must watch your language to make certain that it is communicating your experience clearly to readers. If you are writing about playing soccer, you must decide how much your readers know about this subject, what terms they understand, and what must be explained to them. If they cannot easily read what you have written, they may not finish it, or if they do, they may not understand it. Your commitment to your readers requires that your language be clear.

You must also watch your language to see that it interests and appeals to readers. Because language can be drab or colorful, dreary or lively, boring or sparkling, you should strive to select words that please and delight your readers. Remember that it is easier to put down a newspaper or a book than it is to click off a television set, walk out of a film, or leave a lecture. Therefore, you should be particularly concerned about attracting and holding your readers.

In view of the importance of language, let us consider in detail how it can be used to make personal writing natural, clear, and lively.

NATURAL LANGUAGE

Among the different ways we react to people is on the basis of whether they are natural or affected. Most of us dislike the latter—people who pretend to be what they are not, usually more genteel, cultured, educated, or important than they are. Americans, in particular, favor friendly, informal people, and expect others, even their Presidents, to act this way except on ceremonial occasions.

How do we distinguish between natural and affected people? We judge them mainly by what they say. When they talk, if they use artificial, flowery, pompous, or formal language, we react adversely. The same is true when they write. We respond to their language: favorably to natural language, unfavorably to artificial language.

This stress on natural language may seem to contradict what many students think about writing. Many believe that good writing should be formal and impressive, characterized by unusual or long words. As a result, these students feel inhibited when they write, trying not to sound like themselves but like doctors or lawyers. In the process, they become dual personalities: delightfully interesting, natural, and lively in person; horribly boring, affected, and dull on paper. Here's an example of what we mean from the paper of a freshman writing about returning from a party when she was fifteen:

I recall well one night when, due to my own stubbornness and ignorance, I came prancing home, an hour late. Naturally, my parents were awake and waiting anxiously for my return. I interpreted their anger as distrust of me. A young person does not always comprehend how parental love is shown. I grew bitter that they would be so protective of me. My bold attitude as I answered their queries stirred greater anger with them. The gap of misunderstanding spread wider and we were soon unable to communicate with each other. I felt unfairly treated because they weren't giving me a chance to exert my independence. My attitude towards my parents at this time was hostile.

My parents were at a loss as to what should be done about this situation, which was progressively growing worse. A total lack of understanding existed between us. I felt completely alienated from my parents and tears of frustration overwhelmed me. Well-intentioned discussions resulted in further upsets. There seemed to be no reasonable solution to calm the fires that flared between my parents and me. The tension was not resolved overnight. Only time dissipated the turmoil.

There is no doubt that this paper was written by an intelligent student who selected an interesting experience that was important to her. The passage starts well with the delightful phrase, "I came prancing home." But from this point on, the language does not capture the feelings of a fifteen-year-old girl being shocked, angered, and hurt. Certain words and phrases seem written mainly to impress an English instructor: "stirred greater anger," "the gap of misunderstanding spread wider," "tears of frustration overwhelmed me," "to calm the fires," and "time dissipated the turmoil." The experience is not re-created in language that allows us to see and hear and feel how bitter the girl became, how angry her parents grew, and how unbearable the situation was. Instead we sense that the writer is trying to impress others, attempting to be a Great Author. The paper misses because the language is not natural.

In contrast, here's a passage from a paper by a student who describes her desire to be a loner.

There was that party for me when I was seven. (I have no recollection what the big deal was, probably a birthday.) All I remember of the trial was a superdesire to barricade myself in my room. So I did. Mom was upset later that evening when one of her friends remarked that I was a loner. It was true. But for a seven-year-old, it appeared to be a crime.

Later I developed an even stronger need to dart from the throng. During high school I slowly dropped out of attending parties and dances. Whether in a bustling pep rally or a tightly packed school assembly, I felt strangled. Finally, it came to the point where only a long walk alone out of the sight of the school could enable me to face another busy event. I recall always being the first to my locker in the morning and then up to homeroom so that I could avoid the clamor.

The language is natural to the writer. We can hear her saying, "the big deal," "a superdesire," "So I did," "It was true," and "I felt strangled." As readers, we can feel her sincerity and conviction. We can visualize her sitting in a room, sprawled on a cushion on the floor, looking us in the eye as she chats about herself in relaxed and easy tones. Her voice is distinctive, lively, and natural.

But being natural in writing is about as difficult as relaxing in a dentist's chair. To help you, we offer these two suggestions:

- Rely on short, simple words.
- Listen to every sentence to determine whether it sounds like you.

Let's apply these suggestions to this sentence from a student paper.

It was on the day following high school graduation that I commenced the task of locating employment.

First we'll replace long, formal words with short, simple ones and see how much better the sentence sounds.

It was on the day following high school graduation that I *started* the task of *looking for work.*

Then we might decide that "It was on the day following" sounds stilted and change it to "The day after." And we might think that "the task of" is unecessary. These changes would result in the simple statement:

The day after high school graduation I started looking for work.

Applying the same two suggestions to the student's next sentence, we might change it as follows:

Original: In view of the scarce number of vocational opportunities that appear to be available to members of the feminine sex in the community where I reside, my expectations of success were at a minimum.

Revision: Because few jobs seem to be open to women in my home town, I expected little success.

If you are afraid that short, simple words will make your personal writing sound childish, remember that such words have been used in many of the most memorable statements in our language:

Ask not what your country can do for you—ask what you can do for your country.
—John F. Kennedy

Government of the people, by the people, for the people shall not perish from this earth.
—Abraham Lincoln

I have nothing to offer but blood, toil, tears, and sweat.
—Winston Churchill

We have nothing to fear but fear itself.
—Franklin D. Roosevelt

That's one small step for a man, one giant leap for mankind.
—Neil Armstrong

Unfortunately, some student writers show off by reaching for the long, pretentious word instead of the short, simple one. They believe that *find* is too common so they switch to *ascertain; agree* too unsophisticated so they substitute *concur;* and *put off* too childish so they use *procrastinate.* In some contexts, formal language may work well. But in personal writing, where the written language should closely resemble the spoken one in order to achieve the desired friendly voice, shorter words are generally more appropriate and effective.

CLEAR LANGUAGE

All writing, including personal writing, should be thought of as communication. The purpose of placing words on paper instead of retaining them in your head is to convey ideas and feelings to someone else, whether to a friend, to a stranger, or even to yourself, who, in a sense, will be a different person in six months or six years. Consequently, to communicate effectively, you must describe the subject clearly, selecting words that cannot be misunderstood but that can transmit your ideas from your mind to the reader's with as little distortion or difficulty as possible.

In personal writing you probably have few problems selecting words recognizable to readers. Unless you are writing about complex scientific experiments, unusual hobbies, foreign customs, or other specialized matters, your language will be generally familiar to your readers. But you must always be alert to explain any slang or technical terms that might be puzzling, as in this example:

The teachings of Mr. Muhammad stressed how history had been "whitened"— when white men had written history books, the black men simply had been left out.

> —*The Autobiography of Malcolm X*

Here a short explanation has sufficed; elsewhere, a synonym might do. Treating the problem is not difficult, but being aware of it is; so you must worry constantly about your readers, just as considerate hosts are always concerned about their guests. By always thinking of how readers will respond to your language, you can anticipate problems and adjust for them.

Conveying an experience clearly is far more complex than explaining or defining terms. It hinges mainly upon your ability to describe what has happened in specific words. What are specific words? They are usually concrete words, ones that refer to anything you can see, hear, touch, taste, or smell. Obviously, *camping* does not fit in this category; *tent* does. But though the word *tent* is concrete, it is specific only in a relative sense. It is general when compared with *pup tent* or *umbrella tent*. So words may be concrete but still not as specific as they could be. Effective writing usually requires the writer to be highly specific, getting down to earth instead of floating around in vague generalities. Note how this works in the following example:

General:	I was feeding my *pet.*
Less general:	I was feeding my *dog.*
Even less general:	I was feeding my *small dog.*
Specific:	I was feeding my *poodle.*
More specific:	I was feeding my *white toy poodle.*

The more specific you are, the more information you convey, and the more clearly readers perceive what you are writing about.

Two language authorities, Bergen and Cornelia Evans, consider the use of general instead of specific words to be the most obvious characteristic of ineffective writing. They advise aspiring writers to ask themselves constantly, "Does what I have written cover more ground than I meant to cover?" These authorities contend that remembering this question while writing "will do more to develop a respectable style than all the grammar books and vocabulary builders in the world."[1]

"Covering more ground than I meant to cover" may result not only from using a general word for a specific one (*transportation* for *subway*) but from omitting details. To re-create an experience for yourself or your readers, you must recount all the significant particulars, as if placing everything under a microscope for others to view. Let us illustrate this point by comparing how a student might write about a personal scene with the way that Alfred Kazin treated it at the close of his "Brownsville" chapter in *On Native Grounds.* First, the student's version:

I can remember Mother always working from early morning until late evening. She was always busy, shopping, cooking, or sewing despite her hand that had been pierced and crudely patched together when she was a girl.

Now Kazin's account:

I can never remember a time when she was not working. . . . When I awoke in the morning she was already at her machine, or in the great morning crowd of housewives at the grocery getting fresh rolls for breakfast. When I returned from school she was at her machine, or conferring over *McCall's* with some neighborhood woman who had come in pointing hopefully to an illustration—"Mrs. Kazin! Mrs. Kazin! Make me a dress like it shows here in the picture!" When my father came home from work she had somehow mysteriously interrupted herself to make supper for us, and the dishes cleared and washed, was back at her machine. When I went to bed at night, often she was still there, pounding away at the treadle, hunched over the wheel, her hands steering a piece of gauze under the needle with a finesse that always contrasted sharply with her swollen hands and broken nails. Her left hand had been pierced through when as a girl she had worked in the infamous Triangle Shirtwaist Factory on the East Side. A needle had

[1] *A Dictionary of Contemporary English Usage* (New York: Random House, 1957), p. 6.

gone straight through the palm, severing a large vein. They had sewn it up for her so clumsily that a tuft of flesh always lay folded over the palm.

Note how the details vividly and convincingly describe the endless activity of the writer's mother. We derive a clearer picture of Mrs. Kazin because of the information about her getting breakfast rolls, conferring over *McCall's* (not just a *magazine*) with the neighborhood women, making supper, washing dishes, and so on. Also, observe how the details about her hand create a more graphic and moving account than the student's version did. Throughout, Kazin's specific language enables readers to visualize his mother's ceaseless work.

Without such descriptive details most writing is flat and colorless. Note how the absence of details makes the following student paper seem drab and lifeless.

As we were trotting along, an unsuspecting cottontail crossed our path, startling Betty's horse. The frightened animal dashed off with Betty trying to stop it. Following behind them, I could see that she was getting tired from the way she was riding.

Suddenly, she fell, hitting her head on the broken limb of a tree. I stopped, got off, and raced over to her, wondering what to do. I decided to pick her up and carry her to my car, which fortunately was parked nearby.

She was still unconscious when we got to the hospital. I carried her to the emergency room and waited there for the doctor to examine her.

This incident is related in such general terms that few pictures flash in our mind's eye. We do not see how Betty was riding, what she looked like lying by the tree, where she was placed in the car, what occurred during the drive to the hospital, and how she was admitted there.

A writer should savor an experience as a gourmet does a fine wine. It should not be gulped hastily, but should be sipped slowly to be fully enjoyed and remembered. Details make an experience vivid and convincing, memorable and clear. A person reading only generalities is like a viewer watching a poorly tuned television set with blurred and fuzzy images. Neither has a clear picture of what is happening.

This emphasis on clarity adds up to the importance of finding words to convey your exact meaning to readers in order to let them see and experience what you did.

LIVELY LANGUAGE: THREE PITFALLS

At the risk of annoying you, we shall keep repeating throughout this book the importance of trying to interest readers, whether they be family, friends, teachers, classmates, or even yourself. Some students seem to forget that writing should be lively and engaging, not drab and dull. In talking, you can tell whether or not you are boring people from their expressions, the direction of their eyes, and even the position of their bodies. If you are, you can change your subject or your manner of speaking, or you can just stop talking. No such feedback is available in writing. But even though you cannot see the yawns or the glances at the watch, you can learn to sense them. One way to pep up your prose and make it livelier is to avoid lifeless words. What are they? They consist mainly of what can be referred to as overworked verbs, worn-out nouns, and petrified phrases.

Overworked Verbs

The life of a sentence depends to a great extent on its verb, the word that directs the action. The flow and movement of ideas revolve around the verb, which functions like a quarterback directing the offense. In the following sentences, note how the substitution of lively, specific verbs for the general, lifeless *looked* communicates the writer's meaning more accurately and engages the reader's interest more fully.

The professor *looked* at the student.
The professor *gazed* at the student.
The professor *glanced* at the student.
The professor *peered* at the student.
The professor *stared* at the student.

Looked is the most general word in the list, suffering therefore from the weakness of all generalizations. *Looked* has the added disadvantage of being used so frequently and in so many different senses that it no longer arouses interest. The other verbs, being more unusual, command more attention and convey more information. *Stared* suggests a lengthy look, perhaps at some wrongdoing; *gazed,* a steady look, maybe of admiration or appreciation; *glanced,* a quick look, probably as a check; and *peered,* a searching look, probably through glasses or with squinting eyes.

Looking away from *look,* we find the most deadly of all the overworked verbs: the members of the *be* family. Like termites, they swarm everywhere, gnawing away at the foundations of sentences. Here they are:

am	be
is	being
are	been
was	were

Here's how these termites work and how they can be exterminated:

Before	*After*
Our response was in the negative.	We responded negatively. (*Or:* We declined, refused, and so on.)
He is a player for the Cincinnati Reds.	He plays for the Cincinnati Reds.
I am a worker on the assembly line.	I work on the assembly line.

In each of these simple examples, the overworked, worn-out form of *be* has been replaced with a livelier verb (*responded, plays, work*), thus tightening the sentences and transferring the action where it belongs—to the verb. But remember that *be* functions not only as a main verb but also as a helping verb. When used alone, it may be avoided; when used as an auxiliary, it may not. For example:

Here is how *be* is used as a helping verb.

The *is* form of *be* in *is used* functions as a necessary auxiliary in this sentence. Thus, there are busy *be*'s and lazy *be*'s: auxiliaries that help your sentences, and main verbs that hinder them. Keep the difference in mind, and try to change the lazy *be*'s to lively verbs.

Other worn-out verbs can weaken sentences. A few of the more common feeble verbs are listed here:

do	hold
give	make
got	put
have	take

Here they are in action, or more appropriately, inaction, along with *be:*

My professor *is* in the habit of *being* late, but on Thursday he *got* to our class on time, *giving* as an excuse for his promptness our need to consider the assignment carefully. After *making* a simple diagram of some object on the board, he requested those who *had* some recognition of it to *do* a rough sketch in their notebooks, *putting* the proper label by each part. After a while, I saw him *take* a glance out the window, *give* a look at his watch, *hold* a brief discussion with the graduate assistant, and *take* his leave of the astonished class. I *made* a decision then to *have* a talk with the chairman.

Without the overworked verbs, the paragraph gains vitality:

The professor habitually arrives late, but on Thursday he appeared in our class on time, excusing his promptness by pointing out our need to consider the assignment fully. After diagraming some object on the board, he requested those who recognized it to sketch it roughly in their notebooks, labeling each part properly. After a while, I saw him glance out the window, look at his watch, briefly discuss something with the graduate assistant, and leave the astonished class. I decided then to talk to the chairman.

Worn-Out Nouns

Let's admit it, most of us are basically lazy! If avoiding work is not too difficult or painful or costly or embarrassing, we'll do so. For example, in selecting nouns, we often rely on the same worn-out few, instead of struggling to find the precise one to explain exactly what we mean. At our worst, we may sometimes sound like this:

I took this thing to the store because I needed a new thing to make it work. If they didn't have the right thing, maybe they could find some other thing to put in its place. But the man told me that they didn't have the thing and there wasn't anything else that would do the job. I don't think he cared a thing about helping me. So I told him a thing or two.

Here are some other catch-all words you should try to avoid:

area	fashion	nature
aspect	field	process
case	kind	situation
factor	manner	type

Please don't misunderstand: you cannot always avoid these worn-out nouns. They are particularly necessary when referring to concrete objects, people, or qualities (a *case* of bourbon, the latest *fashion*, the *type* for the newspaper). But often you can eliminate them:

Before: In many *cases*, students fail to learn about career opportunities.
After: Many students fail to learn about career opportunities.

Before: The *nature* of this emergency *situation* called for drastic action.
After: This emergency called for drastic action.

Before: In the *field* of veterinary science, demand exceeds supply.
After: In veterinary science, demand exceeds supply.

Watch for these worn-out nouns and strike them out whenever possible.

Petrified Phrases

Often student writers turn to trite but true phrases that once may have been as pretty as a picture but now are as old as the hills. These students may think they are being as sharp as a tack, but the expressions, to make a long story short, are as dead as a doornail and as ugly as sin, being much the worse for wear. It goes without saying that it is penny wise but pound foolish to let them rear their ugly heads in your writing. If you do, you may even bore your own family although blood is thicker than water. Truer words were never spoken!

Once fresh and striking, hackneyed phrases or clichés, like the ones in the above paragraph, have lost all their sparkle. They pop into our mouths when we talk, and in our haste to express ideas, we find them handy. But in writing we have an advantage: the time to search for other words in the first draft or a later one. Of course, sometimes the clichés cannot be avoided. In a particular context, you may find no effective substitute for "Variety is the spice of life." Use it, but realize that you are not being clever: give it as little emphasis as possible.

Whenever you can, devise your own figurative language—similes, metaphors, or personifications. Here are some examples of these figures of speech:

> Simile: He looked as innocent as a first grader.
> Metaphor: Excessive team loyalty can be a disease that eats away good sportsmanship.
> Personification: Rumor scurried up and down the halls the day before busing began.

All three suggest a comparison. A simile does it explicitly or openly, signaling with the words *as* or *like* ("as a first grader"), a metaphor does it implicitly, not directly expressing the comparison ("can be a disease" = can be like a disease), and personification also works implicitly but by assigning human attributes to an inanimate object or abstraction ("Rumor scurried up and down" = Rumor was like a human being running around).

Of the three figures of speech, personification occurs least often in personal writing because it seems strained and artificial, especially when invoking such lofty abstractions as Life, Time, Nature, and Death. Metaphor is more common, often slipping unnoticed into our daily speech *(the light at the end of the tunnel, a foot in the door, break the ice)*. The test of a metaphor is to determine whether the comparison is literally possible. For example:

He is the captain of our team.

Captain is not a metaphor because its literal meaning is not violated.

He is a rock in times of trouble.

Rock is a metaphor because a human being cannot literally be one.

Metaphors may be as simple as this example or they may be extended to great complexity, like this famous one by John Donne:

No man is an island entire of itself; every man is a piece of the continent, a part of the main. If a clod be washed away by the sea, Europe is the less, as well as if a promontory were, as well as if a manor of thy friend's or of thine own were. Any man's death diminishes me, because I am involved in mankind, and therefore never send to know for whom the bell tolls; it tolls for thee.

—Meditation XVII

Here an abstract concept, the human community, is explained in two related parts of a geographical metaphor; we are not islands; we are parts of a continent.

Metaphor allows a writer to inform readers about something unknown or unfamiliar in terms that are easy to grasp and enjoyable to consider because of their imaginativeness and originality. Unfortunately, in straining for metaphors, writers sometimes produce artificial or mixed ones:

He thought he had a key to the problem, but he found he did not get to the heart of it.

In the first clause, the problem is treated like a lock; in the second, like a human being. The resulting mixed metaphor is disconcerting and confusing.

Similar to metaphors are similes, explicit comparisons signaled by *as* or *like*. The metaphor "He is a rock" becomes a simile when the form is changed to "He is like a rock." Perhaps because they are more obvious and less compressed than metaphors, similes are easier to write, and thus more common, just as cars with automatic transmissions are easier to drive and thus more common.

A SPECIAL PROBLEM: "I"

Having discussed such general features as naturalness, clarity, and liveliness in the language of personal writing, we'd like now to focus on a specific problem—the overuse of *I*. Because you are writing about yourself, chances are that you may overuse this conspicuous pronoun, which can irritate readers. Just as frequent coughing can detract from the impact of an effective speech or a moving concert, so the overuse of *I* can spoil personal writing.

If *I* appears as the first word in several successive sentences, the effect is generally childish. If this is what you wish, fine. It is the effect Malcolm X achieves in the following selection from his *Autobiography:*

One thing in particular I remember made me feel grateful toward my mother was that one day I went and asked her for my own garden, and she did let me have my own little plot. I loved it and took care of it well. I loved especially to grow peas. I was proud when we had them on our table. I would pull out the grass in my garden by hand when the first little blades came up. I would patrol the rows on my hands and knees for any worms and bugs, and I would kill and bury them. And sometimes when I had everything straight and clean for my things to grow, I would lie down on my back between two rows, and I would gaze up in the blue sky at the clouds moving and think all kinds of things.

In this passage, five of the seven sentences start with *I*. The voice is that of a child. If the writer had not wanted to achieve that effect, he might have written the passage this way (our additions are italicized; Malcolm X's words are crossed out):

1. *According to my recollection,* I remember one thing in
2. particular that made me feel grateful toward
3. my mother was the day I went and asked her
4. for my own garden, and she did let me have my
5. own little plot. I loved it and took care of
6. it well, *especially the growing of peas.* I loved
7. especially to grow peas. Having them on the
8. table made me proud. I was proud when we had
9. them on the table. I would pull out the grass
10. in my garden by hand when the first little
11. blades came up *and* I would patrol the rows
12. on my hands and knees for any worms and bugs,
13. killing them and burying them and I would kill
14. and bury them. And sometimes when I had every-
15. thing straight and clean everything was straight
16. and clean for my things to grow, I would lie
17. down on my back between two rows and I would gaze
18. up in the blue sky at the clouds moving and think
19. all kinds of things.

Much of the childish charm of the original has disappeared along with seven of the eleven *I*'s.

If you wish to reduce the number of *I*'s or *we*'s, you can do so by applying any of these techniques that will work effectively in your writing:

1. Change the subject + verb to a prepositional phrase: "I remember" to "according to my recollection." See line 1.
2. Change the subject + verb to an *-ing* phrase: "I loved especially to grow peas" to "especially growing peas." See lines 6–7.
3. Change subject-predicate clauses to *-ing* phrases to act as subject: "I was proud when we had them on the table" to "Having them on the table made me proud." See lines 7–8.
4. Combine sentences with the same subject: "I would pull out . . . I would patrol" to "I would pull out . . . and patrol." See lines 9 and 11.
5. Shift an object to subject position; this can be done by recasting the sentence from active to passive or, as in this case, by changing the verb

36

have to *be:* "And sometimes when I *had* everything straight" to "when everything *was* straight." See lines 14 and 15. (Occasional use of the passive may be less harmful than piling up *I*'s.)

To conclude, feel free to use the *I*, but keep an eye open to see that it doesn't sneak in at the beginning of several successive sentences; let it in only when you wish it to be there.

SUMMARY

This chapter is designed to make you aware of how you can use language to protect your natural voice, to transpose your personality to the written page. To achieve this, we suggested that you substitute specific words for vague, general ones—that you avoid the overworked words and petrified phrases that make your writing voice sound like everyone else's. We suggested that you use, instead, metaphor and simile to add life and color to your papers—figures of speech that *you* create, that reflect *your* personality and voice: the real *I* behind your writing.

Assignments

For Discussion

1   What is your reaction to the language in the following letter written by a college freshman to his aunt?

Dear Aunt Gert,

It is with utmost gratitude that I wish to express my appreciation to you for the splendid dictionary that you gave me. I shall cherish this gift of great utility during my college career and afterwards. I truly hope that this epistle finds you in excellent health and in full and complete enjoyment of life.

Sincerely,

Albert

How would you reword this letter?

2   What will you have to unlearn about using language in order to write about yourself effectively? Specifically, did you believe that all written English should be formal? What or who created that impression? How informal should personal writing be?

3   In the following passages, the writers have used colorful verbs, not prosaic ones. Identify them and discuss their effect. What figures of speech do you recognize?

a You would play upon me, you would seem to know my stops, you would pluck out the heart of my mystery, you would sound me from my lowest note to the top of my compass; and there is much music, excellent voice, in this little organ, yet cannot you make it speak. 'Sblood, do you think that I am easier to be played on than a pipe? Call me what instrument you will, though you can fret me, you cannot play upon me.

—William Shakespeare

b A little while later, the ice accepted the moonlight. The tip of the moon's upper limb was actually shining through miles and miles of piled-up ice! The light rays glittered, splintered, and slithered at odd angles, flashing right across the horizon. Then, slowly, the moon showed herself, her light shining horizontally over the cluttered masses of ice, casting long shadows.

—Tristan Jones

c Her hands trembled among the hooks and eyes, and her eyes had a feverish look, and her hair swirled crisp and crackling under the comb.

—William Faulkner

d The rangy dog darted from between the wheels and ran ahead. Instantly two ranch shepherds flew out at him. Then all three stopped and with stiff quivering tails, with taut straight legs, with ambassadorial dignity, they slowly circled, sniffing daintily.

—John Steinbeck

4 Analyze the language in the following letter from President Abraham Lincoln to General Ulysses S. Grant. Is the language natural, simple, concrete, and concise? How appropriate, sincere, and effective is the letter?

My dear General:

I do not remember that you and I ever met personally. I write this now as a grateful acknowledgment for the almost inestimable service you have done the country. I wish to say a word further. When you first reached the vicinity of Vicksburg, I thought you should do what you finally did—march the troops across the neck, run the batteries with the transports, and thus go below; and I never had any faith, except a general hope that you knew better than I, that the Yazoo Pass expedition and the like could succeed. When you got below and took Port Gibson, Grand Gulf and vicinity, I thought you should go down the river and join General Banks; and when you turned northward, east of the Big Black, I thought it was a mistake. I now wish to make the personal acknowledgment that you were right and I was wrong.

Yours very truly,

5   Create new similes to replace the following petrified phrases:

brown as a berry
cool as a cucumber
fit as a fiddle
drunk as a lord
poor as a churchmouse
sick as a dog

For Practice

1   Rewrite the following sentences, trying to enliven the. language by avoiding overworked verbs, worn-out nouns, and petrified phrases.

a   Her uncle, who is friendly in manner, was able to give her advice about the driving situation in New York.
b   She is one of those types of people who are willing to make a donation at the drop of a hat.
c   Students have the desire to make decisions about the process of selecting their electives.
d   A comparison of various colleges cannot be done by most people in the area of faculty quality.
e   Her friendly nature was the factor that had the result of her being elected class president.
f   The instructor made use of his knowledge of the field of psychology.
g   She made a suggestion that the faculty give consideration to making a change in the regulations.
h   My father had the ability to make an analysis of a situation of the type that would have had the effect of placing most people in confusion.
i   Her mother was a definite influence on my decision to put an application in for a scholarship in the field of mathematics.

2   In the following sentences, substitute each of the verbs in parentheses for the italicized one. Jot down the resulting difference in meaning as we did with the verb *looked* on page 31, consulting a dictionary or synonym book if you wish.

a   When the door opened, she *cried out.* (screamed, shrieked, yelled, shouted, roared)
b   He *turned down* the offer to settle the insurance claim. (refused, declined, rejected, repudiated, scorned)
c   She *saw* her mother getting into the car. (noticed, observed, watched, witnessed)
d   He *fixed* it in about two days. (repaired, corrected, mended, remedied, renovated)

   e   The noise *frightened* me. (scared, alarmed, terrified, terrorized, startled)

3   Examine the language in "Ricky" and "The Carnival" in Chapter 1. List five to ten words in each story that contribute to its effectiveness.

4   Rewrite the following sentences, eliminating as many *I*'s as possible but preserving most of the original wording.

   a   Because I am not accustomed to agreeing with Bill, I would like to point out that I do agree with him on this subject.
   b   I had dolls that talked and cried and opened their eyes, but I never had a doll that I loved as much as I did the Betsy doll.
   c   As I think back on the incident, I can realize now that I was being arrogant.
   d   When I consider how my Sundays are wasted, I know that I could have studied more and I could have gotten higher grades.
   e   I can remember vividly how I felt when I first drove off in the car alone.
   f   I had not seen Terry for several weeks and as I thought about meeting her in an hour, I realized that I was worried about what I would say to her.
   g   One night as I was returning from the library, I looked in the Chemistry Building and I saw a dog on the lab table, sniffing at the test tubes.
   h   I felt I was too weak to continue. I thought I was going to pass out. I was afraid that I would not be found until it was too late.
   i   I estimate that I must have thrown 36,700 newspapers onto porches during the days that I was delivering for the *News*.
   j   I have always felt that if I were to receive an opportunity, I could become a famous spy.

5   Rewrite the following student anecdote, adding specific details and verbs that contribute to the action.

After a collision, when we finally stopped moving, I opened my eyes. I was alive and so was my mother. I tried to get out of the car but my door was jammed. So I had to crawl out the back window. My mom got out finally when someone got her door open, but she couldn't really do anything for herself. The condition of the cars after impact made me feel small and powerless. Our car was not badly damaged, because we had a much heavier car; still the front left side was completely crushed. There was broken glass everywhere, but when I looked at the other car I was completely horrified. It was about half the weight and size of our car. The remains of the vehicle looked like someone had taken parts of it and crumbled, crushed, and thrown these parts into the air to land wherever they pleased. The battery was on one side of the road and the radiator on the other.

Grammar, Usage, and Spoken English

Which of the following sentences would you consider grammatical?

1. Youse guys ain't got no natural smarts.
2. Are you gonna go with us or not?
3. a. Who did you go to the movies with?
   b. Whom did you go to the movies with?
   c. With whom did you go to the movies?
4. The argsters had flinly tooglized the stidments.
5. No dog the bones closet skeletal eats the in.
6. Every day he is asking me the same thing.

If you selected only the three versions in sentence 3, then you would agree with most people. Trained to equate the term *grammatical* with correctness, most people would probably consider sentence 2 sloppy, and would unhesitatingly classify 1 as "incorrect" or "bad" grammar. They would probably find 4, 5, and 6 perplexing and would probably feel uneasy about considering them as examples of English, much less of "good" or "correct" English.

But modern language experts would find all the choices except 5 and 6 grammatical. Why the difference? Obviously, it is a matter of both definition and attitude: whether you consider "grammar" in terms of the whole language or only bits and pieces of it and whether you feel that language must be "correct" to be acceptable. It would be ideal if everyone would apply the same attitudes toward language use that they have about other social conventions, such as styles of clothing. They could then find that some uses are more appropriate in some situations than in others and some are not acceptable at all, not because they are "incorrect" but simply because they don't fit the occasion. Then the choices in example 3 would be analogous to the clothing you choose for public occasions: 3a for everyday, "school" clothing; 3b and 3c for formal affairs when you need a tuxedo or a formal gown. The language used in examples 1 and 2 would compare to wearing blue jeans or cut-offs; that in number 4 to donning a barrel or a large paper bag that others recognize as body covering, but not as clothing. Sentence 5 seems as odd as clothing worn in the wrong places—socks on the hands, a mitten on the ear, a hat on the foot. Example 6 seems to be a foreigner, wearing clothing a little different from our styles. However peculiar someone's clothing might seem, as long as it is not blatantly out of place, most of us are tolerant of such individual differences. However, we are often unable to muster such a relaxed attitude about the way people "wear" their language.

One reason for this reaction perhaps is the grammar traditionally taught in our schools. For the most part, textbooks have been primarily concerned with prescribing acceptable choices among several possible ways of saying the same thing: recommending the "correct" choice between items such as *is/are; who/whom; I/me;* and *like/as.* Thus, grammar textbooks have dealt mainly with isolated language structures and their use, rather than with the total system of the language. For generations, they have instructed American students about whether it is more "correct" for plural subjects to take a singular or plural verb form, as in "Ham and eggs *is/are* good"; or whether pronouns like *somebody* should take singular or plural pronoun referents, as in "Somebody left *his/their* umbrella." Conversely, contemporary language scholars prefer not to classify these concerns about isolated usages as *grammar* but to define the term more carefully than is done in the traditional texts.

GRAMMAR AND APPROPRIATENESS

In contemporary language study, *grammar* has two meanings: it can refer either to the total underlying system or structure of a language (in our case, English), or to a description of that basic system. In the first sense each language has only one grammar or underlying system; in the second, a language may have many grammars, or ways of describing its system. But in each of these current uses, the term *grammar* refers to the whole system of the language, to all the available structures and words that the language contains. Thus, if a statement is within the limits of structure and vocabulary possibilities, it would be considered *grammatical.*

In modern terminology, the term *grammatical* is not synonymous with *correct,* but with *possible.* And who determines what is possible? The final arbiters of the possible are native speakers—those people who speak the language as their "mother tongue."

With this understanding that any language structure possible for native speakers is grammatical, look back at examples 1–3 on page 41. All of these sentences are grammatical in that they are possible choices in English. However, some are considered more appropriate in some situations than in others; some more formal than others. If all the examples were placed on a scale of formality, sentence 1 ("Youse guys ain't got no natural smarts.") would be the most informal. Sentence 2 ("Are you gonna go with us or not?") would be next on the scale, then 3a, 3b, with 3c the most formal. Obviously, the *whom* in the latter two (3b and 3c) would be most appropriate in situations requiring careful use of language, but 3a would certainly be respectable in most cases since the *who* substitution for *whom* in questions has become widespread in the language. Example 2 is grammatical in that it represents a common pronunciation of "Are you going to go with us or not?" It still would be characterized as a casual, informal way of using the language, appropriate to speech or dialogue, but not to most writing situations. Sentence 1, although grammatical in our sense of the word, would be classified by many as inappropriate language or, at best, acceptable only in a jocular or highly informal situation.

What can we make of the two peculiar sentences (4 and 5) in our opening sample? Are they within the possibilities of English? Obviously, neither makes much "sense." But, surprisingly, sentence 4 can be considered more grammatical than 5. True, sentence 5 has well-known English words, but English *word order* is violated. Sentence 4, on the other hand, is made up of nonsense words, but their *order* is true to English structure. The words even contain recognizable word elements: *-ster, -ly, -ize, -ment,* and the plural *-s.* A familiar word like *youngster* is reflected in *argster, quickly* in *flinly, summarize* in *tooglize;* thus all are grammatical in the structure of English. But the words have no meaning to us; therefore, "The argsters had flinly tooglized the stidments" does not communicate. For a sentence to be grammatical, both its structure and its meaning must be possible to the language. In order for the sentence to become completely grammatical, we would have to substitute other words into its grammatical structure; for example, "The youngsters had quickly summarized the arguments."

Sentence 6, on the other hand, makes sense but is ungrammatical because it exhibits a strange verb form. Only a foreigner would say, "Every day he *is asking* me the same thing." Native speakers might use *has asked, asked* or *asks,* but not *is asking* in this context; it is not one of our grammatical options.

In this discussion we have indicated that English speakers have a wide variety of choices available, but factors other than mere concern for structure become involved in our use of language. We have hinted also that our choice of language structures and words must be weighed for appropriateness in certain situations. What influences act on us as we make decisions about language?

USAGE AND SOCIAL VALUES

One major influence on language choice is *custom.* For everyday purposes, we tend to use the language structures that we encounter most frequently at home, work, or play—the ones that seem most natural or comfortable. A second influence is the *situation* in which we use language, and the purpose for its use. Language, after all, is a form of social behavior and is therefore tempered by the forces influencing other kinds of human interaction: the seriousness of the occasion, the demands of established etiquette, the ritualistic character of the event, to cite only a few. Society demands more subdued behavior at a funeral, for instance, than at a Saturday night dance. If we switched these behavioral patterns, our social audience would be uncomfortable.

In language usage, another major influence is the *audience.* When you visit your grandparents, you probably leave your comfortable, faded jeans and sagging T-shirts in the closet and wear clothes more to their liking than yours, clothes that look more formal and that pinch here and there. Perhaps, without realizing it, you also tuck away your wardrobe of comfortable language usage and don a more respectable garb of words and sentences. For the easy, loose, slang vocabulary of your peers, you substitute more generally used words or even switch to the special vocabulary of your grandparents' generation. You may shift from a looser, more relaxed sentence form to a tighter, more concise wardrobe of sentences, substituting complete structures for the short idiomatic phrases and sentence fragments used in conversation with your friends. You consciously avoid usages that your elders would find crude or unacceptable, just as you avoid dressing in a way that might be offensive to them.

Whether you are with your closest friends or your grandparents, whether you are in an intimate, relaxed situation or a formal one, you speak in the English *language;* you use structures of English *grammar;* but the choices you make in any social situation are in the province of *usage.* Let us now consider in more detail the various social influences on language usage. Most of this discussion of usage has centered—and will center—on spoken varieties of English and very little has been said so far about the written forms. But since you learn the spoken form first and use it more frequently, it is the primary form that influences your written language in many, sometimes very subtle ways. It is important, therefore, that as a writer of English, you know and understand some of these influences on your writing habits.

Robert C. Pooley, in *The Teaching of English Usage,* wrote that good usage lies in making choices in spoken or written English that are "appropriate to the purpose of the speaker, true to the language as it is, and comfortable to speaker and listener."[1] As a speaker of English, you should be able to write in your language in such a way that you are not cramped by the discipline of its grammar or the social acceptability of certain usages. But remember, to communicate effectively to your listeners you must adhere to most of the dictates of both grammar and usage.

Students sometimes fail to be concerned about a listener's reaction to their language usage. Instead, they often view their particular way of speaking as something not to be questioned or tampered with. But as a student of composition, you need to realize that language communication is a two-way process, involving a complex set of behavioral patterns. On the one hand, it is highly personal and individualized: each of us has a distinctive way of speaking and writing, just as each of us has a unique set of fingerprints or our own special way of forming letters in our handwriting. In a very real sense, it can be said that your language is *you*—an integral part of your personality and personal identity.

On the other hand, language is not used simply for self-gratification. As the most complex form of all human communication, it must operate with conventional structures and with usages shared by all members of the language community. You might, for instance, find fun in greeting your friends with "Dirky ratafratch" or "Morning to good you," but in doing so you would not be communicating effectively. To do this, you can't make up your own rules, but must respect the generally accepted conventions of language.

However, the demands of communication are not the only social influences on language use. Certain language options may be given greater value than others, even though the preferences may be completely arbitrary and may shift from one generation to another. Language uses, like clothing and hair styles, can lose or win public favor. An example of this is the double negative used for emphasis. The modern English community frowns upon usages like "I ain't got no money" or "I won't go noplace with you," but there was a time when this form was perfectly respectable. In Anglo-Saxon texts written a thousand years ago, the emphatic double negative occurs frequently. As recently as the early seventeenth century, it was permissible for Shakespeare to allow the most aristocratic of his characters to use it. For instance, in *Romeo and Juliet,* Mercutio angrily states, "I will not budge for no man's pleasure." If a modern Mercutio were to utter this challenge, a present-day, aristocratic Romeo would view him as a low-class hothead, rather than the high-class hothead he really was.

[1] Robert C. Pooley, *The Teaching of English Usage* (Urbana, Ill.: National Council of Teachers of English, 1974), p. 12.

Usage changes, and so eventually does the grammar of a language. Major structural changes in language, such as many of those from Old English to Modern English, take place over centuries and not within the lifetime of any one individual; but because usages may become fashionable or taboo within a few years, speakers of language must be prepared to adjust to the new values. The English you will speak when you are older will probably be grammatically the same as that you speak now. But it will be characterized by the loss of some present usages and the additions of others. These individual changes will be strongly influenced by your profession, your geographical location, your educational background, and your social group.

Always, your language communication will be shaped by two major forces, sometimes without your awareness: (1) your subconscious, built-in knowledge of the restraints and demands of English *grammar* (the system); and (2) the usage or choice dictated by a particular social *situation:* a situation that includes the occasion, the purpose of the communication, and the audience. If you wish to communicate effectively, your choice of language must not only fit the patterns possible to English, but must also be acceptable to your social community. As a college student, your social community is the college or university you attend. It will place its own special demands upon your English usage—demands that you may resent at times. But as you become a successful participant in this new language community, you will fashion yet another garment to hang in your usage closet and you will be able to don it comfortably when the situation demands it.

VARIETIES OF SPOKEN ENGLISH: DIALECTS

As we have indicated, although the grammar of a language is fairly static, usage is flexible. We all speak our own brand of English, and this is as it should be. But in writing to a general audience, we must continually decide which of our particular usages will aid communication and which will interfere with it. A knowledge of the forces shaping our language patterns and of the usages peculiar to the different varieties of American English can help us make those choices. In this discussion, we will briefly examine the geographical and social varieties of spoken English that skillful users of the language must be able to recognize.

Like all languages, English is made up of many varieties of speech called *dialects.* These dialects differ in pronunciation, vocabulary, and structure, but they share most of the features of the language, so that the speakers of one can understand the speakers of another with little difficulty. If these dialects are a result of geographical location, they are called *regional* dialects; if they are a result of social differentiation, they are called *social* dialects. Other dialects may be ethnic in origin; that is, they result from the immigration of another language-speaking group, so that some aspects of their native language become fused with the adopted language. Pennsylvania Dutch, the dialect spoken in some areas of Pennsylvania by German immigrants, illustrates such a fusion: aspects of German pronunciation, word order, and vocabulary have become a part of their English as attested by their well-known saying, "We grow too soon old and too late schmart."

Other interesting language varieties may arise from occupations such as jazz, coal mining, railroading, the television industry, and professional sports. But these are not generally considered dialects, since they vary only in vocabulary or jargon.

Each of us is influenced by all these sources. Our speech bears the stamp not only of our home geographical region, but also of our social and ethnic backgrounds, and it may also include elements of specialized jargon. Your own speech may include slang words derived from the particular jargon of your high-school or home community.

Geographical Dialects: Three Main Regions

The English language is rich in regional dialects because of the massive migration of its speakers to many parts of the world. Today, because of separation from the English spoken in homeland Britain and the influence of local languages, many varieties of English exist throughout the world. In the United States, where English became the dominant language despite the many early French and Spanish settlers, three main geographical or regional dialects have evolved. Their distribution and peculiar characteristics are closely tied to the history of the British settlement of the New World and the geographical barriers the settlers encountered. The settlers of New England and the central Atlantic coastal states came largely from the eastern and southern parts of England, while later immigrants to the Piedmont areas came from north and northwest of London. The differences in their original dialects account for many of the present speech variations we encounter in these regions.

In the dialect studies initiated in the 1930s, Hans Kurath and his fellow researchers discovered that three distinct dialect regions exist along the east coast of the United States and that emigrants from these areas carried their speech characteristics with them as they moved across the continent to the west coast. The dialects—Northern, Midland, and Southern—share more language similarities than differences, of course, since all speakers of American dialects understand each other. However, each dialect demonstrates peculiar characteristics of pronunciation, grammatical structures, and vocabulary. But let's look first at their geographical distribution. The accompanying map shows a rough approximation of the main contemporary dialect areas of the United States.

—Adapted from Roger Shuy, *Discovering American Dialects*

Northern Dialect Regions Northern dialect includes both Northeastern Northern (spoken in the New England area north of New York City) and Great Lakes Northern (spoken in the area surrounding the Great Lakes and extending north and west to the Rocky Mountains). The division of Northern into two subclasses results from the difference in the pronunciation of *r*. Northeastern Northern speakers pronounce a word like *party* as *pahty*, whereas those in the Great Lakes region say *party*, pronouncing the *r* sound after the vowel. Some Northeastern speakers also have an intrusive *r*; that is, they include an *r* sound between two vowels, as in John F. Kennedy's highly publicized pronunciation of *Cuber* for *Cuba* in such contexts as "*Cuba*(r) *and* the United States," in which *Cuba* ends with a vowel sound and *and* begins with one.

Midland Dialect Regions Like the Northern, the Midland region is subdivided into two dialect areas, North and South Midland. As the map shows, the Midland region extends from the east coast across the central part of the United States, including the Appalachian region, the Midwest corn belt, and the states on the west coast. The dividing line between North and South Midland is roughly along route 40, formerly the National Highway and now approximate to Interstate 70. The Midland area has been subclassified into North and South Midland mainly because of variant pronunciations in words like *greasy* (North Midland: greasy; South Midland: greazy) and in whether there is a *pin/pen* distinction. South Midlanders tend to pronounce the latter two words exactly alike, so that they often must be asked whether they mean "stickin' pins" or "writin' pins."

Southern Dialect Region   The Southern dialect area not only manifests the most variation within a speech region in the United States, but is also the smallest geographical area. During the nineteenth-century westward migration, Southern settlers were more limited by the laws prohibiting slavery in the new territories than by geographical barriers. If Southern families wished to move west, taking their slaves with them, they were confined to those areas where slavery was legal. The Southern dialect shares the pronunciation of *greasy* as greazy, the lack of *pin/pen* distinction, and similar vowel sounds with South Midland dialect, but lacks the *r* sound after vowels characteristic of Midland varieties.

Differences in Pronunciation, Vocabulary, and Syntax   Whether or not the speakers of a region make a *pin/pen* distinction is only one of the specific ways in which dialects vary. Following is a chart listing a small but significant sampling of dialect differences:

	NORTHERN	MIDLAND	SOUTHERN
PRONUNCIATION FEATURES			
r after vowels	deleted in N.E. present in G.L.	present in all varieties in words like *wash* (warsh)	deleted
intrusive *r*	between vowels in some N.E. varieties	absent	absent
pin/pen distinction	clear distinction	N.—clear distinction S.—no distinction	no distinction
pronunciation of *greasy*	greasy	N.—greasy S.—greazy	greazy
vowel contrast in *on/not*	no contrast (both rhyme with *hot*)	*on* pronounced as in *pond; not* rhymes with *hot*	same as Midland
VOCABULARY ITEMS			
animal with strong scent	skunk	skunk	polecat
small ground animal	chipmunk	ground squirrel	ground squirrel

VOCABULARY ITEMS	NORTHERN	MIDLAND	SOUTHERN
nocturnal insect	firefly (urban) lightning bug (rural)	lightning bug fire bug	lightning bug
wild plants used for salad	————	greens salat (S. Midland)	greens, salad, salat
large sandwich	hoagie	submarine poor boy (S. Midland)	poor boy
SYNTACTICAL STRUCTURES nauseated	sick *to* my stomach	sick *on/in* my stomach	sick *at* my stomach
plural of *pair*	two *pair* of	two *pairs* of	two *pair* of
fifteen minutes before the hour	quarter *to,* quarter *of*	quarter *till*	quarter *till*

Significance of Regional Differences   Obviously, this discussion of American dialects has touched on only a few of the pronunciation, syntactical, and vocabulary differences in regional speech. But even from this small sample of socially acceptable features, it is clear that in the United States there is no one "correct" way of speaking. Instead, each geographical dialect has its own norm; each has its own cluster of pronunciations, its own syntactical and word usages that the majority of that region's people, including the most educated and influential, look upon as respectable English. In their spoken language, Americans do not impose a single "standard" dialect upon their speakers as people in other countries, such as France and England, have attempted to do. True, some Americans training for the stage or national broadcasting may adopt a leveled-off form of American English, sometimes referred to as "CBS" or "network" English, which avoids regional characteristics. But most cultured Americans talk in the voice of their home region, thus helping to preserve the flexibility of speech and the individuality that are so highly valued in our country.

Social Dialects

However strong a factor in language variety it is, geographical variety can account only in part for the complexity of speech patterns in the United States. A second influence, on both spoken and written English, comes from the many social dialects; clusters of language usages that become associated with social prestige and approval. In the preceding discussion of language, we emphasized that speakers place social values on certain usages: some are greatly respected and looked upon as standard; others, less respected, are therefore viewed as nonstandard. This value system seldom has a linguistic basis; it has to do with social snobbery rather than linguistic effectiveness. "Ain't nobody see nothin' " communicates to speakers of English just as effectively as the socially valued "Nobody has seen anything," and both are certainly grammatical possibilities of English. In fact, the former structure undoubtedly carries more emphasis than the latter, particularly when the accompanying intonation features of speech are added. But rightly or wrongly, the people who create the standards of speech in a language—a group made up of the majority of speakers, including the most educated and socially prestigious—would not generally accept as respectable the usage of "Ain't nobody see nothin'."

Thus, each geographical dialect region has a distinctive cluster of features that make up the norm or standard variety of the dialect—the prestigious social dialect. Other varieties within the regional dialect containing a pattern of usages considered socially unacceptable are looked upon as nonstandard. Thus, each regional dialect includes several social dialects: the standard form and a number of variants considered by the "standard" speakers to be "nonstandard." Many critics of this nonegalitarian classification refer to standard dialects as "Establishment English," that spoken by the educated and socially influential people in the community. Nonstandard varieties, on the other hand, are usually spoken by people less educated, less affluent, and generally less influential in the "power structure" of the community. Language use, then, whether we approve of the practice or not, becomes a tool of social prestige. The standard dialects, like a large estate in the country, indicate a more respected social position. The fact that the nonstandard forms, like a three-room house, are just as functional as the standard forms is often obscured by highly emotional factors. Since "nonstandard" carries such snobbish connotations, we prefer to call such forms *community dialects*—subdialects within a regional variety that are limited to tightly integrated, close-knit social groups. The community dialects most thoroughly studied to date are those in the large urban centers settled largely by southern black people who migrated north for economic reasons. Because of their social isolation in the northern city ghetto, they have retained most of the features, both standard and nonstandard, of their Southern and South Midland origins.

The findings of these studies should help dispel some misconceptions about community dialects: (1) that there is only one standard dialect of spoken English and all else is nonstandard; (2) that nonstandard dialects are inferior to the standard in communication and reasoning power; and (3) that nonstandard variants are drastically different from standard dialects. Contrary to these misconceptions, current study has found that like regional varieties, social dialects are alike in more ways than they are different. Also, researchers like William Labov contend that "nonstandard" community dialects are far from being verbally deficient; he offers convincing evidence that they have the same abilities to express logical relationships and to communicate as effectively as do more socially acceptable dialects. In fact, Labov and others claim that some community dialect usages may be superior to standard ones. For instance, a person who creates sentences like "She working" and "She be working" can use them to make distinctions between present action and continuous action that standard speakers cannot make without the addition of adverbial modifiers—"She is working *now*" and "She works *every day*."[2]

The speakers of any community dialect, whatever its characteristics might be, communicate fully with one another. It is only when a community dialect is used outside the group that certain usages might interfere. Just as some regional forms can temporarily impede communication and social interaction, so too can specialized community usages. The broader our personal social base becomes, the more "voices" we need. When we attempt to inform or persuade a widely divergent audience, then we should strive for a voice free of usages that would confuse or irritate some of those people. We should particularly avoid the following usages, claimed by Raven I. McDavid, Jr., to be those universally considered nonstandard throughout the United States.[3]

1. Very few pronunciation features would be considered unacceptable, except perhaps to the most hypercorrect listener. Probably the most universally questioned are the pronunciation of *thing/then* as *ting/den* and of the italicized sounds in *three/brother* as *free/bruvver*.
2. The omission of inflections indicating noun plurals and possessives, as in "Those two boy ran away" and "We found Mr. Smith hat." These would be frowned upon in all regional dialect areas. So too would the deletion of the third person singular -s and of other verb inflections:

   He really bug me. (Omission of third person singular -*s*.)
   He scold me yesterday. (Omission of past tense inflected -*ed*.)
   He'd finish it at home. (Omission of past participle inflection: He'd [He had] finish*ed* it at home.)

3. The consistent omission of any element in a verb phrase, as in:

   He a good boy *for* He *is* a good boy.
   He been drinking *for* He *has* been drinking.
   I going home *for* I *am* going home.

[2] William Labov, *The Logic of Nonstandard English,* Monograph Series on Language and Linguistics, No. 22 (Washington, D.C.: Georgetown University Press, 1969).
[3] Raven I. McDavid, Jr., "A Checklist of Significant Features for Discriminating Social Dialects," *Dimensions of Dialect,* ed. Eldonna Everts (Urbana, Ill.: National Council of Teachers of English, 1967), pp. 7–10.

4. Deviant case inventions:

Those are our'*n for* Those are our*s.*
He told me hiss*elf for* He told me hi*m*self.
Them hot dogs were good *for Those* hot dogs were good.

Although the list is surprisingly short, it is highly significant because it includes those usages that should be avoided by all speakers and writers trying to communicate with a general audience. But, as a student writer, you cannot assume that these are the only items that might be unacceptable to members of your audience, many of whom will have regional preferences, hypercorrect biases, or just plain distaste for certain usages. But if one of these critics, even a teacher, questions a word or its pronunciation, or your use of a grammatical structure, you can expect the objection to be justified on grounds other than that it is nonstandard. For instance, a usage can legitimately be questioned if it does not seem appropriate to your social situation or to your audience, or if it violates the effect you are trying to achieve. Language usage appropriate to one writing assignment could be unacceptable for another: vocabulary perfectly acceptable to your peers, such as in the statement "Seeing that movie is a *must,*" may fall offensively on the ear of a middle-aged English teacher. Or the use of colloquially acceptable idiomatic structures may mar the tone of a paper written to persuade a well-educated audience of doctors or lawyers.

When you write, you should remember that all usages—even those in our nonstandard listing—are relative to the language situation. Just as some standard speakers might be offended by usages they consider nonstandard, so might speakers of community dialects, having many of our listed items as regular dialect features, find "correct" forms offensive. In highly personal interrelationships, we must tailor our language usages to the situation and the moment. But in communicating with a general audience, you as a person committed to effective communication should attempt to avoid generally unacceptable usages and the special vocabulary of community dialects, just as a network TV announcer omits features of specific geographical dialects.

FROM SPOKEN TO WRITTEN ENGLISH

In this section on personal writing, you are expected to write *close* to the way you speak. But you should be aware that the written language is never an exact transcription of the spoken. The first and most influential reason for this is that when you write you lose the face-to-face contact of conversation and all the nonverbal advantages gained from that. As speakers, we use facial expressions, body movements, hand gestures, changes in voice quality, and the intonational features of language to aid our communication. A frown, a wave of the hand, or a change in voice pitch often substitutes for a dozen words. In addition, we "catch" our listeners by literally touching them or by involving them in the conversation through such question devices as "isn't that so?" or "don't you agree?" These verbal "catching" devices often become regional in character, as in the Northern "eh?" and the Southern "ya hear?" Even the ubiquitous "y'know" serves this purpose.

Another reason for the differences in spoken and written English is the kinds of grammatical structures employed. Spoken conversational English is characterized by short sentences, sentence fragments that are often single words, and omission of structural "clues," such as prepositions, sentence subjects, parts of verb phrases. In speaking, we tend to use contractions—*I've, he's, you'd*—and often the sounds represented by *'ve, 's,* and *'d* disappear entirely. In writing, because we cannot rely on visual and vocal aids, and on the closeness of our audience, we must replace many of the missing parts to make communication work.

To get at some of the differences between spoken and written English, let's look at a transcription of an interview with a professional tennis player taped by Studs Terkel for his book *Working.* Next to it is a revised version more characteristic of written English. However, both represent informal style. Note the differences indicated by the italicized words and the omissions indicated by the caret (∧).

ORIGINAL	REVISED
If I go out with *guys* that aren't sports-minded, I feel like a *jock.* ∧ The whole conversation, there's nothing to go on. ∧ *You* go out with a baseball player or something, *you* carry on a normal conversation. But *this one guy* can't get it out of his mind. A female athlete is just so new. It's just like a *kid* growing up to be an astronaut. This *was* never before. . . . I meet *these* fantastically wealthy people I would never have ∧ a chance to meet before. A dentist, *he goes* to a cocktail party, who's gonna talk about *your* teeth? If you're a tennis pro, everybody can talk. There's a common bond. . . . In a way *it's an ugly wealth,* too. ∧ Gaudy diamond rings, ∧ impressing each other. At Miami Beach I stayed at the Jockey Club. I *lucked* out, and three of us got to stay *like* on an eighty-five-foot yacht.[4]	If I go out with *men* that aren't sports-minded, I feel like an *athlete.* Through the whole conversation, there's nothing to go on. If *I* go out with a baseball player or something, *I* can carry on a normal conversation. But *other men* can't get it out of their minds. A female athlete is just so new. It's just like a child growing up to be an astronaut. This never *happened* before. I meet *some* fantastically wealthy people I would never have *had* a chance to meet before. A dentist *goes* to a cocktail party and who's going to talk about teeth? If you're a tennis pro, everybody can talk. There's a common bond. In a way *their wealth is ugly,* too. *With their* gaudy diamond rings, *they* impress each other. At Miami Beach I stayed at the Jockey Club. I was lucky; three of us stayed on an eighty-five-foot yacht.

[4] Studs Terkel, *Working* (New York: Pantheon Books, 1974), p. 379.

54

Keep in mind that Terkel probably edited out a lot of characteristics of the real conversation, such as repeated words, pauses, false starts, the *uh*'s and the *y'know*'s. As you can see, the spoken version is rich in slang: *guys, jock, kid, lucked out.* The omissions include prepositions (*through, with*), conjunctions (*if*), a subject (*they*), and part of a verb phrase (would never have *had*). The repeated subject ("A dentist, *he*"), although common to spoken English, occurs only in realistic dialogue in written English. The impersonal *you* ("*You* go out with a baseball player") is another common feature in speech, but one that should be used sparingly, even in informal writing. Other vague pronouns such as "*these* fantastically wealthy people" and "*it*'s an ugly wealth" are discouraged in written language because there is no chance to explain away confusion.

For greater informality—in a letter, perhaps—the revised version could have retained the slang words, but we attempted to adapt the spoken version to a general audience, retaining only enough slang to sustain an informal style.

As you can see, written English, regardless of how informal, has features that are different from those of a spoken version. In fact, many current language scholars regard written English as a separate dialect—one that all of us, regardless of our regional and social dialects, must learn to master if we are to communicate in writing.

SUMMARY

In this chapter, we have tried to make a clear distinction between the *grammar* of a language and its *usages;* grammar as it refers to the whole language system, usage as the ways we use the pronunciation, vocabulary, and syntactical options available. The usages consistently chosen by a community of people can create a separate dialect—regional or social. However, some usages can become more or less socially acceptable than others, resulting in favorable or unfavorable attitudes toward them. Thus, some usages acceptable to a limited group of people may be criticized by the larger community.

Also, we have indicated differences in spoken and written English—even when both are informal and relaxed. Perhaps a list of these characteristics can summarize most effectively.

Informal Spoken English	Informal Written English in Personal Writing
1. Large number of regional and social usages (vocabulary and syntactical)	Vocabulary and syntactical usages closer to those recognizable to a larger audience
2. Many single words and short sentence fragments	Fragments used sparingly—complete enough to avoid reader confusion

	Informal Spoken English	*Informal Written English in Personal Writing*
3.	Omission of "function" words, such as *at, with, be, have, the, a, because*	Careful inclusion of function words to provide meaning clues for readers
4.	Heavy reliance on tone of voice, intonation features, and body gestures	Substitution of more complete syntactical structures and punctuation devices for speech features
5.	Numerous repetitions and pauses	Careful choice of words to avoid distracting repetitions
6.	Choice of words—slang, profanity, specialized jargon—suitable to a limited peer group	Word choice tailored to a broader audience

Of course, in free, personal writing and in narrative attempting to be realistically accurate, written English is close to spoken and is characterized by regional and social usages. But in communicating with a wide, diverse audience, writers adopt a new dialect, somewhat different from their spoken one—a dialect that has universal features, rather than those of a particular regional and social group. Writers do this even if it means sacrificing some of the individual flavor characteristic of their spoken language because of their commitment to being understood by as wide an audience as possible.

This chapter is designed not to teach you "grammar" or to make you a dialect scholar, but to make you aware of the language options available to you and of how social attitudes can influence your choice of those options. We have replaced the straitjacket of "correctness" with the roomier garment of "appropriateness." We have alerted you to regional and social dialect varieties and to the different levels of language usage, and how audience, purpose, and the occasion influence the level you choose—whether in speaking or writing. Such knowledge can help you realize the relationship of language usage to the commitment you make to yourself and to your readers when you write.

Assignments

For Discussion

1 What distinctions does this chapter make between grammar and usage?

2 According to the definition of *grammatical* developed in this chapter,

which of the following examples are grammatical? Discuss the social acceptability and communicative effectiveness of each example. (Read them aloud before deciding.)

a   Dja eat yet?
b   Where's he at?
c   Ask him where is he.
d   Ain't nobody seen nothin' around here.
e   "Twas brillig, and the slithy toves
     Did gyre and gimble in the wabe."
                                    —Lewis Carroll
f   The question is, who's fooling who?   ·
g   At what are you looking?
h   What are you looking at?
i   He's never at home when I call.

3   Analyze the following three passages. What does the usage in each reveal about the writing situation? How do vocabulary and stucture indicate occasion and audience?

a   I like the spring of the year the best because everything looks as if it is coming to life. In the fall of the year, it looks like it's done everything it is going to do. You see these here things jumping up out of the ground. The trees turning green, like life is coming into things. In the fall of the year, the cold winds begin to blow and the leaves look like they are dying away, don't it?
                    —Craig Evan Royce, *Country Miles Are Longer than City Miles*

b   The ketch *Palawan* is built of aluminum, with one-quarter-inch maximum thickness, so we were very cautious about our predicament. Visions of various Arctic explorers frozen in over a winter; visions of how we would explain to our friends what had happened to our vessel; visions of how a helicopter would have to come from Thule to rescue us; visions of dealing at close quarters with water temperatures of 33 degrees F.—all sorts of unpleasant visions of being considered not intrepid explorers but amateur troublemakers—crossed our minds. We cautiously backed the boat into an open lead, and after three hours of work, were able to get her turned around and headed to the open sea.
        —Thomas J. Watson, Jr., "Sailing in the Arctic Is a New Challenge for a Yachtsman"

c   And so, my fellow Americans: ask not what your country can do for you—ask what you can do for your country.
    My fellow citizens of the world: ask not what America will do for you, but what together we can do for the freedom of man.
    Finally, whether you are citizens of America or citizens of the world, ask of us here the same high standards of strength and sacrifice which we ask of you. With a

good conscience our only sure reward, with history the final judge of our deeds, let us go forth to lead the land we love, asking His blessing and His help, but knowing that here on Earth God's work must truly be our own.

—John F. Kennedy, Inaugural Address

4 Chinese has many varieties, which are often referred to as dialects. However, a number of them, such as Mandarin and Cantonese, are mutually unintelligible. According to our definitions, how would they be classified?

5 Have you ever had difficulty communicating with a person from a dialect region different from yours? Or have you ever been confused by regional names when traveling outside your geographical area? Discuss.

6 Underline or write in the blanks the word you use for the following items. If there is a wide diversity of answers in the class, try to establish the regional source of each word.[5]

   a Halloween greeting: trick or treat, tricks or treats, beggar's night, help the poor, Halloween!, give or receive, _____

   b Landing on stomach when diving: belly-flop, belly-flopper, belly-bust, belly-buster, _____

   c Be truant from school: bag school, bolt, lay out, play hookey, play truant, ditch, flick, flake school, blow school, _____

   d Drinking fountain: cooler, water cooler, bubbler, fountain, drinking fountain, _____

   e Knee-length pants worn by men: shorts, bermuda shorts, bermudas, walking shorts, knee pants, knee knockers, pants, _____

   f Knee-length pants worn by women: shorts, bermudas, walking shorts, pants, _____

   g Location of instruments in automobile: dash, dashboard, instrument panel, panel, crash panel, _____

   h Device for accelerating an automobile: accelerator, gas, gas pedal, pedal, throttle, _____

   i The car needs _____: a grease job, lubrication, a lube job, to be greased, to be lubed, servicing, to be serviced, _____

   j New limited access road: turnpike, toll road, freeway, parkway, post road, tollway, thruway, expressway, _____

   k Place where an audience watches movies in their cars: drive-in, drive-in movie, outdoor movie, outdoor theater, open-air movie, passion pit, _____

7 Compare slang terms for the following items with other members of your class or friends in the dormitory:

[5] Examples taken from Roger Shuy, *Discovering American Dialects* (Urbana, Ill.: National Council of Teachers of English, 1967).

a an automobile		**h** an unpleasant person	
b a policeman		**i** money	
c a party		**j** a homosexual (male and female)	
d an attractive male		**k** marijuana	
e an attractive female		**l** being drunk or high	
f an unattractive male		**m** a conceited male	
g an unattractive female		**n** a conceited female	

8 Why is it difficult to find a social dialect (standard or nonstandard) that would be consistent throughout the United States in vocabulary, syntax, and pronunciation? What are some of the characteristics shared by nonstandard community dialects of American English?

9 Look up the listed items in any two of these three books (available in the reference room of the library). Do they agree? Discuss.

Bryant, Margaret M. *Current American Usage* (1962).
Evans, Bergen and Cornelia. *A Dictionary of Contemporary American Usage* (1957).
Follett, Wilson, *Modern American Usage* (1966).

a *the reason is because*   **e** *can* and *may*
b *ensure/insure*   **f** *lie/lay*
c *hangs, hung/hanged*   **g** *sit/set*
d *dive, dove/dived*

10 Currently, *plus* is increasingly used as a conjunction to substitute for *and* and *in addition to,* as in "They expected their tour of France to be very educational. *Plus* they expected to eat a lot of good French cooking." Check several recent dictionaries to see if this usage is noted. Note all the occurrences of the usage that you encounter over a two- or three-week period. Jot them down on 3 x 5 cards, indicating the age and educational background of the user. Compare your findings with those collected by the other members of your class. Decide on the appropriateness of the usage.

For Practice

1 In the following selections are usages generally considered unacceptable for many writing purposes. Replace the questionable ones with standard forms. Then write a letter to the local school board justifying the original usages.

a The father grunted. "I'll be bound. If there was trouble there, I'll be bound he was in it. You tell him," he said violently, "if he lets them yellow-bellied priests bamboozle him, I'll shoot him myself quick as I would a reb."
—William Faulkner, *Light in August*

59

b David sat down. Fascinated, he stared at the shining cogs that moved without moving their hearts of light. "So wot makes id?" he asked. In the street David spoke English.

"Kentcha see. Id's coz id's a machine."

"Oh!"

"It wakes up mine fodder in de mawning."

"It tells yuh w'en yuh sh'd eat an' w'en yuh have tuh go tuh sleep. It shows yuh w'ea, but I tooked it off."

"I god a calenduh opstair's," David informed him.

"Puh! Who ain' god a calenduh?"

"I save mine. I godda big book outa dem, wit numbuhs on id."

"Who can't do dat?"

"But mine fodder made it," David drove home the one unique point about it all.

—Henry Roth, *Call It Sleep*

c "There was her hens," suggested Mrs. Fosdick, after reviewing the melancholy situation. "She never wanted the sheep after that first season. There wa'n't no proper pasture for sheep after the June grass was past, and she ascertained the fact and couldn't bear to see them suffer; but the chickens done well. I remember sailin' by one spring afternoon, an seein' the coops out front o' the house in the sun. How long was it before you went out with the minister? You were the first ones that ever really got ashore to see Joanna."

—Sarah Orne Jewett, *The Country of the Pointed Firs*

For Writing

1 Write a paragraph describing the dating activities of your high school crowd, using the group's vocabulary.
2 Write a second paragraph describing the same activities but addressing yourself to a general audience.
3 Describe an event typical of your home region that attracts many kinds of people, such as an arts and crafts fair; a drag race; a state or country fair; a street fair or festival. Use words and expressions you hear at home but not in other places.

Sentence Strategies in Personal Writing

WHAT IS A SENTENCE?

The police did not come. In my agitation I found myself beside Ruth First whose article I had not written. She didn't seem to mind at all. Time passed and the knots began to shred away slowly. I joined the head-shaking people making their way to the Anglican Mission in Proes Street, shaking my head as I went. I looked back. There was no one on the pavement outside the old synagogue. The police had also left.

—Alfred Hutchinson, *Road to Ghana*

This passage is taken from an autobiographical narrative describing the release of a number of black political hostages after two years in prison. If you read it aloud, you will find that the short sentences encourage fast reading, thus heightening the sense of action and urgency in the situation. With the exception of a few sentences in the passage, most are what we traditionally call simple sentences. Actually, the term *simple* is a little misleading because it connotes short, simple-minded sentences, and simple sentences are not always that simple. In the above paragraph, there are some short examples: "I looked back," "The police did not come," and "The police had also left." But what of "I joined the head-shaking people making their way to the Anglican Mission in Proes Street, shaking my head as I went"? Although not short, it too fits the traditional definition of a simple sentence—one that consists of only one subject and one main verb.

To better understand simple sentences and their usefulness to personal writing, let's look first at some general characteristics of the sentence. Traditionally, a simple sentence is defined as having a single thought or idea. But in conversations, short phrases or even single words can imply a complete thought, as in this example where John relies on Helen's question to supply the missing information in his answer:

Helen: "Where are you going after class?"
John: "Home."

Obviously, "home" spoken all by itself could not convey a complete thought—other sentence elements are needed. Instead of the traditional definition, let's define the sentence as a language *form* that has two main positions or *slots*. The first slot contains the someone or something that not only participates actively in the situation described, but is usually the instigator of the action. This participant-agent, usually a noun or pronoun, you probably know as the *subject* of the sentence. The second slot in a sentence contains a verb and other words closely related to the verb that indicate the "action" in the sentence and make a comment about the subject. You may remember this from your school grammar as the *predicate,* so called because it predicates (states) something about the subject. In the last sentence of our opening example, "The police had also left," the participant-subject is "the police," and the predicate is "had also left." If we made a graphic model (or frame) of a simple sentence and its parts or slots, it might look like this:

SIMPLE SENTENCE

| *Subject* (participant) "The police" | *Predicate* (comment) "had also left." |

The form of the sentence, then, is closely related to meaning; both slots are needed to really express a "complete thought" and to supply the basic information in the sentence.

WHAT DOES A SENTENCE MEAN?

On the surface, it may seem silly to ask what a sentence means. You might ask, "Doesn't the basic information in the sentence give the meaning?" The answer is, "That depends!" Many things can influence the meaning of a sentence: its words may have several meanings, resulting in several possible interpretations of the sentence. Or its structure may be ambiguous, as in the hoary example "She fed her dog biscuits." But often sentences, even those without built-in ambiguity, mean what we *intend* them to. For instance:

Helen: "My brother used masking tape to fix his water hose when his car broke down on the highway."
John: "That was intelligent."

Helen: "My brother skied over gravel yesterday and broke his ankle."
John: "That was intelligent."

As speakers and writers, we need to be aware that the basic information in a sentence may not mean what it appears to and that we can shape the meaning of any sentence according to our intent. Significant in all speaking and writing situations, this knowledge is especially important in writing dialogue. Spoken, John's sarcasm would be more obviously apparent, because he would have used tone of voice, eyebrow raising, or facial expressions to make sure that his message was received. But writers must find other devices, such as providing adequate information about the situation or shaping sentences, to show special emphasis.

However, when you intend to make an assertion in a direct, straightforward manner, you can best accomplish it with a simple sentence in its most basic form. Then your *intent,* the *basic information,* and the SUBJECT-PREDICATE *form* are all working together to "tell it like it is."

BASIC SENTENCE PATTERNS

Besides the ability to make a direct assertion, basic sentence patterns have other uses in language. Simple sentences stripped down to their basic components of subject and predicate make up the raw materials to build *all* sentences—simple, compound, and complex. We can add descriptive modifiers to one of the basic patterns, reorder its elements, join several together in various ways, or omit parts to produce partial sentences or fragments. Because they are the building blocks of language, basic sentence patterns deserve at least a brief look.

As in all languages, the basic patterns in English are limited in number, but all are made up of subjects and predicates. However, the words in the predicate do not always have the same relationship to each other and to the subject. Always in the predicate, of course, there is a main verb or an auxiliary verb that shows present or past time, such as *wash, was, seems, gave, have, has gone.* But the predicate may include other parts. In some sentence patterns the verb is followed by a noun-phrase complement: Mary washed *the baby;* Billy was *a baby.* In another sentence pattern, an adjective fills the complement slot after the verb: Mary was *happy.* In addition, adjunct words or phrases showing the manner or way the action took place, indicating the time of the action, or specifying the place, can also appear in the predicate. For example, adjuncts such as these show manner: *vigorously, with alacrity, by sheer will power.* These adjuncts indicate place: *there, at the student center, downtown;* while these are examples of time: *now, then, at ten o'clock.*

Although adjunct slots supply additional information to a sentence, they do not change its basic form. In the following examples the italicized portions indicate the adjunct; what is left is the basic sentence pattern.

1. Jimmy washed the dog *with great care.*   MANNER
2. Jimmy washed the dog *in the bathtub.*   PLACE
3. Jimmy washed the dog *in the morning.*   TIME
4. Jimmy was born *in 1969.*   TIME
5. Jimmy is happy *in his hometown.*   PLACE
6. Jimmy was reading *avidly.*   MANNER

Sometimes all three kinds of adjuncts can occur in the same basic sentence. For instance, sentences 1, 2, and 3 can be combined, still retaining the same basic pattern:

BASIC PATTERN

Jimmy	washed	the dog
Subject (S)	*Verb* (V)	*Complement* (C)

ADJUNCTS

with great care	in the bathtub	in the morning.
Manner (M)	*Place* (P)	*Time* (T)

Adjuncts can be combined with sentence 6 in a pattern that has no complement:

BASIC PATTERN

Jimmy	was reading
Subject (S)	*Verb* (V)

ADJUNCTS

avidly	on the couch	last Saturday night.
Manner (M)	*Place* (P)	*Time* (T)

As you can see from the examples, the predicate slot in a sentence can be broken further into other slots, each having a different function. Thus, to reveal all the possible relationships in a sentence, we need to change our earlier sentence frame to something like this:

SENTENCE

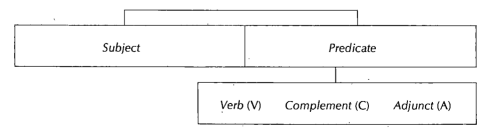

64

Using this frame, we can show the basic sentence patterns of English. Note that the adjuncts are in parentheses, meaning they are optional, not necessary to the basic sentence pattern.

Subject (S)	Verb (V)	Complement (C)	Adjunct (A)
The professor	was jogging		(effortlessly.) *Manner*
The professor	was	happy.	
The professor	became	a Ph.D.	(in 1976.) *Time*
The professor	was carrying	a book	(in her hand.) *Place*

Rarely will you use simple sentences as basic as these, although the opening example paragraph exhibited some: "The police did not come"; "I looked back." But you can combine these patterns in many ways to create the variety of sentences you will need for all kinds of writing. For now, we will be concerned with sentences that contain only one of these basic sentence patterns, even though they may include additional modifiers and adjuncts.

Simple Sentences

In personal writing, as we hinted earlier, you should feel free to use many short, simple sentences. As assertions, they add a tone of directness and sincerity, and they are characteristic of casual, spoken conversation. However, this practice may not be desirable in other writing. And even in personal narrative, too many short simple sentences sound like a "Dick and Jane and Spot" primer. But for some purposes, as in the opening example, piling up a series of simple sentences that closely follow the basic sentence patterns can be very effective to describe a fast-moving, violent, exciting, or suspenseful action and to establish a breathless, dramatic quality. Here's an effective student example using such sentences:

Suddenly we heard a scream. Ahead a man was pulling a young child into a car. We started to run towards it. He slammed the door and started the car. The child continued to cry. We reached the car and banged on the window. Then the car moved away. I saw the license plate: Michigan WN 69837. I kept repeating it aloud: Michigan WN 69837. Michigan WN 69837. Then I dashed to a nearby telephone booth, luckily found a dime in my pocket, dialed "Operator" and told her to write down: Michigan WN 69837. I explained, gave her my name and

65

address, and hung up. Then I burst into tears. I didn't stop until Jane drove me home and Mother hugged me and comforted me. I don't know why I was terrified. Perhaps it was the realization that evil was as close as a passing car.

The first nine sentences in the student paragraph are short simple sentences, some having the adjunct words moved to the beginning. As you can see, the short sentences enabled the writer to re-create the haste, panic, and immediacy of the action.

Reordering Adjuncts

Even with short, simple sentences, however effective they might be for a particular writing situation, variety is desired. A series of sentences all beginning with the subject not only becomes monotonous but provides little opportunity for making transitions or connections from one sentence to the next. By comparing a rewritten paragraph from John Steinbeck's "The Chrysanthemums" with the original, we can illustrate the importance of varying the basic subject-predicate (SP) sentence structure and the special effects that can result. Be aware of the placement of the italicized adjunct phrases in each version.

Rewritten Version	*Steinbeck's Version*
1 The high gray-flannel fog of winter closed off the Salinas Valley from the sky and all the rest of the world. **2** It sat like a lid on the mountains *on every side* and made of the great valley a closed pot. **3** The gang plows *on the broad, level land floor* bit deep and left the black earth shining where the shares had cut. **4** The yellow stubble fields *on the foothill ranches across the Salinas River* seemed to be bathed in pale cold sunshine, but there was no sunshine in the valley now in December. **5** The thick willow scrub along the river flamed with sharp and positive yellow leaves.	**1** The high gray-flannel fog of winter closed off the Salinas Valley from the sky and all the rest of the world. **2** *On every side* it sat like a lid on the mountains and made of the great valley a closed pot. **3** *·On the broad, level land floor* the gang plows bit deep and left the black earth shining like metal where the shares had cut. **4** *On the foothill ranches across the Salinas River,* the yellow stubble fields seemed to be bathed in pale gold sunshine, but there was no sunshine in the valley now in December. **5** The thick willow scrub along the river flamed with sharp and positive leaves.

Both versions exhibit the same basic SP structure in sentences 1 and 5. But the other sentences in Steinbeck's paragraph differ from those in the rewritten version: the place adjuncts appear at the beginning of the sentences. This reordering does not merely vary the SP pattern; it also provides a sense of spatial transition, allowing the reader's "eye" to move in space from one part of the scene to another. This quality of movement is missing in the rewritten version, making it less effective as description.

Time and manner adjuncts can also be moved to the beginning of a sentence to achieve special effects:

On Monday, you report to the Marine Corps office. (time is given special emphasis)

Gingerly, he scraped the egg off his shirt. (gives added importance to the manner in which he scraped the egg)

Compound Sentences

Another useful sentence device is the *compound* sentence, which results from the combining of two simple sentences. As we have noted, simple sentences retain their basic structure regardless of any modification or expansion, as in this sentence from a Hemingway story:

S   P
I   tried not to think and to be perfectly calm.

But in a compound sentence, several SP patterns can be combined, as in this sentence from the same example:

S   P   S   P
It   was hot in the cafe   *and*   the air   was bad.

A compound sentence consists of two or more structures joined by a coordinating conjunction—such as *and, but, for, or, nor, yet*—or occasionally a semicolon. The SP structures can also be linked by a pair of conjunctions—*either/or, neither/nor, both/and, not only/but also*. Structurally, these two compounding patterns look like this:

$$SP \begin{Bmatrix} and \\ but \\ for \\ or \\ nor \\ yet \\ ; \end{Bmatrix} SP \qquad \begin{Bmatrix} either \\ neither \\ both \\ not\ only \end{Bmatrix} SP \begin{Bmatrix} or \\ nor \\ and \\ but\ also \end{Bmatrix} SP$$

         S   P   S   P
Either you mow the lawn *or* we go to the movies.

Neither did you mow the lawn *nor* did we go to the movies.

Notice that the negative quality of *neither* and *nor* forces a change in the position of the subject. Work out a sentence using *not only* to see if a similar phenomenon occurs.

Despite their usefulness in personal and narrative writing, compound sentences formed with *and* might be frowned upon in other kinds of writing because they fail to signal any special relationship between the two joined ideas. For instance, the following *and* sentence merely reports what occurred, leaving it up to the reader to wonder about the connection between the two clauses:

He cut a full cord of birch and his wife called him into the house.

Is there a causal relationship (because he did it) or a temporal one (after he had done it) or what?

It is precisely this imprecision that accounts for the conversational effect of the compound sentence. When we talk we are so busy thinking of what we want to say that we often neglect to furnish the necessary signals. Thus we use many compound sentences (particularly with *and* as the connecting conjunction) and depend upon the situation to supply the relationships. But in writing, too many consecutive compound sentences sound juvenile, as shown in this account by a child:

I was walking to school and a bird hit a tree. I ran to it and it tried to fly away. It could not move and I brought it to school. All my friends were sorry for it but the teacher was angry. She made me take it to the principal's office and he called someone on the phone. He told me the bird would be taken care of and I went back to class. I wonder what happened to it.

Richard Bradford uses the compound effectively in the second and third sentences in the opening paragraph of *Red Sky at Morning:*

We were using the old blue china and the stainless steel cutlery, with place mats on the big oval table and odd-sized jelly glasses for the wine. The good stuff was all packed and stored, and the Salvation Army was due the next day for the leftovers. My mother called this last dinner a picnic, but she didn't wear her overalls to it. She had on the blue hostess gown with the purple flowers.

QUESTIONS AND EXCLAMATIONS

In addition to simple sentences and compound sentences, other sentence types can help to provide a conversational tone in your narrative writing. Questions, particularly, are valuable in achieving a natural and informal voice. Once again, let your own conversation be your guide. Generally, the questions that you and your friends ask are short and direct, often no more than a grunt with a trailing question intonation: "How come?" "Why not?" "How much?" "What then?" "So what?" But in writing, questions should be used sparingly. Like expensive perfume or after-shave lotion, they are most effective when saved for special occasions.

The same goes for exclamatory sentences. You probably sprinkle these throughout letters to close friends to impart the stress and pitch you would use in talking to them. Although they should be used only occasionally in other kinds of writing, what could be more natural than a few exclamations in autobiographical narratives or personal essays? But please use moderation! Like continuous going-out-of-business sales, exclamations lose their effectiveness when overused.

SENTENCE FRAGMENTS

Another device that can be used effectively in personal narrative—when used sparingly—is the sentence fragment. Starting with a capital and ending with terminal punctuation, but usually lacking a subject or a verb that shows tense, these nonsentences can add color and vigor to informal prose. Note how skillfully Dick Gregory used sentence fragments (italicized) in this passage from his autobiography, *Nigger:*

The teacher thought I was stupid. *Couldn't spell, couldn't read, couldn't do arithmetic. Just stupid.* Teachers were never interested in finding out that you couldn't concentrate because you were so hungry, because you hadn't had any breakfast. All you could think about was noontime, would it ever come? Maybe you could sneak into the cloakroom and steal a bite of some kid's lunch out of a coat pocket. *A bite of something. Paste.* You couldn't really make a meal of paste, or put it on bread for a sandwich, but sometimes I'd scoop a few spoonfuls out of a paste jar in back of the room. Pregnant people get strange tastes. I was pregnant with poverty. *Pregnant with dirt and pregnant with shoes that were never bought for me, pregnant with five other people in my bed and no Daddy in the next room, and pregnant with hunger.* Paste doesn't taste too bad when you're hungry.

The fragments here are all effective. In the first, the omission of the subject (*I*) shifts the emphasis from the writer to the reasons for the teacher's opinion of him and achieves a free, natural effect that would have been lost in the traditional counterpart:

The teacher thought that I was stupid because I couldn't spell, read, or do arithmetic.

The emphatic summary declaration of the next fragment ("Just stupid") conveys a decisive note of finality. The next two fragments ("A bite of something" and "Paste") focus attention on the boy's desperate craving for food: first on his urge for just "a bite of something" and then on a highly unappetizing substance—paste. The final fragment ("Pregnant with . . .") is a lengthy one that is in apposition with the previous sentence. Here the ironic repetition of the word *pregnant,* generally meaning fruitfully abundant, emphasizes the boy's barren predicament.

Sentence fragments, if they are to work for the writer, must in some way amplify what is said in the surrounding context. Also, the missing elements should be easily recoverable, as in the rewritten version of Gregory's first sentence. Of course, fragments that are idiomatic, such as "The sooner, the better," present no problems.

Any restrictions on fragments? Yes. Like questions and exclamations, they are dramatic, attention-getting devices and so should be used sparingly. However, some types of fragments unacceptable to most readers should be avoided. Very often in these cases, student writers mistake a verb form in the fragment for a main verb in a sentence. Let's look at some of these puzzlers.

I had a perpetual clash with my mother. *A woman who was as stubborn as I was.*

The italicized fragment is a noun phrase modifying *mother* in the preceding sentence. Unlike the Gregory examples, this fragment detracts from the relationships involved rather than emphasizes them. Confusion of the verb in a relative clause (*"who was"*) for a main sentence verb is the culprit here, as it often is. A comma or dash after *mother* solves the problem.

John lost his driver's license for two years. *For drinking while driving.*

This common type of fragment involves a prepositional phrase. It is often a problem for student writers because its verbal *-ing* form can easily be mistaken for a true verb.

He felt that he was capable of making his own decisions. *Being of sound mind and body.*

Here, use of the *-ing* form may again be at fault. You can avoid such fragments by making sure an auxiliary verb, such as *have* or *is,* precedes the form. Without an auxiliary, the *-ing* verb carries no tense and cannot be a main verb.

He wore a raincoat. *Although it was not raining.*

Here, a subordinate clause (an SP structure introduced by a subordinating conjunction) is the culprit. Subordinating conjunctions, such as *although, because, whether,* and *if,* signal a close and dependent relationship between two sentence elements that logically should not be separated by a period.

Like other language devices, fragments can be highly effective when used properly, but they require that you understand their structure and their limitations. Fragments are certainly helpful in narrative writing as another means of adding the spice of naturalness to your prose. But like other spices, they should be applied sparingly.

ACTIVE VERSUS PASSIVE SENTENCES

In personal writing, particularly in narrative, you can best establish a conversational tone and a sense of immediacy and action by making certain that most of your sentences are in the *active* voice—that the subject is the logical agent for the action in the predicate (the verb + the complement). Look at these three versions of the same sentence and note the difference in the dramatic immediacy generated by each:

1. Tom fearlessly chased the bear raiding the cooler.
2. The bear raiding the cooler was fearlessly chased by Tom.
3. The bear raiding the cooler was fearlessly chased.

You probably agree that example 1 carries more immediate impact. It is an *active* sentence; *Tom* is the agent or initiator of the action shown in the predicate ("fearlessly chased the bear raiding the cooler"). The other two versions are reordered to *passive* form. In both, the object of the verb ("the bear") is transposed to the subject position and the verb form is changed. In example 2 the subject *Tom* has been relegated to a less active role at the end of the sentence. Example 3 is least active of all: because English structure permits it, *Tom* has been completely removed from the action; in 3, there is no apparent human agent.

As you can see from the examples, changing a sentence from active voice to passive alters not only its psychological effect but also its form. The passive form is a result of two changes in the original sentence:

1. Reordering the object to subject position and putting the subject, now introduced with *by*, after the verb. This *by* can be omitted, as in example 3 above.

   Tom fearlessly chased *the bear*.
   (subject)   (object)
          becomes
   The bear was fearlessly chased (by *Tom*).
   (object)   (subject)

2. Changing the active verb to passive by adding a form of *be* before the past participle.

   chased *becomes* was chased

Obviously, this reordering to passive is only possible when the noun complement refers to a different person or thing than the subject does. *Tom* and the *bear* are not the same creatures. Even though the subject and noun complement are reversed, the meaning remains essentially the same. In both, Tom is the one who does the chasing; the bear is the one chased. However, the force of the sentence is diminished when the passive is used. The sense of direct action and the action itself are broken, because the verb is diluted by the added meaningless verb *be*. When used in narrative, these characteristics can obscure or de-emphasize the people involved in the situation. Note how the human activity is subordinated in the passive version of the following example:

Active: Lee slam-dunked the basketball and clinched the win with two points.

Passive: The basketball was slam-dunked and the win was clinched with two points (by Lee).

There is, of course, a time and place for the passive. In scientific writing, in dealing with abstract ideas, or in situations where the subject-agent is unimportant, the passive is preferable to the active. We will discuss effective uses of the passive in later chapters. But to achieve a sense of action and immediacy in your personal writing, you should avoid the passive whenever possible.

DIALOGUE SENTENCES

Using dialogue whenever appropriate is a good idea because it adds life, color, and authenticity to your personal writing. Also, dialogue is more enjoyable to read than long paragraphs of explanation or description, and it can move the events of your narrative or personal essay along at a faster speed. But while it is easy to read, dialogue is anything but easy to write. Done skillfully, however, it creates the illusion of conversation without reproducing all the distracting elements of a real conversation—the false starts, the asides, and the pauses characteristic of speech. When we talk to one another—when we talk, y'know—we often stop—uh—to light up a cigarette—uh—or to think, y'know—uh, we do ramble on at—uh—great length, don't we? As you do, readers would find an exact transcription of a taped conversation such as this insufferably boring. Consequently, you should trim such "fat" from dialogue but retain the often fragmentary characteristics of speech. But too much written dialogue can become distracting or monotonous; therefore you should intersperse it with expository or descriptive passages.

No matter how brief it is, dialogue should depict the personalities of the speakers. Each person should be individualized and characterized by what is said, what is not said, how it is said, and what actions accompany the statements.

Direct Discourse

Let's study the following passage to note some techniques for writing dialogue in personal narrative. In the selection, Rube Marquard, one of the few major league pitchers to win more than two hundred games, who had been disowned by his father ten years earlier when he left home to play baseball, tells about the reunion with his dad.

One day when I was pitching for Brooklyn I pitched the first game of a double-header against Boston and beat them, 1–0. I was in the clubhouse during the second game, taking off my uniform, when the clubhouse boy came in.

"Rube," he said, "there's an elderly gentleman outside who wants to see you. He says he's your father from Cleveland."

"He's not my father," I said. "My father wouldn't go across the street to see me. But you go out and get his autograph book and bring it in, and I'll autograph it for him."

But instead of bringing in the book, he brought in my Dad. And we were both delighted to see one another.

"Boy, you sure are a hardhead," he said to me. "You know I didn't mean what I said ten years ago."

"What about you, Dad?" I said. "You're as stubborn as I am. I thought you never wanted to see me again. I thought you meant it."

"Of course I didn't," he said.

After we talked a while, I said, "Did you see the game today?"

"Yes, I did," he said.

"Where were you sitting?" I asked him.

"Well, you know the man who wears that funny thing on his face?"

"You mean the mask? The catcher?"

"I guess so. Well, anyway, I was halfway between him and the number one—you know, where they run right after they hit the ball."

"You mean first base?"

"I don't know," he said. "I don't know what they call it. I was sitting in the middle there."

"How many ball games have you seen since I became a ballplayer, Dad?"

"This is the first one," he said.

    —Rube Marquard, "I Become a Big Leaguer," in *The Glory of Their Times*

Note the short sentences, the simple words, the question-and-answer rhythms, the frequent omission of tags (words that identify the speaker), and the reliance on the word *said,* a legitimate use of an overworked verb discouraged in other kinds of writing. Three dialogue devices are used in the conversation:

1. Speaker unidentified:
"How many ball games have you seen since I became a ballplayer, Dad?"

This device is particularly useful in dialogue involving only two people. But referring to the participants by name as in example 1 avoids possible confusion about who the speaker is.

2. Speaker identified by a speaker tag:
    a. "Where were you sitting?" I asked him.
    b. "Rube," he said, "there's an elderly gentleman outside who wants to see you."

A speaker tag can effectively indicate the speaker in dialogue involving more than two people. It can also serve to break the monotony of repeated sentences without speaker identification. Interrupting the speech with a speaker tag as in (2b) can prevent distracting repetition of the speaker tag at the end of the statement.

3. Speaker tag included in narrative:
After we talked for a while, I said, "Did you see the game today?"

Many advantages can be gained from the device in example 3: indicating the passage of time, as is done here; serving as transitional material; adding descriptive details.

Indirect Discourse

Thus far we have been discussing the most common form of dialogue, direct discourse, but as you know from Chapter 1, dialogue can also be expressed indirectly. Indirect discourse gains in brevity but loses in vividness, because readers are told about the conversation instead of hearing it for themselves. Here is an indirect-discourse version of the first part of the Marquard passage:

The clubhouse boy told me about an elderly man claiming to be my father who wanted to see me. I knew it couldn't be my father because he wouldn't go across the street to see me. But when the man came in, it was Dad. We were delighted to see each other. He told me that he hadn't meant what he said ten years ago. I was surprised. I said I thought he never wanted to see me again.

Although indirect dialogue usually lacks the freshness and vitality of direct dialogue, it may be especially effective in compressing conversation intended merely to provide a transition between two scenes or to save space for other purposes.

Questions in Direct and Indirect Discourse

It is sometimes difficult to distinguish between direct and indirect questions starting with question words (*who, what, when, where, why, how*).

Direct: He asked, "How much will you sell it for?"
Indirect: He asked how much I would sell it for.

You may have observed that the word order is the tip-off: the inverted word order of a question (question word + auxiliary + subject + verb) signals direct discourse:

Direct: They asked me, *"Where   has   he   gone?"*
                Question word Auxiliary Subject Verb

Normal sentence order after the question word (subject + auxiliary + verb) signals indirect discourse:

Indirect: They asked me *where   he   had   gone.*
              Question word Subject Auxiliary Verb

Note that *whether* nearly always signals an indirect question.

Direct: The young man asked, "Will it be ready on Friday?"
Indirect: The young man asked *whether* it would be ready on Friday.

Whenever you are writing dialogue—direct or indirect—watch for question words to crop up, and when they do, pay particular attention to word order.

A simple problem of this sort should not deter you from writing dialogue. No other single device provides such life to your papers and to the people you write about. Writing dialogue is fun, but difficult to bring off well. The suggestions presented above should assist you with matters of craft, but they will not help much in your developing an ear for the idioms, dialects, phrases, structure, pace, and sounds of speech. To become aware of these, listen carefully to the way people talk and study the dialogue in the fiction of such writers as John Updike, Saul Bellow, Norman Mailer, Philip Roth, Doris Lessing, and Bernard Malamud. If you really want to master dialogue, you might follow Benjamin Franklin's example: copy a passage from a good writer, reproduce it from memory, and compare your version with the original.

SUMMARY

In this chapter we have discussed two types of sentences frequently used in personal writing—simple and compound. We have pointed out that although all simple sentences have the same SUBJECT-PREDICATE structure, a number of basic sentence patterns are possible within that structure. These basic sentence patterns comprise the building materials for constructing all the possible sentences in the language. Although the form of a sentence and its meaning are usually closely related, meaning is also dependent on the writer's intention. Therefore, to convey clearly what you intend to say, you must be aware of the various ways of manipulating sentence structure: by reordering elements, by combining a number of simple sentences, or by converting active sentences to passive and vice versa. Proficiency in sentence construction is perhaps the most important aspect of good writing.

Assignments

For Discussion

1 Using the chart on page 64, identify the subject and the predicate components of the following simple sentences. Which have reordered adjuncts?

   a Emotions play a large part in dancing.
   b Next came the railroads.
   c About three houses down on the opposite side of the street lived a cute little girl named Kathy.
   d The present population of the world is four billion people.
   e Balance is the key factor in skiing.
   f The following year I dropped math.
   g One night I rode my bicycle on the fraternity house roof.
   h Clarke gives us a picture of a world that is similar to today's society.
   i Waterskiing is very easy to learn.
   j I was in the senior band that winter.

2 Identify the simple and compound sentences used in this student narrative of an adventure on a railroad bridge. What advice about sentence choice could you give the student to make any effective description even more exciting? Can fragments be used to advantage anywhere?

HIGH BRIDGE

We parked the motorcycle on the side of the highway and climbed up. The hill was covered with limestone gravel, glittering in the bright sunlight. The loose stones rolled down the incline as our feet sought firm footholds. Finally, my hand grasped the rusted steel railing at the top and I pulled Robin up behind me. We were at High Bridge after a half hour of hard riding and climbing.

    We looked all around us and tried to take in the beauty below us. There was even beauty and grace in the old, black and rusty railroad bridge spanning the open distance between two high rising cliffs. We could see the muddy water of the river below us, moving slowly in its sluggish course. The tall oaks and their neighbors in the river valley tried in vain to reach up to us. We were almost higher than the birds in their own territory.

I held a small rock over the edge and released it. We started to count, one, two, three . . . nine . . . ten, splash! In that brief span of ten seconds the small missile seemed to hang motionless in the atmosphere. I didn't see it move; it just shrank until it crashed into the water. All this time Robin held her breath and ended by just saying, "God!"

It all seemed so serene; we were just suspended in space by a network of steel. Whomp! WH OO MP! As soon as my ears picked up this deep bellow, I experienced a sickening realization. There was a train coming and we were both in the middle of the bridge. The diesel engines were thundering as it came churning ever closer. It was too late to get off the bridge, so we sat down on the catwalk clutching the handrail. Now came the monster . . . the bell was clanging constantly as his white eye flashed back and forth. The bridge began to shake violently to and fro. The metal struts were singing like telephone lines. I wondered if that structure of rusted steel could hold such weight on its back.

I looked around at Robin as if nothing was happening, but I really felt sick. Robin was still there—staring wordlessly at me. The cars rolled by as the caravan of steel picked up speed. All I could see was a blur of colors, letters, and numbers posted differently on every one. The wheels clicked monotonously over the small breaks where the rails had been joined. The springs on the cars creaked as they were pitched from one side to the other. Will this never end? How long have we been hanging here? Then we saw the red caboose. It looked like a small house on wheels chasing after the iron serpent ahead of it. We both knew that our ordeal was finally over. As the fire-breather snake wound back into the hills from where it came, the bridge became quiet and stable. We stood up and made our way back to the motorcycle. Neither of us spoke.

3 Identify the fragments in the following student examples. Be able to provide a possible explanation (other than punctuation) as to why the students may have confused them with complete sentence structure.

a The people are moving out of the cities to own homes with lawns. Places away from the bustle of the cities. Good farm land is being bought up and subdivided. Thousands of new homes are built every year. More and more mouths to feed with less land to produce the necessary crops.

b But if some parents think married students should be on their own and need help financially, then the young couple will have to work, but not make enough money to live adequately and save money, too. Which they will need desperately in the future.

c If we have disagreements about where to go or what to do. My wife does not insist that we do what she has planned.

d The great awakening started back in the 1950s when a mild form of violence made its way into films. For example, the Bogart movies of the 50s.

e The Puritans also had crime and mental disease among their ranks. Disease being the biggest problem they had.

SENTENCE STRATEGIES IN PERSONAL WRITING

f College athletic recruiters are as bad as advertising agents; they both have something to sell. The advertising agent selling his product, the college recruiter selling his school.

g The amateur golf player and the professional both have their own unique character and style of playing. Such as their clothes: one could be fancy and flashy, the other not so colorful. The individual way they swing and hit the ball.

h As I look over the green lush grass of the meadows and fields, I am aware that there are many beautiful things going on. There is new life and excitement everywhere. Rabbits crawling out of their winter homes in the ground. Rabbits taking their first breath of crystal-clear spring air. Also, the trees and flowers trying desperately to show their new beauty.

4 Sentences in the passive voice not only obscure the agent subject but also frequently result in extremely awkward sentence structure. Discuss the problems involved in the following student examples and be able to change them into active sentences.

a Ships were the first form of transportation shown in the film as people were brought to America.

b One wonders if all the campus activities are only carried on during the week.

c The bow and arrow has been replaced by the gun for protection purposes.

d Also, John Lennon is constantly seen barefoot in these pictures and on their album "Abbey Road," which is the way they bury the House of Lords, which all Beatles are a member of.

e Because of the fear one would experience in coping with such extraordinary circumstances, emotions would be stirred.

f The paper must be written by him by tomorrow.

5 Discuss the techniques of dialogue sentence structure in the following examples. What advantage does each give the writer?

a Mr. Martin got to the office at eight-thirty the next morning, as usual. At a quarter to nine, Ulgine Barrows, who had never before arrived to work before ten, swept into his office. "I'm reporting to Mr. Fitweiler now!" she shouted. "If he turns you over to the police, it's no more than you deserve!" Mr. Martin gave her a look of shocked surprise. "I beg your pardon?" he said. Mrs. Barrows snorted and bounced out of the room, leaving Miss Paird and Joey Hart staring after her. "What's the matter with that old devil now?" asked Miss Paird. "I have no idea," said Mr. Martin, resuming his work. The other two looked at him and then at each other. Miss Paird got up and went out. She walked slowly past the closed door of Mr. Fitweiler's office. Mrs. Barrows was yelling inside, but she was not braying. Miss Paird could not hear what the woman was saying. She went back to her desk.
—James Thurber, "The Catbird Seat"

b   "If you go, I'll tell," Jason said.

"We'll have fun," Nancy said. "They won't mind, just to my house. I been working for yawl a long time. They won't mind."

"I'm not afraid to go," Caddy said. "Jason is the one that's afraid. He'll tell."

"I won't tell," Jason said. "I'm not afraid."

"Jason ain't afraid to go with me," Nancy said. "Is you Jason?"

"Jason is going to tell," Caddy said.

—William Faulkner, "That Evening Sun"

c   "Ah, you're—you're—a?" I began as soon as I had mastered my surprise. I couldn't bring out the dingy word "models": it seemed so little to fit the case.

"We haven't had much practice," said the lady.

"We've got to *do* something, and we've thought that an artist in your line might perhaps make something of us," her husband threw off. He further mentioned that they didn't know many artists and that they had gone first, on the off-chance—he painted views of course, but sometimes put in figures; perhaps I remembered—to Mr. Rivet, whom they had met a few years before at a place in Norfolk where he was sketching.

"We used to sketch a little ourselves," the lady hinted.

"It's very awkward, but we absolutely *must* do something," her husband went on.

"Of course, we're not so *very* young," she admitted with a wan smile.

—Henry James, "The Real Thing"

For Practice

1   Rewrite the sentences in exercise 3 above, replacing the fragments with complete sentences or with more effective fragments.

2   Rewrite the following student paragraphs, making use of short simple sentences or compound sentences to add a stronger air of immediacy and urgency to the action. Add details if you feel they would make the narrative more effective.

a   I got a taxi and headed for the National Airport in Washington, D.C. I figured it to be about five miles away—it was more like thirty. "Damnation" was all I kept saying. The driver had been covered with perspiration from waiting outside the cab, but he was cooling off now in the air-conditioned cab, and loving it. I asked him to step on the gas and he did, quite readily. I think that he must have been drunk.

When I arrived at the National Airport, I ran up and down stairs to get to my terminal, dragging my bicycle behind me. A man asked me when I made it there what flight I was to be on. "Eastern Flight 547," I replied. "There she goes!" he said as he pointed out the window at the red tail-lights of my plane disappearing into the black sky. I was only five minutes late.

b Sunday morning at ten o'clock, Tony, Albert, and I were in the canoe ready for the "Great Canoe Race." The gun went off and we were on our way down the river. The first part of the race we were in the lead, but someone had drilled a hole in our canoe. I had to take my shoes off and start bailing the canoe. As we neared the finish it was obvious we would not win so Tony decided to tip the canoe. At which time I lost my shoes and car keys. The water was thirty-six degrees Fahrenheit. My skin turned a pale blue and I thought I was dying. We came in fourth in the "Great Canoe Race" and won absolutely no prize at all, but we did get our picture put in the school newspaper.

Special Topic: Punctuation

Punctuation is often a headache for even the most experienced writers. One reason for this is the often seemingly arbitrary or illogical way punctuation marks are used. A brief look at the historical development of punctuation will help to explain how present-day rules developed, sometimes without reference to the grammatical needs of the language.

Because many early English manuscripts were read aloud to a largely illiterate population, the earliest punctuation marks indicated breath pauses for church lectors or readers. As printing came into use and the literacy rate increased, more and more punctuation devices were invented. In the beginning, they were generally used arbitrarily by the typesetters, rather than consciously by the writers. By the nineteenth century a systematic effort was made to set off grammatical structures by punctuation. Although current punctuation practices are still moving toward that goal, many earlier arbitrary decisions remain a part of the conventions, or rules, of written punctuation. In spoken English, for instance, a breath pause almost always occurs between a long, complicated subject structure and the verb, as in:

The unique characteristic of the generation now passing through adolescence in America is that it is the first to be born into a technological society.
—Barry M. Schwartz

Few people could read this sentence aloud without pausing for breath between the last word in the subject, *America,* and the first verb, *is;* but it is conventionally unacceptable to place a comma between them. The general punctuation practice is not to place a comma between the subject and verb.

Another convention with no relationship to either structure or punctuation logic requires that quotation marks always be placed outside rather than inside a period:

They sang, "Let's all make it, this time around."

Under some circumstances, however, the writer can arbitrarily decide whether to substitute one punctuation mark for another or omit a device altogether. For example, in this sentence from a popular rhetoric textbook, the author rather arbitrarily decided on dashes rather than commas to separate the phrase "the concept of *net force*" from the rest of the sentence:

The subject which the author wished to explain—the concept of *net force*—is unfamiliar to most readers.

—Edward Corbett

The sentence is just as "correct" when commas replace the dashes:

The subject which the author wished to explain, the concept of *net force*, is unfamiliar to most readers.

As you can see, punctuation choices can be difficult and confusing. Often you, like other writers, are forced to bow to the rules of convention even when they seem unreasonable or arbitrary. But gaining a knowledge of the ways that features of spoken language often relate to punctuation can give you more confidence and skill in effective written communication and can release you from some of the perplexity of conflicting rules. By understanding the possibilities inherent in spoken English, you can use punctuation in your writing to aid your readers' comprehension and to create some of the effects achieved in speaking.

THE "PUNCTUATION" OF SPOKEN ENGLISH

Years ago, Victor Borge, the pianist-comedian, devised a comedy routine in which he used oral punctuation. He ascribed to each punctuation mark a verbal equivalent—a grunt, a snort, a click. His audiences found the results hilarious not only because of his own comic antics, but also because he was applying to spoken English those conventions that were devised for written English.

Borge was implying that there is a need for punctuation in spoken English, but obviously he was wrong. We do get along without punctuation in talking—but how? The answer is that we do not speak in consonants and vowels alone. Other vocal noises are present, which end sentences, signal important syntactical structures in the sentence, and help us to indicate the separate words we speak. A brief discussion of these can enable you to understand how we can talk without punctuation.

In English, we rely strongly on the emphasis or *stress* given to individual syllables in words, phrases, and sentences to give meaning to what we say.

You are probably aware that you can change the meaning and function of certain words in the language simply by shifting the stress to another syllable, as in pérfect (adjective), perféct (verb). We can also rely on stress variation to signal differences in sentence meaning:

They are hunting *dógs.* ("They" are looking for dogs.)
They are *húnting* dogs. ("They" are dogs that hunt.)

In addition to stress, we rely on pitch to signal our listeners. By varying the tonal quality of our voices, we can affect the meaning of our sentences. By dropping from normal pitch to a lower one, we can state, for example, "You're the expert," without offending the hearer. But raising the pitch at the end can also raise the listener's temper:

You're the expert. ↘ (statement of fact, compliment)
You're the expert? ↗ (insulting or sarcastic question)

Another intonational signal is a pause. The dramatic effect that a pause can add to meaning is illustrated by an old linguistic joke. With normal question intonation, the question "What's that in the road ahead?" merely asks the listener to identify an object in the road. But when a pause is put before the last word, it indicates a second question mark, and the query then takes on a macabre tone: "What's that in the road? (pause) A head?"

Although our discussion of these complex intonational signals—stress, pitch, and pause—has been very brief, it should help you realize how we depend upon these devices in spoken communication. They are the "punctuation marks" that Victor Borge jokingly found lacking in speech. To compensate for their absence in writing, we often substitute punctuation marks. Like a notational system in music, punctuation can help readers reproduce more accurately the writer's intended language tune.

But intonation is not the only influence on the punctuation of written language. Syntactical structures such as parenthetical phrases, introductory phrases, and long compound words require specific punctuation devices. Sometimes, as we indicated earlier, the mark required and its placement in the sentence are dictated by convention, without logical relationship to either intonation or structure. Therefore, we cannot rely solely on intonational clues to determine what punctuation is needed. As we discuss the different punctuation conventions throughout the book, we will indicate the occasions when intonation can assist.

END PUNCTUATION

The period, the question mark, and the exclamation point are the usual devices of end punctuation; that is, they end a complete statement or a question. These marks are common to all forms of writing, of course, so our discussion here is not limited to their use in personal writing.

The Period

With Sentence Endings   Periods signal the end of a declarative sentence, a command, or a sentence fragment. Two intonational clues can help to determine the need for a period: (1) when the sentence drops in pitch at the end, and (2) when it is not spoken with great emotion.

I'm going to a party tonight. (declarative sentence)
Close the door on your way in. (command)
The keys jangling in the bicycle basket. (fragment)

But the period has another use, often not as obvious as those in our examples above. Personal writing, in particular, often uses special sentence structures with this unusual use of the period.

With Indirect Questions   Indirect questions are frequently used in dialogue and differ from direct ones in structure, as we indicated in Chapter 4. Not surprisingly, they are also punctuated differently, as the following examples show.

He asked me, "How do you think you will do tomorrow?"
(direct—question mark required)

He asked me how I thought I would do tomorrow.
(indirect—period required)

The Question Mark

Questions in English can ask in many ways: some request verification of information; others ask for further information; others expect no answer; and still others express sarcasm, rather than ask a question.

With Yes/No Questions   Questions that seek verification through a *yes* or *no* answer usually end in rising pitch. But the simple-sentence structure (SUBJECT-PREDICATE) is reordered without adding special question words. These two examples indicate how the yes/no question differs from a statement. Watch the auxiliary verb!

Statement: They   *are* planning to take the exam tomorrow.
           Subject   Predicate

Yes/no question: *Are*   they   planning to take the exam tomorrow?
              Auxiliary · Subject   Remaining Predicate

With Additional-Information Questions   Questions that expect additional information in an answer are reordered in the same way as yes/no questions, but we add a question word: *why, when, where, what, how, who.* Intonation is no help here; these questions can end with either rising or falling pitch. Again, let's contrast them with a statement.

Statement: They   *are* planning to take the exam tomorrow.
             Subject   *Predicate*

Question: Why   *are*   they planning to take the exam tomorrow?
            Question Auxiliary   *Remaining Predicate*
            ·Word

With Questions in Statement Form   In speaking this form of question, the only change is intonational—the tell-tale rising pitch at the end that contrasts sharply with the falling pitch of a statement.

Statement: You're really serious about that. ↘ (drop in pitch dictates the period)
Question: You're really serious about that? ↗ (rising pitch indicates need for question mark)

With Complete Question or Fragment Added to Sentence

"Me, I don't study for exams." *or* "Me? I don't study for exams."

Either punctuation is possible, depending upon the intent of the speaker. The comma following "me" corresponds to a drop in pitch in spoken English, producing the effect of a cocky, defiant declaration, while the question mark indicates rising pitch, corresponding to a question such as, "Are you talking to me?"

"Bill—can you believe it?—aced that exam without cracking a book."

Here, the parenthetical question needs a question mark; both the reordered form and the rising pitch would indicate its use.

With Tag Questions

"You heard what I said, *didn't you?*"
"You didn't go to the game last week, *did you?*"

These short questions tagged on to a statement are very common in speech; they are therefore likely to occur in written dialogue. They are set off from the statement with a comma, with the question mark at the end. Notice this peculiarity: if the statement is positive, the tag is negative. If the statement is negative, the tag question is positive: "You didn't hear what I said, did you?"

With Questions in Direct Dialogue   Direct dialogue can create some problems in questions when a speaker tag is used. If the speaker tag comes first, there is no real difficulty.

Sylvia asked, "How did it go?"

But when you wish to add variety by putting the speaker tag after the question, this punctuation is required.

"How did it go?" Sylvia asked.

The Exclamation Mark

Because it signals such a wide variety of vocal possibilities, the exclamation mark is used more often in personal writing than in any other kind. Its presence usually suggests a speaking voice filled with strong emotion or agitation, sounding generally higher, more intense, and perhaps louder than the one used in normal conversation. Hence, sentences that might otherwise end in periods or question marks are given an exclamation point to signal strong emotion to the reader.

Excessive use of exclamation suggests a scatterbrained writer, one who is as irritating as a hard-sell car salesman on TV. But used judiciously, the exclamation mark can be helpful in dialogue when speakers interject comments ("Oh!"), talk in emotional fragments ("If I'd only known!"), or exclaim whole sentences ("You shouldn't have done it!"). But even in dialogue, you should avoid the exclamatory excesses of the comic strips ("Wow!!") or ("Lucy, why don't you get back in center field where you belong!!!"). When not writing dialogue, be certain you have sufficient reason to use an exclamation mark!

INTERNAL PUNCTUATION OF SPECIAL IMPORTANCE IN PERSONAL WRITING

Internal punctuation is more closely related to syntactical structure and to arbitrary convention than to intonation. Because English intonation allows for great variety, a direct relationship between intonation and internal punctuation is often difficult to establish. Also, several punctuation marks may be used in the same situations; for instance, commas can often be substituted for dashes; semicolons for commas. Let's look only at the internal punctuation problems most common to personal writing: extensive use of the dash to replace other, more conservative punctuation marks and the conventions of handling quotations. Other internal punctuation devices follow the same rules in all forms of writing, and will be treated in later chapters and in the Reference Guide.

The Dash

The dash is indeed a dashing mark, dramatically signaling an interruption, surprise, or shift in thought. Frankly, we could get along adequately without the dash—as some writers do—because it serves mainly as a substitute for other punctuation marks, usually the comma. But the dash produces a stronger, more forceful pause than the comma. Note how the dash functions in the following statements from Claude Brown's *Manchild in the Promised Land,* making them more effective than their "dashless" counterparts:

Replacing the Comma

They wouldn't put any good cops down there—if there is such a thing as a good cop.	Dash adds emphasis.
They wouldn't put any good cops down there, if there is such a thing as a good cop.	Comma could separate clauses, but shorter pause diminishes importance of second clause.

Replacing the Colon

This was a real Sunday morning—a lot of blood and vomit everywhere and people all dressed up and going to church.	Dash highlights explanation.
This was a real Sunday morning: a lot of blood and vomit everywhere and people all dressed up and going to church.	Colon could signal explanation, but accompanying drop in pitch more widely separates the two sentence elements.

Replacing Parentheses

Mr. Stillman—everybody but me called him Silly—had tiny red eyes that looked at people in a mean way from way back in his head.	Dash calls attention to interruption.
Mr. Stillman (everybody but me called him Silly) had tiny red eyes that looked at people in a mean way from way back in his head.	Parentheses could enclose this optional aside. Here, the effect is visual rather than intonational.

Replacing the Semicolon

But then I thought, aw, hell, it wasn't their fault—as a matter of fact, it was a whole lotta fun.	Dash accents idea.
But then I thought, aw, hell, it wasn't their fault; as a matter of fact, it was a whole lotta fun.	Semicolon could connect short, related ideas, but signals drop in pitch, thus sacrificing the immediacy of the relationship.

These examples illustrate how the dash can replace other punctuation marks and add emphasis. In addition, the dash has a few special—but rare—uses. In dialogue, it may indicate that the speaker is fumbling for words or is interrupted:

"If you don't stop talking about the dash, I'll— I'll—." The student's voice faltered. Then she shouted, "You know what you can do with the dash? You can—." "That's enough," the instructor interrupted.

We do not want to dash off without some final comments. As our examples indicate, the dash can replace any other internal punctuation; however, every time it does, a different effect is produced. Because it does add a dramatic note, the dash is often used in personal writing. But elsewhere, use it with caution.

Quotation Marks

In narrative writing, quotation marks appear mainly to enclose spoken words in dialogue. Their use is illustrated in the following passage from Ernest Hemingway's "The Short Happy Life of Francis Macomber."

"We're going after buff[alo] in the morning," he told her.
"I'm coming," she said.
"No, you're not."
"Oh, yes, I am. Mayn't I, Francis?"
"Why not stay in camp?"
"Not for anything," she said. "I wouldn't miss something like today for anything."

We hope that in reading the selection, you have not missed these points about quotation marks in narrative writing:

1. They enclose only the actual words of the speaker, not any words about these words.

2. The closing quotation mark appears after (not before or above) the other punctuation marks. Note the placement of the commas, periods, and question marks in the passage.
3. Quotation marks must be used again each time the speaker's actual words are interrupted. Note how this practice is followed in the last sentence in the dialogue.

When a lengthy statement continues for more than one paragraph, a special convention is used to help the reader. To signal that the same speaker is talking, use quotation marks to introduce each new paragraph, but use quotation marks only at the end of the last paragraph.

In your first attempts at writing dialogue, check your drafts carefully against the instructions given here. After a while, you'll be able to use quotation marks with confidence.

SUMMARY

In this chapter we have tried to help you with some punctuation problems that might arise in your personal writing. Because personal writing is closest in style to spoken language, we have pointed out areas where written punctuation corresponds with intonational features of spoken English. Other punctuation devices that are common to all writing and that are not so closely related to stress, pitch, and pause will be discussed in later chapters or in pages 499–509 of the Reference Guide. If you have any questions about punctuation not included in this chapter, check those pages.

Assignments

For Discussion

1 In the following sentences, discuss whether punctuation use was determined on the basis of established convention, arbitrary decision, or in response to breath pause or other intonational factors. Note the cases where the writer's punctuation forces you to read the sentence in a particular way.

a Betrayal between strangers? A very unlikely idea. But does a kiss on the cheek make the persons less than strangers?

—Paul Velde

b Yet yesterday when Huldah told me all this she had just left a basket of strawberries—Lillian not being visible—at Mrs. Burnham's house.

—Edmund Wilson

c Looking back through the long past we picture the beginning of the world—a primeval chaos which time has fashioned into the universe that we know.

—Arthur Stanley Eddington

d Human life does not "work," either.

—Herbert Gold

e Therefore, I, for one, choose not to leave.

—Richard G. Hatcher

f We often ask ourselves why life must be like this.

g Sometimes I think I heard Waneko telling me, "It's almost over, baby, it's almost over—we got it beat."

—Piri Thomas

h At this extreme of polarization, movies won't even be called movies anymore, but cinemah or filluhm (as in Philharmonic Hall).

—Andrew Sarris

i Everything disappointed him [Lee Harvey Oswald]; nothing gave him a feeling of his own distinct being; he tried over and over again to find a situation in which he could experience himself as alive, productive, a person of consequence; and one of the most interesting clues to his personality lies in the odd fact of his always writing about his actions (in the Historic Diary) in the present tense.

—John Clellon Holmes

j It is almost as if while taking a walk through a green field, I espied a blade of grass with manure on it, and bending down to that obscure little blade I said to it scoldingly, "Naughty! Naughty!"

—Henry Miller

k So many decisions in life are of this kind: they fall in between.

—Joseph Fletcher

2 Discuss what punctuation is needed in the following passage:

This sentence and the following one give you an idea of the difficulty of reading a passage without punctuation marks reading would be even more difficult than it now is if we had no way to signal the end of clauses and sentences indeed under such circumstances reading and particularly oral reading would be almost impossible.

For Practice

Punctuate the following examples (in each of which dialogue is used). Justify your punctuation choices.

1   In the annals of Zen there are many cryptic answers to the final question What is the Buddha which in our terms means What is the meaning of life What is truly real For example one master when asked What is the Buddha replied Your name is Yecho Another said Even the finest artist cannot paint him Another said No nonsense here And another answered The mouth is the gate of woe My favorite story is about the monk who said to a Master Has a dog Buddha-nature too The master replied Wu which is what the dog himself would have said.

—Gilbert Highet

2   Ain't she cute Red Sam's wife said leaning over the counter Would you like to come be my little girl No I certainly wouldn't June Star said I wouldn't live in a brokendown place like this for a million bucks and she ran back to the table Ain't she cute the woman repeated stretching her mouth politely Ain't you ashamed hissed the grandmother

—Flannery O'Connor

3   I have heard said he you will not take this place any more sahib What are you going to do with it Perhaps I shall let it again Then I will keep it on while I am away

—Rudyard Kipling

STRATEGIES FOR REVISING PERSONAL WRITING

Organization

1. Can you improve the organization by shifting paragraphs or changing the sequence of events?
2. If narrative, can you add or delete anything that would unify the essay around its opening statement?
3. Can the ending be improved?

Narration

1. Can you improve characterization by adding details?
2. Is there sufficient information about setting but not too much?
3. Should suspense be increased?
4. Should any descriptive passages be dramatized or vice versa?

Language

1. Are the voice and language of the narrator consistent, or should some words and phrases be altered?
2. Can you improve the language to make it clearer, livelier, or more natural?
3. Can you add specific details to describe the action more effectively?
4. Can you eliminate any details or passages because they are irrelevant?
5. Are there too many *I*'s or *we*'s?
6. Do your sentences contribute to your purpose? by adding suspense or urgency? by signaling the passage of time?

These are the kinds of questions you should have in mind as you review your paper. Often you may have to delete some sentences or passages you considered clever, a heroic action requiring you to sacrifice your pets to the waste basket. On other occasions, you may have to go back to the drawing board to provide a new introduction or conclusion, or to add several completely new sentences or paragraphs. We know what it's like. We've done it on practically every page of this book, reworking third and fourth drafts, deleting, adding, changing, touching up here and there. It's hard and painful work. It's part of the commitment that good writing requires.

But so far we've been talking mainly about major revisions. You must also be alert to others involving usage, vocabulary, spelling, punctuation, capitalization, and the like. These matters may seem like petty details, but if not attended to they can distract and annoy readers, spoiling the effect of your writing. Why take the chance of wasting all your hard work?

In particular, we advise our students to take one tour of their papers with only a single thought in mind—to underline any word whose spelling they would not bet five dollars on. For various reasons, many people—students and adults—spell poorly. And, perhaps illogically, most people, of clauses and sentences indeed under such circumstances reading and particularly oral reading would be almost impossible.

For Practice

Punctuate the following examples (in each of which dialogue is used). Justify your punctuation choices.

1   In the annals of Zen there are many cryptic answers to the final question What is the Buddha which in our terms means What is the meaning of life What is truly real For example one master when asked What is the Buddha replied Your name is Yecho Another said Even the finest artist cannot paint him Another said No nonsense here And another answered The mouth is the gate of woe My favorite story is about the monk who said to a Master Has a dog Buddha-nature too The master replied Wu which is what the dog himself would have said.

    —Gilbert Highet

2   Ain't she cute Red Sam's wife said leaning over the counter Would you like to come be my little girl No I certainly wouldn't June Star said I wouldn't live in a brokendown place like this for a million bucks and she ran back to the table Ain't she cute the woman repeated stretching her mouth politely Ain't you ashamed hissed the grandmother

    —Flannery O'Connor

3   I have heard said he you will not take this place any more sahib What are you going to do with it Perhaps I shall let it again Then I will keep it on while I am away

    —Rudyard Kipling

91

Revision of Personal Writing

WRITERS AND REVISION

Good writing results from careful, thoughtful, painstaking revision. Although it is probably the most important step in the writing process, most students overlook revision, apparently feeling that papers can be dashed off at one sitting and then copied in a neat final draft. Experienced writers know better. Tolstoy wondered how anyone could write without rewriting everything over and over again, a conviction that no doubt accounts for the fact that he revised *War and Peace,* his monumental masterpiece, five times. James Thurber has told of rewriting a short story fifteen times; Hemingway of redoing the last page of *A Farewell to Arms* thirty-nine times. James Michener never even writes an important letter in one draft, because he considers himself to be "not a good writer" but "one of the world's great rewriters." Innumerable other professional writers testify about the importance of revision.

Why then do most student writers fail to rework their papers? It may simply be that they do not realize the importance of revision. They may not understand that writing is a process, a system of achieving an objective through a series of step-by-step operations much like other processes, such as performing a lab experiment or preparing a meal. The writing process consists of five steps: selecting a subject, planning it, writing, revising, and proofreading. Newspapers and newsmagazines assign these steps to different people: an editor selects the subject, a reporter writes about it, a rewrite person revises it, and a proofreader checks it. You must play all these roles yourself. The first three roles will be considered later. Here we will be concerned with revision and proofreading.

BLOCKS TO EFFECTIVE REVISION

The main obstacles to effective revision are psychological ones. After you have received a writing assignment, stewed about it, labored over it, and eventually turned out an acceptable quantity of words, chances are that you will be elated. How great to be rid of that nagging worry about the assignment! Why fuss and fret further? Why not copy the paper neatly, and then dash off for a date, a beer, or a movie?

Added to this euphoria of completion is the satisfaction derived from the act of creation. Certainly there is a special joy in creating something with your own mind and hands, whether it is a sandcastle, a candle, a poem, an omelet, a piece of pottery, or a writing assignment. But often, in our enthusiasm, we are blind to our creation's imperfections. And so, blinded by pride and hope, we turn in a completed—but unrevised—paper. It is done—the impossible has been accomplished! And we are usually content.

APPROACHES TO EFFECTIVE REVISION

How to combat these two paralyzing psychological blocks—the euphoria of completion and the satisfaction of creation? The answer lies in transforming yourself from author to editor. In other words, you must reread your paper as you would someone else's. You must, in a sense, become another person, detached and objective, one who will not be kind, considerate, or generous about the writing, but will scrutinize it closely, noting every error, flaw, weakness, awkwardness. This transformation from author to editor can best be accomplished by getting away from the first draft for a period of time and by adopting a particular critical frame of mind.

The first draft should cool for as long as possible so that you can see it as others will. Like pie from the oven, its taste can't truly be judged while it's hot. The best suggestion is to write the first draft long before your deadline and get away from the paper for a day or two. But if you're working at the last minute, as most of us do, take a break to walk, make a phone call, watch TV, or work on an assignment for another course. When you return, you will be more likely to read your paper as a stranger. Then you can see what you have actually written instead of what you intended to write. The longer you stay away from your first draft, the more likely you are to find faults.

And find faults you must. If you view revision as a perfunctory chore to be completed quickly, then don't waste your time. You must consider revision as a valuable opportunity to catch your errors, find your weaknesses, improve your strengths—in sum, to turn a so-so first draft into a first-rate paper. It means being harsh, ruthless in refusing to settle for less than perfection. It means consciously searching for imperfections, trying to spot weaknesses. Only in this frame of mind can you revise effectively.

STRATEGIES FOR REVISING PERSONAL WRITING

Organization

1. Can you improve the organization by shifting paragraphs or changing the sequence of events?
2. If narrative, can you add or delete anything that would unify the essay around its opening statement?
3. Can the ending be improved?

Narration

1. Can you improve characterization by adding details?
2. Is there sufficient information about setting but not too much?
3. Should suspense be increased?
4. Should any descriptive passages be dramatized or vice versa?

Language

1. Are the voice and language of the narrator consistent, or should some words and phrases be altered?
2. Can you improve the language to make it clearer, livelier, or more natural?
3. Can you add specific details to describe the action more effectively?
4. Can you eliminate any details or passages because they are irrelevant?
5. Are there too many *I*'s or *we*'s?
6. Do your sentences contribute to your purpose? by adding suspense or urgency? by signaling the passage of time?

These are the kinds of questions you should have in mind as you review your paper. Often you may have to delete some sentences or passages you considered clever, a heroic action requiring you to sacrifice your pets to the waste basket. On other occasions, you may have to go back to the drawing board to provide a new introduction or conclusion, or to add several completely new sentences or paragraphs. We know what it's like. We've done it on practically every page of this book, reworking third and fourth drafts, deleting, adding, changing, touching up here and there. It's hard and painful work. It's part of the commitment that good writing requires.

But so far we've been talking mainly about major revisions. You must also be alert to others involving usage, vocabulary, spelling, punctuation, capitalization, and the like. These matters may seem like petty details, but if not attended to they can distract and annoy readers, spoiling the effect of your writing. Why take the chance of wasting all your hard work?

In particular, we advise our students to take one tour of their papers with only a single thought in mind—to underline any word whose spelling they would not bet five dollars on. For various reasons, many people—students and adults—spell poorly. And, perhaps illogically, most people, except for English instructors, believe that spelling is a true indication of how well you write and how intelligent you are. Nothing—but absolutely nothing—is more certain to irritate your readers and cause them to belittle you as poor spelling. Therefore, spend ten or fifteen minutes checking every doubtful spelling in a dictionary or spelling handbook. Actually, you don't have to know how to spell. You do have to know that spelling is important, that you can't consider it beneath your artistic temperament, or excuse yourself because you have always been a miserable speller. Mainly, it's a matter of laziness, isn't it? We have many suggestions in the Reference Guide for students with serious spelling problems, but our best advice for everyone is—look it up!

We also advise a second tour of your paper, this time reading it aloud to yourself or a friend. You'll be amazed at what the eye will miss but the ear will find. You will stumble over difficult sentences, catch awkward phrases, note rough passages, and discover other weaknesses. Naturally, when reading aloud, you must listen to yourself, concentrating on improving your paper.

Perhaps you can understand now why revision requires a major effort on your part and why many writers consider it to be the most important step in the writing process. You should plan to allow sufficient time for it, work conscientiously and painstakingly on it, and realize that only then will your papers represent the best work you can produce. You should be committed to nothing less.

PROOFREADING

So you've worked hard to revise your paper; you should be finished. You should be able to turn it in, confident you've done your best. But you can't. Still another step lies ahead: the fifth and last one, proofreading.

Proofreading a paper before turning it in is like glancing in the mirror before an important date to make sure that you look your best. But good proofreading requires more than a glance. Although this inspection is slow and tedious, it is an important step in all writing.

It's difficult to decrease your reading speed to about five miles an hour to scrutinize your final copy, making sure that no words are missing, no letters are omitted or transposed, no words have accidentally been repeated at ends and beginnings of lines and pages, and so on and on and on. It is easy to race through a paper, skim it quickly, and think that it is proofread. But it is arduous to inch through a paper patiently and painstakingly. You may find it helpful to read it aloud again slowly to yourself, or start at the end and go through the paper backward, sentence by sentence, as some professional proofreaders do, or redot every *i*. Also, even though you may have proofread your paper the previous night (or early morning!), do it again

The Informative
Voice:
Descriptive
Writing

My task . . . is, by the power of the written word, to make you hear, to make you feel—it is, before all, to make you see.

—Joseph Conrad

This is precisely the purpose of descriptive writing: to share with readers some object, scene, activity, person, or mood that you have experienced. When you re-create it in writing, you are trying to capture the way it is or the way you saw it, heard it, felt it, tasted it, or smelled it. How does this differ from personal writing? In that form, you focus directly or indirectly on yourself in order to reveal something about your life or character. In descriptive writing, you shift the emphasis to some other person, object, or scene in order to provide information about it. The distinction is one of purpose and perspective. When would you write a description? You might do so either in a separate work or as part of a personal, expository, argumentative, critical, or other essay. For example, you might describe the pollution of a stream in a political pamphlet, the attractiveness of a rug in an advertising brochure, the nature of a person in a businesss recommendation, the beauty of a campsite in a college newspaper article, the taste of food in rating a restaurant, the outcome of a laboratory experiment in a scientific report, the damage to a car in an accident report, or the features of a person in a letter. Whether or not they are aware of it, people are constantly describing, and often their descriptive ability determines whether they are interesting or dull people. Some of your friends can go on a vacation and enthrall you afterward with a lengthy, vivid account of magnificent natural settings or quaint, charming towns; other friends can tell you little more than that they had fun.

In addition to informing and interesting others, description adds to our enjoyment of life. We experience the world through our senses, and as we increase or heighten our sense perceptions, so we enrich our lives. Much of the beauty in the world comes from nature—from the oceans, mountains, lakes, trees, birds, flowers. As we increase our awareness of nature—become more sensitive to its delicate and subtle colors, its graceful and lovely patterns—we appreciate more of what life has to offer and we live more fully and richly.

Descriptive writing, therefore, should not be considered solely as an academic exercise fostered by English instructors. It can help you improve your skills as a writer: you will develop a more discriminating sense of language by realizing the descriptive qualities of words, understanding the importance of selecting the right one, and recognizing the different effects created by their different shades of meaning. Descriptive writing calls for numerous details; consequently, you will learn how to expand sentences, rearrange elements, and reword for greater sentence variety.

In the following chapters, we will suggest ways to treat the different forms of descriptive writing, examine particular language considerations, discuss appropriate writing voices, note some special sentence strategies, and improve a few pertinent revision techniques. Throughout, our purpose is to help you with your writing of description.

The Forms of Descriptive Writing

What exactly is description? What forms does it take? What are its characteristics?

Let's start with the philosophers, who have argued for centuries whether an object really exists or exists only in the mind of someone perceiving it. This metaphysical speculation gave rise to the classic question: Does a falling tree make a sound in the forest if no one is around to hear it? We mention this philosophical problem not to confuse you but to relate it to the two basic forms of description: factual and personal.

Factual description assumes that material substances exist independently of the beholder. It follows that people, places, animals, buildings, objects, and scenes can be accurately and objectively described as they truly are, regardless of the personal perceptions, associations, and impressions in the mind of a particular writer. What is important in such factual descriptions is fidelity to the subject. As a writer, you try to present the subject not as it seems to you alone, but as it exists to any objective observer. A factual description of toads, for example, would enable readers to recognize and learn about them. It would not mention your squeamishness about them. All such personal reactions should be omitted from factual descriptions. In a nutshell, the factual description proclaims: This is the way it *is.*

Not so the personal description. It assumes that material substances have no true reality because each is transformed by the minds and senses of people. Therefore, we each are entitled to our own reactions, responses, impressions, feelings about anything we see, hear, smell, taste, or feel. In the process of describing, we may reveal much about ourselves as well as our subjects. In another nutshell, the personal description proclaims: This is the way it is to *me,* the writer.

The distinction between a factual and personal description is somewhat like that between photographs and paintings. Although photographers do select the angle, light, composition, lens opening, and shutter speed, their freedom is greatly limited by the subject. And generally their purpose is limited: to represent the subject as it exists to most people. But in paintings, artists portray only what they observe and choose to represent. They may enlarge, diminish, discolor, or otherwise distort or transform the subject as they wish. The photograph is similar to factual description; the painting to personal description.

Let's look at a couple of examples. Here is an excerpt from a factual description of the praying mantis:

The praying mantis, a member of the family Mantida, order Orthoptera, derives its name from the prayerful position it assumes with front legs raised while the mantis is waiting to attack its prey. A full-grown mantis varies from 2 to 5 inches in length, resembles in color the plants on which it rests. Behind the small, freely movable, triangular head with a biting mouthpiece is a long and thin prothorax, which is held almost erect. The rest of the body is thicker, although the general shape is long and slender. The wings are short and broad. The forelegs have sharp hooks for capturing and holding the prey, which consists mainly of injurious insects.

The purpose here is to present information objectively and clearly. The writer's attitude toward the insect is not revealed: the tone is matter-of-fact, the language simple, clear, exact. Anyone with a knowledge of the mantis might have written this description; there is no flavor to it, nothing personal, distinctive, individualistic.

Quite the opposite is this paragraph from Jean Henri Fabre's captivating descriptive essay about the praying mantis:

Apart from her lethal implement [the forelegs], the Mantis has nothing to inspire dread. She is not without a certain beauty, in fact, with her slender figure, her elegant bust, her pale-green coloring and her long gauze wings. No ferocious mandibles, opening like shears; on the contrary, a dainty pointed muzzle that seems made for billing and cooing. Thanks to a flexible neck, quite independent of the thorax, the head is able to move freely, to turn to right or left, to bend, to lift itself. Alone among insects, the Mantis directs her gaze; she inspects and examines; she almost has a physiognomy.
　　　　　　　　　　　—Edwin Way Teale, ed., *The Insect World of J. Henri Fabre*

The purpose here is to convey an impression of the insect, particularly how this writer feels about it. To most people, the mantis is sinister; to Fabre, the mantis resembles an attractive, slender woman with an elegant bust, a dainty mouth, a head that turns to inspect and examine, and almost facial features. In the factual description, the mantis was referred to as *it;* here the mantis is *she.* Fabre provides his readers with a fresh, distinctive way of thinking about and visualizing the mantis. This personal description is distinctive, individualistic, interpretative, although it includes some facts, as do nearly all personal descriptions. And, in language that is rich and suggestive (*elegant, ferocious, like shears, billing and cooing*), the description contains elements of both irony and droll humor as it points out the contrast between appearance and reality.

The nature of description, like other forms of discourse, is determined by the purpose, audience, and occasion. In much scientific, industrial, government, and business writing, the purpose of description is to present the facts to an audience interested in learning them; such descriptions occur in speeches, reports, articles, memorandums, and books—all usually serious and formal. In novels, short stories, plays, poems, and personal narratives, the purpose is usually to evoke an experience to an audience interested in feeling and perceiving it under circumstances that are more relaxed and less formal. And in other writing—nonfictional books and articles about places, scenes, objects, people, and the like—the purpose is to interest and inform an audience in ways that vary considerably, from the light and casual to the serious and significant. Thus writers approach description differently and use it—occasionally alone, but usually in narrative, informative, and persuasive works—according to their purpose, the audience's interests, and the communication situation.

What this means to you is that you need to weigh these three factors before writing a description. For example, if you describe your dorm room to your mother so that she can make curtains for it or bring you some furniture, you should stick mainly to the factual. If you describe it for a high-school friend, you should present your personal impressions, although including some actual details.

At this point, you might find the following outline helpful as a summary to remind you of the differences between the two main types of descriptions.

	Factual	*Personal*
Purpose	To present information	To present an impression
Approach	Objective, dispassionate	Subjective, interpretative
Appeal	To the understanding	To the senses
Tone	Matter-of-fact	Emotional
Coverage	Complete, exact	Selective, some facts
Language	Simple, clear	Rich, suggestive
Uses	Writing in science, industry, government, professions, business	Novels, short stories, plays, poems, personal narratives, some essays

PERSONAL DESCRIPTION

In the introduction to this section about description, we mentioned that personal description is similar to personal writing but differs in emphasis and purpose. Both deal with your response to the external world; both are concerned with your impressions and feelings. In personal writing, however, you are center stage; in personal description, something else is. In personal writing, your main purpose is to reveal something about yourself. In personal description, your main purpose is to portray something else. These distinctions are real, even though they may be slight in some instances. What may be more apparent are differences in organization, style, and tone.

Organization

Personal narratives are generally organized chronologically from past to present, while personal essays are organized around an introductory focusing statement. Personal descriptions begin similarly with an expression of the writer's main impression. For example, Fabre began his description of the praying mantis with the statement that she "has nothing to inspire dread."

In the following sentences from Edgar Allan Poe's "Fall of the House of Usher," note how he presents his main impression and tries to evoke the same response from readers:

During the whole of a dull, dark, and soundless day in the autumn of the year, when the clouds hung oppressively low in the heavens, I had been passing along, on horseback, through a singular dreary tract of country; and at length found myself, as the shades of evening drew on, within view of the melancholy House of Usher. I knew not how it was—but, with the first glimpse of the building, a sense of insufferable gloom pervaded my spirit.

In these two beginning sentences, Poe has created a mood of oppressive melancholy and stated his dominant impression, one of "insufferable gloom." This early statement of a dominant impression is a fine example for you to follow in your personal descriptions. Occasionally, however, you may withhold your impression for the conclusion to give the effect of a summary.

In addition to stating the dominant impression, you must consider point of view, whether you wish to be a static or moving observer. If static, then you should select and follow consistently some logical order, just as in factual descriptions. If moving, then you must clearly signal readers with phrases or sentences that mark the shift from one location to another. To illustrate, here are some of the introductory sentences from paragraphs in John Ruskin's description of St. Mark's Cathedral in Venice:

And now I wish that the reader, before I bring him into St. Mark's Place, would imagine himself for a little time in a quiet English cathedral town, and walk with me to the west front of its cathedral.

Think for a little while on that scene. . . . And then let us quickly recollect that we are in Venice. . . .

We find ourselves in a paved alley. . . .
A yard or two farther, we pass the hostelry of the Black Eagle. . . .
Let us enter the church.

—John Ruskin, *The Stones of Venice*

Whether static or moving, writers of description generally organize their material spatially, describing the subject from top to bottom, left to right, or in some similar way. But occasionally, writers will rely on a time sequence, often depending on a before-and-after contrast. In *Life on the Mississippi*, Mark Twain begins his description of the excitement generated by steamboats arriving at a Mississippi town with an introductory sentence signaling this organization: "Before these events, the day was glorious with expectancy; after them, the day was a dead and empty thing." However, even within such a time framework, the details may be organized spatially.

Style

In personal description, you should be concerned about how to interest readers. Strong, dramatic, intriguing, controversial, or provocative statements in the introduction or at the beginning of paragraphs can help. Note how Tom Wolfe creates interest by his paragraph-openers in *The Pump House Gang*:

Her walk-up flat was so essentially dreary. . . .
They have missed the Off Broadway's most extraordinary show, however, which is in the kitchen.
The boys have the new Los Angeles car kids' look.
One afternoon, however, about 2 p.m., I came back into the room, and boy, it was chaos in there.

Each of these sentences should arouse readers' interest, prodding them to satisfy their curiosity by continuing to read. The writer's enthusiasm or strong personal feeling can also spur readers on. The following examples from Henry David Thoreau's *Walden* are softer and more serene than Wolfe's, befitting the silence and solitude of life in the woods by Walden Pond, yet the sentences in the context motivate readers effectively:

This is a delicious evening, when the whole body is one sense, and imbibes delight through every pore.
I rejoice that there are owls.
The scenery of Walden is on a humble scale, and, though very beautiful, does not approach to grandeur, nor can it much concern one who has not long frequented it or lived by its shore, yet this pond is so remarkable for its depth and purity as to merit a particular description.

Whatever the technique used, you should try to interest readers, arouse their curiosity, and compel them to want to share your experience. Never assume that everyone is waiting breathlessly to read about the squalor of a city ghetto, the commotion of a church picnic, the frenzy of a rock concert, or the elegance of a high-school prom. Remember, good writers take pains to interest readers.

Attracting their attention is the first step; maintaining it is the second. To do so depends mainly on presenting details, recording the small, individual sense impressions that combine to create vivid images in the readers' minds. Consequently, you must be alert to the sights and sounds and odors and tastes and textures of the world around you. In the following student paper, note how details graphically depict the scene:

POND CREEK

Lucy Lubbers

Walking through a hazy, warm October afternoon, in my mind I could see Pond Creek in the July sun as clearly as if I had been there only yesterday instead of years ago. Now, in another year, another season, and another place, the memory of Pond Creek comes sharply into focus and once more I feel that I'm ambling along its banks in a warm, redolent, unhurried midsummer afternoon.

It seems that days were never anything but beautiful at Pond Creek, or at least my memories always picture them so. It was always warm, but in a special way. I don't recall it being uncomfortably humid. Rather, there was a dry enveloping kind of heat that wrapped itself around you and seemed to dispel all memories of winter chills with its gentle pervasive warmth. It used to come in soft, sweet-smelling breezes that would tousle you like huge children ruffling up a puppy's fur and then swirl you about lethargically. All this glorious warmth seemed to be confined within a tent of sky that was perpetually the color of chicory blooms, a clear, soft, unobtrusive blue that seemed to have absorbed some of the warmth of the day into itself. The sky was an important part of Pond Creek and is prominent in my memories of the place. I can see it now, vaulting high above the whole scene, glowing in the warm July sunlight, and gathering the whole valley under its buttresses.

I could never quite figure out whether this sky held the hills about Pond Creek with its edges to keep them from undulating away like benign green sea monsters or whether the hills reached up and clung to the skirts of the sky to hold it and keep if from lifting away. At different times both have seemed appropriate. These hills about the creek weren't really outstanding as far as hills go but they always seemed to have a personality. Their green rounded forms always reminded me of old, old creatures who have seen, experienced, and understood much life and who are patiently waiting for whatever the future has to distribute over their sinewy, weathered coils. These long, low-lying giants were always marked by a soft blue haziness that perhaps hid many scars that were evident of their having existed eons ago.

Bound among the coils of these ridges were the wide, rocky, grass-covered fields through which wound Pond Creek. Sloping from the hills to the very waterline of the creek, the land as I remember it teemed with things that stimulated every sense. I can remember vividly the sweet dusty fragrance of hot dry grass; the acrid, alive smell of sweating horses and cattle; the sharp tang of wood sorrel and the blandly sweet taste of honeysuckle nectar; the whipping of the blowing grass against my jeans; the playful snatching of the matted blackberry vines at my hands and ankles; and the exhilarating loss of balance as I trip in some hole or over a root; the warm contented chirring of the cicadas, the rustle of the tall grasses and the squeaky munching of the horses—all in a world of golds, browns, and greens interspersed with the brilliant flowers of later summer that are just beginning to bloom.

But most of all, I remember Pond Creek itself, flowing in a long, lazy, almost unvaried curve through these grassy fields. Even now I hear it babbling like a small baby as it trundles busily among the round brown stones of its bed, a kind of clear sparkling brown in color that catches the gold colors of the grass and reflects them back brightly. A coolness always seemed to rise off its waters as they'd pass beneath an overhanging bank, bringing with it the peculiar odor of mossy stones and water reeds and the suggestion of hidden crannies where minuscule animals cling in the dark to cool wet rocks, safe from the sun's intrusion. The creek then deepens in the sunshine and takes on a more majestic flow, or rather a slower one, for Pond Creek was always a bit of a baby and never able to summon the dignity necessary for majesty. It then disappears around the bend, under the single-laned bridge and out of memory.

It's strange how real Pond Creek's memory is. I haven't seen it in a long while but the day, the season, the hills, the grass, and especially the creek are recalled whenever I experience the warm, hazy afternoons similar to those at Pond Creek.

Much of this description's effectiveness stems from its wealth of detail. Note how the writer has relied on all the senses:

Sight
clear, soft, unobtrusive blue sky
green rounded hills
wide, rocky, grass-covered fields
round brown stones

Hearing
the warm contented chirring of the cicadas
rustle of the tall grasses
squeaky munching of the horses
babbling of the creek

Smell
soft, sweet-smelling breezes
sweet dusty fragrance of hot dry grass
the acrid, alive smell of sweating horses and cattle
the peculiar odor of mossy stones and water reeds

Touch
the dry enveloping heat with its pervasive warmth
the whipping of the blowing grass
the playful snatching of the matted blackberry vines

Taste
the sharp tang of wood sorrel
the blandly sweet taste of honeysuckle nectar

In addition to this abundance of detail, the description gains its effectiveness from its rich language. The writer's feeling for Pond Creek is conveyed in large part through similes (the breezes "that would tousle you like huge children ruffling up a puppy's fur," the hills that might undulate away "like benign green sea monsters"); through metaphors ("heat that wrapped itself around you," "long, low-lying giants"); and through the alliterative repetition of initial sounds ("the soft, sweet-smelling breezes," "the contented chirring of the cicadas," and "trundles busily among the round, brown stones of its bed"). The richness of the language adds not only vitality and interest to the description but evokes feelings of pleasure, enabling readers to share the joyful mood of the author as she describes memories of Pond Creek.

Also contributing to this effect are the sentences that often ramble lazily like the creek itself. Many flow on to great length, adding phrase upon phrase, packing in details, pointing out specific sights, impressions, sounds, and smells, all suggesting how meaningful and moving were the writer's summer days at Pond Creek and how poignant are her recollections of it.

Such well-developed sentences, along with the evocative language, the sensory details, and some attempt to create and maintain reader interest, are stylistic qualities of personal descriptions. This is not to say that every personal description must contain all these elements (note, for example, that "Pond Creek" does little initially to attract reader interest); but most of these characteristics may be found in effective personal descriptions and all can help you in your writing.

Consequently, before writing, you should list all the details you can, jotting down everything that caught your eye, came to your ears, and affected your other senses. Then add adjectives and adverbs so that through suggestion and association you arouse in your readers the same mood that you experienced. Finally, with this list as a guide, write the first draft of your paper.

Tone

In personal descriptions, your tone must clearly indicate your attitude toward your subject. Your writing "voice" may be filled with disgust and bitterness about filthy, rat-infested, underheated housing for the poor; with sadness about the destruction of grass and bushes and trees for a new highway; with irony about the gaudy taste of the newly rich; with compassion about the infirmities of the aged; with reverence about a crocus blooming; or with excitement about a circus, rock concert, or championship game. Listen to the voice of crusty old Squire Bramble, Tobias Smollett's eccentric but lovable character in *Humphrey Clinker,* describing the pollution in London in 1771:

I am pent up in frowsy lodgings, where there is not room enough to swing a cat; and I breathe the streams of endless putrefaction, and these would undoubtedly produce a pestilence, if they were not qualified by the gross acid of sea-coal. . . . I go to bed after midnight, jaded and restless from the dissipations of the day—I start every hour from my sleep, at the horrid noise of thundering at every door . . . and by five o-clock I start out of bed, in consequence of the still more dreadful alarm made by the country carts, and noisy rustics bellowing green peas under my window. If I would drink water, I must quaff the mawkish contents of an open aqueduct, exposed to all manner of defilement, or swallow that which comes from the river Thames, impregnated with all the filth of London and Westminster—Human excrement is the least offensive part of the concrete, which is composed of all the drugs, minerals, and poisons, used in mechanics and manufacture, enriched with the putrefying carcasses of beasts and men; and mixed with the scourings of all the washtubs, kennels, and common sewers, within the bills of mortality.

As Squire Bramble registers his disgust at the dirt, noise, and discomforts of London, he becomes more and more emotional, undoubtedly exaggerating as we all do in such circumstances, pouring his fury out in a surging, powerful piling up of phrases, each providing more stomach-turning details as he rages on and on. But the tone is conveyed above all by his words.

FACTUAL DESCRIPTION

As we said earlier, the information in factual descriptions needs to be presented clearly and objectively. To achieve these qualities, keep in mind the following recommendations about organization, style, and tone.

Organization

Factual descriptions are mainly concerned with physical data, although other information may be included. Sometimes the organization is prescribed, following a pattern established by a particular publication, company, or discipline. The following description of the cardinal from Roger Tory Peterson's well-known *Field Guide to the Birds* illustrates such an organizational scheme dictated by the demands of a profession and a publication form.

CARDINAL   RICHMONDENA CARDINALIS

Field marks:—*The only all-red bird with a crest.* Smaller than Robin (8–9). Male:—All red except for black patch at base of bill. Female:—Yellowish brown, with a touch of red; at once recognizable by its crest and heavy bill.

Similar Species:—Summer Tanager (no crest); Special Tanager (black wings).

Voice:—Song, a series of clear, slurred whistles diminishing in pitch. Several variations: *what-cheer, cheer, cheer,* etc.: *whoit whoit whoit,* etc. Note, a short thin chip.

Range:—United States e. of Plains and n. to s. New York, Lake Erie (s. Ontario), s. Minnesota, and se. South Dakota; towns, farms, roadsides, edges, swamps, etc. Non-migratory.

This pattern (field marks, similar species, voice, range) would present you with no organizational problem: once you had established the sequence, you would simply follow it. In other factual descriptive assignments, realizing that sight is the main means of perception, you might use some form of spatial organization like top to bottom (see the description of the praying mantis on page 109, left to right, main feature to less important ones, foreground to background. Like a cinematographer letting the audience observe every detail clearly, you should focus on each part before moving in an expected direction rather than confusing the audience by jumping back and forth unpredictably. But unlike the camera operator, you can reveal more than meets the eye and ear. The preceding description, for example, contains information about where cardinals may be found.

Style

You can assume that readers are already interested in the subject of your factual description and wish to be informed about it as accurately, clearly, and completely as their needs indicate. Consequently, you need not attempt to arouse their curiosity or otherwise motivate them. But you should keep their purpose and reading interests in mind. The description of the cardinal, for example, was written mainly for people who just want to be able to identify a strange bird and learn a little about it. Of course, in such general factual descriptions, there are no imaginative opening lines like "Most glorious of all the winged creatures is the magnificent shocking-red male cardinal." And there are none of the scientific facts about eating, breeding, and the like that ornithologists would need.

In keeping with the objective approach, the language in factual descriptions is specific and simple. Naturally, an account of a breeder reactor producing plutonium would be couched in more technical terms for nuclear physicists than for nonscientists. But usually in the nontechnical language of factual descriptions, the sentences are relatively simple and short, featuring mainly forms of *be* and other common verbs, beginning with subject-verb combinations, and omitting the first-person pronoun (*I*). Observe these characteristics for yourself in the following passage about the sassafras from Alfred Carl Hottes' *Book of Trees:*

The leaves are usually one- to three-lobed and turn orange-scarlet in the Autumn. The bark is a cinnamon-gray, and is deeply furrowed. The twigs are hairy when young, and yellowish-green, aromatic, and with very unequal internodes. The scanty fruits are bluish-black, with red stems, and surrounded at the base by thick, scarlet calyx.

Hottes presents only the facts, using precise adjectives and concrete nouns and emphasizing the details by avoiding almost any other verb but the colorless *be.* In some circumstances, verbs are so unimportant that they are omitted, as they were in the description of the cardinal.

Tone

The tone used must be appropriate to the objective, straightforward presentation of the material. Readers should be unaware of the writer. No judgment should be rendered, no opinion stated, no feeling expressed. A driver may smell of alcohol (a fact), but unless the results of a breath test are available, he or she should not be described as drunk (a judgment).

Complete objectivity is difficult but necessary if readers are to rely on what is written. This factual, impartial quality is best achieved by a matter-of-fact tone with no excesses, no emotions. Because the subject is serious, the attitude of the writer should be serious. Thus a factual description— whether of an eye, a rock formation, a television tube, or an engine—may be quite formal, even dull and dry. But otherwise it may not be trusted. The voice heard in the writing should be that of an authority speaking soberly and calmly, not that of an average person expressing opinions and emotions. Perhaps factual descriptions, as a result, do not make for exciting reading, but they do serve important, useful functions when readers need reliable information. And generally, if readers are at all curious about a subject, they will be interested in any intelligent, clear, carefully written description of it. Consequently, in this form of description, which implies "Here are the facts," only a sincere, straightforward, matter-of-fact tone is effective.

HINTS FOR WRITING PERSONAL AND FACTUAL DESCRIPTIONS

Here is a checklist of suggestions that may be helpful to you in writing personal and factual descriptions.

Personal Descriptions

- Organization: Logically organized by space, time, or both. But opening statements should attract readers and establish the dominant mood. The writer may be static or moving; if moving, clearly notify readers of position changes.
- Style: Details are essential in picturing whatever is described. Also vital are rich and suggestive words and phrases to evoke emotional responses in readers. Listing details according to their sensory appeals is helpful. Sentences may be lengthy and involved, and the first-person pronoun may be used.
- Tone: The description should be written with feeling. The writer's voice—casual, warm, enthusiastic, caustic, bitter, or whatever—should be heard. The implication: here is how I feel about it.

Specifically, you might ask yourself these questions before writing:

1. What details shall I include?
2. How shall I organize them?
3. How can I interest my readers?
4. What is the dominant impression I wish to convey in my personal description?
5. What tone should I adopt?

Factual Descriptions

- Organization: Usually spatial: top to bottom, left to right, large to small, and so on. Be logical, consistent: do not shift back and forth.
- Style: No need to attract reader interest. Language should be simple and specific. Technical words that readers would understand may be used. Emphasis on nouns, adjectives—not verbs. The passive may be effective, the first-person pronoun ineffective. Sentences should be short and simple.

- Tone: Factual, serious, formal. The writer's voice should not be heard. The description should sound as if it were written by a scientific, objective, detached authority. The implication: here are the facts, only the facts.

Naturally, no list of suggestions or questions can solve all your writing problems. But by checking here before you write, you may be reminded of one or two helpful hints.

DESCRIPTIONS OF PEOPLE

Writing factual descriptions of people requires no techniques different from those just discussed. But these descriptions are rare, occurring mainly in official records and documents. These descriptions consist of certain statistical information (height, weight, age), visible characteristics (color of hair, skin, eyes), and recognizable marks (scars, birthmarks). Probably the most familiar factual description of people appears in post offices under the word *"Wanted."*

The Character Sketch

Writing personal descriptions of people is more common and more difficult. Usually called character sketches, such descriptions may also be referred to as profiles, literary portraits, or biographical sketches. As its name indicates, a character sketch delineates a person's main personality traits. In the process, it may include some factual details about a person's appearance, but it does more than tell what people *look* or *seem* like; it shows what they *are.*

A character sketch may be about a type rather than an individual, revealing the characteristics common to the members of a group, such as campus jocks, cheerleaders, art students, religious fanatics, television devotees. The purpose of writing about a type may be serious or satirical, either to inform readers about the group or to poke fun at it. In the following opening paragraph from Milton Birnbaum's article "Professor Scylla and Professor Charybdis," you can observe how a character sketch can be used for humorous effect to caricature a "mod" young professor:

Professor Scylla is still in his thirties but likes to think of himself as much younger looking in appearance. He tries to reinforce this impression by adopting the latest sartorial innovations—bell-bottom pants, vivid-colored striped shirts, worn open at the collar, ankle-top shoes; although tending to baldness, he lets his remaining hair grow below the neck and has recently sprouted some formidable looking sideburns. There is a sparkle to his eyes, a new spring to his gait, a general feeling of "it's good to be alive" exuding from his demeanor. He's never seen alone on campus. He's always followed by a coterie of admiring students; he eats with students instead of his colleagues, and his office is never closed; memoranda of seemingly grave import from students and to students are tacked onto the bulletin board outside his office. His home likewise is an oasis for the exchange of ideas and calls to action. He smilingly denies the allegation that he condones the use of pot and asserts that, after all, pot is not nearly so damaging to one's health as are cigarettes and alcohol.

In such character sketches about types, you should treat the subject as a composite of most members of the particular group. For example, if you were to write about "The School Bus Driver," you should include in this portrait the characteristics of most drivers, not a particular one. Descriptions of types, therefore, require more generalization than do descriptions of individuals, but both rely on essentially the same rhetorical techniques.

These techniques include narrative and expository as well as descriptive devices. Anecdotes, personal narrative, and dialogue are all important in vividly portraying someone or some type. One incident demonstrating a person's stubbornness is far more effective than a flat statement that the person is stubborn. But the character sketch often relies on expository techniques in presenting and illustrating an individual's most striking or memorable qualities. Thus, a character sketch has a rather formal structure, generally being organized into three parts: an introduction, body, and conclusion.

Introduction   When a character sketch is not part of another literary work, such as a novel or essay, but an independent piece, the introduction should serve both to interest readers in the person and to present his or her most striking characteristic. In the following student examples, an intriguing or provocative opening paragraph catches the reader's attention and also establishes the person's dominant trait.

I guess the most exciting fellow I've ever known was a six-foot guy everybody called Little Stevie.

Tough and mean. That's the best way to describe Bill Evans. When babies are born, they're sweet, soft, and cuddly. Not Bill Evans. He was probably fighting and clawing and scrapping from the start.

After six hours of being locked up in a classroom with a teacher during the class day, most kids don't want to have anything more to do with her. They beat it out of the room as fast as possible. But in Room 145 the kids linger after the school buzzer sounds. That's where Carol Sicars teaches. She's wonderful.

Sometimes the dominant quality about a person is presented in an opening anecdote, which by its very narrative form usually interests the reader. The following account by Carmen Mendez describes how she entered the Guatemala American Hospital as a fifteen-year-old girl just out of high school and met an unforgettable man.

A wiry little cricket of a man in old work clothes. . . . He was about 30 and stood only five-foot-seven, even counting his plume of black hair. He couldn't have weighed more than 110 pounds. His grin was the biggest thing about him.

Thinking that he was probably a hired man, I found it unexpectedly easy to ask, "Whom should I see about studying to become a nurse? My pastor says it's a good career."

"I think that you should see *me*," he answered with mock gravity, not in the least self-conscious about his poor Spanish with its heavy American accent. His light blue eyes twinkled. "And yes. How could anyone have a better, more satisfying career than to serve in the medical-missionary field, where the need is so great."

Thus, in the first moment of meeting Dr. Charles Albert Ainslie, I heard his favorite prescription for attaining the good and happy life—the formula that was to make him one of our country's most valuable and beloved medical pioneers.
—"My Most Unforgettable Character," *Reader's Digest*

The key idea in each of these introductions commits the writer just as "I've got a funny story to tell you" commits the speaker. Each of the students has a clear assignment: to show why Little Stevie was so exciting, Bill Evans was tough and mean, and Carol Sicars was wonderful. And Carmen Mendez has also indicated her thesis: to demonstrate why Dr. Charles Albert Ainslie was a valuable and beloved medical pioneer.

Body   The second part of the character sketch—the body—should be organized according to either a chronological or an analytical pattern. If the introduction describes a first meeting, then it would be logical to follow with a discussion of how this initial impression was later supported, modified, or reversed. Or the flashback technique could be used to review the subject's birth, family, and early life. But this biographical approach should be used cautiously because often it is uninteresting, inappropriate, or irrelevant. A paper about a teacher, for example, should generally not include such material unless it is unusual or illuminating. Yet you could still use the chronological plan by beginning with your first school day with this teacher and proceeding to the last, or starting with the last and flashing back to the first, or introducing a striking anecdote from a Christmas party and then flashing back to the first day and moving forward from that point.

The second option for organizing a character sketch, the analytical pattern, consists of dividing the main trait into parts and elaborating on each. The student paper about the exciting Little Stevie, for example, was divided into three sections: his spectacular athletic feats, his impulsive whims, and his search for daring experiences. The writer thus organized his material by dividing it into units, each showing one aspect of why Little Stevie was exciting.

Failure to use either the chronological or analytical pattern can confuse and irritate the reader. Despite some fine touches, the following paper illustrates how poor organization can weaken a character sketch.

Gail is a friend I wish I hadn't known so well last summer—wish I hadn't known at all. She has long brown hair falling gently over her shoulders. Her sparkling hazel eyes twinkling above an almost perpetual set smile make her very tempting.

Gail is different from most girls. She seems to be very grown up but is really two-faced. You're great when you're with her but behind your back, you're not so great.

Gail wants to be popular so she'll go with anyone to be seen in the right places by the right people. She used people like a ladder, walking over them until she reached the top—vice president of the class, homecoming queen, and various other honors.

Gail makes people feel good with her dumb honest manner, asking lots of questions, pretending that your're so smart, complimenting you and acting modest. It's a game which she plays well. After you know Gail, you'll know how to play it well too.

Some clear organizational pattern would have been helpful here, either a before-and-after plan, setting forth Gail's apparently attractive qualities and then exposing them, or an analytical approach, breaking down her deceitfulness into the ways she beguiles, dupes, and uses people.

Poor organization is not this paper's only weakness. Writers are obliged to show *why* they feel as they do. It is not enough to state their opinion: they must make readers realize the reasons for it. Lawyers do not go into court and merely declare their client is innocent. They prove it. Similarly, you must prove that the subject of your character sketch is foolish or fascinating, compassionate or cruel, shy or sophisticated. It is not enough for the student writer to tell us that Gail is a phony; he should have shown us. Why not some dialogue illustrating how Gail asks lots of questions, plays dumb, and showers compliments? Or some evidence to support the statement that she wants to be seen in the right places by the right people? Or an example about how she used people to become homecoming queen? The failure to show Gail in action not only results in a weak depiction of her but also makes us question the accuracy of the portrayal. We wonder whether the writer is just bitter because Gail wasn't interested in him. In sum, the lack of specific detail, proof, and evidence results in an unconvincing paper.

Conclusion   Although it may consist of only one or two paragraphs, a conclusion to your character sketch is necessary to give readers a sense of completion and a final glimpse of the character's main trait. Keep these objectives in mind while worrying about and planning your paper. Perhaps you will want to save an apt quotation, a short anecdote, or a brief observation for the conclusion. Here's an illustration from the end of a character sketch about Donald W. Nyrop, the highly active chairman of Northwest Airlines:

Recently, a clear-plastic plaque appeared on Nyrop's desk. A gift from a compatriot at another airline, it reads: "Along the way . . . take time to smell the flowers." The recipient does not appear to be heeding the sentiment. The plaque faces those seated in front of him.

—Hugh D. Menzies, *Fortune*

Other popular techniques consist of a reference to the subject's future or to the introduction of the sketch, thus making it come full circle. For example, the opening sentence about Nyrop relied on a cowbody metaphor: "Like a bronco rider of old, Donald W. Nyrop . . . is willing to dig in his spurs and take his lumps in order to stay on top of everything that affects his beloved bottom line." A full-circle ending might have taken this form: "Despite labor problems, increasing competition, and the lure of fishing, Don Nyrop enjoys being in the saddle and gives little evidence of giving up the rough ride to settle back in the comfort of the old corral."

Whatever technique you use in your wrap-up, strive for an effective conclusion: an appropriate last glimpse of your subject and a clear signal of the ending. These are difficult to achieve, probably requiring as much work as your introduction. But readers are particularly apt to remember your final words, so the conclusion is important.

Conviction in a character sketch is significant because the sketch is not an academic exercise concocted by English teachers to plague students but a valuable, practical writing experience. Chances are you will be writing letters about new friends; examinations and term papers about illustrious people; statements in behalf of other students for social and academic honors; recommendations for jobs or promotions; and testimonials for relatives, friends, or company or civic leaders. The importance of being able to write interesting and informative character sketches should certainly be evident when you consider how often you talk about people. And people are what character sketches are all about.

SUMMARY

This chapter has dealt with the forms of descriptive writing: personal and factual description and the character sketch. In personal description, you present your impression of some place or thing to interest and inform your readers. This description often begins with a focusing statement of the dominant feature, and then proceeds according to some spatial plan of organization, which includes an indication of the point of view or position from which the description is being written. To convey feelings strongly and evocatively, personal description should be rich in details, precisely chosen words, and varied sentence structures.

Factual description is designed to furnish information—usually about the physical appearance of some person, place, or thing. Organized spatially, it usually is serious, factual, and formal in tone, using simple, specific language and short sentences, while avoiding personal pronouns.

Although a character sketch may describe a person, it should mainly characterize that individual. To do so, it may incorporate narrative and expository elements along with descriptive ones. Its usual three-part organizational structure consists of an introduction to catch the reader's attention and state the person's main trait; a body to furnish amplifying information; and a conclusion to provide a sense of finality and, often, to restate the dominant impression.

Assignments

For Discussion

1   Read the following paragraphs from George Orwell's essay "Some Thoughts on the Common Toad," and then answer the questions that follow.

Before the swallow, before the daffodil, and not much later than the snowdrop, the common toad salutes the coming of spring after his own fashion, which is to emerge from a hole in the ground, where he has lain buried since the previous autumn, and crawl as rapidly as possible towards the nearest suitable patch of water. Something—some kind of shudder in the earth, or perhaps merely a rise of a few degrees in the temperature—has told him that it is time to wake up; though a few toads appear to sleep the clock round and miss out a year from time to time—at any rate, I have more than once dug them up, alive and apparently well, in the middle of the summer.

At this period, after his long fast, the toad has a very spiritual look, like a strict Anglo-Catholic towards the end of Lent. His movements are languid but purposeful, his body is shrunken, and by contrast his eyes look abnormally large. This allows one to notice, what one might not at another time, that a toad has about the most beautiful eye of any living creature. It is like gold, or more exactly it is like the golden-colored semiprecious stone which one sometimes sees in signet rings, and which I think is called chrysoberyl.

For a few days after getting into the water the toad concentrates on building up his strength by eating small insects. Presently he has swollen to his normal size again, and then he goes through a phase of intense sexiness. All he knows, at least if he is a male toad, is that he wants to get his arms around something, and if you offer him a stick, or even your finger, he will cling to it with surprising strength and take a long time to discover that it is not a female toad. Frequently one comes upon shapeless masses of ten or twenty toads rolling over and over in the water, one clinging to another without distinction of sex. By degrees, however, they sort themselves out into couples, with the male duly sitting on the female's back. You can now distinguish males from females, because the male is smaller, darker and sits on top, with his arms tightly clasped around the female's neck. After a day or two the spawn is laid in long strings which wind themselves in and out of the reeds and soon become invisible. A few more weeks, and the water is alive with masses of tiny tadpoles which rapidly grow larger, sprout hind-legs, then fore-legs, then shed their tails; and finally, about the middle of the summer, the new generation of toads, smaller than one's thumb-nail but perfect in every particular, crawl out of the water to begin the game anew.

I mention the spawning of the toads because it is one of the phenomena of spring which most deeply appeal to me, and because the toad, unlike the skylark and the primrose, has never had much of a boost from the poets. But I am aware that many people do not like reptiles or amphibians, and I am not suggesting that in order to enjoy the spring you have to take an interest in toads. There are also the crocus, the missel thrush, the cuckoo, the blackthorn, etc. The point is that the pleasures of spring are available to everybody and cost nothing.

a   What is the basic organizational pattern?
b   How has Orwell tried to interest his readers?
c   What rhetorical device does Orwell use twice in the second paragraph zo make the toad seem attractive? What transition does he use to move from one device to the other? Could this descriptive paragraph appear earlier or later? Is it most effective here? Why or why not?
d   What is the dominant impression Orwell wishes to convey about toads in the third paragraph? Does this impression serve any descriptive function? What transitions does Orwell use to switch from toads to tadpoles?
e   What is the rhetorical function of the first sentence in the fourth paragraph? From your reading of this paragraph, what do you think is the tmesis of Orwell's essay? Why is his description of the toad particularly effective in view of this thesis?

2   Writers are occasionally faced with the problem of how to provide a great deal of statistical descriptive information in an interesting manner. How does Ted Morgan try to accomplish this in the following paragraphs? Which details do you think best indicate the enormity of the luxury liner S.S. *France*? To what extent is the description factual? To what extent personal? Discuss its organization, tone, style.

"To give you an idea of the size of the *France*," a ship's officer said, "it is the only ship in the world where you can travel with your wife and your mistress with the assurance that they will never meet."

The *France* is 1,035 feet long, almost as long as the Eiffel Tower, and 110 feet wide. It weighs 66,348 tons, can do better than 30 knots, and can carry up to 2,044 passengers. It has eight boilers that develop 90 tons an hour of steam pressure and four propeller shafts driven by a set of turbines that can deliver up to 160,000 horsepower. Each propeller weighs 27 tons. It has two autonomous engine compartments, with 14 watertight bulkheads—so that no damage can deprive the ship of more than half its propulsion machinery—and two pairs of antiroll stabilizers. Its red and black smokestacks, with fins that drive soot away from the ship, weigh 45 tons each.

All the fresh water, including the water for the boilers, is produced in four distillery plants capable of converting 300 tons of sea water in 24 hours. The ship has long lines and a terraced silhouette like the *Normandie*. The curves of her hull are so graceful that below the waterline there is not a single flat plate. The plates are welded, not riveted. There are 22 elevators serving 11 decks, and telephones in each cabin, linked by 18,000 miles of wiring. There are 46 miles of sheets, cut up into useful lengths; two padded cells; one prison cell; a hospital; a refrigerated morgue; a printer who stocks 80 different models of engraved invitations; 13 full-time firemen, and stainless steel kennels with wall-to-wall carpeting and five-course meals, and imitation fire hydrants for homesick American dogs.

On the two-class North Atlantic run, the segregation is horizontal. First-class passengers use the upper decks. The passengers in tourist class, which is called *Rive Gauche*, are spared the humiliating barriers with "first class only" signs as they take their turns around the deck.

3   Discuss each of the four student papers that follow, pointing out the strengths and weaknesses of their tone, style, and organization, and indicating exactly what the writer might work on in revision.

a   During the first few weeks of school, a student's roommate can greatly influence his or her outlook on college life. Many students, including myself, leave for college without knowing a single person going to the same school. If such is the case, it is of utmost importance to like and get along well with that person whom you are spending so much time with. I consider myself most fortunate in this respect. Judy has proved to be much more than just a roommate to me. She is already a really close friend. I have been very content here at school, and I am sure that Judy is one of the factors which add to my contentment.

b   My roommate is definitely a unique character. He has a life style strictly limited to one human being—Jim Beard. I think no other person has such a combination of peculiarities as Jim does. Since I've known him, I've become accustomed to being prepared for anything. From my experiences of the last few weeks, there is nothing he could do that would shock me.

In appearance he seems to be average enough—six feet tall, straight blond hair and blue eyes. However, quite often his actions are to the contrary.

For example, the average college student living in a dorm normally sleeps on a bed, but not my roommate! Instead, he prefers to sleep on the floor without a mattress. He uses his mattress for lounging around in the daytime but not for sleeping.

Another peculiarity I'm becoming accustomed to is to see him walking down the corridors of the dorm at all hours of the night doing John Wayne imitations while dressed only in his underwear and cowboy boats. On our floor we have people from all over the country, but no one but Jim walks around at midnight in such attire!

Jim has a variety of odd eating habits to go along with his unusual clothing styles. He seems to be the only person I know who combines sweet pickles and beer, herb tea and pizza, and bananas with black coffee.

In addition to strange eating habits he constantly redecorates the room. He changes posters so often I barely have time to become accustomed to one before he changes it. His latest addition to the room is a black light which he uses to send Morse Code to the girls in Donovan Hall.

Jim may have some odd personal habits, but he is a decent person to have for a roommate. Very seldom is he unhappy, and he's one of the best-liked fellows on Haggin Hall's B-3. In spite of some of his more distinguishable habits, I feel I couldn't have found a better person with whom to share such close quarters.

c In a student's lifetime, hopefully he will be fortunate enough to have one teacher who dedicates his whole being to his pupils. In high school, we were blessed with a man like this. Mr. Fiorucci taught biology and chemistry, and he made the whole realm of these courses come alive for every student. He made each class hour a fascinating new discovery into a world of science none of us knew or understood before. Mr. Fiorucci sincerely loved the students and wanted them to realize the total value of education. His influence certainly changed the lives of many teenagers. Many students went eagerly on to college because he had touched their lives. I myself am here today with inner thoughts of someday teaching students with that same thrill for learning Mr. Fiorucci always gave.

d My roommate, in my opinion, happens to be a unique person with a well-rounded personality. Not one day goes by that I do not learn something new about him. He has an engaging sense of humor and can find something amusing about almost any situation. I do not stay depressed when he is around because of his positive disposition. He can always point out the brighter aspects of whatever may be bothering him. He is rarely discouraged but easily hurt. My roommate is sensitive to the feelings of other people and tender and kind to anyone who needs help. He has a logical solution to most problems that arise and is usually able to look at things objectively. I have chosen to present only his best personality characteristics, although as he is a human being, he does have a few imperfections. It is obvious that I admire him and in case you haven't guessed, he is not only my roommate, but also my husband.

For Practice

1   Choose one of the following and write paragraphs according to the instructions.

   a   You probably had or have some toy, object, or other "security blanket" that you were or are attached to. Write a factual description of it; then write a personal description.

   b   If you have ever been in an automobile accident, write three factual descriptions of it: first, your own view as you might write it to your insurance company; second, the other driver's account as he or she might write to his or her company; third, the policeman's report.

   c   Write a paragraph-length factual description of your doctor's or dentist's office; then write a personal description of how it looked to you as a nervous patient.

2   Using any of the following or similar sentences as your opening statement, write a descriptive paragraph:

   a   It was thrilling to be there.
   b   For the first time, I was truly stirred by the beauty of nature.
   c   People's disregard for the environment was evident everywhere.
   d   On a clear day you can see _____.
   e   The _____ was out of place in those surroundings.
   f   Bedlam broke loose after the game.
   g   It looked like a wreck.
   h   The old neighborhood had changed.
   i   At night my childhood room was filled with terrifying shapes and shadows.
   j   I had expected it to look different.
   k   Town springs to life on Saturday.
   l   I had looked at it many times but never really seen it before.
   m   Summer nights are a symphony of sound.

3   One of your friends has applied for a summer job as a camp counselor, giving your name as a reference. As a result, you have just received a letter from Mr. Outdore, Director of the Whispering Pine Camp, asking you to write a recommendation for your friend. Write the letter; do not worry about its business format.

For Writing

Personal Description

1   Select an activity and write a personal description of it, recording all the sights, sounds, odors, and other sense impressions. Among subjects you might choose are a rock concert, a country fair, a church picnic, a

high school dance, the locker room after the game, lunch in the school cafeteria, or Sunday night at the high school hangout.

2 Write a personal description of a place. If one does not come quickly to mind, perhaps the following questions will help. If you could spend the next few hours anywhere, what place would you choose? Where is the most beautiful place you've ever been? The ugliest? The most disturbing? Most peaceful? Noisiest? Happiest? Most inspiring? Most terrifying? Most ornate? Dingiest? Oldest? Most charming? Most comfortable?

3 As a child, you probably had some favorite hideaway where you could be all alone. Describe it, explaining your feeling of comfort and seclusion.

4 Most of us are creatures of routine, walking or driving the same way from our room to class every weekday. Write a personal description of what you see, hear, smell, touch, and experience as you proceed from door to door.

Factual Description

5 Write a factual description of the same place you selected in assignment 2 or the route you selected in assignment 4.

6 Write a factual description of a stereo-radio, the attire worn for some sport, or you English classroom.

7 Write a facual description of something related to a hobby or activity you are interested in: for example, a tropical fish, a breed of dog or cat, a musical instrument, a make of automobile or motorcycle, jogging shoes.

Character Sketch

8 Write a character sketch about a certain type of person at high school—student, teacher, administrator, or other employee. Be certain to discuss at some length the appearance, interests, mannerisms, likes, and dislikes of such a composite individual, and to portray him or her in some characteristic incident. Your paper may be serious or satirical.

9 From your experience in a summer or other job, write a character sketch about some person or type. For example, if you worked as a waiter or waitress, you might want to describe your boss or someone you worked with, or such customers as The Big Spender, The Indecisive Individual, The Wine Connoisseur, or The Spoiled Brat.

10 Write a character sketch either about a favorite relative, teacher, neighbor, minister, friend, employer, or about someone you dislike or detest. Be sure to provide sufficient evidence to support your opinion.

11 Write a description of the most unforgettable character you have ever met. It might be someone you have encountered only once—on an airplane, perhaps, or at a concert.

Language in Descriptive Writing

HOW DOES A WORD MEAN? DENOTATION AND CONNOTATION

A man was killed and his son was seriously injured in an automobile accident. The boy was rushed to a hospital. The surgeon took one look at him and said, "This is my son! I can't operate on him!" How could the boy have been the surgeon's son?

Most people are baffled by this question. Some reply with a timid, "The boy was adopted?" Others rack their brains, then give up. The answer is quite simple: the surgeon was the boy's mother. The reason people are puzzled is that they are so accustomed to thinking of a surgeon as a man, they do not consider the possibility that it could be a woman. According to the dictionary, the word *surgeon* refers to any physician, male or female, who "diagnoses and treats injury, deformity, and disease by manual and instrumental operations." This definition gives us the word's *denotation,* or dictionary definition. However, the total meaning of a word is not necessarily limited to its denotation. *Surgeon* conjures up in the minds of most people the word's associations, or its *connotation*—an image of a male, usually white, usually middle-aged, probably above average in height, garbed in a gown with a mask over his mouth and nose. But, obviously, surgeons can also be female. Thus, the connotation of a word may lead people astray, as it does in this story.

The advocates of women's liberation are right on target in showing how language can corrupt thought. But in most instances, such as the word *surgeon,* the fault lies not in the word but in society, perhaps the medical society in particular, for traditionally limiting the admission of women to medical schools. So it is natural to think of men when we talk about

123

surgeons, or about pilots, professors, politicians, and business executives, just as we visualize women when we talk about nurses, secretaries, librarians, and housekeepers. But as times change, so will connotations and language. Our guess is that *mankind, countrymen,* and *freshmen* will not be replaced by *peoplekind, countrypeople,* or *freshpeople,* but as more women have moved into traditionally male occupations, we are finding common acceptance of *policewoman, newspaperwoman,* and *chairwoman,* or perhaps even their unisex equivalents, *policeperson* (or *police officer*), *newspaperperson* (or just *journalist*), and *chairperson* (or *chair*). The dictionary already includes *Ms.;* other changes will follow.

Which brings us back to the dictionary and its definitions. To be fair and accurate to lexicographers, those alert and sagacious word-watchers, dictionaries are concerned with both denotations and connotations. The part of a dictionary entry that explains the meaning of a word is denotative. But the discussion of a word and its synonyms involves connotations, or the associations people have with words. Note how this concept is illustrated in the following discussion from the *American Heritage Dictionary* about words that have the same denotations as *fat* but different connotations:

Synonyms: *fat, obese, corpulent, fleshy, stout, portly, pudgy, rotund, plump, chubby.* These adjectives mean having an abundance of flesh, often to excess. *Fat* always implies excessive weight and is generally unfavorable in its connotations. *Obese* is employed principally in medical usage with reference to extreme overweight, and *corpulent* is a more general term for the same connotation. *Fleshy* implies an abundance of flesh that is not necessarily disfiguring. *Stout* and *portly* are sometimes used in polite terms to describe fatness. *Stout,* in stricter application, suggests a thickset, bulky person, and *portly,* one whose bulk is combined with an imposing bearing. *Pudgy* describes one who is thickset and dumpy. *Rotund* suggests roundness of figure in a squat person. *Plump* is applicable to a pleasing fullness of figure, especially in women [note that dictionaries are not immune to sexism]. *Chubby* implies abundance of flesh, usually not to excess.

EUPHEMISMS

Euphemisms—words with overly favorable connotations—are often used to conceal what might be offensive or disturbing. The word *prison* is being replaced by *penal institution* and *correctional facility,* suggesting places less harsh and dehumanizing than those in which we actually incarcerate violators of the law. Another social problem is being made less poignant because the words *indigent, inner-city,* and *low-income* are commonly substituted for *poor,* a term with more explicit connotations. And we no longer have *poor* children; they are *disadvantaged, underprivileged,* or *culturally deprived.*

Euphemism, or "language pollution," or "doublespeak," as some call it, is often intended to obscure or hide the real situation. Bureaucrats are especially skillful in selecting terms with inoffensive connotations, as was evident in the Watergate affair: the Watergate defendants' perjury and destruction of evidence were referred to as *stonewalling;* their unethical procedures as *game plans.* Government officials are not the only ones at fault. Big business no longer *lays off* workers, it *furloughs* them. And labor engages in *work stoppages,* not *strikes.*

Occasionally, but only occasionally, language pollution is reversed, the offensive terms replacing the more polite ones. More newspapers now report that women are *raped* instead of *criminally assaulted,* a word substitution that may contribute to greater public concern about this offense. Similarly, *syphilis* and *gonorrhea,* formerly taboo words, are replacing the polite term *venereal disease* in an effort to arouse public concern.

Sometimes euphemisms are harmless. Like white lies, they may be kinder than the literal truth. One of our ugliest words for people is *crippled;* a pleasanter one is *handicapped.* To many people, being considered old is a terrifying experience, so they sometimes prefer to be called *senior citizens* instead of *old people.* And to give individuals a greater sense of prestige and importance in their work, we often refer to *hair stylists* instead of *barbers, beauticians* instead of *hairdressers, custodians* instead of *janitors, realtors* instead of *real estate salesmen,* and *morticians* instead of *undertakers.* These substitutions and others like them do little harm and make life more tolerable for the people involved. But you should be so alert to the use of words that you recognize euphemisms and generally avoid them in your writing.

EFFECTIVE USE OF WORDS IN DESCRIPTIVE WRITING

At this point, you may be wondering what all this talk about connotations, denotations, and euphemisms has to do with writing, particularly descriptive writing. The general answer is that good writing always depends on the effective use of words. In personal description, words play a dual role: to communicate and to evoke, to let readers both perceive and feel. This twofold purpose is evident even in such a practical and common form of writing as an advertisement. Read the following two passages and decide which one ran as an ad in *Playboy* (compare words in italics*)*:

COPY A	COPY B
Whether *speeding* on the highway or *driving over curving country roads,* the Jaguar E-type *is the best.*	Whether *cruising* on the highway or *deftly stalking through twisting country roads,* the Jaguar E-type *dominates all it surveys.*
It is so handsome that it has been *shown* at the Museum of Modern Art.	*Its styling is so classically distinctive* it has been *displayed* at the Museum of Modern Art.
Beneath that *attractive exterior*	

are engineering features that have enabled it to win at the 24-Hour Race of Le Mans.

Jaguar's independent suspension front and rear *lets the car keep its four wheels on the road even when it's rough.*

The four wheel disc brakes are ventilated in front and mounted inboard in the rear. All E-types are complete with Dunlop Sport 70 whitewall belted radials.

The *excellent* Jaguar V-12 aluminum alloy engine is *exceptionally smooth.* Its 326 cubic inches of capacity is *much* smaller than the 468 cubic inches of capacity of the average American luxury V-8.

In addition to the luxury, comfort and instrumentation that you expect in a Jaguar, there is that *something else* in the Jaguar E-type that gave this automobile its name. Jaguar, *a fine animal, fierce but in full control of itself, excitable but restrained.*

Beneath that *sculptured surface lurks engineering that traces its breeding to the legendary Jaguar victories* at the 24-Hour Race of Le Mans.

Jaguar's independent suspension front and rear *lets the graceful cat keep all four feet on the ground, silky even on rough terrain.*

The four wheel disc brakes are ventilated in front and mounted inboard in the rear. All E-types are complete with Dunlop Sport 70 whitewall belted radials.

The *incredible* Jaguar V-12 aluminum alloy engine *gives the word "smoothness" a new standard to live by.* Its 326 cubic inches of capacity is considerably smaller than the 468 cubic inches of capacity of the average American luxury V-8.

In addition to the luxury, comfort and instrumentation that you expect in a Jaguar, there is that *indefinable quality* in the Jaguar E-type that gave this automobile its name. Jaguar, *a magnificent beast, wild of spirit but in full control of its powers, exuberant yet disciplined.*

Copy A describes a fine machine; Copy B (which is the version that appeared in *Playboy*) suggests an experience, an opportunity to own a car that will make driving an adventure and will win the admiration and envy of others. What creates the difference is the use in B of language that is rich in suggestiveness. From the opening "Whether cruising on the highway or deftly stalking through twisting country roads" to "wild of spirit but in full control of its powers, exuberant yet disciplined," the copy has been directed to the reader's imagination, implying that the Jaguar car is as alive, powerful, graceful, and exciting as the animal itself. Note the references to *stalking, breeding, cat, feet,* and also the evocative quality of the final sentence. Just the contrast between "a fine animal" in Copy A and "a magnificent beast" in B illustrates our point. Although *fine* expresses approval, *magnificent* suggests much more, conveying the idea that something is exalted, superlative, impressive, imposing. Similarly, *animal* is a vague, neutral term, while *beast* conjures up the picture of a powerful, wild creature, prowling for prey, alert for adventure, action, danger, excitement. Given the choice of buying a car that is likened to "a fine animal" or "a magnificent beast" (assuming that money is no object), most people under thirty would opt for the latter. That's what the Jaguar manufacturers are hoping.

Connotative and figurative language are important in nearly all forms of writing, but particularly in personal descriptions. There, as in the Jaguar example, a writer is conveying an experience, trying not only to present information about an automobile but also to show how it feels to own and drive that car. In such descriptions, words rich in associations are more effective than those that mainly transmit information.

However, words and phrases rich in their ability to convey experiences vividly and imaginatively have no place in factual descriptions. In scientific and technical writing, language should be exact and precise, selected to convey a specific meaning, designed to communicate information, not feeling. A factual description of the Jaguar would indicate details about overall length and width, interior headroom and legroom, and engine and trunk space, as well as numerous mechanical specifications. Indeed, there are times and places for words and phrases with little imaginative appeal.

How do you learn to use words skillfully—the right words in the right places? You can't learn in several simple steps. To begin with, it takes a commitment to finding the precise word instead of settling for the first one that pops into your mind. For example, if you were trying to describe the odor in a room, would it occur to you to use any of the following?

stale	smoky	spicy	rancid
musty	fragrant	rich	burnt
greasy	cloying	pungent	sour
damp	heavy	dusty	acrid

It takes a little extra time and effort to look for one of these lively, colorful words instead of just writing "The room smelled good," or "The room smelled bad." But to write effective descriptions, you must take the trouble to search for the exact word that expresses what you have experienced.

If you can't find a suitable word, try a figure of speech. What did the room smell like? Like a crowded bus? A damp basement? A musty attic? A sweaty locker room? A department store perfume counter?

And then there are dictionaries or synonym books. They can be helpful if used cautiously. But either select a synonym you know well or one that is defined thoroughly, like those in our previous dictionary example of *fat*. And be careful if you use a thesaurus, a reference book containing synonyms but no discussion of their meaning. The danger is that you might look up *fat*, for instance, and substitute for it the listed term *voluminous*, an apt word for a fat book but not a fat person. Consequently, use words you know well or words defined precisely for you.

How can you learn more words? This book is no place for a lengthy discourse on vocabulary-building, but we do suggest that you open your eyes and ears to the words in your books, magazines, newspapers, and textbooks, and in the talk, lectures, and conversations of friends, professors, and articulate television commentators. You might jot down some words that interest you, check them in the dictionary, and try them out soon in your conversations to fix them in your memory.

You can also expand your vocabulary through your experiences. If you're around horses at a farm, track, or show, you should pick up from others the meaning of such terms as *foal, colt, yearling; gelding, mare, filly; palomino, roan, pinto*. Or if furniture interests you, antique dealers might help you understand such different styles as Chippendale, Duncan Phyfe, Victorian, Louis XVI, Queen Anne. To write knowledgeably about these and other subjects, you need to be familiar with their specialized terminology. Vocabulary-building is both a bookish activity and one involving a knowledge of the life around you.

But you also need to generate a zest for words, cultivate an interest in them, acquire a feeling for them, struggle and play with them. If you do, in time you will develop a larger and more discriminating vocabulary that will enable you to become a more effective speaker and writer.

Remember that your task, particularly in descriptive writing, is to find the right word, one that says exactly what you mean. It should be primarily denotative for factual descriptions, richly connotative for personal ones. By using the right word to describe what you have seen, smelled, tasted, heard, and felt, you will improve your next paper and future ones. And by noting and considering and developing a fascination for words, you will improve as a writer.

SUMMARY

In descriptive writing, perhaps more than in any other form, effectiveness depends on the skillful use of words. To make others aware of what you have experienced and to communicate your impressions to them, you must choose words that convey exactly what you mean. Consequently, you should have a vocabulary suitable for your subject, and a knowledge of the denotations and connotations of the words you use. A dictionary, synonym book, or thesaurus can help, but what you basically need is a commitment to learning words and to finding the precise one to express your exact meaning.

Writing effective descriptions depends on other factors such as careful observation and meaningful details, but especially important is the skillful use of language. Generally, the greater your knowledge of words and the more careful your selection of them, the better your descriptions will be.

Assignments

For Discussion

1 Explain the following statements:

   a Words do not have meanings; only the people who use them have meanings.

   b If the language is debased or misused, if the meaning of words is obscured, the basis for common judgment is undermined, if not destroyed.

   —Eugene McCarthy

   c People go to dictionaries to find out what words mean while lexicographers (people who write and edit dictionaries) go to people to find out what words mean.

2 In *Confessions of an Advertising Man*, David Ogilvy stated that the two most powerful words a copywriter can use in a headline are *free* and *new*. His research indicates that other effective words include *important*, *sensational, miracle, bargain, hurry, last chance*, and *wanted*. Why do you think these words are appealing? What other words would you add to the list?

3 What do you think are the ten most beautiful words in the language? (Some suggestions: *dawn, mother, murmuring, nevermore*.) The ten ugliest? (Some suggestions: *scab, mud, gonorrhea*.) The saddest? Happiest?

4 Find a term in sports that has a different meaning in another context. In addition, suggest why the term is used as it is in sports. For example, the word *diamond* obviously refers to the shape of the playing field in baseball, but how would you account for *bullpen, dugout, strike*, and numerous other terms?

5 With the trend toward writing comments on report cards instead of giving grades, teachers have learned how to use euphemisms. For example, instead of telling parents that their child is cheating, a teacher might write that the child needs guidance in learning how to abide by the doctrine of fair play. What euphemisms can you suggest for the following qualities: *dirty, fights frequently, lies, steals, disliked by others, lazy, rude, selfish, noisy, usually late*?

6 Fill in the blanks and point out the connotation of each added term:

   a When you tell me to do it, it's nagging; when I tell you to do it, it's

   _____.

   b When you talk to your friends, it's idle chatter; when I talk to mine, it's _____.

   c When you don't like something, you complain; when I don't like something, I _____.

   d My dog is playful; yours is _____.

e I offered helpful suggestions; you offered _____.

f Our basketball team plays an aggressive game; your team plays

_____.

g I am broad-minded; you are _____.

Can you make up any additional sentences?

For Practice

1 Write a response to either of the following:

  a Ed Lane, minister of the Unitarian Church in Westport, Conn., in the church newsletter *Echoes*:

Symbols are important and have their place, yet there is danger of focusing so much on a symbol that it becomes more important than the reality it represents. . . .

In these terms, and in support of women's liberation, de-genderizing language is a diversion into trivia rather than a raising of consciousness and a mutilation of language rather than an accomplishment of equality in status.

The straw that broke the camel's back was the substitution of "chairperson" for "chairman." . . .

"Chairman" did not ever have a sexual connotation for me. Because the word was neutral it was preceded by "Madame" or "Mister" when addressing a particular individual, just as "Jones" is sexually neutral unless preceded by Mr., Miss, etc. . . . and the last syllable of "chairperson" is just as masculine as that of "chairman." . . .

And while we're at it, why discriminate against last syllables? I'm sure that words like *man*agement, *man*date, and *man*datory had their origin in an era in which men made the decisions and gave the orders, so those will have to go also.

Imagine a world with no *brother*hood, hu*man*ness, and not even ro*man*ce.

  b Harriet Duzet, letter in *Intercom*, a newsletter of the Society for Technical Communication:

I would like to go on record as a proponent of "chairperson" because it is, indeed, sexually neuter. In the business and professional world, I believe that women would prefer to be regarded as "people" and not given sexual or marital labels. Yes, the word "chairman" has survived many decades of use because it was apt in a male-dominated world. Now, however, a substantial proportion of the population working outside of the home is female. Semantic changes are overtaking us and what sounds strange today will be commonplace tomorrow. Who would have thought a year ago that "Ms." would not only be accepted but popularly used today?

I object to the terms "chairlady" and "chairwoman" for various reasons. My first objection is that their use forces you to distinguish by sex between chairpersons. My second is that the terms appear similar to the worn-out expressions "charlady" and "charwoman," who performed the most menial of tasks. Further, use of "chairlady" suggests corollary use of the term "chairgentleman," which is obviously absurd.

2 In *Language in Thought and Action,* S. I. Hayakawa points out that, connotatively, words can be neutral—can "purr" (have a favorable effect), or can "snarl" (be insulting to the audience). These three sentences, all describing the same church breakfast, demonstrate how word choice can add different emotive color to description.

> Neutral: Every Sunday, between the church services, the women of the congregation serve a breakfast of scrambled eggs, bacon, grits, biscuits, juice and coffee for $1.25.
>
> "Purr": Every Sunday, between the inspiring services, the untiring ladies of this charming congregation offer an appetizing brunch of fluffy scrambled eggs, crisp bacon, butter-laden grits, light, hot scones, fresh frothy nectar, and steaming *café au lait* for a reasonable $1.25.
>
> "Snarl": Every Sunday, between the deadening services, the female do-gooders of this sleepy congregation ladle out a nauseating mess of leathery scrambled eggs, limp hogback, soggy hominy, heavy, cold buns, stale, flat, juice-flavored water, and tepid java for a presumptuous $1.25.

Write three paragraphs describing something from your own experience—a place, a person, something that has special meaning to you—describing it first in neutral language, then with "purr" and "snarl" connotations. As in the first examples, make use of adjectives and synonyms to accomplish your purpose.

The Varieties of Written English

In Chapter 3, we discussed the varied voices of spoken English—the dialects of different geographical regions and different social communities. We also pointed out that you, as a speaker of English, have many personal voices available to you—one for chatting with close friends, another for conversing with parents or grandparents, another for talking to strangers. Depending upon your audience and the circumstances, you shift freely back and forth among these different modes of speaking. Most of the personal writing you were asked to do in Part 1 of this book was in a style close to conversational English. But the chances are that as you moved through the assignments from journal writing to personal essay, your writing style automatically changed. Your voice came closer to the one you reserve for strangers: a voice characterized by relative freedom from regionalisms and community usages. In other words, you moved closer to another variety of English: the dialect of written English. As you change from the intimate audience of your personal writing to a more public one, you will need to operate more and more in that dialect.

In Chapter 3, we also exemplified some of the differences in the characteristics of casual spoken English and writing that emulate a conversational essay style. Many of the distinctions we made between written and spoken English will apply to any writing situation, no matter how informal or formal. Written English pays closer attention to sentence and paragraph structure. The rambling disjointedness characteristic of our speech must be replaced by tighter structures in writing: modifiers should be placed near the words they modify; transitional or connecting words should be added and carefully placed in the sentence; more careful word choice should be exercised. And as we pointed out, written English avoids regionalisms, using instead universally accepted vocabulary and syntax. But even though you are expected to use more conservative and formal sentence structures, you do not need to write in the same style for every situation, any more than you speak in the same manner at all times. Just as spoken English permits a variety of styles, so does written English.

This variety, however, does not result from the same factors affecting your spoken language. We have seen that even in spoken English the "distance" from the audience can be an influence. If speaker and listeners are close in age and interests, the speaker uses a different level of language than that used when talking to parents, teachers, or strangers. But in written English, this separation is not only generational and social, but physical. Gone is the face-to-face contact of speaking; your concrete, live audience is replaced by an abstract, hypothetical one. What you write is the only contact you will have. But it is hard to address someone who is not there; therefore, you need to imagine an audience, one that may be as sympathetic as your friends, as indifferent as a stranger, or even as hostile to your ideas as the registrar when you ask for an extension of fee payment. Then you can choose the kind of writing that is acceptable to a particular audience, as well as one that is appropriate for your purpose in writing, and for the writing occasion.

CASUAL, GENERAL, AND SPECIALIZED ENGLISH

An analysis of three examples can help to clarify the relationship of audience, purpose, and occasion in determining appropriate usage.

1. Well, you just sour your dough. You start it off with a little yeast and flour and water, and you set it up close to the stove with the lid off, 'cause they say there's so much wild yeast in the air. Then you just set it up there and you leave it sit for thirty-six hours or so. And it gets a tang to it. And then when you get ready to make your pancakes, you pour a little bit of this in a bowl, the way I do it. Now most of the people don't do it this way. I keep quite a little sour dough on hand. Most of the people, just a cupful.
—Quoted in Carol Hill and Bruce Davidson, *Subsistence U.S.A.*

Even though taken out of its social situation, this paragraph contains clues to it. The purpose here is to give another person a general idea of how sourdough is made. The highly conversational tone almost suggests a face-to-face relationship between writer and audience; the choice of everyday, simple vocabulary and the use of the personal pronouns *I* and *you* add to the intimate tone. In the statement, "You pour a little bit of this in the bowl," the use of *this* indicates that the speaker is pointing to the mixture—speaker and listener are almost sharing the experience. This close relationship is additionally signaled by the simple sentence structure throughout and the fragment at the end, which convey only minimal information. Sentence introducers, such as *now, well,* and the clipped word *'cause,* also bear

133

witness to the informal, conversational quality characteristic of close social contact. All of these combine to produce a distinctive style of writing: a written variety that we call *Casual English.*

2. Sourdough ranks among the world's most controversial foods. Like fried chicken or spaghetti sauce, it has its factions and fanatics, each of whom knows more about it than the next fellow, or thinks he does. There is the old-fashioned type who believes that the only real and effective starter is made from hops, water, and flour, and must be at least a couple of decades old—a kind of eternal flame that should never be extinguished. And then there is the type of aficionado who is convinced that potato water makes a better starter . . . with a boost from today's active dry yeast, and, though he will concede that a starter *can* improve almost indefinitely as it ages, he tosses his out at the end of each year. About the only point on which Phil and the others agree is that a starter should not be kept in a metal container, for its ingredients corrode almost all metals; thus Phil's kitchen boasts the ubiquitous earthenware crock of the true sourdough devotee.

—Dale Brown, *American Cooking: The Northwest*

Again on the subject of sourdough cookery, this paragraph has markedly different characteristics from the preceding one. The purpose is still to inform the audience about the topic, but the writing situation is obviously not similar. Here, the writer speaks to a distant audience: a stranger in the room. He cannot point to one sourdough batter and then another. Instead, he is forced by the situation to supply information, and in doing so must use more precise language. And in order to convey details, the sentence structure takes on complexity and length. The longest sentence in the previous example of Casual English contained twenty-three words, but, with the exception of the first, all sentences in paragraph 2 exceed that—the longest having forty-four.

Further evidence of the writer's distance from his audience is in his use of the neutral third-person pronouns, resulting in a more formal tone than was projected by the *you* of the first example. However, some writers prefer to use the second-person impersonal *you* to establish a more intimate relationship with a general audience than is possible with the third person.

Other features of the second example that add formality and distance are the choice of words and the lack of conversational sentence openers such as *Well.* Although most words in the passage are suitable for a general audience, others are addressed to one with a fairly high level of education (note especially the words *aficionado* and *ubiquitous*). Formal grammatical structures such as *each of whom* also point to an educated audience.

Taken together, all these factors create a style of writing distinctively different from that of Casual English, one we call *General English.*

3. For the manufacture of yeast, most authorities have recommended that subsequent to the treatment with malt the mash should be "soured" by the action of lactic acid bacteria, a culture of which is added in the final stages of the process and allowed to act for a period of 12 to 15 hours at a temperature of 59° C. The precise effect of this treatment is obscure. It is claimed on the one hand to bring about a hydrolysis of the proteins present in the grain extract and thus render them more readily available for yeast growth.

—Magnus Pyke, "The Technology of Yeasts"

Again, essentially the same topic is dealt with, but purpose, audience, and occasion are drastically changed. The purpose of this excerpt from a scientific text is not to give a practical, general description, but a detailed technical explanation of the process. The social context is a classroom or laboratory. The audience is not a general one, but highly specialized, familiar with the scientific jargon. Note that the writer expects his readers to understand 59° C and *hydrolysis*. In addition, the writer usually separates himself from the audience as much as possible: *authorities* recommend, not the author; his quotation marks around *soured* almost apologize for the near-casual tone of this commonplace usage; impersonality is also conveyed by introductions such as "It is claimed" or "This researcher has observed," instead of "I have observed." In such writing, *I* is used sparingly, if at all.

To convey precise information, the sentences are long and involved: the first sentence alone contains fifty-eight words. Most of the verbs are passive —"should be soured," "is added . . . and allowed," "is claimed"—contributing not only to the complexity of sentence structure but adding an even greater tone of impersonality by removing any human agents.

This paragraph represents a variety of written English characteristically different from the other two, one that we call *Specialized English.* In this book, any writing utilizing a special vocabulary as in this example, or that makes artistic use of figurative language (as in literary writing), will fit this category. In other words, Specialized English is a variety aimed at a particular audience with a special educational background or written primarily to appeal to the artistic senses of the audience in order to delight as well as inform.

MIXING STYLES

We do not intend to imply that all writing falls neatly into these three categories; human nature and language usage do not permit such simplicity. But these are convenient starting points of classification. Little writing will be purely one variety or another. Instead, as do regional and social dialects, the three varieties tend to overlap.

This overlapping occurs when a writer who is using predominantly one style or variety dips into another to deal with a special problem or purpose. Particularly in dialogue sections, many autobiographical narratives are predominantly written in Casual English, but may exhibit some characteristics of General English in expository passages. Personal essays written to a

WRITTEN VARIETY	USE IN WRITING
CASUAL ENGLISH	Limited use: personal narrative and essays, dialogue, letters to friends and relatives, writing addressed to peers
GENERAL ENGLISH	Unlimited use: magazine writing, books appealing to a mass audience, newspaper writing, term papers, nontechnical reports, letters to editors and business people, argument papers, written examinations, most college assignments, literary writing
SPECIALIZED ENGLISH	Limited to a particular subject and audience. Specialized technical or professional writing; academic writing; theses and dissertations; legal drafts and documents; literary writing

general audience, like the Bombeck example on pages 18–19, are basically in General English with a few features borrowed from Casual. In addition, autobiographies such as Eldridge Cleaver's *Soul on Ice* make extensive use of such a mix. Many quasi-scientific articles written for magazines with popular appeal, such as *Psychology Today* and *Scientific American,* are usually in General English, interspersed with some vocabulary items of Specialized English. This textbook, for example, is mostly in General English,

AUDIENCE	LANGUAGE FEATURES	VOICE
Familiar: close in some way to writer, mutual knowledge and experience	Vocabulary: simple words, slang, and localisms. Sentences: short, simple sentences; fragments; compound, coordinate sentences. Punctuation: individualized and relatively free from conventional rules	Subjective: personal, intimate, friendly tone; use of first-person pronouns and references
General: distant, but acknowledged. Audience needs informative details	Vocabulary: generally recognized and current. Sentences: longer and more complex than in Casual English; coordinate and subordinate structures. Punctuation: tighter adherence to rules, less individualized choice	Neutral: generally third person; impersonal *you*
Select audience: distant from writer. Audience has specialized background	Vocabulary: specialized technical jargon; literary devices. Sentences: long and highly complex; high percentage of subordinate-coordinate structures. Punctuation: rigid adherence to rules	Objective: highly impersonal and formal; third person; strict avoidance of personal pronouns

with some characteristics of Casual—the use of the impersonal *you* and the occasional direct references to you as audience. Because we are writing to a general audience, we avoid technical jargon as much as possible, being careful to define any technical terms that are necessary.

As a student of writing, you should not only be aware of the general characteristics of each variety of written English, but you also should realize that each can be mixed with the others. To become an effective writer, you should be able to judge when mixing varieties is beneficial to your purpose and when it is detrimental. For instance, the word *soured* in the example of Specialized English did no real harm to the tone and level of its language usage. Likewise, a few slang words interjected into a paper written in General English might add life and interest, but an excess could seriously change the style you are attempting to establish. If you wish to maintain consistency, you must take care that the written variety you have chosen is not overshadowed by the inclusion of too many items from the others.

FEATURES OF THE VARIETIES OF WRITTEN ENGLISH

The chart on pages 136–37 can help you to become familiar with the general characteristics of the three written varieties. But remember that even though writing can be broadly categorized, no two pieces of writing are exactly the same. Each bears the stamp of a writer's own style.

SUMMARY

In Chapter 3 we pointed out that narrative writing permits a wide range of language usage. In the writing of realistic dialogue all the stylistic options of spoken English are available, including regionalisms, slang, and even usages generally considered nonstandard. As a rule, the scope of language in descriptive writing is not that broad, except perhaps in descriptions narrated by a literary character. The colorful descriptions in *Huckleberry Finn* exemplify this possibility; because Huck is the narrator in the novel, the descriptive sections are expressed in his unique manner with the same social and geographical dialect characteristics of his dialogue.

Other descriptive writing, however, particularly factual or objective description, calls for an idiom characterized by standard usages, by avoidance of regionalisms, and generally by features closer to those of Casual or General written English than to those of free, conversational spoken English. But because you are often asked to write for a broader audience than you were with personal narratives, you are then committed to a more general use of vocabulary and grammatical structures. The voice in the writing should remain yours, but should not be the intimate one reserved for your journal or your closest associates. Strive instead to reproduce the voice you reserve for a friendly but less familiar audience, such as for an aunt or uncle you like.

To resolve confusion about appropriate language use, you might think of the varieties of written English as operating on a continuum from very informal usage to extremely formal usage:

Informal $\longrightarrow \longrightarrow \longrightarrow \longrightarrow \longrightarrow \longrightarrow \longrightarrow \longrightarrow \longrightarrow$ Formal

Casual $\longrightarrow \longrightarrow \longrightarrow$ General $\longrightarrow \longrightarrow \longrightarrow$ Specialized

On the continuum, the language style of most descriptive writing is closer to General than is much narrative writing. However, you should not find moving from one language style to another difficult in written English. You do it many times a day in spoken English. Remember how easily you shift from the intimate, relaxed style of your conversations in the hall to a more formal usage in classroom discussions? With practice, you will become equally proficient in changing modes in written English.

Assignments

For Discussion

1 Specify the written variety of each of the following passages and explain your choice.

a   America is rather like life. You can easily find in it what you look for. If you look for skyscrapers or cowboys or cocktail parties or gangsters or business connections or political problems or women's clubs, they will certainly be there. You can be very hot there or very cold. You can explore the America of your choice by plane or train, by hitch-hike or on foot. It will probably be interesting, and it is sure to be large.

    —E. M. Forster, *Two Cheers for Democracy*

b   For a number of days before the nymph is ready to leave the water, gross morphological changes take place. The nymph gradually darkens in color, from a mossy green to an opaque brown; the wing sheaths swell until they stand above the abdomen, an outward sign of the massive growth of powerful flight muscles; the compound eyes progressively enlarge until they meet in the center of the head; and as the tissues of the specialized labium degenerate, new mouthparts form to suit the adult's feeding habits.

    —John Farrar, "Emergence of the Green Darner," *Natural History*

c   Look around you; what do you see? Long, stringy, greasy, smelly, lice-infested hair, patched and torn and patched again blue jeans and tie-dyed tee shirts. On which sex? Both! Unless there is a prominent mustache or beard, the males and females look the same. These kids think they are "cool" and "hip to the trick." They sit around and meditate or protest on the Court House steps for love and peace instead of war. They rebel against our established and wonderful way of life and try to destroy it. We who love our life style have to conquer the hippies.

    —Student paper

d Like their relatives—leafhoppers, spittlebugs, cicadas, aphids, and scale insects—most of the treehoppers that one encounters in the United States are fairly ordinary-looking insects, the sort of things all but a naturalist or an orchard owner would very likely overlook. But move south towards the tropics and these insects become an array of elaborate monstrosities. They remain, in essence, the same humble insects, but carry around on their backs extravagant structures, the purposes of which are by no means clear to scientists.

—Lewis L. Deitz, "Mild-mannered Minimonsters"

e Before I had gone that 50 yards, I noticed an uneasy feeling. Then, just as I realized I was getting dizzy, I fell. Sitting there in two feet of water, I couldn't get up. The world seemed to be moving back and forth. What I had not noticed before I began to walk was that the entire sheet of water was moving—mostly out, but with small undulations, unrippled. The moving water and the still land around had collided in my eyes and bounced off the ear balancers, so all I could do was fall. I sat there several moments, smiling into the sea, relieved to know why I was soaked.

—Charles Jones, "A Place Apart"

f In children the infection [osteomyelitis] is caused by organisms such as the staphylococci and less commonly by streptococci or pneumococci. The germs usually reach the bone through the bloodstream from a focus elsewhere in the body. Osteomyelitis can also be caused by direct spread from infected tissue in the vicinity of bone, or as a result of a wound or open fracture.

—Adrian E. Flatt, "Bones and Muscles and Their Disorders,"
Family Medical Guide

g Acute osteomyelitis of children starts as a localized infection of the yet-uncalcified ends of the shaft of a growing bone. This infectious process rapidly extends to the medullary cavity of the shaft whence it may perforate through the cortex to the periosteum separating the latter from the bone by formation of a subperiosteal abscess; or it may dissect through the epiphysis (the end of the bone, developed separately as part of a joint, and which later unites with the shaft) into the near-by articulation, causing a purulent arthritis.

—Charles Phillips Emerson and Jane Elizabeth Taylor, *Essentials of Medicine*

h *What* and I had an unpleasant time of it during my childhood. Like many of us I was told never to respond with "What?" "Tommy?" "What?" was to be replaced by "Tommy?" "Yes, Sir?" or "Tommy?" "Yes, Ma'am?" or to my peers, "Tommy?" "Yes?" "What?" meaning "What did you say?" was another no-no. I was told to say, "I beg your pardon?" I never understood why I should beg the pardon of someone if *he* was mumbling.

—Thomas H. Middleton, "What's What"

2 Why must writers be concerned about their audience when they choose a written variety of English?

For Practice

1 Write two brief character sketches of yourself: one to include in a letter to a new pen pal who is your age and a freshman at another college; the second to include in an application to the Peace Corps. (Review the chart on pages 136–37 for the characteristics of Casual and General English.)
2 Write two descriptive paragraphs of an eyesore on your campus: one for inclusion in a letter to a friend or relative; the other to be included in a letter to the president of the college.
3 Using the three examples on sourdough as models, write three contrastive paragraphs—one in Casual, one in General, and one in Specialized English—about a topic or activity that interests you. The first two paragraphs may be personal description; the paragraph in Specialized English should be factual description.

Sentence
Strategies
in Descriptive
Writing

As we indicated in Chapter 4, one way to achieve sentence variety is to move adjunct phrases indicating manner, place, or time to the beginning of the sentence. You can move other sentence structures as well: to add special emphasis, to achieve greater clarity, to break the monotony of too many similar sentences. You can also provide clarifying or colorful details by adding modifiers to elements of the subject or the predicate, or to the sentences as a whole. The latter—the addition of modifiers to a simple sentence that serves as the base clause of an expanded sentence—can be accomplished in two ways. One is to pile up modifiers before the base clause, resulting in what is usually called a *periodic* sentence, as in this example where the base clause is italicized:

> When the students have left, and when few staff members are around, *the campus is serenely beautiful.*

Another way to add sentence modifiers is to state the base clause first, then pile up modifiers after it:

> *They were silent and intent,* facing the wind, feathers ruffling, eyes turned upward.

A sentence in this form is called a *cumulative* (or *loose*) sentence; most sentences follow this pattern, perhaps because we usually think of the main idea first.

Expanded or complex sentences are used in all kinds of writing. For the purposes of this chapter, however, we will examine the ways in which short simple sentences can be combined to carry the rich details that add life and color to description.

COMBINING SENTENCES BY INSERTION

Combining sentences is a creative process; we not only change a simple sentence to a more complex one, but we can combine a given set of sentences in various ways. Let's look first at how we might add descriptive details to the subject noun:

The dog is a German Shepherd.
The dog is large.
The dog is black.
The dog is menacing.

These short sentences would not be effective in any kind of writing; to the contrary, they create a childish tone, a "primer" style. Since the subject and the verb are the same in all four sentences, the repeated information, superfluous and distracting, can be eliminated, leaving modifiers that we can add to the base sentence. The process goes like this:

The dog is a German Shepherd. (base sentence)
~~The dog is~~ large. (insert sentence: subject, verb deleted)
~~The dog is~~ black. (insert sentence: subject, verb deleted)
~~The dog is~~ menacing. (insert sentence: subject, verb deleted)

With the deadwood gone, we can expand the base sentence by inserting the remaining material in a number of ways:

a. The large, black, menacing dog is a German Shepherd.
b. The dog, which is large, black, and menacing, is a German Shepherd.
c. Large, black, and menacing, the dog is a German Shepherd.
d. The dog is a German Shepherd—large, black, and menacing.

All these are possibilities; you choose any one of them on a given occasion depending on what you want to emphasize. Sentence *b* gives the least amount of importance to the dog's characteristics, concentrating instead on its breed. Sentences *c* and *d* emphasize the dog's description; the placement of these characteristics at the end in *d* results in the most menacing statement of all.

The process for adding modifiers to the predicate is similar to that for expanding the subject, as this example demonstrates.

The man carves animals. (base sentence)
The man carves patiently. (insert sentence)
The man is sitting on his porch. (insert sentence)
The man is chewing tobacco. (insert sentence)
The man has a sharp knife in his hand. (insert sentence)

143

Here, the subject "the man" is the same in all sentences and many of the verb forms are needlessly repetitive; all predicates can modify the verb *carves*. Eliminating them and inserting what remains into the base sentence can result in these possibilities:

The man patiently carves animals, sitting on his porch, chewing tobacco, a sharp knife in his hand.

The man carves animals patiently, sitting on his porch, chewing tobacco, a sharp knife in his hand.

A sharp knife in his hand, the man patiently carves animals, sitting on his porch, chewing tobacco.

Chewing tobacco, the man patiently carves animals, sitting on his porch, a sharp knife in his hand.

See how many more you can do without creating ambiguity. Notice that "sitting on his porch" deals with place; "patiently" says something about the manner in which the man carves. Thus, they can be moved as freely as the adjuncts discussed in Chapter 4.

Several college-level books about sentence-combining techniques are available if you wish to pursue this writing device. We want only to touch on the general principles here, hoping to make you more aware of this sentence-expanding process. In talking, you subconsciously rely on these techniques. But in writing, you may often play it safe by sticking to short, simple sentences. Consequently, when revising your first draft, search for such sentences, particularly successive ones that repeat subjects or elements in the predicate, or contain references to them. Then experiment in combining your sentences to form richer and more sophisticated ones.

Bound and Free Modifiers

In English, we can take a number of liberties with the positions in a sentence that added modifiers can hold. But not all modifiers are equally movable. Some are *bound;* that is, they are tied to the head word they modify—the subject noun, the object noun, or the main verb. Others are *free,* easily movable like those in our sentence-combining example about the man carving. When speaking, you are intuitively aware of these restrictions; otherwise you would have trouble communicating. But in writing, we often tune out our language sense, failing to listen to what we write. We need, therefore, to set up conscious warning signals alerting us to the wealth of language ability we already have. Let's look at a few examples of bound modifiers to jog your unconscious memory:

1. Noun-head modifiers:

> *ten little purple*   marbles
> (noun modifiers)   (noun head)

Try to shift any of these italicized modifiers without adding a breath pause. If you cannot, that means they are bound to their position before the noun head. And bound they are.

2. Verb-head modifiers:

> He *completely* forgot the assignment.

Again, extensive reordering proves difficult; *forgot completely,* or *forgot the assignment completely* are both possible; but we can't reorder *completely* to the front of the sentence, as we can adjuncts; it must stay close to the verb in the predicate.

These examples should make you aware that we cannot freely move modifiers about, that there are grammatical restrictions on rearranging some elements in a sentence. But what of the ones that can be shifted?

Not all free modifiers are equally free, and some are more restricted in some contexts than in others. In general, noun-head modifiers can be placed before or after the noun head, but cannot be moved to another position in the sentence. Let's look at some of the possibilities of several kinds of phrases that can serve as noun modifiers:

> A large man *with a sneer on his face* threatened the porter.

Prepositional phrase modifying noun-head *man*—normal word order.

> *With a sneer on his face,* a large man threatened the porter.

Prepositional phrase moved to front position for special emphasis.

> The man *standing near the door* held a gun on the crowd.

Here, an *-ing* verb phrase (participal phrase functioning as an adjective) modifies the noun-head *man,* and appears in normal word order.

> *Standing near the door,* the man held a gun on the crowd.

This placement, desirable in some instances to put special emphasis on the location of the man, is not always possible. If the expanded noun phrase occurred in the context of the following sentence, the *-ing* phrase would be bound to its position after *the older man:*

> The young man at the teller's desk demanded the money; the older man *standing near the door* held a gun on the crowd.

Here, the phrase is restrictive—that is, it is bound to the position after the noun phrase *the older man* because its main function is to distinguish him from the other man rather than to give his location in the bank.

> Billie Jean King, *flushed with victory,* jumped the net to console her opponent. (past participle phrase modifying the noun head *Billie Jean King*)
>
> *Flushed with victory,* Billie Jean King jumped the net to console her opponent.

Moving the italicized phrase to the front of the sentence merely gives it greater emphasis; it still modifies *Billie Jean King.*

> Attempts *to reorder infinitive phrases such as this* are generally unsuccessful.

Can you logically reorder the italicized infinitive phrase, which modifies the noun head *attempts?* Is it bound or free?

You can probably see from these few examples that a good rule of thumb is to keep noun modifiers close to the head they modify. The same holds true for modifiers bound to the verb: they should not lose their heads.

Some modifiers, however, logically seem to modify the sense of the whole sentence, rather than just a single element. These *sentence modifiers,* as they are sometimes called, have almost unlimited flexibility, depending upon your purpose, as in this example:

> Martha sobbed soundlessly, *standing there in the rain.*
> *Standing there in the rain,* Martha sobbed soundlessly.
> Martha, *standing there in the rain,* sobbed soundlessly.

The normal word order—placement of the italicized modifier at the end—gives it only the same status that any other adjunct of place would have in the sentence: "Martha sobbed soundlessly *there, under the tree, by the car,*" and so on. In the second sentence, placing the modifier before the base clause gives added importance to the location where the sobbing was done, an emphasis only slightly lessened in the third version, in which *Martha* receives the positional emphasis.

These brief discussions of inserting modifiers by combining sentences and of arranging these insertions in various ways in a base sentence suggest how you can create more complex sentence structures. By so doing, you can add a wealth of descriptive detail to each sentence. However, there are pitfalls to this process. Too many modifiers added to a noun or verb head can make the sentence heavy and difficult to read. Although these insertions may result in effective description by appealing to the reader's senses —sight, hearing, taste, touch, and smell—too many can produce sentences that are almost unreadable:

> All the ten thousand "catch-as-catch-can" spectators, old and young alike, standing with their heads thrown back and their mouths dropped in awe, emitting not a sound, not even the shuffle of feet nor the rustle of

clothing, watched in frozen silence, a silence that seemed almost an entity in itself, the drama of life and death, of hesitation and despair, being enacted on the bridge.

As you can see, this sentence is rich in detail, but it contains so many inserted modifiers between the subject and the predicate that the base sentence—*all the spectators watched the drama being enacted on the bridge*—almost gets lost. When you wish to add this much detail, you would do well to use the cumulative sentence we mentioned earlier, which the late Francis Christensen, in his work on sentence analysis, suggested was perhaps the best vehicle available for carrying a heavy load of modifiers.[1] In a cumulative sentence, the base clause is kept intact and modifiers are added after it, as in this example:

> *Writing is often a frustrating task,* demanding long hours of thought, requiring us to sharpen both wit and pencil, forcing us to discipline ourselves to inevitable criticism—personal and public.

As you can see, the italicized base sentence is followed, rather than interrupted, by a series of modifiers. This arrangement gives you the same advantage of clarity and focus possible in basic simple sentences, but at the same time allows you to add much detailed information at many levels of generality.

Levels of Generality

Since the term *levels of generality* may seem new and confusing, let's analyze some examples. We have seen that modifiers can add more specific information to a fairly general statement, permitting us to move in the sentence from general to specific. A basic sentence pattern operates at only one level—a very general level—while an expanded sentence with many modifying structures can include many levels or layers—general modified by specific, modified by more specific, modified by even more specific, and so on. Let's look at an expanded noun phrase so that you can see the principles involved. We will start with the basic noun phrase *a cow* and add these modifying phrases:

black and white
with a bell around her neck
that jangled raucously with every step

---

[1] Francis Christensen, "A Generative Rhetoric of the Sentence," *Journal of the Conference on College Composition and Communication,* October 1963, pp. 155–61.

147

We can diagram the expanded phrase like this:

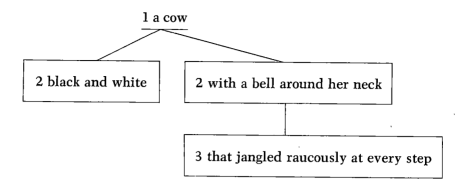

The numbers indicate the levels of generality of the various phrases. *A cow* is the noun head in the expanded phrase and is its most general part, so we have labeled it level 1; *black and white* and *with a bell around her neck* both provide specific information about the head, *a cow*, so they are at level 2. *That jangled raucously at every step* results in even greater specificity by giving detailed information about the bell; because it modifies *bell* rather than *cow*, it is at level 3.

Now let's consider levels of generality in sentences, particularly in cumulative sentences. Here is a diagram of our earlier example of a cumulative sentence:

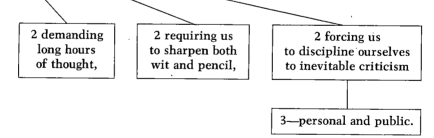

The main subject-predicate (SP) clause, as the sentence head—the structure to which modifiers can be added—contains the most general information. The three *-ing* phrases at level 2 add specific details. Because all three modify the base clause (note that any of them can be omitted without damaging the logical sense of the sentence), they are all at the same level of generality. But the phrase "personal and public" refers to "criticism" rather than to the base clause and therefore adds a third dimension of detail—a third level of generality—to the sentence. Let's look at the same sentence arranged as Christensen suggests to indicate the movement from general to specific:

1 Writing is often a frustrating task,
   2 demanding long hours of thought,
   2 requiring us to sharpen both wit and pencil,
   2 forcing us to discipline ourselves to inevitable criticism
      3—personal and public.

You are probably wondering, "Why make such an issue of all this?" Certainly, you have no difficulty in creating highly modified sentences laden with many levels of generality. But being aware of *how* you move from general to specific in your sentences can help you to provide signals to your readers that will enable them to sort out your sentence structure and understand your meaning more easily. For instance, in our example, all the items at level 2 have the same basic structure, each beginning with an *-ing* verb form; this parallelism in their structure indicates that they are at the same level of generality. Because not all of us have the innate sense of style to produce such parallelism consistently, some conscious knowledge of the modification levels and their relationship to writing style can improve our writing.

Varying Cumulative Sentences

Many variables are possible within the basic pattern of the cumulative sentence:

BASE CLAUSE *Modifier 1, Modifier 2, Modifier 3,* etc.

Let's analyze some of them.

First, here is a sentence arranged to show its two levels of generality:

1 They [the Indians] are covered in the corn,
   2 swamped in the oil,
   2 hidden in the coal of Franklin County,
   2 run over by the trains,
   2 turned phantom by the stockyards.

                                    —Saul Bellow

Note that here, as in the preceding example, the author has relied upon parallel structure to signal that the modifiers (past participle phrases) are equal to each other or *coordinate.* One way to test if modifiers are coordinate is to see if one can be omitted without substantially changing the meaning. Another test is to see if the modifiers can be switched. For instance, can the third phrase precede the first without serious change in meaning? Obviously it can. When modifiers are not dependent on each other for meaning

149

and when they have a parallel relationship to the main clause, they are said to be in *coordinate sequence.*

But what about this sentence?

```
1  Then the pair moves on,
   2  leaving the eggs to the sea,
      3  which gently stirs them and packs the sand about them,
         4  grain by grain.
```
—Rachel Carson

In this cumulative sentence, the modifiers are *subordinate* to each other. The meaning of each is dependent upon the modifier preceding it: the relative clause introduced by *which* in level 3 adds description to the noun head *the sea* in level 2; *grain by grain* of level 4 refers to *packs the sand* in level 3. Because none can be reordered or (with the exception of level 4) omitted without the one following it, the modifiers are in *subordinate sequence.* The writer does not use parallel structure here; it would falsely indicate the possibility of coordinate relationship.

Both of these sentences are fairly uncomplicated examples of cumulative sentences: the first limited to coordinate modifiers and the second to a series of subordinate ones. But cumulative sentences can be very complex and characterized by mixed sequences, as in this student example:

```
1  The Berlin street was alive with activity—
   2  everywhere people walking or riding,
   2  Volkswagens swarming like flies,
      3  black and noisy,
   2  young children with red cheeks playing on the sidewalk,
   2  elderly women walking slowly,
      3  huddled in their woolen coats
         4  clutched tightly against the bitter wind,
   2  all ages riding bicycles.
```

Notice the student's effective use of parallel structure to keep the level 2 coordinate modifiers sorted out: each has a noun-phrase subject followed by an *-ing* verb form.

As with other sentence types, one way to achieve variety in cumulative sentences is to start the sentence with a transitional phrase:

```
Transitional phrase And for the players themselves,
   1  they seem expert listlessly,
      2  each intent on a private dream of making it—
         3  making it into the big leagues and the big money,
            4  the own-your-own bowling alley money;
```

```
1   they seem specialists like any other,
  2   not men playing a game
    3   because all men are boys
      4   time is trying to outsmart.
```
—John Updike

This sentence also illustrates another means of varying cumulative sentences: by stringing them together as compounds, using a comma and a conjunction or (as here) a semicolon to join the main clauses.

So far, we have been showing you how to analyze sentences already created by other writers. How can you create a richly textured cumulative sentence in your own writing? Suppose in your first draft you have written this basic sentence:

She was practically brought up at the tennis club.

In revising, you decide that this sentence is vague and anemic. What to do? First, you might insert a modifier to the subject:

The daughter of two tennis pros, she was practically brought up at the tennis club.

Then some to the verb:

The daughter of two tennis pros, she was practically brought up—*first with tolerance, then with encouragement*—at the tennis club.

Then you might change the basic structure to a cumulative form:

The daughter of two tennis pros, she was practically brought up—first with tolerance, then with encouragement—at the tennis club, *playing in a sandbox, taking lessons, working as a ball girl, and eventually winning club tournaments.*

Finally, you would need to insert modifiers in some of these:

The daughter of two tennis pros, she was practically brought up—first with tolerance, then with encouragement—at the tennis club, playing in a sandbox *within sight of the courts,* taking lessons *all year round,* working as a ball girl *in her spare time,* and eventually winning club tournaments.

You would now have a sentence that is rich in descriptive detail but that, despite its length, is not at all awkward or hard to understand.

Our purpose in these analytical discussions of the inserting process and the cumulative sentence has not been to make you an expert at analyzing sentences, but to give you the background you need to employ these devices for sentence expansion and variation in your own writing. In the next chapter, we will look at some of the pitfalls you should avoid in creating richly modified sentences. But now, let's look at some other complex sentence structures that are useful in description and many other kinds of writing: two clauses joined by words that indicate something about the logical relationship between the ideas in the two.

COMPLEX SENTENCES: SUBORDINATE SEQUENCES

In Chapter 4, we indicated that one way to join sentences or clauses was to compound them by adding coordinate conjunctions such as *and* or *or*, formulated thus:

SP *and* SP *and* SP.

In compound sentences, as you recall, the SP clauses are independent, or base, clauses, restricted only by a relationship of chronological or logical order. All the clauses are at the same level of generality; none serves to modify any other, as in:

1 The pitcher stepped up to the mound *and*
1 the fans fell temporarily silent as he started his wind-up *and*
1 by the time he released the pitch, he had whipped them into a crescendo of sound.

Although superficially similar in structure to compound sentences, complex sentences differ greatly in the relationships established between clauses. If you experiment a bit with the following examples, you can see why sentences with subordinate clauses are called "complex." Decide which choices are possible and which are not.

1. The weather was very bad; (Base clause)
   - therefore,
   - so,
   - however,
   - but
   - nevertheless,
   - as
   - otherwise,
   - furthermore,
   - whether,

   the men did not hesitate to go fishing. (subordinate clause)

2. The men did not hesitate to go fishing, (Base clause)
   - therefore,
   - moreover,
   - however,
   - because
   - although
   - in spite of
   - the fact that
   - whether

   the weather was very bad. (Subordinate clause)

You probably discovered that only these choices are logically possible for the first example:

The weather was very bad; $\left\{\begin{array}{l} \text{but} \\ \text{however,} \\ \text{nevertheless,} \end{array}\right\}$ $\left.\begin{array}{l} \text{the men did not} \\ \text{hesitate to go} \\ \text{fishing.} \end{array}\right.$

Conversely, none of these possibilities is appropriate for example 2, which permits only these:

The men did not hesitate to go fishing, $\left\{\begin{array}{l} \text{although} \\ \text{in spite of} \\ \quad \text{the fact that} \end{array}\right\}$ $\left.\begin{array}{l} \text{the weather was} \\ \text{very bad.} \end{array}\right.$

Even from this simple exercise, you should realize that you do not have free choice of joining possibilities: that some subordinators work better for some purposes than for others.

Using the same examples, let's look at some of the other peculiarities of subordinate sentences. Asking yourself these questions will help you to write this kind of sentence more effectively.

1. Can the final clauses in both these examples be shifted to initial sentence position? Obviously not; it works for the second, but not for the first.

   However the men did not hesitate to go fishing, the weather was very bad.
   Although the weather was very bad, the men did not hesitate to go fishing.

   You can see from the examples that shifting the clause beginning with *however* is not grammatically possible; shifting the *although* clause is no problem.

2. Can the subordinator be moved to positions other than the initial one in the clause?

   The weather was very bad; the men, *however,* did not hesitate to go fishing. *Or* The weather was very bad; the men did not hesitate to go fishing, *however.* (Both are grammatical possibilities.)
   The weather was very bad; the men, *although,* did not hesitate to go fishing. (not grammatical)
   In these examples, *however* has a property that subordinators like *although* do not: it can be moved freely within the clause.

   As you can see, clauses can become subordinate in different ways, depending on the subordinator. We will refer to the two types of subordinators as *subordinating conjunctions* and *transitional adverbs.*

Subordinating Conjunctions

Subordinating conjunctions can be moved only by taking the whole clause; the most common ones are *after, although, as, because, before, since, if, whether,* and *while.* Remembering that all subordinators signal that a complete SP clause follows, let's look at an example (the subordinating conjunction is italicized):

The Indians appear rather doll-like in the radiance of the present moment *when* you force your mind to summon them.

When you force your mind to summon them, the Indians appear rather doll-like in the radiance of the present moment.

—Saul Bellow

The conjunction *but* behaves like a subordinating conjunction, but the subordinate clause it introduces cannot be shifted to initial position.

There is Saturday, *but* Saturday is not much better than Monday through Friday.

—Tom Wolfe

but not:

But Saturday is not much better than Monday through Friday, there is Saturday.

Transitional Adverbs

A transitional adverb relates two clauses somewhat differently than do the subordinating conjunctions previously discussed. Although still in subordinate sequence to the base clause, the added clause introduced by a transitional adverb can become an independent sentence. Also, a transitional adverb can be moved freely within the clause, but we cannot shift the whole clause to initial position, as these examples show:

A month after the egg laying the embryos will be ready for life; then the high tides of another full moon will wash away the sand of the nest.

—Rachel Carson

or:

A month after the egg laying the embryos will be ready for life; the high tides of another full moon will *then* wash away the sand of the nest.

but not:

Then the high tides of another full moon will wash away the sand of the nest, a month after the egg laying the embryos will be ready for life.

However, the two clauses can be separated into two independent sentences, but the sequence must remain the same as in Carson's original sentence:

A month after the egg laying the embryos will be ready for life.
Then the high tides of another full moon will wash away the sand of the nest.

Even when separated, the idea expressed in the second clause is subordinate to that in the first.

As you have probably noticed, these two types of complex sentences require different punctuation devices. Here are the possibilities:

Clause 1 , subordinating conjunction clause 2.
Clause 1 ; transitional adverb, clause 2.
Clause 1 ; subject, transitional adverb, predicate.
Clause 1 ; clause 2 , transitional adverb.

Relationships Established by Subordinators

English is rich in words that function as joiners, particularly subordinators. Although we use relatively few of these in everyday, spoken English, we lavish them throughout our writing. Because they are fairly specialized, you should realize the kinds of relationships they signal. The following list does not include all the joiners, nor does it indicate all their complexities, but it should help you in making decisions about appropriate choices.

Relationship	Subordinating Conjunction	Transitional Adverb
Information about the topic in addition to that given in the main clause		also, furthermore, likewise, morever
Separation or exclusion of the main clause material from that in the added clause	else, lest, whereas	otherwise, alternatively
Contrary condition or alternate possibilities	but	however, nevertheless, on the contrary, on the other hand
Causal	so, because, since, as, for	therefore, for this reason, then, consequently, thus

155

	Subordinating	*Transitional*
Relationship	*Conjunction*	*Adverb*
Purpose	that, in order that, so that, for the purpose of	
Limitation or restriction	though, although, in spite of the fact that, notwithstanding that	
Time	after, as, as soon as, while, before, until, since, when	
Special conditions	if, whether	

SUMMARY

In this chapter, we have discussed many ways to combine simple sentences in order to create more complex ones. We have also indicated that the structure of the cumulative sentence—a base clause followed by a series of modifiers—is a useful vehicle for carrying a heavy load of descriptive details. Of course we are not suggesting that *only* cumulative or complex sentences be used in description, nor are we suggesting that they are not useful in other kinds of writing. Like a string of simple, basic sentences, too many cumulative or complex sentences can become monotonous and artificial, and they can interfere with communication and style, rather than enhance them. Descriptive writing, like other forms, is most effective when the sentences are varied and tailored to the needs of the writer and the reader, as in this student paragraph, the first sentence of which we quoted earlier:

The Berlin street was alive with activity—everywhere people walking or riding, Volkswagens swarming like flies, black and noisy, young children with red cheeks playing on the sidewalk, elderly women walking slowly, huddled in their woolen coats clutched tightly against the bitter wind, all ages riding bicycles. Near a corner a small crowd stood waiting for the next bus. Along both sides of the street many sundry shops and pubs, gaily adorned in the typically Old German style, attracted wide-eyed tourists. The noise of construction was distinctly audible in the background. Here and all over the city new buildings were going up, new tunnels dug for the U-Bahn, and better "Strasse" paved.

The paragraph is effective because the student has employed many of the sentence devices discussed in this chapter to re-create the scene on a

Berlin street as he remembers it: combining sentences by inserting noun and verb modifiers, reordering some of those modifiers, and making effective use of the cumulative sentence.

Assignments

For Discussion

1 In the following descriptive sentences, identify first the base sentence, then the modifiers. Do they modify noun heads or verbs? Are the modifiers free or bound? (Hint: look for the head word being modified and test for reordering.)

    a The water skier, his life-jacket a bright orange band, swerved suddenly.

    b Disgusted with the turn of events, the cyclist propelled her machine toward the hills, purple in the distance.

    c The silent birds sat motionless in the sand.

    d He felt the impact of the blow throughout the length of his arm, jarring his flesh lightly.

                                       —Richard Wright

    e Silently we unlatch the door, letting the drift fall in, and step abroad to face the cutting air.

                               —Henry David Thoreau

    f They are feeding it on to the conveyor belt, a moving rubber belt a couple of feet wide which runs a yard or two behind them.

                               —George Orwell

    g Over a mouthful of spaghetti—delicious spaghetti—I peer at Janie with her newly red hair, the butterfly effect penciled out from the eyes, those pants, the gold chain dangling from hips to pelvis.

                               —Rasa Gustaitis

    h The big cottonwood tree stood apart from a small grove of winterbare cottonwoods which grew in the wide sandy arroyo.

                               —Leslie Chapman Silko

    i It had an amber tree against a blue-green background, resplendent with fruits and flowers and the all-important roots.

                               —Jane Howard

    j During the climb, I had seen the moss-covered boulders mottled by shafts of bright sunlight which fell through the canopy of green leaves overhead.

                               —Student paper

157

For Practice

1 Using sentence combining, expand the following base sentences in as many ways as possible with modifiers from the insert sentences under them. Remember to match up the heads you modify with the subjects of the insert sentences.

a Mountains surround the lake. (base sentence)
The mountains are high.
The mountains rise in peaks.
The mountains are gray granite.
The peaks are covered with snow.
The lake is blue.
The lake is cold.
The lake is deep.

b The porcupine lay beneath the tree. (base sentence)
The porcupine was still.
The porcupine was cold.
The porcupine had been warm a moment ago.
The porcupine had been alive a moment ago.

c The two people pitched their tent. (base sentence)
The two people were young.
The two people were intent on their task.
The two people were pounding in the stakes.
They (the two people) were pulling on the ropes.
They were adjusting the poles.
They were building a shelter.
A shelter protects them from the weather.
The weather is cold.
The weather is rainy.
The weather is windy.

2 Add sentence modifiers to the following base clauses to produce descriptive cumulative sentences in coordinate, subordinate, or mixed sentences. Try to use parallel structures to indicate levels of generality, and watch your punctuation.

a The girl walked slowly toward him . . .
b· He gazed out pensively at the passing landscape . . .
c I remember my grandfather well . . .
d On the balmy spring evenings, I must force myself to the library . . .
e _____ Hall is the most unusual building on campus . . .
f I looked around at my classmates . . .
g I sauntered into the campus grill for breakfast . . .
h I wearily carried the last load of clothing to my new dormitory room . . .

158

i The sun suddenly broke through the clouds . . .
j I dove into the cold water . . .

3 In the following paragraphs, combine sentences so that detail-bearing modifiers make them more vividly descriptive. Use the cumulative sentence and the other sentence devices discussed in this chapter, including reordering and inserting.

a He paused at the corner to watch the work of the wrecking crew. The great metal ball swung at the walls. Everything it touched wavered and burst. There rose a cloud of plaster dust. The afternoon was ending. There was a fire in the area of demolition, fed by the wreckage. Moses heard the air, felt the heat. The workmen threw strips of molding. Paint and varnish smoked. The old flooring burned gratefully. Scaffolds walled with doors quivered as the trucks carried off fallen brick. The sun was surrounded by gases.
—adapted from Saul Bellow's *Herzog*

b The skier started down the slope. The main mountain range was behind him. He veered down the steep grade and he picked up speed as he went. He felt the cold air on the parts of his face exposed by the ski mask. The sun shone on the snow. The atmosphere and the exertion made him gasp for air. He gathered speed and experienced a sense of flying. Trees seemed to be rushing off in the opposite direction. He swerved to a stop at the bottom. He felt a sense of satisfaction and returned to the chair lift for another run.

4 Using the following pairs of clauses from Wendell Berry's *The Unforeseen Wilderness*, construct as many different complex sentences with each pair as possible. From the limitations you encounter, identify the kind of subordinator. Be sure you punctuate accurately.

a There is nothing to be found
When I slip up and examine the spot
b You would hardly notice that it is water
If it weren't for the shadows and ripples
c Some of the duller trees are already shedding
Though the slopes have not yet taken on the bright colors of the autumn maples and oaks
d When the time comes I prepare supper and eat
Then I wash kettle and cup and spoon and put them away
e I no longer had the faintest shadow of a wish to go any farther
Yet my pride held on to my intentions a while longer
f It drove down onto the comb of the rocks and was torn apart
Then it gathered back into the single strand of itself, to be torn apart again
g It was my own strangeness that I felt
For I was a man out of place

h The last of the sunlight glows on this rock and then slowly rises away from it
While we make camp
i The day is warm and overcast
But it seems unlikely to rain

5 From a descriptive paper you have written for class, choose one paragraph or sentence that you wish to make more colorful and richer in detail. Expand the sentences according to the principles outlined in this chapter.

10

Special Topics

Like most useful things, the complex, expanded sentence can create problems. Ambiguity or double meaning can result from adding modifiers; punctuation becomes more difficult than with simple statements or questions. However, learning to handle these problems is part of learning to write and part of your commitment to readers to write as clearly and interestingly as possible.

AMBIGUITY IN EXPANDED SENTENCES

Modification Booby Traps

Is there anything peculiar about these sentences?

1. The mayor is a dirty street fighter.
2. A girl with a flag that was waving at us looked very familiar.
3. Rodolphe sent Emma Bovary a note that he was leaving town in a basket of apricots.
4. He knew Brahms as a young man.
5. Pedaling frantically and watching the bus barrel down on you from behind, a raucous·voice pierces the air: "Don't you know what bicycles are for?"

You're right. They're all a little weird. In 1, the mayor could fight dirty streets or fight dirty in the streets. In 2, either the girl or the flag could wave at us. In 3, Rodolphe may have discovered a new way to travel—in a basket of apricots. In 4, are you sure that *he* was a young man, or was it *Brahms?* And 5 presents the mind-boggling possibility of a raucous voice pedaling a bicycle down the street, dodging buses.

Though these sentence problems can be humorous, we rarely set out to create them; in fact, we often find them embarrassing—a slip of the pen, so to speak. Not only are these ambiguous structures disconcerting, they also seriously interfere with clarity of meaning. Therefore, we try to avoid these kinds of booby traps, all of which involve ambiguous or dangling modifiers. But they often occur accidentally as a result of inserting modifiers into noun phrases, verb phrases, and sentences as a whole, because we tend to place structures into sentence positions natural to spoken English. In written English, unlike spoken English, we cannot adequately indicate the stress, pitch, and pause features that keep us from being ambiguous when we speak. Understanding these structural ambiguities can help you to avoid them.

Ambiguous Noun-Phrase Modifiers

As in examples 1 and 2, a very common source of ambiguity is the expanded noun phrase. The kind of double meaning illustrated in example 1 ("The mayor is a dirty street fighter") would not cause problems in spoken English. The speaker's intonation would clearly indicate the meaning intended. In writing, however, to clarify such structural problems, we must either rewrite the phrase or use punctuation devices to substitute for the intonation. The hyphen is useful for this purpose:

The mayor is a dirty-street fighter.

or

The mayor is a dirty street-fighter.

In both of these versions, the hyphen indicates which compound the writer intended. Any remaining ambiguity stems from the multiple meanings of *dirty,* rather than from the structure.

This kind of ambiguity booby trap can be a problem in the process of adjective insertion because the resulting expanded noun phrase can be interpreted in more than one way. For this reason, when you insert an adjective into a noun phrase, you should be especially wary of the structure Adjective + Noun + Noun Head (*dirty + street + fighter*).

Another cause of crossed wires in a noun phrase is possessive nouns. The ambiguity in a statement like "Smith is an old women's college" arises from two structural possibilities:

(Adjective + Possessive) + Noun Head
    (old women's)   (college)   = a college for old women

Adjective + (Possessive + Noun Head)
    (old)   (women's college)   = an old college for women

Here, rewriting can solve the problem.

Modifiers following the noun head can also cause trouble. In the noun phrase of example 2, "A girl with a flag *that was waving at us,*" the italicized relative clause could have been derived from either of these insert sentences.

A girl was waving at us.

$\longrightarrow$ that was waving at us

A flag was waving at us.

The proximity of the relative clause to *flag* and the use of the neutral *that* exaggerate the ambiguity. A more careful choice of relative pronouns solves this problem:

A girl with a flag *who was waving at us.* (*who* is used to refer to humans)
A girl with a flag *which was waving at us.* (*which* is used to refer to non-humans and inanimate objects)

Ambiguous Free Modifiers

If such a strong risk of ambiguity lurks in noun modifiers, which are not easily moved, imagine the dangers inherent in the highly movable modifiers. One of the tricks that these can play on unwary writers is illustrated in example 3:

Rodolphe sent Emma Bovary a note that he was leaving town *in a basket of apricots.*

Ordinarily, a place adjunct can appear at the end of a sentence without much danger of ambiguity, as in:

John give her an engagement ring *at the Country Fair.*

No problem here. There is no question about where John gave her the ring. But this end-of-sentence position can cause ambiguity if other structures are added between the main clause and the adjunct, giving it another modifying possibility, as in:

John gave her an engagement ring he had purchased *at the County Fair.*

Now there is confusion: did John *give* her the ring at the fair, or did he *purchase* the ring at the fair? In both examples, the basic problem is the same: the place could have originated in either the base or the insert sentence.

John gave her an engagement ring *at the County Fair.*
   (base sentence)
John had purchased the ring *at the County Fair.*
   (possible insert sentence)

Rodolphe sent Emma Bovary a note *in a basket of apricots.*
   (base sentence)
Rodolphe was leaving town *in a basket of apricots.*
   (possible insert sentence)

You can use this device to spot ambiguity, then solve the problem simply by placing the modifier close to the verb.

> Rodolphe sent Emma Bovary a note *in a basket of apricots* that he was leaving town.

> The same positional influence operates in example 4:

> He knew Brahms *as a young man.*

However, the modifier would create no problem in this position if the noun preceding it could not possibly serve as its head, as in:

> He knew her as a young man.

In cases like this, moving the modifier to initial position removes the danger of double meaning:

> *As a young man,* he knew Brahms.

Dangling Sentence Modifiers

Perhaps the structural booby trap that most jeopardizes writers is the dangling sentence modifier, the culprit in example 5:

> *Pedaling frantically and watching the bus barrel down on you from behind,* a raucous voice pierces the air: "Don't you know what bicycles are for?"

What makes these structures especially hazardous is that, unlike the other ambiguous modifiers we have been discussing, the problem may not be limited to the internal modification of a single sentence. Rather, with dangling initial modifiers, the preceding sentence may play a big part in creating the ambiguity. Let's look at this example as it appeared in the context of a student paper on the dangers of bicycling:

> Motorists will actually vie for the honor of having you and your machine entangled in their front grills as trophies of a good day's work. *Pedaling frantically and watching the bus barrel down on you from behind,* a raucous voice . . .

The use of *motorists* as the subject of the first sentence sets up the expectation that *pedaling* and *watching* will refer back to it. Indeed, structurally they seem to do so, but logically they cannot; instead, they dangle.

Traditional grammar requires that any modifiers placed before the main clause be logically tied only to the subject. However, recent recognition that such movable modifiers can be related to the whole main clause has caused us to realize that not all traditionally identified "dangling modifiers" dangle. But how can you know when a sentence modifier really dangles? Often good sense will signal you. But another test is to change the *-ing* structure into a sentence that could be an insert sentence. If the subject of the insert sentence is different from that of the main clause, the modifier dangles. Let's look at an example:

> *Driving down the Interstate,* the moon followed us at the same rate of speed.

Here, we can change the *-ing* phrase to an insert sentence:

> We were driving down the Interstate.

We is the logical subject underlying the *-ing* phrase; this is signaled by *us* in the main clause. But *moon* is the subject of the main clause, so the relationship of the modifier to the rest of the sentence is illogical and thus ambiguous. Note that both our examples involve *-ing* phrases, the guiltiest structure in dangling modification—so guilty that it is often set apart by a special label: dangling participle. Writers need to be especially vigilant about these and other subjectless verbal phrases. Remember, if the subject of the insert sentence is different from that of the main clause, the modifier dangles.

Although not as troublesome as the *-ing* participle, the infinitive phrase, one that contains *to* + verb, often creates ambiguity:

> *To become a violinist,* a good teacher is needed.

Restoring the deleted subject of the main clause remedies the ambiguity:

> To become a violinist, *Jack needs a good teacher.*

Does the following sentence seem ambiguous to you?

> *After the bill was passed,* Congress recessed for a week.

Only the most puristic critic would deem this a dangling modifier. Although *bill* seems to be the subject of the passive modifying clause, the logical subject (*Congress*), lost when the insert sentence was made passive, is still implicit in the sentence.

> Congress passed the bill. (insert sentence) ⟶
> The bill was passed (by Congress). (changed to passive)

Normally in such situations, ambiguity is not a problem because readers automatically supply the logical subject.

There are many instances when the logical subjects in the main clause and in the sentence modifier are different, but no ambiguity results because some other grammatical device signals the relationship. Look at this example.

> *When John was twenty-one,* his father decided to retire.

Here, the possessive pronoun *his* shows an unambiguous relationship to

John. But in the next example, we can't be sure whether *he* refers to John or to his father.

When he was twenty-one, his father decided to retire.

Many times ambiguity can be eliminated by very simple devices. Here are a few additional tips that may help you.

● Sometimes you can add gender signals (*his, her, its*):

Ambiguous: The boy on the horse with a patch over one eye
    Clear: The boy on the horse with a patch over one of *his/its* eyes

● Occasionally you can change the verb form to show singular or plural (*is/are; was/were*):

Ambiguous: one of the football players who seemed exhausted
    Clear: one of the football players who *was/were* exhausted

● Sometimes a coordination signal (*and, but, or*) can be added:

Ambiguous: a car that was parked in front of a garage that needed paint
    Clear: a car that was parked in front of a garage *and* needed paint

All this does not mean that you should avoid using certain structures just because they may result in ambiguity; they are much too valuable for that. If you are alert to ambiguity and apply the suggestions given here, you can avoid these modification booby traps.

PUNCTUATION OF EXPANDED SENTENCES

As you create more complicated sentences, you become more committed to furnishing punctuation aids to your readers. In a long, involved sentence, punctuation is needed both to indicate grammatical structures—such as the limits of the sentence—and to clarify meaning. So far in this chapter we have examined some types of ambiguity that can arise when sentences are rearranged and expanded; now let's turn to some of the punctuation problems that can also arise in the process.

Reordered Elements or Sentence Introducers

Free modifiers placed *before* the main clause are usually set off by a comma:

His face had been a long time healing *after the accident.* (normal order, no comma needed)
After the accident, his face had been a long time healing.
                                                    —Dorothy Canfield

We dipped the oars into the lake *occasionally*. (no comma needed)
Occasionally, we dipped the oars into the lake.

Occasionally a comma is not used after a single-word sentence introducer like *occasionally*, nor after a short reordered adjunct or modifier:

For about ten years astronomers have been observing sites in the sky that are powerful emitters of x-rays.

—Ben Bova

However, if the omission of the comma in such instances results in ambiguity, leave it in:

In ten years time will have eroded away their youth.

Here, the reader may be forced to reread the sentence because of an initial confusion whether the opening adverbial is "in ten years" or "in ten years time." A comma solves the problem:

In ten years, time will have eroded away their youth.

Parenthetical Elements

Parenthetical elements, phrases that do not contribute directly to the meaning of a sentence but provide incidental information or function as transitional devices, are usually set off by commas:

The snow, *as we could see,* had covered all landmarks.
We could not, *of course,* find the way back to the lodge.
The fawn, *unfortunately,* stumbled into the trap.

Elements in a Series

Noun Phrases in a Series   Commas may be used to separate each noun phrase in a series from all the others or to separate all but the last two:

The breakfast table was laden with *steaming coffee, fresh fruits, orange juice, and delicate crepes.* (commas separate all four noun phrases)
The breakfast table was laden with *biscuits, fruit juices, jams, ham and eggs.* (no comma between the last two items)

Omitting the comma in the second example creates the sense that the last two items are a unit, rather than separate entities. Consequently, if they are not a unit, we prefer a comma before the *and,* though some instructors and editors consider it optional.

Instead of commas, semicolons are sometimes used to set off lengthy, complex items in a series. This helps to avoid confusion with other commas

167

used for punctuation inside a lengthy modifier. This punctuation device is perhaps found more in expository writing than in description:

On the contrary, the trend to encourage the crash programs to get quick answers—like the Manhattan project, which turned the laboratory discovery of uranium fission into a cataclysmic bomb in six years; the Computer/Automation Revolution; the Space Program; and now the Bioengineering Revolution, with its possibilities not only of spare-organ plumbing but of changing the nature of living things by gene manipulation . . .

—Lord Ritchie-Calder

Noun Modifiers in a Series Modifiers following the noun head are always set off by commas:

Valley children, with sunken, impudent eyes, quick tongues and singing voices, chests thin as shells, gathered around the Punch and Judy.

—Dylan Thomas

However, modifiers preceding the noun head do not need commas if they occur in normal word order, as in this example:

The big bright summer sun shone in her eyes.

Appositives

An appositive element functions as a device of definition or identification when inserted into sentences after noun phrases. An appositive may take the form of a noun phrase, as in "Beethoven, *the composer* . . .," or of a relative clause, as in "Beethoven, *who wrote nine symphonies*. . . ." These appositives are set off by commas only if they add information that is not necessary to the logical meaning of the sentence. (Appositives can also be set off by dashes and parentheses. See the Reference Guide, pages 502–507.) Appositives not directly tied to the meaning of the sentence are called *nonrestrictive;* those necessary to the meaning are *restrictive,* as in this example:

Patterson Tower, *the recently completed office building,* is a monument of concrete ugliness. (Information in the appositive is not necessary for identification; it merely adds details—set off by commas.)

The recently completed building *Patterson Tower* is a monument of concrete ugliness. (Here *Patterson Tower* is the appositive, needed for identification—no commas used.)

Identifying restrictive and nonrestrictive appositives can be difficult and confusing. If you remember these three points, you can avoid most of the punctuation problems that these structures pose:

- You as the writer must decide how you want the reader to "hear" and understand the sentence. If you wish to make the appositive nonrestrictive, you must provide the punctuation to set it off completely from the rest of the sentence. If you wish to make the appositive restrictive, omit the commas.
- Read the sentence aloud and listen for breath pause, or juncture. If you produce juncture on both sides of the appositive or only one juncture following it, set the appositive off with commas.
- If the appositive is a relative clause beginning with *that,* use no commas.

The distinction between restrictive and nonrestrictive elements can be difficult to make when relative clauses are involved. For a full discussion, see the Reference Guide, page 503.

PUNCTUATION OF CUMULATIVE SENTENCES

Cumulative sentences require punctuation between the base (SP) clause and the added sentence modifiers. The punctuation can be a comma, a dash, or a colon.

Comma: It is a difficult country, where the goats must drink seawater and the finches drink blood, where the people drink rainwater collected on roofs or brackish water drawn from wells near the sea.
—Kenneth Brower

Dash: By day there were flies everywhere—flies in the soup, flies in the tea; at night the buzz and bites of mosquitoes in the small, warm, overcrowded tents.
—Ernest Hemingway

Colon: Though the clock on the living room sideboard says only 4:20, darkness has come: dark carpets, thick drawn drapes, dead wallpaper, potted plants crowding the glass on the side that has windows.
—John Updike

Assignments

For Practice

1 All of the following sentences are ambiguous. Explain the source of the trouble in each and rephrase to clarify.

   a They are now experimenting on food to be shot with atomic rays that can stay under water as long as the submarine.

169

b They named me Marian Buford after a heated debate.

c Reminiscing about 1964, my father had a heart attack and was taken to the hospital.

d In its concentrated form, a teaspoon could kill 30 million people.

e Looking down the waterway some more boats appear, adding more confusion and excitement which amazes the tourists.

f Ever since grade school, I had looked forward to this occasion when I, with all my fellow classmates, moved my tassel from the right to the left.

g Since the magic ring was devised by an evil power, it inevitably corrupted anyone who used it in the end.

h The drinking age had really nothing to do with the context of his letter, and it left me as one reader hanging on a short note.

i A woman was petting a horse with a big cartwheel hat.

j To get a good view of the stage, a box seat is needed.

k While a small child, my grandfather carried me on his shoulder.

l Driving through the Smokies, a bear stopped our car at a garbage can.

m He didn't see how a woman had the ability to run the office without someone helping her like a man.

n I sit here writing my autobiography, weighing two hundred and forty-five pounds.

2 Punctuate the following descriptive sentences from Sally Carrighar's *Home to the Wilderness*. Be able to justify your punctuation.

a Looking smaller this was the little creature who a few moments earlier had been up on the bough wrapped in sunshine enjoying life.

b Their leaves as they tossed and swung seemed to be cutting the sky into bits to be scattered as scraps of sunlight along the ground.

c Compare a park only a few spaced-out trees were allowed to grow their dead branches were pruned away the flowers were all in neat beds the grass was kept mowed never allowed to become weeds or "grasses."

d With a feeling of cowardice shrinking back I wanted to leave to return to the wide placid lake.

e Sometimes I walked about but more often sat under one of the trees which were firs and quivering aspens listening to the songs of the birds and watching them and a squirrel who was always there.

f I held a blue flower in my hand probably a wild aster wondering what its name was and then thought that human names for natural things are superfluous.

Revision
of Descriptive
Writing

At the end of Part 1, when we discussed the revision of your personal writing we urged you to reread your paper to find its weaknesses. We suggested a two-step process: a first reading for such general qualities as organization, development of ideas, voice; and then a second for specific items like spelling, punctuation, sentence structure, and choice of words. Use the same two-step process when you revise your descriptive writing, keeping the following questions in mind.

FIRST REVISION

Organization

1. Have you organized the description according to some logical and appropriate plan? If it is a character sketch, have you generally followed the three-part structure?
2. Whatever your plan, have you followed it consistently throughout?
3. Whether your relationship to the subject involves space, time, or personal acquaintance, is the relationship clear?
4. Can you improve your introduction? Could it be more interesting? Could the dominant impression be clearer?
5. Can you improve your ending? If you've written a character sketch, does the ending provide a sense of finality and completion?

Development

1. Can you add some details to improve your descriptions? Are some details unnecessary?
2. Have you relied on all your senses in writing the description—hearing, smelling, tasting, touching, seeing?

3. If you've written a character sketch, should you add a short anecdote or two?

Voice

1. If factual description, does the paper sound formal, serious, factual? Have you deleted all value judgments, personal references, and personal expressions of feeling?
2. In other descriptions, do you convey some impression of yourself to readers? Are you satisfied with this impression? Does the tone of your writing voice suggest your feelings? Can you add or change words, phrases, or sentences to make the writing sound more like you?

SECOND REVISION

Language

1. Do any words seem awkward, inappropriate, or misleading?
2. Can you sharpen some general adjectives like "good," "nice," or "bad" by substituting more precise ones?
3. Should you check a few words in the dictionary or synonym book for their exact meaning or to find more effective ones?
4. Would a figure of speech in some places help to evoke an impression?

Sentences

1. Can you improve your sentence variety by shifting modifiers?
2. Can you avoid successive short sentences by combining them?
3. Can you improve your sentences by making them cumulative?
4. Have you avoided ambiguous modifiers? Dangling sentence modifiers?

Spelling

1. Is every word spelled correctly? Are you sure?
2. To be absolutely positive, shouldn't you check a few in the dictionary?

Punctuation

1. Undecided about some of your commas? Before *and* and *but?* Before *which?* Any others? Why not check them in the chapter or the Reference Guide?
2. Are you unsure about any other punctuation marks? Colons, semicolons, quotation marks? Shouldn't you check them in the Reference Guide?

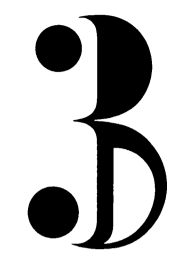

The Explanatory Voice: Expository Writing

You've been writing and speaking exposition all your life! Of course, you haven't called it that. You have probably thought of it as explaining, or informing, or sounding off. But all these are forms of exposition. Look at the term *exposition* itself. In a general sense, it means "a setting forth." You may recall that a World's Fair is often referred to as an exposition, a place where nations set forth their artistic or industrial works. In fiction, the author sets forth the background of the characters in the exposition. In a fugue or sonata, the composer sets forth the themes in the exposition. In your papers, when you set forth your ideas or opinions or views, you are engaged in exposition.

You may be wondering: Why not simply refer to expository writing as informative writing? Why not use the common word instead of the specialized one? Is there some distinction, and does it matter?

There is a distinction, and it does matter. Nearly everything you write could be classified as informative: an account of your attending the wrong class the first day of college, a poem expressing your feelings toward a loved one, a letter describing your dorm room to your mother, or a handout urging students to vote for your friend in a campus election. Exposition differs from these informative writings because its purpose is not primarily to narrate, describe, or persuade; its main purpose is to explain. It does so in numerous ways: by classifying, defining, analyzing, exploring, interpreting, and evaluating, to mention a few.

In the process of writing exposition, you may be concerned with one extreme or the other: the relatively objective or the highly subjective. An expository paper about kitchen knives, for example, would be mainly objective: it would probably include general information about paring, boning, slicing, and carving knives and perhaps about a few others, such as cook's knives, butcher's knives, cheese knives, filleting knives, and Chinese chopping knives. But a paper evaluating your high school or explaining why young people have lost faith in most politicians would be mainly subjective: it would reflect your personal opinion. Of course, in a strict sense, every expository paper states your personal opinion, whether about the uses for kitchen knives or the quality of your high school. But in the following chapters we will treat exposition more generally, viewing it as usually comprising the factual (process description, classification, definition) and the personal (analysis).

Exposition differs from the other kinds of writing in that it tries to draw a distinctive response. After reading narration, readers usually say or think, "We enjoyed that"; after description, "We saw, heard, and felt that"; after persuasion, "We're convinced of that." But after exposition, "We understand that."

Now that you understand what exposition is, you should realize why it is important to master this form of writing. In college, you will be called upon to write essay examinations, critiques, analyses, case histories, lab reports, abstracts, and research papers explaining what you think, know, found, or learned. After college, whether you work as a lawyer, engineer, sales person, manager, teacher, or nurse, you will have to write letters, memorandums, reports, and papers explaining what you did, found, accomplished, proposed, concluded, or recommended. In a sense, expository writing is the writing of the working world and the writing that enables the world to work. It does this by providing answers to such vital questions as these:

What is _____?
What is the purpose of _____?
What are the causes of _____?
What are the effects of _____?
What is the value of _____?
How does _____ work?
How effective is _____?
How should _____ be evaluated?
Why is _____ important?

In answering these questions, writers may include narration or description, but they rely mainly on exposition.

To help you improve your expository writing, we will discuss the characteristics of its various forms, provide a method to develop a logical outline, indicate ways to construct effective paragraphs, consider language problems, and examine several special features. Naturally, in these chapters as in earlier ones, when we explain these various points, we are writing exposition.

The Forms
of Expository
Writing

Jack: Taken in any of the flicks in the Silent Film Festival at the Student Union?

Jim: Just the old Keystone comedies. The movie auto chase boggles my mind. You know, the Keystone Kops really began all that.

These two students are starting a discussion that could involve the common expository forms used in explanation. Jack could be knowledgeable about the way the car chase is filmed and explain the process to Jim. Or Jim might divide movie auto chases into several subtypes, classifying them according to purpose: building suspense, illuminating character, or satirizing the American preoccupation with fast cars. During the conversation, Jack might mention a trucking shot, a term unknown to Jim, and then be called upon to define it, to tell what it means in this context. Or Jim might briefly describe the steps in producing an effective chase scene, or show the relationship of the chase scenes to the plot, or he might express his opinion about why these movie devices have always been popular.

Even in such an everyday discussion as this one, Jack and Jim are using expository forms that their subject and purpose naturally require. In dealing with *how* scenes are shot, Jack produces a *process description;* his *what* explanation requires *classification* or *definition*. When Jim expounds on *why* chase scenes are important or on *why* he holds an opinion about some aspect of movie auto chases, the result is *analysis*.

In all these expository forms—process description, classification, definition, and analysis—you will be called upon to perform a dissecting task, to divide your subject into parts so that you can explain to your readers how those parts operate, what relationships they have to each other, why they function as they do, or why they result in a particular effect.

PROCESS DESCRIPTION

In describing a person or a place, you write about physical appearance or characteristics of the subject. But in describing a process, you trace the steps involved. To illustrate the difference in the two types of description, you might physically describe a screwdriver as a hand tool made up of a metal rod or dowel that is flattened at one end to fit the slot in the head of a screw. The other end is inserted into a wooden or plastic handle designed to fit comfortably in a hand. But a description of how to use a screwdriver would require you to consider the steps involved so that another person could successfully follow your directions. Such a description might include the following steps:

1. Choose the right-size screwdriver for the job.
2. Make a hole where the screw is to be set in order to hold the screw secure.
3. Grasp the screwdriver in one hand while holding the screw steady with the other.
4. Insert the flat end of the screwdriver into the slot in the head of the screw.
5. Turn the screwdriver in the direction of the threads of the screw until the screw head is flush with the surface.

Every process, even one as simple as using a screwdriver, involves a unique set of steps. Describing how to change the oil in a car, for instance, requires a different approach than describing how to choose a tennis racquet, or how to select a mate. But there are some general questions that can help you to organize your thoughts before you begin to write a process description. Throughout, remember that your primary purpose is to answer the question *how*. Here is a set of questions to ask yourself before writing a process description:

1. What are the essential steps in the process?
2. What chronological order must they have?
3. What is the purpose of each step?
4. How does this process relate to other similar processes?
5. Do I have to describe any items for my readers?
6. What is the end result?

Like the outline for using a screwdriver, most process descriptions are usually arranged chronologically; first this is done, then that, and so on. Determining the logical starting point is important. In describing an effective tennis serve, for example, you would not need to describe the racquet or explain how to obtain a court. But you would need to indicate how one step relates to the next—hand grip on the racquet, stance, ball toss, swing, and follow-through.

A process description is usually factual, but can be personal. Choosing the approach you take depends to a large extent on the subject. For instance, telling someone how to avoid a blind date or how not to succeed as a bridge player might call for a personal, even humorous, approach. But if, as is usually the case, you set out seriously to tell someone how to do something, then an objective, factual approach is best. When you are assembling a tricycle for your little brother's birthday, you want straightforward, clear directions, not entertainment. Here is an example of such directions—a brief, factual description of how to read a road map and improve navigational skills.

HOW TO READ A ROAD MAP

Julie Candler

When the family vacations by car, custom puts father behind the wheel and someone beside him reading the road map. If you can be a front seat navigator who guides the driver with clear and accurate directions you can make the trip safer and more pleasant. As a solo driver, you head for a happier trip if you know the safest way to be a combination automobile pilot and navigator.

Whether traveling alone or with the family, take along a few map-reading accessories to make your work easier. A magnifying glass helps in distinguishing minute symbols, a flashlight illuminates the map for night reading and a marking pen or crayon of a light, see-through tint is useful for circling daily destination points or interesting side trips.

As for the map itself, make certain yours is the latest available by checking the date at the bottom of the legend (the space in which map symbols are explained). Mapmakers issue new road maps every six months to one year. Last year's maps lack thousands of miles of new national interstate highway system, hundreds of new towns and other details which may help you on this year's trip. . . .

If you prefer to plan your own route, begin on a map showing both your starting point and destination. It may require a multistate or even a national map. Use the map index to check locations of unfamiliar cities. Most map indexes utilize a reference system which divides the map into imaginary or faintly-outlined squares. They are formed by lines running from grid marks spaced around the four edges of the map. Letters identify the areas between grid marks along the sides, while numerals mark spaces between grids at top and bottom. To find a town indexed A-5, check the square formed by lines running from grid marks on either side of A and 5. Once you have located the places you want to visit, rule a line between them. Then plot your course via the major highways running closest to your straight line. For the safest and fastest trip, route yourself whenever possible onto the national interstate highway system (where you are three times safer). Next best choices are U.S. or principal state highways.

Before you map your own or embark on a course charted by experts, study the legend. Road maps direct by sign language and the legend teaches you to translate. Once you learn it you can recognize national interstate, U.S., state, and proposed highways at a glance. You can spot the locations of auto ferries, interchanges, mountain peaks and time lines. On some maps tiny symbols tell you where there is a park, with or without camping sites, an airport, college, fish hatchery, golf course, United States national monument or point of interest. But understanding the legend on one map may not help you with another because legends and symbols vary from mapmaker to mapmaker.

For safety's sake, remember that limited or controlled access can mean that an occasional railroad or highway crosses the multilane divided highway on the same grade level. Therefore you must remain alert to the possibility of traffic or a train crossing your high-speed path. Do not drop your guard against an occasional crossing unless you are certain that access is *fully* controlled.

Legends tell you how to read another important map message: your mileage. Maps always show a scale, usually about one inch to fourteen actual miles. You can therefore estimate your miles with a tape measure or a piece of paper onto which you have transferred the scale. An easier way is to total up the mileage figure alongside your route. The figures tell you the mileage between towns, arrows or stars, whichever the legend lists as the break-off point. Most maps include a table or inset which tells the exact mileage between major cities. When you know how to estimate mileage, you can help the driver by saying, "We just passed highway 83. That means that highway 53, where we exit to the south, is about four miles ahead." At a mile a minute, that gives the driver four minutes' warning. . . .

Some helpful information for mapreaders: an alternate route such as 66A forks off a regular route, sometimes to skirt city traffic, other times to carry traffic into a city the regular route passes. Eventually, both routes rejoin. A route marked B.R. or "city route" takes you to the heart of the business district. A bypass or loop route takes you around a city. A truck route usually passes through the outskirts of a city where traffic is lighter.

Once they are studied, road maps, as every traveler knows, are harder to fold back to their original state than a fancy bow on a Christmas gift. After extensive research we have found that all road maps accordion-fold. Open smaller maps to their fullest, hold the two sides and let the folds accordion-pleat into place. Then fold over once. With larger maps the folding-over is done first. Refold the two or three horizontal creases, then accordion-fold from side to side.

Even with the map folded away, you can be a good front seat navigator for the driver beside you. Keep him in a happy (and safer) frame of mind by avoiding arguments, help him to stay awake and alert and spell him at the wheel if he gets drowsy. If you change places with him, give him the navigating responsibility and remind him to take it seriously. A good map reader is important to a good trip and a safe one.

In this process description, Candler follows the usual form for such a paper: (1) introduction of the process; (2) discussion of special materials needed; (3) steps in the process. Steps move in chronological order; in paragraph 6, even the safety tip that seems to digress adds information about the process. To show the chronology, the writer uses words like *before, once, when, then, first.* (Another common device to indicate order is enumeration: *first, second,* or *one, two,* and so on.) Note, too, that many of the sentences are imperative, omitting an unnecessary subject: "Then plot your course . . . ," "Open smaller maps . . . ," "Refold the two. . . ."

CLASSIFICATION

The Uses of Classification

We have said that process description—explaining *how* something operates—demands sorting out the steps involved. So too, classification—explaining *what* something is composed of—requires dividing a broad subject into its component parts. Although often merely a part of expository papers, classification can be an end in itself. For instance, an agriculture student might write a paper classifying the corn plants available to farmers; or a Xerox executive might prepare a report that lists and describes that company's copiers. In both projects, classification is the main purpose and thus the only rhetorical form needed. Classification is often an important aspect of definition (pages 183–88) and other forms of expository writing. In defining *investments,* for example, it would be informative to include a brief classification of the various kinds, such as savings accounts, savings certificates, Treasury bills, stocks, and bonds. Classification can also be useful in papers in which evaluation is the objective. If you were rating cars, you'd be wise to classify them first according to price, horsepower, gas mileage, and safety features. Here again, classification would be used not as a separate form, but as a means to some other rhetorical end.

The Techniques of Classification

Suppose you have been asked to submit a report to the dean that involves classifying the professors at your college. You should recognize that the subject "professors at X College" constitutes a generally accepted and well-defined *class.* The next step is a dividing procedure: categorizing "professors at X College" into *subclasses.* But first, you must decide on a basis for the classification. If the report is to be used to help make promotion decisions, you would subclassify on the basis of teaching ability and knowledge of subject matter. But if the report is to be used to make awards for advising students, then you would subclassify on the basis of personality, interest in students, and ability to relate to them. As you can see, your purpose in writing the paper will determine the classification.

In planning your classification scheme, keep these suggestions in mind:

1. You should have a clear-cut basis for establishing *class*. For instance, "professors at X College" as a class could include only people who teach full time; you could not validly include deans, registrars, teaching assistants, or counselors.
2. You should be able to divide your class into at least two subclasses. For example, suppose you decide to make the sex of the teacher your basis for classification. If all the professors at your college are males, then a subclassification by sex becomes logically impossible. You can deal only with male professors. "Male professors at X College" in your discussion thus becomes a separate class; no subclasses are possible.
3. You should determine subclasses according to the subject matter and the purpose of your paper, as previously explained.
4. You should include all pertinent subclasses. For example, it is distressing that many articles classifying drugs omit the most widely abused drug, alcohol.

Let's apply these four suggestions to a classification of bike carriers for cars, which might be the basis for a paper informing students about the advantages and disadvantages of each type.

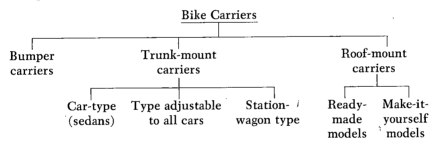

Now to apply the four suggestions:

1. Is there a clear-cut basis for establishing class? Bike carriers could include only those devices used specifically to carry bicycles. Boat and trailer carriers could not be included.
2. Is each class divided into at least two subclasses? In the diagram, the class *bike carriers* is divided into three subclasses, two of which are divided into at least two subclasses. If the student wished to include information about chrome and aluminum models, then each subclass could be further divided.
3. Are the subclasses determined by the subject matter and the purpose of the paper? All subclasses include types that students might consider in buying a bike carrier.
4. Are all pertinent subclasses included? All types of bike carriers available on the market have been included.

The following student paper is a humorous classification of different kinds of toothpicks. See if you can determine the classification scheme used.

A PICKY CHOICE

Joseph Coomer

Have you ever been "up to the teeth," been "in the teeth," "showed your teeth"? Ever fought "tooth and nail," had a toothache, used a toothbrush? Ever been called toothy or even toothsome? Well of course you have, and you should really be able to get your teeth into this essay unless, of course, you're toothless.

The toothpick is usually a small stick of softwood used for extracting bits and pieces of food from between the teeth after a meal. Invented by the legendary Seymour Tooth in the fifth century B.C., it is a time-tested answer to molar infestation. But like other products in our technical society, the tooth pick industry has saturated the market with fascinating varieties, unthought-of advances since Seymour's era. Five different types dominate the modern world, each with a specific purpose: the common or round toothpick, the flavored toothpick, the flat toothpick, the colored toothpick, and the prickly toothpick. An explanation of each and its specific use follows:

Often seen jutting from the lips of America's "tough" youth is the common toothpick. Round in nature, the Volkswagen of the toothpick kingdom, its purpose is implied by its name—you pick your teeth with it. Grasping one end between the index finger and thumb firmly, you insert the pick in your mouth to the location of that tough piece of gristle and deftly dislodge it with the free end of the pick. Then, according to your disposition, you may either chew up the morsel or spit it to the ground. Ashes to ashes and dust to dust.

The second toothpick discussed herein is the flat, or utilitarian toothpick. Due to its flat, easy-to-glue surface, this toothpick is generally used in the construction of various elementary school art projects such as Indian forts. Of course, it may also be used as a toothpick, but this is considered rather gauche, and should be done only in extreme cases, or when no one is looking.

The colored toothpick is a variation of the common toothpick. This variety comes in yellow, red, blue, and green; occasionally a mutation will slip in, resembling a tie-dyed shirt. However, these are considered rare in collector's circles and if found should be placed in an air-tight container and rushed to the Seymour Institute for inspection. Returning to the subject, the colored toothpicks are widely used for decoration purposes. They are not used by the tough youths of America as they are considered not cool.

The flavored toothpick is the Cadillac of toothpick technology. Intimately packaged in twos they are found in small, out of the way, romantic restaurants and are used in place of after-dinner mints.

Finally we have the prickly toothpick. With their brightly colored "skirts," these toothpicks are used to make unsavory hamburgers look savory. The makers of these picks have been accused of trying to put an air of show business into the toothpick industry, an accusation to which they have pleaded "nolo contendere." It is my opinion that these "showy" picks will become obsolete, owing to their only having one end that serves as a conventional toothpick.

Thanks to these explanations of each toothpick and its purpose, anyone should be able to pick the precise pick for the purpose. Toothpick etiquette has remained one of the few major social institutions left in this modern world, a tradition of which we should all be proud.

DEFINITION

As the preceding section indicated, classification is a relatively uncomplicated process when there is general agreement about the scope and meaning of a term; thus the term as a *class* has already been determined. But often a term has several possible meanings, depending on the situation and the audience. In such cases, the writer or speaker must isolate and clarify the meaning intended. For instance, a professor in a psychology or education course might frequently use the phrase *exceptional children*. Without knowledge of the specialized definition, you might assume that the term refers to highly intelligent or gifted children. Other students might think the children are mentally retarded. Neither assumption would be accurate here. Thus your professor is obligated to explain that the specialized definition applies to *any* child who does not meet the criteria for "normal." True, the term *exceptional children* does include both bright and mentally retarded children. But its specialized meaning in education and psychology also includes children with birth defects, children with acquired physical handicaps, and emotionally disturbed children.

The definition of a word or term, then, is often crucial to clear communication. And, as our examples and earlier discussion implied, the connotative meaning of a word depends on numerous factors: context, age of the user, geographical dialect, use in specialized language. To write clearly, especially in exposition, you will often have to define your terms, particularly abstract, technical, and key words. So you should be aware of the different ways of handling definition. Your choice depends on your purpose and the word's complexity, or difficulty.

Synonym Definition

We used this technique in the preceding sentence by adding *difficulty* to indicate the meaning of *complexity*. This simple method of defining by adding one or more similar terms can clarify an unfamiliar word quickly and easily. Synonym definition is particularly helpful in supplying a brief explanation for those readers who need it without boring or offending those who do not. Synonym definition, however, should not be used with key or complex terms because such words require more complete explanations.

Illustrative Definition

This definition relies on examples to explain the term. Often it consists of naming or pointing to a specific person, place, or thing to illustrate the meaning: "110 pocket cameras, such as the Kodak Instamatic, are convenient." An illustrative definition may also explain an unfamiliar term by referring to a familiar one, as when New England town meetings are used as an example to explain the direct democracy of ancient Athens.

Negative Definition

It is often necessary to define a term by indicating what it is not, as with *widow:* a woman whose husband is not living and who has not remarried. But except in such cases, negative definition should be combined with other forms of definition. For example, in a paper about equal employment opportunities for minorities, you might define *minorities* as referring not to religious minorities (Jews) or national minorities (Japanese-Americans), but to economically deprived minorities (blacks, Indians, Chicanos).

Formal Definition

Frequently, in writing a paper, you will need a more accurate and precise definition of a term than the ones just described. This is particularly true when you use a word in a very special or limited sense. Let's select as an example our previous term, *exceptional children,* this time to refer to highly intelligent or creative children. In such a situation, a formal definition would be helpful.

If you were classifying *exceptional children,* you would subdivide it into its parts—the gifted, the handicapped, and so forth—and further subdivide them. In definition, however, although you classify, you do it differently. You begin by describing your term as part of a larger group and then indicate how it differs from other members of that group. Exceptional children, therefore, are members of a group of children who are not ordinary or average. As you plan to use the term, exceptional children differ from other members of that group by possessing such qualities as high IQ, unusual problem-solving ability, a high degree of creativity, and mature motor-development. Thus you have first related the term to be defined to a larger group (non-average children); then you have explained how your use of the term possesses qualities that distinguish it from other members of that group. You have performed these two steps:

1. Related the term to its larger group or class.
2. Indicated how it differs from other members of that group or class.

Here's another example to show you how formal definition works. Suppose you wish to define the term *university* accurately in a paper. First, you should determine the larger class the term belongs to, in this case *institution of higher learning*. However, there are other institutions of higher learning; you must now determine what distinguishing features a university has that are not shared by other members of its larger class—four-year colleges, junior colleges, community colleges—all of which, like universities, award some kind of undergraduate degree or diploma. But a university is different in some ways from a college. An organizational scheme for a formal definition that includes these differences could look like this:

1. Item to be defined: *university*
2. Larger class: *institution of higher learning*
3. Distinguishing features that make it different from other members of the class:
   a. Includes a number of colleges.
   b. Awards degrees at the master's and doctoral levels.
   c. Awards advanced professional degrees (such as law, medicine, engineering).
   d. Places great emphasis on research.

The following brief formal definition, which clearly establishes *university* as a class, could be written from this scheme:

> A university is an institution of higher learning that is made up of not one, but many colleges. A university awards degrees, not only at the bachelor's level, but also at the master's and doctoral levels. In addition, it trains advanced professional people in such fields as law, medicine, and engineering. Unlike other institutions of higher learning, it places a high premium on research in all fields.

Note that the example follows certain procedures recommended in writing a formal definition:

1. It uses a form of the verb *be:* "A university *is* . . ." (Occasionally, verbs such as *means* or *refers to* are used.)
2. The definition statements are positive. They avoid the vagueness often resulting from negative statements: "A university is not a four-year college."
3. A synonym for the term or the term itself is not used in the definition. Taboo: "A university is a *university* of higher learning." Or "A university is a *multiversity* of higher learning."
4. A definition avoids figurative language. Defining a university as "a haven where dreams are realized or shattered" tells nothing about the function of a university.
5. A definition should not show personal bias: "A university is allegedly an institution of higher learning."

It may be fun to write comic, caustic, or witty definitions such as "Love is a warm football date." And it may be easy to dash off inaccurate generalizations like "A university is a place where people go to attend football games." But it takes hard and painstaking work to define a term accurately and logically in a formal definition.

Extended Definition

Occasionally you will need to develop a more complete, detailed explanation of a term than you can achieve in a formal definition of a few sentences. Let's say you are asked in a history course to write about the legislative branch of the American government. Extended definition is one form that such a paper could take. Your first task is to identify the larger group it belongs to: *legislative branch of government*. Then you need to distinguish between the American form and other legislatures, such as the British, Canadian, or French, to show what distinguishing features the American form has that are not shared by the others. In doing this, you are using the techniques of formal definition. Now that your class term has been clearly explained, you can expand the formal definition by subclassifying the term into the legislative branches of federal government, the state governments, and local governments. The result would be an extended definition, a rhetorical form with two main parts:

1. Establishment of class. As we have said, this involves the methods of formal definition, introducing the term and setting up its distinguishing features. Two common methods of separating a particular meaning of a term from other possibilities are to examine the historical origin and meaning of a word (its derivation), and to examine some crucial aspect of the item in great detail. For instance, in your extended definition of the American legislative branch of government, you might include the derivation of the word *legislature* from the Latin *lex,* meaning "law."
2. Extended discussion of the term. A term can be more fully explained in a number of ways: subclassification, discussion of the history of the word, extensive comparison with a similar item, historical or sociological analysis of the term, or examples. Any one or combination of these can be used in an extended definition.
   a. Subclassification. This involves subcategorizing the members of the class, as in classification. You can simply enumerate them, compare and contrast them, furnish an extensive description of them, or subdivide them into more subclasses.
   b. History of the word. This will involve using a dictionary with information about the origin and history of a word, as we suggested earlier for *legislature.* Such information is not only helpful to the definition of a term, but adds interest and life.

c. Comparison. This device is especially useful when defining a new term or one that has many connotations. In defining *detective story*, for example, you might pinpoint your definition of the term by comparing it to other kinds of mystery stories.
d. Historical or sociological analysis. This approach would be especially applicable to subjects like our legislature example. Giving a brief history of the development of legislative forms of government, starting perhaps with the Greek and Roman forms, could help explain the peculiar characteristics of American legislatures.

Some of these techniques are exemplified in the following example—an extended definition written by a student.

HOLLERS

Benita Joy Riley

First-time visitors to southern Appalachia are often left perplexed when told that someone lives "two miles up the holler"; or that to reach their destination they must "go to the mouth of the holler and turn right." Directions such as these only leave strangers asking themselves and others, "What's a *holler?*" or "What's a *mouth?*"

Introduction
Introduces the term to be defined

The word *hollow* would have little meaning to most native mountaineers in a region where the colloquial pronunciation and spelling are so prevalent that they are assumed to be correct. So, for the purposes of this paper, the more familiar word "holler" will be used.

Explanation of the word form

To say that a holler is simply a narrow valley between two hills completely denies the true essence and life of the term. Hollers reveal social standing, exemplify voluntary social segregation, represent family clans, and provide a sense of community. In physical fact, a holler is a very narrow valley beginning at the part known as the "mouth" and terminating at the "head." Usually the mouth of the holler is closest to one of the small towns scattered throughout the hills, or is found leading onto a main, paved road. Also, many times, a small branch of a creek, or "crick," runs into a larger body of water at the mouth of the holler. The source of the smaller creek usually can be found at the head of the holler where the water trickles slowly and constantly out of the hills be-

Formal Definition
States distinguishing features of a holler as a social entity and as a physical place

hind. At the head, the holler abruptly ends and fades into the wooded mountains.

To the people who populate the hollers, the location of their homes is very important. Almost always the more affluent families occupy the larger, nicer homes found at the mouth of the holler, closest to the store, post office, and main road. Farther up the holler, visitors find the more poverty-ridden and substandard living conditions. The mountain phrase, "she acts like she comes from the head of a holler," has definite negative connotation in Appalachia.

Sociological Analysis

But frequently the holler population represents a family clan with numerous relationships spanning several generations. In such cases of social segregation, the family name is almost always given to the holler and fierce loyalties flourish within these clannish groups. It is very doubtful that a stranger could make it to the head of "Hall Holler," for example, without meeting up with several Halls inquiring about the nature of the visit.

Subclassification
a. Family clans
b. Diverse but close-knit communities

Even people in a holler filled with diverse, unrelated families are united by a sense of belonging together. It's hard to keep a secret in a holler, especially since there is only one road and it goes by everyone's house. All comings and goings are noticed by neighbors who sit on their front porches during the evening hours.

Comparison

There are no signs in the mountains saying "This is a holler." But the hollers are there, at every turn—narrow valleys of life and lore, a part of the lifeline that is Appalachia.

ANALYSIS

The Uses of Analysis

We said earlier in the chapter that process description deals with *how*, while classification and definition deal mainly with *what*. In handling these forms you should be objective—reaching outside your personal observations to the public domain of facts and knowledge. But analysis papers concerned with *why* demand that you rely on your personal domain as well—drawing inferences, making judgments, expressing your opinions about the subject.

Like classification, analysis is a sorting process, dividing an item into its component parts. But as we have implied, analysis goes one step further; it deals with the relationships each part has to the others and to the whole. In a classification paper about the student organizations on your campus, for instance, you would merely list the different types—Greek organizations, religious clubs, service-oriented goups, academic societies, and so on—and briefly describe their activities. But in writing an analytical discussion of the same subject, you would include material on how you find them similar to or different from each other; you would express your views on why they exist, what their contributions are to students, or why you think they are important to campus life.

In writing an analysis paper, then, you need to go beyond public knowledge of the subject and apply your own critical skills by asking such questions as these:

Why is each part or step important to the others? How related?
In what ways are the parts similar? In what ways different?
Do they have an effect on _____? Why?
Why are the parts important to the whole?

Describing Relationships in an Analysis

As you might have guessed from the previous questions, the two most common methods of relating items in an analysis are (1) by comparing and contrasting, and (2) by showing the causes for a certain effect. The first involves pointing out the similarities and differences of the items that make up the subject, or comparing them with items more familiar to your audience. For instance, in writing to a general audience about a complex subject like the federal deficit, you might compare it to a family's use of credit. The second common method, pointing out causes for a specific effect, might be useful in a paper on freshman alienation. The sense of isolation experienced by many students in a large university (an *effect*) might be attributed to the university organization. Deans, department heads, or faculty members may not show enough interest in students' emotional adjustment to school. And the student government may be elitist, concerned only with a small clique. In your opinion, these could be two valid reasons (or *causes*) why freshmen feel lonely and isolated.

Cause-and-effect analysis is often used in reporting a scientific experiment or observation—for example, in explaining chronic inflation or the failure of something to function. But it is also used when writers set forth their opinion about something; essentially they are saying "I hold this opinion because. . . ." In such a paper the opening paragraphs express the opinion (the effect) and the remainder deals with the reasons (the causes) for the formulation of the opinion. The following essay analyzes the student

189

writer's opinion about enforced retirement, a policy that has been legally modified since the writing of the paper.

MANDATORY RETIREMENT

Paula Mahoney

In many Asian countries the older people are considered to be very important members of society because they are thought to hold the wisdom and knowledge that only the experience of living can give. In our society we believe that wisdom comes from a college degree, not from years of living. Age does not bring wisdom, only senility. As a result of our views, the aging people of society have to a large extent lost their productive value. One practice that clearly illustrates this lack of respect is mandatory retirement, which requires people at the age of 65 to retire from their jobs.

Introduction
Introduces the problem, mandatory retirement. States the writer's opinion about the problem: the effect.

Mandatory retirement wastes valuable human resources and talents. There are many reasons why older people should be kept working as long as possible. They have gained the stability and responsibility that comes from maturity. Because they have many years of experience behind them, they are usually good leaders and have steadier work habits. Studies made by the Bureau of Employment Security have found that older workers account for less absenteeism and waste less time on the job than younger people. The agency feels that older workers are less distracted by outside interests and influences, and have fewer family problems. In addition, older women are not likely to take time off to bear and raise children.

Body
Discusses three reasons for the writer's opinion— the causes:
1. Causes a waste of resources

Our society abounds with examples of older people who have continued to make important contributions after the age of 65. Agatha Christie was in her eighties when she died, but continued writing up to her death. The famous conductor Leopold Stokowski was still active at 94. Margaret Mead, the noted anthropologist, continued her research, lecturing, and writing until her death at 77. Ten percent of the members of Congress are over 65. It is easy to see how human talent and knowledge would be wasted if these people were forced to stop working.

In addition to wasted human resources, mandatory retirement also causes economic problems both for those who must retire and for the rest of the working and tax-paying population. Retired persons often find it difficult, if not impossible, to survive on their Social Security pensions, even if they are supplemented by some company plan. If a person is getting money from a company pension, other workers must contribute to the retiree. However, the most detrimental economic effect is on the Social Security system, already in trouble, because it must pay out more than it receives.

2. Causes economic problems

Lastly, mandatory retirement also causes emotional problems which often lead to physical ones. When people are forced to retire they often feel that their freedom of choice, their pride, and their value to society are stripped from them. An older man may become obsessed with minor ailments that can stem from boredom, and from a self-fulfilling prophecy that since he is no longer able to work, his health must be declining. He becomes senile because that is expected of him. It has been reported that there is a disproportionate death rate among those forced to retire, compared to that of those who choose to retire.

3. Causes health problems

In view of these human and economic problems, mandatory retirement does not appear to be a viable solution for aging people. Allowing people to work until ready for retirement seems not only a humane approach, but a solution to many economic problems as well. All of us grow old; surely we should be allowed to do it with dignity.

Conclusion
Restatement of opinion

Even in such a relatively simple discussion as this one, causal analysis can become quite complex. Not only can we view the waste of human resources, economic problems, and health problems as causes contributing to the writer's conclusion about retirement; but retirement could also be the cause behind the effects of wasted lives, ill health, and economic problems of the aged. As you can see, causal relations involve not only writing concerns, but logical thinking processes as well: thus, we will deal with this kind of analysis at greater length in the section on argumentation.

Here, we are interested only in introducing you to the techniques for organizing the kind of analysis in which you present the causes or reasons for your opinion or attitude about a subject.

SUMMARY

In the previous pages, we have looked at the most commonly used methods of exposition: the ways that writers explain and order knowledge and experience so that an audience can receive the message clearly. The structures outlined in the relatively objective forms—process description, classification, and definition—can serve as an organizational pattern for writing your own papers. These are the "game patterns" established for these rhetorical forms.

Papers that involve analysis, however—whether for the purpose of comparing, of predicting the effect of a particular phenomenon, or of giving the reasons why you hold a certain opinion about something—must rely more heavily on the logical relationships of the material. For such a paper, therefore, you need a strategy that goes beyond a mere outline. In Chapter 12, we will explore the techniques that you can use in the pre-writing stage of a comparison-and-contrast paper or one dealing with the causes for an opinion.

Assignments

For Discussion

1   Discuss the steps required for writing a process description of the following:

   a   Buying a car
   b   Making a dress
   c   Getting a date
   d   Getting a good grade
   e   Tuning up a car
   f   Washing clothes at a coin laundry

2   Work out the classification scheme used in "A Picky Choice," pages 182–83.

3   Discuss the different classification approaches that might be used for the following:

   a   Cafeterias
   b   Hamburgers
   c   Jocks

   d College bands
   e Rock-band stars
   f TV situation comedies

4 Indicate whether the following statements are adequate or inadequate as formal definitions and why:

   a A chair is an object that a person sits on.
   b A holiday is when you don't have to work.
   c Communism is the form of government they have in Russia.
   d A free person is not a hungry puppy.
   e Love is the most beautiful emotion.
   f Happiness is a warm puppy.
   g A schlemiel is a person who falls on his back and breaks his nose.
   h Obscenity is the state of being obscene.
   i Life is just a bowl of cherries.
   j Discord is disharmony.

5 Consider the following statements about war to determine their adequacy as formal definitions and also to note whether they contain anything that would be helpful to you in writing an extended definition of the subject.

   a War, more ancient than any history, is the outcome of passions, follies, fallacies, misconceptions, and defective political institutions common to the great mass of men. They are not incurable misconceptions, not incurable follies. But they may well become so if we persist in assuming that they don't exist.

            —Sir Norman Angell

   b For a war to be just, three conditions are necessary—public authority, just cause, right motive. . . . But those wars also are just, without doubt, which are ordained by God himself, in whom is no iniquity, and who knows every man's merits.

            —St. Augustine

   c War is a racket.

            —Smedley Butler

   d To my mind, to kill in war is not a whit better than to commit ordinary murder.

            —Albert Einstein

   e War is delightful to those who have had no experience of it.

            —Erasmus

   f Warfare is the means whereby the members of a parasitic ruling class of alien origin endeavor, while exploiting their own subjects, to dominate those surrounding peoples who produce wealth in a tangible and desired form.

—Havelock Ellis

g We have no adequate idea of the predisposing power which an immense series of measures of preparation for war has in actually begetting war.

—William E. Gladstone

h I have never advocated war except as a means of peace.

—Ulysses S. Grant

i War is a science, a series of mathematical problems, to be solved through proper integration and coordination of men and weapons in time and space.

—George Zhukov

j War alone brings up to its highest tension all human energy, puts the stamp of nobility upon the peoples who have the courage to meet it.

—Benito Mussolini

6 The following passage is from the Student Code of the University of Kentucky. Analyze it as an extended definition. Which of the steps recommended in this chapter does it include?

PLAGIARISM

All academic work, written or otherwise, submitted by a student to his instructor or other academic supervisor, is expected to be the result of his own thought, research, or self-expression. In any case in which a student feels unsure about a question of plagiarism involving his work, he is obliged to consult his instructor on the matter before submitting it.

When a student submits work purporting to be his own, but which in any way borrows ideas, organization, wording or anything else from another source without appropriate acknowledgement of the fact, the student is guilty of plagiarism.

Plagiarism includes reproducing someone else's work, whether it be a published article, chapter of a book, a paper from a friend or some file, or whatever. Plagiarism also includes the practice of employing or allowing another person to alter or revise the work which a student submits as his own, whoever that other person may be. Students may discuss assignments among themselves or with an instructor or tutor, but when the actual work is done, it must be done by the student and the student alone.

When a student's assignment involves research in outside sources or information, he must carefully acknowledge exactly what, where, and how he has employed them. If he uses words of someone else, he must put quotation marks around the passage in question and add an appropriate indication of its origin. Making simple changes while leaving the organization, content, and phraseology intact is plagiaristic. However, nothing in these rules shall apply to those ideas which are so generally and freely circulated as to be part of the public domain.

For Practice

1 Write a paragraph describing a simple process such as those illustrated in this chapter. Be sure to include all the necessary steps in their chronological order.

2 Write a one-sentence formal definition of one of the following:

    a A blind date
    b A turnover (basketball)
    c An easy grader
    d Thumbing a ride
    e A roadie
    f A dormitory

3 Write a paragraph expressing and briefly supporting an opinion you have about something.

For Writing

1 Using the techniques of classification suggested in this chapter, write a paper of classification on one of the topics in Discussion Exercise 3 or on one of the following:

race cars	recreation vehicles
male chauvinists	tents
feminists	back-packers
fishing lures	a type of popular music
bicycles	college roommates
TV heroines	campus dates
cola ads	TV heroes

2 Choose one of the following terms or one of your own and, using the method recommended in this chapter, write an extended definition of it.

designated hitter	sexism
screen pass	ripoff
phase elective	bugging
back-packing	X-rated
high-school senioritis	condominium
Black Power	tachometer
school spirit	funky
phony	sisterhood
ghetto	cheating

Pre-Writing
and Exposition

The art of writing consists of more than the act of writing. Already you are familiar with revising and proofreading, two necessary and important steps occurring *after* writing a first draft. Now we wish to discuss pre-writing, another key part of the writing process, which, as its name indicates, occurs *before* writing a first draft.

Pre-writing involves four steps:

1. selecting a topic
2. limiting the topic
3. formulating a thesis statement
4. developing a plan or outline

In writing your personal and descriptive papers, you may have engaged in these activities. But you probably found it relatively simple to select and limit your topic and organize your paper. It was probably easy to recall interesting experiences or memorable scenes, to limit your paper to what you could relate vividly in a short paper, and to arrange your material in either a time or space sequence.

In expository writing, these matters are more difficult. Often you can't think of anything to write about. Or if you decide on a general subject, like television or education, you can't determine how to restrict it to a manageable topic you can explain intelligently in a short paper. Then when you do select a topic, you find it difficult to organize your ideas because neither time nor space arrangements will do the trick. Also, in writing expository papers you are bound by another convention. Because readers expect explanation rather than entertainment, they want to know early what your paper is about. Consequently, you need to provide a thesis statement, expressing the thesis or main idea, somewhat like the focusing statement in descriptions or personal essays.

Therefore, expository writing is usually more difficult and demanding than personal and descriptive writing. Consequently, you should spend more time and energy in the process of pre-writing, thus preparing yourself more completely for writing your paper. To help you, we will consider in some detail each of the four steps mentioned previously. We have arranged these steps in chronological order, even though not everyone follows this order. But the final three steps are always dependent upon the first.

SELECTING A TOPIC

Quite often, in college and later, at work, you will be assigned a topic. Your history, sociology, or psychology instructor will suggest certain ideas or problems, or your boss at work will ask you to get out a memo or letter about a specific matter. And your English instructor may assign topics from an essay collection, this book, or another source. But what if you have to come up with one of your own? Or what if one is assigned, but it leaves you blank?

You can wait for an inspiration, but you may wait for months. If one comes while you are daydreaming through a lecture or listening to music, fine. So much the better. But what if it doesn't? What then? Try one or both of these methods: brainstorming and inventing.

Brainstorming

Brainstorming requires your writing down any feasible idea that comes to mind. It necessitates concentrating for about thirty minutes to produce a list of ideas. During this time, search through your bag of interests, hobbies, gripes, likes, and worries. Think about whatever preoccupies your friends, father, mother, brother or sister, aunt or uncle, grandparents, neighbors, high school teacher, coach, doctor, clergyman, druggist, mailcarrier, or any of the other people you customarily talk to. What do you converse about after the weather and their health? Write down any possible subject. Then think about the conversations you've had during the past few days with friends. List again. Also review recent class lectures and discussions that interested you. List them. Finally, flip through some newspapers or magazines for ideas. List, list, list. And in the process, write down any related ideas. A thought that hardly any TV characters worry about money might lead you through association to such other omissions as the relative lack of handicapped, old, fat, or divorced people on television. What is important is to generate ideas. Afterwards you can discard the unappealing or impractical ones.

Invention

If brainstorming fails to produce an interesting topic, try inventing one. Here's one way to go about it. Select some broad subject of interest, such as automobiles, camping, medicine, or sports. Then narrow your focus somewhat—say, from sports to football. Finally, run this subject through the perspective of various academic disciplines. Here's how to go about it, using football as an example:

Academic discipline	Topics
Agriculture:	Comparison of grass field and artificial turf
Architecture:	Football stadiums: covered or open; design; sight-lines; comfort; accessibility; parking arrangements
Art:	Pageantry of college football games
Economics:	Cost of tickets, food, parking; expense of football team
Engineering:	Machines used in practice or exercise; computer-aided defense
Health:	Football injuries
History:	The game past and present; rule changes; change in top teams
Music:	Unappreciated role of bands; marching bands; half-time performances
Law:	——
Literature:	Depiction of football players in novels, films, plays
Religion:	Nature and purpose of opening prayer; football and character-building
Science:	Application of scientific principles to training; off-season conditioning

And, for good luck (or good ideas) you might throw in these additional perspectives, or some of your own:

Social life:	Tailgating; football dating; victory parties
Future:	Changes in the game
Feminism:	Football for women; women playing on men's teams
Contrast:	Football and soccer, baseball, tennis
Comparison:	Football and big business; coach as corporate executive
Children:	Danger of children playing football
Television:	Impact of TV on football games

This invention system comes with no money-back guarantees. You may strike many blanks, as we did with Law. Or you may hit on many ideas but none that suit your fancy. But either invention or brainstorming should be far more helpful than waiting for an inspiration, wringing your hands, or moaning, "I can't think of anything."

Also, nothing is sacred about these methods. You will not be graded on how many categories you can fill or how many ideas you can develop. Use them any way you wish to find and decide on a topic or to generate additional ideas. They are ways to help you when you feel helpless.

The Final Choice

So far we've been concerned with generating ideas for a topic. Assuming you have found several, which one should you choose?

One important consideration in choosing a topic, of course, is your purpose—writing the paper. Many of the topics that have been generated here lend themselves better to certain kinds of exposition than to others. Because "tailgating," for instance, in the sense of picnicking from the tailgate of a station wagon, is a relatively new use for this word, you might want to give your readers an extended definition of the term. The topic under Architecture suggests a classification, while the two under Science seem to necessitate a process description. Others seem more appropriate to analysis: comparison of grass field versus artificial turf; the historical changes; attitudes or opinions you might have about injuries or women's participation in football.

Another important consideration in choosing a topic is the kind of audience you plan to address. Readers who are football players would be more interested in technical aspects of the game than in the stadium parties; teachers or parents might find a paper on the character-building potential of football more to their liking than a discussion of football as big business.

But important also is that the topic appeal to you, as well as to your readers. If you are not interested in a subject, you will find it difficult to interest others, which is part of your writing commitment. Sometimes we suspect a national student conspiracy to bore freshman English instructors because they are a captive audience required to read all papers. We urge instead a campaign to interest all readers—instructors, classmates, and others.

A related consideration is the complexity of a topic. No matter how much it interests you, if you don't know quite a bit about a topic and don't have the time to do research, forget it. On the other hand, don't feel you have to be an expert. Whether you realize it or not, you bring a different perspective and fresh thoughts to a subject even though you may not know everything about it. If you are reasonably informed about it, you can say something interesting and worthwhile.

199

RESTRICTING THE TOPIC

Thus far in our discussion of pre-writing, we've tried to suggest a method and to set up some criteria for choosing a topic. Next you must consider whether the topic is suitable for your purpose, or whether it is too broad for a short paper.

Most students err in selecting a topic too huge to handle. Understandably, they feel more secure with a broad subject, confident they can grind out a paper long enough to fulfill the assignment. Thus it seems safer to write about cooking than about a more restricted subject like crockpot cookery. But remember, the aim of writing an expository paper is to explain something in great detail. In a short paper, no writer can do justice to a subject as vast as cooking.

One way to test the scope of your topic is to write a rough draft. If you can only come up with one page, the topic is too restricted; but if you find yourself writing four or five pages on one aspect, the subject is obviously too broad. Another way is to see how many main ideas you would have to discuss in order to cover the subject thoroughly. If three or four main points are adequate, then you are safe to assume that your topic is sufficiently restricted. However, more than that indicates that you need to narrow the subject further—to shift to a more specific, particular treatment.

For example, let's say you want to write a paper about the growing popularity of sports. Because that subject includes both spectator and participant sports, you can see that to deal with both would require a volume. You would be well advised to narrow it to one or the other. Taking participant sports, you might consider the growing popularity of sports that fit the classification: golf, tennis, running, cycling, soccer, volleyball, and so on. Aha! you think. There certainly is enough here to write about. But can you explain about each sport, relate it to other participant sports, and express your views about them? Not in a short paper. True, you could write a classification paper, but if your purpose is to express an opinion or present a viewpoint about the subject, the topic is still too broad; any explanation would be highly superficial. And so you need to narrow your topic still further. Choosing one sport to talk about would solve your problem. Consequently, you might decide to write on the growing popularity of soccer.

Your next step, then, is to generate three or four main points that you would like to make. For instance, you could write about the availability of soccer fields, the comparatively low cost of equipment, the relatively low risk of serious injuries, the ease of learning to play, or the fact that it is a team sport, enjoyable for all. Out of these, you can choose the three or four main points that you feel best explain the growing popularity of soccer. Thus, you have now restricted your subject to a workable length. By the time you have finished this second step, you are well on your way to the third—formulating a thesis idea.

FORMULATING A THESIS STATEMENT

The Function of the Thesis Statement

Formulating a thesis statement is considered by many to be the most important part of the pre-writing process. Many composition teachers who do not require a formal outline from students do demand a concise, straightforward summary of the main idea to be dealt with in the paper. Such a thesis not only summarizes what the paper is about, but shows the restriction of the topic. For instance, the thesis statement "Football injuries could be alleviated by better training practices" limits the writer to dealing only with those injuries and training practices occurring in football. Switching to a long discussion of injuries in baseball or basketball would not be feasible under the restrictions of this thesis.

The main function of the thesis, then, is to indicate your subject and to provide you with a "rudder" for maintaining restriction and focus; with it you can steer clear of the muddy shoals of indecisive and disorganized writing. In order to guide you safely through a paper, your thesis should include the following characteristics:

1. The thesis statement should be a simple, declarative sentence, stating only the main idea of the paper. In order to be as concise and straightforward as possible, you should avoid a complex sentence full of subordinate ideas, which can often trap the inexperienced writer. Here's an example:

   In spite of the danger that many guilty parties may go unpunished by law because the resulting publicity may make a fair trial impossible, *the Senate is justified in holding public hearings on wrongdoings in government.*

   As you can see, there are two possible subjects included in the sentence: (1) guilty parties may go unpunished, and (2) the Senate is justified in holding the hearings. However, the italicized material is the main idea in the thesis and the one your readers would expect you to write about. But too often, inexperienced writers get mired down in a long discussion of such subordinate material as "many guilty parties may go unpunished," and then as an afterthought sail quickly through the real subject in the last paragraph or so. A simple declarative sentence that expresses clearly the main idea of the paper can usually prevent this false emphasis.

2. The thesis statement should suggest both what you intend to do in the paper and your attitude toward your subject. Inexperienced writers often feel that they must hit their readers over the head by starting with such phrases as "My purpose in this paper is," or "I intend to show that," or "It is my opinion that."

Except when writing scientific or technical papers, sophisticated writers generally avoid a bald statement of purpose. And unless they are trying to establish themselves as an authority or to justify an unpopular opinion, they also avoid overtly stating their opinion, letting other devices indicate their bias toward the subject. Let's look at two examples, to see the difference between explicit and implicit statements of purpose and opinion.

Example: *My purpose in this paper is to support the view* that a college education is a lifelong benefit.

Revision: A college education is a lifelong benefit.

The first version is wordy, formal, and somewhat pretentious, perhaps projecting a condescending tone. In the revised statement, the purpose or intent is still there; the reader expects the writer to support this view. Here's an example of opinion overkill:

Example: *I think that* strip-mining is only a short-term, environmentally destructive solution to the long-term problem of fuel shortages.

Revision: Strip-mining is only a short-term, environmentally destructive solution to the long-term problem of fuel shortages.

The revised version expresses the writer's opinion as forcefully as the first; the emotionally charged words, such as *environmentally destructive,* and restrictive devices, such as "only," sufficiently indicate the writer's attitude toward the subject.

3. The thesis statement should be expressed in specific, concrete language. You should avoid using figurative or emotional language that is vague and inexact.

Example: Documentary dramas on television are *like figures in a wax museum.* (figurative)

Example: Documentary dramas are *absurdly deceiving.* (highly emotional)

Neither tells much about the main idea, and to a great extent both would be difficult to support with examples, reasons, or facts. The first makes an analogy, but the purpose of the comparison is not clear. The second expresses a strong, emotional opinion that cannot provide the kind of focus and restriction demanded of a thesis statement. A better version for both might be:

Revision: Documentary dramas frequently mislead audiences into accepting a distorted view of history.

By making sure that your thesis statements satisfy these three criteria, you can be reasonably certain that you have focused and restricted your subject and expressed your attitude toward it.

The Thesis Statement and Expository Form

Thesis statements should be designed to fit your writing assignment. A process description or classification often needs only an introductory statement similar to the focusing statement of a description or personal essay. For instance, in a paper explaining how to study, a thesis such as this would suffice:

Study skills are necessary for academic success.

As we mentioned in the last chapter, an extended definition usually opens with a brief formal definition, which then serves as the thesis statement:

"TV sportsaholics" are sports fans who watch TV sports programs with a compulsion beyond their control.

As you can see, these thesis statements are closely related to the organizational schemes for writing process descriptions, classifications, and extended definitions. But the thesis required for an analysis paper is in a sense an inference statement—a conclusion based on some kind of evidence or observation. An inference thesis can take several forms and can generate different kinds of analysis papers. Here are some examples:

1. Inference thesis for analysis of an opinion or viewpoint.

   a. The financial plight of the big cities may be a serious national economic threat.

A conclusion drawn from evidence, this thesis demands extensive information about the reasons why the financial problems of big cities will adversely affect federal taxes and spending.

   b. Television commercials have become a pop art form.

A conclusion drawn from observation and perhaps requiring definition of "pop art," this example nevertheless requires the writer to draw largely from personal experience and opinion.

   c. Congress needs to reform committee structure, committee assignments, and subcommittee activity.

Although an inference thesis whose main statement is "Congress needs reform," this thesis differs by including a brief outline of the three main points. Sometimes referred to as an "analytical" thesis, this form is useful for long papers or for complex subjects. However, it does impose some restrictions on the writer: (1) the points must be stated in parallel structure and must be parallel in idea; (2) the writer must decide in advance how the points will be presented in the paper.

2. Inference thesis for comparison-and-contrast analysis.

Fly rods are superior to casting rods in fishing for trout.

This is an inference drawn to a great extent from the writer's own experience and opinion. However, the form of the thesis requires the paper to demonstrate the superiority of the fly rod over the casting rod by discussing their similarities and differences.

One last word of advice: your thesis statement at this time is not binding. As you work through the planning stage or your first draft, you might find the statement inadequate. Feel free to make changes. But remember that any changes you make in the thesis should be reflected throughout the final draft of your paper.

DEVELOPING AN ORGANIZATIONAL PLAN

Just as in most human activities it pays to plan ahead, so in writing it pays to develop a skeletal plan or to outline your ideas. Some writing experts have recently claimed, however, that you don't really realize what you know about a subject until you express it. Therefore, after you select and restrict your subject, and formulate a tentative thesis idea, they suggest that you write out everything you know about it. Then from this first rough draft, you can rearrange your ideas into logical order, discard some digressions, and add material at certain critical points. There is merit in this approach—provided you are willing to work hard on your second draft and probably even write a third. Obviously, this process takes a great deal of discipline—a discipline that even the writers of this text often lack.

If you also lack this discipline, then you would benefit from drawing up a tentative outline in advance of your first draft, so that less revision will be necessary. After following our brainstorming and invention tactics this far, you certainly should have some ideas about your subject that you can jot down, categorize, and arrange in logical order for a workable plan. Then, as you write, this plan will free you from worrying about what to say next, and will allow you to concentrate on explaining the idea at hand. This way, you can select your words carefully, and create the most effective sentences and paragraphs.

But there is a danger in a preconceived plan. You may feel compelled to follow it slavishly, not allowing for relevant ideas you may think of as you write. So treat your plan as tentative. Remember that it is a way to help you organize your ideas, not a barrier to the discovery of new ones. In the rest of this section, we'll show you two extended examples of how to prepare such a plan—the first for a cause-and-effect analysis, the second for a comparison-and-contrast analysis.

Cause-and-Effect Organization

Assuming that you have selected your topic, restricted it, and formulated a tentative thesis idea, you are ready to generate the knowledge you have about the subject. Suppose you have decided to express your opinion that popular music is a more vigorous art form than it used to be. Using brainstorming tactics, you can then start randomly jotting down previous ideas and search for others. Your list might look like this:

1. Increase in record sales
2. Popularity of country music
3. Many kinds of rock music
4. Universal appeal
5. Protest music of the sixties
6. Use of electronics in modern music
7. Recent popularity of ballads
8. More sophisticated musical arrangements
9. Experimentation beginning with the Beatles
10. Revival of jazz and swing
11. Influence of soul music

From this list, you can move to categorizing, the next step in the process. Items 1 and 4 seem to relate to the popularity and vigor of pop music; items 6, 8, and 9 could fit into a general category having to do with its maturation or growing sophistication; while all the others attest to its present variety— country, rock, ballads, jazz, swing, and soul music. With this step, we have grouped many fairly particular ideas into three workable categories of major and minor points.

Ordering, the next step, involves arranging the ideas. One of the numerous factors to be considered has to do with the purpose you hope to achieve in the paper. By saving your most important point until last, you can make a powerful impression and fix the information more firmly in your reader's mind. Another factor, of course, is the audience. College-age readers might be more interested in the variety and in the performers of each type of music. Older people might be more impressed with information about the vast increase in record sales. Both these audience concerns should be considered before you make your final choice of order. A third factor is the material: if it is highly controversial, you might wish to present your most unacceptable point last. However, reader opposition does not seem to be a problem with popular music.

A first topic outline might look like this:

Thesis: Popular music is a more vital art form today than ever before.

    I. Popularity
       A. Universal appeal
       B. Increase in record sales
   II. Increased sophistication of popular music
       A. Advanced electronics
       B. More sophisticated arrangements
       C. Experimentation with new forms and instruments
  III. Wide variety of music
       A. Country
       B. Rock
       C. Ballads
       D. Jazz and swing
       E. Influence of soul and protest music.

Note that all the main items (numbered I, II, and III) have some direct relationship to the thesis idea. Of course, those relationships might be more clearly revealed if the topic phrases were full sentences, but even as expressed, they carry ideas that support the idea of popular music as a vital art form. In like manner, the items listed under the Roman numerals are related directly to the ideas expressed in their main point.

At this stage, specific examples could be added to the outline under each subtopic (A, B, etc.). For instance, Rock could be broken down into acid, punk, country, hard rock, and soft rock. You should recognize that this step is similar to a classification process. For many writers, this topic outline would be an adequate plan from which to write the first draft.

However, other writers might wish to show more clearly the relationship they wish to make with the points. In such a case, they would expand the main points of the topic outline into a sentence outline. Note that the word *because* could be inserted before each point, thus indicating the causal relationship.

        Thesis: Popular music is a more vital art form today than ever before.

(Because) I. The popularity and appeal of pop music are at an all-time high.
       A. Universal appeal
       B. Increase in record sales

(Because) II. The musical quality and sophistication are vastly improved over earlier forms of pop music.
       A. Advanced electronics
       B. More sophisticated arrangements
       C. Experimentation with new forms and instruments

(Because) III. The wide variety indicates that pop music is a healthier art form today.
- A. Country music
- B. Rock music
- C. Ballads and revivals
- D. Jazz and swing
- E. Influence of soul and protest music

(Some instructors may prefer that all points be stated in sentence form to indicate clearly all relationships.)

With either of these tentative outlines, you can begin writing a first draft, confident you have solved some of the problems inherent in dealing with cause-and-effect analysis. As you begin this draft, concentrate more on what you want to say than how you are saying it—stylistic revisions can come later. If you have a pertinent new point or if you even feel the need for a new category to justify your opinion, add it. Or, if you decide that a discussion of earlier influences on today's music is not relevant, omit it. At every step of the process—pre-writing, writing, and revising—writing should be creative and inventive so that you can learn and discover. Only then does it become an exciting and enriching experience.

Comparison-and-Contrast Organization

In organizing a comparison paper, you can follow all the pre-writing steps outlined earlier in the chapter. But in this kind of paper, you have both an advantage and a disadvantage in the organizational stage. The advantage is that you can follow a standard plan; the disadvantage is that two such plans are available, requiring therefore that you select the best one for your subject, audience, and purpose. Your choice is between the item-by-item comparison and the point-by-point comparison. To illustrate, suppose you want to compare the students of the '60s with those of the '70s, considering such matters as their educational interests, extracurricular activities, and social customs. Here are your two options:

Item plan	Point plan
I. '60s Students	I. Educational interests
A. Educational interests	A. '60s students
B. Extracurricular activities	B. '70s students
C. Social customs	II. Extracurricular activities
II. '70s Students	A. '60s students
A. Educational interests	B. '70s students
B. Extracurricular activities	III. Social customs
C. Social customs	A. '60s students
	B. '70s students

207

Deciding on whether to use the item or point plan is difficult. Each has its drawbacks. The weakness of the item comparison derives from the fact that the reader is apt to forget about the first subject (the '60s students) when reading about the second (the '70s students). The weakness of the point comparison stems from a ping-pong effect, causing the reader to bounce back and forth and perhaps to lose a sense of the whole.

And each plan has its strengths. The first is usually easier for writers because they can deal first with one subject, then another. Also, if the second item is more important than the first, the item plan will permit readers to remember it best. But usually, the point-by-point comparison is more effective because it brings into sharp view the ways that the items are similar to or different from each other. However, it would be almost impossible to use this plan to compare more than three items, say, the students of the '40s, '50s, '60s, and '70s.

USING THE OUTLINE

When you read the following points about using an outline, realize that it deals with the ideas presented in the *body* of your paper. The introduction and conclusion are separate parts with different rhetorical functions, which are discussed in Chapter 16. In longer papers or research papers, however, you may want to include ideas for your introduction and conclusion.

1. The outline, whether it is in topic or sentence form, is a *tool* to help you. Constructing an outline after writing the paper in order to satisfy an instructor's requirement is useless—unless you do the outline after the rough draft to catch weaknesses in your logic. But student writers are usually not proficient enough to do that, nor can they often bring themselves to completely rewrite a poorly organized first draft. It is almost always best to develop an outline before writing.

2. For convenience, the thesis statement is isolated from the rest of the outline. But in the paper, the thesis idea should be worked into the introduction. Only in scientific writing do you ever encounter a professionally published article with an isolated thesis. In such a case, the thesis serves as a brief abstract of the article.

3. The outline is the substructure of your final paper. If your paper is merely your outline put into paragraph form, then you are misusing this valuable tool. The outline can help you to organize your ideas, to indicate the major sections of the paper, and to set up logical relationships, but it is still only a skeleton. In writing the paper, you should add the flesh and form that make your subject aesthetic and exciting. A paper that goes no further than the outline is about as interesting and informative as someone else's botany notes.

4. The outline should not hamper or restrict you. Although your instructor

may require it, the outline exists not as an end in itself but as a means to help you improve the final product, your paper. As you are writing, for example, if you are smitten with some inspiration, feel free to add the new idea. But do check the outline carefully to see that such a change fits logically into the organization of your paper.

SUMMARY

In this chapter, we have discussed the subject of pre-writing, showing you how to generate a subject, restrict it, formulate a thesis statement, and organize an analysis paper. These pre-writing techniques may be used in any writing assignment, from the most precise scientific description to the most highly imaginative science fiction. Although each writing task presents its own individual problems, each requires some search for ideas, restriction of the subject, formulation of a main point, and concern about a plan of presentation. The more systematic your use of these pre-writing processes, the more effective your papers are likely to be.

Assignments

For Discussion

1   Here are some broad subjects that could lend themselves to opinion analysis, using either cause-and-effect or comparison-and-contrast organization. Apply the tactics of brainstorming and invention to generate ideas for paper topics. Then determine which would work best as cause-and-effect papers and which as comparison-and-contrast.

Advertising	Automobiles
Animals	Money
College	Movies
Crime	Hobbies
Drugs	Education

2   Discuss why each of the following sentences is inadequate as a thesis statement for an expository paper of opinion. Reword each to make it an effective, workable thesis.

a   The pollution caused by our technology has had an effect on everyone.

b   Classes are the toys of college freshmen, and drop-add is the traumatic procedure they must go through to purchase their toys.

c   Sports are a deciding factor in the actions and behavior of many people.

d   There has been a great need for organized labor because working conditions were bad, with long hours, low wages, and few vacations.

209

    e Should we grant amnesty to all, or should we grant amnesty with punishment, and who should make the final decision on amnesty?

    f Riding a bicycle to, from, and on the campus can be disastrous.

    g Football and soccer are alike in many ways.

    h In selecting a college, students consider academic reputation, social atmosphere, and costs.

    i Because college freshmen have a hard time adjusting, they need to live in a dormitory and be forced to attend class.

    j The registration system at this college is lousy.

3 Using the list in Exercise 1, generate a topic, restrict it, and formulate a thesis statement.

For Practice

1 Using the following list of ideas, develop a topic outline for an opinion-analysis paper. Formulate a thesis sentence and use only the items that seem relevant to your opinion about the subject.

Student loans	Tax rebates for educational
Scholarships	purposes
Government support for	Students with part-time jobs
students	Parental support
Free tuition for gifted students	Grant-in-aid scholarships for
Special scholarships	athletes
	Low-interest loans to students

2 Using the following list of ideas, formulate a thesis statement and develop a plan for comparing and contrasting several items. Use either the item plan or the point plan (pages 207–08 and be prepared to give reasons for your choice.

Home cooking	Vending-machine sandwiches
Cafeteria food	Picnic fare
Fast-food restaurants	TV dinners
Health food	Airplane food
Junk food	Chinese food

For Writing

1 Write a cause-and-effect paper, using the outline developed on pages 205–07 in this chapter. Or, if you prefer, develop an organizational plan on a subject of your own choosing.

2 Write a comparison-and-contrast paper. You may use one of the subjects outlined on page 207 or develop an organizational plan on a topic of your own choosing.

The Form
of the Expository
Paragraph

WHAT IS AN EXPOSITORY PARAGRAPH?

Earlier, in discussing personal and descriptive writing, we were more concerned with sentence structure and word choice than with paragraph structure. Paragraphing in personal forms of writing has few conventions. Writers shape their paragraphs to the needs of the task at hand: creating realistic dialogue, giving special emphasis, or often bowing to personal whim. Obviously, the relatively loose quality of personal and descriptive writing permits much variety and individuality. But paragraphs in expository papers, like the expository forms themselves, are generally more tightly constructed. However, that is not to say that all expository para-graphs are exactly alike.

In books, magazines, and newspapers, paragraph length varies greatly, often controlled more by the medium than the message. For instance, newspaper paragraphs tend to be short; that is because newspaper articles are usually reportive, containing only the essential facts about an incident or situation, and because newspaper columns are narrow, so that long paragraphs would seem endless on the page. If you examine a variety of magazines and books, you will probably find that their paragraph length often reflects the audience the material is aimed at. Magazines for general audiences, like *Time* and *Newsweek,* tend to have shorter paragraphs than those written for more educated readers, like *Harper's* and *Atlantic Monthly.* Defining the nature of expository paragraphs is further complicated by the practice of interspersing short paragraphs for emphasis or transition, even in scholarly articles or books.

In spite of its elusive character and its infinite variety, the paragraph, like the sentence, does seem to be a recognizable convention of the language. Even though linguists and rhetoricians continue to debate the fine points of sentence definition, most people agree on what a sentence is. So, too, with expository paragraphs.

Try this simple experiment. Read this passage from a freshman paper, indicating where you sense that paragraphing is indicated. Then check your results with those of your classmates to find whether most of you agree.

1. To a speleologist the excitement of cave-exploring seldom grows stale. **2.** There are thousands of sights and variations in the underworld and each trip below entices new adventure. **3.** Although every cavern is different, it is possible to classify most caves. **4.** The most inspiring type of cave to "spelunkers" is the virgin cave. **5.** It is a cave that is still in its natural state and has never been explored. **6.** Its interior is alive with the wonders of the Dark Frontier; untouched and unmarred by the searching hands and trudging feet of curious visitors. **7.** The virgin cave is delicately beautiful, walls covered with brilliant crystalline gypsum flowers and onyx streaks, ceiling draped with stalagmites and stalactites, ice-water pools filled with mysterious life forms. **8.** Probably the rarest type is the ice cave. **9.** It is usually nothing more than a large hole in an iceberg or a crack in the frosty Arctic land formations. **10.** But for the dedicated spelunker who is willing to cope with the severity of the sub-zero weather, it offers a wide variety of sights and adventures not found in other caverns. **11.** A third type is the "living" cave—one that is actively affected by flowing water that enlarges its passages, or by seepage water that leaves deposits. **12.** In this evolving cave is found the widest variety of formations and wild life and usually it presents the most difficult exploring passages known to spelunkers.

The chances are that you and your classmates will generally agree on where the writer began each new paragraph. This experiment has been tried successfully so many times with such a variety of forms, including nonsense-word paragraphs, that considerable evidence now exists that the paragraph is indeed a generally recognized convention of the written language.

Let's analyze the student example to see why you paragraphed as you did. Since most definitions of *paragraph* emphasize meaning as the basic concern in paragraphing, let's look first at the meaning clues. Sentences 1-3 introduce the term that the student intends to classify: *caves.* At sentence 4, discussion of the first subclass or type of cave begins. Sentences 4 through 7 all relate to the idea of virgin caves. Sentence 8 introduces a new idea—the ice cave—discussed in sentences 8-10. A third type is mentioned in sentence 11 and the discussion of it extends through sentence 12. Each of these meaning units comprises a separate paragraph. Thus, sentences 4, 8, and 11 might be referred to as topic sentences, which, as you may know, generally state the paragraph's central or summary idea in much the same way that thesis statements present the main idea of a paper. What has occurred, therefore, is that we have responded to meaning clues in determining the scope of the paragraph. But meaning is not a sufficient criterion for paragraphing. By examining printed paragraphs, you could find numerous examples of a single idea discussed throughout several paragraphs instead of being confined to one, as paragraphing by close meaning relationships would indicate that it should be.

Consequently, many rhetoricians now rely more on structural signals than on meaning as paragraph indicators. In our student example, even though the writer lacks the sophistication to supply the number and variety of structural devices employed by more skillful writers, we can still isolate some that you responded to, perhaps subconsciously. Words like *most* and *rarest,* for instance, signal the ranking often used in separating ideas or items; pronouns such as *it* (sentences 5, 9, 10, 12) and *one* (sentence 11) make clear reference to the specific type of cave being discussed. Words like *its* (sentence 6) and *this* (sentence 12), in positions commonly occupied by the less specific articles *a* or *the,* establish a close relationship between the material in these sentences and the ones that precede them. Reordering of elements, as in sentence 12 ("In this evolving cave"), helps to hook the sentence ideas together.

So you see that in spite of the wide variations in paragraph length and content, there is evidence that the paragraph is a recognizable unit of discourse. Using our observations about the example and other writings, we can construct the following formal definition:

A paragraph is a unit of discourse containing a sequence of sentences closely related in structure and meaning. The main, or subject, idea may be expressed implicitly or explicitly; in the latter case, the subject idea generally takes the form of a topic sentence. A paragraph is also characterized by a complex set of structural or formal signals that help to establish relationships between the sentences.

The rest of this chapter will extend and develop more fully this formal definition to show you how to write effective paragraphs. You might keep in mind that we will be discussing the attributes of an ideal paragraph—sometimes referred to as a textbook paragraph. As you will see, good paragraph writing can result from the struggle to attain this ideal.

THE COMPONENTS OF THE PARAGRAPH: SUBJECT, RESTRICTION, AND ILLUSTRATION

A. L. Becker's research indicates that modern paragraphs consist of three components: *topic* (or *subject*), *restriction,* and *illustration.*[1] Becker and his colleagues concluded that a paragraph is a unit characterized by the presence of certain kinds of "slots": one that introduces a topic, one that limits or restricts it, and a third that illustrates or develops the restricted topic.

[1] A. L. Becker, "A Tagmemic Approach to Paragraph Analysis," *College Composition and Communication* (December 1965), pp. 237–43.

To clarify this theory, let's briefly glance back at sentence structure as discussed earlier. In a highly generalized sense, the components of a sentence (subject, predicate) can be viewed as functional slots that can be filled with many different items. Here are a few examples:

Subject	Predicate
Freshmen	study composition.
Over the fence	is out.
Whoever believes that	is naive.
To be or not to be	is the question.

Like the sentence, the paragraph can be thought of as a language form, can be analyzed at a very general or abstract level, and can be schematized as having certain functional slots: subject, restriction, and illustration (SRI).

These correspond to the component parts of an expository paper: the introduction of the essay, which states the subject of the paper restricted to a workable scope, corresponds to the subject and restriction slots of the paragraph; the body of the paper, in which the supporting and illustrative ideas are presented, is analogous to the illustration slot of the expository paragraph.

Expository Essay	Expository Paragraph
Introduction————————	⎰Subject
(statement of thesis)	⎱Restriction
Body———————————	Illustration

Having briefly looked at how paragraph structure relates to a smaller unit, the sentence, and to a larger one, the essay, let's examine the paragraph itself. Earlier in the chapter, the paragraph was defined as a unit of discourse containing a series of sentences and having as a central, focal point a topic or main idea, generally an explicitly stated topic sentence. How then does this summarized definition relate to paragraph *form*? Let us examine the following paragraph from the middle of a *Time* magazine article about current marriage experiments.

Versions of the 50–50 marriage are cropping up all over the country. In Detroit an industrial relations — **Subject / Restriction**

specialist does all the cooking and his social worker wife keeps the family books. In Berkeley a research economist quit his job so his wife could continue working as a radio program coordinator while he takes care of their two children. A Boston lawyer feeds and dresses his children each morning because his wife often works late for the National Organization for Women. — **Illustration**

In this paragraph, the opening sentence is the topic sentence, establishing both the subject—"50–50 marriage"—and the restriction of the subject —"versions . . . are cropping up all over the country." As is often the case, the paragraph subject refers back to the subject of the whole essay—in this case, cooperative marriages. The restriction is directed toward the paragraph itself. In longer, more complex paragraphs, the writer may use two or three sentences to establish subject and restriction, as in this example from an article whose general subject is competitive sports:

The competitive-sport experience is unique in the way it compresses the selection process into a compact time and space. There are few areas of human endeavor that can match the Olympic trials or a professional training camp for intensity of human stress. A young athlete often must face in hours or days the kind of pressure that occurs in the life of the achievement-oriented man over several years. The potential for laying bare the personality structure of the individual is considerable. When the athlete's ego is deeply invested in sports achievement, very few of the neurotic protective mechanisms provide adequate or sustaining cover. Basically, each must face his moment of truth and live with the consequences. The pro rookie usually gets only three or four chances to demonstrate ability before he is sent home. What sort of personality structure supports the person who can face this blunt reinforcement of reality?

> Subject
> Restriction
> Illustration

—Bruce D. Ogilvie and Thomas A. Tutko, "Sport: If You Want to Build Character Try Something Else," *Psychology Today*

Both these sample paragraphs provide examples in the illustration slot to develop the topic idea set forth in the beginning. Thus, in these examples, as in all well-constructed paragraphs, there is a discernible flow: the material in the paragraph moves from a general statement of the topic (subject) to a more specific restatement of it (restriction) and then to a concrete discussion that often includes examples (illustration). In traditional rhetoric a paragraph characterized by this movement from general to specific is called *deductive*. But some paragraphs reverse this order: they begin with a series of sentences containing specific material, move to a general statement about the content, and then to an indication of that statement's relationship to a more general topic. Traditionally, this order is called *inductive*. Here's an example:

Under a canopy of hickory and oak trees file people of all ages and sizes, some neatly dressed in street clothes formal enough for lunch at the Tavern, others in sloppy jeans and fringed jackets, with huge, floppy, hand-crafted leather hats on their heads, and here and there, some older women in the long gingham dresses and sun-bonnets characteristic of the Appalachian farm wife. They file past booths topped with red, yellow, and blue-striped canvas and filled with the hand-crafts traditional to this fair: thin, beautifully polished wooden trays, brightly colored enamel-ware, rainbows of cornstalk flowers, and macramé wall hangings sharing the limbs of trees with sand-castle candles. Near the gate the loud clatter of a corn-meal grinder can be heard, interspersed in the quiet pauses between customers with the plucking of dulcimer strings and the soft crooning of mountain singers. This Mardi Gras scene, greeting the newcomer to the Berea Arts and Crafts Fair, } Illustration
is an annual rite of spring. This gentle orgy, one of several in the area, is a reaffirmation that tra- } Restriction
ditional craftsmanship is alive and well and still flourishes in Appalachia. } Subject

This kind of inductive, or IRS, paragraph can be used effectively to break the monotony of a long series of SRI paragraphs and often provides an interesting way to structure opening or closing paragraphs.

Other possibilities for ordering these components exist. You can restrict, illustrate, and then state your subject (RIS); or you can restrict, state the general subject, and then illustrate (RSI). You can follow the pattern of the sports paragraph (SRI plus transition to the next paragraph); or you can restate the subject at the end (SRIS). Besides the SRI forms, other discernible but less frequently used paragraph types occur: problem–solution, obviously, describes a paragraph that opens with a statement of a problem and then proceeds to suggest solutions; question–answer follows a similar pattern. However, the SRI form seems most favored by modern writers. But the important thing to remember about any paragraph form is not that the components are restricted to any particular order, but that you must include all components if your paragraphs are to be complete and well developed.

The workhorse paragraphs in your expository papers—that is, the informative and explanatory paragraphs—should be especially well developed. If any of the component slots is empty or only half-filled, your paragraphs will be anemic. However, at times, like other writers, you may deliberately delete some parts of the paragraph for specific purposes. More about these possibilities later.

PARAGRAPH DEVELOPMENT

Earlier in the chapter we mentioned that a variety of fillers can occupy the functional slots—subject, restriction, and illustration—of the SRI workhorse paragraph. The nature of these fillers and their relationship to the overall structure of expository SRI paragraphs might be diagramed like this:

Subject: General subject matter of both the paragraph and the paper. May be mentioned in a transitional sentence or in a topic sentence that takes the form of a generalization, a statement of opinion, or an inference.

Restriction: The main, specific point of the paragraph. May be included in the topic sentence with the subject or restated in a generalization, opinion statement, or inference. Definition of terms used. Clarifying materials—background, history, orientation information.

Illustration: Supporting material to demonstrate the validity of the restriction:

Example	Classification
Statistics	Definition
Reasons or causes	Comparison
Authority	Anecdote

Inadequate Paragraph Development

We suggested previously that failure to provide enough material to fill any of the slots can result in a poorly developed paragraph. Let's consider inadequate development in each of the three basic paragraph slots.

Development Lacking in the Subject Slot

At the turn of the twentieth century the American Indians were a demoralized people. Their population had decreased because of war, disease, and famine. This led to an increased belief that the Indians were unable to take care of themselves, and, in 1849 the Bureau of Indian Affairs was established to aid the Indians and help them improve their way of life. The Bureau is now in a difficult fix: from many outside sources comes pressure to make the Indians self-sufficient. But inside the Bureau, many employees see their role as paternalistic, and their main function to show the Indians the error of their ways.

Because this transitional paragraph introduces the paper's restriction (the conflict in the Bureau of Indian Affairs), the lack of illustration here is acceptable. But what is needed (and never supplied anywhere in the paper) is an explanation of the subject, the Bureau of Indian Affairs. The student assumes more knowledge about this organization than a general audience could be expected to have. Four or five detailed sentences of explanation would have not only developed the paragraph but improved the effectiveness of the entire paper.

Development Lacking in the Restriction Slot

By now everyone knows of the serious energy and fuel problems facing the United States today. Many ways out of the "energy crisis" have been proposed; however, little if anything has been done by our government to pursue the most attractive proposal of all, the use of hydrogen. Hydrogen is undoubtedly the fuel for the future.

Here, the student's restriction of the subject of solving the fuel problem is the use of hydrogen, but he assumes that the audience is familiar with all the properties of hydrogen that make it an ideal substitute for the fossil fuels. Developing "hydrogen" more fully in the opening paragraph could help to catch readers' interest, convince them that the writer is authoritative, and at the same time provide better development for the paragraph.

Development Lacking in the Illustration Slot

Illustration is the most frequently underdeveloped paragraph slot. One of the most frustrating tasks in writing is deciding how much development is enough. How many examples are needed? How many authorities should be cited? How many statistics are necessary? These questions can be answered only in light of the writing context, the nature of the material, and the needs of your audience. Generally, complex or controversial material requires a great deal of supporting or explaining illustration. If you are writing about a specialized subject to a general audience, you should also supply more information than would otherwise be necessary.

Methods of Developing the Illustration Slot

The following student paragraphs illustrate some of the devices available for developing the illustration section of a paragraph.

Development by Example

Information can be obtained from school catalogues to help a student select a college. After receiving a catalogue, the student can begin to flip through it for general details. For example, in scanning one from a large university and one from a small private school, he would find several differences. Two of these are costs and academic requirements. He would notice that the cost at the state university is approximately half the cost at the private college. In academics, the student who plans to enter the state university is required to take the American College Test (ACT) while many small colleges require the Scholastic Aptitude Test (SAT) plus several achievement tests. The catalogue also provides a general description of the academic subjects offered. From glancing over these, the student is able to get a general idea of the courses that suit his intended major. A student interested in medicine or home economics could tell by the catalogue of the small college that these two areas are not stressed as much as in the large university. A large university is designed to meet the needs of all students, so the programs are extensive, offering almost every course and discipline. The smaller, private colleges are designed for a general education, even though majors are offered in traditional fields.

Compare the extensive use and explanation of examples in the last paragraph with the skimpiness of this one:

The laws concerning marijuana are out of date. They are vague and hard to enforce. They need to be strengthened in some areas and completely changed in others.

The instructor's comment beside this papagraph was, appropriately, "What laws? Be specific. Laws vary from state to state." Some of these laws cited as examples and some discussion of the *ways* they should be changed or strengthened would have improved the paragraph. Note how statistics, reasons, and use of authority serve as illustration in the following student examples.

Development by Statistics

The air pollution of this area is largely due to the recent vast increase in the local population. The 1960 census showed the population of the city of Lexington to be 62,180 persons, but this has increased to well over 100,000 according to the 1970 figures, a 46 percent increase in the city alone. Fayette, the county to which Lexington belongs, has had the same proportionate increase as the city. All this does not include the university students residing here, which adds anywhere from 15,000 to 20,000 more people to the population. This huge influx of people along with their cars, fireplaces, and other pollutants has direly affected the purity of the local air.

Development by Reasons or Causes

It should be realized that Zero Population Growth is not an immediate answer. It will take time for its effects to become apparent. As Jacoby states, there will be 300 million people living in the U.S. by A.D. 2050 if Zero Population Growth is started in 1975. But even three hundred million people polluting the earth is preferable to the population possibilities if Zero Population Growth is not realized. As for Jacoby's economic fears, a large population inhibits economic growth, rather than enhances it. The United States has always been a leader in economic growth, while having a relatively small population when compared to poorer, more crowded countries, such as China and India. Obviously, the resources of India cannot handle the large population; starvation and disease are rampant there as a result. India and China provide vivid warning signs that should be considered by opponents of Zero Population Growth before they raise their voices against it.

Development by Authority

This paragraph cites several expert sources to make its point.

The in-patient program does not have a lot of these problems, i.e., the patient's dropping out of the program, or being thrown into constant association with drug pushers. It was reported in *U.S. News and World Report* that "one weapon against today's narcotics epidemic is to *lock up* drug users while they undergo treatment." A study was done for the federal government by psychologists of the University of California at Los Angeles. The survey indicated that confinement, combined with follow-up care, may be the most effective way to treat heroin addiction. Another study on the in-patient program was done by Dr. George Vaillant, a Harvard University psychiatrist. He traced for twenty years the activities of 100 New York City heroin addicts who had been patients at the U.S. Public Health Service Hospital in Lexington, Kentucky. The study, Dr. Vaillant said, disclosed that only 3 percent of the patients released in less than nine months kept away from heroin. The abstinence rate rose to 13 percent for those who served nine months or more, and shot up to 66 percent for those confined for more than nine months followed by parole. Another psychiatrist, Dr. Bejerot, of Sweden, also agrees that the only way to cure heroin addiction is to isolate drug addicts in treatment centers away from the urban areas and keep them there until authorities judge it is safe to return them to society.

Development by Classification

Whether they like it or not, Americans are spending more time in queues. We now expect to queue for library books, cabs, movies, ski lifts, tees, subway tokens, and even campsites in the wilds of our national parks. Doctors, dentists, barbers, and employment interviewers line us up. So do headwaiters, sales clerks, cashiers, bank tellers, income tax adjusters, and the few remaining meat cutters. Lawn services line our lawns up for mowing. Plumbers line our emergencies up for fixing.

—Caroline Bird, *The Crowding Syndrome*

Here, on a smaller scale than in a classification paper, the class or group (queues) is divided into the kinds of lines Americans are expected to endure: those for entertainment services, for food, for professional services, and so on.

Development by Definition

The greenhouse effect is probably the most serious longterm pollution problem that we face. When any hydrocarbon, such as wood, oil, natural gas or coal, is burned, carbon dioxide is produced as one of the end products. It enters the atmosphere and reflects heat back to Earth that would normally be radiated out into space, much as the glass roof of a greenhouse traps heat. Meteorologists worry that large-scale coal burning, even with "ordinary" pollutants removed from the smoke, will eventually result in drastic changes in the Earth's weather.
—James S. Trefil, "Wood Stoves Glow Warmly Again in Millions of Homes"

In this paragraph, the writer defines the term "greenhouse effect" by explaining what causes it. Any definition device may be used in individual paragraphs to develop the illustration slot.

Development by Comparison

. . . Christianity is a complex faith, and its consequences differ in differing contexts. What I have said may well apply to the medieval West, where in fact technology made spectacular advances. But the Greek East, a highly civilized realm of equal Christian devotion, seems to have produced no marked technological innovation after the late seventh century, when Greek fire was invented. The key to the contrast may perhaps be found in a difference in the tonality of piety and thought which students of comparative theology find between the Greek and the Latin churches. The Greeks believed that sin was intellectual blindness, and that salvation was found in illumination, orthodoxy—that is, clear thinking. The Latins, on the other hand, felt that sin was moral evil, and that salvation was to be found in right conduct. Eastern technology has been intellectualist. Western technology has been voluntarist. The Greek saint contemplates; the Western saint acts. The implications of Christianity for the conquest of nature would emerge more easily in the Western atmosphere.
—Lynn White, Jr., "The Historical Roots of Our Ecologic Crisis"

In this comparison of Eastern and Western Christianity, the writer emphasizes the contrasts between the two, using the point-by-point scheme. Note that sometimes the comparison is made in adjoining sentences; at other times in the same sentence. The illustration slot begins with the words "The key to the contrast . . ." and moves to the end where the paragraph subject is stated as an opinion.

221

Development by Anecdote

This anecdote paragraph in IRS form was an opening paragraph, with the final sentence acting also as the thesis statement for the paper.

Four boys were driving home from the Kentucky State Fair one summer night. They were all a little drunk. About three miles from their homes they were pulled over because one of the headlights was out. Immediately the police detected the alcohol and quickly called another patrol car. Then began a series of ridiculous happenings which convinced me that at least some of the rumors about police treatment of teenagers are true.

Paragraphs developed by anecdote or by narrating a case study very often lend themselves readily to the IRS form.

We have listed several ways of developing paragraphs in expository writing. Other specific methods of paragraph expansion will be discussed in Chapter 20.

Deciding about the kind and amount of development you need is frustrating. It is easy to look at another writer's solution, but the sobering knowledge remains: you must still grapple with these problems alone with your pen or typewriter. The only real advice we can offer, once you have familiarized yourself with the possible kinds of solutions, is this: you must place yourself in the role of your readers. Then ask yourself these questions as you read over what you have written:

Where did you find this out?
How do you know this?
Why is it true?
Who says so?
Can you give an example?
What led you to this conclusion?

Remember that you obviously believe and accept what you have written. But your readers need to be convinced. You can get them to accept your opinion or explanation only by fully developing the illustration slot of your paragraphs. Use examples, anecdotes, statistics, reasons, authorities, or enumeration to drive your point home.

FUNCTIONAL VARIETIES OF PARAGRAPHS

As you become more aware of paragraph structure and are exposed to more college-level prose, you will realize that there are several varieties of paragraphs besides the previously discussed "workhorse" paragraph, in which all the component slots—subject, restriction, and illustration—are filled.

As we have indicated, there are times when writers employ a short, isolated paragraph to emphasize an important point that might be buried if it appeared within a fully developed paragraph. Sometimes writers break up a lengthy enumeration paragraph into several short, simple paragraphs, each containing a reason, cause, or other enumerated item. Writers also occasionally use short paragraphs to help readers by signaling an important transition, particularly when moving from one major idea to another in a lengthy paper. The following discussion will show you when, how, and why you should employ these paragraph forms, which are characterized by the absence of material in one or two of the function slots—subject, restriction, or illustration.

Transitional Paragraphs

A transitional paragraph has an empty illustration slot. It usually performs two functions: it summarizes or evaluates previous material, and it foreshadows subsequent material.

A transitional paragraph introduces both subject and restriction, as this example shows:

> And that's why welfare is a women's issue. For a lot of middle-class women in this country, Women's Liberation is a matter of concern. For women on welfare, it's a matter of survival.
>
> —Johnnie Tilman, "Welfare Is a Women's Issue"

The first sentence summarizes the reasons presented in preceding paragraphs. The phrase "women on welfare" in the last sentence picks up the overall subject of the article. And "a matter of survival" introduces the restriction to be discussed in the paragraphs to follow.

Sometimes a transitional paragraph takes the form of a question, which moves readers from one idea to another and has the added advantage of making readers confront the material. Two examples follow:

> How real and how general does the confusion seem actually to be?
>
> —Joseph Wood Krutch

This one-sentence paragraph bridges the writer's preceding discussion of the subject, "confusion," and the restriction of the discussion to follow, indicated by "how real" and "how general."

In the next sample a question is asked and then the writer indicates the nature of the subsequent discussion by observing that no answer has been previously sought.

What happens inside the mind of a woman struggling with such a conflict? Since it has not been properly acknowledged until now, the question has remained unaddressed.

—Vivian Gornick

Our final example of a transitional paragraph states a value judgment pertaining to the previous discussion and then introduces the subject of the forthcoming paragraphs, indicated by the italicized words:

But not even those wonderful clergymen who pray in behalf of Congress, expressway ribbon cuttings, urban renewal projects, and testimonial dinners would pray for a demolition derby. *The demolition derby is,* pure and simple, a *form of gladiatorial combat* for our times.

—Tom Wolfe, *The Kandy-Kolored Tangerine Flake Streamline Baby*

Emphatic Paragraphs

A paragraph of emphasis consists of short declarative sentences (sometimes only one sentence) generally intended to shock readers, elicit a gut reaction from them, or ensure that they get the message, clear and unadorned. This example from a student publication probably accomplishes all three:

The last frontier is indeed gone—but this time it's not the dinosaur or the buffalo who are in danger of extinction, it's man himself, and at his own hand.

—Linda Hanley

Sometimes the emphatic paragraph effectively ends a paper, providing an impact not easily achieved by a longer paragraph. Here is an effective two-sentence final paragraph that also serves as a general summary of the student paper's subject:

The Greek system has grown up, moving from a "teenie-bopper" mentality to a seriousness of purpose more appealing to young adults. Because of all the changes in the system, more students are choosing to be Greeks rather than freaks.

Introductory and Concluding Paragraphs

Paragraphs that serve as openers and closers of a paper have many of the formal characteristics of the other kinds of paragraphs discussed in this section. Because they present unique problems, they are treated separately and at length in Chapter 16.

Enumerative Series of Paragraphs

Frequently in papers with complex subject matter, you may have to deal with several aspects of a problem, such as a recital of the factors that, contributed to United States involvement in Southeast Asia. Or you may be faced with a situation like that of one student writer whose final paragraph was reprinted above: listing the reasons for the recent renewal of interest in fraternities and sororities. If you discuss each factor or reason in detail, the resulting paragraph with its many items will be too long to be read easily. What to do? The most common device is to divide the paragraph material into a series of paragraphs. For instance, the subject and restriction can be introduced in a short paragraph that is followed by a series of paragraphs, each dealing with separate aspects of the illustration materials. Here's how one student, writing on America's use of the atomic bomb, solved the problem:

In spite of much information from reliable intelligence sources that Japan's defenses were rapidly weakening, President Truman listened to the pro-bomb advocates and went ahead with the bombings. There were several major factors which were considered by the pro-bomb factions as overwhelming reasons for the use of the bomb.	First paragraph in the series introduces subject and restriction
The first was that the entire research and building projects had been geared toward their eventual use. [Factor 1: supported in the rest of the paragraph.]	Second paragraph in the series: illustration 1
The second factor was the cost in money and resources which the production of the bombs had required. [Factor 2: developed in the rest of the paragraph.]	Third paragraph in the series: illustration 2

In this section of the book we have explained some of the ways in which the various paragraph forms can be used. Paragraphs in which only one or two of the function slots are filled can serve important rhetorical functions—to provide a bridge from one idea to another, to emphasize an important point, to enumerate a list of items, to summarize, or to introduce a new aspect of the paper.

SUMMARY

In this chapter, we have indicated that the paragraph, at least in written English, is a recurring structure, just as the sentence is. As a language form, the paragraph ideally has three "slots": one that introduces the subject; one that restricts it; and a third that develops or illustrates the restricted subject. However, far from being a rigid form, the paragraph permits great flexibility in ordering these components. Nor must all paragraphs contain all the slots. Some paragraphs, introducing a complex idea that will require extensive discussion, may simply state the subject and its restriction. Others may contain only material that expands and develops an idea stated earlier in a transitional paragraph. Variety is possible, too, in the many ways that writers can choose to handle development—example, statistics, causal analysis, citing of authority, classifying, defining, comparing and contrasting, using anecdotes. As in other aspects of writing, the length and complexity of paragraphs is determined by the writers' purpose and their commitment to their audience.

Assignments

For Discussion

1 Find the subject-restriction-illustration partitions in the following student paragraph. What devices has the student used in developing the paragraph? Does he convince you that his opinion is valid?

WHO'S BOSS?

Men are more capable for being the head of a household than women. As men are stronger than women it is only right that the responsibility of such a position should be upon their shoulders. A man should be the dominant influence of the family and have the final word on important matters. A man is less timid than a woman and as it takes a certain amount of boldness to face any authoritative job, a man's brisk manner is called for. A man is better able to cope with the many business matters essential to the efficiently run home. In business details a man has the upper hand due to a working knowledge of such things as mortgages, banking procedures, insurance premiums and numerous other items in business. A man is the best decision maker because he is less gullible, doesn't get hysterical, or do things rashly as women do. A man shows more protective qualities towards his family and home and is concerned with its well-being as a whole. If back in pioneer days a woman took matters into her own hands and set herself up over her husband as head of the household, she might suddenly find herself homeless, because the husband had built the house and it was rightly his to be boss in. The pioneer wife was a woman who knew she was lucky to have a roof over her head and was content to keep house and not to be the head of it. Although there are exceptions the usual situation finds that the man is the head of the household and until the reverse becomes true, this proves man is the better boss.

2 Do the weaknesses inherent in the following student paragraph result

from faulty paragraph organization, weak development, or both? What kinds of materials could the writer have used to develop his ideas?

One might say our ambition has been hampered by the idol of security. Security has beome our ultimate goal. Our existence revolves around our new idol and gives us nothing more than a stable job and group security. We conform to group standards and find ourselves being expressed through a group rather than individually. Everything is thought out and laid before us so no individual mental exertion is necessary.

3 Identify the organizational technique used in each of the following paragraphs. Is it SRI, IRS, SRIS—or is one slot missing? Can you determine the subject of each paragraph's essay? Are they paragraphs of development or transition?

a In the past two decades, however, a combination of new technology and sociopolitical changes has overturned the classic balance of privacy in the United States. On the technological front, microminiaturized bugs, television monitors, and devices capable of penetrating solid surfaces to listen or photograph have dissolved the physical barriers of walls and doors. Polygraph devices to measure emotional states have been improved as a result of space research, and increased use has been made of personality tests for personnel selection. The development of electronic computers and long-distance communication networks has made it possible to collect, store, and process far more information about an individual's life and transactions than was practical in the era of typewriter and file cabinet.
—Alan F. Westin, "Privacy"

b The sinister fact is not that most citizens are taking drugs; people have always done that, although never as many or as much. The real terror implicit in our current drug culture is that so many, incredulous about official pronouncements, are experimenting, sometimes lethally, with very dangerous ones.
—Joel Fort, "The Drug Explosion"

c For a time, the television industry comforted itself with the theory that children listened to children's programs and that, if by any chance they saw programs for adults, violence would serve as a safety valve, offering a harmless outlet for pent-up aggressions: the more violence on the screen, the less in life. Alas, this turns out not to be necessarily so. As Dr. Wilbur Schramm, director of the Institute of Communication Research at Stanford has reported, children, even in the early elementary school years, view more programs designed for adults than for themselves; "above all, they prefer the more violent type of adult program including the Western, the adventure program, and the crime drama." Experiments show that such programs, far from serving as safety valves for aggression, attract children with high levels of aggression and stimulate them to seek overt means of acting out their aggressions. Evidence suggests that these programs work the same incitement on adults. And televiolence does more than condition emotion and behavior. It also may attenuate people's sense of reality. Men murdered on the television screen ordinarily spring to life after the episode is over: all death is therefore diminished. A child asked a man last June where he was headed in his car. "To Washington," he said. "Why?" he asked. "To attend the funeral of Senator Kennedy." The child said, "Oh yeah—they shot him again." And such shooting may well condition the manner in which people approach the perplexities of existence. On tele-vision the hero too glibly resolves his problems by shooting somebody. The *Gunsmoke* ethos, however, is not necessarily the best way to deal with human or social complexity. It is hardly compatible with any kind of humane or libertarian democracy.

—Arthur M. Schlesinger, Jr., *Violence: America in the Sixties*

d What about the interactions among social organizations, world order, and human nature?

—Elisabeth Mann Borgese, "Human Nature Is Still Evolving"

For Practice

1 Using the following as opening sentences that contain the subject and restriction of the paragraph, add illustration, using the method of paragraph development indicated in parentheses.

a In our society, automobiles are both a delight and a curse. (comparison)

b Women's purses serve many important functions in their lives. (classification)

c Every CB'er has a distinctive "handle." (definition)

d Surely something can be done to make college registration less traumatic to students. (anecdote)

e Clean air can become a reality if industry is affected economically by an irate citizenry. (examples; perhaps statistics or authority)

f Many freshmen withdraw from my college during the second semester. (reasons or causes)

g Many buildings on campus are in serious need of renovation. (examples)

2 Rewrite the following paragraph, developing it by adding detailed information that would make the statements apply to your own college's catalog.

The Catalog is a fantastic collection of information that is at least one year old and is organized to confuse and bore almost everyone. The course descriptions are occasionally partially accurate. The stated requirements are not up to date and you should check with your advisor for changes (practically every undergraduate college in the University changed its requirements in some way during the past year and NONE of this is reflected in the Catalog).

3 Choose one of the opening statements in Practice Exercise 1 and develop a paragraph, using one of the methods discussed in the chapter; perhaps one that requires enumeration of reasons, causes, or subclasses will work best.

4 Choose another and construct a paragraph using authority, examples, or definition.

For Writing

1 Write a well-developed paragraph, using SRI form, agreeing or disagreeing with a paragraph in exercise 3 in the Discussion section.

2 Choose a topic about which you have some opinion. Develop a topic sentence and write two paragraphs, using the same topic sentence and supporting material—one in SRI form and the other in IRS form.

The Movement of the Expository Paragraph

THE INTERNAL STRUCTURE OF THE PARAGRAPH

An architect must consider not only the external shapes, colors, and relationships that make a building attractive but also the internal features that make it comfortable, pleasant, and functional. Similarly, writers should be aware not only of the basic external form of the paragraph but also of the internal organization, particularly the direction of movement or modification within the paragraph and the part played by the relationships between sentences.

Francis Christensen, whose concept of levels of generality in sentences was discussed in Chapter 9, sees the paragraph as a series of sentences that move from general to specific—from one level of generality to another—in much the same way that sentence modifiers do. In our earlier discussion of sentence sequence, we outlined cumulative sentences with modifiers in *coordinate* relationship as follows:

1 The swallows fed on insects, (main clause)
  2 swooping down at breathtaking speeds, (sentence modifier)
  2 wheeling back to dizzying heights, (sentence modifier)
  2 and soaring aloft for the next dive. (sentence modifier)

Modifiers occur in *subordinate* relationship in sentences like:

1 The swallows fed on insects, (main clause)
  2 swooping down at breathtaking speeds (sentence modifier)
    3 that dazzled the watchers (modifier)
      4 —the envious humans below. (modifier)

As you remember, both these sequences can be combined in a single sentence—resulting in a mixed sequence.

This principle can also be applied to paragraph structure, since sentences in a paragraph exhibit relationships to one another similar to those that sentence modifiers have. We can analyze paragraphs by the same method used earlier to analyze sentences. The number 1 signifies the most general level in the paragraph (usually the topic sentence); 2 less general; 3 even less; and so on. Just as a sentence modifier labeled 2 meant that it modified the main clause (1), so too, sentences at level 2 in a sense "modify" the main idea or topic sentence of a paragraph. Let's look at the various kinds of paragraph structures.

Coordinate Sequence

Paragraphs in coordinate sequences usually have only two levels of generality. Let's look at a paragraph by a professional writer, in which the last sentence is a restatement of the first and acts as a transitional bridge to the next paragraph.

1(a)   The evil that has produced what we now call the "environmental crisis" is arrogance or, to use the ancient Greek term that is more accurate, *hubris,* the assumption by men of divine prerogatives.

    2(a)   It is the willingness to use more power than one can control.

    2(b)   . It is the ignorant use of power.

    2(c)   It is a sin the consequences of which are invariably visited upon the descendants of the sinner, as the Greek myths tell us over and over again.

    2(d)   It is the reason why humility and modesty and self-restraint and temperance have been recognized as essential virtues through all of human history.

1(b)   The man who assumes and uses the powers of the gods must in his ignorance inevitably reduce the common fund of life and fortune on which his children will have to live.

             —Wendell Berry, *The Unforeseen Wilderness*

The first sentence is the topic sentence for the paragraph and contains both subject ("environmental crisis") and restriction ("arrogance or . . . *hubris*") and is the most general statement in the paragraph. The subsequent series of 2 sentences, even though they are all coordinate to one another—that is, at approximately the same level of generality—are less general than the topic sentence is and together serve as illustration. Berry's topic sentence introduces the idea of *hubris;* the subsequent 2 sentences serve as an extended definition of the term *hubris.* However, none is dependent upon any of the others; deletion of any of them would not seriously impair the meaning or logical arrangement of the paragraph, but only thin it out. Also, there is a certain amount of flexibility in the order. 2(a) and 2(b) could easily be reversed, as could 2(c) and 2(d), without changing the meaning or tampering too seriously with the climatic effect of the series. As you can see, the writer frequently has a choice in the internal arrangement of the coordinate paragraph.

A striking characteristic of this and many other coordinate paragraphs is the parallel structure used for the "modifying" sentences, here four beginning with "It is. . . ." Parallelism of structure is one of the devices used by good writers to convey meaning accurately.

Experienced writers apparently use coordinate-sequence paragraphs for rather limited purposes. However, writers occasionally use this paragraph arrangement in defining a complex or controversial idea, in driving home an important point, or in a concluding paragraph when they wish to summarize their points.

Subordinate Sequence

A paragraph in subordinate sequence contains sentences at diminishing levels of generality, each dependent upon the preceding one for meaning. Here is a paragraph containing such a sequence:

1 The tolerant attitude of the state government in Pennsylvania has helped to guarantee the continued presence of the Amish community at Lancaster.
2 The state constitution, modeled after Penn's Articles, ensures that no religious practice of the Amish or any other sect will be interfered with.
3 Although there is a national law which states that a child must attend school until the age of 16, Pennsylvania tends to favor its state law where the Amish children are concerned.
4 Consequently, in Pennsylvania, the Amish are permitted their own schools, usually taught by one of their own sect, where attendance is anything but mandatory.
5 When the children are not needed on the farm, they are sent to school to learn enough reading to be able to read the Holy Bible, enough writing to be able to write their names, and enough arithmetic to be able to keep household and farm accounts.
6 This is in accordance with the Amish belief that the only real education their children need is in the ways of God and of the sect and this is best discovered in the ways of keeping a house and working a farm.
7 These things are best taught at home.

Here we are concentrating on the meaning relationships; later in the chapter we will discuss the structural, or formal, devices of paragraph unity. Note, however, that despite the differences in the internal organization of these two sequence types, both exhibit the same overall form: both are SRI paragraphs. In the example of subordinate sequence, the first sentence introduces the subject ("tolerant attitude"); the second states the restriction (Pennsylvania follows state rather than federal law); and the remaining sentences constitute a detailed illustration. Note, too, that unlike the Berry example, deleting a sentence or reordering the levels here would interfere with meaning and logical relationships.

Paragraphs in subordinate sequence are especially useful for the full development of a single idea. But what of the many times when you want to write about a fairly complex idea or to show the relationship between two ideas? Obviously a more complex paragraph organization would be necessary. Writers solve this problem by mixing the two sequences within a single paragraph.

Mixed Sequence

Consider this student paragraph:

1 In general, men share the same attitude about sex.
    2 For men, sex is only an animalistic drive.
       3 Man looks for sex to ease his animal nature.
    2 Man loves to dominate woman and uses sex to accomplish this.
       3 He experiences a superior feeling when he engages in the sex act.
          4 The phrases "She melted in my arms," or "She was like a puppet on a string," or "I wore her out" emphasize the way in which a man uses a woman to build up his own ego.
       4 It is common knowledge that when a man does "conquer" a woman, he tends to boast about his "victorious campaign."
         5 The act itself sometimes doesn't give a man enough of a superior feeling, so he must tell others about his venture.
            6 In this way, he makes up for any lost feeling of superiority by courting the envy of his male counterparts.

The sentence numbers indicate how the internal organization of this paragraph combines coordination and subordination. Note also that here we have a more complex version of the SRI paragraph, with the writer dividing the restriction into two sentences and two segments of the paragraph (marked by level 2) and providing some illustration for each. Our example is fairly simple, but you should realize that mixed sequences can become very complex.

We suggest that you try your hand at analyzing some of the paragraphs in the exercises at the end of the chapter. However, the purpose of the discussion and the exercises is not to instruct you how to analyze other people's paragraphs, but to make you aware of the inner workings of the paragraph so that you can improve your own. An understanding of paragraph structure can help you to see that paragraphs are not made up of randomly ordered sentences, but contain sentences clustered and arranged according to their relations to one another and to a central unifying idea, the subject. The levels of generality that a writer assigns to sentences help to maintain the integrity and unity of the paragraph as a rhetorical form.

PARAGRAPH UNITY

We have discussed the roles of both contextual meaning and levels of generality in establishing paragraph unity—the sense of cohesiveness necessary to identify a unit of discourse as a paragraph. Both of these center more on the meaning of the content than on the structure (although it is sometimes very difficult to separate the two). However, we suggested that there are other structural, or formal, devices of paragraph unity that readers respond to, sometimes without consciously realizing it. Parallel structure is certainly one clue to paragraph unity, but there are others. Before categorizing these formal paragraph signals, we would like you to try a simple experiment: try to reconstruct the following paragraph as the student writer originally wrote it, placing the scrambled sentences in proper order. (One hint: the paragraph is in SRI form with sentences arranged in mixed sequence.)

1. This erosion removes precious topsoil, making the ground unfit for anything to grow—not rabbit's tobacco, not sassafras, not corn, not beans.
2. But now the pasture is filled with boulders from the strip mine up the hill, and never again will cattle graze nor meadow birds nest there.
3. I have seen creeping soil banks topple towering oak trees and cover the lush shrubs and vines carpeting the ground.
4. The land dies.
5. Finally, I know of a pasture where partridges once nested after the cattle were removed.
6. Not only the waterways but the land itself has been a victim of strip mining.
7. And because there is no ground cover, erosion occurs.
8. Rabbits also lived there, as did many other ground creatures.
9. Erosion, in the form of monstrous landslides, resulting from locating strip mines close to highways, blocks the roads and makes it impossible for school children and workers to reach their destinations.
10. Because the trees are toppled, squirrels, birds, and possums can't nest there and the habitats of the wildlife are crowded; more squirrels must nest in fewer trees.

You should not have had too much trouble unscrambling this paragraph. Except in sentence 4, the student writer has provided you with many formal signals. Here is the original paragraph with the signals marked to show how the various elements are linked to chain the sentences together.

6 Not only the waterways but the land itself has been a victim of strip mining. **3** I have seen creeping soil banks topple towering oak trees and cover the lush shrubs and vines carpeting the ground. **10** Because the trees are toppled, squirrels, birds, and possums can't nest there and the habitats of the wildlife are crowded; more squirrels must nest in fewer trees. **7** And because there is no ground cover, erosion occurs. **1** This erosion removes precious topsoil, making the ground unfit for anything to grow—not rabbit's tobacco, not sassafras, not corn, not beans. **4** The land dies. **9** Erosion, in the form of monstrous land slides, resulting from locating strip mines close to highways, blocks the roads and makes it impossible for school children and workers to reach their destinations. **5** Finally, I know of a pasture where partridges once nested after the cattle were removed. **8** Rabbits also lived there, as did many other ground creatures. **2** But now the pasture is filled with boulders from the strip mine up the hill, and never again will cattle graze nor meadow birds nest there.

Note that the circled words are synonyms for or refer in some way to *land* in the topic sentence; these are then woven throughout the paragraph, creating a unifying chain. Rectangles enclose words that tie together clusters of sentences having significant relationships: *erosion* in 7 to *erosion* in 1 to *erosion* in 9, for example. Both circles and rectangles indicate a general class of paragraph unity signals that use words generally equivalent or related in meaning. We will refer to these signals as *meaning links.*

The underlined words in the student paragraph do not function as vehicles of meaning. Instead, they provide transition from one idea to another (*not only . . . but, and*) or allow the reader to move from one relationship to another (*because, also*). Other underlined words act as signals of time or place: *there, now, never again, finally.*

In summary, structural, or formal, signals of paragraph unity can be classified thus:

1. Meaning links.
   Series of words having equivalent meaning: synonyms, pronouns, and the demonstratives (*this, these, that, those*) are most common.
2. Transitional words.
   a. Subordinate conjunctions such as *because, if, when, thus, although.*
   b. Coordinate conjunctions—*and, or, either . . . or* are most common.

     c. Transitional phrases or adverbials such as *furthermore, for example, in other words, on the other hand.*

3. Signals of time or place.

     a. Time: *now, then, later, sooner, previously.* Also prepositional phrases such as *at that time, in the past, in the future, last week.*

     b. Place: *Here* and *there.* Also hundreds of prepositional phrases such as *over the hill, in that place, outside the window.*

4. Verb sequences.

We did not discuss this in reference to the student example, but frequently a shift in verb tense is a signal that a new paragraph is needed. In our sample paragraph (except where the student writes about the past condition of the meadow), all the verbs or auxiliaries of the main clauses are marked for present tense: *"has* been," *"is," "blocks."* But suppose the student had added this sentence at the end of the paragraph: "Strip mining *was* outlawed in Illinois." You as the reader would have immediately responded as much to the shift to past tense as to the abrupt shift in content; you would have been disturbed that the writer included this statement as part of the paragraph. This may help to explain why English professors react to this in your papers by writing "tense shift" in blood in the margins of your papers.

The omission or skimpy use of these signals is an easy trap for any writer to fall into, but it is especially hazardous for inexperienced writers. Because, as you write, you are mentally aware of the relationships you intend, you may not feel compelled to supply helpful signals to your reader. But this is a part of your commitment to your readers. You have an obligation to help them quickly discern your meaning, unhindered by the illogic and the fuzzy references that so often result from omitting these signals.

Writing unified paragraphs, then, is especially a matter of communication, and effective communication can result only from sending out and receiving clear signals. If you, the writer, provide the proper signals, readers should get the message loud and clear.

SUMMARY

We have seen that the sentences in a paragraph can relate to each other in much the same ways that sentence elements do. Following the opening or topic sentence, the subsequent sentences may be coordinate, all relating directly back to the subject of the paragraph. Or each subsequent sentence may, in a sense, "modify" the one that precedes it, thus having subordinate function. Because paragraphs are longer than sentences are, special devices are required to maintain focus on the main idea in the paragraph: meaning links, transitional words and phrases, signals of time or place. Even consistent verb sequences can help a paragraph "keep its act together."

Assignments

For Discussion

1   Following is a paragraph in which the sequence of sentences has been scrambled. Try to put it back together as the student wrote it. State what form the paragraph takes (SRI, IRS, or whatever) and indicate its level of generality. If you find that, like Humpty-Dumpty, it can't be put together again, analyze the weaknesses of the paragraph that prevent the reassembly.

1   The members of the group all go to a designated place and sit in a circle around the fire.
2   Each member then partakes of the peyote and goes through his "experience."
3   These ceremonies always follow a set pattern.
4   This was described in a brief statement on how the ceremony is set up.
5   Peyotists do not deviate from this pattern, unless absolutely needed, and then only rarely.
6   He starts the group through by chanting songs and prayers to Mescalito, who is the god of peyotism.
7   These experiences or "trips," as the modern drug culture terms them, are how a peyotist learns from his religion.
8   There is a leader to guide the group through the ceremony.
9   The ceremony usually breaks up in the morning when the ceremonial feast is eaten.

2   What sentence sequence does each of the following three paragraphs exhibit—coordinate, subordinate, or mixed?

a   Adopting the Korean pattern of waging war without declaring it, of nominating only a few to do the killing while the rest stayed home to make a killing, we corrupted a whole generation. Young men were openly counseled in ways to beat the system; innumerable college men took education courses so they could become elementary-school teachers when they had no vocation for such work but only a desire to evade the draft. The poor went to war and the rich stayed home. Ghetto youths were sent to Vietnam while members of professional athletic teams were provided with escape hatches. Young men joined the National Guard to avoid service overseas, and girls were coached on how to marry quickly and become pregnant even more quickly so as to help their men beat an evil system.

—*New York Times Magazine*

b   However, one important aspect of the college that is often considered early in the planning stage is the particular college's general reputation. This general reputation is made up of the picture ones sees of the college

237

in academics, sports, and social life. The image that is thus presented of what the school is like is quite often a prerequisite to trying to find out more about the college. For example, perhaps a young man in junior high school read an article in a sports magazine about the outstanding athletic program at college "X." After reading it, he decided that this school was one that interested him. So, he then tried to learn about other aspects of the college. In a similar manner, what a student has read or heard about a school's academic, athletic, or social life can be the initial factor in his beginning to select a college.

c   The grading system also contains penalties and rewards, but that's what makes people tick. Would any student write a term paper, read a textbook, or attend a lecture in a field outside his interest if he were not motivated by grades? Because studying and learning are hard work, students need penalties and rewards. Of course, this results in pressure. Certainly, this produces competition. But without them, few people would strive to let their learning exceed their intellectual reach. Oh yes, there are a few students who are highly self-motivated and are genuinely interested in learning. But most students would rather see a basketball game, rap in the Grill, or watch a movie. Let's face it—that's why we need the present grading system. Anything else would result in a lowering of the standards and a fifth-rate university.

3   Classify the various kinds of focusing signals—meaning links, transitional words, signals of time or place—in the three paragraphs in exercise 2.

For Practice

1   Choose three paragraphs that you've recently written and expand them, experimenting with coordinate, subordinate, and mixed sentence sequences.

2   Write a paragraph-length extended definition of the word *scholar*, using the following distinctive features:

a   a seeker of truth and knowledge
b   a possessor of an insatiable curiosity
c   a practitioner of critical thinking
d   a citizen of the world of discovery

First write the paragraph in coordinate sequence. Then add descriptive details to each distinctive feature, creating a mixed sequence. Then check to see if parallel structure helps the reader to determine the levels of generality. Last, revise for effective use of the structural signals listed on pages 235–36.

15

Language in Expository Writing

Excellent ideas, organization, paragraphs, and sentences do not a fine expository paper make. The effective use of language is also essential. In this chapter, we discuss the need for clarity, accuracy, appropriateness, and economy in the selection of words.

THE NEED FOR CLARITY

Clarity—the word should be uppermost in your mind as you search for language to express your thoughts in expository writing. After all, the main purpose of this form of writing—to explain—can not be achieved if your language is murky or misleading. In a sense, writing exposition is like showing someone your ideas through a glass window. If the glass is dirty or distorted, the reader cannot see clearly. But replacing a pane or cleaning the glass may be easier than attaining clarity in writing. In fact, the word itself—*clarity*—is anything but clear. Just what do we mean?

In the mid-eighteenth century, the great English letter writer Lord Chesterfield advised his son to write *clear* business letters and explained what he meant by adding that "every paragraph should be so clear and unambiguous that the dullest fellow in the world may not be able to mistake it, nor obliged to read it twice in order to understand it." We wouldn't go as far as Chesterfield does in requiring that "even the dullest fellow in the world" be able to understand your writing. Instead, we urge you to write so that your readers do not have to struggle over your words, or reread them, or wonder what you meant, or be misled.

But once again, who are your readers? Your answer to this question is crucial because what is clear to an adult might not be to a child; what is clear to a nurse might not be to an engineer; and what is clear to a college student from a Wyoming ranch might not be to one from Detroit's inner city. Thus you must first realize who your readers are and aim your writing at them.

Sometimes we like to talk about the writer as a quarterback aiming a message at the reader cutting down field. The writer is successful only if the message gets across to the reader. It is of little interest whether the writer stays in the pocket, or scrambles, throws when set or on the run, flips a hard or soft pass. The readers must catch on. If they don't then the effort is worthless; there is no gain—in yardage or understanding. That is why we have emphasized repeatedly that you must write for your readers, which requires you to think about who they are.

Often you do know who your readers are. But in other writing situations, you may know little about them and have to guess more. What should you do? How much can you take for granted about your audience? How high or low should you aim?

There is no all-purpose answer. Often you must make an educated guess at the schooling, interests, experiences, life styles, and backgrounds of readers. Then we suggest that you write just below this level, thus not taking too much for granted. It's better to err on the side of simplicity than complexity, as this old example illustrates:

> A plumber wrote to a Washington government department asking whether any damage was done to sewer pipes that he had cleaned with hydrochloric acid. He was informed that "The efficacy of hydrochloric acid is indisputable, but the corrosive residue is incompatible with metallic permanence." The plumber thanked the department for letting him know that no damage had been done. The department replied in dismay: "We cannot assume responsibility for the toxic and noxious residue of hydrochloric acid and suggest you use an alternate procedure." Again the plumber thanked them for approving. Finally, the department wrote the plumber, "Don't use hydrochloric acid. It eats hell out of the pipes."

You may not wish to give your readers hell and you may be leery of writing so simply as to seem to be talking down to them. If so, you might use some of the following devices instead to make certain that your writing is clear.

1. The explanatory *such as*.

> Critics of business assert that it is stacked in favor of private goods, *such as* food, cars, cigarettes, hair sprays, soaps; and against public goods, *such as* parks, libraries, beaches, clean air.

2. The explanatory *or.*

> Passive restraints (*or* air bags, as they are commonly called) may add hundreds of dollars to the price of retail cars.

3. The flattering *which, as you know.*

> Plea bargaining—which, as you know, is the practice of pleading guilty to a less serious offense instead of being tried for a more serious one—is increasing in our overburdened courts.

You might ask whether the simpler words could not always be used. Why such specialized terms as *private* and *public good, passive restraints,* or *plea bargaining?* Sometimes such terms are necessary because no suitable synonyms exist. For instance, we use *a fair catch* in football to refer to the act of signaling by the receiver of a kicked ball to indicate that he will not run with it and to notify opposing players that they will be penalized if they interfere with him. Imagine having to use this explanation instead of the specialized term!

But using such terms poses a problem—specifically, whether to define them or not. When informing do-it-yourself carpenters how to frame a basement or attic wall, you could assume that they would be familiar with such terms as *studs, plumb line, toenailed, joist,* and *lag screws.* You could assume that camera buffs would understand such terms as *XL cameras, reflexes, automatic metering, zoom lens, fixed-focus lens,* and *built-in exposure meters.* But if you were writing for beginning carpenters or photographers, you would need to clarify these words.

You may argue that all these examples are for real people in the real world and have little to do with you in freshman English, writing assignments for your English instructor. In one sense, you are correct: your English instructor will evaluate your paper. But generally your instructor will ask you to write for your classmates or people like them. These readers should be easy for you to identify with because most of them are about your age, have many of your interests, share many of your ideas. But they are also different—in career plans, attitudes, values, knowledge, family relationships, political views, life style, aspirations, and morals. You must be aware of these differences and consider them when you write to these readers.

Of course, you can't explain everything to every one of them. But you can try to make your ideas clear to most of them. This means being careful not only about specialized terms but also about any other troublesome ones. For example, we used to talk about bright, lively people as being *gay;* now, because of its recent change in meaning, we do not use the word so freely. Perhaps more prevalent than such misleading words are obscure ones that may be troublesome to some readers. To show you what we mean, we have rewritten the following paragraph from *The New York Times Magazine* to make it clearer to high school students. The changed words are in italics.

Original	*Revision*
Although the beaver is an air breather, it is beautifully adapted to an *amphibious* life. Its oversized liver and large lungs enable it to hold its breath for as long as 15 minutes. Its ears and nose are *valvular* and can be shut off at will. A *transparent membrane* protects its eyes when it dives. Its mouth is constructed so that fur flaps close behind its front *incisors,* allowing it to chew wood underwater without choking.	Although the beaver is an air breather, it is beautifully adapted to *a life in the water as well as on land.* Its oversized liver and large lungs enable it to hold its breath for as long as 15 minutes. Its ears and nose *work like valves* and can be shut off at will *like a faucet. A thin layer of tissue* protects its eyes when it dives. Its mouth is constructed so that fur flaps close behind its front *cutting teeth,* allowing it to chew wood underwater without choking.

Some of these changes might be unnecessary for high school students. You must be the judge. The important point to remember is that you must write to your readers and for them. This requires that you develop a double vision, looking inward to see what the words mean to you and outward to see what they mean to your audience. You may do this when writing your first draft or when revising. But you must do it, and you must see to it that your readers see clearly what you mean.

THE NEED FOR ACCURACY

But words may fail to communicate clearly for reasons other than that they are difficult or specialized. Sometimes we fail to use words accurately, selecting not the proper one but one almost like it. This may be done, as it often is by Archie Bunker ("You're invading the subject") for comic effect in the tradition of Mrs. Malaprop, the humorous character in Sheridan's eighteenth-century play *The Rivals.* But if you inadvertently create malapropisms such as *respectfully* for *respectively, condone* for *condemn, irreverent* for *irrelevant,* then you will be laughed at, not laughed with. The trick in avoiding errors of this sort is not to submit a paper until you have checked every word whose meaning you have any doubt about. We have found that our students usually admit they had been unsure of words they misused, but hadn't bothered to check them. Recklessness in some human endeavors may be desirable, but not in writing. Our advice: take a minute to check doubtful words, in either the writing or revising stage.

Flaubert, the great French novelist, told how he spent hours searching for *le mot juste* (the precise word) when writing. You will not have the time or the inclination to do that, but you can strive for accuracy, particularly in revising, by trying to substitute a more precise term for the one that popped into your head while you were writing your first draft. Consulting a thesaurus, a synonym dictionary, or a regular dictionary may be helpful. But remember to be careful about using a thesaurus, because it merely lists words and does not distinguish their connotations or different shades of meaning. A dictionary or synonym dictionary is safer and more helpful.

THE NEED FOR ECONOMY

Most Americans hurry. Whether driving, eating, shopping, dancing, vacationing—or reading—we seldom do it slowly. While we may read narration and description at something approaching a slow pace, savoring the experiences they convey, we generally speed through exposition. In looking at information about assembling a bicycle, buying insurance, or enrolling in summer school, Americans want it to be to the point.

That's what is meant by economy. In our writing and teaching, we used to try to convey this concept with words like *conciseness* and *brevity.* But the trouble with these terms is they suggest that writing should be concise or brief. They imply that all sentences should be short, simple sentences, rather than the expanded ones we have discussed. But that's not what we mean by economy. Your writing must be complete enough to communicate everything necessary to help your reader understand the subject fully, but it's almost equally important to omit anything unnecessary. Achieving sentence economy is like dieting: the purpose of both is to remove fat. What's left should be strong, firm, and muscular. To diet, you've got to cut down on calories; to achieve sentence economy, you've got to cut down on words. You can do that by remembering this:

Omit any and all words for which you do not have any use.

Or, economically stated:

Omit useless words.

And here are questions to ask yourself while revising to achieve economy:

1. *Can I omit the relative pronouns* which, who, *or* that? These three little words—*which, who, that*—are likely to clog your sentences unless you are alert. Note that one or two words are saved in the revised version of each of the following sentences, making each that much more economical.

Original: The fumes *which* come from millions of cars fill the air with pollutants.
Revision: The fumes from millions of cars fill the air with pollutants.

Original: Thousands of people *who* want to own luxury cars borrow at high interest rates from banks and finance companies.
Revision: Thousands of people wanting to own luxury cars borrow at high interest rates from banks and finance companies.

Original: Many automobile parts *that* are now made of plastics and other synthetic materials do not last long.

Revision: Many automobile parts now made of plastic and other synthetic materials do not last long.

Note when the relative pronouns are omitted, we also delete part or all of the verb phrase in the clause as in the first and third examples. Another common device is to change the verb to an *-ing* form, as in the second example.

Of course, you cannot always delete *which, who,* and *that* because sometimes they are essential to your desired effect. But when you can remove them, do so. Your writing will be more economical and more vigorous.

2. *Can I remove the introductory* there is, there are, *or* it is? Just as inexperienced writers often lead up to the subject of their papers slowly, so they do with the subject of their sentences, resulting in the unnecessary introducers—*there is, there are,* and *it is.* Sometimes you may need them for stylistic purposes, but usually they can be eliminated.

Original: *There is* an increase in membership in sororities and fraternities this year.

Revision: Membership in sororities and fraternities has increased this year.

Original: *It is* one of the new policies of student government to encourage civic projects.

Revision: One of the new policies of student government is to encourage civic projects.

The savings in eliminating *there is, there are,* and *it is* may be small in each sentence, but this reduction and others will achieve significant overall economies in your paper.

3. *Can I delete prepositions?* Prepositions will swarm all over your papers unless you are vigilant. Most dangerous is *of,* a creature that has to be as carefully screened out as the housefly. But also be on guard against *in, on, by, to,* and *with.* Here's how they operate:

Original: At the time *of* registration, students are required to make payments *of* their fees.

Revision: At registration time, students are required to pay their fees.

Original: Because of the increase *in* enrollments, some classes *in* sociology are closed by early *in* the morning.

Revision: Because of increased enrollments, some sociology classes are closed by early morning.

Note that often the remedy for eliminating these prepositions involves changing the post-noun prepositional phrase into a pre-noun modifier, as in the first example. Other times, as in the second example, the problem can be solved by using a verb form rather than a noun derivative.

You should also guard against some prepositional phrases. They come in clusters: the *fact* cluster, the *regard* cluster, and the *reference* cluster are the main ones to watch out for. Here are all three clusters in one monstrous sentence:

> *Due to the fact that* she inquired *with reference to* the dormitory hours, specifically *in regard to* when the girls had to return at night, we sent her a copy of the new regulations.

Here is the sentence without the prepositional clusters:

> Because she inquired about the dormitory hours, specifically when the girls had to return at night, we sent her a copy of the new regulations.

In reference to this subject and in regard to these prepositional phrases, and in view of the fact that you can improve your writing by eliminating most of them, do so!

4. *Can I omit any* -ion *words?* Unfortunately, the desire to impress others in writing often results in the piling up of the sonorous sounding *-ion* words. But they are all sluggish, overweight dreadnoughts likely to sink readers, sentence and all.

Original: The chair made a recommendation that students should be given an invitation to provide information to faculty members about proposed new courses.

Revision: The chair recommended that students be invited to inform faculty members about proposed new courses.

5. *Can I combine sentences and omit repetitious material?* Using the techniques of sentence combining discussed on pages 143–47, you can combine a series of short sentences:

Original: I decided to attend the university because of its fine academic program. The university has a good faculty. Athletics at the university are also excellent, particularly basketball. And the university has a lovely campus.

Revision: I decided to attend the university because of its fine academic program, good faculty, lovely campus, and excellent athletics, particularly basketball.

6. *Can I eliminate dead nouns?* Worn-out, meaningless nouns, such as *kind, manner,* and *nature,* were listed and discussed on pages 33–35, so we won't bore you by repeating them here. But we do want to remind you of them and point out that they too cause waste.

7. *Can I do away with deadwood?* After you have provided money for certain regular items in your budget, such as room, food, clothing, and fun,

245

numerous miscellaneous expenses still exist. Although we have already classified six regular wordy patterns, numerous others elude these categories, so we have adopted a miscellaneous category termed *deadwood*.

Deadwood is so prevalent in freshman papers that it constitutes a serious fire hazard. We'd like to have a Coke for every time we've cut the ponderous "in this modern world of today" down to "today" or else crossed out the entire phrase. Why is it that expressions involving time bring out the wordiness in us?

> By the time that the end of our vacation arrived, we were completely exhausted. (By the end of our vacation . . .)
>
> In this day and age of inflated prices, five dollars does not go far. (In these inflationary times . . .)

And then there are those phrases using *number* ("five in number"), *color* ("blue in color"), *shape* ("round in shape"), and the like. Also on the deadwood list are certain unnecessary modifiers, particularly *very* and *really,* which can provide emphasis in speech but lose their effectiveness in writing. See for yourself:

> Original: It is really necessary to return the library book very soon.
> Revision: It is necessary to return the library book soon.

The unnecessary modifiers have probably emigrated from advertising, a world of raucous excesses. Law may have provided us with another form of deadwood—doublets or synonym twins. First and foremost, you should be on the lookout for these, anxious and eager to eliminate each and every repetitious word. We know you get the idea.

Most deadwood defies classification. Thus you must become economy-minded, scrutinizing your sentences to strip the waste away. Naturally, you can't adopt a telegraphic style, but you can attack your sentences as if you were being charged for each word. Here's how we reduced one student sentence:

> Original: He contracted in the sociology course to fulfill the requirements for an *A* grade as established by the professor.
> First revision: He contracted in the sociology course to fulfill the professor's requirements for an *A* grade.
> Second revision: He contracted in the sociology course to fulfill the professor's requirements for an *A*.
> Third revision: He contracted to fulfill the sociology professor's requirements for an *A*.
> Fourth revision: He contracted for an *A* with the sociology professor.

Perhaps, in some other contexts, the pruning might have stopped at the second or third cut. Sometimes, for stylistic or semantic reasons, all deadwood cannot be completely cut away. That's a conscious decision you should make after becoming aware of the unnecessary words and phrases in your own papers.

What is most important is to keep your eyes and your mind alert to wordiness. If you do, you will find numerous opportunities to economize in your work. The seven questions, repeated here for your convenience, should serve as guidelines:

1. Can I omit the relative pronouns *which, who,* or *that?*
2. Can I remove the introductory *there is, there are,* or *it is?*
3. Can I delete prepositions?
4. Can I omit any *-ion* words?
5. Can I combine sentences and omit repetitious material?
6. Can I eliminate dead nouns?
7. Can I do away with deadwood?

. The key factor in achieving sentence economy is your frame of mind. You must realize that it's not the number of words you write that matters, but what you say. If you clutter your work with unnecessary words, you will probably confound your readers, resulting in their either deciding not to finish your paper or else finishing it and being finished with you. That's how aggravating it is to read padded prose. So don't be wasteful—eliminate any unnecessary word. Doing so may almost kill you, but it will bring life and clarity to your writing.

THE NEED FOR APPROPRIATENESS

Remember that in personal writing and in much descriptive writing, you either write directly to yourself or to someone else from a highly personal point of view. But in exposition you would not be likely to write a comprehensive explanation to yourself. Therefore, an extensive written explanation presumes an audience—one rather far removed from your immediate personal circle. In order to communicate with that audience, you as a writer are forced to search for words whose meaning is generally recognized. In addition, you must use more complex paragraphs and sentences and more widely accepted language usages. Your explanatory writing then takes on the character of General English (see the chart on pages 136–37). You shift from the relaxed language dress of Casual style to the more conservative General English required for a general audience—the language apparel you don along with a clean shirt and take to the classroom or office with you.

In expository writing, you must be especially aware of the words you use. Breezy, colloquial words such as *kid, guy, loony, dude,* and *chick* or in-group slang terms like *freaked out* and *spacy* are appropriate to Casual English when your audience is a peer group. But you are committed to using more generally acceptable words when writing to a broader audience and for a serious purpose. Writing in the vocabulary of General English will lessen your chances of irritating or alienating your readers and help you to explain your ideas more clearly.

Your problem is in determining how to distinguish when certain words or phrases are appropriate to the writing situation. One way to make sure is to check our glossary at the end of the book. Another is to use a dictionary, most of which indicate the relative formality of a word: *slang, colloquial,* or *informal.* Items marked with one of these labels should be avoided unless you wish to use them for special effect, as illustrated in this paragraph, taken from an explanation of how people change as they grow up:

> I suppose that I see the world as made up of "them guys" who choose to not take chances, to work 40 hours a week at a boring job, drink lots of beer and watch "Let's Make a Deal" on television; and "us guys" who are willing to take chances, speak up, move, drink wine, eat cheese and read lots of newsmagazines. Along the way a number of "them guys" have been my friends, and they have admitted that they are jealous of the way I choose to approach my life. I now wonder if I'm a little jealous of some of what they have as well.
>
> —Martin L. Krovetz, "Going My Way"

Note that the writer has placed the colloquial words in quotation marks to signal to readers that he does not ordinarily use them to a general audience.

If you have any doubt about whether you should use a word, then avoid it. Find another one. In your search, you will not only find a more effective word, you may increase your vocabulary as well.

SUMMARY

Selecting words that are clear, accurate, appropriate, and economical is no easy task. Usually you cannot achieve it in your first draft while striving to express your ideas. But in revising your paper, when you have an opportunity to scrutinize every word, you can keep asking, "Is it clear?" "Is it accurate?" "Is it appropriate?" "Is it economical?" By doing so and following the suggestions in this chapter, you can do much to fulfill your writing commitment.

Assignments

For Discussion

1 We often think of specialized words as strange new terms, but sometimes they are simple words used in new ways. Here, for instance, are the opening sentences of a political editorial.

Congress may be getting ready to do a better job on the long-neglected task of legislative oversight. It would be a mistake to expect too much. Strong practical and institutional barriers remain. Nonetheless, new chairmen, new members, new rules and new grass roots pressures all push in the direction of an expanded oversight effort.

—*Wall Street Journal*

What does *oversight* mean to you? To the writer? If you do not know, see if you can figure out the meaning from the following sentence, which appears later in the editorial:

The new effort also stems from a belief that closer oversight of agencies and programs may help rebuild public trust in government, persuading many citizens that someone up there is at last fighting their battles.

If you were writing the editorial, would you substitute another word for *oversight*? If so, what?
2 Many words in sports, like the term *stealing* as used in baseball, have entirely different meanings in other contexts. See how many you and your classmates can think of. For example, a *diamond* in baseball isn't a girl's best friend, and a *shortstop* isn't a brief layover at an airport.
3 One of the most colorful and imaginative forms of slang is that used by short-order cooks. We were startled at breakfast one morning to hear our waitress cry out, "Wreck two and roast the English!" Soon afterward we received our two scrambled eggs and English muffins. Are you familiar with contexts other than sports where slang terms can be misleading to outsiders?
4 Many words and phrases mean almost the opposite of what they say. For example, "Speed Zone" really means slow zone and "heads up" means to duck, or put your head down. What other examples can you think of?
5 What does this statement mean: "When he throws a party, he throws a party"? How do you know what it means? How can any meaning be conveyed by the same words as the words being explained?
6 Discuss the following:

The word *love* has by no means the same sense for both sexes, and this is one cause of the serious misunderstandings which divide them.

—Simone de Beauvoir

7 A pun is a play on words, often creating an effect of pleasure (or pain) from different meanings of the same word. For example, in *Romeo and Juliet*, the dying Mercutio quips, "Ask for me tomorrow and you shall find me a grave man." Do you know any pungent puns that illustrate how dual meanings can produce humor?

249

8 How would you rephrase the following statements if you were using them in a talk to a club of retired people not familiar with current college slang?

   a Students with a three-point average have developed good study habits.
   b Some soc. courses are snaps.
   c One of the joys of the library is wandering around in the stacks.
   d A few profs like to give pop quizzes.
   e Many of the first-year courses are taught by teaching assistants.
   f If we started Thanksgiving vacation on Tuesday, students would probably cut on Monday.

9 What is the meaning of the word *round* in each of the following sentences?

   a He rounded off the bill at $23.
   b The bout ended in the tenth round.
   c The round trip cost $47.
   d He bought chuck instead of round.
   e He paid for the round of drinks.
   f Just then he came round the corner.
   g The earth turns round.
   h He was a funny, round fellow.
   i The library is open all year round.

For Practice

1 Remove the unnecessary words from the following sentences and indicate the technique used; omitting the relative pronoun, removing the introductory words, deleting prepositions, avoiding the *-ion* word, combining clauses, eliminating dead nouns, doing away with deadwood, or any combination of these.

   a There are two screws, which are included in the package, that attach the handlebars to the frame.
   b In some cases, students do not know whether they will have enough money to pay for registration at the university next semester.
   c The chairman received your letter in which you informed him that due to the fact that you were ill, you did not take the final exam.
   d I wish to invite you to the first meeting of the Philosophy Club this year. This meeting will be held in the conference room of the Student Center. It will occur on Wednesday, September 20, and start at 8 p.m.
   e He gave consideration to the recommendation that students should submit their applications before spring break.

f   In view of the fact that few women apply to the College of Engineering, there are few women students admitted.

g   It is the opinion of most women employees that the university is engaged in discrimination against them.

h   Many faculty members who have had extensive experience at other schools claim that discrimination of this kind also exists there.

i   The investigator conducted an examination of the records in a hurried manner.

j   The number of applications to the College of Education is on the decrease.

k   The president addressed the faculty with regard to this matter of decreasing enrollments.

l   He was doing well in the course until the time during the semester when the research report was due.

For Writing

1   Write a letter home explaining why you need a car; why you didn't make the dean's list; why you need money; why you want to get married; or some other explanation. Make effective use of subordinators in your paper.

2   Write a paper explaining how you have become a waster of words, perhaps including a few sentences or phrases that you especially regret. Make use of complex sentences.

3   Draft a letter to the author of a textbook, pointing out how he or she might have eliminated unnecessary words from a particular paragraph and urging the author to write more economically in the future.

4   Find a "fat" paragraph in a newspaper, article, or book. Write a paper for your instructor, showing how you would replace the paragraph and identifying the techniques you would use.

Special Topics

CHOOSING TITLES

Writers begin with the first word of the first sentence, but readers start with the title—and sometimes get no further. If the title is not attractive, engaging, or catchy, or if it does not appeal sufficiently in some other way, readers may not proceed. That doesn't mean you must start by writing the title. It does mean you should devote some time and thought to it, usually after your first draft unless you have an inspiration sooner.

What we want to emphasize is that a title should be chosen with care, not indifferently slapped on. As an attractive hairstyle dresses up a person, so an attractive title enhances a paper. But the title should also provide some inkling about the content. And it should be brief. We can't tell you how to come up with a short, informative, and attractive title, but we can provide some types and models for you, and offer some general advice.

Type	Model
The Question	"What's Wrong with Cocaine?"
Modified Saying	"Eat, Drink, and Be Thin"
What-to-Do + Surprise	"What to Do before the Crab Grass Comes"
Controversy	"The Student Football Ticket Dilemma"
Humanizing Non-Human Things	"Keep House Plants Smiling"
Word Play	"Some Words about Words"
Imperative	"Don't Be a Cheerleader!"

You, your classmates, and your instructor may think of others that might be helpful. But whatever you do, avoid the single-word, general-subject title ("Ballooning") or its cousin with an article ("The Hairpiece"). If you can't come up with a title that's short, snappy, and says something about your subject, then state your thesis in question or abbreviated form: "Is Career

Planning Necessary?" or "The Importance of Career Planning." Or, in desperation, resort to the *and* title, such as "Cars and Rust" or "Kids and Crime."

You may have noticed that not all the words in a title are capitalized. For valuable information about that tricky subject, see page 511.

WRITING INTRODUCTIONS

Starting papers usually seems as difficult as getting the first squirt of ketchup out of a new bottle. That's why many people postpone writing until the deadline is about to strangle them. But once you perceive what options are available and what pattern you will follow, writing the opening paragraph should not be so nerve-wracking.

Although long articles and term papers may call for introductions of several paragraphs, short papers usually require only a one-paragraph introduction. Yet these introductory four or five sentences are so exasperatingly painful to write that some teachers suggest that you postpone the torture, waiting until you've completed your paper. You may do this if you're in a bind about getting started. As for us, we've always liked the Red Queen's advice in *Alice in Wonderland:* "Begin at the beginning, keep on going until you get to the end, and then stop." We've found that skipping the opening paragraph and returning to it later is like starting a meal with the main course and eating the appetizer afterward.

What complicates the introduction are the decisions required and the challenges posed. Here are some of the questions you usually have to consider:

1. How can I get my readers' attention?
2. How can I interest my readers?
3. How should I state my thesis?
4. Should I state the plan of my paper?
5. What voice should I employ?
6. What point of view should I use?

Let's tackle these one by one.

How Can I Get my Readers' Attention?

The opening sentence is somewhat like the introductory "tease" in a television commercial: both hope to attract people's attention so they will not turn away. Although advertising writers may rely on such standard visual devices as ravishing girls, virile athletes, appealing children, or breathtaking scenery, expository writers have none of these options. But they have others. By considering these other choices, you may find one that strikes your fancy if your own inspiration fails. Here are some possible attention-getting approaches:

1. A controversial statement

   Some students swear that graduate teaching assistants are inexperienced, ignorant, and uninteresting; others insist that they are enthusiastic, friendly, and inspiring.

2. An element of surprise

   That slightly older guy, garbed in jeans and sweatshirt, sometimes with beard, often with pipe, nearly always with a sack of books, who strides in late the first day of freshman class, is neither student nor professor but a peculiar species known as a graduate teaching assistant.

3. A note of contradiction

   Graduate teaching assistants are neither fish nor fowl, neither completely students nor teachers, neither really graduates nor assistants.

4. A short, dramatic statement

   Beware of graduate teaching assistants.

5. The use of statistics

   Most of the two million freshmen entering colleges and universities this fall will be instructed by graduate teaching assistants.

6. A figure of speech (simile or metaphor)

   A graduate teaching assistant is like a pilot on a new route: each is capable, but each is unfamiliar with the course.

7. The use of quotation

   "Although they are inexperienced, most graduate teaching assistants are generally effective instructors because they relate well to their students," state the authors of *The Writing Commitment*.[1] [In an endnote you would cite the source of this quotation. See the discussion of endnotes in Chapter 24.]

8. A reference to a current event

   The recent debate in the freshman dorm about graduate teaching assistants was almost as heated as the one at the United Nations about the Third World.

9. Proof of your authority

   Having had seven graduate teaching assistants in my first two semesters at college, I feel well qualified to discuss their strengths and weaknesses.

These nine openings may not at all be appropriate for your subject, your readers, or the occasion of your paper, but they do suggest some possibilities. If not, here are three others to consider: the rhetorical question, the definition, and the anecdote.

We separated these three from the others because they require some discussion. The *rhetorical question* has been employed so frequently that many sophisticated readers resent it as condescending or trite. Our advice is to use it only in a pinch, and then not as a single question but as a series. The danger with the single question is that it represents a desperate gamble. If readers reply "Yes" to the question, you've got them; but if "No," you've lost them. Here's what we mean:

> Have you ever thought about what it would be like to have a graduate teaching assistant for an instructor?

Because most readers haven't thought about this—and don't see any reason why they should—they might discard the paper instead of reading further. With a series of questions, however, the odds on hooking your readers' interest increase:

> Should you sign up for a course taught by a graduate teaching assistant? How effective are they? How do they grade? Are they interested in their students? Do they have time to see students in conferences?

The multiquestion approach may not always succeed, but the chances that it will are greater.

Another possible opening involves the *definition*. Here, too, some words of caution. If we had a dime for every paper we've read that began with "According to Webster," we could retire to Hawaii tomorrow. Definitions are deadly unless you're addressing highly educated readers or unless the subject lends itself to an interesting use of a definition. For example:

> Patriotism is generally defined as love of country, but to Samuel Johnson it was "the last refuge of scoundrels."

> The dictionary definition of a graduate teaching assistant as "a graduate student with part-time complete or partial college teaching responsibilities" says a lot but explains little.

The third possible opening that warrants a word of caution is the *anecdote*. Most readers enjoy jokes and short narratives, but these are effective only when they relate to the subject being discussed. In other words, the point of the anecdote must be closely related to the thesis of the paper. After-dinner speakers often violate this injunction with their "While I was coming to this meeting tonight. . . ." But after-dinner speakers have a captive audience. You don't.

Up to this point we've been discussing ways to write an attention-getting introduction. Now we'd like to mention what not to do. Here are some ways to turn readers off:

1. The apology

> Although I don't know much about graduate teaching assistants, I thought that I'd write a paper about them.

(Says the reader, "You may write it, but I'm not about to read it.")

2. The complaint

> I started thinking about this paper after dinner and couldn't come up with an interesting subject because we were told that we could write about anything, but I finally decided to discuss graduate teaching assistants for lack of something else.

(Says the reader, "Dullsville. I'll skip this one.")

3. The platitude

> Some graduate teaching assistants are good and some graduate teaching assistants are bad.

(Says the reader, "Some papers are good but this one sounds bad.")

4. The reference to the title

> The title of this paper, "Graduate Teaching Assistants," indicates that it is concerned with graduate students who are teaching in college while also pursuing their own graduate work.

(Says the reader, "So what else is new? Why waste time reading this?")

And there you have it—what to do and what not to do to gain the attention of readers. Do you always have to be concerned with getting their attention? No; there are some occasions when you can assume that people will be highly motivated to read what you've written. But generally you'd be wiser not to take your readers, even your instructor, for granted.

How Can I Interest My Readers?

Let's assume you've written that horrendously difficult first sentence or so and are confident that it will get your readers' attention. Now to develop readers' interest in your subject. This requires answering these questions: Why is my subject important? Why should people read about it? How will it benefit them?

In our earlier discussion about selecting an interesting subject, we talked about the importance of appealing to readers. You may assume that most people would like to save time, effort, or money; to improve their knowledge, looks, and health; and to gain prestige, praise, and popularity. Does your subject appeal to any of these motivations? Or, can you suggest why a reasonably intelligent person should be concerned about it? For instance, not everyone is interested in cats, but most readers have developed a fondness for some pet at some time in their lives. You can build on this interest in writing about cats.

But you must keep your specific readers clearly in mind. If you were writing about graduate teaching assistants to a general audience of taxpayers, you would appeal to their curiosity in one way; to parents, in another; to entering college students, in a third. Unless you have your readers' interests at heart, you may be unable to attract their minds.

How Should I State My Thesis?

In Chapter 12, we discussed the thesis statement and suggested how to formulate it. But we did not discuss specifically where to place it in the paper or how to introduce it. We shall deal with these matters here.

As we mentioned, the formal statement of thesis is usually appropriate only in scientific or formal papers, such as research reports or dissertations. It is generally signaled by the words *subject* or *purpose:*

It is the purpose of this paper . . .
The subject that I plan to discuss . . .

Because your purpose generally is to treat the subject less formally, the thesis should be stated or implied without such explicit signals.

Next, where should it appear? Many students state it as the first sentence as if it were too hot to hold on to longer. But the introduction should function to introduce a subject graciously, not to dump it on readers. You probably wouldn't introduce two friends to one another by simply saying, "Mary Anderson, I want you to meet Fred Clarkson" and then leave them alone. You'd undoubtedly mention their mutual acquaintances or interests to indicate why they should enjoy knowing each other. Similarly, you should introduce your thesis to readers rather than merely announcing it in your opening sentence and leaving it practically alone in a skimpy paragraph.

Instead, conceive of an introduction that consists of three parts: (1) a hook or attention-getting device, (2) reference to the significance of the subject, and (3) statement of the thesis. In longer papers, writers often add a fourth part to the introduction: mention of the main points to be covered. By following this pattern, you start with an attention "grabber" and then move on to the thesis, as in the following opening paragraph:

DON'T LET THEM FOOL YOU!

Television commercials are often as irritating   Attention-getter:
as an unanswered ringing telephone. Although any   figure of speech
of the millions of viewers can turn off the blasting
advertisements for deodorants, detergents, denture

257

adhesives, girdles, or hair washes, dyes, and lo-
tions, most people endure them or flee to the refrigerator for a snack. If commercials were only
annoying, perhaps serious complaints could not
be registered. But what is wrong affects not
people's taste but their pocketbooks. *Television
commercials misrepresent products by employing
deceptive devices.*

Interest:
appeal to mutual dislike;
then to pocketbook

Thesis

Should I State the Plan of My Paper?

Particularly in writing a long paper or one with a complicated organizational plan, you would be wise to indicate the plan to your readers. This
practice is helpful because the plan serves as a road map, showing readers
where you are taking them. For example, the following sentence could be
added to the preceding example:

These commercials rely on trick photography, misleading experiments, and false testimonials.

This statement helpfully notifies readers that your paper will deal with
these particular subtopics and in the order announced. Although most
readers welcome such help in long or complicated papers, it is usually
unnecessary in short ones. Let common sense be your guide.

What Voice Should I Employ?

Occasionally you're introduced to a stranger—a friend of a friend, an
acquaintance of your parents, a teacher, or the parents of the person you are
dating. Usually you adapt your manner to theirs: if they are polite, reserved,
and detached, then you are too. But in writing, you call the shots. You must
establish in the first paragraph, and to some extent in the first sentence, the
voice that sets up the relationship between you, your subject, and your
readers. We've already talked about this subject of voice several times,
pointing out how it depends on numerous factors such as choice of words,
sentence structure, verb form, and pronoun choice. What is important to
realize now is that in the introduction you will need to decide *which* voice to
use. For example, the following opening sentences are arranged in the order
of increasing formality. Note how each launches readers into the subject in
a slightly different way.

1. So you're getting ready to go on vacation.
2. If you want to make a clean getaway to your vacation hideaway, here is a
   way to do it.

3. The best-laid vacation plans need not go astray.
4. Before you go on vacation, you should spend some time planning.
5. Most people can't wait to go on vacation.
6. Though the daily activities of people in various stages of life may differ, nearly all engage in the ritual of relief and relaxation known as a vacation.
7. It is my opinion that people must not only plan their vacation but plan what must be done before they leave.
8. One should be aware that preparations for departure on a holiday may assume an importance proportionate to the deliberations for the holiday itself.

Whichever voice you choose, it must be maintained throughout your paper. Decisions, decisions—but that's what writing is all about. And while you may sweat over a few initial sentences, trying to establish just the appropriate voice, remember the plight of the great historian Edward Gibbon, who three times rewrote the entire lengthy first chapter of his classic work *The Decline and Fall of the Roman Empire,* searching for just the proper tone of voice to introduce readers to his monumental study.

What Point of View Should I Use?

In Chapter 1 we indicated that you have several choices of point of view in narrative writing. In expository writing you have three possibilities—first-, second-, or third-person pronouns and their noun antecedents.

First Person—*I* Generally, the first-person *I* or *we* strikes a personal, intimate note, which is especially appropriate when your experience lends authority or credibility to what you are saying about the subject. If your parents are divorced and you are writing about the effects of divorce on children, then by all means use *I* in referring to your own reactions. Take care, however, because, as Chapter 2 pointed out, one *I* can lead to many *I*'s, distracting and annoying readers, who may consider you egotistical or turn away from the subject to speculate about you, the writer. To avoid *I*, some students resort to such bloated substitutes as "your reporter" or "the author of this article," which are usually more distracting. There is nothing wrong with using *I*. If you choose it, stick with it—but be temperate.

Sometimes *I* may be employed less personally, as when you present yourself as representative of a group:

Like other college students, I am concerned about the scarcity of jobs.

Here and in similar situations, you are writing as a member of a group, not as a unique person. You may be tempted to slip into *we* on these occasions, but remember that the use of *we* instead of *I* in a personal context is affected:

> Sitting in our room, we stared at the walls, looking for a subject for our paper.

This editorial *we* is acceptable in editorials, where it usually represents the views of the editors, but it should be avoided elsewhere, particularly in situations where it may establish a condescending tone. Just remember the teacher who always annoyed you by saying, "We are going to do our arithmetic homework" or the nurse who insisted, "We will take our medicine now."

These warnings do not mean that *we* is out. It can be perfectly proper and effective when used for two major purposes—to establish writer-reader togetherness:

> We all struggle in writing the first sentence of a paper.

and to refer to an actual group:

> As new freshmen on campus, bewildered by the strange buildings, dazed by the hordes of students, and confused by new routines, we felt lost and unimportant.

The "togetherness" *we* establishes a natural, friendly relationship. The "group" *we* is less personal but still far from formal. Occasionally, a third situation calling for *we* arises: when two or more writers are collaborating— as we are so well aware in this book.

Second Person—*You* The second-person *you* is highly controversial. As you may know, many instructors forbid students to use it in their papers. We're usually on their side even though we ourselves use *you* throughout this book and accept it in some student papers. What's wrong with *you?* For one thing, it establishes a note that may often be too informal for exposition. Readers may resent being addressed as *you,* which sometimes they visualize as a finger pointing at them as in the old recruiting posters, "Uncle Sam wants YOU!" Then, too, the *you* viewpoint is closer to speech usage and is thus considered less formal and acceptable than the third-person pronoun. Therefore, some instructors feel that students need the practice of writing in the more demanding formal style required in their work in other courses and often in business, industry, and the professions. Some instructors also feel that because much high school writing calls for *I* or *you,* college writing should require the third person. Finally, *you* is dangerous, subject to being "over-yoused." Like *I,* one *you* frequently leads to many more:

> If you will take my advice, you will find that you do not have to spend much of your time studying for your final exam.

In defense of *you,* it is perfectly acceptable and effective when used sparingly and skillfully. It need not grab the reader ("Hey, you!"), but it can serve as a valuable impersonal or indefinite reference:

As citizens interested in the community, you should inquire into the policies, practices, and politics of the zoning board.

In this textbook, we have generally employed *you* in this generic sense, hoping that you would find it a refreshing and pleasant departure from the dreary solemnity and impersonality of most college textbooks.

Third Person—*He, She, It*   The last point of view, the third-person pronouns or their antecedents, is the one used most frequently in expository writing. The subject itself—poets, garbage collectors, birth control pills, or organic farming—stands in the spotlight, attended by its appropriate personal or indefinite pronoun (*he, she, it, they, anyone, each, everybody,* and so on). The main warning when using this point of view is to avoid the stilted, deadly *one.* When one is writing exposition, one often wishes to impress others by showing how important one can sound. But after one has encountered this use of *one* in one's reading, one would plead with others to shun it entirely or else resort to it only when one is without any viable alternative. You can see how *one* can drive a reader up the wall.

Something that drives women up the wall these days is to read about themselves as males. This occurs frequently with the pronoun *he,* traditionally used generically to refer to both males and females. But women rightfully object, because language, as we pointed out earlier, can corrupt thought. Therefore, beware of third-person pronoun constructions like the following:

If a student wishes to make an appointment, *he* should see the department secretary.

Anyone wishing a copy should write for one on *his* company's stationery.

In the last sentence, many people in talking use *their,* ignoring the problem of reference to a singular pronoun (*anyone*). This practice is currently unacceptable in expository writing. Therefore, the sexist use of pronouns should be corrected by changing the subject and pronoun reference to the plural.

If students wish . . . *they* should see . . .
Individuals wishing . . . should write on *their* . . .

In other situations, you may be unable to shift to the plural. Try then either to change the construction to the passive, to repeat the noun, or to substitute a synonym for it, instead of using a pronoun.

Example: When the professor arrives, he will take care of the problem.

Passive: When the professor arrives, the problem will be taken care of.

Example: A doctor should be called in such cases. He will be able to determine whether the patient should be hospitalized.

Noun
Repetition: A doctor should be called in such cases. The doctor will be able to determine . . .

In an emergency, you may resort to the cumbersome *he or she* or *he/she*, which becomes monstrous with their oft-accompanying *him or her*, but try anything else first. And don't look for any help from coinages like *shem* or *ter/tem*. Numerous words enter our language, but not pronouns.

A last recommendation about point of view: after determining your point of view, stick to it throughout your paper. Ralph Waldo Emerson stated that "A foolish consistency is the hobgoblin of little minds," but in writing, there is nothing foolish about maintaining consistently the point of view established in your introduction.

A Final Word about Introductions

After this discussion of getting readers' attention, maintaining their interest, stating the thesis, announcing the plan, establishing a voice, and deciding upon a point of view, you can realize why the introduction is so agonizingly complicated to write. But don't despair. Most experienced writers struggle too. Probably the best advice is to jump in and get started, remembering that you can always return to polish up the introduction later. And in an emergency, if you can't get started, skip the introductory paragraph and begin by writing the second paragraph. It's more important to get going than to wait until you have hit upon the perfect beginning, because it may never come.

WRITING CONCLUSIONS

The conclusion of a paper serves two functions: it signals the end and leaves readers with something important to remember. The first is necessary for readers' sense of completeness, suggesting that they have just finished a well-planned, carefully conceived paper. The second is necessary for readers' sense of the subject, leaving them to think about what is important and appropriate. To fulfill both these functions in only a few sentences is no mean achievement.

Perhaps the first point to make is that the conclusion should not be long.

Lingering goodbyes may be enjoyable with a loved one, but they bore readers. In short papers, a conclusion may even be omitted when enumerating a series of reasons in climactic order, the most important being reserved for last. In other instances, about three or four well-worded sentences should do the trick.

You may look either backward or forward in these concluding sentences. In looking backward, you may return to some metaphor or other motif in the introduction, restate the thesis, or, in longer papers, summarize the main points. In looking forward, you may forecast the future, call for action, discuss implications, or point out the significance of the ideas. Here are some examples of these options.

Looking Backward

1. Return to the introduction (the italicized words refer to a comparison made in the introduction).

    Despite all these suggestions, finding a summer job may still be as difficult *as locating an inexpensive apartment near campus.* But at least you can be confident that you have gone about it efficiently and looked into all the possibilities. The rest is up to luck.

2. Restate the thesis.

    You can see that looking for a summer job need not be a hit-or-miss process. It can be conducted in a systematic, efficient manner that should produce results. Almost always, it will.

3. Summarize the main points (only in longer papers).

    What is important is to start looking for a summer job early and to follow the specific suggestions noted here. You may not want to investigate all the possibilities—employers overseas, federal agencies, local or state governments, industries in other areas, and local businesses. But you should realize it is better to have too many opportunities than too few. That is why all these suggestions have been offered.

Looking Forward

4. Forecast the future.

    Despite these suggestions, you may not find summer work. The growing demand for these positions and the diminishing supply of them means that many young people will be unemployed. The result may be a return to the campus to attend summer sessions, which could double present enrollments. The end product might well be many three-year bachelor's degrees. And that is what the future may hold.

5. Call for action

> The important point to remember is to get started looking for that summer job today. You can write letters to federal agencies, check into local and state government possibilities, get a copy of the *Summer Employment Directory,* and follow the suggestions about seeking work in local businesses. They who hesitate may be lost this summer.

6. Discuss implications.

> The implications of these suggestions should be apparent. Summer jobs will be more difficult to find this year than last. You may wait for Lady Luck to smile upon you or roll up your sleeves and start searching for yourself. You may follow these suggestions or your own. You may even decide to chuck the idea of getting a job—and enroll in summer school.

7. Point out the significance of ideas.

> Perhaps what is more significant than these specific suggestions is that even such an undertaking as finding a summer job can be carefully researched and planned. Some people go through life haphazardly, meeting problems with hastily conceived, last-minute answers. Other people anticipate problems and study how to meet them. To do so is usually more rewarding.

These examples suggest how the same paper might be concluded in various ways. Obviously, depending on the context, some would be more appropriate than others. Before concluding this discussion about conclusions, let us note a few rhetorical considerations brought about by the examples.

1. Not one of the examples starts with the overworked words *In summary* or *In conclusion.* We suggest that you discard these feeble mechanical signals. They can be as monotonous to your audience as a repeated TV commercial.
2. No apology is offered, no afterthought included, no extraneous note sounded. The conclusion should be like a parting handshake: firm and brief. Both present a final impression. It should be favorable.
3. In several examples, short sentences end the paragraph. These are effective in snapping it to a close. Sometimes an uncommon sentence pattern is also helpful, as in the last sentence of example 7, which begins with an infinitive. Even punctuation, such as the dash in example 6, can be utilized to achieve a sense of finality.
4. Another effective way to conclude is with a rhetorical question or with a catchy statement, as attempted in example 5. A possibility not exemplified here is to use an anecdote, but keep it short and make certain it is pertinent.

These suggestions should help you in writing the concluding paragraph of your paper. If you're stumped, look through them to find one that strikes your fancy and work it appropriately into your paper. After writing the paragraph, check to determine whether it conveys a sense of finality and leaves the reader with something vital to remember.

WRITING ESSAY ANSWERS

The previous discussion about titles, introductions, and conclusions assumes they are required in all writing assignments. Not so. One exception is an essay exam answer. In addition to having no title, introduction, or conclusion, it is organized differently than other expository forms.

While you may be called upon to define, classify, or describe a process in an essay exam, usually the questions require you to compare, explain causes or effects, or discuss. And essay exams usually provide little time for pre-writing or revising. In fact, many students have difficulty completing these exams by the end of the period because they digress too much, filling space with everything they have memorized about the subject instead of providing the exact information the questions call for.

Consequently, you should adopt an efficient procedure for taking essay exams. We suggest the following:

1. Select the questions.
   Read all the questions to obtain a sense of the exam. Note how many questions must be answered and make the necessary choices.
2. Plan your time.
   Consider the value of each question or the time suggested for each. Plan your time accordingly.
3. Select the order of your answers.
   If you do not have to answer the questions in order, begin with the most important unless it appears too difficult. If so, let it percolate in your subconscious while you answer easier ones. Often while writing, you will think of some points to use in answering the difficult questions.
4. Reread each question.
   Before writing, reread each question carefully, considering exactly what information is asked for. Note whether you are asked to define, explain, compare, discuss, or outline. Jot down a few points on the exam sheet.

These four steps will take only a few minutes but should pay big dividends.

Writing an exam answer is much like writing a newspaper story: both should begin with the important information in the opening sentence, or immediately thereafter. In journalism, this organizational plan is referred to as an "inverted triangle" because it places the vital facts (who-what-when-where-why-how) at the top and then narrows down to other facts or details in order of decreasing importance. Similarly, you should begin your essay with a one- or two-sentence response that directly and clearly answers the question. You don't need an attention-getting opener or a paragraph about the significance of the subject. You do need to repeat some words in the exam question, but they can often serve as a thesis statement. Make your main point quickly and clearly. Then support it with additional points or with information and examples according to the question. Here's how your inverted triangle should look:

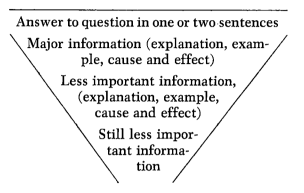

Answer to question in one or two sentences

Major information (explanation, example, cause and effect)

Less important information, (explanation, example, cause and effect)

Still less important information

And here's an example of how the inverted triangle works in an essay answer. (Note how the question is incorporated into the thesis idea.)

Question: Do prejudice and discrimination always occur together? Explain.

Answer: Because prejudice is a state of mind while discrimination is a form of behavior, the two are distinct and need not always occur together. Prejudice refers to people's attitude; discrimination to their action.

People may be prejudiced against others but still not discriminate against them. An employer might not like men with beards but still might hire one out of a sense of fairness. A department chairman might not care to have a woman faculty member in his department but might seek one, even discriminate in favor of one, to comply with affirmative action regulations. On the other hand, people without prejudice can discriminate, as illustrated by homeowners who might be reluctant to sell their houses to blacks due to concern for their neighbors. (Sometimes this might be an excuse to rationalize a prejudice.)

In this example, the two terms were briefly defined, the question answered, and then further information and examples provided the explanation that the question asked for.

In an answer to a question calling for causes or effects, all should be mentioned first, followed by a discussion of them in decreasing importance as illustrated here:

Question: Why was the Battle of the Bulge crucial in World War II?

Answer: The Battle of the Bulge was crucial because it resulted in the defeat of Hitler's major reserves, the end of his plan to win the war, and a psychological boost to the Allied forces.
 Discussion of first reason with supporting evidence.
 Discussion of second reason with supporting evidence.
 Discussion of third reason with supporting evidence.

You can better understand the importance of writing according to the inverted triangle plan by placing yourself in the role of your readers. Instructors generally do not look forward to grading essay exams because of the time and effort required. They are often irritated as they pore over page after page, often barely able to decipher the hasty scrawls and to follow the rambling explanations. Therefore, if you use the inverted-triangle plan, you should make a good impression. Of course, what you know about the subject is important, but as long as a human being rather than a computer is reading your paper, both its form and its content will be taken into account.

If you have any time left at the end of the exam, revise your paper. Correct any errors neatly; add information where needed and draw inserting arrows. Resist the temptation to finish quickly and to leave for more relaxing places. Stay as long as possible to make your paper as perfect as possible.

Assignments

For Discussion

1 Discuss the writing situations in which it is not necessary to attract the attention of readers.

2 What appeals would you use to interest the following groups of readers in the essays below: high-school seniors; homemakers; retired people?

Hypertension Is Deadly
Safety Tips for Bike Riders
Cable Television in the Future
Confused about Tires?
How to Eat Less and Like It
Give the President a Six-Year Term!
A Review of No-Fault Auto Insurance

3 Analyze the introductions to chapters in this book or in other textbooks you have with you in class. To what extent are they successful in gaining the reader's attention? Discuss, supporting your conclusions with reasons.

4 Evaluate the following introductions from student papers:

a The automobile, a four-wheeled transportation vehicle, was initially a great blessing. It was a source of pleasure for people and an indication of one's prosperity. Its invention has allowed society to become very mobile and distant places to become far more accessible. The auto industry has been a tremendous boon for the economy of the United States over the past one hundred years. Yet today it is a menace.

b There is always at least one television commercial on your set that will disgust you. When you come home after a hard day's work and flip on your TV set, the last thing you want to see is a lady caressing and singing to her box of detergent. I've watched people practically ram their feet through an expensive color portable just because a certain obnoxious commercial was on the air. The television commercial is an ineffective means of advertising a product.

c Even though freshman dormitory hours are a much debated issue among new students at the university, I feel they are essential.

d Surveys and statistics show that there has been an increase in the number of people who have experienced college life, and this is due in part to the fact that a college education has become more and more vital in succeeding in today's world. Because of the increase in recent college enrollment, more people have become informed about the Greek system and its advantages. People today realize there's more to get out of a college education than knowledge from books, and a fraternity or sorority helps a student to acquire this knowledge.

5 Compare your past instructions from teachers and your own attitude about the use of *I, we,* and *you* with the views presented in this chapter.

6 What are the two functions of the conclusion? Why are they both important?

7 Evaluate the following conclusions from student papers:

a Considering both the advantages and disadvantages of the automobile today, it is evident that the country needs to develop a mass transit system to relieve traffic in and around the major cities. This system will take years to build, and much time and effort will be needed to persuade people to use it. In the meantime, they will continue to curse at and be cursed with the automobile.

b Insulting, shocking, and deceiving the public should not be effective ways of selling products. Yet products sell or else they would not continue to be advertised on television. Perhaps the continued use of these deplorable techniques says something about the American public. Perhaps people are not as intelligent as we would like to think they are.

c For these reasons I feel freshmen should be required to be in their dorms at certain hours from the opening days of school until the Thanksgiving vacation.

d According to a recent survey, there has been an increase in membership in social sororities and fraternities, so apparently more and more people have come to believe that the Greek system is good. Knowledge obtained from books is important, and just as important is the Greek system in promoting character, scholarship, and student involvement.

For Practice

1 Rewrite one of the introductions in discussion exercise 4 and the corresponding conclusion in exercise 7 and add a statement explaining why your revision is more effective.

2 Write an analysis of several attention-getting devices used in television commercials or magazine advertisements.

3 Write three introductory paragraphs, one for each of the audiences mentioned in discussion exercise 2, about any subject.

4 Write three different conclusions for a single subject, using a different technique in each.

5 Select one of the topics in discussion exercise 2 and write at least six opening sentences for it, each modeled after a different approach suggested in this chapter.

6 Choose one of the introductions in discussion exercise 4 or write one of your own on any topic. Restate the introduction several times, using an increasingly formal tone, as exemplified on pages 258–59.

Revision of Expository Writing

Revision is a process not available to you when you speak. True, as you talk, you can stop to correct a grammatical error or replace a mispronounced word, but the advantage of writing over speaking is that you have the time to bring your critical judgment to bear. You've surely experienced the embarrassment after a party of remembering something that you wish you hadn't said and wishing that there were some way to take it back. Writing, on the other hand, allows you to reconsider, to return, to redo. You hold all the cards: to stand with what you have written, to revise, to revise again, to return to the original version, or to the second, or to revise yet again. Whatever you finally decide to use will result from deliberate, conscious thought, which is almost always superior to impulse. Certainly, as you rework and rework material, it may lose its novelty and effectiveness in your own mind. But a reader, encountering it for the first time, will view your final draft as a fresh one and probably think that it appears on the page as it originally poured out of your mind.

Of course, it didn't—just as this book didn't pour out of our minds but resulted from planning, making several false starts, writing, revising, and revising again and again. And because this book is an example of expository writing, we had certain questions in mind as we revised each chapter. These questions not only may help in revising your expository papers but also should provide a summary of much of the material discussed in this section on exposition. We have omitted some general questions about the subject— about its appeal, breadth, and complexity—because we assume that with the paper already written, you would probably decide to go with it at the revision stage instead of writing a completely new one. Here are the questions:

1. Audience
   Is the paper directed effectively to a particular audience?

Are there any assumptions about the audience's knowledge that might be erroneous?

Is the tone appropriate for the audience?

Has an effort been made to interest the audience?

2. Form

Does the paper mainly fall under one general category: process description, classification, definition, analysis?

If the paper consists of several of these or only one, does it adhere to the discussed techniques appropriate to the form?

3. Logical organization

If the paper was based on an outline, does it follow the outline fairly closely, so that its organization is logical?

If the paper was not based on an outline, would an outline reveal that it had been logically organized?

Is the thesis sentence clearly stated or implied?

4. Paragraphs

Do most of the paragraphs fit some variation of the SRI format?

Is the development (illustration) sufficient?

Have all the appropriate resources been used for developing paragraphs—examples, statistics, authorities, and so on?

Do the paragraphs have various levels of generality? Or do they all follow the same basic pattern with only two or three levels?

5. Sentences

Does the sentence structure help to emphasize and focus the subject matter?

Are clear relationship signals provided for the audience?

Could any of the sentences be written more economically?

Is it possible to eliminate any *who, which,* or *that* constructions, *There is* or *There are* sentence openings, *-ion* words, or any of the other unnecessary words and phrases discussed on pages 244–47?

6. Language and usage

Are words with special meanings defined?

Are usages avoided that would be restricted to a particular group?

Have the meanings of any difficult words been checked?

Have any idioms been used that might confuse or irritate members of a general audience?

7. Introductions and conclusions

Is the introductory sentence attention-getting?

Does the rest of the paragraph contain a general exploration of the broad subject to interest readers?

Does the thesis appear near the end of the introduction?

Does the conclusion indicate that the paper is ending?

Does the conclusion leave readers with an important idea to remember?

You may feel by now that we are overemphasizing the importance of revision. But revision in writing is like ripping apart a sewing project or repainting one wall of a room because it does not yet meet your standards of excellence. It's how you go about improving a piece of writing. Granted, there are times—examinations, in-class themes, routine letters—when you can't revise. Realize, however, that under such conditions, you are not writing at your best. You can do that only when you revise. And you can revise effectively only when you properly psych yourself up for the job and when you develop a systematic approach to it. To revise or not to revise? In writing, that is the crucial question. Your answer will determine whether you write your best. It's your choice.

Revision Exercise

Revise a written paragraph that you prepared in a hurry and that received a grade you're not satisfied with. As you revise, recopy the paragraph so that you can use it later for comparison purposes. Put it away for a few days and then revise the revision, again recopying it as you go. Now analyze the three versions as we did the student sentences on pages 246–47. List the major changes made. Which seems more fluent and spontaneous? Ask your composition instructor to evaluate your final draft.

The Argumentative Voice: Persuasive Writing

Mastering the art of persuasion can be very rewarding and satisfying to you in your academic, social, and career roles. In college classes, papers, and exams, you will often confront controversial issues that require you to present an effective argument. In your social life, you will often want to stake out a position on a number of subjects—political, economic, cultural, educational. In less serious moments, you will try to persuade your parents and friends to accept your taste in such things as pets, clothes, eating places, and television programs. And after college, no matter what field you enter, you will spend much of your time trying to sell people some product, service, or idea, whether it be to accept an out-of-court settlement, to buy an annuity, to follow a diet more carefully, or to contribute to some worthwhile cause. And when you "sell" people, you persuade them. Persuasion, therefore, is a form of communication that attempts to change the attitude or behavior of others by appealing to their reason or emotions. It differs from exposition, particularly opinion, in that the focus of the message shifts from writer to reader. In exposition, writers explain their opinions, indicating why they think as they do, with only a minimum of concern for the needs of readers. In persuasion, however, the aim is to convince readers that something will benefit them in some way. In persuasion, then, the reader or audience becomes paramount; writers must shape and design their convictions about a subject to appeal to a particular group of readers. Effective persuasion papers, or arguments, must do more than clearly explain a problem or the reasons for the writer's opinion about an issue. Effective arguments must persuade readers to adopt a new attitude toward the issue and, sometimes, to act in support of it.

In writing persuasive papers, therefore, you must be concerned with what readers know and need to know about the subject, and also with how they feel about it, why they feel that way, what their general values and attitudes are, and even how they will relate to you. For example, trying to persuade the faculty to call off classes the Wednesday before Thanksgiving would take entirely different tactics than trying to convince Student Government to support such a proposal. Because readers are central in the persuasive process, additional planning to consider their beliefs, attitudes, and values is vital.

But all the planning in the world about how to persuade others cannot accomplish miracles. Facts and predispositions may thwart even the most effective arguments. After all, you can't persuade your father to give you a million dollars if he doesn't have it—and even if he did he might have a few other uses for the money. Nor can you talk teachers into giving you an A for a course if you haven't earned it. Their professional commitment to evaluate your work honestly would predispose them against granting your request.

You should realize that no logical argument or emotional appeal can change the minds or actions of some people on some subjects. Readers strongly committed to an opposing position generally cannot be reached unless you can show that conditions have changed since they formulated their views. Usually, therefore, you are concerned about those mildly opposed to your argument, those uncommitted, or those committed but needing reinforcement. Because you probably cannot convert those strongly opposed, you must seek to understand the needs, desires, and motivations of those you can convince.

You can understand now why writing effective persuasive papers is not easy. To help you master this complex art, we will discuss in the following chapters the organization of persuasive papers, the tactics of persuasion, the uses and abuses of logical reasoning, and sentence and paragraph strategies for persuasion.

As you read these chapters, remember that the study of persuasion is not unrelated to your life but very much a part of it. To speak, write, and think logically, to analyze skillfully, and to reason effectively are skills you will need throughout your life, whatever your major is, and whatever career plans you have.

The Forms of Persuasive Writing

As with other kinds of writing, the form of persuasion you choose depends on what you want to accomplish in your paper. You might wish to convince your community that it would benefit from an arts center or a professional hockey team. Or you might hope to persuade others to adopt your political or religious views. In such cases, you would write a proposition argument, organizing your ideas in much the same way as in expository papers: a thesis stating your proposition, followed by supporting reasons and evidence. But unlike the emphasis in expository papers, your emphasis here would be on how readers would benefit.

A second form, the problem-solution argument, involves stating a problem and then convincing readers your solution would be best. If, for instance, you think the system of grading on a curve is unfair to students, you might write a letter to the university president, pointing out the problems it causes, and then suggest a solution that would be acceptable and beneficial to both students and faculty members. Or you might write a letter to the Faculty Senate, explaining the problems arising from inadequate parking facilities on campus, urging the implementation of your solution, and perhaps indicating weaknesses in other solutions.

Both types of persuasion make use of the tactics of logical reasoning: they appeal to the interests and intelligence of the reader, they cite reputable authority, and they include evidence. Not every persuasive paper uses all three tactics, but along with clear organizational principles, they are the raw materials of effective argument.

PRE-WRITING

Choosing a Subject

Like expository writing, arguments may often be assigned—either in your college classes or in your career. And they often arise naturally from some controversial situation in your community, your church, or your job. For instance, your community government may formulate a plan for clearing the streets of snow, but ignore the issue of cleaning them. As an avid jogger, you feel compelled to write a letter to the local newspaper, urging that some action be taken on this issue. Or you may be asked to write a statement to convince a prospective employer that you are particularly qualified for an available position. In such cases, you would not need to search for a subject.

But let's assume that you encounter a situation where you must find a topic—a classroom assignment, a request for an after-dinner speech, or an article for your firm's newsletter. How do you go about it? We'd advise you to use the brainstorming approach discussed in Chapter 12. However, you should be aware of certain considerations peculiar to persuasive writing before you begin this process or before you roll up your sleeves and leap into combat.

First, avoid subjects that can be determined immediately by available factual material. Arguing about whether George Washington was six feet tall or not is a waste of time when the answer can be found quickly in an encyclopedia. Issues such as the resale value of used cars, or the number of atomic submarines owned by Russia and the United States, are also poor subjects for a persuasive paper because they can be resolved by referring to sources available in most homes or libraries. However, you could argue that George Washington defined and established the model for the United States presidency, or that used car dealers be required to list any flaws an individual car might have, or that more atomic submarines are needed by the United States.

Other subjects to avoid are "no-win topics," those for which no conclusion can be reached. These often involve matters of personal taste ("Blue is a prettier color than green" or "My dog is more beautiful than your dog"). Arguments based on such personal judgments may be fun, but you are not likely to resolve the issue or persuade your audience. However, you could argue that one artist was greater than another if you establish some objective criteria for your evaluation.

In addition to avoiding subjects dealing with facts or personal judgments, you should also avoid those that would not interest your readers. What kind of people are you trying to reach? Obviously, you don't need to waste time convincing people who already agree with you; the main purpose of argument is to persuade people who disagree or are indifferent to the subject. Also, the reader must derive some benefit from your proposal: a PTA group would not ordinarily be interested in or perceive any personal benefits from a beautifully organized and logical argument that the trading of financial futures on the stock market should be abolished. But they would find relevant an argument about sex education or the need to immunize their children against disease.

Restricting the Subject

In persuasive papers, as with expository writing, the restriction of your subject will largely depend on your audience and your purpose for writing the argument. In urging better architectural planning in your community, for example, you should restrict the subject to public buildings if your audience is the city council. But if your readers are home builders, then their particular interests would demand that you restrict it to residential buildings. Dealing with all the facets of architectural planning would force too general a discussion for effective persuasion.

Of course, every subject has its unique restriction problems, but these questions may help you in making decisions about restriction:

- What idea do I want accepted? What proposal adopted?
- How will my readers relate to this idea or proposal? Will they benefit in any way?
- Can I construct a detailed, complete argument from this restriction?

As with expository pre-writing, brainstorming to find supporting points can also indicate whether your topic is too broad or narrow for a short paper.

PROPOSITION ARGUMENTS

As we stated earlier, one type of argument paper involves a thesis sentence in the form of a proposition: a conclusion reached about a controversial subject, a suggestion or recommendation for reform or action, a strong personal stand on an issue. But remember, a proposition reflects the biased convictions of the writer and unlike a factual statement may or may not be true or verifiable. A statement such as "The earth revolves around the sun" is factual; scientific evidence may be used to verify it. But a statement such as "The United States should not become involved in the internal affairs of other countries" is a personal conviction; the writer can only give reasons—can only present arguments that will logically lead readers to the writer's conclusion, which may or may not be true.

The "Therefore" Relationship

Writers of argument, therefore, are less concerned with fact than with showing how the proposition thesis logically follows from a set of conditions and relationships. Ideally, in argument, of course, you persuade your reader to accept your conclusion by bringing into play factual evidence, a genuine belief in your proposition, and the ability to argue convincingly. To best accomplish the latter, your thesis should have a *"therefore"* relationship to your main points or premises. For instance, suppose you plan to write a paper on the issue of student aid. Your proposition might be this:

The system for granting student aid should be reformed.

One supporting argument might be:

The present student-aid policies discourage student initiative.

As you can see, the proposition follows logically from the premise:

The present policies discourage student initiative; *therefore,* the system should be reformed.

Because this organizational tactic may involve special reasoning skills, we will discuss them in detail in Chapter 18. But for the purposes of organizing your persuasive paper, the attempt to establish a "therefore" relationship between each main point and the thesis should be your first step in creating reasoned argument.

Like the thesis statement in exposition, the proposition in a persuasive paper serves as a focusing device. While it can offer a solution to a problem or make a recommendation, it also acts as a logical conclusion derived from the presented evidence or supporting material. Let's see how this can work in organizing a paper on pass-fail courses.

In the preceding pre-writing step, you have narrowed the subject, and you intend to convince the Faculty Senate that freshman courses offered on a pass-fail basis could help eliminate the stigma of the low grades often earned by freshmen with high academic potential. The proposition is stated as simply and directly as possible in the form of a strong recommendation that can double as a logical conclusion:

Freshman courses should be offered on a pass-fail basis.

Now let's randomly list possible supporting points or evidence—factors that could result in poor grades in the freshman year:

1. The shock of a freshman transition from home to college life
2. Change from high-school courses to college courses
3. Lack of motivation

THE FORMS OF PERSUASIVE WRITING

4. Indecision about career plans
5. Psychological pressure of grades
6. Lack of self-discipline

You now have the beginning of a topic outline. You might combine 1, 2, and possibly 6; you also note that 3 and 4 seem related and could be generalized as one main point. The result is a topic outline:

Proposition: Freshman courses should be offered on a pass-fail basis.
  I. The difficulty of adjusting to college.
 II. Lack of career motivation.
III. Psychological pressure of grades.

This outline provides the general points, but what of their logical relationship to the proposition—and to one another, for that matter? In a topic outline no relationship is indicated, but if the points are made into statements that serve as premises in an argument, each can have a "therefore" relationship to the thesis. Here is one possibility:

  I. The letter-grade system unnecessarily penalizes those freshmen having difficulty adjusting to college. (*Therefore*) Freshman courses should be offered on a pass-fail basis.
 II. The letter-grade system unnecessarily penalizes those freshmen with unformulated career plans. (*Therefore*) Freshman courses should be offered on a pass-fail basis.
III. The letter-grade system unnecessarily penalizes those freshmen suffering from the psychological pressure of grades. (*Therefore*) Freshman courses should be offered on a pass-fail basis.

As you can see, the thesis statement follows logically from each point; each passes the "therefore" test. Each of the three main points in complete sentence form serves as a possible reason why it would be advantageous to offer freshman courses on a pass-fail basis. So much for the logical concerns for our paper on pass-fail grades. Let's look now at the organizational problems you must solve in writing any persuasive paper.

Organizational Scheme for Proposition Argument

A persuasive paper, like an expository one, is divided into three main parts: an introduction, a body, and a conclusion. But unlike exposition, effective arguments usually answer any possible counterarguments to the points made in the paper. This refuting of conflicting viewpoints can be handled at any stage in the paper. They might be included as part of the background material in the introduction, or they might be more effectively used in the discussion of your main points. Occasionally, writers save them until the conclusion, especially if the refutation of them is especially relevant to the writer's plea for action. Here is an organizational model that accounts for all these rhetorical concerns:

INTRODUCTION

Orientation: Introduction to your restricted subject. Why is it important to your readers?

    Thesis: Statement of proposition
             Counterarguments (optional)

BODY

   I. First supporting argument
     A. Evidence or supporting material
     B. Evidence or supporting material
     C. Counterarguments for Point I (optional)
  II. Second supporting argument
     A. Evidence or supporting material
     B. Evidence or supporting material
     C. Counterarguments for Point II (optional)
 III. Third supporting argument
     A. Evidence or supporting material
     B. Evidence or supporting material
     C. Counterarguments for Point III (optional)

CONCLUSION

Restatement of the proposition
Appeal for action
Counterarguments (optional)

You realize, of course, that not every persuasive paper will exactly follow this model. Some subjects may be so familiar to the readers that only a brief introduction to the subject is needed; others will require extensive background or history for orientation. Some subjects may require only two main points; others more than three. Some may benefit from a long, extended summary; others need only a brief, dynamic statement at the end. Nor must you always deal with dissenting views. Noncontroversial subjects require less attention to your readers' opinions than will hotly debated issues. Also, you need not always state the proposition in the introduction. To achieve a climactic effect, you may save it until the conclusion. As you can see, this model is not intended as a restriction on your writing, but as a guide for structure. Let's look now at a short argumentative paper written by a college adviser, based on the proposition that students should not be advised against majoring in fields with a tight job market. In our comments, we indicate how the paper fits the organizational scheme we provided earlier.

SELF-KNOWLEDGE FOR STUDENTS

Harriet C. Seligsohn

Having been an academic adviser and the administrator of an advising unit for almost eight years, I faced this question [whether to advise students against majoring in fields where job potential is poor] as part of my daily routine. Generally speaking, I would have to answer "no." In practice, however, I have advised students to analyze their reasons for selecting a particular major; to evaluate their own potential for that field; to talk with people already employed in appropriate fields; to consider willingness to relocate; and to obtain some exposure to related working environments either by doing volunteer or paid work or simply by obtaining permission to observe those employed. Very often, the student who has made an uneducated selection decides the major was a poor choice. The initial selection is typically based on reasons such as, "My parents want me to be a ———," with no consideration of the student's own motivations and abilities. Also, the freshman student comes to the university or college with little knowledge of the world of work and has stereotyped impressions of what is involved in common careers. Or the student has no idea what he or she wants to do and, if pressured to select a major, picks something popular among peers.

Once the student has learned how to investigate major fields, the activities and functions involved with careers in those fields, and the job market—and it is critical that the student understand the chances of obtaining a position in a selected field at a given educational level—then motivation should be the determining factor. A student who is willing to work hard and excel in order to compete in a tight job market should not be discouraged if all other indicators point in the direction of that major. A student who does not have the drive to compete should be discouraged from entering a highly competitive field.

However, any student who wishes to compete in a crowded field should be further advised to get

Introduction

Proposition

Body
  I. *Main Point:*
    advise students
    how to make intel-
    ligent choices.

  II. *Main Point:*
    motivation as the
    determining
    factor

  III. *Main Point:*
    second major

282

preparation in a second area either as an alternative or as a complement to the first. It could also be helpful for the individual to develop some specific skills appropriate to lower-level positions as a means of entering the appropriate environment with the prospect of advancement. This could be particularly valuable if there is less competition at levels just below the one at which the student desires employment.

In all cases, students should be encouraged to have a broad general education. I'm not sure if I'm one of a dying breed which believes in the value of general education or if I'm part of a new movement to reinstate the concept as an important part of education. But in regard to the present issue, since it is not possible to predict long-range market trends with any degree of precision, it is my strong belief that the person who "learns to learn" and is well educated in the broad sense will be better situated to take advantage of future opportunities than a person who overspecializes.

Perhaps the most valuable function educators can perform in helping students select a field of study is to assist them to know themselves, to investigate career options, and to match the two. Knowledge of job prospects is only one of many elements that must be considered toward this choice.

IV. *Main Point:* need for a broad general education

Conclusion: appeal to educators.

By paraphrasing the main points in the paper, we can see their logical relationship to the proposition:

I. Students given the ability and information will make wise choices of major.
II. Highly motivated students should not be discouraged from competing in tight market situations.
III. A second major can give students an alternative for the job market.
IV. A broad general education provides students with extensive flexibility.

Therefore: Students should not be advised against majoring in fields where job prospects are poor. (thesis proposition)

Because the writer is addressing educators, she does not go into as much detail about some of the points as she might in writing to students. In that case, she might present a more persuasive case for Point IV.

PROBLEM-SOLUTION ARGUMENTS

As we indicated earlier, problem-solution argument involves the explanation of a current or future problem and the proposal of a solution. Any time you seek to change the way things are or will be, the problem-solution approach can be adopted. The basic outline for this type of persuasive paper is simple:

I. The problem
   A. Explanation
   B. Analysis of causes and effects
   C. Relevance to readers
II. The solution (thesis-proposition)
   A. Explanation
   B. Relation of solution to problem
      1. Effect of solution
      2. Practicality of solution
   C. Superiority of solution over others

Of course, this outline can be modified according to the nature of the problem, the readers, the situation, and the purpose of the writer. For example, if a problem is evident, such as the need for more student parking, then little should be said about it. But if a problem is complex, such as the necessity of making the campus more accessible for wheelchair students, then it must be explained in detail with perhaps criteria stated to show what any proposed solution should accomplish. Also, if numerous solutions are to be considered, they might be presented and discredited before the proposed one is advanced, as we suggested in the model for the proposition argument:

II. The solution (thesis-proposition)
   A. Explanation and weakness of solution 1
   B. Explanation and weakness of solution 2
   C. Explanation and weakness of solution 3
   D. Superiority of proposed solution

In addition, a final step might be added to some persuasive papers to inform readers how to implement the proposed solution. As with the proposition-argument model, you can modify the basic problem-solution outline.

Note how the following newspaper editorial generally follows the proposed outline although it devotes much space to explaining the problem and little to relating its dangers to readers. The reason is obvious: most readers are aware of the community's pollution problems but relatively few understand the effect of unleaded gas on emission controls. Thus the writer has adapted the problem-solution scheme to the nature of the subject and the readers.

USE OF LEADED FUEL IMPERILS EFFORT TO CLEAR WORSENING AIR

Lead in gasoline is one of the dangerous pollutants in the poisonous haze that envelops our urban areas whenever the air is stagnant. But it's an even more serious matter that leaded gasoline quickly destroys the usefulness of the catalytic converters that are today's principal tool for cleaning up auto emissions.

That's why it's alarming that a new study released by the federal Environmental Protection Agency shows that as many as fifteen percent of post-1974 car owners are illegally using cheaper leaded gasoline rather than unleaded gasoline in their cars. After a tankful or two, the late-model car belches pollution just like the older vehicles with no emissions controls.

If nature takes its course, that percentage will rise as the newer cars reach second owners, who usually are more economy-minded than new-car buyers. Some surveys indicate that this trend already is under way. So everybody from the American Petroleum Institute to the Environmental Policy Center agrees that something must be done to assure that owners of 1975 and later models use the fuel for which the cars were designed.

Unfortunately, the petroleum industry likes least the only one of several ideas for discouraging fuel-switching that would work quickly enough to do any good. That plan is a curb on the industry's current practice of making a high-profit item of unleaded fuel and a low-profit sales-builder of leaded fuel.

Unleaded fuel costs only a half-cent to two or three cents more per gallon than leaded to produce and distribute, depending on who's telling the story. But the gap has been rising ever since unleaded fuel went on the market. It's now as high as eight or ten cents a gallon in many locations. A recent survey of Washington-area stations by the

I. The Problem
 A. Explanation of
  the problem

 B. Present and
  future causes and
  effects

285

Center for Auto Safety showed differences of up to fifteen cents.

That's enough to tempt almost anyone to tamper with the easily defeated device automakers have installed to prevent leaded fuel from being used in cars with catalytic converters. And the size of the price spread has no apparent explanation other than marketing convenience. Essentially, buyers of unleaded fuel are subsidizing the leaded-fuel buyers so that dealers can attract business by advertising a rock-bottom price for the latter.

C.   Relevance to readers

If we're serious about clean air, or at least having air no worse than at present, the subsidy, if there must be one, should be reversed. The Department of Energy wants to eliminate gasoline price controls, which is fine, since the controls aren't functioning in any useful way. But there's a strong case for a new form of temporary control that would tie together the prices of leaded and unleaded gas, while letting both move freely up or down.

II.   Proposed solution—thesis

The Center for Auto Safety suggests a one-cent differential in favor of leaded gas. Others have proposed a differential of two or three cents, while some critics suggest the two should be priced equally.

A.   Explanation of proposed solution

Allowing some differential in favor of leaded fuel makes sense, since pricing both gasolines at the same level might discourage investment in new equipment to produce unleaded gas. A small difference would tempt only the more perverse to use the illegal fuel.

B.   Relation of solution to problem
1.   Practicality
2.   Effect

Closing the price gap is only one of four possible solutions to the problem being considered by the Environmental Protection Agency. But the other three have little prospect of getting any results in the near future.

Probably the most hopeless method is the idea of imposing fines on motorists who illegally use unleaded fuel. At present, they're subject to no penalty. Gas station owners already are subject to fines of up to $10,000. About 40 have been fined an average of about $1,000 each. But penalties on motorists would be largely unenforceable, and

C.1.   Another solution: "unenforceable"

would generate resentment against the whole anti-pollution effort.

A requirement that auto makers install tamper-proof necks on gasoline tanks, instead of the present easily removed barriers to the larger leaded-gasoline nozzles, is a good idea and should be adopted. But nothing can be done before the 1980 models appear. That leaves five years' production of cars subject to easy tampering.

2. Another solution: good, but it takes too long to implement

The other plan is to push ahead with a nationwide inspection and maintenance program to make sure that emissions controls stay effective. That needs to be done, beginning in urban areas, whether or not other measures to prevent tampering are taken. But any effective nationwide inspection program is years away.

3. Another solution: implementation is "years away"

By that time, the fuel-switching problem should have solved itself. Unleaded gas already claims about a third of the market, having moved up from zero in 1975. Unless high prices prevent it, unleaded gas will be the dominant fuel in three years or so. Higher-octane unleaded fuel will have replaced today's premium leaded gasolines. That should end whatever fuel-switching is based on performance rather than price.

4. Argues that a short-term solution is necessary

Then, most likely, unleaded gas will be getting the heaviest promotion, and the price problem will take care of itself. That reportedly already is beginning to happen in a few affluent areas where new cars are the rule rather than the exception.

Until then, however, there seems to be little practical alternative to closing at least some of the price gap. That's the course the EPA should pursue.

Conclusion: Restatement of solution

As you can see from the example, the problem-solution approach is simple to follow and effective to use. Its main advantages are threefold: it allows writers (1) to establish rapport with their readers; (2) to relate the subject to their readers; and (3) to delay mention of their ideas until readers are sympathetic to the need for them. Each of these is important.

Readers are certainly persuaded by what you write, but they are also convinced by the image you project in your paper. If they are attracted to you, believe what you say, and have faith in your intelligence and character, they are more apt to trust and accept your solution. The first part of your paper, an analysis of the problem, enables you to establish yourself as such an informed, sensible, sincere person. In addition, it enables you to identify with readers because the problem confronts them as well as you. The fact that you both share some form of misery or dissatisfaction creates a bond, thus generating good will for you. As a result, the analysis of the problem serves both to prepare for the solution and to impress readers with your good sense, will, and character.

The analysis also allows you to involve readers in the subject. Because you must explain how the problem directly or indirectly affects them, readers should become interested and concerned about what you write. On the one hand, this means that you must aim your persuasive message at your readers in terms of their particular age, income, education, social interests, or other characteristics. On the other hand, it means that readers are more apt to become involved because the problem is stated in terms that are meaningful and pertinent to them.

The problem-solution outline requires you to withhold mention of the solution until readers have some opportunity to understand the problem and to become acquainted with you. As a result, few readers will be immediately turned off, as they might be if your paper began with a statement of your thesis. Your readers have to wait, so they are more apt to be receptive to what you propose, especially if you can impress them with your knowledge of the subject and your good judgment. Since your readers are almost committed to hear you out, the problem-solution scheme provides you with a good opportunity to convince them—even those who are apt to react unfavorably.

HANDLING COUNTERARGUMENTS

In classical rhetoric, the argument had a rigid, conventional form: counterargument, or refutation (*refutatio*), was usually dealt with early in the argument before the writer's own views were presented. As we have indicated, modern writers can take care of the opposing views early in the paper; they can deal with them one by one as they present their own views; or they can present them in the closing paragraphs. Each approach has its advantages. The first, making refutation a part of the introduction, is most effective when writing on highly controversial subjects. More commonly, however, writers deal with counterpositions side by side with their own opinions and proofs. This approach is seen in the following paragraphs, taken from the body of a persuasive article, which introduce possible opposing views in a series of questions immediately following the writer's own plea for action on environmental pollution:

We can have anti-pollution auto engines, but they will still have to run on some kind of energy, which will require mining or offshore oil drilling or electric plants. Can we really afford to let individuals have cars at all? Or all the cars they buy?

We can build lower-pollution electric power plants at acceptable cost, very probably, for a while. But even they will cause some pollution and require smokestacks that tower over landscapes and peaceful rivers. U.S. power needs are now doubling every ten years, far faster than the population. Can we really let everyone consume all the electricity he wants—for electric typewriters, electric pencil sharpeners, electric can openers, hair driers, knife sharpeners, shoe polishers? Do we really need endless miles of neon signs, scarring the roadsides and confusing the drivers as well as eating up scarce energy? Do we really need air conditioning on days in the pleasant 70's, just because big buildings are now being erected with sealed windows (to keep out the pollution that this overuse of energy causes)?

—Victor Cohn, "But Who Will Pay the Piper and Will It Be in Time?"

Note that Cohn begins each paragraph with a possible solution to the problem of pollution (first, anti-pollution auto engines; then, lower-pollution power plants) and goes on in each paragraph to present a counterargument to that solution (first, that energy to run anti-pollution auto engines will result in another kind of environmental pollution; then, that smoke pollution and increasing use of electrical appliances will nullify the advantages of lower-pollution power plants). Also note Cohn's use of questions, which flatter his readers by appealing to their rationality and intelligence; with these questions he guides his readers to his way of thinking, rather than forcing it upon them.

The third way to handle refutation is to conclude with it. This approach, less common than the others, is most effective when the audience is uninformed or neutral and there is little danger of alienating them from your position. Occasionally a summary of the counterarguments you presented earlier can add to the effectiveness of your conclusion.

As these examples indicate, you choose the method of dealing with counterarguments according to your material, your purposes, and, most important, the attitude of your audience. But remember that you are likely to be most persuasive when you can show some immediate or future benefit to your reader. Establish a common bond between you and your readers before you attack their views.

SUMMARY

As in expository papers, argument papers consist of an introduction, a body, and a conclusion. The introduction gives background and stimulates the reader's interest in the problem or proposal. But in argument, you must also convince your readers that they can trust you and that they can benefit from your proposition. Without these considerations, your readers are unlikely to be persuaded. The writer of the problem-solution paper on unleaded gasoline appealed first to his readers' self-interest: their health problems arising from air pollution.

The body of the paper, too, must reflect your commitment to your readers. The ordering of your points, the kind of evidence you present, the appeals you make, all should reflect your concern for the needs of your readers. The organization of your paper should enhance your reasoning processes and your persuasive tactics. Supporting evidence can consist of statistics, authority, analogy, facts, case studies, historical or social background, or explanation of causes. These should be so presented that, along with the language you use and the way you order the material, they help you develop your argument as forcefully as possible.

The conclusion should summarize the argument and restate the proposition. In addition, to be most effective, it should make an appeal to the readers for whatever action may be appropriate. This appeal can be emotional, capitalizing on the sympathy or indignation that you have stirred in readers. Or you may appeal to the decency and fairness of your audience. In some instances, you can present them with a choice: either this must be done, or this will be the consequence. Another effective concluding device is to point out some benefit to your readers—how your proposition can affect them.

We have presented organizational models for two kinds of persuasive papers. But we remind you again that these outlines are only tools, not straitjackets.

Assignments

For Discussion

1   The following are thesis statements—expanded and rephrased propositions—from argument papers. State each one as a proposition. What advantages does the writer of each gain from the original, expanded version?

   a We are precipitated into a war which, I think, cannot be justified, and a war which promises not a benefit, that I can discover, to this country or the world.

   —William Ellery Channing

   b A great many folks admit that many of the people in jail ought to be there, and many who are outside ought to be in. I think none of them ought to be there.

   —Clarence Darrow

c   Legislation against manufacture and export of DDT, particularly in the United States, can bring a major international disaster: the return of malaria epidemics—suffering and debilitation from hundreds of millions of cases—deaths from tens of thousands of them.

—James W. Wright

d   It seems to me that our ideals, laws and customs should be based on the proposition that each generation, in turn, becomes the custodian rather than the absolute owner of our resources—and each generation has the obligation to pass this inheritance on to the future.

—Charles Lindbergh

2   It is often necessary in a persuasive paper to provide factual information as support for your argument. Students sometimes find it difficult to design such material so that it is persuasive rather than merely explanatory. Examining the following pairs of examples and determining which is argumentative and which expository will help you with this writing problem. Determine the characteristics of each that influenced your identification.

a   The usual explanation, that the stone giants were moved to their present sites on wooden rollers, is not feasible in this case, either. In addition, the island can scarcely have provided food for more than 2000 inhabitants. (A few hundred natives live on Easter Island today.) A shipping trade, which brought food and clothing to the island for the stonemasons, is hardly credible in antiquity.

—Erich Von Daniken, *Chariots of the Gods?*

One explanation for the Easter Island statues is that large numbers of people rolled the huge stones to their present sites. But it is believed that the island itself could not have supported so many people, nor could merchants from another place have brought food and supplies to the stonemasons on the island.

b   The act provided that after every Indian had been allotted land, the remainder would be put up for sale to the public. But the loopholes with which the act was punctured made it an efficient instrument for separating the Indians from this land. The plunder was carried on with remarkable order. The first lands to go to whites were the richest—bottomlands in river valleys or fertile grasslands. Next went the slightly less desirable lands, such as those that had to be cleared away before they could produce a crop. Then the marginal lands were taken, and so on, until the Indian had left to him only desert that no white considered worth the trouble to take. Between the passage of the Allotment Act in 1887 and a New Deal investigation in 1934, the Indians had been reduced to only 56,000,000

291

acres out of the meager 138,000,000 acres that had been allotted them—and every single acre of the 56,000,000 was adjudged by soil conservationists to be eroded. At the same time that the Indians were being systematically relieved of their lands, their birth rate rose higher than the mortality rate, and so there were more and more Indians on less and less land.

—Peter Farb, "The American Indian: A Portrait in Limbo,"
Man's Rise to Civilization

The act provided that after every Indian had been allotted land, the remainder would be put up for sale to the public. But the many provisions in the act permitted the separating of the Indians from the land. The first lands to go were the richest—bottomlands in river valleys or fertile grasslands. Next went the slightly less desirable lands, and then the marginal lands. Finally, the Indian was left with desert land that no one else wanted. Between the passage of the Allotment Act in 1887 and a New Deal investigation in 1934, the Indians retained only 56,000,000 eroded acres out of the 138,000,000 acres that had been allotted to them. During this same period, the birth rate rose higher than the mortality rate, so there were more Indians on less land.

c All men are capable of procreation. Besides the power to think and will, man has the ability to create new life. These generative powers are possessed by all normal men and women for the purpose of perpetuating the human race. It is axiomatic that those who bring such life into existence should assume responsibility for it. And since this obligation is not a light one, mankind must be encouraged to assume it and be rewarded for doing so.

—John S. Banahan, "What a Catholic Wishes to Avoid in Marriage"

Besides the ability to think and will, all normal people have the ability to procreate. However, human reproduction involves heavy responsibility.

For Practice

1 Outline the following short arguments. What is the implicit proposition for each? The main arguments? Is the appeal emotional, logical, or a combination of the two? How is refutation handled? How effective is the conclusion? What kinds of proofs does the writer rely on?

a Autos are the number one cause of air pollution, as well as energy wastage. They kill 50,000 to 60,000 people a year—needlessly, from unsafe design. Highways and parking lots drain available agricultural and industrial land. The exercise of which they deprive us (walking, bicycling) is a major contributor to death from heart disease. The 7.6 million we throw away each year, like beer cans, clog our landscapes and city dumps. The steel, rubber, glass, plastic and energy used in building eight to ten million new ones each year squanders scarce resources.

Urban design, inadequate public transportation and physical health make automobile transportation a necessity for many Americans. We can't forbid their sale. But how about a ban on advertising cars? Isn't it incongruous for a nation claiming concern over energy to spend millions of dollars (especially on television licensed to serve "the public interest") encouraging the consumption of more and more thirteen-mile-per-gallon autos?

Half of all auto use is for distances under five miles. Bicycle sales (fifteen million a year) have already soared ahead of the sluggish auto market. Once the auto ads are banned, how about building on this citizen sensibility with a media campaign (à la World War II bond sales) to encourage further walking and bicycling—thereby saving our air and our health as well as our oil? (Reports and public-service spots on cars' gas mileage would be useful, too.) It worked (while we tried it) with anti-smoking spots on TV. . . .

—Nicholas Johnson, "Ban Auto Ads"

b Ten years ago this month the U.S. surgeon general brought forth his Report on Smoking and Health. The report climaxed ten years of controversy over the relationship between cigarettes and lung cancer, and it precipitated a second decade of controversy on the same issue. The story merits a backward look.

In truth, the controversy over smoking and health probably dates from the time that Columbus first saw the Indians puffing their tabacas. Efforts to ban smoking can be traced to the edicts of James I against the "sot weed." From time immemorial, little boys have been warned against coffin nails. The cigarette has had many lovers, but very few friends.

Even so, it wasn't until the mid-'50s that statistical evidence began to accumulate on the cigarette-cancer relationship. By the time Dr. Luther L. Terry's study commission went to work, some 10,000 professional papers were available. From these papers—the commission did no independent research of its own—came the conclusion that heavy smokers are more likely to die of lung cancer than nonsmokers. Six additional reports have followed the first report of 1964, each of them identifying new perils and raising new warnings.

These cries of alarm have wrought considerable changes within the cigarette industry and within the advertising industry also. Back in 1963, the ten leading brands, headed by Pall Mall, included such non-filter labels as Lucky Strike and Chesterfield. Now Pall Mall has slipped to third, behind Winston and Marlboros; sales of Camels have dropped in half; Luckies and Chesterfields have disappeared from the top ten, and some new brands, relatively low in tar and nicotine, have taken their place. Cigarette advertising has vanished from radio and television; smokers are exhorted in public service announcements to "kick the habit" instead.

The anti-smoking campaign also has led to the ignored and familiar statement on every package and in every magazine ad: "Warning: The Surgeon General Has Determined That Cigarette Smoking Is Dangerous to Your Health." The decade has seen airlines divide their passenger compartment into sections for smokers and nonsmokers. The man or woman who lights up in public has become acutely self-conscious of the offense that may be inflicted on others.

Yet these years of intensive effort have had little effect on the smoking habit. Per capita consumption in 1963 amounted to 217 packs; last week it was 205 packs. Over the decade, cigarette sales have increased from 524 billion to 583 billion. Ironically, sales of cigars and pipe tobacco, thought to be less harmful, have significantly decreased in this period.

Why has the typical smoker been so indifferent to the warning and appeals? One answer may lie in the unconvincing nature of the evidence. After ten years, scientists have yet to identify what substance in the cigarette, if any, causes cancer. They have yet to demonstrate how smoke or tar or nicotine converts a normal cell to a malignant cell. The one major effort to prove that cigarettes cause cancer in dogs produced a publicity splash four years ago, but the experiment has run into professional criticism and has not been replicated.

The palpable fact remains that most smokers die from causes apparently unrelated to smoking. There may be lessons in all this, in terms of the power of government to control the personal habits of the people. Such a lesson should have been learned in the long, dark night of Prohibition. The nation even now is receiving instruction in such areas of the law as marijuana, homosexuality, and pornography: criminal sanctions may have some suppressive effect, but on the whole, not much. So, too, with tobacco: Men have smoked it for 500 years, and whole platoons of Surgeons General are not likely to dissuade them now.
—James J. Kilpatrick, "Government Meddling Can Be Hazardous to Freedoms"

c A letter in Time magazine a few weeks ago, from a reader who opposes gun laws, was typical of the kind of illogical thinking that supports such arguments. The letter said:

"A gun has no will of its own. A gun does only what its owner causes it to do. The root of the problem is within the human heart. Cure the cause rather than treat surface symptoms."

Let me transpose this argument to a similar term to demonstrate how absurd it is:

"An automobile has no will of its own. An automobile does only what its driver causes it to do. The root of the problem is within the human heart. Cure the cause rather than treat surface symptoms."

Therefore, dispense with automobile laws. No more speed limits, no more traffic signals, no more registration of cars, no more tests for drivers, no more fines or jail terms for offenses.

Instead, we try to reform and change human nature. We work at making most people kind and considerate and attentive and rational and model citizens.

Meanwhile, what is happening on the streets and highways? Slaughter, that's what's happening. While we're slowly "curing the human heart," we're speedily killing thousands of human bodies.

Why bother to make cars safer, either? Since it's obviously the motorist, and not the car, that causes accidents, let's also dispense with stronger bumpers, roll-over bars, seat-belts, impact-bags, or anything else designed to protect in a crash. When people's hearts are warmer, the highway homicide rate will go down to practically nothing.

All we have to do is improve the human race—it may take a few thousand years—and the auto will be no more of a threat, or fatal weapon, than the tricycle.

This is what the gun people imagine is rational thinking. Another of their themes is "infringement of liberty." But what would they think of a drunk driving a car down the road, without a license, without plates, without the slightest responsibility or obligation to others?

The automobile, at least, serves a useful purpose when its ownership and operation are carefully supervised. The handgun serves no purpose except the taking of human life.

True; guns don't kill—but people with guns do. And far too often.
—Sydney J. Harris, "Illogical Thinking in Gun Law Debate"

2 Rewrite the parts of the following topic outlines, first as an organizational scheme for a proposition argument, then as a problem-solution argument. State the thesis idea and the main points as complete sentences so that the latter reflect a "therefore" relationship to the thesis.

a Legalized gambling
   I. Alternative to income tax
   II. People always gamble
   III. Possibilities for revenue for charitable organizations

b Banning of automobiles in national parks
   I. Pollution damage
   II. Overcrowding
   III. Preservation of wild life

c School busing
   I. Concept of neighborhood schools
   II. Integrated housing
   III. Fuel crisis
   IV. Educational advantages

3 Determine which groups in your audience would be most likely to be hostile to your views about the subjects in exercise 2. What refuting arguments might you have to deal with?

For Writing

1 From the following lists of topics, determine which would be best suited for a proposition argument and which for a problem and solution. Choose one of each, decide on the audience you plan to write to, restrict the subject, and construct two outlines for persuasive papers: one for proposition-argument form, the other for problem-solution form.

a Inequities of student-aid programs
b Poverty in the United States
c The role of the media in government
d The effect of television on children
e Social change
·f Enforced busing
g Marijuana legalization
h Drug education for young people
i Conformity and American education
j Competition for grades
k Coed housing on campus
l Academic records—private or public information?
m Women and the ERA
n Gun control
o Birth control for teenagers
p Cults
q The energy crisis and possible solutions
r Striking—a tool for teachers?

2 Write a 1000–1500-word argument based on one of your outlines.

Logical Reasoning and Persuasion

Effective persuasion requires a well-organized argument, but it also necessitates logical reasoning. True, eloquent orators have often played successfully on the emotions of an audience. And true, advertisers and others rely on similar appeals in print. But in most situations you would be wise to consider your readers as being as intelligent as yourself. That means you should mainly depend on logical reasoning, although you certainly may include emotional appeals if the subject and situation warrant them.

The basic study of logic is covered in a college course that deals with far more than we can touch on in this chapter. But we can consider some of the fundamental principles of logical reasoning and we can help you construct persuasive arguments that are sound and valid.

PROBABILITY AND CERTAINTY

Arguments come in three shapes: inductive, deductive, and a combination of the two. Induction and deduction differ in that they arrive at conclusions from opposite starting points in the thinking process. *In*ductive reasoning begins with an observation or an example—an *in*dividual *in*stance; *de*ductive reasoning proceeds from an already *de*termined generalization. To illustrate:

Induction

Individual instance	This supermarket-brand item is cheaper than its comparable name-brand item.
↓	Each of these other seventeen supermarket-brand items is cheaper than its comparable name-brand item.
Conclusion	Supermarket-brand items are cheaper than comparable name-brand items.

Deduction

Determined   People who live in huge homes, have servants, and
generalization   drive expensive cars are wealthy.

                The Johnsons live in a huge house, have servants, and
                drive an expensive car.

Conclusion   The Johnsons are wealthy.

Which reasoning method is better? The answer depends on several factors, but in one sense inductive argument is weaker. Induction can lead you to a conclusion that is *probable* but may not be *certain*. For example, in the illustration cited, unless you compare every supermarket-brand item with every name-brand equivalent, you cannot know that all of the former are cheaper. Therefore, even though inductive arguments are certainly effective and carry great persuasive force, their conclusions should be stated cautiously and should reflect the evidence examined. For instance, it would be more accurate to state the previous inductive conclusion in this form: *Usually,* the supermarket-brand items in this store are cheaper than comparable name-brand items.

Deductive reasoning, on the other hand, can result in more persuasive argument, leading to conclusions that are not only *certain,* but valid and true. However, these valid and true conclusions must be based on self-evident or accepted generalizations, and the argument itself must be constructed properly, as we shall discuss later. At this point, we want only to explain how inductive and deductive reasoning differ by starting either from individual instances or from determined generalizations, and how they also differ by arriving at conclusions that are probable, as in induction, or certain, as in deduction.

Now let's look at each of these reasoning processes in greater detail, noting the forms and characteristics of each.

THE METHODS OF INDUCTIVE REASONING

Whether you realize it or not, you practice inductive reasoning every day of your life! For example, if after comparing prices, you conclude that your bookstore charges more than your friend's, you are reasoning inductively. Or if you decide to eat at a particular restaurant because your friend, a connoisseur of good food, has recommended it, you are reasoning inductively. Or if you selected a new book because you liked an earlier work by the same author, you are reasoning inductively. Or if you surmise that your unhealthy plant is doing poorly because it is the only one not getting light, you are reasoning inductively. All these examples involve the process of generalization in which the following problems might arise: in providing evidence, using of authority and analogy, and showing causal relations.

The Use of Evidence

In the previous example about textbook prices, you concluded as a result of the comparative evidence that your bookstore was more expensive than your friend's. You use similar generalizations in numerous arguments. But, as we said earlier, you should be cautious about these generalizations, basing conclusions on sufficient evidence, and providing your readers with a large enough "sampling" of individual instances so that they can accept the probability of your conclusions.

Faulty argument resulting from insufficient evidence or sampling is so common that this fallacy is known as a *hasty generalization,* the conclusion having been arrived at so quickly that not enough evidence was considered. But what constitutes sufficient evidence? How many swallows make a summer? Must you sample every apple in a bushel of green apples before concluding that they are sour? There is no simple answer to the question of how much evidence is sufficient because much depends on your subject and readers. However, you should investigate a reasonable number of instances. In comparing bookstores, you should compare at least a dozen textbooks from a variety of courses before you can convincingly persuade others that your store's prices are higher. Even then, remember to qualify your conclusion, because inductive reasoning leads to the probable, not the certain. Unless you examine every book in the stores, you cannot know for certain that the prices at one bookstore are higher than another. Nor can you predict that your conclusion will be true tomorrow or next week. We repeat that you should be cautious; say something like: *In general,* the prices in the Collegiate Bookstore are higher than those in the College Bookstore.

Stereotyping is one of the unfortunate results of generalizing about people. Many of our prejudices about minorities arise from observing an insufficient sample of people in the group—a single individual or a small number—and then leaping to a conclusion about all its members. Blacks, women, Jews, Poles, Indians, and others have been victimized for generations by such reasoning. These prejudices are difficult to dispel because some individuals may seem to fit the stereotype. The fallacious reasoning, therefore, may result not only from insufficient evidence but from emotional attitudes about the people involved.

For example, suppose you observed in high school that girls did not do well in math. And because your mother and aunts always have difficulty with figures, you conclude that women are poor in math. But while there is some evidence to support your view, you need to question your conclusion. Is there something inherent in women's nature that results in their being poor in math, or is it a matter of their being conditioned at home, at school, and in society to believe that math is for men? In view of the many women students, encouraged by the women's movement, who are now excelling in math, we realize that cultural conditioning is the culprit.

Thus we should be particularly careful in generalizing about human beings, remembering that each person is a unique individual, influenced by many factors—but not solely determined by any one of them. We should subject these and all generalizations to the most intense scrutiny, requiring that they be based on a sufficient number of cases, be examined with understanding and knowledge, and be stated with the necessary qualification.

Authority

An inductive argument may also be based on evidence provided by an *authority,* a reliable person or source that is well informed about the subject and completely impartial about it. The problem here is that we are prone to use statements by well-known individuals who may be authorities in their own subject but not the one at hand, or who have some self-interest that causes them to be biased. In our previous example about your selecting a restaurant on the authority of a gourmet friend, you might have been misdirected if your friend's parents owned it. For similar reasons, you should be wary about relying on assertions against cutbacks in defense spending by Pentagon officials, against strip-mining restrictions by coal companies, against cable television by television stations, and against national health insurance by doctors. These people and organizations find it difficult to be impartial about such issues because their profits, salaries, lives, and futures are involved in decisions about them. Because the truth may be obscured by self-interest in any situation, relying on information from a particular source can be dangerous unless you know something about the source's relationship to the subject.

You should also be careful about using authorities outside their field of expertise. This frequently occurs when well-known figures in one field issue statements about others. For example, athletes frequently provide testimonials in advertisements for products. But there is no reason why a professional quarterback should be a greater authority on razor blades than other men or why a tennis star should know more about deodorants than other women. Of course, if she endorses tennis racquets, balls, or shoes, that's another story. But even then, we should remember that she's being paid for her testimonial and therefore cannot be impartial. Of course, athletes are not the only culprits. Film stars speak out on politics, economists about education, doctors about crime, lawyers about traffic problems, clergymen about economics, and college professors about everything. All these people are entitled to an opinion, but we should question their authority in one field when their reputation has been made in another.

The purpose of this discussion about authorities is not to steer you away from using them in your persuasive arguments. We want to stress only that you should be careful, checking to determine whether your authority passes the tests of being well informed and completely impartial. If so, then the use of authority can add great persuasive power to your arguments.

Analogy

Another form that inductive reasoning can take is *analogy,* a comparison between two entities that are alike in some respects and that therefore are inferred to be alike in another. Earlier, for instance, we mentioned your selecting a new book because it was written by the author of a book you had liked. In this case, you can safely assume that the second book will have much in common with the first. Thus, analogies, to be sound and effective, must compare things more alike than different: a federal hospitalization plan may be logically compared with individual hospitalization insurance, but not with welfare programs.

As you can see, analogies can be unsound; they can also mislead by oversimplifying a complex situation. For example, it has been argued that because the United States placed a man on the moon, we should be able to eliminate poverty. Or, because the President is like the captain of a ship, he alone should determine the direction of foreign policy. Or, because you can't teach an old dog new tricks, senior citizens should not be allowed to attend college. Like all inductive reasoning, analogies should be checked and stated carefully. In the preceding examples, the analogies are faulty because senior citizens are not like dogs, the United States is not like a ship, and the social, economic, and political problem of eliminating poverty is not like the scientific problem of landing a man on the moon.

Often analogies are not logically sound because what is true of something at some time in some place may not be necessarily true of something similar at another time and in another place. Yet even faulty analogies can be quite convincing, as this letter to *Newsweek* by James C. Simmons illustrates:

Death, taxes, and the prohibitionists are always with us. The last naively believed they could cure a host of social vices by outlawing liquor, gambling, prostitution, drugs, and pornography. They were wrong, of course. And if gun control goes on the books, the result will be the same: people who want guns for illegal purposes will have no difficulty getting them—they will simply pay more on the black market.

The suggestion here that gun control must fail because controls of liquor, gambling, prostitution, drugs, and pornography have failed is a clever use of analogy but is logically unacceptable. The analogy is an oversimplification: prohibitionists are not necessarily "wrong"; the laws have not been properly enforced. The analogy, like many others, is effective only because it oversimplifies the situation.

Analogy can add interest and color to your persuasive papers, and can effectively illustrate your arguments. But don't depend on it for your sole, logical proof and don't insult your readers' intelligence by making unsound comparisons.

Causal Generalization

Inductive reasoning is also used to establish causal relationships. In a previous example, we mentioned that all the house plants were healthy except one, because it received no light. Here is how we might have arrived at the conclusion that light is necessary.

Observation 1: This sick plant receives no sunlight but otherwise is treated like all the other plants.

Observation 2: These healthy plants receive sunlight.

Conclusion: This plant is sick because it receives no sunlight.

Like other forms of inductive reasoning, causal generalization is fraught with dangers. In our example, the causal connection was simple and direct. In other instances, the relationship may appear to be causal but may only be temporal, coincidental, or correlative; or it may indeed be causal but the cause may not be the only one or not a direct one.

Most common of all the dangers inherent in causal generalization is the relationship that appears to be causal but is actually *temporal.* Popular superstitions best illustrate this point. A student who fails an exam on Friday the 13th blames the failure on the date. Another who walks under a ladder on the way to class and later stumbles on the stairs, bruising a knee, blames the injury on the ladder. Millions of people consult their horoscope every day, believing that a causal relationship exists between their birthdate and their daily fortunes. Such examples may seem silly, but many people swear by these and other superstitions. Unfortunately, they remember only the instances when there was a *coincidental* relationship. How often, for example, has the horoscope been wrong, Friday the 13th passed without incident, or no accident resulted from walking under a ladder?

Superstitions are examples of one kind of faulty causal relationship. If one occurrence follows another closely, the first is interpreted as the cause of the second—a type of faulty, or fallacious, reasoning so common that it bears a special name, *post hoc* (abbreviated from the Latin *post hoc, ergo propter hoc,* meaning "after this, therefore because of this"). *Post hoc* reasoning is exemplified not only in superstitions but in other situations, even medicine. For centuries, ill persons were subjected to the practice of bleeding. Because many of them responded well to this treatment, bleeding was believed to have caused their recovery. This *post hoc* reasoning and "the cure" were finally abandoned when the medical profession realized that patients recovered from diseases because of their bodies' natural recuperative powers or because the disease had run its course, not because of the bleeding. But even today many people credit various patent medicines or folk remedies with curing common colds when they would probably recover in the same time without any treatment except resting and drinking extra liquids.

One way to test causal relationships is to determine whether they are regular—that is, whether a particular cause always produces the effect. Here are three questions to ask:

1. Does the cause always produce the effect?
2. Without the cause, is the effect different?
3. When the cause varies, does the effect change?

Now to apply these as a test for causal relationships. Let's say that for several Christmas holidays you've given your friends loaves of fruit bread made from your mother's old recipe with yeast, cinnamon, eggs, flour, raisins, citron, maraschino cherries, and other goodies. This year you decide to experiment: you omit the yeast entirely from one loaf, add only one package to another, and use the regular two packages in a third. After you've given the dough time to rise, you note that the one with the right amount of yeast has doubled in bulk, the one with half the amount has increased somewhat, and the one without yeast has not risen at all. Under these circumstances, assuming that each loaf otherwise contained the same ingredients and was treated the same, you could conclude inductively that the yeast caused the fruit bread to rise.

But, alas, some conclusions, particularly those involving people, are not this simple and do not readily lend themselves to this test. Let's take a look at some examples.

As you know, there is a link between cigarette smoking and lung cancer. A recent HEW study finds that a high proportion of both men and women who smoke heavily die of this disease, a lesser proportion who smoke moderately contract the disease, and relatively few nonsmokers are afflicted. Statistics indicate, therefore, that the cause (heavy smoking) often produces the effect (cancer), that without the cause the effect is different (those who do not smoke seldom get lung cancer), and that when the cause varies (light smoking) the effect changes (few cancer deaths). In this and similar situations, scientists and other careful observers call the relationship a *correlation* rather than a cause because a direct causal connection has not been proven. There is a possibility, for example, that some third factor —physiological or psychological—may be responsible both for the desire to smoke and for lung cancer.

Mention of this third factor suggests another problem in dealing with causal relationships: a cause may not be the only one or the direct one or even a possible one. Recent figures about rape in our country reveal that this crime has been increasing greatly. But some authorities wonder whether the increased number of rapes is due to more rapes being committed or more rapes being reported. Formerly, authorities estimated that only one rape out of ten was reported to the police. Recently, as a result of the consciousness-raising efforts of the women's liberation movement and more sensitivity by the police in dealing with rape victims, more victims may be reporting the crime and the incidence of rape may not have increased significantly.

Finally, our tendency to oversimplify sometimes results in a failure to perceive that a cause may not be the only one or the direct one. Too often we rush in with simple answers to complex problems. We might talk of a friend's dropping out of school because of low grades, a person's divorce because of financial problems, or our country's economic difficulties because of increased oil prices. These may all be examples of oversimplification. The friend's dropping out of school could stem from financial problems; the divorce may have resulted from sexual tensions; and the inflation may have been caused by numerous other factors, particularly government spending during the Vietnam War. Or, in one of these examples, the apparent cause may have been only an indirect one. Low grades may have been a cause for your friend's leaving school, but the direct cause may have been his lack of money, which required that he work forty hours a week, leaving him too tired to study or attend classes regularly. In this situation, your friend's financial problem is the direct cause, his poor academic record the indirect cause.

The tactics of inductive reasoning are often necessary in effective persuasive writing. Therefore, be cautious and critical when reasoning inductively and when analyzing the inductive arguments of others. Your arguments will be more sound if you avoid the perils of hasty generalizations, the dangers of incompetent or biased sources, and the pitfalls of analogy. Avoid too the hazards of causal generalizations: the temptation of *post hoc* reasoning; the confusion of a correlation with a cause; or the failure to identify the nature of the cause—whether it is the only one involved, or the one directly responsible, or merely an indirect one.

THE METHODS OF DEDUCTIVE REASONING

Although induction and deduction may be combined in complex arguments, each is a distinct process. In inductive reasoning, we rely on specific evidence discovered or believed to be true. For example, we relied on studies of tobacco smoking to come to the generalization that heavy smokers frequently develop lung cancer. But as we pointed out, this generalization, like all inductive conclusions, is only probable. In deductive reasoning, on the other hand, if a conclusion is based on generalizations or premises considered true, then it too can be considered true.

To be most effective, deductive reasoning must not only start from true premises and lead to true conclusions, but the reasoning process must be *valid.* Validity requires that the pattern of reasoning used in deduction must satisfy certain logical criteria. The concept of validity is so crucial to effective deductive argument that we will discuss it in detail.

But first, we assume you have a common-sense knowledge of truth and you understand that true premises are necessary in deductive argument. These points are important because it is possible to construct a valid argument based on false premises. Here's how:

All student who turn in typed papers automatically receive an A.
All the students in Professor Brown's class turned in typed papers.
Therefore, all the students in Professor Brown's class automatically receive an A.

There's nothing wrong with the reasoning here; the argument *form* meets the criteria for sound reasoning: a conclusion based on premises whose terms are logically related. Therefore, the argument is valid. Yet the conclusion is worthless because it has been derived from a false premise: all typed papers do *not* automatically receive A's. Thus a deductive argument can be valid but false. Keep in mind as you read this discussion that we assume deductive reasoning is based on *true* as well as valid premises.

Now to the concept of validity, a subject considered in such detail by Aristotle and later logicians that a thorough study usually requires at least an entire semester. Consequently, we can only introduce you to the fundamentals, enough to help you in writing effective persuasion.

The Categorical Syllogism

We mentioned earlier that deductive reasoning follows a particular pattern or form that consists of a series of statements: one or two premises, followed by a conclusion. This form is called a *syllogism,* and deductive argument is often referred to as syllogistic reasoning. Although syllogisms can take several shapes, the most common is the *categorical syllogism.* Made up of three statements, the first (the major premise) sets forth the general terms, the second (the minor premise) a more particular term, and the third (the conclusion) makes a statement about the minor-premise term. Our earlier example about typed student papers follows this form. To illustrate that a syllogism's validity depends not on the information conveyed in the statements but on the form itself and the relationships between the statements, syllogisms are often expressed in shorthand. The following example illustrates the three parts of a categorical syllogism with its shorthand counterpart:

	Categorical syllogism	*Shorthand form*
Major premise:	All freshmen are dorm residents.	All A's are B's.
Minor premise:	All the members of the Athletic U. tennis team are freshmen.	All C's are A's.
Conclusion:	Therefore, all the members of the tennis team are dorm residents.	All C's are B's.

Sometimes, to show how a syllogism works and to test its validity, circle diagrams are used. Here's how a syllogism having the form of ours looks in circles:

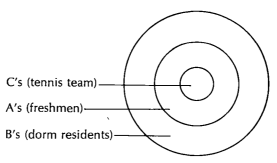

All the C's are included in the A's circle, which in turn is included in the B's circle. Thus, the conclusion is valid.

If you find circles confusing, perhaps this picture version will help:

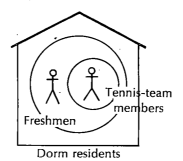

Although such visual devices are often helpful in determining validity, understanding of the reasoning process involved will be more important to you in writing sound arguments, particularly since the process is closely related to the form of the simple sentences that serve as the premises of a syllogism. Earlier, in Chapter 4, we pointed out that such sentences are made up of a subject (participant-agent) and predicate (comment). In deductive logic the subject and predicate make up the *terms* of a syllogistic statement; the logical interactions of the subjects and predicates are involved in the reasoning process. Looking again at our sample syllogism, we can see how it works. Note that the three statements contain only three terms.

	Subject	Predicate
Major premise:	All freshmen (Term 1)	are dorm residents. (Term 2)
Minor premise:	All the members of the tennis team (Term 3)	are freshmen. (Term 1 repeated)
Conclusion:	All the members of the tennis team (Term 3 repeated)	are dorm residents. (Term 2 repeated)

All the terms in a syllogism must deal either with a whole group, or only part of a group. This is important in the reasoning process, because we cannot conclude anything about all of a group from premise terms that deal with only a part of that group. For instance, you would be guilty of unsound reasoning if you concluded that because *most* dogs bark, *all* dogs do. But you would be on safe grounds to assume that if *all* dogs have four legs, then *any* individual dog has four legs.

Determining whether the subject term deals with the whole or only a part of a group is relatively simple: "all freshmen" and "no freshmen" indicate that the whole group is included; "some freshmen," "many freshmen," and "most freshmen" obviously refers to only part. The predicate term, however, is more complex. Perhaps outlining the four basic syllogistic statements can help you understand better:

1. All freshmen / are dorm residents.   All A's are B's.
   (whole group)   (part of the group)

Here, the predicate term "dorm residents" deals only with those stipulated as freshmen; older dorm residents are not included in the argument, but they do exist. The empty space in our "dorm" in the drawing indicates non-freshmen.

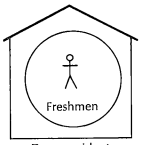
Dorm residents

2. *No* freshmen / are dorm residents.   No A's are B's.
  (whole group)   (whole group)

Because the subject and predicate terms are separated by the negative
no, they are two separate groups—no inclusion and no overlapping.

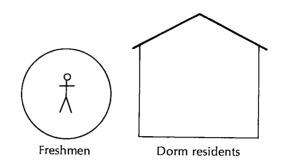

Freshmen   Dorm residents

3. *Some* freshmen / are dorm residents.   Some A's are B's.
(part of the group)   (part of the group)

Obviously, *some* indicates that the subject term is not whole. As in statement 1, the predicate term *dorm residents* includes people other than freshmen; therefore, it does not comprise the whole group.

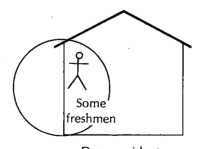

Dorm residents

4. *Some* freshmen / are *not* dorm residents.   Some A's are not B's.
  (part of the group)   (whole group)

As in statement 2, *some* freshmen are outside the dorm, not in with the
other residents, including the remaining freshmen who are dorm dwellers.
The *some* freshmen in the subject are not included in the predicate term.

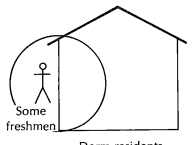

Dorm residents

With this background, let's move to some other valid syllogisms.

Major premise:	No graduate students are dorm residents. (whole) (whole)	No A's are B's.
Minor premise:	Carol Smith is a graduate student. (whole) (whole)	All C's are A's.
Conclusion:	Therefore, Carol Smith is not a dorm resident. (whole) (whole)	All C's are not B's.

Because Carol Smith is one of a kind she comprises a whole group. The syllogism is valid because the conclusion about Carol as a whole group follows logically from the whole group "Carol Smith" in the minor premise. Here's a picture of it:

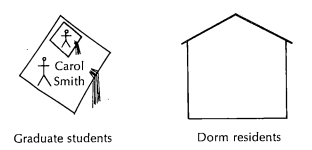

Graduate students   Dorm residents

Let's move on to another syllogism, one using the "some" form of statement 3 above as the minor premise:

Major premise:	No graduate students are dorm residents.	No A's are B's.
	(whole) (whole)	
Minor premise:	Some older students are dorm residents.	Some C's are B's.
	(part) (part)	
Conclusion:	Therefore, some older students are not graduate students	Some C's are not A's.
	(part) (whole)	

This syllogism is valid, again because the conclusion about the part of the group "some older students" follows logically from the part in the major premise. Here's how it looks in a drawing:

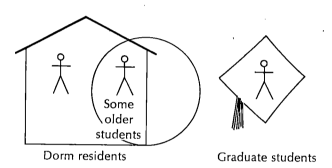

Dorm residents   Graduate students

As we indicated earlier, syllogistic reasoning is invalid if the conclusion attributes qualities to a whole class or group when the premises have assigned these qualities only to a part of the class or group. Some examples will clarify this fallacy:

Major premise:	All property owners favor reduced real estate taxes.
	(whole) (part)
Minor premise:	Janet favors reduced real estate taxes.
	(whole) (part)
Conclusion:	Therefore, Janet is a property owner.
	(whole) (part)

As you can see, the "middle" term—the one that occurs twice in the premises (favor reduced real estate taxes)—never deals with the whole group. Others besides property owners favor reduced real estate taxes; thus, Janet need not be a property owner. For the conclusion to be valid, then, the repeated middle term must include the whole group at least once. You can understand the illogic of this fallacy by laughing at it in this nonsense syllogism:

310

Major premise: All goats have beards.
Minor premise: Santa Claus has a beard.
    Conclusion: Therefore, Santa Claus is a goat.

It's easy to see the faulty reasoning here but often harder to spot it in unethical advertising copy or a political speech, such as the following:

All the misguided liberals in the country applaud the recognition of Red China and the SALT agreement with the Russians. My opponent has supported the President's stand on these issues. If you want a Congressman who will take a "get-tough" attitude, vote for me.

The political opponent here, like Janet and Santa Claus in the previous examples, has been falsely associated with a group when he shares only one characteristic of that group.

A related fallacy occurs in this form of syllogism:

Major premise: All faculty members belong to the Credit Union.
                 (whole)   (part)
Minor premise: All faculty members belong to the Faculty Club.
                 (whole)   (part)
    Conclusion: Therefore, all Credit Union members belong to the Faculty Club.
                            (whole)   (part)

The conclusion here is not valid because nothing in the premises states anything about *all* Credit Union members. Of the three groups mentioned there (*faculty members, Credit Union,* and *Faculty Club*), we know something only about all faculty members. Possibly, members of the business office could belong to the Credit Union but not the Faculty Club, while administrators like assistant deans could belong to the Faculty Club but not to the Credit Union. We cannot know from the premises. Consequently, this form of syllogism, which contains an *all* statement about a class or group (Credit Union members) in the conclusion, cannot be valid unless the whole group appears. This simpler example should help you to spot this fallacy:

Major premise: All rings are luxuries.
Minor premise: All rings are small, circular metal bands.
    Conclusion: Therefore, all luxuries are small, circular metal bands.

The Conditional Syllogism

In a categorical syllogism, validity stems from the logical relationships between the terms in the subject and predicate components of the two premises in the conclusion derived from them, as in:

All cats have the ability to purr.
Mopsie is a cat.
Therefore, Mopsie has the ability to purr.

There are other kinds of deduction involving syllogisms in which certain conditions are set up; if these conditions are met, the conclusion is valid. One of these is sometimes known as an *if/then* syllogism:

If the stadium is finished, *then* the team will open its season there.
The stadium is finished.
Therefore, the team will open its season there.

Another kind of "conditional" syllogism is the *either/or* type:

Either the Common Market succeeds *or* Europe falls.
The Common Market is succeeding.
Therefore, Europe will not fall.

Both these forms are tricky and can be valid only if the conditions and the alternatives as stated in the syllogism are scrupulously met. We need not go into great detail about them here; we mention them only because they occur so often in written argument. Because they are frequently at the core of fallacious reasoning, we will deal with them at greater length in our discussion of other logical fallacies in Chapter 19.

Validity, Truth, and Form

Just as you naturally express your thoughts and ideas in certain sentence patterns, so too you naturally formulate arguments in logical patterns. But in persuasive writing, mere ability to create logical patterns is not enough. As you probably realize by now, logical form—here illustrated by the syllogism—has persuasive power of its own, aside from the information or conclusion that it carries. As we've indicated, even a nonsensical or blatantly false argument appears persuasive if presented in a valid, logical form. You might say that using logical deductive argument without realizing the power inherent in its form is like firing a gun without knowing whether it's loaded or not. In like manner, people can easily be deceived if they do not know that there is a difference between truth and validity. Who knows, for instance, how many people are persuaded by the "truth" of a slogan like "If guns are outlawed, only outlaws will have guns," when they are really responding to the persuasive force of a valid syllogism? The form camouflages other obvious possibilities; after all, policemen also carry guns. Many experienced writers capitalize on the persuasive force of syllogistic reasoning; but responsible writers, in addition, avoid using deductive reasoning for unethical purposes. They are careful to arrive at conclusions that are both valid and true.

In order for a syllogistic argument to be sound, the conclusion must stem from true premises; truth is not dependent on the validity of the syllogism. Nor does validity necessarily result in sound argument. Sound argument must be reasoned validly from true premises to a true conclusion; it requires both truth and validity. To demonstrate, let's look at this syllogistic argument:

All feminists are against motherhood.	All A's are B's.
Joan is a feminist.	All C's are A's.
Therefore, Joan is against motherhood.	All C's are B's.

The reasoning is ironclad; it proceeds validly from premise to premise to conclusion. But because the major premise is false—a gross over-generalization—the conclusion is false. However, because it "sounds logical," the unwary might be convinced that the conclusion is true, just from the force of the logical argument. And it is precisely this characteristic of deductive reasoning that demagogues and unethical advertisers exploit. Making their task simpler is the fact that validity is always easier to establish than truth—even when the audience understands the mechanical processes of deductive reasoning. Perhaps that is because "truth" is so elusive; people hold radically different attitudes about abstract ideas such as religion, love, socialism, and justice. Therefore, in your own writing, you are probably on safer logical grounds to operate from premises that can be supported by factual concrete evidence. The following syllogism demonstrates some of the problems confronted in reasoning from abstract ideas:

All things derived from God are capable of love.	All A's are B's.
Human beings are things derived from God.	All C's are A's.
Therefore, human beings are capable of love.	All C's are B's.

Even though they might recognize such a syllogism as valid, your audience could accept the conclusion as true only if they believed that (1) God exists, (2) all things are derived from God, and (3) all things, including human beings, are capable of love. So you see, when we speak of "truth," we can speak only in relative terms; thus we can surely argue more effectively if we avoid abstract premises whose truth can be questioned.

The aim of this discussion has been to show you that in deductive reasoning, truth and validity are two separate entities, but they are equally important. Unlike love and marriage in the once-popular song, you *can* have one without the other. But you should realize that you can achieve maximum persuasive force only when your arguments are both valid and true. Otherwise, you will be guilty of reasoning that is either untrue or unsound. In either instance, your reasoning will be unacceptable.

SUMMARY

In this chapter, we have been concerned with the formal aspects of logical reasoning. We have briefly compared the two main types of reasoning—inductive and deductive—in terms of the conclusions they lead to. In inductive reasoning, we come to a *probable* conclusion by generalizing from individual instances—from sampling evidence, from citing authority, or from making analogies. In deductive reasoning, by starting from already accepted generalizations or premises, and by using sound syllogistic argument, we are able to arrive at a *certain* conclusion. Of course, certainty depends on whether the premises are true and whether the reasoning process was valid.

Persuasive writing requires these reasoning processes. You must reveal the logical relationships between your evidence or main points and your conclusions or recommendations, so that your readers will accept them. In the next chapter, we will discuss how logic and language interact in persuasive writing.

Assignments

For Discussion

1 In the following examples, determine whether the writers depend on inductive or deductive reasoning. Remember, induction comes to a generalization based on the evidence of individual instances; deduction arrives at a conclusion based on generalizations accepted as true.

a The reputed lush jungles of Central America exist in only a few places, where enough rain falls to support heavy vegetable growth, and even there soils are notoriously poor. Most of Central America is high, rugged and mountainous. In these regions there are only two seasons—wet and dry—and the dry is searing. No rain falls for six months, streams dry up, vegetation withers, and agriculture and vegetable growth in general come to an end. This type of high and seasonably dry mountain country is sadly depleted by erosional processes. It is in this area where ignorance and indifference are causing the plunder of these nations.
—James B. Packer, "Slash and Burn Below the Border"

b The primary function of a university is to discover and disseminate knowledge by means of research and teaching. To fulfill this function a free interchange of ideas is necessary not only within its walls but with the world beyond as well. It follows that the university must do everything possible to ensure within it the fullest degree of intellectual freedom. The history of intellectual growth and discovery clearly demonstrates the need for unfettered freedom, the right to think the unthinkable, discuss the unmentionable, and challenge the unchallenged. To curtail free expression strikes twice at intellectual freedom, for whoever deprives another of the right to state unpopular views necessarily also deprives others of the right to listen to those views.

—Yale Committee, ''Freedom of Expression at Yale''

c Each year over four million Americans take ''aptitude,'' ''achievement'' and ''proficiency'' tests. They include 1.8 million high-school students who take the College Board exam required by most colleges for admission; 500,000 students seeking admission to graduate schools, law schools, and business schools; and people seeking certification or placement in more than 20 different occupations and professions—teachers, architects, auto mechanics, CIA agents, medical technicians and policemen. Their performance on these tests will determine, largely or in significant part, the schools they will attend and the professions they will enter.

—Ralph Nader, ''Reports''

d But if those skills were more than salable, if the study made them better citizens and made them happier to be human beings, they have not been cheated. They will find some kind of job soon enough. It might even turn out that those humanizing and liberating skills are salable. Flexibility, an ability to change and learn new things, is a valuable skill. People who have learned how to learn, can learn outside of school. That's where most of us have learned to do what we do, not in school. Learning to learn is one of the highest liberal skills.

—Robert A. Goodwin, ''Should College Teach Salable Skills?''

Induction

1 Discuss whether the following persuasive paragraphs rely primarily on emotional or logical argument. What audience would they best appeal to?

a In the philosophy of semantics there is a standard rhetorical question: Is it progress if a cannibal eats with a knife and fork? Similarly, if society is sexist is it altered when its language is revised? Or do its attitudes remain when its platitudes change? The prognosis is not good. Words, like currency, need to be reinforced with values. Take away the Federal Reserve and its dollar bill is waste paper. Take away meaning and a word is only noise. Changing chairman to chairperson is mock doctrine and flaccid democracy, altering neither the audience nor, in fact, the office holder. Despite its suffix, chairman is no more sexist than the French designation of boat as masculine, or the English custom of referring to a ship with feminine pronouns. Chairman is a role, not a pejorative. Congressman is an office, not a chauvinist plot. Mankind is a term for all humanity, not some 49% of it. The feminist attack on social crimes may be as legitimate as it was inevitable. But the attack on words is only another social crime—one against the means and the hopes of communication.

—Stefan Kanfer, "Sispeak: A Msguided Attempt to Change Herstory"

b Teachers are overworked and underpaid. True. It is an exhausting business, this damming up the flood of human potentialities. What energy it takes to turn a torrent into a trickle, to train that trickle along narrow, well-marked channels! . . . Do not blame teachers if they fail to educate. The task of *preventing* children from changing in any significant way is precisely what most societies require.

c Thus Women's Lib may achieve a more peaceful society on the way towards its other goals. That is why the Swedish government considers reform to bring about greater equality in the sex roles one of its most important concerns. As Prime Minister Olaf Palme explained in a widely ignored speech delivered in Washington this spring: "It is *human beings* we shall emancipate. In Sweden today, if a politician should declare that the woman ought to have a different role from man's, he would be regarded as something from the Stone Age." In other words, the most radical goal of the movement is egalitarianism.

If Women's Lib wins, perhaps we all do.

—Gloria Steinem, "What It Would Be Like if Women Win"

d The political struggles ahead are for increasing shares of government largesse. The opposed forces are numerous. On one side are powerful lobbies such as the industrial-military complex, the argo-business lobby, and the highway lobby. These have powerful spokesmen. The poor, the unemployed, and the disemployed are opposed—and they are not well organized.

The use of violence as an instrument of persuasion is therefore inviting and seems to the discontented to be the only effective protest.

—William O. Douglas, *Points of Rebellion*

e Such a rally here will serve not only to organize for the national fight, but also to show tangible support for the embattled Black students whose very right to enter certain parts of this city has been challenged. It will say to them that "you are not alone in this national struggle." It will encourage their parents to hold on. It will make all those who would gather in mobs to intimidate our children think twice.

Today only 80 of Boston's schools are involved in desegregation. In September all 200 will be involved. We have already been told by the antidesegregation forces that they will renew their opposition and their resistance this spring, and that their numbers will grow. I believe them.

If school desegregation cannot be brought about in Boston, then it won't happen anywhere else in the North. That's why this fight *must* continue. And that's why we must win.
—Thomas Atkins, Speech before the National Student Conference Against Racism

2 Identify the inductive weaknesses (weak analogy, unreliable information, inductive leap) in the following:

a Many students who dislike and fear courses in mathematics have learned to respect mathematical theory in logic courses. Therefore, students who are not proficient in languages might profit from a general linguistics course.

b Ralph Nader has quoted the president of the Educational Testing Service as saying that "charging the tests with bias against minority and poor students is like criticizing the bathroom scales because some people are fat and others don't get enough to eat."

c After interviewing the women on the third floor of the women's dorm, I concluded that most students drive home for the weekend.

d The Army Corps of Engineers and the law firm representing the investors in a proposed marina issued figures that "proved beyond doubt" that a new dam would be an economic asset to the state.

e Every summer, the academically motivated new freshmen register early. Composition classes offered at prime times—9:00 a.m. to 12 noon—close out first. Therefore, these classes will have a higher grade average than classes offered at unpopular times.

f Jobs for history graduates are almost impossible to find. My brother, who graduated last year, hasn't found a job yet.

g The president of a national fraternity reported that students who live in fraternity houses have a happier college experience than those who reside in dormitories.

3 Examine the causal relationships in the following passages. Identify the effect and the cause or causes. Does the writer consider the cause(s) the direct one, the only cause, or merely a correlation?

a Ironically enough, this sinister and threatening phenomenon [overpopulation] has been caused by the beneficent and praiseworthy activities of medical science and public health in preserving life. It is the result of death control. Mortality has gone down, especially infant mortality, which not so long ago in many countries accounted for the deaths of a third or even a half of all babies born before they had reached the age of one. The expectation of life of a Roman citizen even at the height of the Empire was only 30 years; in tropical countries less than a century ago, it was often only 20. Today it is rising everywhere, and in some Western countries is over 70.

—Sir Julian Huxley, "The Age of Overbreed"

b All the federal legislation in the world won't help this country if its citizens are not aware of their invaluable function to keep our communities safe. Many of you are aware of some strange trends which have developed in this country. There are people willing to overlook crimes which imperil us each and every day. Many shirk their responsibility for the crime rise by "scapegoating" the police and other law enforcement officers.

—Congressman Bill Chappell, "Some Call It Dissent"

c Clearly *Playboy's* astonishing popularity is not attributable solely to pin-up girls. For sheer nudity its pictorial art cannot compete with such would-be competitors as *Dude* and *Escapade*. Rather, *Playboy* appeals to a highly mobile, increasingly affluent group of young readers, mostly between eighteen and thirty, who want much more from their drugstore reading than bosoms and thighs. They need a total image of what it means to be a man. And Mr. Hefner's *Playboy* has no hesitancy about telling them.

—Harvey Cox, "*Playboy's* Doctrine of Male"

d Even Winston Churchill, who is looked upon by older whites as perhaps the greatest hero of the twentieth century—even he, because of the system of which he was a creature and which he served, is an arch-villain in the eyes of the young white rebels.

—Eldridge Cleaver, *Soul on Ice*

e As you can readily hear, if you listen to any jazz performance (whether of the Louis Armstrong, Benny Goodman, or Charlie Parker variety), the rhythmical effect depends upon there being a clearly defined basic rhythmic pattern which enforces the expectations which are to be upset. That basic pattern is the 4/4 or 2/4 beat which underlies all jazz. Hence the importance of the percussive instruments in jazz: the drums, the guitar or banjo, the bull fiddle, the piano. Hence too the insistent thump, thump, thump, thump which is so boring when you only half-hear jazz—either because you are too far away, across the lake or in the next room, or simply because you will not listen attentively. But hence also the delight, the subtle effects, which good jazz provides as the melodic phrases evade, anticipate, and return to, and then again evade the steady basic four-beat pulse which persists, implicitly or explicitly, thoughout the performance.

—John A. Kouwenhoven, "What's American About America?"

Deduction

1 The following statements could serve as major premises in a categorical syllogism. What kind or kinds of inductive reasoning—sampling, analogy, or causal generation—might have contributed to each generalization? Add a possible minor premise and conclusion to each to form a deductive categorical syllogism.

a   All public school teachers are people certified by state education departments.
b   All cold-blooded animals are hibernating creatures.
c   All West Point cadets are eligible for combat duty.
d   Constitutional laws are those laws that ultimately can be approved by the Supreme Court.
e   Home-canned food is a potential health hazard.
f   Disease can be eradicated by educating people about it.
g   Undergraduate men's colleges tend to overemphasize sports.
h   Great literature is a mirror of human relationships.
i   Hippies are nonconformists.
j   A martyr's cause is never lost by an assassin's bullet.

2   Decide whether the following categorical syllogisms are valid. If a syllogism is invalid, explain why.

a   All human societies are doomed to deteriorate.
    America is a human society.
    America is doomed to deteriorate.
b   No philosophers are evil.
    Some Greeks are philosophers.
    Some Greeks are not evil.
c   All students are eligible for student government.
    No teachers are eligible for student government.
    No teachers are students.
d   No Republicans are Democrats.
    Some Republicans are supporters of George Wallace.
    Some supporters of George Wallace are not Democrats.
e   All barbiturates are drugs.
    Marijuana is not a barbiturate.
    Marijuana is not a drug.
f   All rational people are believers in rule by law.
    Some rational people are college professors.
    Some college professors are believers in rule by law.
g   All women are potential mothers.
    Betty is a potential mother.
    Betty is a woman.
h   God is love.
    Love is blind.
    Homer was blind.
    Homer was God.

For Writing

1 Suppose you received the following letter from your brother in high school. Answer the letter, explaining the significance of "truth" and "validity" in reference to his reasoning.

> Dear _____,
>
>   Life at home is really a hassle these days. Mom and Dad treat me like an infant—hassle me every time I go out at night, set time limits and wait up for me. Mom is constantly at me for not eating right. Then I go to school and it's the same scene—the teachers act as if I'm a baby freak. I guess the truth is that all grownups think teenagers are babies. The only valid conclusion I can come to is that Mom and Dad are just like all the other grownups in the world. Teachers too. Sometimes I feel like splitting the whole scene. You are sure lucky to be in college where you get treated like an adult.

The inherent syllogism here is:

Mom and Dad (and teachers) are grownups.
They treat teenagers like babies.
All grownups treat teenagers like babies.

Remember, "truth" and "validity" are difficult concepts—define them carefully.

19

Language and Logic in Persuasive Writing

LANGUAGE AND PERSUASION

Even though some persuasive devices such as logical syllogisms can be reduced to abstract formulas, effective persuasion is best accomplished through effective use of language. You can achieve maximum persuasive force only after you have learned to express your logical reasoning in language that can attract your audience to the problem, can convince them that your viewpoint is valid, and can appeal to their self-interest, their sense of justice, or their pity. This task requires not only a writing commitment, but also an ethical one. Making use of tactics that are persuasive because they appeal to the baser instincts of readers, or somehow deceive them, is dishonest. Unscrupulous politicians who deliberately play upon their constituents' racial or ethnic hostilities to sell themselves as candidates, and advertisers who exploit their readers' desires to be socially or sexually attractive, are using unethical persuasive tactics. Usually these involve calculated and deliberate methods.

But often there is a narrow distinction between honest and dishonest persuasion. You want to shape your ideas and language so that they best present your argument, but if you carry this too far, omitting or obscuring information, then dishonesty can be the result. You do want to appeal to the emotions of your audience—to foster sympathy, respect, or appreciation toward the subject of your argument—but too strong an emotional appeal may obscure the logical reasoning in the paper. Obviously, the best way to make sure that your arguments are presented rationally and ethically is to be aware of the ways that persuasive language can be used and abused. In this chapter we will examine some of these ways.

Shaping Your Ideas to Your Audience

One of the tactics of persuasive writing is that of shaping your language and ideas to most effectively enhance your particular viewpoint about a subject. Used wisely, it can help you to place your ideas clearly before your readers. Unfortunately, however, shaping can also be used unscrupulously, as shown in this speech by a fictitious congressman. Which side is he really on? He slants his views so blatantly and unethically that they are completely lost.

CONGRESSMAN OILEY'S POSITION ON WHISKEY

I had not intended to discuss this controversial subject at this particular time. However, I want you to know that I do not shun a controversy. On the contrary, I will take a stand on any issue at any time regardless of how fraught with controversy it may be.

You have asked me how I feel about whiskey.

Here is how I stand on this question:

If when you say whiskey you mean the devil's brew, the poison scourge, the bloody monster that defiles innocence, dethrones reason, destroys the home, creates misery and poverty, yes, literally takes the bread from the mouths of little children; if you mean the evil drink that topples the Christian man and woman from the pinnacles of righteous, gracious living into the bottomless pit of degradation and despair, shame and helplessness and hopelessness, then certainly I'm against it with all my power.

But if when you say whiskey you mean the oil of conversation, the philosophic wine, the ale that is consumed when good fellows get together, that puts a song in their hearts and laughter on their lips and the warm glow of contentment in their eyes; if you mean Christmas cheer; if you mean the stimulating drink that puts the spring in an old gentleman's step on a frosty morning; if you mean the drink that enables a man to magnify his joy and his happiness and to forget, if only for a little while, life's great tragedies and heartbreaks and sorrows; if you mean that drink whose sale pours into our treasuries untold millions of dollars which are used to provide tender care for little crippled children, our blind, our deaf, our dumb, our pitiful aged and infirm, to build highways and hospitals, and schools, then certainly I am in favor of it.

This is my stand and I will not compromise.

Do you really know which side Oiley is on? No, because he has effectively kept his own position from you by exploiting to the fullest the connotative possibilities that words have. Playing on their emotional effects, he employs words and phrases to support and heighten first one position, then the other.

In aligning himself with the temperance advocates, he woos their support by such words of condemnation as "devil's brew," "poison scourge," "misery and poverty," "evil," and "topples Christian man and woman from the pinnacles of righteous, gracious living." But to ensure the vote of his drinking constituents, he shifts to language of approval: "oil of conversation," "Christmas cheer," "when good fellows get together," "stimulating drink that puts spring in an old gentleman's step." Manipulating language in this way is dishonest. Oiley is deliberately deceiving his audience; he is guilty, in a literal sense, of doublespeak.

Argument, to be effective, must be shaped to your readers, but you should retain your own integrity in the process. Your aim, after all, is to convince your readers to accept your ideas, not deceive them about what you are saying. Responsible shaping involves (1) organizing your material—that is, selecting and arranging supportive information; (2) constructing your sentences so that their structure helps to emphasize your main points; and (3) choosing language that will set the mood and tone best suited to your audience and to the purpose of your argument.

In Chapter 7, we talked of the importance of considering the connotations of words in writing vivid descriptions. In persuasive writing, you need to be even more alert to the effect of words on your audience. In descriptive writing, you made word choices for aesthetic reasons—reasons that required no ethical decisions on your part. But in persuasion, there is often a fine line between using words to achieve responsible shaping and twisting words to cater to the prejudices of the audience.

The following paragraphs from a newspaper demonstrate some of the degrees of shaping that are possible on a single controversial subject—in this case, the Equal Rights Amendment. The first is from an editorial:

The equal-rights business just doesn't make sense when screened against tradition and mores and personal identity. But ERA agitators are hell bent for action, and as Alexander Pope said, "Oh woman, woman! When to ill thy mind is bent, all hell contains no fouler fiend."

For the record, one does not quarrel with such ERA concepts as equal pay for equal ability. Nor does one take exception to the basic precept in the amendment's terse language: "Equality of rights under the law shall not be abridged in the United States or by any state on account of sex." . . .

What bothers us are the interpretations being placed on the proposition of equal rights and what this is doing and will do to our traditional way of life. Family, marriage, morality—these, for example, are threatened by libertinism already being practiced in the name of freedom.

These paragraphs, though colorful, are obviously biased in favor of the "woman's place is in the home" point of view. Words and phrases like "business doesn't make sense" and "ERA agitators are hell bent for action"; the derisive quote from Alexander Pope; and the appeal to fears that the

ERA threatens "our traditional way of life"—all are unfairly slanted. The highly emotive language begs for confrontation, not compromise.

The second example, from a response to the editorial, uses more neutral language, but still expresses a strong opinion—this time on the other side of the issue. The writers, a group of newspaperwomen, attack the editor's contentions rather than relying upon emotive language. The shaping in this instance is less offensive, being more dependent on content than on language: the language is neutral; no single word or phrase would elicit a strong emotional response.

[The editor] mentions "the best of all possible worlds" in reference to the traditional view of women. Some women prefer this, and we respect them for that, but some women today question whether they should have "easier jobs" because they are thought to be the weaker physically. We question the assumption that a physical job is harder than a nonphysical job.

Most professional jobs are not easy jobs, neither are they physical jobs. They are jobs demanding integrity, ability to assimilate, innovation and imagination: a fine mind. We question the assumption that men's minds are of a higher quality than women's or vice versa. We concur that there will always be minds greater and lesser than all people's, but some will belong to men and others to women.

Here, the writers respond to the editor's concern about women's traditional role by expressing respect for a point of view that conflicts with their own—the preference of some women for that traditional role. Then they turn to another point that the editorial stressed—that women need to be excluded from certain kinds of "physical jobs" for their own protection. Generally, the writers' plea is a rational one: that men and women be hired according to individual ability instead of disqualifying women because of their supposed inferiority. The writers achieve responsible shaping by restraining the emotional impact of the language and relying on rational, logical content.

As in this example, language use should be responsible and disciplined, thus enhancing the writer's voice and the logical tactics of the argument. You certainly may use emotive language, but it should appeal to the reasonable and humane instincts of your readers. It should not insult them, or taunt them, or appeal to their basest emotions. The latter tactics may occasionally have a dramatic impact. But their persuasive force is greatly limited, and with many readers, they may backfire.

Ambiguous Language

In persuasive writing, clarity is of primary importance. In addition to defining any uncommon terms, you must also take care that each word has exactly the meaning you intend; words used in ways that permit several interpretations can weaken the force of your argument. Word ambiguity can derive from two main sources:

1. The word may have several dictionary meanings and appear in a context that gives no clues to the intended meaning, as in this sentence from a student argument paper:

    The want of independence is a common urge within us that often tends to make some people act hastily and without proper thought.

    Here, the problem is with *want*, which can be a synonym for either *desire* or *lack*. Even if the context provided clues to the intended interpretation, the reader still might puzzle over it or be amused—resulting in a break in the communication track.

2. A word may have more than one function (for example, some words can function as either a noun or a verb, or as an adjective or a verb), and appear in a context where its intended function is unclear, as in this sentence:

    In the early 1970s, campus unrest about the Vietnam War reached a desperate peak; everywhere students were revolting.

    Here, *revolting* creates ambiguity because it can function either as an adjective or as a verb. Often this kind of word ambiguity is inadvertently humorous and may seriously undermine the effectiveness of your argument.

Vague Language

Vagueness results from either the overuse of abstract language or the use of poorly defined words. This student paragraph from a paper persuading students to seek a liberal education demonstrates both characteristics:

The rags to riches ideology that Horatio Alger instituted in the 1900's has been perpetuated past reality. Climbing the "ladder of success" can no longer begin on the bottom if one hopes to reach the top. And a college degree is a means of starting in the middle. The increased technological advancements and growth of bureaucratic business have complicated our lives to the point that a specialized education is of paramount importance if one hopes to live with a certain degree of financial security and luxury. A student's primary concern is succeeding within America's economic system after graduation. Students, for the most part, are no longer interested in studying the humanities, but only what is able to qualify them for a good job. The purpose of education at the university level has been altered; the quest for knowledge is secondary and the quest for a degree is primary. In viewing a major university's faculty–student relationship one can see that education has been atomized and organized to the point that it has almost become a commodity.

Even though the paragraph is potentially effective, it is so vague that you might have had to read it several times to get the message. Ask yourself whether an argument can be convincing if the reader is forced to reread and decipher meaning, in the meantime losing track of the point being made. Highly abstract terms such as *increased technological advancements, bureaucratic business, paramount importance,* and *financial security* combine with poorly defined terms such as *humanities, atomized,* and *commodity,* producing a vague, weak statement and confusing the issue.

In this revision, we substitute more specific, concrete words wherever possible and provide some definition of specialized terms.

The Horatio Alger "rags to riches" concept has invaded the realm of college education. Unlike the Horatio Alger heroes, we can no longer start at the bottom rung on the ladder of success. Instead, we must start in the middle in order to reach the top. A college degree is a way of starting in the middle. But the demands of an ever-expanding technology and an international business system have forced many students to seek not a liberal education, but a highly specialized one. Pre-med students, for instance, must specialize early in the natural sciences—chemistry, biology, anatomy—if they are to assimilate the number of scientific discoveries and techniques they will encounter in their graduate work. Without a specialized education, there is little chance of getting a professional job and making a decent living. Therefore, to achieve financial security, students search out the professional courses, not the courses in literature, music, philosophy, and language that have traditionally been the core of the humanities. Thus, the purpose of education at the university level has been altered: the quest for knowledge is secondary to the quest for a certifying degree. Even faculty—student relationships reflect the change; instructors and students alike look upon education as a commodity—a package of merchandise to be bought over the counter and resold in the marketplace.

Notice that in the revision we have not altered the student's meaning nor strayed very far from the original wording. The "ladder of success" metaphor has been more specifically related to the topic; a specific example (pre-med students) has been provided; brief definitions have been added; specific courses have been mentioned to indicate what is meant by professional and humanities courses; the word *degree,* which could cover all college degrees, is now limited in meaning by the addition of "certifying"; and *commodity* has been explained by adding a descriptive phrase. Not only is the point made clearer, but the concreteness of the paragraph adds authority to the writer's voice. In persuasive writing, then, as in narrative and description, concrete language generally better serves your purpose than words that are so abstract or so general that they mean nothing in particular.

LOGIC AND PERSUASION

Logical Fallacies

In a world where you are constantly bombarded with advertising slogans and political speeches, you may well challenge our contention that valid logical reasoning, along with responsible shaping of your material, is the best aid to persuasive force. After all, the public is persuaded to buy everything from disposable diapers to waterproof coffins every day—persuaded by argumentative devices that are logically fallacious. But logical fallacies, despite their persuasive force, should be avoided in reasoned argument. They are the tools of the advertising con artist, the political demagogue, and the unscrupulous evangelist. Anyone persuaded by these tactics will sooner or later feel cheated and belittled—hardly the relationship you want to establish in persuading someone to your point of view.

Logical fallacies derive from several sources. One involves deductive validity, as we saw in the discussion of deductive reasoning in Chapter 18; these "formal" fallacies occur when there are more than three terms in a syllogism or when the conclusion does not logically follow from the premises. Other kinds of logical fallacies occur in inductive reasoning; three of these—insufficient sampling, hasty generalization, and *post hoc*—were also discussed earlier. A third kind of fallacy, the most blatant abuse of logical reasoning, involves an appeal to the emotions of the audience. These "emotional" fallacies are probably most damaging to a reasoned argument, but ironically are most persuasive. The following lists of additional logical and emotional fallacies can help you to recognize and avoid them in your writing.

Non Sequitur *Non sequitur* (Latin for "it does not follow"; pronounced "non se'kwiter") is evident in a statement like this: "X will make an excellent President because he's a good family man." Underlying this is the syllogism:

All good family men make excellent Presidents.
X is a good family man.
Therefore, X will make an excellent President.

The problem lies in whether being a good President logically follows from the premise about family men. In actuality, the very qualities that make a good President—strong leadership, decisiveness of action, single-mindedness of purpose—might be disastrous to family relationships. When tempted to use *non sequitur,* remember that this fallacy is Edith Bunker's stock in trade.

Begging the Question   You commit this fallacy when you present questionable premises as uncontestable truth. The premise "Abortion is wrong, because it's murder," is obviously not accepted as truth by everyone in modern society; otherwise, there would be no court cases trying to decide the issue. When the major premise is questionable, the conclusion is also.

The most common form of begging the question is the circular argument. A categorical syllogism constructed from the "abortion" premise illustrates this:

Abortion, a form of murder, is wrong.
All forms of murder are wrong.
Therefore, abortion is wrong.

Arguing in a circle, the question-begging conclusion echoes the question-begging premise.

You can also beg the question and argue in a circle using an *if/then* form. In this statement from a letter to a newspaper editor, the writer both assumes that everyone accepts the truth of his reasoning and restates the major premise in the conclusion: "If God is left out of the schools completely, then the schools will be without God."

Either-Or   This fallacy results when two conditions or positions are falsely presented as the only possible alternatives. This fallacy (sometimes called False Dilemma) can be highly persuasive, as in Patrick Henry's famous "Give me liberty or give me death!" But it can also lead to dangerous oversimplification, as in the slogan, "America—love it or leave it." Another example of this is an argument presented by the Army Corps of Engineers to justify the building of a dam that would destroy a uniquely scenic area: "Either build the dam or have yearly destructive flooding."

There might be other alternatives in these three situations or any other. Your argument will have greater strength if you recognize all the alternatives and discuss them, rather than relying on the *either-or* fallacy.

Emotional Fallacies

Emotional fallacies appeal directly to the human frailties of the audience: some to their prejudices, some to their vanity, some to their national pride, others to their desire to emulate people they admire. Because of this, they exert great persuasive force. These fallacies should be avoided in writing for essentially the same reason that you shun slanting: they deceive your readers. Remember how often you have felt cheated because an advertiser convinced you to buy an expensive, ineffective product by playing on your desire to be attractive to the opposite sex. Using such tactics in argument can only have short-range effectiveness; your commitment should be to make a lasting impression on your readers.

Ad Hominem   *Ad hominem,* or an appeal "to the man," involves attacking a person instead of that person's stand on an issue. A politician who, when challenged by an opponent to discuss military spending, instead accuses the opponent of alcoholism is arguing *ad hominem.*

Ad Populum   *Ad populum* is an appeal "to the people"—particularly to their prejudices or fears—rather than to the merits of the issue. A politician who exploits the racial hostility generated in a community over an explosive busing issue is guilty of this fallacy.

Name-Calling   When Valerie Solanas wrote her *S.C.U.M. Manifesto,* her name-calling tactics helped to polarize the women's liberation movement: "He (the male) is a half dead, unresponsive lump, incapable of giving or receiving pleasure or happiness; consequently he is at best an utter bore, an inoffensive blob, since only those capable of absorption in others can be charming." This kind of verbal attack really persuades no one: it repels rather than attracts. Engaging in this kind of name-calling, however, may be less reprehensible than resorting to names intended to trigger an automatic negative response: *commie, pinko, Nazi, fascist,* and racial and ethnic slurs —*nigger, kike, Cannuck,* and the like.

Glittering Generality   A glittering generality is a stock statement or phrase that appeals to the patriotic or family feelings of an audience: "the American way of life," "life, liberty, and the pursuit of happiness," "the joys of motherhood," "the American dream," are all perfectly acceptable when used in a relevant context and clearly defined. But when used specifically to elicit an emotional response, they become fallacious devices.

Bandwagon Appeal   How many times in high school did you persuade your dad to let you have the car to go to a party because "everybody else" was going? Similarly, many advertising slogans urge readers to jump on the bandwagon—to buy something so that they become associated with the majority of people or with a particular prestigious group: "Beer belongs," "Camels aren't for everybody (but then, they don't try to be)," "Join the Pepsi generation," "The car for the people who think."

THE SYLLOGISM IN PERSUASIVE WRITING

Syllogisms are all around us, in newspaper and magazine letters and editorials, in advertising, in public speeches, in ordinary conversation, on bumper stickers, and even in poetry. But rarely are they obvious. The syllogisms discussed in Chapter 18 are the forms that logicians use; in written discourse, however, syllogisms can appear in many forms. With only a little practice, you can see through their disguises and recognize them as *bona fide* logical syllogisms.

Occasionally syllogisms are complete; but their three-statement form is perhaps disguised by some added explanatory material, or their conclusion worded differently from the main premise, or their statements arranged in an order that differs from the usual logical form. Most frequently, however, syllogisms are either shortened in form or expanded to include several syllogisms within one paragraph. Let's look first at two passages that contain complete, three-statement syllogisms.

The Complete Syllogism

Our society has moved illogically in this direction by virtually institutionalizing adultery; a growing number of spouses permit each other complete sexual liberty on the conditions that there shall be no "involvement" and that the extracurricular relations are not brought to their attention. It is beginning to institutionalize ritual spouse exchange.

—Alex Comfort, "Sexuality in a Zero-Growth Society"

Here the form of the syllogism is hidden in a reordering of its essential elements: the terms of the major premise appear in the opening and closing sentences of the argumentative sequence. Here's one way to put it into a tighter syllogistic form:

A society that encourages ritual spouse exchange is a society that institutionalizes adultery.
Our society is a society that encourages ritual spouse exchange.
Our society is a society that institutionalizes adultery.

A valid, and probably true syllogism. Here's another, supported by specific experiences, that has an underlying syllogism:

The cases of Adolf Beck, of Oscar Slater, of the unhappy Brooklyn bank teller who vaguely resembled a forger and spent eight years in Sing Sing only to "emerge" a broken, friendless, useless, "compensated" man—all these, if the dignity of the individual has any meaning, had better have been dead before the prison door ever opened for them. This is what counsel always says to the jury in the course of a murder trial and counsel is right: far better to hang this man than "give him life."

—Jacques Barzun, "In Favor of Capital Punishment"

Here's how the syllogism might be constructed:

An experience that takes away individual dignity is worse than death.
Long imprisonment is an experience that takes away individual dignity.
Therefore, long imprisonment is worse than death.

The Shortened Syllogism and the Hidden Assumption

On Washington's Birthday, a man interviewed by a roving reporter was asked if he thought George Washington was really truthful. His answer was, "Of course not, he was a politician, wasn't he?" This cynical reply was actually a shortened syllogism with the main premise missing—but easily supplied.

Major premise: (All politicians are untruthful—unstated)
Minor premise: George Washington was a politician. (stated)
Conclusion: Therefore, George Washington was untruthful. (stated)

This is a common shortened syllogism, one in which the major premise is missing, but in spite of that omission it still carries logical force. In fact, one of the reasons that shortened versions occur so often in writing is that they frequently carry more persuasive power than complete, explicitly stated syllogisms do. This power stems mainly from their dependence upon hidden assumptions—the assertions missing along with the omitted statement. In this dependence lies both the strength and the danger of shortened syllogisms. These abbreviated forms can be persuasively effective because they flatter your audience: your readers can demonstrate their knowledge and logical facility when you permit them to supply the missing part. But shortened syllogisms can also obscure premises or conclusions that are invalid or untrue; in a very real way, they often beg the question. For instance, in our George Washington example, are you really willing to accept as absolute truth the hidden assumption in the missing premise— that *all* politicians are untruthful? We hope not.

Hidden assumptions accompany all variants of the shortened syllogism. Let's look at some of these possibilities and their underlying hidden assumptions:

Shortened form	*Syllogism* (unstated premises italicized)	*Hidden assumption*
Of course he writes poorly—he's a football player.	*Football players write poorly.* He's a football player. He writes poorly.	All football players write poorly. (sweeping generalization)

Shortened form	Syllogism (unstated premises italicized)	Hidden assumption
"Folger's coffee is mountain-grown."	*Mountain-grown coffee is the best coffee.* Folger's is mountain-grown coffee. *Folger's is the best coffee.*	All coffee grown in the mountains is superior to other coffee. (begging the question)
Part-time students don't get free football tickets; and poor Connie's a part-time student.	No part-time students get free football tickets. Connie is a part-time student. *Connie won't get a football ticket.*	Projected conclusion that Connie is analogous to all other part-time students and won't get a free ticket. (probably valid)
CAUTION: WOMAN DRIVER (bumper sticker)	*All women drivers demand caution. This driver is a woman driver.* This driver demands caution.	All women are dangerous drivers. (stereotyping)

As you can see, any part of the categorical syllogism may be missing. Your task in writing and analyzing arguments is to realize this, probe for the hidden assumptions, and check the complete syllogism for both truth and validity.

The Expanded Syllogism

Occasionally, it is necessary to reason through a series of syllogisms in order to arrive at a valid conclusion or to illustrate an argument more vividly. At such times you can combine several syllogistic forms. Let's look at such a situation:

The man who is not at peace with himself cannot be trusted to lead his fellow-men in the ways of peace. The unbalanced leader is certain to unbalance the society in which he functions. Even the leader who is intent on the side of the good but who is a fanatic will stimulate fanaticism in his followers, arouse dogmatism and bigotry, and induce oppression and cruelty. When he is on the side of evil, he will lead his followers into such excesses and wickedness as will shame all humanity, and which even the innocent will wish to forget as soon as possible.

—Marten Ten Hoor, "Education for Privacy"

The assertion made in the first sentence establishes the major premise for all the syllogisms implicit in the sentence. First we construct a formal syllogism from the first two sentences. This then supplies an underlying major premise for the others:

Syllogism 1

Major premise: *The man not at peace with himself is unable to lead.*
Minor premise: The unbalanced man is a man not at peace with himself.
Conclusion: The unbalanced man is not able to lead.

Syllogism 2

Major premise: (Same as above)
Minor premise: The good leader who is a fanatic is a man not at peace with himself.
Conclusion: The good leader who is a fanatic is unable to lead.

Syllogism 3

Major premise: (Same as above)
Minor premise: The man on the side of evil is a man not at peace with himself.
Conclusion: The man on the side of evil is unable to lead.

As you can see from this example, the expanded syllogism is a handy stylistic device; once the major premise and the form are established, you can expand the idea and at the same time retain the full persuasive force of the categorical syllogism. And you can avoid unnecessary repetition by letting one premise work for several syllogisms.

SUMMARY

The purpose of our discussion on the logic and language of argument is not to make you a master of all the intricate devices of formal argument. Actually we've touched on only a few. Instead, in this chapter we have looked at some pitfalls to avoid: the language slanting, the logical fallacies, and the hidden assumptions that bypass rational processes and appeal directly to people's emotions and fears. However, emotional appeal is effective and certainly does have a place in persuasive argument, but it should be used judiciously and responsibly. Remember, the most effective argument comes from combining sound, logical reasoning with fair-minded appeal to readers' compassion or decency. The more adept you become at recognizing the methods of argument, the more proficient you will be in using these argumentative devices to persuade other people to accept your ideas.

Assignments

1   In these examples, identify the words or phrases that signal the writer's opinion or bias about the subject.

a   Grades are the play money in a university Monopoly game. As long as the tokens are offered, the temptation will be largely irresistible to play for them. Students are so busy taking notes, doing tests, and getting tokens that they have forgotten to ask: Of what worth is all this? Or perhaps they ask and the grade is their answer.

One certainly learns something in the passive lecture-note-read-note-test process: how to do it all more efficiently next time (in the hope of eventually owning Boardwalk and Park Place). As Marshall McLuhan has said, we learn what we do. In this process most students come to view learning as studying and remembering what other people have learned. They assume that knowledge is logically and for practical reasons divided up into discrete pieces called "disciplines," and that the highest knowledge is achieved by specializing in a discipline. By getting good grades in a lot of disciplines they conclude they have learned a lot. They have indeed, and it is too bad.

Such harsh judgment seems unjustified to many professors. From their viewpoint a great deal of thinking goes on; they generate most of it themselves and then hear their own echo, often disguised, on tests and papers.

—Roy E. Terry, in "Dialog," *Change*

b   And I noted a recent Congressional committee's report pointing out that for comparable services New York's cost of doing business is roughly the same as that of most large American cities. But that is not what is really important to me now, any more than is the knowledge that weaknesses, mistakes and mismanagement in frontline city government have long been there and still are.

What *is* important is the appalling insensibility of the leader of our country to such a major part of American life as the American city. One would hope that such myopia is only confined to this one critical aspect of America and its history. Mr. Ford has never faced a large and diverse constituency. A safe and homogeneous Congressional district is hardly the school of hard knocks.

Twenty-five years in the marbled cocoon of the House of Representa-

tives can be a far more isolating experience than that of the average person trying to "make it" in almost any neighborhood in America today. And being on the Committee on Armed Services for most of that 25 years is worse than confinement in a cocoon—it's being sealed in a tank, unless one is to adopt the unsafe and uncomfortable course and ask hard questions of the Pentagon and its management, its uses, and abuses. Enormous cost overruns of taxpayer-funded contracts, millions in waste, to say nothing of Vietnam and other exorbitant junta alignments and adventures, were none of Mr. Ford's critical concern for waste, mismanagement or policy; from him, we got only unquestioning and uncritical support.
> —John. V. Lindsay, "Speaking Up for New York"

c Of the products of the human intellect, the scientific method is unique. This is not because it ought to be considered the only path to Truth; it isn't. In fact, it firmly admits it isn't. It doesn't even pretend to define what Truth (with a capital T) is, or whether the word has meaning. In this it parts company with the self-assured thinkers of various religious, philosophical, and mystical persuasions who have drowned the world in sorrow and blood through the conviction that they and they alone own Truth.
> —Isaac Asimov, "When Aristotle Fails, Try Science Fiction"

d The murders within five years of John F. Kennedy, Martin Luther King, Jr., and Robert F. Kennedy raise—or ought to raise—somber questions about the character of contemporary America. One such murder might be explained away as an isolated horror, unrelated to the inner life of our society. But the successive shootings, in a short time, of three men who greatly embodied the idealism of American life suggest not so much a fortuitous set of aberrations as an emerging pattern of response and action—a spreading and ominous belief in the efficacy of violence and the politics of the deed.
> —Arthur M. Schlesinger, Jr., *Violence: America in the Sixties*

e A university, as a center of learning rather than as a manipulator of land, is a place of realism and ferment. Inevitably, performance of the academic mission has an effect on students who claim that knowledge has a moral force which dictates action. Naive as this claim is, it has led to a lot of earnest effort—if poorly planned and often bungled—toward changing the anteroom.
> —William Ellet, "The Overeducation of America"

2 Identify the main weakness of the following sentences: vagueness or ambiguous language. Try to reword each so that the meaning you think the writer intended is more clearly expressed.

a Many attempts have been made to force athletic teams to drop nicknames and mascots symbolizing the Indians.

b The people are the church, but in their fear of involvement they have ironically used the church as a hideaway.

c One reason for people's loss of faith is their inability to relate to the intangible.

d Nurse Ratched is McMurphy's persecutor. She turns him into a vegetable but his essence still lingers on.

e Almost all prejudicial views yield a lack of knowledge of the facts about prejudice.

f Talking about sex dealing with children, people and parents should be more open-minded.

g I think that the highest appreciation should be given to parents, because what they have done for their children was done because they wanted to and not because they had to.

h The Russian divisions advance toward Berlin as the Eighth Army push bottles up the Germans.

i While there is accent on skills and methods, as there would be for any disciplined studies, the aims are to come to an understanding of language as fundamental to what it means to be human, and to the ability to synthesize and utilize that understanding in a variety of human concerns.

j Does your business suit fit the needs of modern merchandising?

k More schools have failed dropouts than dropouts have failed schools.

l When these gun control laws failed to control crime, these groups, instead of looking toward the real cause of the problem, simply asked that more of the same type laws be passed as if the number of laws would aid in fighting crime.

3 Identify the logical or emotional fallacies in the following examples:

a I was with the FBI for twenty years. My son can't be a bigot.

b The Imperial Wizard maintained in a newspaper interview that the Ku Klux Klan was the best organization in America—the only one organized for the purpose of maintaining Americanism.

c American taxpayers are going to have to support the reorganization of our rail system in terms of mergers, abandonments and the elimination of parallel trackage and redundant yards, or they will be saddled first with subsidies and soon thereafter by a nationalized rail system.

d If the Pope were a woman, he'd be for abortion.

e It all adds up to the fact that throughout history women have preferred at heart to paddle their own canoe, having what might better be called a mind of their own, however poorly it may work. Do we really want to change the interesting, exciting and beautiful nature of women through legislation, by ratifying the ERA?

—Letter to the editor

336

f It's the foxiest station-wagon on the road.

—Ad for Audi Fox

g Finally, say those who want weather war outlawed, even the most limited uses of weather modification tend to open up a Pandora's Box of horrors. If we accept weather modification as a very limited battlefield weapon, the next step is a slightly less limited operation—and the next step is the use of the same techniques to alter the climate of an entire country.

—Phil Stanford

h Rare taste. Either you have it or you don't.

—Scotch ad

i There is a certain kind of person who knows how to live. He knows how to get just a little extra out of every precious minute.

—Boat ad

j In this friendly, freedom-loving land of ours, beer belongs—enjoy it.

—Beer ad

k Middle America is concerned about law and order.

l Making [basketball] points wasn't always easy for a girl. But now you can do anything. Make the team or color your hair.

—Hair dye ad

m Bob True, in my opinion, is the best qualified candidate. I have known him since 1963, and in my opinion, he is an honorable, Christian man, an upstanding family man.

—Letter to the editor

n Men are all alike: selfish creatures who every weekend plant themselves in splendid isolation in front of a TV set. They substitute vicarious touchdowns, birdies, chip shots, and home runs for family participation and fun.

o The pinkos and weirdos at the state university naturally are against my legislative programs.

4 Below are examples of shortened and expanded syllogisms. Complete the syllogisms and state the hidden assumption in each.

a Wars are not "acts of God." They are caused by men, by man-made institutions, by the way in which man has organized his society. What man has made, man can change.

—Fred M. Vinson

b All those millionaires who pay no income tax can eat their hearts out; they won't get any rebate.

—Newspaper filler

337

c Football coaches can't expect to hold the job forever. After all, they weren't elected by the people.

—Newspaper filler

d Determination comes from keeping one's mind on something. This determination can result in good or ill but there's no doubt that without determination and drive, little greatness would have come out of this civilization.

—Letter to the editor

e Everything positive is accomplished in terms of negatives. You can become branch manager by not sticking your neck out. You can make it to the vice-presidency of the corporation by not contradicting and by not being too egghead grammatical. The man who knows says nothing controversial.

—Eve Merriam, "The Matriarchal Myth"

f But legislation which would funnel money to families who adopt [handicapped or retarded] children is not the right way of getting them into homes. People could start adopting children because of the money rather than because they really want a child. Children with special defects need special love and attention, and a subsidy from the federal government is not the way to get it.

—Newspaper editorial

g The real job will have to be done by the public. If it won't seek out and elect candidates capable of making moral distinctions, it's fated to continue being victimized by a system in which the ends too long have justified the means.

—Newspaper editorial

h "Milk-drinkers make better lovers."

—Bumper sticker

i The company may discharge any employee whose conduct on the job is disruptive. Joe's conduct is certainly disruptive.

j Of course he was under surveillance. Anyone with a job in government who dates foreign women is suspect.

k I could not love thee, Dear, so much,
Loved I not honour more.

—Richard Lovelace, "To Lucasta, Going to the Wars"

l Of course freshman English is boring; it's a required course.

m The tax cuts sound good until we grasp the over-all picture. Energy is industries' life-blood. When the oil industry is burdened with added tax to compensate for some of our tax cuts, not only will gasoline prices soar, but personal tax cuts will be re-collected threefold through more energy costs involved in producing all commodities.

—Newspaper editorial

For Practice

1 Choose one of the following syllogisms (or construct one of your own) and write a paragraph that incorporates the syllogism. Reword the syllogism so that it is not so obvious.

a The guarantee of a stable society is a desire of middle-class America.
Enforcement of law and order is a guarantee of a stable society.
Enforcement of law and order is a desire of middle-class America.

b All people are members of the human family.
Blacks and whites are people.
Blacks and whites are members of the human family.

c All forms of marriage are risky.
The commune marriage is a form of marriage.
The commune marriage is risky.

d No people should be victims of oppression.
The American Indians are people.
No American Indians should be victims of oppression.

e All societies educate their children in compliance with societal values.
The people of the United States are a society.
The people of the United States educate their children in compliance with societal values.

f If congressional steps are not taken soon, then the governmental weaknesses exposed by Watergate can destroy our country.

For Writing

1 In the following editorial, the writer exposes a hidden assumption in an argument to ban commercials on candy and soft drinks. Write a similar brief exposé of an advertising or campaign slogan.

JUNK FOOD ADS

The Federal Trade Commission recently turned down a request from a consumer group that wanted a ban on commercials for candy and other sugar-laden foods on TV programs aimed at children. The petitioners claimed that such products pose a health hazard, but the FTC ruled that it would defer any action until the Food and Drug Administration completes its current review of the sugar question.

The nation's nutrition obviously would improve considerably if children could be persuaded to eat fruit, vegetables and nourishing snacks, rather than sugar-coated cookies, candy and cakes. But claiming that these are a health hazard, except in the very narrowest sense, is stretching the meaning of that word pretty far.

The gist of this argument seems to be that children exposed to such ads soon start clamoring for the advertised products, a not unreasonable assumption. But the tacit premise of all this is that parents are then obliged to cater to Junior's wishes by buying junk food they know is of little value.

TV may well raise expectations that youngsters would be better off without, but adults who can't firmly dampen those expectations will have parental problems far worse than the effects of bad nutrition.

2   Write a paper discussing the use of emotional fallacies in advertising. You may choose to concentrate on one kind of ad—automobile or liquor ads, for example—or on advertising tailored to a specific magazine—*Playboy, Ms., Gourmet,* or *Ebony,* for example.

20

Special Topic: Focusing

FOCUSING DEVICES AND THE AUDIENCE

You are probably familiar with the old story about the farmer who had much success in persuading his mules to perform their mulish duties. When asked his secret, he replied that there was no magic involved: before telling the mules what to do, he hit them over the head with a stick to get their attention. Argumentative writing requires a similar tactic; but the "stick" is the point of view you are trying to impress your audience with. Your success in persuading your audience will be largely a result of your ability to stimulate and sustain their interest in your argument. But they must also be convinced. This requires supporting evidence—statistics, examples, authority, comparisons, facts—any material that can add to the persuasive force of your argument. Adding such information, however, can often lead writers astray because the proposition can be easily lost in a mass of information. Developing skills in maintaining focus can help you write more effective arguments.

USING PARAGRAPHS TO FOCUS THE ARGUMENT

Opening Paragraphs

Opening paragraphs in persuasive papers, like those in expository writing, should catch your readers' interest. But to be most effective, they should also contribute to the argumentative force of your paper. Sometimes this can be done by anticipating counterarguments and soothing your readers' possible hostility toward your subject. At other times, you might wish to start with a description or anecdote that appeals to the emotions. In the introduction, examples can also be effective in supporting problem-solution arguments, as this opening paragraph from a student paper illustrates. The writer uses examples to add persuasive force to the depiction of the problem and to prepare for his solution that the Alaskan Lands Acts must be passed:

> At one time in this country, many years ago, there lived an animal whose numbers were staggering; literally millions of them covered the Great Plains. Then came modern man with his rifle. Not only were they shot indiscriminately for food and sport, but often just the tongue and skins were taken from the dead animals. Skinned carcasses lay piled by the hundreds, left to rot in the sun. After twenty years of intensive hunting, this animal, the American bison, disappeared from the plains. Today, only a few private herds remain. Unfortunately, however, this is not the only example of ecological destruction resulting from human callousness. The bald eagle, the grizzly bear, the peregrine falcon, and the timber wolf are all perilously close to extinction in the continental United States.
>
> But there is still a chance to preserve these species from man-induced pressures. At present before Congress is an act to set aside in Alaska an area of land the size of California for wildlife preserves and national parks. In order to preserve America's last true wilderness, the Alaskan Lands Act must be passed.
>
> —Carl Marshall

As you can see, the student's lengthy description of the senseless slaughter of the bison both appeals to his readers' sense of outrage and implies the same kind of irresponsible killing for the other animals mentioned. This appeal then helps to focus the problem and justify the need for legislation.

Supporting Paragraphs

In the body of the paper, you must concentrate on adding support, and at the same time, perhaps, you must handle conflicting views. Therefore, it is often most difficult to keep the readers' attention on your proposition or solution. This is particularly true when you attempt also to handle a demanding paragraph structure—showing causes and effects, making comparisons and contrasts, or drawing an analogy. All of these take careful attention to focusing devices. Here are some examples of each.

Cause-and-Effect Paragraphs   For some purposes in a logical argument, you may want to support a point by dealing mainly with particular effects, as Marvin M. Katz does in this paragraph from his essay "What This Country Needs Is a Safe Five-Cent Intoxicant." As you read, note that he moves from a discussion of the diverse human needs for drugs (cause) to the diverse effects of drugs.

Man's needs, it turns out, vary in kind and in pattern from person to person and within the same man. In view of this diversity of needs the accomplishments in drug development have been remarkable. The span of effects man can attain with drugs extends from such minor alterations as relief from tension, to major psychological changes that include escape from lethargy, from boredom and from aggressive inhibitions and, ultimately, to altered states of consciousness. They may even transport a person to an entirely different emotional or psychological state.

Cause

Effects

In another paragraph from the same article, Katz discusses at length one cause projected for the use of marijuana (effect):

The most parsimonious of explanations, however, comes from sociologist Howard Becker. In discussing possible reasons for the use of marijuana he proposes that there is nothing unusual or deviant about the motives that lead to its use; it is rather the use that may lead to deviant behavior. He proposes that a person usually comes upon marijuana by chance and experiments with it simply out of curiosity. He maintains the habit only if he derives pleasure from it. Becker concludes that if someone learns to derive pleasure from marijuana, more complex explanations are unnecessary; he continues to use marijuana simply because it is a new kind of pleasurable experience.

Effect

Cause

You can see that cause-and-effect paragraphs can move from effect(s) to cause(s) or from cause(s) to effect(s). In a long, complex argument, the effect may be introduced in a separate paragraph followed by a series of paragraphs, each dealing with a single cause. Note also that the writer maintains the focus of his paper (satisfaction of human needs) by speaking directly of needs in the first paragraph, by referring to a particular one in the second.

Comparison-and-Contrast Paragraphs   Individual paragraphs in the body of a paper can follow the same comparison schemes that we discussed for expository papers in Chapter 12 (see pages 207–08). The following paragraph compares the two sides of America (A: the America of Lincoln and

Stevenson; B: the America of Teddy Roosevelt). The author uses this scheme: Point 1: A, B; Point 2: A, B; and so on.

There are two Americas. One is the America of Lincoln and Adlai Stevenson; the other is the America of Teddy Roosevelt and the modern super-patriots. One is generous and humane, the other narrowly egotistical; one is self-critical, the other self-righteous; one is sensible, the other romantic; one is good-humored, the other solemn; one is inquiring, the other pontificating; one is moderate, the other filled with passionate intensity; one is judicious and the other arrogant in the use of great power.

—J. William Fulbright, *The Arrogance of Power*

Note that the focus on the comparison is maintained by the author's careful sentence structure: "one" statements refer to Lincoln's America; "other" to Roosevelt's. Repeating in the last sentence the phrase "arrogant in the use of great power" pulls the reader back to the focus of the book as revealed in the title.

Analogy Paragraphs   In the following analogy, the student writer compares the current problem of high-salaried players in baseball to a problem arising from an unfortunate rule in the Articles of Confederation.

The root of the salary problem is the owners' disunity. These men are basically facing the same difficulties that plagued the new-born United States 200 years ago. The owners could be compared to the individual states; the commissioners' office that regulates the game is like the ineffective weak central government under the Articles of Confederation. One of the archaic rules the National League lives by is the requirement of unanimous vote for any major change. The reason the National League couldn't expand in 1977 as the American League did is that it couldn't get approval of all twelve owners. One owner feared a new team would be a threat to his territory, so he cut the throats of the other eleven. That's what Rhode Island did in 1784 when it failed to ratify the Robert Morris tax amendment, although it had been supported by all the other colonies. To eventually strengthen the federal government, the founding fathers had to replace the Articles of Confederation and its unanimous vote rule in favor of a constitution that could be amended by two-thirds of the states approval. Baseball owners must now take similar action with the salary problem.

—Phil Chaney

To support his argument that the rules must change, the writer uses a characteristic common to both situations, the ability of one constituent to have veto power over the majority. Obviously, his analogy would not be valid on all points of comparison. Note that the reference to the "salary problem" in the opening and closing sentence maintains the focus of his paper.

Concluding Paragraphs

In your concluding paragraphs, you should not only summarize, but bring the full force of your argument to close the paper. You can make a last appeal, and often strongly restate your proposition. In the following brief paragraph, the student writer restates his proposition, picks up a phrase from the quotation about the kaleidoscope that started his paper, and appeals to his readers' pride of community and home:

With the proper planning of housing, we can surround ourselves with creative architecture and beauty. And, just as the mirrors of a kaleidoscope create beauty out of a jumble of pieces, builders can use planning to create beautiful neighborhoods and areas of housing that we can be proud of in years to come.

In the next student example, the writer uses comparison and contrast to set up a subtle *either-or* situation. Note that he, too, appeals to the readers' sense of responsibility and pride in country. By not overtly restating his proposition, he flatters his readers by allowing them to arrive at that conclusion.

So there it is. The issue is laid out; sides have been chosen. One side represents life and the preservation of a fragile and beautiful world. The other stands for the exploitation of natural resources to the fullest extent, consequently supporting the destruction of the last wilderness in America. We, the people of America, are thrown into the middle to choose. We have the power to kill; we have the power to preserve. We have a responsibility to life and a decision to make: whether to preserve life or to destroy it. The balance rests in our hands.

USING SENTENCE STRUCTURE TO FOCUS THE ARGUMENT

Because your purpose is to sway your audience, you should be very conscious in persuasive writing of how the order of sentence elements can add to the effect your writing will have on the reader. Often, simple reordering of sentence elements will create greater argumentative force by better focusing on the points you wish to emphasize. Particular sentence types, too, can do this more effectively than others. Let's see how these work:

Reordering Sentence Elements

In the first example in this chapter, the student paragraph on animals nearly extinct, the final sentence originally looked like this:

The Alaskan Lands Act must be passed in order to preserve America's last true wilderness.

By reversing the order of the two clauses in the sentence, the student achieved better transition from the ideas expressed in the rest of the paragraph, and added persuasive force by placing his proposition last, leaving readers with that idea.

In order to preserve America's last true wilderness, the Alaskan Lands Act must be passed.

Another effective reordering situation arises from a sentence type commonly used in argumentation: the *if . . . then* sentence. However, students often write it as follows, losing much of its possible syllogistic force:

Many endangered species will become extinct if strict enforcement of the laws is not practiced.

Look at the difference in persuasive force when the sentence elements are reordered to state an *if . . . then* syllogism:

If strict enforcement of the laws is not practiced, (then) many endangered species will become extinct.

Logical Transitions

Another sentence strategy useful in argumentation is the use of transitional adverbs. In Chapter 9, we pointed out that transitional adverbs (*however, therefore, thus*) not only show logical relationships within a sentence, but can also be used for this purpose between two sentences. Here's an example of how they can function:

Such differences [in the mathematical ability of boys and girls] could, of course, be genetic. *However,* it seems equally or more plausible to suggest that they are related to social pressures operating differently on women and men to mold them into the adult roles they are assigned by tradition to play.
—Marijean Suelzle, "Woman in Labor"

In addition to subordinators such as *however,* other adverbs can bridge relationships between two sentences: *in addition (to), obviously, fortunately, in truth, conversely, in fact, in much the same way, in similar fashion*—these are but a few of the most widely used adverbial idioms. Good writers, however, avoid overusing them and rely instead on supplying short sentences to act as meaningful bridges and on reordering sentence elements to serve as transitional devices.

When you employ these transitional devices in your writing, you need to be aware of the conventions of punctuating them. Such devices are almost always set off from the rest of the sentence by commas, regardless of what position they have in the sentence:

Initial: *Moreover,* they were unable to determine a cause for the epidemic of measles.

Middle: They were unable, *moreover,* to determine a cause for the epidemic of measles.

Final: They were unable to determine a cause for the epidemic of measles, *moreover.*

Passive Sentences

In an earlier discussion of the passive, we pointed out that active sentences are more effective in narrative writing. In persuasive writing, if the passive construction is not abused, it places strong focus on the topic when other devices are inadequate. It can also be useful in other ways. In the following example, the writer effectively uses the passive for subject-focusing. But in addition, note the subtle diplomacy resulting from the omission of the agent *by*-phrase and how it contributes to the persuasive power of the sentence. By the use of the passive, the writer can imply blame but not place it on a definite agent, thus avoiding a defensive reaction from the men in her audience.

The journeywoman [in a union] *is given* less training [than a journeyman], her promotional ladder is shorter or nonexistent, and she *is paid* less.
—Marijean Suelzle

The following sentence demonstrates another advantage of the passive: the omission of the agent when it is unimportant to the point. This results in added emphasis to the reordered subject.

Women *were asked* to write a story. . . . Men *were given* the same task.
—Marijean Suelzle

This use of the passive, when added to the many active sentences in the argument all beginning with the word *women* or *men,* helps the writer to keep constantly before her audience the contrast basic to her argument— the discrepancy between men and women in employment opportunities.

Used wisely and sparingly, passive sentences can be a valuable tactic for subject-focusing, particularly when the agent is unimportant or unnecessary.

Cumulative Sentences

In persuasive writing, all sentence types are brought into play—simple sentences for stark emphasis; compound for listing causes, relationships, and proofs such as statistics; complex for indicating logical relationships, particularly those in which the clauses are joined by *if . . . then, either . . . or, therefore,* or a dash. But one type of sentence that is of special use in argumentation is the cumulative sentence.

In descriptive writing, you used cumulative sentences for handling colorful details. But the structure of the cumulative sentence can also be advantageous in persuasion: the main clause at the beginning can carry an uninterrupted, emphatic statement of a supporting argument, which is then strengthened by the additional proofs or alternatives that follow:

Ask yourself what might happen to the world of tomorrow if there is complete automation, if robots become practical, if the disease of old age is cured, if hydrogen fusion is made a workable source of energy.

—Isaac Asimov

The cumulative structure can also enable a writer to add descriptive details that qualify the stated point without breaking up the close grammatical relationships of the main clause:

The treatments are worse than the sickness: insulin shock, electroshock, and even psychosurgery, during which the frontal lobes of the brains of unmanageable patients were quickly disconnected.

—Wesley C. Westman

Periodic Sentences

As you see, the cumulative sentence can be an effective persuasive tool, but its use in argument is limited. Of greater advantage for some persuasive purposes is the periodic sentence. Unlike the cumulative sentence, which presents the main statement first, the periodic sentence either places the modifiers at the beginning and the main clause at the end, or places the subject first, then the modifiers, and finally the rest of the main clause. This structure's value in argument is that its climactic effect can enhance persuasive force: it gives the same advantages as inductive organization does. Note in the following examples how the message in the italicized material gains importance throught the piling up of convincing details beforehand.

As long as students whisper among themselves, look at their watches, read newspapers, and write letters in class, *little learning can take place.* (Main clause at end)

But the widely publicized estimates that one in seven, one in four, or one in two of the seven million college students in America can be considered a "drug abuser" *are vastly exaggerated.* (Subject at beginning; predicate at end)

—Kenneth Keniston

The main weakness of the kind of periodic sentence in the second example is that the interruption between the subject and predicate can make it difficult to read and comprehend. So use it only when you want the climactic emphasis it offers.

Balanced Sentences

A balanced sentence can take the form of two main clauses that are equal in content, length, and grammatical structure, such as Pope's:

To err is human; to forgive, divine.

Or the balance may be between the subject and the predicate:

The difference between tragedy and comedy is the difference between experience and intuition.

—Christopher Fry

The balanced sentence can be used to emphasize a point, as in the Fry example, or it can permit the counterbalancing of two opposite points—which is probably its greatest contribution to argument. Using balanced sentences in this way also lends a psychological dimension to persuasion: the symmetry of the sentence form can lend an air of rationality and logic to the argument contained within. For this reason, perhaps, many writers like to use a balanced sentence to close an argument paper or to dramatize a central point.

SUMMARY

The strategies in this chapter for using sentences and paragraphs to provide support or focus can be added to your ever-expanding stock of writing skills. Because of the importance of appealing to an audience in persuasive writing, you should strive to gear everything in your argument to the particular needs of your audience. Remember, your paper will carry strongest persuasive power if your logic, organization, language, and sentence and paragraph structure all work toward the same end. Difficult? Yes. But the satisfaction of creating a piece of writing that influences others is well worth the effort.

Assignments

For Discussion

1 What kind of audience is each of the following introductory paragraphs addressed to? Does the writer consider the audience neutral, supportive, or antagonistic? How does each writer appeal to the audience? Is any supporting information included?

   a If I looked at jails and crimes and prisoners in the way the ordinary person does, I should not speak on this subject to you. The reason I talk to you on the question of crime, its cause and cure, is that I really do not in the least believe in crime. There is no such thing as a crime as the word is generally understood. I do not believe there is any sort of distinction between the real moral conditions of the people in and out of jail. One is just as good as the other. The people here can no more help being here than the people outside can avoid being outside. I do not believe that people are in jail because they deserve to be. They are in jail simply because they cannot avoid it on account of circumstances which are entirely beyond their control and for which they bear in no way responsibility.
   —Clarence Darrow, "Crime and Criminals"

   b People of Yale University! What's happening around you? I'm becoming convinced that the rampant, out-of-touch intellectualism in which you immerse your daily lives is leading you down the path of inert oblivion. In the two and a half years I've been here, I have never seen so many people out of touch with themselves, their bodies, and maybe even life itself.
   What good is your jammed-up intellectualism to you when you can't relate together the things that are happening around you, the things that are shaping your lives? I have never seen a place with so many talented people where inaction is actually valued, where people think that they can control their lives by thinking out something devoid of action. To think that this docile, jammed-up institution is to produce "1000 male leaders per year"! If so, then someone should seriously consider what it is that we will be leading.
   —Robert Wesley, "All About Production"

   c Speaking of the different kinds of treatment accorded to the affluent and to the marginal citizen, as I was the other day, reminded me that Barry Goldwater has lately come out for gentler penalties against marijuana offenders.
   This hardest of hard-liners in the law-and-order field admitted that his view of the subject had been changed by "personal considerations." All this can mean is that somebody close to him was puffing on pot and got his hand caught in the act.
   —Sydney J. Harris, "Pot Moves Up in Class"

2 The following are cause-and-effect paragraphs. Identify whether they move from cause to effect or from effect to cause. How is each focused toward the argument inherent in the paragraph?

a The pursuit of excellence in scholarship is inherently a lonely business and traditionally college life compensated by providing intimacy-producing relaxation, clubs, and other activities. As universities and colleges have grown at an explosive rate, creating an uprooted environment in the process . . . as they have become more depersonalized with television lectures, machine grading, and compulsory ID cards . . . as they have drawn more and more students from distant places . . . and as clubs have become less a part of the college scene, much of the old intimacy of college life has disappeared.
—Vance Packard, "Collegiate Breeding Ground for Transients"

b In place of the traditional family has come the activist family in which each member spends the majority of his time outside the home "participating." Clubs, committees, and leagues devour the time of the individual so that family activity is extremely limited. Competition among clubs is keenly predicated upon the proposition that each member should bring his family into its sphere. Thus Boy Scouts is made a family affair. PTA, the YMCA, the country club, every activity, competes for total family participation although it demands entry of only one member of the family.
—Vine Deloria, Jr., "Indians and Modern Society"

c The militancy of young people, both white and black, eager for social change is often accounted for by saying that they have lost faith in the slow processes of democratic discussion and decision-making. This argument seems to me highly questionable. It is my impression that militant young people, far from being "disillusioned" with democratic processes, are totally unacquainted with them, since they are rarely shown on television. To be sure, national conventions are shown on television every four years, but the arduous, day-to-day debates, fact-finding, and arguments by which social decisions are arrived at by every democratic body from town councils to the Congress of the United States are never shown.
—S. I. Hayakawa, "Who's Bringing Up Your Children?"

3 In the following comparison-and-contrast paragraphs, identify the type of comparison scheme used.

a The device used to limit competition is that of assigning different roles to the different groups within the American society. White males have assigned to themselves such roles as President of the United States, corporate executives, industrialists, doctors, lawyers, and professors at our universities. They have assigned to white women roles such as housewife, secretary, PTA chairman, and schoolteacher. Black women can now be schoolteachers, too, but they are most prominently assigned to domestic roles—maid, cook, waitress, and baby-sitter. Black men are thought to be good porters, bus drivers, and sanitation men.

—Shirley Chisholm, "The Politics of Coalition"

b Those who are for busing at all costs simply don't give a hang about the hostility, hatred, disaffection, and indifference generated among people who are expected to implement the educational and racial gains that are wanted: they are, typically, inclined to say that "at least we have an improved balance in the classroom." Consequently, they are miracle workers, do-gooders of the worst sort, who dream of transforming the country in accord with their entirely admirable vision, by means of cumulative but purely formal and administrative arrangements. Just bus them and the education of blacks as well as race relations will be improved—or, at any rate, a measurable gain will be added to previous, comparable gains, and the objectives will be brought a step nearer. Nonsense! On the other hand, those who are against busing at all costs simply don't give a hang for whatever deterioration appears within their own communities as a result of their imposed isolation, rigidity, and resistance to any but selected local concerns. Just throw the carpetbaggers out, keep the old traditions, let the neighborhoods manage their separate affairs, and education and relations between the races throughout the country will flourish in their most natural way. Again, nonsense!

—Joseph and Clorinda Margolis, "Busing"

4 **How has the writer used analogy for support in each of the following paragraphs? How is focus maintained?**

a Living together without any sense of permanency or legality is no more like marriage than taking a warm shower is like shooting the rapids in your underwear.

—Sydney J. Harris

b But the area of urban and suburban planning is only one instance of environmental crusaders rushing in where more reasonable men would tread more warily. In just about every aspect of American life, the environmentalists are imposing their regulations with all the indiscriminate enthusiasm of Carrie Nation swinging a baseball bat in a saloon. Common sense seems to have gone by the board, as has any notion that it is the responsibility of regulators and reformers to estimate the costs and benefits of their actions.

—Irving Kristol

c The only way to promote freedom is to devise a set of rules and thus construct a pattern which the various members of that society can follow. Each can then determine his own acts in the light of his knowledge of the rules. On this basis each can predict his field of action in advance and what results are likely to ensue from his acts; and so he gains freedom to plan and to carry out his plans. The more you attempt to administer society, however, the less free it becomes. There is opportunity for freedom of choice only in acting subject to the rules, and then only if the rules are freed of any element of will or dictation. If these rules are just rules that tell you what method or act will yield what results, like the rules of a game, you can then freely determine your own play. You can use the rules to win the game. The more abstract and objective the rule, the freer is the individual in the choice of his alternatives. The rules must be so written as to cover every possible eventuality of choice and action.

    —A. Delafield Smith, "Law as a Source of Notions of Freedom"

5 Discuss the effectiveness of the following conclusions. What kind of appeal is made? Is any syllogistic reasoning involved?

a From an argument for reopening the Kent State case:

By the time the Kent cases are completed, the ACLU and its foundation will have expended well over $100,000 in the quest to hold public officials accountable for their acts. Whenever someone asks why we are devoting so much time and effort and so many resources toward accountability for events that happened so long ago, I tell them that just four months ago—a few days before he was again sworn in office after a mandatory four-year hiatus—Governor Rhodes was questioned under oath by ACLU attorneys. He was asked, whether, in retrospect, there was anything he would have done or would now do differently at Kent.

    His reply: "None whatsoever. . . . Nothing."

    —"Kent State Five Years Later," *Civil Liberties*

b From an argument for learning the history of black people in the United States:

We weep for the true victim, the black American. His wounds are deep. But along with their scars, black people have a secret. Their genius is that they have survived. In their adaptations they have developed a vigorous style of life. It has touched religion, music, and the broad canvas of creativity. The psyche of black men has been distorted, but out of that deformity has risen a majesty. It began in the chants of the first work song. It continues in the timelessness of the blues. For white America to understand the life of the black man, it must recognize that so much time has passed and so little has changed.

—William Grier and Rice M. Cobbs, *The Shadow of the Past*

c **From an argument against the pursuit of status:**

Finally, I think we must learn to transcend the pettiness of scrambling for the symbols of status. We should recognize the true strength that lies in being individuals who think for themselves and are independent in mind and spirit. We would all lead more contented and satisfying lives if we judged people not by the symbols they display, but by their individual worth.

—Vance Packard, "The Pursuit of Status"

d **From an argument that the space age can bring about a twentieth-century spiritual and social renaissance:**

The choice is ours, it must be made soon, and it is irrevocable. If our wisdom fails to match our science, we will have no second chance. For there will be none to carry our dreams across another dark age, when the dust of all our cities incarnadines the sunsets of the world.

—Arthur C. Clarke, "Space Flight and the Spirit of Man"

6 Identify the kinds of sentences below (cumulative, periodic, or balanced) and discuss their effectiveness in achieving the writer's purpose.

a He calculated that if only one star in a thousand of these had planets at a suitable distance, and if an atmosphere developed on only one in a thousand of these, and if the right chemicals were present in the oceans and atmospheres of only one in a thousand of these, we would still be left with a hundred million planets suitable for life.

—John P. Wiley, Jr., "Don't Bet Everything on the Big Bang"

b The earth rotates on its axis at one thousand miles an hour; if it turned at one hundred miles an hour, our days and nights would be ten times as long as now, and the hot sun would then burn up our vegetation each long day while in the long night any surviving sprout would freeze.

—A. Creasy Morrison, "Seven Reasons Why a Scientist Believes in God"

c If one person alone refuses to go along with him, if one person alone asserts his individual and inner right to believe in and be loyal to what his fellow men seem to have given up, then at least he will still retain what is perhaps the most important part of humanity.

—Joseph Wood Krutch, "The New Immorality"

d We no longer think of our life span as a steady, desperate accretion of money, but more as an arc, after a certain point tapering down into easy retirement.

—Thomas Griffin

e There, for approximately a week, this teeming, milling mass of sun and sex worshippers swims, sleeps, flirts, guzzles beer, sprawls and brawls in the sands.

—Alvin Toffler

f You are not in charge of the universe; you are in charge of yourself.

—A. Bennett

g American parents, to the extent that they are Americans, expect their children to live in a different world, to clothe their moral ideas in different trappings, to court in automobiles although their forebears courted, with an equal sense of excitement and moral trepidation, on horsehair sofas.

—Margaret Mead

h To have a quiet mind is to possess one's mind wholly; to have a calm spirit is to command one's self.

—H. Mabie

i Style, to define again by example, is when a brother is wearing his gators (alligator shoes), fine vines (clothes), a slick do (process), in the old days, or an "uptight" natural today; style is having a heavy rap (verbal display), like the preacher, the young militant and the pimp (three strong and admired characters in black communities); style is driving an Eldorado; style is standing on a street corner looking cool, hip and ready; style is diggin on Yutsef Lateef rather than Johnny Cash; style is the way a black man looks at a woman and says, "Come here with your bad self."

—Johnnetta B. Cole, "Culture: Negro, Black and Nigger"

For Practice

1 The following statistics are a result of a survey of college students taken by George Gallup in 1975. Construct a comparison-and-contrast paragraph using the figures.

"Do you think the use of marijuana should be made legal or not?"

	Yes	No	Don't know
Freshmen	47%	49%	4%
Sophomores	46	49	5
Juniors	58	36	6
Seniors	64	30	6

"Do you drink alcoholic beverages?"

	Yes	No
Freshmen	64%	36%
Sophomores	72	28
Juniors	83	17
Seniors	88	12

2 Write a persuasive paragraph using analogy as your main tactic.
3 Write a paragraph discussing the causes of some condition in your community—for example, air pollution, water pollution, poor support of public schools, or the high dropout rate in the local high school.

Revision of Persuasive Writing

Throughout the book, we have been offering you all kinds of suggestions for revising your papers, so by now you should be aware that revision is important. If you have practiced good revision habits throughout, you should be able to identify mechanical errors, question your choice of words, and in general criticize your papers more objectively than you could at the beginning of the course. These are skills that you can apply to any writing assignment. But since persuasive writing involves a new set of writing tactics, this checklist of questions may help you in revising an argument paper.

Organization and Support

1. Is my thesis in the form of a proposition?
2. Do my main points have a "therefore" relationship with the proposition —that is, does the proposition logically follow from the main points?
3. In the problem-solution plan, have I clearly presented the problem and explained the practicality and advantages of the solution?
4. Have I supported my arguments with significant evidence?
5. Have I kept my audience in mind, refuting contrary opinions where necessary?

Logic

1. Have I relied on sound logical reasoning?
2. Have I used analogy? If so, is it reinforced by other kinds of evidence?
3. Is my syllogistic reasoning valid and true?
4. Have I avoided unethical slanting and ambiguous language?

Sentence and Paragraph Structure

1. Does my sentence structure help me make my points clearly and forcefully?

2. Have I effectively used comparison-and-contrast and cause-and-effect paragraph structure when needed?

Check through your paper, asking yourself these questions. If you can answer "yes" to each, then you can be reasonably certain that you have written a successful argument.

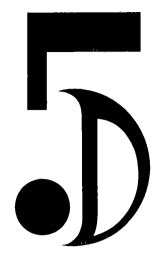

The Critical
Voice:
Writing About
Literature

tudents frequently complain to English teachers that they can't see why a story or poem has to be discussed in class. "Why," they ask, "can't we just read it to enjoy it?" Let's make an analogy with eating to find an answer to the question. How do you "enjoy" eating? Do you walk into a restaurant and instruct the waiter to bring just anything on the menu? Of course not. You *choose* the foods you enjoy—you browse through the menu to find something you have developed a discriminating taste for. To some extent, this discrimination is personal; it results from years of sampling different foods. But it is also a guided, learned preference; the people you have eaten with—your parents, brothers and sisters, friends—have all influenced your choice in foods.

So with reading. The critical analysis of a literary work does not necessarily mean a negative or disapproving interpretation. Rather, the term *critical* as used here refers to the making of discriminating evaluative judgments. Even a glutton for reading, one who indiscriminately reads everything, should eventually acquire some taste for a really fine literary meal. A faster way to develop this taste is through critical discussion in English class. Here you have the opportunity to sample the dishes savored by the teacher and your fellow classmates.

"We can see that," our reluctant students might answer, "but why do we have to take literature apart? Why can't we just respond emotionally to it?" The answer is that emotional pleasure is only one aspect of the enjoyment of anything. We appreciate a literary work just as we appreciate any human accomplishment: by understanding what the problems are and how they are solved. In baseball, we can admire a shortstop's artistry as he takes the throw on a dead run from the second baseman, touches the bag, veers off slightly to dodge the base runner, and then manages to throw to first base in time to complete the double play. Only by analyzing what he has done, by becoming aware of each decision he makes, and by realizing all the possibilities involved in the situation can we fully and truly appreciate the feat. You can apply a similar analysis to any human activity that requires skill. When a master does something, it looks easy. But master critics know that this ease is an illusion because they are aware of the artistry and effort required at each step of the process. Just as judges of diving events analyze the way divers handle the approach and other aspects of a dive, so critical readers examine the parts of a literary work. To evaluate the parts, they must take the work apart.

Before you can write critically, you must read critically. How to start? We offer two suggestions: read closely and carefully; inquire constantly as you read.

But before pursuing these tips, let's return to the ball game analogy for a moment. The baseball fan notes the second baseman or shortstop edging toward second, depending on whether the batter is right- or left-handed. Then with the crack of the bat and the sight of the ball bouncing out to second, the fan watches the shortstop scoot to the bag, take the toss in stride while touching the bag, and evade the runner while throwing to first. The knowledgeable fan observes every action on the diamond: the casual spectator misses most of it. Similarly, the critic is alert to every detail and nuance in the literary work; the casual reader misses most of it.

Analytical discussion of literature, along with critical writing, can generally improve both your reading and writing skills. In your English class, you are introduced to the methods of critical reading by an expert "coach," a teacher who is trained in the special reading skills needed for literature. In discussion, you practice the analytical skills that can aid in gaining an intelligent understanding of the art and craft of the literary writer. As you may know from experience with other activities, when intellectual awareness is heightened, so is pleasure. But learning critical techniques can do more than increase your enjoyment of reading; it can add a new dimension to your understanding of other art forms, such as television programs, films, music, and even painting and sculpture. It can also add a new dimension to your understanding of the real world and the motivations of the people you know. This humanizing effect is possible because literature is real—real in the sense that its people and events are believable even though they don't "really" exist.

As you participate in class discussion, you will discover that different people will interpret works differently. You and each of your classmates will bring to a work an individual, personal interpretation. In that sense, critical writing about a creative work is in itself a creative process. To help you with that process, a critical reading approach will be presented in this section to enable you to develop skills for effective critical writing. Then that approach will be applied to a short story to indicate the kinds of critical papers you might write.

Even though after college you may never write such papers about literature, or film, or music, or the other arts, by doing so here you will acquire valuable skills to take to other analytical tasks: weighing the worth of something, evaluating its quality, drawing inferences from various observations, establishing criteria for judging excellence, and presenting your critical opinions clearly and convincingly to others. In later life, you may use these skills to analyze a television program or a baseball game, to evaluate a house you wish to purchase, or to weigh the platform of a political candidate. But whether you use them for artistic or practical purposes, critical skills are an important aspect of your education. They are an essential part of your commitment to becoming a discriminating, literate, articulate, and sensitive person.

21

Approaches to Critical Writing

After finishing a book, viewing a television drama, or seeing a movie or play, we usually have an overall feeling of liking or disliking it, enjoying or not enjoying it, considering it time well spent or wasted. To translate this gut reaction into specific subjects to discuss or write about you must analyze the work. This process of analysis, as you will recall, involves dividing the whole into its parts, so that you can focus on one or several aspects of a subject. One analytical approach to literary works is to start with some of the following questions, modeled on the journalist's lead to a news story: *who, what, where, when, why,* and *how.* Then you can use the inverted-triangle method we described on pages 265–66.

The questions	*The areas*	*The issues*
Who?	Character	The function, traits, and credibility of the people in the work
What?	Plot	The series of related actions involving some problem that builds to a crisis and is resolved
Where?	Setting	The physical location and the general environment, including the social, political, and other conditions affecting the characters
When?	Time	The time structure of the work and the period it is set in
Why?	Theme	The central or controlling idea that is conveyed mainly through the character and plot
How?	Technique	The author's use of language devices to gain an effect

The value of this approach is that it will suggest ways for you to consider a literary work and questions you can ask yourself to stimulate your thinking. In applying this method, we have limited literary works primarily to novels, short stories, and dramas, although many poems might also be analyzed in this way.

CHARACTER (WHO?)

Other people—on the screen, stage, page, or in life—fascinate us. Observing them in literature may be most absorbing because we can know characters better than friends. You should realize that you never learn exactly and fully what your friends are thinking and you seldom, if ever, see their private selves, the side they prefer not to expose to others, perhaps not even to themselves. But literature allows us to tap into the characters' minds and souls, enabling us to understand and know people better than we do in real life.

Yet we need to raise some questions about literary characters that we would not about real people. Real people exist and are what they are, for genetic, environmental, and other reasons; literary characters exist and are what they are for literary reasons. These questions should help us to realize what those reasons are:

1. What is the character's function?
2. What traits does the character reveal?
3. Does the character change?
4. What is the overall impression of the character?
5. How credible is the character?

Let's discuss each of these questions in turn.

What Is the Character's Function?

Literature is memorable for the characters who have walked from its pages into our cultural consciousness, appearing frequently in our minds, discussions, and writings. For example, how many of the following have you heard about: Oedipus, Antigone, Hamlet, Macbeth, Tom Jones, Heathcliff, Oliver Twist, Huck Finn, Captain Ahab? Like most central characters, all were involved in and generally dominated by a series of events from which they emerged either winner or loser, happy or unhappy, richer or poorer, better or worse; but all were wiser for the experience and became somewhat more admirable people even in death or defeat. Because these literary personages are compelling, we speak of them informally as heroes and heroines, but the more appropriate term is central character or, if you wish, main or principal character. In such a category would appear Mark Antony, Antigone, or Gatsby, yet we would not think of these characters as individuals of great nobility, nor even as worthy of emulation. But insofar as they are prominent in a literary work and command our attention and interest throughout most of it, to some extent we identify with them, feel sympathy toward them, and are attracted to them. Occasionally, a central character may repel us, as does Jane Austen's Emma, who in the early part of the novel is snobbish, malicious, and overbearing. Sometimes, a work will have not one but several main characters, such as the Joad family in *Grapes of Wrath.* Usually the title of the work indicates the main character, but there are exceptions: Brutus, for example, dominates *Julius Caesar;* Captain Ahab is the hero of *Moby Dick.* Our point is that central characters come in all sizes, shapes, sexes, races, and creeds. In popular escape literature, they are golden heroes and heroines, the good guys and the good gals, who win out and live happily ever after. In serious literature, they are absorbing individuals who command our interest and attention, though not necessarily our admiration. Their function is obvious because without them there would be no literary work. But what about the other characters?

They may serve various roles, which you can best determine by asking what would be missing if they were not present in the story. Always remember that authors are creators, determining everything that appears on the printed page. Every character and every character's thoughts, feelings, words, and actions have been created by an author for some purpose. Being aware of that purpose will enable you to better understand the characters and the work itself. Exactly what do we mean?

Some characters serve as foils, whose actions, feelings, and opinions contrast with those of the central character, often in parallel situations that reveal much about both. So it is in *Don Quixote* that the practical Sancho serves as a foil to the impractical Don Quixote, and, in *Huckleberry Finn,* the clever Tom Sawyer to the naive Huck.

Other characters function like accessories, helping to portray the main character. *The Catcher in the Rye,* for instance, is populated with minor figures who reveal Holden's compassion for others. They range from the innocent and virtuous (the nuns) to the shrewd and vicious (Stradlater and the bellboy, Maurice). Unlike these characters who enter in one scene and later exit forever, other literary characters, like the slave Jim in *Huckleberry Finn,* appear throughout most of the novel.

Characters may also serve a plot function. The ghost in *Hamlet* causes the prince to suspect his uncle Claudius of murder; Mr. Mason in *Jane Eyre* stops the heroine's marriage to Mr. Rochester. These and other characters primarily create plot complications that add to the action of the story.

Characters can also function as spokespeople or representatives of the author's views. In *Crime and Punishment,* Raskolnikov's sister Dounia and his friend Dmitri personify the author's beliefs in salvation through love and generosity. And in *The Catcher in the Rye,* Mr. Antolini appears to express Salinger's ideas. However, concluding that a character represents or speaks for an author should be decided only after a careful consideration of the reliability of that person and other evidence in the work.

Then there are background characters who add to the setting, providing an illusion of the real world. They are usually the common folk: the citizens in Shakespeare's *Julius Caesar*, the seamen in Melville's *Moby Dick*, the rustics in Hardy's Wessex novels. Such characters help to create a sense of place and atmosphere.

Somewhat similar are characters who perform solos, who provide a few moments of relief or laughter or interest, although they contribute little to the development of plot or an understanding of other characters. Among these characters, who are truly "characters," are the porter in *Macbeth*, many of the clowns in Shakespeare's other plays, and Dickens' eccentrics, notably Mr. Micawber in *David Copperfield*. Such characters contribute to the tone of a work.

Characters, therefore, may play various roles: main figures, foils, accessories, plot functionaries, representatives or spokespeople for the author's views, and contributors to the setting or the tone. Determining how characters function will enable you to analyze a literary work with greater insight.

What Traits Does the Character Reveal?

Once you have determined the function of characters, the next step is to analyze them individually. To do this, you should consider the evidence revealed about them in these five ways: (1) their thoughts; (2) their statements; (3) their actions; (4) the reactions of other characters to them; and (5) the author's evaluation of them.

This fifth way is found more frequently in older novels, where the author introduces characters to readers as Dickens does Mr. Bounderby in *Hard Times:*

He was a rich man: banker, merchant, manufacturer, and what not. A big, loud man, with a stare, and a metallic laugh. A man made out of coarse material which seemed to have been stretched to make so much of him. A man with a great puffed head and forehead, swelled veins in his temples, and such a strained skin to his face that it seemed to hold his eyes open, and lift his eyebrows up. A man with a pervading appearance on him of being inflated like a balloon, and ready to start. A man who could never sufficiently vaunt himself a self-made man. A man who was always proclaiming, through that brassy speaking trumpet of a voice of his, his old ignorance and his old poverty. A man who was the Bully of humility.

The description proves apt: Bounderby is an obnoxious braggart in the novel, a perfect bounder; the storyteller is reliable. But as we have mentioned, this may not always be so. In D. H. Lawrence's *Sons and Lovers*, the portrayal of Walter Morel is one-sided, showing him to be a coarse, insensitive, brutal husband but giving little attention to his filthy, dangerous, bestial labor in the mines, and his wife's lack of understanding. In literature, as in life, we must collect all the evidence but give more weight to what we ourselves see and hear, and carefully consider the source of all other information.

In amassing this information, you might find it helpful to jot down some notes. For example, if you were writing about Brutus in *Julius Caesar,* here are some traits you could note:

1. Foolishly trusting, naive (fooled by Cassius; tricked by Antony)
2. Respected (all conspirators originally pay tribute to him; becomes leader)
3. Irritable (quarrels with Cassius; peevish with poet)
4. Tender, kind (loving husband to Portia; considerate of Lucius)
5. Idealistic (duty to Republic; failure to plan for successor)

And so on. Notes of this sort help because they force you to base your opinions on evidence within the work.

Does the Character Change?

You may have assumed from this discussion of character traits that people in literature are the same at the end of a work as they were at the beginning. Not at all. Some characters, particularly most central ones, change as a result of their experiences. Young people initiated into the realities of life gain maturity and insight, as Gene (*A Separate Peace*), Henry Fleming (*The Red Badge of Courage*), and Frankie Addams (*The Member of the Wedding*) all attest. And older people are altered—from kings (Oedipus) to housewives (Nora in *A Doll's House*). Look for a change, determine whether and how and why it takes place—or does not—and you will obtain more insight into the character.

Note, however, that some central characters do not learn from their experiences. One such is Harry Angstrom, the former high-school basketball star, who is trapped in his marriage, his job, and his community in John Updike's *Rabbit, Run.* But like his nickname, Rabbit, he is more unthinking animal than responsible human, running away at the beginning of the novel only to return, wreck the lives of his lover and wife, and then run away again—no better, no wiser, no different—as the novel comes full circle.

What Is the Overall Impression of the Character?

After determining a character's function, traits, and change, you are ready to run a tally. What does it all add up to? Is the character admirable or not, or, more crudely, does the character belong with the good guys and gals or the bad ones? Sometimes the answer is simple. Obviously, Fagin in *Oliver Twist* is a villain and Antony in *Julius Caesar* is a hero. But most central characters and those in conflict with them are not pictured as black or white, all good or all evil. Most are drawn in shades of gray. Trying to arrive at some conclusion about them, therefore, forces you to analyze them in some depth.

A case or two in point. Earlier, we mentioned that Updike's Rabbit is irresponsible. Yet he is far from being completely unlikable. An individualist, he refuses to accept his sorry plight and seeks instead to recover the lost glory and the ideal life he enjoyed as a basketball star. Like many writers, Updike portrays his character in gray; often we find ourselves sympathizing with Rabbit in spite of his immature qualities.

More difficult to reach some conclusion about is "the noblest Roman of them all," Brutus, whose traits we itemized earlier. What do they add up to? Do his honorable motives excuse his dishonorable act? Is his sincerity sufficient? Can a noble death compensate for ignoble deeds? The answers are not simple; great literary figures have the same complexity as real people.

So, as judge and jury, you should find for or against your characters, see them as complete human beings at the end of a literary work, and arrive at some verdict about them, just as you arrive at conclusions about your friends on the basis of your knowledge and observations of them.

How Credible Is the Character?

So far we have been concerned primarily with the nature of characters, suggesting a method for you to follow in analyzing what they are like. Our purpose is to enable you to understand the characters—and, of course, the work—better. Now we suggest that you consider how well the characters are depicted. Essentially, this requires that you determine how realistic they are.

Because this textbook is designed for a course in writing and not in literary study we shall skip over tricky theoretical problems about the nature of reality and suggest that in considering whether characters are credible and realistic, you apply some of the traditional, common-sense views about people: that they have motives for their actions, are reasonably consistent, and are essentially individualistic. Not all the characters in literature must demonstrate all three of these qualities, but the central character and other important ones should do so to be credible. Let's consider each of these aspects of credibility.

Motivation   Readers must be able to understand why characters act as they do. And actions must stem from probable causes, not possible ones. Life is stranger than fiction partly because people's true natures are hidden. Several times a year, for example, we read about gruesome murders committed by quiet young men who have led exemplary lives as Boy Scouts and Sunday School teachers. In literature, such characters would be unbelievable unless there was some previous suggestion of their potential hostility and violence. In other words, characters must be adequately motivated for readers to view them as credible.

Usually the crucial point for examining motivation occurs late in a work when the central character is confronted with a decisive choice. In popular escape literature—westerns, gangster and cop stories, cheap romances, and the like—often some accident occurs or some character changes for no valid reason. The villain suddenly turns good, allowing the hero to wed his sweetheart or kiss his horse and ride off into the sunset as virtue triumphs. Certainly, people may change in life, but if they do in literature, the transformation should occur over a period of time and the reasons should be both apparent and plausible. Generally speaking, selfish people just don't suddenly become unselfish—unless it's in their own self-interest to do so. But we can accept the change in a character like Arthur Dimmesdale in Hawthorne's *The Scarlet Letter,* having seen him wrestle with his conscience until finally, unable to bear his guilt any longer, he confesses his adultery from the pillory.

Consistency   Although characters may change, we still expect them to be as consistent as real people. Generally, we know how our friends will respond in new situations. Similarly, we should be able to anticipate what characters will usually do. In *Sons and Lovers,* we realize that Paul Morel cannot marry either Miriam or Clara because of his strong attachment to his mother. To be consistent, Paul cannot love anyone but her. While readers may prefer literature to end happily, it would have been out of character for Paul to marry Miriam or anyone else. Characters must be true to themselves: this consistency is necessary if they are to be credible.

Individuality   If consistency is carried too far, characters will lack the complexity necessary for individuality. People are born equal, but they are also born different. Good literature portrays people as individuals, bad literature as stereotypes. We can recognize them at a glance: the cleancut cowboy, the bearded villain, the mad scientist, the old-fashioned schoolmarm, the brusque businessman, and so on and on. Sometimes different stereotypes emerge: gangsters have been portrayed as loving family members (*The Godfather*), and police as alienated loners (*Serpico*).

Although in good literature central characters are complex individuals, most of the supporting and background characters usually cannot be treated in such great depth, particularly in brief works such as plays and short stories. But occasionally in longer works these characters are portrayed with such vividness, flavor, and intensity that they take on individuality.

Dickens' comic and satirical characters come readily to mind, as do other memorable figures like the Duke and King in *Huckleberry Finn* and Juliet's nurse in *Romeo and Juliet.*

PLOT (WHAT?)

The related actions or episodes in a literary work are called its *plot* (although this term is not generally applied to poetry). When someone asks us what a work is about, we tell them its story—its plot. But as a critical reader writing about literature, you should be able not only to summarize the plot but to analyze its structure.

The Elements of a Plot

Most plots follow the traditional pattern diagramed here:

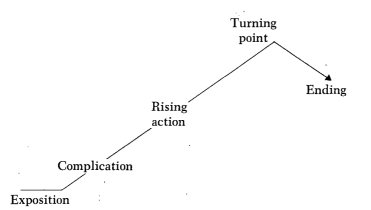

Let's first define the terms used in the diagram and then discuss and illustrate them.

1. Exposition: introduction of characters, establishment of relationships, setting of scene, creation of atmosphere, presentation of point of view.
2. Complication: the initial incident that creates some problem, conflict, difficulty, or change.
3. Rising action: the heightening of interest, excitement, or involvement as difficulties increase.
4. Turning point: the crisis or climax, the point of greatest emotion and interest, when the difficulty or problem is confronted and resolved.
5. Ending: explanation of events, how characters were affected, and what happened to them.

The *exposition* exposes you to the world of the literary work, providing information about the characters and their relationships, the setting, and the time. It allows you to discover where you are, who these people are, and what kind of physical, social, and cultural surroundings they live in. And, equally important, it informs you about the narrator's point of view.

The *complication* closely follows the exposition because readers require that some problem or conflict become apparent soon to stimulate interest. Thus the conspirators plan to kill Caesar, or Romeo and Juliet fall in love despite their feuding families. Something occurs or someone arrives to disrupt the routine and to intensify the lives of the characters.

Rising action is a term that describes the increased emotional effect created by additional events or ramifications of the original one. Theoretically, our interest rises as the action does. For example, in *Romeo and Juliet* we become more involved as major events occur: Romeo kills Tybalt, the wedding of Paris and Juliet draws near, Juliet swallows the potion, Romeo hears about her "death," Romeo kills Paris.

The *turning point,* or *crisis* as it is often called, is the decisive incident that resolves the problem or conflict. Usually the point or scene of greatest interest, it is exemplified in popular escape literature by the courtroom trial; the "let's re-create the crime" episode in detective stories; the big game, match, or meet in sports stories; the showdown at high noon in cowboy yarns; the shootout chase in cop films; and so on. It is the point of no return; once reached, the outcome is settled. The central character usually makes a choice from which there is no escape; Romeo drinks the poison, Laertes fatally wounds Hamlet, Dimmesdale confesses.

The *ending* may be presented in a paragraph, a page, a chapter, or more, depending on what is needed to explain previous events and to account for what happens later to various characters. It is used for tidying up, straightening out, unraveling, cleaning up. There may literally be dead bodies to be hauled away (four in *Hamlet*), or a death to be revealed (Huck's father), a marriage (Eppie to Aaron Winthrop in *Silas Marner*), or other events signaling a termination or resolution.

Of course, no formula can be applied to all literary works, and the preceding simple diagram does not provide for episodic plots, subplots involving supporting characters, and other complexities. And just as readers interpret literature differently, so they may differ in diagraming a plot's structure. It would be possible to show, for example, that the turning point of *A Separate Peace* occurs when Finney falls from the tree limb instead of when he falls down the stairs.

As mentioned, episodic plots are different, consisting of incidents involving a central character but with no rising action or turning point. Usually they are constructed around a central character who goes from adventure to adventure with little change, much like Lou Grant or Hawkeye Pierce in television serials, who never seem to be affected by their previous experiences.

Evaluation of a Plot

Having understood the plot and realized its structure, you should be ready to consider how skillfully it is conceived. Your evaluation should take into account such factors as foreshadowing, reliance on chance, unity, and the plausibility of the ending.

Foreshadowing The word *foreshadowing* becomes self-explanatory when you think of the way people's shadows can appear in front of them, so that others are alerted to their approach. In literature, foreshadowing is a device to prepare readers for what follows. It may take the form of a strange remark, a prophecy, or some foreboding note. The terrors of childhood in the opening section of *Portrait of the Artist as a Young Man* foreshadow the problems of young Stephen; the supernatural signs and warnings early in *Julius Caesar* foreshadow his fate. To what extent is foreshadowing necessary? Obviously, in a detective story in which a plumber kills a homeowner, you would feel cheated if you never heard of the plumber until the last chapter. As a rule of thumb, the greater the element of surprise in the story, the greater the need for foreshadowing.

Reliance on Chance Another factor to consider in evaluating the plot of a work is the extent to which authors rely on chance to manipulate the lives of characters. Chance may take the form of unusual and unpredictable occurrences (death, automobile accident, sudden fortune, and the like) or coincidences (unexpected meetings, lucky or unlucky timing, discovery of unknown relationships, and so on). While we realize that chance plays a role in all our lives and anything can happen to any of us at any time, we expect a literary world to be more probable than the real world. If fact is stranger than fiction, then fiction must be more normal than fact.

This does not entirely rule out chance from literature; it simply suggests that you question its use. Generally, chance may be accepted at the beginning of a work to develop the complication. And it should not be disapproved of in the rising action unless the author had unrealistically used death or some other device as a pat solution to some plot problem. There should be little concern, for example, that Jim O'Connor in Tennessee Williams' *The Glass Menagerie* turns out to be Laura's high-school idol, because this coincidence does not materially change the action in the play. But it is highly implausible that Pip's benefactor in Dickens' *Great Expectations* proves to be the escaped convict, and this coincidence does significantly affect what happens at the end of the novel.

Particularly at the turning point and the ending, we must deplore an author's resorting to chance. When one member of a romantic triangle is killed in an auto accident, when an unknown wealthy uncle dies leaving the desperately poor main character a fortune, or when the villain drowns, we should indeed find fault. Ideally, chance should play little or no role in a literary work. Characters should meet under certain circumstances and the work should unfold, generated from the conflict created by this initial situation.

But in literature chance may certainly play a major role when the author's intention is to show that chance is the controlling influence in the lives of people. In the novels of Thomas Hardy, for example, the forces of nature constantly plague men and women; strange, often improbable events and unlucky meetings also occur to spoil their happiness. In his works and those of writers with similar views, chance is almost the central character, playing a major role in affecting human destiny.

Unity   A third matter to consider in evaluating a plot is unity, whether all the episodes in a plot are necessary and contribute to its development. In popular escape literature and films, there is a tendency to add juicy sex scenes. We should ask whether they serve any function. Do they disclose something important about the characters involved, or are they included only to appeal to people's sexual instincts and thus to sell more copies or tickets? Generally, a work of literature should not contain digressions of any kind, unless included for some comic effect. The work should be as well unified as your themes.

Plausibility of the Ending   A final plot consideration is the ending of the work. It should be both logical—growing naturally out of what has gone before—and satisfying—concluding the issues raised in the work. You should be particularly wary of happy endings brought about illogically by chance or by sudden character transformations, like the convenient rehabil-itation of a drug addict or the sudden religious conversion of a hardened criminal. And you should question the use of marriage to end a plot happily. After all, how many weeks would you give Cinderella and the prince? Let's not settle for marriages in which the couple will probably live unhappily ever after.

In this section we have raised a number of issues to help you understand the structure of plots and to enable you to evaluate them better. Let's summarize this material in these questions you should ask about a literary work:

1. How effectively is the exposition handled?
2. What is the complication? What issues does it raise?
3. What other issues or problems are developed in the rising action?
4. Where is the turning point? What is resolved and how?
5. Are events, particularly surprising ones, properly foreshadowed?
6. What role does chance play? How acceptable is the use of chance?

7. Is the work unified? Are there scenes or characters that could be eliminated?
8. Is the ending logical and satisfying? Has the author resorted to chance or sudden character transformations to bring about the ending?

SETTING (WHERE?)

Every literary work takes place in a particular setting consisting of a physical place (house, community, region, country) and the beliefs and values (social, moral, economic, political, psychological) of the people there. In few works, if any, is setting insignificant, but its importance may vary considerably according to the extent of an author's belief that environment shapes and controls human lives or that a work should depict the manners and morals of people.

On a simple level, literary works derive a vivid sense of realism from the inclusion of descriptions of such details as the natural surroundings, the architecture of a house, the decor of rooms, and the dress and physical appearance of characters. Most authors supply enough graphic details so that readers can experience, for example, a battlefield in *The Red Badge of Courage,* the farm labor camps in *The Grapes of Wrath,* Harlem in *The Invisible Man,* and Civil War Tara in *Gone with the Wind.*

The setting can also create an atmosphere, playing on the feelings we experience about a location. In many of Edgar Allan Poe's short stories, the strange surroundings contribute greatly to the suspense and to the mood of gloom, melancholy, and apprehension. Emily Brontë's description of the moors and their wild storms in *Wuthering Heights* provides a background conducive to the tragic, tempestuous love of Heathcliff for Catherine.

The setting of a work can serve an even more important function: as a force in conflict with human desires and endeavors. Often the struggle is an emotional one between people and nature. In James Dickey's *Deliverance,* men battle the Cahulawassee River as well as one another, and in *The Old Man and the Sea,* Santiago fights nature and its creatures. In Thomas Hardy's *The Return of the Native,* Egdon Heath might be viewed as the central character, dominating the work as an evil force: some people are the heath's victims, dying from drowning and snakebite, while others become its disciples by practicing witchcraft and succumbing to the primitive emotions it evokes.

Setting is not confined to the physical location of a work; it also includes the human environment. Characters are born, raised, and live among other people. The values of these other people—in the family, the community, the schools, the churches, and businesses—may influence a character's behavior. As discerning readers, we should be aware of the part environment plays in shaping the characters' lives. The twentieth-century world of F.

Scott Fitzgerald's *The Great Gatsby* reflects a materialistic society that cares only about a person's wealth, not how it is obtained. Jay Gatsby is a product of his age; in another society he might have been a different person with different values.

Such considerations give rise to the following questions, all of which should be asked in evaluating the setting of a literary work.

1. Could the setting be changed without seriously affecting the work?
2. Does the setting contribute significantly to the lifelike quality of the work?
3. Does the setting contribute to the atmosphere of the work by establishing a particular mood?
4. Does the setting play an important role in shaping or controlling the lives of the characters?

TIME (WHEN?)

Time in a literary work is important in two respects: (1) the time sequence in which the author presents the story; and (2) the historical time (day, year, period, century) in which the characters live.

Authors may present stories either straight forward in natural chronological sequence or may use a flashback device. The former is obvious: the work begins at some point in time and continues to a later point. The flashback device is more complex, as it can be used in several ways. Often authors begin their stories at or near the ending, then flash back to earlier scenes. This happens in *The Catcher in the Rye* when Holden begins by talking about his sanitarium and then explains the preceding events that caused him to be sent there. A familiar opening flashback device is used in movies such as *To Kill a Mockingbird,* which starts with a courtroom scene to gain attention and heighten suspense, and then flashes back to reveal the reason for the murder trial.

Flashbacks may occur later in a story, following the *in medias res* ("in the middle of things") technique of the epics, such as the *Odyssey,* which begins with Odysseus returning home almost ten years after the Trojan War. Later in the work, he stops at a banquet to recount his many adventures during the nine preceding years. After this flashback, he continues his travels home, where numerous other trials and struggles confront him. Similarly, in *Wuthering Heights,* following the dramatic opening scene involving the strange members of the household and the weird events, a housekeeper relates in a flashback what had happened there many years before, providing an explanation for the apparition at the broken window. After her story about the three generations of the Earnshaw family, the novel continues.

An even more intricate use of the flashback occurs in other works when a character's mind at numerous times is triggered by some association to recall something or someone in the past. This occurs, for example, in Arthur Miller's play *Death of a Salesman,* where the action takes place in only two days. During this brief time, however, Willy Loman and others think about events as far back as sixteen years, which are represented on the stage but not in chronological order. The study of how and why an author handles time may not be as interesting or significant as it is in this play, yet you should always consider it in analyzing a literary work.

The second important use of time is the age or period when the action occurs. Kurt Vonnegut, Jr., a prisoner of war in Dresden, Germany, when it was fire-bombed by American planes in 1945, included this incident in his 1969 novel *Slaughterhouse-Five* as the kind of senseless apocalyptic event that typifies human experience and may well bring about the end of the world. The time of the action in *A Separate Peace* is similarly significant because Gene's aggression toward Finney parallels the aggression between nations in the Second World War, which disrupts the peacefulness of the isolated prep school and affects the lives of all its students.

An author must decide both how to handle time in the work and at what time to set the action. By considering the following questions, you should understand the significance of both:

1. How does the author handle the movement of time in the novel? Which of the two main time sequences is used—chronological or flashback? What are its advantages or disadvantages?
2. In what period of time does the work take place? What difference would it make if the work were set in another time? What is the significance of its being set at that time?

THEME (WHY?)

Authors may write for money, fame, self-fulfillment, or other reasons, but what they write expresses some idea about the human condition. This theme may be stated directly or indirectly, it may be philosophical, psychological, or social, and it may be revealed by an examination of the characters, plot, setting, or some other aspect of the work. The question "Why?" as it applies to literary analysis commits you to examine the ideas, particularly the main idea, in a work to determine what statement it makes about life. Does every work contain some such statement? If so, how do you discern it?

Even the simplest nursery rhyme or story can have a thematic message: "Jack and Jill" shows how dangerous life's routines can be; "Little Red Riding Hood" indicates the need for vigilance against disguised evil. Every work, no matter how slight, contains some basic observation about the nature of people, the freedom of the individual, the opportunity for happiness, the role of society, the importance of love, the discovery of self, the existence of evil, or some other aspect. On a simple level, if the central character finds happiness, then the view of life is optimistic; if not, it is pessimistic. But usually it is far more important to analyze *why* and *how* the work ends as it does rather than merely to note the ending.

The theme grows out of the ending—or, more specifically, out of how the turning point is resolved. Often at this point, either the action may exemplify the central idea or a favorably presented character may express it. In *The Grapes of Wrath*, Tom Joad talks to his mother about the universal soul after the Christ-like preacher Casy has been murdered.

> Guess who I been thinkin' about? Casy! He talked a lot. Used ta bother me. But now I been thinkin' what he said, an' I can remember—all of it. Says one time he went out in the wilderness to find his own soul, an' he foun' he didn' have no soul that was his'n. Says he foun' he jus got a little piece of a great big soul. Says a wilderness ain't no good, 'cause his little piece of a soul wasn't no good 'less it was with the rest, an' was whole. Funny how I remember. Didn' think I was even listenin'. But I know now a fella ain't no good alone.

In Anthony Burgess' *A Clockwork Orange*, an admirable minor character (the husband of the raped woman) utters the thematic statement to Alex, the central character:

> You've sinned, I suppose, but your punishment has been out of all proportion. They have turned you into something other than a human being. You have no power of choice any longer. You are committed to socially acceptable acts, a little machine capable only of good. . . . A man who cannot choose ceases to be a man.

Thus, thematic statements usually are expressed by characters who are portrayed favorably, whether the central character or some other, including the omniscient narrator. Occasionally, the theme may be stated or reinforced ironically by an unattractive character. For example, when the odious Bounderby in Dickens' *Hard Times* argues strongly in favor of all work and no play and deplores anything that appeals to the imagination instead of the reason, the reader realizes that almost the opposite is being advocated.

How do you come to such a realization? And how can you support your opinion about a work's theme?

Nearly everything within a work should point to and contribute to the theme. In *The Grapes of Wrath*, Tom's statement, quoted previously, sums up the change from the Joad family's concern only for themselves to concern for others: first for the Wilsons, then for the people in the government camp, and finally in Rose of Sharon's giving the milk of her breast to the starving stranger. In *Hard Times*, Bounderby is exposed as a cruel man and a fraud, and as a result of his daughter's unhappiness, his son's crime, and the kindness of Sissy and the circus people, Tom Gradgrind realizes that there is more to life than learning facts. Just as you can check an answer in algebra, you can check a theme in literature by applying it to incidents and character changes. And quite often in literature the theme will be suggested symbolically or literally in the title (*The Red Badge of Courage, Pride and Prejudice, For Whom the Bell Tolls*).

In some works, thematic ideas are not stated by characters or suggested in titles. What then? Your task is more difficult—but not impossible. Asking yourself these questions should help:

1. What happens to the central character and why?
2. Was what happened the character's own fault or due to forces beyond control?
3. If it was the character's own fault, what weakness did it reveal?
4. If the character overcame the difficulty, what new realization or trait did the resolution require?
5. Did other characters have similar problems? What do their actions reveal?
6. If the central character's problem cannot be attributed to human weakness, what was it due to?
7. Can this force be overcome? If so, how? If not, how can human beings cope with it?
8. Are people portrayed as basically evil or good, selfish or unselfish, kind or cruel?
9. Do the characters find happiness? If not, why not? If so, why? How?
10. Is nature favorable or unfavorable to people?
11. Does the literary work make any statement about ethical, religious, economic, social, political matters?
12. Does the work provide any insight into psychological problems about sex, love, death, guilt, alienation, and so forth?

Applying these and similar questions to a work to perceive its ideas should help, but you must be cautious in deciding on answers. Remember that a work—particularly a novel—may contain numerous ideas, but the theme is like a thread, tying together most of what occurs. *The Grapes of Wrath,* for example, contains numerous views about big business, charities, religion, private ownership of property, and the role of the government. But only the theme of human community runs throughout and sums up the entire work.

In deciding on a theme or stating it, you should avoid the imperative. The theme is not a moral, a commandment, a directive about how to live or what to do. Rather, it is a statement about life and people, an observation, a pronouncement, a verdict. Ralph Ellison's *The Invisible Man* points out how white people fail to see and treat blacks as human beings, using and exploiting them instead. George Orwell's *1984* shows how the human desires for love, freedom, and dignity can be eliminated or suppressed in a totalitarian society that controls communication and technology. And the theme of

Robert Frost's poem "The Road Not Taken" is that a choice made at a crucial point in life may affect everything that happens to one afterward. These works are not sermons exhorting us to action. They are representations of people and life that we may not have experienced before. We should, therefore, enjoy the literary work as we enjoy other experiences; but at the same time we should become wiser from reading it just as we become wiser from our significant real-life experiences.

Of all the elements in a literary work, the theme is the most difficult to perceive. The problem stems from the work's presentation of specifics: certain characters in certain places at certain times engaged in certain actions. On the other hand, the theme is an abstraction, a generalization. Consequently, you need to consider all the other elements in a work to arrive at its theme. You should do this cautiously, testing your conclusion against specific characters and events in the work. Only when you have done this thoroughly should you feel confident about your interpretation.

TECHNIQUE (HOW?)

No analysis of a literary work would be complete without a study of the writer's technique, the artistic devices that shape the content. There are too many of these devices to include here, so we shall limit our discussion to three: point of view, irony, and symbolism.

Point of View

In writing a story, the author must decide whether to narrate (tell) it in the first person, as one of the characters, or in the third person, either as a character involved in the plot or as a narrator outside of it.

First Person The first-person point of view is easily recognized by the recurrent use of "I," the voice being that of a character, not the author, telling the story. Sometimes you may tend to equate the "I" with the author, but you should resist this inclination, realizing the clear distinction between authors, who write stories, and characters, who tell them. Often this difference is clear, as in the following example from the beginning of Mark Twain's *Huckleberry Finn:*

You don't know about me without you have read a book by the name of *The Adventures of Tom Sawyer;* but that ain't no matter. That book was made by Mr. Mark Twain, and he told the truth, mainly. There was things which he stretched, but mainly he told the truth.

Like Huck Finn, first-person narrators are characters and should be analyzed like other characters. When the "I" narrator is the main character, you should be especially careful to determine whether that person's views are reliable. For example, in the fourth book of Jonathan Swift's *Gulliver's Travels,* Gulliver relates his adventures in the land of the horses, whom he admires because they base their lives and society on reason, excluding any emotion. Gulliver presents them as far superior to the human-like creatures in that country who live solely by their emotions. But a close reading of the ending reveals that Gulliver is an unreliable narrator, truly gullible, because the evidence there indicates that the rational horses are also flawed. Society needs a balanced combination of reason and emotion.

Our previous examples may have erroneously suggested that the "I" narrator is always the central character. Often an author uses a minor character, as Joseph Conrad does in *Lord Jim* and *Heart of Darkness,* both told mainly by Marlowe; or as F. Scott Fitzgerald does in *The Great Gatsby,* related by Nick Carraway. When such minor characters narrate the story, you must determine not only their reliability but also the plausibility of their being present at various scenes and their knowing what they do about the other characters. For example, you might question whether Nick Carraway becomes the confidant of nearly everyone because he is so likable and trustworthy or whether Fitzgerald contrived these convenient relationships so Nick could tell the story.

The advantage of the first-person point of view is that the story appears to be real because it seems autobiographical in its presentation. The disadvantage is that the writer is limited to relating what the "I" character can naturally see, understand, and be in a position to witness, either as the central character in the story or a minor one.

Third Person   The third-person point of view is handled in one of two ways: the *omniscient* (all-knowing) or the *limited* narrator. In the omniscient form, the godlike narrator observes all the action and describes all the thoughts and feelings of the characters, using third-person pronouns or proper nouns throughout ("he felt," "she thought," "Bill was astonished"). Of course, when the characters speak, they do so with the first person "I," but otherwise the narrator uses the third person as in the characterization of Bounderby (see page 365).

This omniscient point of view is the oldest and most common way to tell a story. You would use it in relating a joke or anecdote in which you played no part. Its advantages are its convenience and freedom. As author, you can tell your readers whatever you wish—you can present the ideas, feelings, beliefs, motivations, and deeds of all the characters, without any limitations. Its disadvantage is that readers become aware that someone outside the story is telling it. As a result, some readers find it difficult to lose themselves in the fictional world, hearing always the voice of the storyteller telling the tale.

This advantage is eliminated in the limited third-person point of view. By telling the story through the mind and eyes of one character, authors remove an outside narrator from their work, and create the authenticity and realism of life. In such a story, you watch people and events from the viewpoint of a single person, just as you yourself might experience them. In the following example, for instance, the first sentence of Irwin Shaw's short story "The Eighty Yard Run," you become part of the action.

The pass was high and wide and he jumped for it, feeling it slap flatly against his hands, as he shook his hips to throw off the halfback who was diving at him.

You should be warned, however, that from the first sentence alone, you could not accurately discern whether an author is using the third-person omniscient or limited point of view. But because Shaw tells the entire story through the football player's mind, the point of view is limited. If Shaw had informed his readers what other characters were thinking and feeling, then the point of view would be omniscient.

A further word of caution: when omniscient narrators tell a story, you should not automatically assume that they represent the author, although they usually do. But you should determine their reliability just as you should with first-person and limited third-person narrators. Remember once again that authors create and narrators narrate. As a reader, you must distinguish between them.

Another complexity stems from the fact that some writers combine point-of-view techniques. In *Lord Jim,* Conrad uses an omniscient narrator and a first-person narrator. In *Emma,* Jane Austen tells nearly all the story through the limited third-person viewpoint of Emma, her central character, but switches (in one chapter) near the end to the viewpoint of another character. Understanding the function of these and similar changes, as well as being aware of the way authors generally have handled point of view in their stories, can lead to greater insight and better understanding of literary works.

In dealing with point of view in a story or novel, you might consider these questions:

1. Has the author used the first-person point of view? If so, is the narrator a major or minor character? If not, has the author chosen the omniscient or limited form of the third-person point of view?
2. What is the function or particular effect of the point of view?
3. What personal traits and ethical standards does the narrator have?
4. Is it plausible for the narrator to know and see what he or she does?
5. Is the narrator reliable and trustworthy?

Irony

Irony is achieved by incongruity: a pairing of opposites or perspectives, one of which may mask or reveal the real truth. It can be created by relying on a single statement (verbal irony). Or language and situation may work together to create it (situational irony).

Related to sarcasm and innuendo, verbal irony can be achieved through understatement or exaggeration. Sometimes the writer uses words of praise to imply criticism or censure, much as you may do when you say to a boastful friend, "Don't be so modest!" In situations such as this, irony is distinguished from sarcasm mainly by tone: the tone of irony is wryly humorous; sarcasm is biting and sharp. Another technique for creating verbal irony is through a reversal or twist; the writer, by exploiting the connotations inherent in the language, creates an expectation of one thing, then presents the opposite—as this student poem shows:

> Coke
> Cold, good,
> Refreshing, reviving, quenching,
> Drive-ins, picnics, snacks, all the good times,
> Pimples.

Situational irony often depends upon the interplay of language and event; in such cases ambiguity plays an important role. For instance, in *Oedipus Rex,* the blind seer speaks in ambiguous riddles to Oedipus—"Today you will see your birth and your destruction"—making an ironic play on the word *see.* The riddle masks the real meaning that Oedipus' true identity, his birthplace and his parents, will be revealed (seen) and he will realize that he has murdered his father and committed incest with his mother. At another level, the word *see* ironically reminds the audience, already familiar with the legend, that Oedipus will lose his sight. When he finally "sees" what he has done, he blinds himself.

Dramatic irony can be enhanced by the language use of verbal and situational irony throughout the story. In Ibsen's *A Doll's House,* for instance, the central irony results from the fact that Nora's loving sacrifice for her husband Torvald leads unexpectedly to her disillusionment in him. This change is reinforced by frequent verbal and situational irony, such as Torvald's fatuous praise of Nora's industry in creating Christmas ornaments for the family—an activity that becomes offensive to him when he discovers she has been selling them to repay an illegal loan.

As you can see, irony, like other literary devices, does more than contribute to tone; it becomes an integral part of the meaning of the work as well. Other language devices not only serve this dual function but also become tools for creating imagery.

Symbolism

Symbols are not restricted to literature: humans are symbol-making creatures, and symbols play an important role in our everyday lives. In addition to the symbolic characteristics of language itself, we are surrounded by objects that have taken on abstract meaning and value. A wedding ring, for instance, is a widely accepted symbol in our culture: its meaning moves out from our literal, concrete concept of it as a circular finger band made of silver or gold to a symbol of marriage and all its attendant connotations and values—love, marital happiness, close companionship, fidelity, family, romance, commitment. Even colors become symbolic: red in our society is associated with heat, anger, passion; white with innocence and purity; green with life and growth. These are some of the many symbolic associations shared by most people in our society; these are called *public symbols.*

Literary writers use such public symbols, but they also create *private symbols,* which are significant to the particular work: the green light on Daisy's dock across the bay in *The Great Gatsby* suggests Gatsby's will-o'-the-wisp search for acceptance in high society; the shark who battles the old fisherman for his catch in Ernest Hemingway's *The Old Man and the Sea* becomes representative of the forces of nature against which humans must often pit themselves. The writer creates these private symbols to achieve a particular purpose and transmits their imaginative meanings to the reader by situation or association with certain characters or behavior. But to be effective, these private symbols must have some relationship to public ones; otherwise, they may have meaning only to the writer. Also, to be effective, they must be part of the realistic telling of the story: the shark is a natural predator in the waters where the old man fishes; thus the attack is a logical possibility as well as being representative of the symbolic associations of survival of the fittest, struggle for existence, and human encounter with unpredictable and overwhelming problems. If private symbols are well conceived, you as a reader will not need to go on a symbol hunt; they will make themselves known to you as you read. But to confirm their presence, be aware how they're used each time—what the circumstances are, what characters are involved—so that you can realize all the possible levels of meaning.

Occasionally, in a literary work, a symbol will be so important and dominant that it becomes a central, unifying force. In Conrad's *Lord Jim,* Stein's butterfly-collecting mania supplies the central symbol for the novel: the butterfly chase becomes symbolic of the romantic striving for an elusive and unattainable ideal—the striving that brings about Jim's destruction. Occasionally, the title of a work gives a clue to the central symbol: Joseph Heller's title *Catch-22,* for instance, refers to a fictitious Air Force rule that by the end of the novel has become a symbol of the stupid workings of bureaucracy and the frustration of trying to cope logically and reasonably with the corporate mind. Thus the central symbol can be used to communicate the writer's "message" in a way very similar to the operation of a shortened syllogism—by permitting the reader to supply the missing material and the logical connections.

SUMMARY

In this chapter we have presented a method for you to follow in writing papers about literature. The "who-what-where-when-why-how" approach is certainly not the only effective one, nor has our discussion of its various elements been complete. We have not had space to discuss myth criticism or other approaches, for example. But now you do have a simple, clear, and handy way to analyze a literary work, to develop stimulating theme subjects, and to write interesting, informative critical papers. Our purpose in this chapter was not to involve you in literary study as such. If you enjoy reading and discussing stories, plays, and poems, we suggest that you enroll in an introduction to literature course or one of the other literature courses offered by your English Department. Our purpose was to help you to understand literature in order to write more intelligently and effectively about it.

Assignments

For Discussion

1 Consider the following passages, taken from literary works and representative of the narrative device used in each. Identify the kind of narrative point of view used in each.

a Gene's brow wrinkled again in irritation; he thought she was deliberately not helping him, whereas in truth she did not know he wanted her help.
"The point is, Mother, I haven't the money to go."
Now for something as important to him as this Ruth would never have denied him the money, and Gene knew it. But Ruth herself did not know it, though he thought she did. He thought not only that she knew it but that the long process of reasoning herself into it, which she always went through, was a method of reproaching him. She had nothing like reproach in her mind; though she did not know it she was providing her conscience with good reasons for giving this money to him.
—George P. Elliott, "Children of Ruth"

b Yesterday afternoon the six-o'clock bus ran over Miss Bobbit. I'm not sure what there is to be said about it; after all, she was only ten years old, still I know no one of us in this town will forget her. For one thing, nothing she ever did was ordinary, not from the first time that we saw her, and that was a year ago. Miss Bobbit and her mother, they arrived on that same six-o'clock bus, the one that comes through from Mobile. It happened to be my cousin Billy Bob's birthday, and so most of the children in town were here at our house. We were sprawled on the front porch having tutti-frutti and devil cake when the bus stormed around Deadman's Curve. It was the summer that never rained; rusted dryness coated everything; sometimes when a car passed on the road, raised dust would hang in the still air an hour or more. Aunt El said if they didn't pave the highway soon she was going to move down to the seacoast; but she'd said that for such a long time. Anyway, we were sitting on the porch, tutti-frutti melting on our plates, when suddenly, just as we were wishing that something would happen, something did; for out of the red road dust appeared Miss Bobbit. A wiry little girl in a starched, lemon-colored party dress, she sassed along with a grownup mince, one hand on her hip, the other supporting a spinsterish umbrella. Her mother, lugging two cardboard valises and a wind-up victrola, trailed in the background. She was a gaunt shaggy woman with silent eyes and a hungry smile.

—Truman Capote, "Children on Their Birthdays"

c But though my mother and I felt that I was fulfilling my part of the bargain all right, Lothar Swift's promise that I would go to Chicago with the band seemed far less reliable. There were rumors going around that he was having plenty of trouble raising money to move his horde so far, let alone to shelter them once he got them to the city.

Presently a form letter came for me. It said that band members had been put on either an *A* list or a *B* list, according to merit. While it was still the band's intention to pay travel and lodging expenses for all its members, it appeared necessary to ask that all *B* members sell two excursion tickets to "band supporters" who might wish to go along to Chicago. The tickets cost $47.50 apiece: Naturally, of course, I was on the *B* list.

—R. V. Cassill, "The Biggest Band"

d Tom remembered that outside the hospital under the stone and brick carriage porch of the *Sanitarium,* on the newly curving and richly planted driveway which the old self-taught doctor had just had redone commemorating that his one son had just graduated from Harvard Medical School, the men had shouldered into their topcoats in the chilly September night and got into their cars, switched on their lights and pulled away. His father had been the last to pull away, in his brand new Studebaker. As he did, his wife, Tom's mother, had begun to sob and cry again. She had hated the old man, the grandfather, ever since she had first met him; and he had equally disliked and detested her. Tom and his sister had whispered together in the backseat about this new state of things where they were no longer grandchildren. They knew all about the active dislike between their mother and the grandfather, since she had told them over and over how miserable and unhappy he made her life having to live so close to him, so they did not put too much stock in her weeping and grief. They were much more interested in where people went when they died.

—James Jones, "The Ice-Cream Headache"

2 In his play *Desire Under the Elms*, Eugene O'Neill gives an explicit, detailed description of the setting he wishes for the play and for each scene. Here is the setting description for the opening scene, followed by the appearance of one of the main characters. What can you surmise from it about O'Neill's use of setting in the play?

Exterior of the farmhouse. It is sunset of a day at the beginning of the summer in the year 1850. There is no wind and everything is still. The sky above the roof is suffused with deep colors, the green of the elms glows, but the house is in shadow, seeming pale and washed out by contrast.

A door opens and EBEN CABOT *comes to the end of the porch and stands looking down the road to the right. He has a large bell in his hand and this he swings mechanically, awakening a deafening clangor. Then he puts his hands on his hips and stares up at the sky. He sighs with a puzzled awe and blurts out with halting appreciation.*

EBEN. God! Purty!

He spits on the ground with intense disgust, turns and goes back into the house.

Special Topics

SUBJECTS FOR A CRITICAL PAPER

In the last chapter, we discussed in general terms the ways you can go about analyzing literature: points to consider, questions to ask yourself as you read. Now, let's tackle a specific assignment together to see how you should proceed. First read this short story by Guy de Maupassant, a famous nineteenth-century French writer.

THE NECKLACE

Guy de Maupassant

She was one of those pretty and charming girls who are sometimes, as if by a mistake of destiny, born in a family of clerks. She had no dowry, no expectations, no means of being known, understood, loved, wedded by any rich and distinguished man; and she let herself be married to a little clerk at the Ministry of Public Instruction.

She dressed plainly because she could not dress well, but she was as unhappy as though she had really fallen from her proper station, since with women there is neither caste nor rank; and beauty, grace, and charm act instead of family and birth. Natural fineness, instinct for what is elegant, suppleness of wit, are the sole hierarchy, and make from women of the people the equals of the very greatest ladies.

She suffered ceaselessly, feeling herself born for all the delicacies and all the luxuries. She suffered from the poverty of her dwelling, from the wretched look of the walls, from the worn-out chairs, from the ugliness of the curtains. All those things, of which another woman of her rank would never even have been conscious, tortured her and made her angry. The sight of the little Breton peasant who did her humble housework aroused in her regrets which were despairing, and distracted dreams. She thought of the silent antechambers hung with Oriental tapestry, lit by tall bronze candelabra, and of the two great footmen in knee breeches who sleep in the big armchairs, made drowsy by the heavy warmth of the hot-air stove. She thought of the long *salons* fitted up with ancient silk, of the delicate furniture carrying priceless curiosities, and of the coquettish perfumed boudoirs made for talks at five o'clock with intimate friends, with men famous and sought after, whom all women envy and whose attention they all desire.

When she sat down to dinner, before the round table covered with a table-cloth three days old, opposite her husband, who uncovered the soup tureen and declared with an enchanted air, "Ah, the good *pot-au-feu!* I don't know anything better than that," she thought of dainty dinners, of shining silverware, of tapestry which peopled the walls with ancient personages and with strange birds flying in the midst of a fairy forest; and she thought of delicious dishes served on marvelous plates, and of the whispered gallantries which you listen to with a sphinxlike smile, while you are eating the pink flesh of a trout or the wings of a quail.

She had no dresses, no jewels, nothing. And she loved nothing but that; she felt made for that. She would so have liked to please, to be envied, to be charming, to be sought after.

She had a friend, a former schoolmate at the convent, who was rich, and whom she did not like to go and see any more, because she suffered so much when she came back.

But one evening, her husband returned home with a triumphant air, and holding a large envelope in his hand.

"There," said he. "Here is something for you."

She tore the paper sharply, and drew out a printed card which bore these words:

"The Minister of Public Instruction and Mme. Georges Ramponneau request the honor of M. and Mme. Loisel's company at the palace of the Ministry on Monday evening, January eighteenth."

Instead of being delighted, as her husband hoped, she threw the invitation on the table with disdain, murmuring:

"What do you want me to do with that?"

"But, my dear, I thought you would be glad. You never go out, and this is such a fine opportunity. I had awful trouble to get it. Everyone wants to go; it is very select, and they are not giving many invitations to clerks. The whole official world will be there."

She looked at him with an irritated eye, and she said, impatiently:

"And what do you want me to put on my back?"

He had not thought of that; he stammered:

"Why, the dress you go to the theater in. It looks very well, to me."

He stopped, distracted, seeing that his wife was crying. Two great tears descended slowly from the corners of her eyes toward the corners of her mouth. He stuttered:

"What's the matter? What's the matter?"

But, by violent effort, she had conquered her grief, and she replied, with a calm voice, while she wiped her wet cheeks:

"Nothing. Only I have no dress and therefore I can't go to this ball. Give your card to some colleague whose wife is better equipped than I."

He was in despair. He resumed:

"Come, let us see, Mathilde. How much would it cost, a suitable dress, which you could use on other occasions, something very simple?"

She reflected several seconds, making her calculations and wondering also what sum she could ask without drawing on herself an immediate refusal and a frightened exclamation from the economical clerk.

Finally, she replied, hesitatingly:

"I don't know exactly, but I think I could manage it with four hundred francs."

He had grown a little pale, because he was laying aside just that amount to buy a gun and treat himself to a little shooting next summer on the plain of Nanterre, with several friends who went to shoot larks down there, of a Sunday.

But he said:

"All right. I will give you four hundred francs. And try to have a pretty dress."

The day of the ball drew near, and Mme. Loisel seemed sad, uneasy, anxious. Her dress was ready, however. Her husband said to her one evening:

"What is the matter? Come, you've been so queer these last three days."

And she answered:

"It annoys me not to have a single jewel, not a single stone, nothing to put on. I shall look like distress. I should almost rather not go at all."

He resumed:

"You might wear natural flowers. It's very stylish at this time of the year. For ten francs you can get two or three magnificent roses."

She was not convinced.

"No; there's nothing more humiliating than to look poor among other women who are rich."

But her husband cried:

"How stupid you are! Go look up your friend Mme. Forestier, and ask her to lend you some jewels. You're quite thick enough with her to do that."

She uttered a cry of joy:

"It's true. I never thought of it."

The next day she went to her friend and told of her distress.

Mme. Forestier went to a wardrobe with a glass door, took out a large jewel-box, brought it back, opened it, and said to Mme. Loisel:

"Choose, my dear."

She saw first of all some bracelets, then a pearl necklace, then a Venetian cross, gold and precious stones of admirable workmanship. She tried on the ornaments before the glass, hesitated, could not make up her mind to part with them, to give them back. She kept asking:

"Haven't you any more?"

"Why, yes. Look. I don't know what you like."

All of a sudden she discovered, in a black satin box, a superb necklace of diamonds, and her heart began to beat with an immoderate desire. Her hands trembled as she took it. She fastened it around her throat, outside her high-necked dress, and remained lost in ecstasy at the sight of herself.

Then she asked, hesitating, filled with anguish:

"Can you lend me that, only that?"

"Why, yes, certainly."

She sprang upon the neck of her friend, kissed her passionately, then fled with her treasure.

The day of the ball arrived. Mme. Loisel made a great success. She was prettier than them all, elegant, gracious, smiling, and crazy with joy. All the men looked at her, asked her name, endeavored to be introduced. All the attachés of the Cabinet wanted to waltz with her. She was remarked by the minister himself.

She danced with intoxication, with passion, made drunk by pleasure, forgetting all, in the triumph of her beauty, in the glory of her success, in a sort of cloud of happiness composed of all this homage, of all this admiration, of all these awakened desires, and of that sense of complete victory which is so sweet to a woman's heart.

She went away about four o'clock in the morning. Her husband had been sleeping since midnight, in a little deserted anteroom, with three other gentlemen whose wives were having a very good time. He threw over her shoulders the wraps which he had brought, modest wraps of common life, whose poverty contrasted with the elegance of the ball dress. She felt this, and wanted to escape so as not to be remarked by the other women, who were enveloping themselves in costly furs.

Loisel held her back.

"Wait a bit. You will catch cold outside. I will go and call a cab."

But she did not listen to him, and rapidly descended the stairs. When they were in the street they did not find a carriage; and they began to look for one, shouting after the cabmen whom they saw passing by at a distance.

They went down toward the Seine, in despair, shivering with cold. At last they found on the quay one of those ancient noctambulant coupés which, exactly as if they were ashamed to show their misery during the day, are never seen round Paris until after nightfall.

It took them to their door in the Rue des Martyrs, and once more, sadly, they climbed up homeward. All was ended, for her. And as to him, he reflected that he must be at the Ministry at ten o'clock.

She removed the wraps, which covered her shoulders, before the glass, so as once more to see herself in all her glory. But suddenly she uttered a cry. She had no longer the necklace around her neck!

Her husband, already half undressed, demanded:

"What is the matter with you?"

She turned madly towards him:

"I have—I have—I've lost Mme. Forestier's necklace."

He stood up, distracted.

"What!—how?—impossible!"

And they looked in the folds of her dress, in the folds of her cloak, in her pockets, everywhere. They did not find it.

He asked:

"You're sure you had it on when you left the ball?"

"Yes, I felt it in the vestibule of the palace."

"But if you had lost it in the street we should have heard it fall. It must be in the cab."

"Yes. Probably. Did you take his number?"

"No. And you, didn't you notice it?"

"No."

They looked, thunderstruck, at one another. At last Loisel put on his clothes.

"I shall go back on foot," said he, "over the whole route which we have taken to see if I can find it."

And he went out. She sat waiting on a chair in her ball dress, without strength to go to bed, overwhelmed, without fire, without a thought.

Her husband came back about seven o'clock. He had found nothing.

He went to Police Headquarters, to the newspaper offices, to offer a reward; he went to the cab companies—everywhere, in fact, whither he was urged by the least suspicion of hope.

She waited all day, in the same condition of mad fear before this terrible calamity.

Loisel returned at night with a hollow, pale face; he had discovered nothing.

"You must write to your friend," said he, "that you have broken the clasp of her necklace and that you are having it mended. That will give us time to turn round."

She wrote at his dictation.

At the end of a week they had lost all hope.

And Loisel, who had aged five years, declared:

"We must consider how to replace that ornament."

The next day they took the box which had contained it, and they went to the jeweler whose name was found within. He consulted his books.

"It was not I, madame, who sold that necklace; I must simply have furnished the case."

Then they went from jeweler to jeweler, searching for a necklace like the other, consulting their memories, sick both of them with chagrin and anguish.

They found, in a shop at the Palais Royal, a string of diamonds which seemed to them exactly like the one they looked for. It was worth forty thousand francs. They could have it for thirty-six.

So they begged the jeweler not to sell it for three days yet. And they made a bargain that he should buy it back for thirty-four thousand francs, in case they found the other one before the end of February.

Loisel possessed eighteen thousand francs which his father had left him. He would borrow the rest.

He did borrow, asking a thousand francs of one, five hundred of another, five louis here, three louis there. He gave notes, took up ruinous obligations, dealt with usurers and all the race of lenders. He compromised all the rest of his life, risked his signature without even knowing if he could meet it; and, frightened by the pains yet to come, by the black misery which was about to fall upon him, by the prospect of all the physical privations and of all the moral tortures which he was to suffer, he went to get the new necklace, putting down upon the merchant's counter thirty-six thousand francs.

When Mme. Loisel took back the necklace, Mme. Forestier said to her, with a chilly manner:

"You should have returned it sooner; I might have needed it."

She did not open the case, as her friend had so much feared. If she had detected the substitution, what would she have thought, what would she have said? Would she not have taken Mme. Loisel for a thief?

Mme. Loisel now knew the horrible existence of the needy. She took her part, moreover, all of a sudden, with heroism. That dreadful debt must be paid. She would pay it. They dismissed their servant; they changed their lodgings; they rented a garret under the roof.

She came to know what heavy housework meant and the odious cares of the kitchen. She washed the dishes, using her rosy nails on the greasy pots and pans. She washed the dirty linen, the shirts, and the dishcloths, which she dried upon a line; she carried the slops down to the street every morning, and carried up the water, stopping for breath at every landing. And, dressed like a woman of the people, she went to the fruiterer, the grocer, the butcher, her basket on her arm, bargaining, insulted, defending her miserable money sou by sou.

Each month they had to meet some notes, renew others, obtain more time.

Her husband worked in the evening making a fair copy of some tradesman's accounts, and late at night he often copied manuscript for five sous a page.

And this life lasted for ten years.

At the end of ten years, they had paid everything, everything, with the rates of usury, and the accumulations of the compound interest.

Mme. Loisel looked old now. She had become the woman of impoverished households—strong and hard and rough. With frowsy hair, skirts askew, and red hands, she talked loud while washing the floor with great swishes of water. But sometimes, when her husband was at the office, she sat down near the window, and she thought of that gay evening of long ago, of that ball where she had been so beautiful and so fêted.

What would have happened if she had not lost that necklace? Who knows? Who knows? How life is strange and changeful! How little a thing is needed for us to be lost or to be saved!

But, one Sunday, having gone to take a walk in the Champs Elysées to refresh herself from the labor of the week, she suddenly perceived a woman who was leading a child. It was Mme. Forestier, still young, still beautiful, still charming.

Mme. Loisel felt moved. Was she going to speak to her? Yes, certainly. And now that she had paid, she was going to tell her all about it. Why not?

She went up.

"Good-day, Jeanne."

The other, astonished to be familiarly addressed by this plain goodwife, did not recognize her at all, and stammered:

"But—madam!—I do not know—You must be mistaken."

"No. I am Mathilde Loisel."

Her friend uttered a cry.

"Oh, my poor Mathilde! How you are changed!"

"Yes, I have had days hard enough, since I have seen you, days wretched enough—and that because of you!"

"Of me! How so?"

"Do you remember that diamond necklace which you lent me to wear at the ministerial ball?"

"Yes. Well?"

"Well, I lost it."

"What do you mean? You brought it back."

"I brought you back another just like it. And for this we have been ten years paying. You can understand that it was not easy for us, us who had nothing. At last it is ended, and I am very glad."

Mme. Forestier had stopped.

"You say that you bought a necklace of diamonds to replace mine?"

"Yes. You never noticed it, then! They were very like."

And she smiled with a joy which was proud and naïve at once.

Mme. Forestier, strongly moved, took her two hands.

"Oh, my poor Mathilde! Why, my necklace was paste. It was worth at most five hundred francs!"

If you were asked to write a paper on Maupassant's story, what possible subjects could you consider? We shall suggest several here by following our "who-what-where-when-why-how" approach, but you should realize that a longer and more complex literary work like a novel or play would provide more fruitful and numerous topics.

A Paper About Character (Who?)

1. *The character sketch*

   An analysis of the central or major character, pointing out traits, discussing motivation, arriving at an overall evaluation, and commenting on Maupassant's skill or lack of it in depicting the character.

Examples: "Mme. Loisel—Pride Goeth after the Loss"
"Character Growth in Mme. Loisel"

2. *The function of a secondary character*

Examples: "The Plausibility of the Wealthy Friend"
"The Role of M. Loisel"

3. *Character comparison*
A description of two characters to show how they are similar or different, and an exploration of the relationship between them.

Examples: "M. and Mme. Loisel—Realist and Romanticist?"
"Mme. Loisel and Mme. Forestier—Contrast in Values"

4. *The values of the central character*
An analysis of the central character's attitudes toward people and life, to provide a better understanding of her nature or actions.

Examples: "Mme. Loisel's Desire for Status"
"Materialism Today and Mme. Loisel"

5. *The language of the central character*
A close examination of Mme. Loisel's language as a means of revealing her nature.

Example: "From *I* to *We* in 'The Necklace' "

A Paper About Plot (What?)

1. *Plot structure*
An analysis of the organization of the story, in whole or in part, to provide a better understanding of it.

Examples: "The Nature and Importance of the Exposition"
"Compression in 'The Necklace' "

2. *Plot evaluation*
A consideration of the artistry of the plot.

Examples: "The Many Uses of Chance in 'The Necklace' "
"The Ending—Satisfying or Not?"

3. *Theme and plot*
An examination of how the theme develops from the action in the story.

Example: "The Ending—Happy or Unhappy?"

A Paper About Technique (How?)

1. *Point of view*
   A discussion of Maupassant's handling of point of view to show how it contributes to the effectiveness of the story.

   Example: "The Self-Imposed Limitations of the Omniscient Narrator"

2. *Irony*
   An analysis of verbal and situational irony, considered together or separately, as keys to the meaning of the work and the artistry of the writer.

   Example: "The Ironic Ending of 'The Necklace' "

3. *Symbolism*
   A discussion of the use of symbolism, particularly if it contributes significantly to the work.

   Example: "The False Necklace and False Values"

We realize that some of these subjects would not result in comprehensive or substantive papers about Maupassant's story. Our purpose is merely to suggest the scope of the possibilities in writing about literature by applying the "who-what-where-when-why-how" approach. Most of these topics would certainly be appropriate for a short paper, and several of them might be combined for a longer one. In any case, we hope we have answered the question that you might ask after reading this or any other literary work: "What shall I write about?"

THE ORGANIZATION OF THE CRITICAL PAPER

Papers about literature take the same forms as those on nonliterary topics. Although the subject matter is literary, the critical paper is essentially descriptive, expository, or argumentative. As we indicated with the Maupassant story, you might decide to write a character sketch (similar to those in Chapter 6) of one of the leading characters, choosing descriptive details from the work itself to produce a compressed picture of a character. Or you might employ the techniques of analysis discussed in Chapter 11 in tracing a theme or examining technical aspects such as the use of irony, imagery, or symbolism. Or you could develop an interpretation inferred from your reading and support it with those "facts" from the work that led you to it, using the organizational skills recommended in Chapter 12. Still another possibility is to convince your readers that your interpretation is valid even though it might be controversial; then you should couch your paper in argument form as illustrated in Chapter 17. Yet another approach is to compare several aspects of the work, extending the techniques suggested earlier for the comparison-and-contrast paper. So you see, the rhetorical problems involved in writing about literature are basically the same as those for other subject matter.

Thesis and Support

As with all well-organized writing, the critical paper needs a controlling thesis, or central idea. This can take the form of an inference statement that reflects a strong opinion or conviction you derive (infer) from the work. Let's look at some student examples of critical thesis statements, discussing the kinds of support and organization each requires.

1. Inference thesis requiring a character sketch of a main character for support:

In *The Bridge over the River Kwai,* Colonel Nicholson's dedication to military discipline and duty saves the morale of his men but results in his treason to the British cause.

> This "opinion" thesis requires that the writer support both contentions: Nicholson's dedication saves morale and leads to treason. Attitudes of other characters toward Nicholson and incidents portraying his growing fanaticism about the building of the bridge are necessary in developing a causal framework that explains the ultimate effect—treason of a dedicated, loyal soldier.

2. Inference thesis requiring comparison-and-contrast techniques for support:

The language of the schoolboys has both an identifying and an excluding power in Kipling's *Stalky & Co.* and in Knowles' *A Separate Peace.*

> Here, the thesis sets up a four-fold writing assignment for the student: to show how each of the two novels uses language to provide group identity and to exclude outsiders.

3. Inference thesis requiring techniques of analysis for support:

The turtle in *The Grapes of Wrath* is symbolic of the Joad family and their fight for survival.

> This thesis idea requires an analytical paper—a classifying of the adventures and characteristics of the turtle that are related in some way to the plight of the Joads. Remember that adequate support of an interpretation involving symbolic meaning requires strong supporting evidence from the text.

4. Argument thesis:

Despite Tolkien's denials, *Lord of the Rings* can be interpreted symbolically as a Christian struggle between good and evil.

This argumentative thesis requires strong support from the novel backed up perhaps by the opinions of reputable critics. Since the author himself refutes the proposition, the student writer must prove that Tolkien's use of symbols, conscious or unconscious, leads the reader to this interpretation. Careful citation of such symbols is of course required to substantiate the proposition.

Student Paper: Tracing a Central Theme Through Character Analysis

In the following paper, the student demonstrates the most effective use of character analysis: not merely to describe a character, but to relate the character to a major theme in the work. In this case, the student develops a limited character sketch choosing only those aspects that support her inference thesis: that a postwar conflict of values is a major theme in Ernest Hemingway's novel *The Sun Also Rises*. The student's organizational scheme is indicated at the side.

JAKE BARNES' LOSS OF VALUES IN *THE SUN ALSO RISES*

Gail Gardenhire

One of the most overwhelming problems that Jake Barnes, the major character in Ernest Hemingway's *The Sun Also Rises,* has to face is adequately stated by a somewhat minor character in the book when Count Mippipopolous advises Jake, "That is the secret. You must get to know the values." Indeed, it seems that throughout this novel, Jake constantly searches to define his values and to see which ones will survive.

Inference thesis

Perhaps the greatest influence on Jake's increasing loss of values is his "old grievance." There are, however, several connotations that could apply to this phrase, the most obvious being Jake's impotence produced by an injury incurred "on a joke front like the Italian." Lady Brett Ashley might be another of Jake's "old grievances," which drags him farther and farther away from a definition of his values. Brett's "circle" of friends and

I. Jake's sexual impotence and his love for Brett contribute to his loss of values.

even her very presence seem only to reinforce Jake's realization that he is incapable of enjoying or satisfying any physical "value" which he might hold, and this, consequently, leads him to seek superficial values as substitutes for human ones.

Also essential to Jake's search is his exposure to a varied set of values characterized by two types of people in the novel and to the transition that these values undergo as these people are introduced to new situations. Perhaps the best example of this idea is the abrupt change in the values of the peasants when confronted with a fiesta in which "everything became quite unreal finally and it seemed as though nothing could have any consequence." These peasants, with their pure and simple ties to the soil and the uncomplicated measure of values in yield of crops or animals raised, quickly lose their pure and simple values, though perhaps only temporarily, when they become involved in the fiesta. Before, "money still had a definite value in hours worked and bushels of grain sold," whereas, "Late in the fiesta it would not matter what they paid nor where they bought." They have assumed the values of the city.

Similarly, Jake goes through some transition in what he thought to be things most dear to him prior to this fiesta. His enthusiasm for bullfighting had been most precious to him and served as his greatest emotional involvement. As the fiesta progresses, however, and Jake becomes involved in the decaying values of all those about him, he loses, due to his bitterness about inability to give Brett sexual satisfaction, the last of his "precious" values.

As a result, Jake is forced to redefine his values in terms of money. Here lies the power he lost in his war accident. Here lies a way to satisfy his senses, through adequate food and plentiful wine to dull his inner awareness that these new values are meaningless. Jake reaches the conclusion that life is, after all, "just exchange of values." Everything that life has to offer must be paid for "by experience, or by taking chances, or by money," but "the bill" always comes. If you strive to "pay

II. Shifting values of others in the novel contribute to his moral confusion.

III. Jake reexamines his values.

IV. Jake redefines his values.

your way into enough things," then you'll eventually enjoy life and "get your money's worth."

In essence, Jake has learned that in order to make friends, and in order to survive in this hopelessly "lost generation," one must value only things that can be replaced. Money can be replaced. Friends or acquaintances can be replaced through the use of money, and superficial needs can easily be satisfied with money. Jake has finally decided that he must *not* value his once-in-a-lifetime love for Brett or his enthusiasm for bullfighting, because these are values that cannot easily be replaced with a "simple exchange."

V. Jake exchanges his value system for that of Brett's "circle."

Sadly enough, any glimmer of hope for the survival of values honestly valuable to Jake is lost by the time the fiesta is over, and he succumbs to all of the "lost generation" by admitting that "I did not care what it was all about. All I wanted to know was how to live in it." He makes that final compromise, that final exchange of a life of substance for one of mere existence.

Conclusion: Restatement of thesis and the theme of values.

Note that the student writer not only works in significant quotes from the novel throughout her own prose, but effectively introduces her subject with one—a reference to the values that have thematic importance in the novel.

The Influence of the Audience

Because students usually write critical papers about works that their fellow students have also read and discussed, and are also writing about, they sometimes assume that all their readers know the work and need no explanatory materials. This assumption, however, can breed dangerous writing habits. Unless your teacher directs otherwise, you should write to your classmates, but should include among your readers some outsiders who may have only a cursory knowledge of the book. Such an audience will keep you from boring your classmates with too much plot summary, but will force you to provide enough information to enlighten the outsiders. You should:

1. Identify the work early in the paper, as the student example does. Generally, the author's name is also given.

2. Provide only enough plot information to illustrate the points you make. Resist the common trap of beginning the paper with an extensive plot

summary before launching into the real subject of your paper. Unless the assignment is to write a plot summary, such detail can be kept to a minimum. The student example strikes a happy balance in this respect. Including details for the less knowledgeable readers also serves the purpose of providing specific evidence to support your inferences.

3. Define or explain unusual terms or concepts. This is as necessary in critical writing as in other forms of writing. Use any of the methods of brief definition suggested in Chapter 11.

SOME TECHNICAL ASPECTS OF CRITICAL WRITING

In general, critical writing follows the same patterns as other forms of writing and commits the writer to the same considerations. Only the subject matter and the specialized skills and vocabulary of literary criticism differ. Organizing the material, maintaining focus and logical relationships throughout the paper, and sustaining awareness of audience and purpose are as much a part of literary criticism as they are of extended definition or an argument. But literary writing does demand special attention to some technical aspects absent in other forms. Let's look at two of the most important of these.

Handling Tense

Often in telling a personal anecdote to a friend, you have doubtless used the present tense: "Then the car salesman *says*, 'Why don't you take it out for a test drive?' He *knows* he *has* me hooked." In a more formal situation or in writing, you probably would substitute past-tense verb forms for *says, knows,* and *has* (*said, knew, had*). But regardless of the tense you use, your friend knows that the event took place in past time. Because of this ability of the present tense to mean past time or even timelessness, many contemporary critics use it in talking about a book or movie. However, some problems of tense accord are involved in critical writing. Here are two examples, one using present tense, the other past, to tell about a plot:

Present tense: The movie *Superman begins* on the planet Krypton, where Marlon Brando *is* trying to convince the council that cosmic forces *will* demolish it.

Past tense: The movie *Superman began* on the planet Krypton, where Marlon Brando *was* trying to convince the council that cosmic forces *would* demolish it.

From the examples, you can see why most writers prefer the literary present over the chronological past for talking about plot: it makes the action more immediate. But note that both examples are consistent in the use of tense; they do not shift from one to the other.

These are your options—the literary present or the chronological past—in relating what occurs or in discussing the ideas in the work. Of course, in direct quotations, you are obliged to use the author's exact words, as illustrated here:

> The action in John Cheever's novel *Falconer* occurs in a dark and depressing prison world. "The bars had been enameled white many years ago." Farragut notices soon after he arrives, "but the enamel had been worn back to iron at the chest level, where men instinctively held them."

Here, the writer of the critical essay uses the literary present as indicated in *occurs, notices,* and *arrives.* The past tense forms (*had, held*) are the forms in the quotation from the novel.

Frequently, critical writers will use the literary present for talking about the book itself, but employ the chronological past when discussing the author's life, achievements, and the like. In the following book-review excerpt, note the use of the past tense (italicized) in references to Flannery O'Connor herself, and the use of the present tense in references to the book, an edition of her collected letters.

> Editor Sally Fitzgerald has performed a labor of love and an act of model scholarship. When factual information is needed, she gives it succinctly and then stands back. This record of a remarkable life is an occasion for sadness, a reminder of wisdom cut off much too soon. But the emotion that Flannery O'Connor *conveyed* most often *was* joy, and this survives intact. Once a correspondent *had suggested* that someone would write a life of the author. Flannery *pooh-poohed* the idea: "There won't be any biographies of me because, for only one reason, lives spent between the house and the chicken yard do not make exciting copy." This book proves her wrong.
>
> —Paul Gray

To sum up, this is the way tense is employed by most modern critics:

1. To describe the action of the work, use the present tense in preference to the past tense.
2. To make a quotation, use the verbs in the work, copying the author's words exactly.
3. To describe what the author does in the work, use the present tense.
4. To discuss the author, use the past tense.
5. Be consistent.

Handling Quotations

In critical writing it is often necessary or useful to quote directly from the literary work. If you wish to use supporting material for a controversial interpretation, the author's original words might carry more weight than your own. Or sometimes, lengthy quotations are used for comparison purposes: a critic may wish to compare a segment of the author's published version with an earlier draft, or contrast two passages from the same work that has had several translations. But for most of your assignments, brief quotations incorporated into your own discussion about the work will be sufficient and effective. Here are some examples from student papers that demonstrate a few of the ways quotations can be effectively worked into critical papers.

1. To demonstrate a representative theme in the work:

Toward the end of D. Keith Mano's *The Bridge* a character observes: "Shakespeare was wrong: there are only two ages of man. Childhood and senility. Savage youth or a self-hating, self-destructive civilization. In between, a few moments—no more, a few—when the balance is held, when he is a god." That glum judgment is at the core of *The Bridge,* and like a number of the novel's thematic assumptions is highly debatable.

> Note that because this quotation of several lines has been made an integral part of the student's comments about the novel, it is not necessary to separate and indent it, as is normal for longer quotes.

2. To support an interpretation (again discussing *The Bridge*):

In a literal interpretation of the communion, Priest developed a craving for "blood and flesh," and it was this hunger that reawakened his determination to survive. When Priest reached home, he found that Ogilvy, the state guard who had provoked the anger that sent him to prison, had killed his wife and child. Insane with grief, Priest jumped on the tormentor and devoured his arm "to the sweet flesh around its bone." Not only was Priest literally partaking of communion, but enacting the "eat or be eaten" law of the jungle. By this, Priest reasserted his right to live, not as a man whose cannibalism is only symbolic in communion, but as a beast who literally devours another. It was only in the most reductive natural context that he could find any support for the desire to live.

> Here the quotations are phrases incorporated into the sentence structure without "example signals"—*such as, for instance, like, Priest says,* and so on. Instead, the quotations flow naturally into the student's prose and only the quotation marks indicate that they come from the work itself.

401

Assignments

For Discussion

1 What kind of critical paper should result from each of the following student thesis statements: character sketch, comparison and contrast, analysis, argument, other? What are the key terms in the statements that require discussion and support? What weaknesses do they manifest?

    a The Joad family in *Grapes of Wrath* possesses the same kind of unselfish love that the biblical Good Samaritan had.

    b In the novel *The Bridge,* the baptism of Priest serves as a transitional bridge from the ending of one era to the beginning of a new one.

    c In *Waiting for Godot,* Samuel Beckett explores Christian symbolism in the guise of garment and nature imagery to support the central themes in his play.

    d In "Bright and Morning Star," Richard Wright illustrates the maturation of the protagonist by contrasting two rebels—one old and one young.

    e In *The Secret Sharer* the young captain as an outsider struggles to overcome his external isolation by correcting his internal, self-imposed isolation.

    f In *Matryona's House,* both Matryona and the narrator are quiet social rebels.

    g In Salinger's *The Catcher in the Rye,* Holden Caulfield can be seen both as a social rebel and as a victim of society.

2 Compare the use of quoted materials in the following three student paragraphs. Which do you think is most effective? Why?

    a Vladimir and Estragon, representing the metaphysical couple, have no society-oriented relationship. They are simply of equal status in a friend-to-friend relationship. Their relationship shows no class distinction or consciousness. This friend-to-friend relationship can be seen in two passages. The first passage is when Estragon falls asleep.

        (Estragon sleeps, Vladimir gets up softly, takes off his coat and lays it across Estragon's shoulders, then starts walking up and down, swinging his arms to keep himself warm. Estragon wakes with a start, jumps up, casts about wildly. Vladimir runs to him, puts his arms around him.)

    The second passage showing Vladimir and Estragon's relationship is in the scene where they talk about their relationship.

        ESTRAGON: You see, you feel worse when I'm with you. I feel better alone too.

> VLADIMIR: Then why do you always come crawling back?
> ESTRAGON: I don't know.
> VLADIMIR: No, but I do. It's because you don't know how to defend yourself. I wouldn't have let them beat you.

b The most obvious indication of Henry's insignificance is apparent from the beginning of the novel. It seems rather ironic that the primary character is not actually introduced until a large portion of the book has been covered. We know him only as the "youth." He has earned no name, no "badge" of distinction or accomplishment and, thus, no identity. While struggling with his initial anxieties about bravely facing combat or shamefully fleeing, the youth is merely one of a multitude of soldiers, "a part of a vast blue demonstration." Only when he is actually confronted with battle and succumbs to what he had feared, are we allowed to meet him as Henry Fleming. He has finally taken some definite action, perhaps not particularly admirable, but nevertheless decisive; and for this, he has earned some form of identity. He, in fact, now fears that everyone knows him as a coward. He is "a slang phrase."

c Humanity has lost its will to live by 2035. Man has been ordered to terminate his own life. Walters, Priest's fellow inmate at Yankee Stadium, states, "It's been coming to this. Dead by our own free will. Thank God—we didn't deserve to live." Xavier Paul and Priest witness a mass suicide on their way to New Loch. Xavier Paul "hates these people who hate their own lives. People who are guilty when they breathe with the lungs God gave them, who have no way to expiate their guilt. The world's polluted with despair. They deserve to die."

For Practice

1 The following excerpts from student papers contain errors in tense accord. Find the errors and revise them.

a Hawthorne's tales usually end with a moralistic view of life. Each character learns something about human nature that virtually destroys him. Sin is inevitable and is deeply rooted in human experience. Father Hooper in "The Minister's Black Veil" recognizes this and is obsessed by it. At his death he felt that every person wears a "Black Veil" to conceal his innermost thoughts and feelings from the rest of the world. Young Goodman Brown found that people wear hypocrisy as a veil to cover their evil natures. Yet each man at his death will have to bare himself to his Maker and face the consequences. Aylmer in "The Birthmark" and Ethan Brand are similar in that both end in having found an ultimate truth. Aylmer should have accepted the imperfection of life and been content with the anticipation of the perfect future. Ethan Brand searched the world over for the "Unpardonable Sin" and finally found it in himself. He discovered it to be egotism, which tends to separate man from his fellow man. Roderick Elliston in "Egotism; or, The Bosom Serpent" suffers from a terrible egotism which stems from jealousy. It manifested itself in the form of a serpent which was eating out the heart. Feathertop alone immediately recognized himself for what he really was, "a wretched, ragged, empty thing," and resolved that he would "exist no longer." Many such others live in "fair repute" and "never see themselves for what they are."

b Gandalt could be called a Christ-figure. In the beginning he has limited power, he is still learning. After the duel with Balrog, Gandalf is transformed and appears in white: "I have passed through fire and deep water, since we parted." Gandalf had returned to life, more powerful than ever. He was beyond all harm: "Indeed, my friends, none of you has any weapon that could hurt me."

The Authoritative
Voice:
The Research
Paper

he thought of writing research papers is frightening to many students. Some avoid courses requiring them; others drop the course at term paper time. True, writing these papers does require more sustained work and intellectual effort than other papers do. True, they demand that a writer work more efficiently and organize material more skillfully. But—also true—research papers are more rewarding. Writing them can be interesting, stimulating, and satisfying. They offer a unique opportunity to learn. And learning how to write research papers is one way to learn how to learn. Let us explain.

From time to time this semester or week, you've probably speculated about some person, event, issue, problem, or subject you wish you knew more about. It might be China, the price of gasoline, child abuse, cable television, personal computers, solar heating, the electric car, or television advertising aimed at children. Whatever you are curious about, wonder about, or want to know more about can be your subject for a research paper. By doing research, you are learning what you want to know about the subject. And by learning how to locate, select, arrange, evaluate, and present information about this subject, you are learning how to learn.

And learning is rewarding. Whether it merely satisfies your curiosity or builds your ego, learning makes life more interesting to you and makes you more interesting to others. You become the local expert, specialist, authority on some subject. Whatever the subject, you probably will know more about it after writing your research paper than do others in your class or perhaps in the entire freshman class.

The research process is not entirely new to you. You have probably already conducted or been involved in some research. You may have combed the newspaper classified ads before looking for a regular, part-time, or summer job. You may have consulted consumer guides and spoken to numerous people before buying a stereo, television set, or used car. You may have boned up on automobile insurance before deciding what coverage to get, how much to buy, and what company to deal with. In these and similar pursuits, you were engaged on a small scale in the same information-gathering activity that goes into a research paper.

Just as the process of research is not an academic exercise confined to English classes, neither is the writing of research papers. Chances are that in other college courses during the next few years you will be asked to investigate a subject and communicate your findings. And after college you may join the many people constantly doing research and writing about it: government experts, lawyers, journalists, business executives, engineers, scientists, economists, and others in such professional fields as medicine, education, social work. Of course, your research differs from what some of these people do. That's why the research paper should more accurately be termed a *library* research paper, because your information is derived from books, magazines, journals, newspapers, and similar library materials. Non-library research papers may be based on interviews or questionnaires, or examinations of things animate or inanimate in their natural environment or laboratories. These studies generally involve observing, measuring, experimenting, formulating and testing hypotheses, and verifying. Library research involves working with primary and secondary sources. The former consists of consulting original documents such as official records, diaries, letters, manuscripts, and fictional and nonfictional works. The latter involves consulting second-hand sources—in other words, reading what others have written about a subject. Since you will be writing this second type of research paper in your composition course, you may wonder what there is for you to do besides string together information you have gleaned.

Much depends on whether the purpose of the research paper is to summarize or persuade. In the summary paper, you are a collector and clarifier, amassing facts and opinions from different sources, sifting through and evaluating them, and presenting them clearly and interestingly for your readers. You perform a valuable service by enabling readers to understand all aspects of a subject or issue, information that might be otherwise inaccessible or incomprehensible. For example, people might wonder why public school teachers are paid according to seniority rather than merit. Why aren't superior teachers given higher salaries? Why should more money go to those with longer rather than better service? A reading of the literature on this subject—both pro and con—could result in an interesting, informative paper presenting the arguments on both sides.

Or, as many instructors prefer, the research paper could be persuasive: you spell out the reasons for and against payment of teachers according to merit and then advocate a particular position on the issue. But whichever paper you write—summary or persuasive—you take a fresh look at the existing facts and opinions, filtering this information through your mind, and presenting the subject in an original way. Writing a research paper is like furnishing a room: both involve selecting, assembling, arranging, adapting, treating, and presenting items according to your own particular taste. Like the room, your paper is an original creation.

Your paper is also original because it is shaped to the needs and interests of your audience. Your instructor should indicate whether you are writing to all the students in class, students majoring in your field of study, or some other group of readers. Whoever your readers are, you will have to consider their needs, interests, and knowledge in order to adapt your paper to them. How much background information will they require? What can they be counted on to know? Which terms must be defined? How much will they want to learn? Your answers to these and similar questions demand you make certain decisions that contribute to the paper's originality.

You can see that the research paper is like the expository and persuasive papers you have written. However, it is longer, more difficult to organize,

Preliminary Steps in Preparing the Research Paper

There is never enough time. At least, not for the research paper. Even though you may have two or three or four weeks, it will vanish in a twinkling unless you cherish every moment. That means you must get started, ignoring the nearby distractions and the comforting thought of the faraway deadline. And it means getting started by setting up a schedule for the ten-step process like this sample three-week one:

The process	*The schedule* (3 weeks)
Preliminary Steps	
1. Subject Selection	Days: 1–2
2. Preliminary Reading	3–4
3. Preliminary Bibliography	5–6
4. Preliminary Outline	7
Writing	
5. Note-taking	8–11
6. Final Outline	12
7. First Draft	13–16
8. Revision of First Draft	17–18
9. Final Draft	19–20
10. Proofreading	21

By dividing the work for the research paper into a series of steps and by establishing and meeting a deadline for each, you will write a better paper with less work. And you'll sleep well the night before it is due. Let's go through the process one step at a time. We'll cover the preliminary steps in this chapter and the writing steps in the next one.

STEP 1: SUBJECT SELECTION

Selecting a subject may be a snap for you. Perhaps your instructor will assign one arbitrarily or let you choose from a list. Perhaps you have something on your mind that you would like to explore. For example, at this writing, Cleveland is on the brink of bankruptcy. We wonder whether any city has ever actually gone bankrupt, and if so, what happened. That might be our subject. But what if no subject is handy?

Subject Search

We suggest that you spend a day or two thinking, reading, listening, questioning, and writing down any interesting possibilities. Think about issues and people in the news or anything associated with them; arguments you've had with friends, relatives, family; historical events or persons you have been curious about; famous people you admire; ideas, movements, opinions, beliefs that have puzzled or concerned you. Glance through newspapers, magazines, books, textbooks with the idea of hitting upon a subject. Listen to what people around you are talking about, to what personalities on radio or television are discussing, to what instructors in your classes are lecturing about. Raise questions in your mind about places you have been or wanted to go to, hobbies you pursue or would like to, careers you are interested in or fascinated by, unusual experiences you have had or heard about. And whenever you have a scintilla of an idea, scribble it down before it slips your mind. If you stay alert to possibilities, brood about finding a subject, sit down and concentrate for periods of time, or discuss the problem with a friend, we think you'll have at least several topics in a day or two.

Subject Suitability

When reviewing these subject possibilities, you should eliminate any that do not lend themselves to library research, such as personal subjects and descriptions of processes or places. The former could not be located in any source; the latter would be easily available in a single source. In addition, most libraries probably would not have sufficient materials for research papers on very recent or local events. What you should keep in mind when considering subjects is the need to select one that will lend itself to various interpretations or different opinions—that is, the need to obtain information from different sources. For example, the operation of the Wankel engine would be an inappropriate subject: the necessary information could be found in one book or article. But the advantages, disadvantages, and future of this engine would require gathering information from various sources and thus would be an appropriate subject for a research paper.

You must be practical, therefore, and select a subject that can probably be researched. But even after you have decided on one, you must answer two questions before making it your final choice: (1) Does the library contain sufficient information about the subject? (2) Does the library contain so much information that the subject should be restricted in scope? To answer these questions, move to Step 2.

STEP 2: PRELIMINARY READING

The purpose of preliminary reading is to obtain an overview of your subject so that you can zero in on it. You may know, for example, that you want to write about the Pearl Harbor disaster in the Second World War, but you may be uncertain whether to tackle the problem of military unpreparedness there or the United States general unreadiness for war. And you also need to learn, as we just mentioned, whether there are too few or too many available sources.

For answers to these questions (and to numerous others, as you can see from the illustration on page 412), go to the library. And prepare to live there for the next week or so in writing your research paper.

Reference Works

Your first goal is to obtain additional knowledge or an overview of your subject. Consequently, you should head for the reference room, where certain standard works are kept: dictionaries, encyclopedias, biographical dictionaries, almanacs, yearbooks, and indexes.

Dictionaries   You probably don't think of a regular dictionary as a reference work, but often it is the fastest and most convenient source. If you were considering that paper about the Japanese attack on Pearl Harbor, a dictionary would provide the location and date; for one on Greta Garbo, it would furnish her original surname, date of birth, and occupation. A dictionary is far more than a spelling book, pronunciation guide, or synonym source; it is a storehouse of information about a wide range of knowledge— historical, biographical, geographical, mathematical, scientific, medical, and linguistic, to mention a few.

You should own a recent edition of an abridged dictionary (one that contains about 150,000 words in contrast to the huge unabridged dictionaries of about 450,000 words). But make certain you know how your dictionary is arranged. For example, in *Webster's New Collegiate Dictionary,* biographical and geographical names, and foreign words and phrases appear in separate sections at the end; this information is included with the regular entries in other dictionaries. In the *American Heritage Dictionary,* the central meaning of a word is given first; in most other dictionaries, the earliest meaning is first. For example, in the *Webster's New World* and the

How to bathe a boa.

Who we should call Ishmael.
Who won the battle of Culloden.
Who discovered Cleveland.
Who invented schnapps.
Who said, "Cogito ergo sum."
Who that actress was.
Who Gutenburg was.
Who Beau Brummel's tailor was.
Who invented aspirin.
Who has class.
Who Lincoln's first date was.
Who plays for the Who.
Who put Saks on Fifth Ave.
Who has a job for you.
Who plays tackle for Detroit.
Who said, "Don't give up the ship"
Why outhouses have moons.
Who the Jazz Singer was.
Who invented gunpowder.
Who wrote Shakespeare.
Who makes parts for your Stanley.
Who the Zealots were.
Who wrote that TV show.
Who Carl Reiner's first boss was.
Who Peach Melba was named after.
Who stood in the snow at Canossa.
Who invented the calendar.
Who figured out arithmetic.
Who signed the Mayflower Compact.
How to fix your car.
How to build a telescope.
How to bake a cake.
How to make a million.
How to get into college.
How to sew a dress.
How to do your taxes.
How to forge a Rembrandt.
How to beat Bobby Fischer.
How to raise gloxinia.
How to fix a leak.
How to land a man.

How to land a woman.
How to get a raise.
How to understand Faulkner.
How to buy a house.
How to train your dog.
How to get a patent.
How to type a letter.
How to find Borneo.
How to buy stocks.
How to ride a horse.
How to wash your house.
How to write a poem.
How to bathe a boa.
How to get a job.
How to throw a party.
How to run for Congress.
How to cut a diamond.
How to build a tepee.
How to blow glass.
How to predict the weather.
How to cast a horoscope.
How to find God.
Where they keep the Hope Diamond.
Where Bora-Bora is.
Where Murano glass comes from.
Where they teach palmistry.
Where gypsies live.
Where the world came from.
Where "The Night Watch" is.
Where Capt. Cook was going.
Where Haley's Comet goes.
Who Cookie Lavagetto is.
Where they speak Esperanto.
Where St. John went.
Where Astroturf is made.
Where the yellow went.
Where to go on vacation.
Where the world's
  tallest structure is.
Where the sun goes at night.
Where they made "Ben Hur."

Where to get a deal.
Where to find gold.
Where to dig for worms.
Where they speak Swahili.
Where to grow mushrooms.
Where they have dog races.
Where Sonnets from the
  Portuguese were written.
Where to get your Nikon fixed.
Where to get a business loan.
Where to take a date.
Where to have a party.
Where to complain about potholes.
Why $E = MC^2$.
Why the sky stays up.
Why Ike won.
Why deserts are dry.
Why bread rises.
Why litmus changes color.
Why England slept.
Why the Mets won in '69.
Why Peter Pan never grew up.
Why Falstaff was a coward.
Why the ocean is blue.
Why the dollar was devalued.
Why the Beatles split up.
Why the Tower of Pisa leans.
Why they eat spaghetti in China.
Why the Dodgers left Brooklyn.
Why the sword was in the stone.
Why Lincoln grew a beard.
Why Chicago is the Windy City.
Why there is smog.
Why it rains.
Why leaves are green.
Why sugar tastes good.
Why John Wayne is called "The Duke."
Why they created West Virginia.
Why outhouses have moons.
Who said, "Don't give up the ship"

Your library has all the answers. Stop in.

American Library Association 1975

Webster's New Collegiate (the word *Webster* is not copyrighted and appears on many dictionaries less respected than these), *saloon* is first defined as a large room or hall for receptions, exhibitions, or entertainments—the word's earliest meaning. A later definition indicates that it is a bar—the central meaning today. But in the *American Heritage Dictionary,* the first definition gives this latter meaning. Our purpose in pointing out these differences is not to recommend one dictionary over the others but to alert you to the importance of reading the explanatory notes or guide to whichever dictionary you own.

An unabridged dictionary, such as *Webster's Third New International,* not only contains more words, especially scientific and technical terms, than an abridged dictionary but also provides more information about each word. Another useful dictionary is the *OED (Oxford English Dictionary),* a work developed on historical principles to show when, in what form, and with what meaning a word originally appeared in the language and how it has changed since. This information is particularly helpful in understanding the use of a word at a particular time between 1150 and 1933.

Among other dictionaries in the reference room are specialized ones on slang, quotations, rhymes, clichés, and acronyms.

Encyclopedias   An encyclopedia will provide more information about a subject than a dictionary will. But you should realize that different encyclopedias are written for different readers. The *World Book,* for example, is generally designed for high-school students. Its simple explanations of difficult scientific concepts are particularly helpful. Also useful are its cross references to related subjects, suggested readings, and short descriptions of books about the subject. The *Encyclopedia Americana,* written for college-educated readers, features American subjects and recommends supplementary readings. Especially important is its Index Volume, which lists not only the main subjects presented in the alphabetically arranged articles but minor subjects discussed in these articles, as well as other references to the main subject. The most scholarly and respected general encyclopedia is the *Britannica.* Formerly it was organized alphabetically and, as such, its ninth and eleventh editions are held in particularly high esteem. The latest edition, the fifteenth, is divided into three sections: (1) the *Propedia,* a one-volume subject index and outline of knowledge; (2) the *Micropedia,* a ten-volume set of short articles; and (3) the *Macropedia,* a nineteen-volume set of long, detailed scholarly articles. Thus you can check the *Propedia,* turn to the *Micropedia* for a short article on your topic, and then consult the *Macropedia* for a lengthier examination of it. Although more difficult to use at first, the new *Britannica* can be especially valuable in providing a broad perspective on a subject.

Numerous other general and specialized encyclopedias may be found in the reference room. Among the most valuable are encyclopedias of education, philosophy, social sciences, science and technology, and world art.

413

Biographies If your subject is a living person, you might find it most helpful to turn to biographical reference works. *Current Biography,* issued annually and in monthly supplements, provides information about living people, including their addresses and a list of articles and books about them. Another source of information about living people is the *Who's Who* series, which appears in different volumes according to classification, ranging from individual countries (*Who's Who in America*) to sex (*Who's Who of American Women*) to subject area (*Who's Who in Art*). Two other biographical sources that deserve mention are *Contemporary Authors* and *American Men and Women of Science.*

The most helpful works about people no longer living are the *Dictionary of American Biography* (1958) and the *Dictionary of National Biography* (British, 1950). Naturally, both these works are limited to individuals who died prior to the publication dates of the main volumes and supplements.

Almanacs For statistical information, chronological listings, major developments in science and technology, and summaries of political events, almanacs are useful. Facts abound about athletics, climate, economics, employment, farm prices, famous people, foreign countries, and innumerable other subjects in these handy paperback volumes with their tissue-thin pages jammed mainly with figures, charts, tables, and lists. Two of the most helpful, the *World Almanac* and the *Information Please Almanac,* are published annually. The former probably contains more data; the latter more interesting articles, particularly because of its review of the year's events. To some extent, the *Information Please Almanac* is more like the annual yearbooks published by the encyclopedias mentioned previously, and the informative digest *Facts on File.*

Our purpose in discussing these reference works has been to suggest how you can obtain a general knowledge of your subject. But we do not want to imply that these books should be used only for that purpose. Often in working on minor points in your paper, you can locate significant information quickly by consulting dictionaries, encyclopedias, biographical sources, almanacs, and yearbooks. And of course, all of these works need not be examined in your preliminary reading; perhaps only one or a few will give you a sufficient overview of your subject.

Now you may be able to decide whether the subject should be restricted in scope. Let's suppose that you've been curious about Galileo, who you have been told was the creator of the modern scientific method. After looking at the material about him in several reference books, you may realize that this subject is too broad and that you had better limit it to his work with the telescope.

But general reading may be helpful mainly in increasing your knowledge of the subject. And so, whether you have decided to limit your topic or not, you should next check on the adequacy of the library's information about it. You have a choice: the card catalog or the indexes, or both. If your subject is likely to be treated in a book, which usually takes at least a year to write and publish, then start with the card catalog. If your subject has been in the news more recently, consult the indexes (*New York Times Index:* one-month lag; *Reader's Guide:* three to six months). Of course, you may end up examining both the card catalog and the indexes.

The Card Catalog

No doubt you already know something about the card catalog from your public library or from your high-school days. But since your college library probably contains many more cards, you can save time and unearth information more easily by learning more details about how to proceed.

You should first find out whether your college library has one card catalog, with all cards listed alphabetically, or two catalogs, one for author and title cards, the other for subject cards. If all the cards are in one place, relax. But if they are divided (which does make life easier once you've learned the system), then you must decide where to turn first. For a paper on the geodesic dome, you would consult the subject catalog; for a book by its inventor, Buckminster Fuller, you would look in the author-title catalog. The only trick is to realize that if you wish a book *about* Buckminster Fuller—not by him—then you must turn to the subject catalog. If you do not discover a card there about your subject, do not panic. Instead, consult the huge index volume—*Subject Headings Used in the Dictionary Catalogs of the Library of Congress*—to determine the heading used for your topic. For example, if you were seeking books about writing, you would not find them under that heading. By looking in the index, you would learn that these books appear under the heading "Authorship."

Realize that you might find the same card in both subject and author-title catalogs because at least two and often three or more cards are made for each book. These cards not only inform you where the book is shelved in the library but also provide numerous helpful hints once you understand and interpret the notations on the card. Look at the sample author-title card on page 416. What information does it provide? Let's list some points that may not be obvious.

1. The author is still living if card is accurate (birth date but no death date). Biographical information about him should be available in current indexes.
2. The number of pages (303—see "Descriptive information") suggests that this book treats the subject in some detail.
3. The date of publication indicates that the work should be based on recent materials.

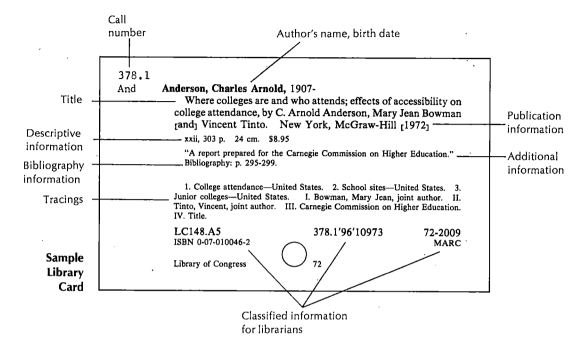

Call number

Author's name, birth date

Title

Descriptive information

Bibliography information

Tracings

Sample Library Card

378.1
And   **Anderson, Charles Arnold,** 1907-
         Where colleges are and who attends; effects of accessibility on
         college attendance, by C. Arnold Anderson, Mary Jean Bowman
         ₍and₎ Vincent Tinto.   New York, McGraw-Hill ₍1972₎
         xxii, 303 p.   24 cm. $8.95

         "A report prepared for the Carnegie Commission on Higher Education."
         Bibliography: p. 295-299.

         1. College attendance—United States.   2. School sites—United States.   3.
         Junior colleges—United States.   I. Bowman, Mary Jean, joint author.   II.
         Tinto, Vincent, joint author.   III. Carnegie Commission on Higher Education.
         IV. Title.

         LC148.A5   378.1'96'10973   72-2009
         ISBN 0-07-010046-2   MARC

         Library of Congress   72

Publication information

Additional information

Classified information
for librarians

4. The inclusion of a five-page bibliography points to a scholarly treatment. This list of source materials could be helpful in your own further research.

5. The Arabic numbers in the "Tracings" refer to information about the main focus of the book (college attendance and school sites), the scope of the treatment (United States colleges only), headings in the subject catalog under which additional material can be found (college attendance, school sites, junior colleges), and, in some instances, the reading level (not pertinent here). The Roman numerals refer to additional catalog cards for the same work (joint author cards, title card).

When used thoughtfully, the catalog card can be more helpful than you might have realized. It can save you time and effort by eliminating certain sources from consideration. And it can suggest certain other sources. It's all in the cards.

Indexes

Indexes do for newspapers and periodicals what the card catalog does for books. A novice researcher can use the catalog; you must be a veteran to know your way around the indexes.

It's mainly a question of what you want to know and in what type of publication it may be found. If your subject has probably been treated in a widely read magazine, the most helpful index is likely to be the *Reader's Guide to Periodical Literature,* which catalogs 160 publications, such as *Atlantic Monthly, Time, U. S. News, Redbook, Art News, Hot Rod,* and *Sports Illustrated.* The entries in this invaluable work may seem baffling at first, but a thoughtful study of several of them for a few minutes and a reading of the introductory guide in the front of the book should clear up any problems. Here's how one entry looks:

Tuition dilemma: a new way to pay the bills. Tuition Advance Fund. J. R. Silber. Atlantic 242:31−2+ Jl, 78.

The entry begins with the title and the author's name. The rest of the information indicates that the article appeared in the July 1978 issue of *Atlantic Monthly* magazine, volume 242, pages 31–32 and the following pages. It's simple when you know how!

The *Reader's Guide* began publication in 1900; for information in nineteenth-century periodicals, see *Poole's Index to Periodical Literature.* And for more specialized articles in scholarly journals, consult the appropriate subject index, several of which are listed below:

Applied Science and Technology Index: A subject index to about 225 periodicals in aeronautics and space science, chemistry, electricity and electronics, engineering, mathematics, physics, and related fields.

Art Index: An author-subject index to about 150 periodicals and museums' bulletins about archaeology, architecture, art history, arts and crafts, fine arts, graphic arts, industrial design, interior decoration, photography and films, planning and landscape design, and related subjects.

Biological and Agricultural Index: A cumulative subject index to about 150 periodicals in agricultural chemicals, economics, and engineering; animal husbandry; bacteriology; biology; botany; ecology; forestry; conservation; and related fields.

Business Periodicals Index: A cumulative subject index to about 170 periodicals in accounting, advertising, banking, economics, finance, management, taxation, and related fields.

Education Index: An author-subject index to about 240 educational periodicals and other materials. Indexed according to professional areas (administration, pre-school, elementary, exceptional children, and so on) and academic fields (arts, applied science and technology, business, and so on).

Social Sciences Index: An author-subject index to 263 periodicals in anthropology, archaeology, economics, environmental science, geography, law and criminology, political science, psychology, religion, sociology, and related fields. Formerly, the *Social Sciences and Humanities Index.*

These and indexes like them in other fields are designed mainly for specialists, but you may find some articles valuable and illuminating.

Another helpful reference tool is the newspaper index, the most widely available, up-to-date, and useful being the *New York Times Index*. Published twice a month and also in a cumulative volume once a year, the index not only refers to news articles, speeches, editorials, essays, and reviews in the *Times,* but also often summarizes their contents. The index entries will look mystifying at first, but the introductory guide should help to unravel them. For example, the citation "D 27, 8:2" simply means "December 27, page 8, column 2." Also, once you find out the date of an event from the *Times Index,* you can use it to consult other newspapers or newsmagazines for their treatment of the story. As you may be aware, the *Times* is not just an excellent newspaper; it is a valuable historical document with its thorough national and international news coverage, comprehensive biographical obituaries; complete texts of speeches and important statements; reviews of books, films, concerts, plays; and its own fine Sunday magazine.

We should also mention some specialized indexes:

The Book Review Digest: presents a list of selected book reviews and excerpts from a few of them. Also, states lengths of reviews.

The Book Review Index: no excerpts but a more complete list of reviews.

Essay and General Literature Index: subjects treated in essays, chapters, or sections of books. Particularly valuable in the humanities and social sciences.

Biographical Dictionaries Master Index: guide to nearly one million people listed in over fifty current *Who's Who* and other biographical works.

Biography Index: indexes biographical information appearing in over 1,000 magazines, books, and newspapers. Complements *Master Index*.

Consumer's Index: lists of articles from 100 periodicals about the financial or physical well-being of consumers. Includes test reports.

Abstracts

Similar to the index but often even more helpful is a reference tool you may know little about—the abstract journal. Published mainly for scholars who do not have adequate time to read all the articles in their field, the abstract journals provide summaries of articles. Among the ones you might find useful are the following:

Abstracts of English Studies: summaries mainly about literature from articles in American and English periodicals.

America: History and Life: A Guide to Periodical Literature: summaries of articles on the history of the United States and Canada.

Historical Abstracts: summaries of articles on political, diplomatic, economic, social, cultural, and intellectual history.

Sociological Abstracts: summaries of national and international books and articles.

Psychological Abstracts: summaries of national and international articles, books, reports, and dissertations.

Pamphlets and Government Publications

Finally, let's mention two other sources of materials: pamphlets and government publications. Because these are often handled differently in various libraries, your reference librarian will help you locate information in these sources. Incidentally, if you are ever stumped about finding anything, consult the reference librarian. This person is professionally trained to help students and scholars use the library and usually enjoys working on research problems.

And now where are you? With these suggestions about how to obtain a general knowledge of your subject and how to find what information the library has about it, you should be able to zero in on your subject, knowing whether sufficient material is available for a research paper. In an afternoon or two, you should be able to check the encyclopedia, find and flip through some books and articles, and decide where you're going. In glancing through books, check the table of contents, preface, and introductory and concluding chapters. For articles, start with the most recent long ones.

To begin, suppose you're interested in politics. A library check reveals numerous books and articles about this subject. Obviously, it is too broad and must be limited. As you poke through the sources, you discover some interesting facts about American voting habits. For example, a smaller percentage of Americans vote than of people in many other countries. You wonder why. Then you notice that only about 20 percent of our 18-to-20-year-olds said they voted in 1978. This shocks and surprises you. How could the figure be increased? As you read, you find several suggestions: postcard registration, registration at the polls on election day, weekend voting. You have a few ideas of your own. And so your research paper is born: "Let's Get Out the Youth Vote."

Once you have limited your subject and discovered what information the library has about it, you are ready to step ahead.

STEP 3: THE PRELIMINARY BIBLIOGRAPHY

The word *bibliography* sounds impressive, but it refers simply to a list of sources about a subject. You could have compiled one in your preliminary reading if you had definitely selected a subject. But assuming that you have only hit upon a topic after some general reading, you are now ready to work on your preliminary bibliography.

We refer to it as a "preliminary" bibliography to distinguish it from the final bibliography that usually appears at the end of research papers. The preliminary one helps you to pinpoint sources that might prove valuable. Because the final bibliography must be typed in alphabetical order, we recommend you do your preliminary work with 3″ by 5″ cards or similar slips of paper that you can rearrange easily as you discover additional sources. Frankly, for your relatively short freshman English paper, you could get by with notebook paper; but by working with the cards or slips, you will be learning the most efficient method for writing the lengthier papers required in advanced classes.

Before this step, you mainly wanted to know whether sufficient material about your subject was available. Now you want to select the most informative books, articles, or other publications about it. Remember to discriminate by thoughtfully studying the catalog cards, as we discussed previously. In looking for magazine articles in indexes, note the title, date, and number of pages, as well as the name of the publication. Exercise some judgment. For example, a seven-page article in *Scientific American* about teaching chimpanzees to use language would undoubtedly be more informative than a four-page condensation in *Reader's Digest* or a one-page account in *Newsweek.*

Also, learn to snoop around a bit, play detective. Investigate related topics, say the family and friends of your subject, or similar subjects. For a paper on the presidency of Ulysses S. Grant, scan the biography of his wife. For one titled "General Patton—Hero or Heel?" look through autobiographies or biographies of his colleagues—Eisenhower, Bradley, Clark, Gavin, and Montgomery. For a paper on state-operated lotteries, check into such related topics as the Irish Sweepstakes, state-run off-track betting, English soccer pools, and lotteries in European countries. A glance at the index of a book on a related subject might unearth a treasure of information.

Whenever you find a promising source, jot it down, one to a card. Most handbooks and rhetoric textbooks advise you to transcribe the bibliographical information according to the complicated form prescribed for the final bibliography (see pages 442–44). You can follow that form or, for the moment, you can use any form you like, but you must note all of the following:

Book	*Article*
Name of author, editor	Name of author
Title	Title
Subtitle	Name of publication
Edition (if more than one has been published)	Volume of professional or scholarly publication
Place of publication (first city listed, if several are given)	Date
Publisher	Page numbers
Date	

This information is generally available from the catalog card if the publication is a book, or the index entry if it is a periodical.

Three helpful hints about your preliminary bibliography.

1. Write the author's last name first to help you in alphabetizing later.
2. Copy down the call number and, if it might be a problem later, the location of the work. You may have to check something in it at the last moment—like the spelling of a name or the exact words of a quotation.
3. Write a comment or two about the material either from the information on the catalog card or from your glancing through it. This note may help later after you have examined many sources and wondered about some you looked at a week or two earlier.

The preliminary bibliography will probably keep growing as you keep reading. One reference source may refer you to another or mention a related subject to investigate. Some may prove to be dead ends, seemingly worthless. But jot down your evaluations and file the cards because you may see new possibilities in these references later.

You may wonder at this point whether you could have combined the previous step—the subject selection—with the compilation of the preliminary bibliography. You might have if you were sure of your subject and confident that materials about it were available. But our experience indicates that most students initially select such broad subjects that they must be trimmed and trimmed again. It might be wasteful to work up a preliminary bibliography before checking the library and doing some reading.

And now, armed with your subject and a stack of bibliography cards, you are almost ready to enter the writing stage. But first, to give direction to your reading and note-taking, we recommend a preliminary outline.

STEP 4: THE PRELIMINARY OUTLINE

As its name indicates, the preliminary outline is a tentative plan for your paper, a general roadmap showing where you are going and how you think you will get there. As you proceed, you may want to alter your trip: detouring here, staying longer there, skipping some places entirely. For example, in view of rising tuition costs, you decide to write a paper about the financial condition of colleges and universities. After some preliminary reading, you might draw up this preliminary outline:

I. Income sources
   A. State and local institutions
      1. Independent junior and community colleges
      2. Universities
   B. Private institutions
      1. Church-affiliated schools
      2. Independent institutions

    II. Expenses
        A. State and local institutions
        B. Private institutions

But after further reading, you realize that because private schools consist of such different types as large universities and small liberal arts colleges, you should further subdivide section I-B-2.

Your preliminary outline is not a binding contract; it can be changed and changed again. But it gets you started. And that's helpful because it's easy to just keep reading and postpone any commitment. The preliminary outline pins you down and forces you to think about organizing your reading and your ideas. But you are still free to make some changes. In our previous example, for instance, you might wind up with a paper restricted to the financial condition of only the private institutions, organized like this:

    I. Church-affiliated institutions
        A. Sources of income
        B. Expenses
    II. Large universities
        A. Sources of income
        B. Expenses
(and so forth)

As we've demonstrated, your preliminary outline might be only preliminary, or it could be your final one. Either way, it will help you get started and get organized.

Another advantage of a preliminary outline is that it can also help you in taking notes. That skill and others relating to the actual writing of the research paper will be discussed in the following chapter.

Assignments

For Discussion and Library Research

1 How appropriate would the following topics be for a research paper?

The Recent Retirement Law	The Future of Solar Energy
Cheating at Your College	The Impact of TV Advertising on Children
Women's Athletics	How No-Fault Insurance Works
Child Abuse	Movies Are Sexier than Ever
Life Today Is Better	Affirmative Action in Your Community

2 How many of the following would you expect to find in an abridged dictionary?

Months of the three principal calendars (Gregorian, Hebrew, Moslem)

422

Diagram of beef cuts
Table of alphabets (Hebrew, Arabic, Greek, Russian)
Currency of foreign countries
Geologic time scale
Diagram of car ignition
Manual alphabet for deaf-mutes
Proofreader's marks
Map of the United States
Books of the Old and New Testaments
Periodic table of chemical elements
Metric system
Morse code
Ship's bells
Zodiac signs
Radio frequencies
List of U.S. colleges and universities
Punctuation guide
Tables of weights and measures
List of capital cities of the United States

3   What information is missing from the catalog cards on pages 423–25?
What hints can you glean from information on the cards?

```
410
Bo1    Bolinger, Dwight Le Merton, 1907-
           Aspects of language / Dwight Bolinger. — 2d ed. — New
       York : Harcourt Brace Jovanovich, [1975]
           xvii, 682 p. : ill. ; 24 cm.
           Includes bibliographies and index.
           ISBN 0-15-503868-0




       P106.B59   1975              410            74-25091
                                                   MARC
       Library of Congress         75
```

616.8
Fre   **Freud, Sigmund,** 1856-1939.
            Sigmund Freud and Lou Andreas-Salomé; letters. Edited by
       Ernst Pfeiffer. Translated by William and Elaine Robson-Scott.
       [1st American ed.]   New York, Harcourt Brace Jovanovich
       [1972]

            "A Helen and Kurt Wolff book."
            Translation of Sigmund Freud, Lou Andreas-Salomé: Briefwechsel.

            1. Freud, Sigmund, 1856-1939. 2. Andreas-Salomé, Lou, 1861-1937.   I.
       Andreas-Salomé, Lou, 1861-1937. II. Pfeiffer, Ernst, ed.

       BF173.F85A43713   1972   616.8'917'0924   72-79922
       ISBN 0-15-133490-0   [B]   MARC

       Library of Congress   73

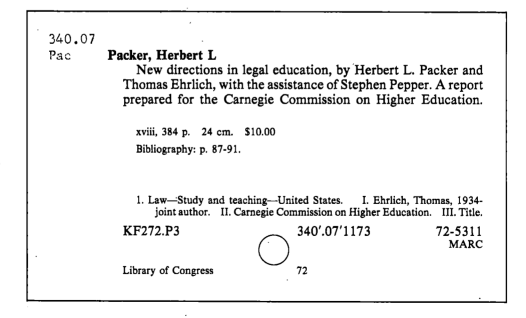

340.07
Pac   **Packer, Herbert L**
            New directions in legal education, by Herbert L. Packer and
       Thomas Ehrlich, with the assistance of Stephen Pepper. A report
       prepared for the Carnegie Commission on Higher Education.

            xviii, 384 p.   24 cm. $10.00
            Bibliography: p. 87-91.

            1. Law—Study and teaching—United States.   I. Ehrlich, Thomas, 1934-
            joint author. II. Carnegie Commission on Higher Education. III. Title.

       KF272.P3   340'.07'1173   72-5311
                                                                   MARC

       Library of Congress   72

Rutherford, William E
    Modern English / William E. Rutherford. — 2d ed. — New York : Harcourt Brace Jovanovich, c1975-

      v.   : ill. ; 24 cm.

  Includes index.
  ISBN 0-15-561059-7

  1. English language—Text-books for foreigners.   I. Title.

₍PE1128.R83   1975₎   428'.2'4   75-10765
                                      MARC

  Library of Congress   75

---

4 Name some possible reference sources for material about the following subjects. Your instructor may also wish you to determine whether your library contains sufficient information for a research paper about one of them.

Mass transit	School competency testing
Day-care centers	Soviet Jews
Women in the clergy	Social Security problems
Illegal immigrants	Nuclear wastes
Gay rights	Campaign finance reform
World famine	Socialized medicine
Polygamy today	New U.S. political alignments
Gambling	Fair trade laws
Hypnosis	Venereal disease

5 In what specialized indexes might you find information about the following? Your instructor may also wish you to determine whether your library contains sufficient material for a paper about them.

Dutch elm disease	Student recruiting in college
Acne remedies	Design and construction of school buildings
Video records	CATV (Community Antenna Television)
Psychiatric nursing	Effect of sexual activity on academic performance
Television advertising	Collective bargaining for public employees
Tax shelters	Military applications of lasers

425

Solar batteries	Giacometti exhibits
Educational games	Attitudes of college students
Cold remedies	Feeding of sheep

6 Suppose the following people are coming this year to speak on your campus. As a student working in the public relations office, you have been asked to prepare biographical sketches of each. What sources would you consult? Your instructor may ask you to write a biographical sketch about one of the speakers.

Edmund G. (Jerry) Brown, Jr.	Walter Cronkite	Zubin Mehta
	Valéry Giscard d'Estaing	Pete Rose
William F. Buckley, Jr.	Jane Fonda	Anwar el-Sadat
Warren Burger	Edward M. Kennedy	John Travolta
Anthony Burgess	Coretta Scott King	John Updike
Johnny Carson	Henry Kissinger	Cyrus Vance

Writing the Research Paper

Most students writing a research paper at a typical high school suffer through the agony of copying lengthy passages from books and magazines, and then frantically try to gather the passages and their own thoughts together in an all-night typing ordeal. A nightmare of an experience.

Sound familiar? If your high-school experience was like this, lack of sleep was only one of the things that was wrong. First, innocently or not so innocently, you probably plagiarized. Second, you were disorganized, having to scramble through pages and pages of notes looking again and again for information that you knew was there but could never find when you wanted it. Third, you probably turned in a mishmash of statements, indirect quotations, direct quotations, and plagiarized passages, few of them integrated with connecting transitions, all designed to fulfill the assignment and satisfy the teacher, but not written to interest readers or to clarify the subject for them.

If your high-school experience was different, fine: you are better prepared than most of your classmates to tackle the research paper. But even so, you can benefit from a review of the techniques that numerous scholars have developed to save time and to improve papers. The writing of a well-organized, worthwhile research paper begins with note-taking.

STEP 5: NOTE-TAKING

As your notes go, so goes your paper. If you learn to take notes carefully and thoughtfully, you should have little trouble writing a fine paper. But skillful note-taking requires an efficient system and disciplined habits.

The Mechanics of Note-Taking

Effective note-taking involves setting up an information retrieval system that enables you to find a particular note easily. To accomplish this, we recommend using 4″ by 6″ cards (to avoid confusion with the 3″ by 5″ bibliography cards) or slips of paper; we urge you not to use notebook pages. Because the note-taking process requires that a single note contain information from only one source about only one aspect of the subject, many notes will consist of only one or two sentences. Using a sheet of notebook paper for each is impractical and cumbersome.

The note-taking process may seem wasteful, but in practice it may save hours. As an example, for a paper about the Babe Ruth legend, you might read that his funeral was one of the largest ever held in New York City. After writing this information on a note card, you would check your preliminary outline to see where it would best fit and then identify the note with a "slug," a shortened subdivision heading from your outline. For the Ruth example, your slug might be "Folk Hero—Death." Later, when you have read all the source materials, you would sort the cards into stacks according to their slugs, arrange the stacks in the order of the outline, and begin your paper. When you reach a particular section, such as "Folk Hero—Death," there are your notes, sitting in a stack, waiting for you. The efficiency of this system results from your organizing the notes while writing them. Consequently, you no longer need endure the frantic search through page after page of a notebook for missing information, a chore that becomes harder as papers grow longer.

Sample note card

Slug————

Note————

First Draft- Getting Started

"Faced with the need to write, most people (including practiced writers) experience a strong and strange impulse to put off beginning."

Barzun and Graff p. 350

Identification

In addition to the slug and the note, each card must contain some indication of the source. Usually the last name of the author and page number is sufficient (see the sample note card below) because complete information is already available on the bibliography card. But if you are using sources by two authors with the same last name or if one author has written two sources cited in the paper, then add a first name or a short title to avoid confusion. Or follow any other system you find helpful and accurate; the notes are for your use only.

In summary, each note card should contain three entries: a subject heading, a note, and an identification of its source. So much for the mechanics of the system; now for the techniques of note-taking.

The Art of Note-Taking

At the beginning of the chapter we mentioned plagiarism. A lengthy definition of it appears on page 194, but simply stated, plagiarism involves using someone else's words or ideas without acknowledging the debt. Actually, plagiarism is stealing—improperly taking someone else's property, someone else's written work. This problem is especially likely to develop in a research paper because you rely on what others have written. Consequently, you may think, everything in your paper is plagiarized in a sense. Not so. You are entitled as a researcher to include common knowledge without documentation (citation of its source). If certain information is generally known, as is evident by the fact that it appears in several sources or in an encyclopedia, then you need not document it unless you use the author's exact words. For example, numerous anthropology sources relate that the bones of prehistoric Peking Man were discovered in a quarry outside the Chinese capital in 1926, and in 1941 were sent to a U.S. Marine base near Chingwangtao, where they were stolen or lost when the Japanese invaded during the Second World War. This information is common knowledge and need not be documented. But opinions about the significance of Peking Man should be. As you can realize, this principle of common knowledge means that you will have to exercise your judgment. As a guide, when in doubt, document anything that could be controversial or questionable. And, of course, document also all other phrases, sentences, and ideas that are not your own, using quotation marks for exact quotes and a raised number ([1]) to acknowledge the source. Realize that even paraphrased material must be documented.

That's why careful note-taking is important. If you copy passage after passage exactly as they appear in your sources, your paper may consist of a mass of quotations that make dull reading. Such papers may even result in inadvertent plagiarism. It's so easy to convince yourself when you finally sit down to write that there is no other way to state the author's idea without using the author's words. But there probably is, as you will discover if you follow our advice in compiling notes: use either telegraphic style or summarize the material.

Telegraphic Notes   You probably are already proficient in telegraphic style from your experience in lecture courses. Here's how to use it in note-taking:

Original passage

Another popular explanation for declining test scores is that desegregation has forced previously all-white schools to lower their academic standards in order to accommodate nonwhite students with fewer academic skills. But desegregation has been confined largely to the South and to a few big northern cities. Test scores, in contrast, have dropped off throughout the nation. In many cases the decline is even greater in the North than in the South. Both Iowa and Minnesota are more than 98 percent white, yet they report marked declines in high school scores. Whites cannot, then, blame their troubles on desegregation.
                              —Christopher Jencks, "What's Behind the Drop in Test Scores"

Telegraphic notes

Another explanation—declining test scores—desegregation. But desegregation largely in South—few northern cities. Test scores down nationally. Some declines greater in North. Iowa and Minn—98% white—test scores down greatly. Whites cannot blame desegregation.

From such telegraphic notes, you would find it relatively easy in your first draft to rewrite the ideas in your own words along the lines of the following:

Rewritten version

According to Jencks, lower test scores cannot be blamed on desegregation, which has occurred only in the South and in some northern cities. But test scores have declined nationally. Also, some scores have declined more in the North than in the South, and in two practically all-white states, Iowa and Minnesota, scores dropped significantly. Thus desegregation does not seem to be the cause of lower scores.[1]

Summary Notes   When you are reading, summary notes take more time and effort to compose than do telegraphic notes, but save time when you are writing because the work has been done. Read the material at least once, digest it, close the book or magazine, write the summary in your own words, and then check it for accuracy and completeness. It sounds time-consuming but it is not because you generally can use the summary in your first draft either as is or with only a few changes.

The trick in writing a summary is to exclude all examples, secondary comments, unrelated references, and superfluous words, and to concentrate on the topic idea. Here's an example of a summary note:

Original quotation

Research has shown that it is all but impossible to develop mental fatigue by studying, even by studying hard. We get "tired" readily enough but this happens because we are bored with the subject, not because bodily wastes accumulate in the brain, or even in the muscles. You may push away a textbook with the comment, "I'm exhausted! I can't read another word," then casually pick up a magazine or newspaper and read avidly, without any signs of fatigue, for an hour or so. Obviously, we have confused *fatigue* with *boredom.*

—Walter Pauk, *How to Study in College*

Summary note

According to research, it is almost impossible to become mentally fatigued by studying hard. People think they get tired, but actually they become bored.

Observe that the summary is not a paraphrase, a sentence-by-sentence rewording of the original. Instead of changing a few words here and there you would be as well off quoting the author's work, which most likely is stylistically better. And because the paraphrase requires nearly as many words, what is its advantage?

The summary, on the other hand, is shorter than the original and requires a thorough understanding of it. Usually you can obtain this by focusing on the topic sentences, which we have italicized for you in the following example:

Original quotation

Two things were outstanding in the creation of the English system of canals, and they characterize all the Industrial Revolution. *One is that the men who made the revolution were practical men.* Like Brindley, they often had little education, and in fact, school education as it was then could only dull an inventive mind. The grammar schools could only teach the classical subjects for which they were founded. The universities also (there were only two, at Oxford and Cambridge) took little interest in modern or scientific studies; and they were closed to those who did not conform to the Church of England.

The other outstanding feature is that the new inventions were for everyday use. The canals were arteries of communication: they were not made to carry pleasure boats, but barges. And the barges were not made to carry luxuries, but pots and pans and bales of cloth, boxes of ribbon, and all the common things that people buy by the penny-worth. These things had been manufactured in villages which were growing into towns now, away from London; it was a country-wide trade.

—Jacob Bronowski, *Ascent of Man*

431

Summary note

Two unique qualities characterize the English canal system and all the Industrial Revolution: the inventors were practical people often with little formal education, and their inventions were designed to serve practical, everyday needs.

You could have worded this summary differently, of course; nothing is sacred about our version. But the point and the beauty of a summary note is that it forces you to read carefully and thoughtfully, requires that you write about the information while it is fresh in your mind, and results in your having written a statement that can be easily integrated into your paper later without your having to rewrite it then. But remember—even though the words are yours, the idea belongs to another. Consequently, you must indicate the debt by citing your source.

Should you ever copy a passage down word for word? Yes, when quoting from a literary work, such as an autobiography, play, or novel, or in special instances when the wording is particularly striking, memorable, or colorful. It would be a shame, for example, to redo Mary-Claire Van Leunen's cogent argument against overquotation:

When you are writing well, your sentences should join each other like rows of knitting, each sentence pulling up what went before it, each sentence supporting what comes after. . . . Quotation introduces an alien pattern—someone else's diction, someone else's voice, someone else's links before and afterward. Even necessary quotations are difficult to knit smoothly into your structure. Overquotation will result in something more like a bird's nest than like fine handiwork.

—A Handbook for Scholars

We agree. The fewer the quotations, the more readable the research paper. And especially, avoid long quotations. They may help you pad but they bore readers. Remember the Golden Rule of Writing: write unto your readers as you would have them write unto you. And just as you often skip over long quoted passages in your own reading (and may have done just that with our example), so you should be cautious about including them. The crucial time to decide not to use them is in note-taking. Later, when writing, you may not have the strength and time to resist inserting quotations to pad your research paper. So—take notes in telegraphic style or write summaries, and save word-for-word copying for irresistible passages.

STEP 6: WRITING THE FIRST DRAFT

Writing the first draft of a research paper is similar to writing any other first draft, except it is even tougher to get started. That's because you know the task ahead is harder, so the temptation is greater to postpone it in order to acquire more information—or to wait for inspiration. But start you must. Once you settle down to it, you are likely to be so full of the subject and so well organized that the writing will be easier than you thought. But the opening sentences are always excruciating! Just plod ahead, realizing that if you do not like them, you can redo them later.

Depending on your own inclination and the length of your paper, you might either write the first draft at one sitting or space the work over several days, perhaps allowing, for example, an evening for each one of your three main divisions. Some writers complete their first draft of one part of the paper before they even do research on others. For example, in a paper on the bombing of Hiroshima, the section about the military situation in the summer of 1945 might be written before doing the research about the decision to drop the atomic bomb and the opposition to it by prominent scientists. If you can block out your paper in this way, you might find it easier to research and write each section of the paper individually. Usually, however, people postpone the writing as long as they can, either because their topic does not lend itself to such neat division or because they want to delay the moment of truth. We recommend that you write as much as you can, as early as you can. You can always revise later.

Quotation Techniques

When you do want to use some quotations in your paper, remember to keep them as short as possible. For long ones that you cannot or do not want to summarize or express in your own words, try the processes of assimilation or reduction.

Assimilation   The process of assimilation consists of using summary along with key words and phrases from the original quotations. You present the idea in your own style, but weave in a few short phrases from the original because of their unusual force and flavor. In the following illustration, note how the assimilated version preserves the main point of the original in about half the words.

Original quotation

When the oriental mystery cults took root in Greece, one of the hallmarks of that era was the turning away from objective knowledge and the rejection of the rational, twin tendencies apparent in this country at least since 1948, when ouija boards first outsold Monopoly games by a substantial margin. Wrenched apart by profound changes in attitudes and custom, Greek civilization with all its complex ambivalence provided fertile ground for the mystery cults, and the parallels between that ambivalence and our own present us with an ominous message from the past: Faith in the occult flourishes in societies that are crumbling, endangered, or in the throes of radical change.
            —Marjorie Clay, "The New Religious Cults and Rational Science"

Assimilated version:

Like the ancient Greeks, according to philosopher Marjorie Clay, we are turning away from objective knowledge and rationalism. Just as their "complex ambivalence provided fertile ground for the mystery cults," so, she claims, have our similar attitudes made us ripe for belief in the occult. Such a faith "flourishes in societies that are crumbling, endangered, or in the throes of radical change."

Reduction Another useful technique for dealing with quotations involves using ellipses to reduce them. This punctuation device allows you to substitute three dots (...) to inform readers that words have been omitted. When the omitted words appear at the end of a sentence, the three dots follow the customary period. In the Van Leunen example on page 432, for instance, we deleted this sentence: "(That's how I think knitting works.)" This parenthetical aside was unimportant so we substituted ellipses. In the following example, ellipses are used to shorten a sentence:

Original quotation

Yet surely it takes only a little common sense to see that some sort of world history is the only way a college can do justice to students who live in a world where events in Asia, Africa, and Latin America are as likely to involve the United States in critical actions as anything happening in Europe or North America.
     —William H. McNeill, "Studying the Sweep of the Human Adventure"

With ellipses

Yet surely ... some sort of world history is the only way a college can do justice to students ... in a world where events in Asia, Africa, and Latin America are as likely to involve the United States . . . as anything happening in Europe or North America.

Depending on your purpose, audience, and the number of other quotations in your paper, you might not want to reduce a sentence like McNeill's. But you should realize that ellipses can be used in this way.

When you use ellipses, you should be careful not to distort the original. This occurs frequently in advertisements for films, plays, books, peformances, and the like. Here's how it's done:

Original review:	In his latest, the author takes aim at the finance business and hits that fat, juicy target with a feather, failing to dent it.
Ad with ellipses:	In his latest, the author takes aim at the finance business and hits that fat, juicy target. . . .
Original review:	The film is pretty silly, but it captures a certain scruffy, seamy side of big city life.
Ad with ellipses:	The film ... captures a certain scruffy, seamy side of big city life.

Quotations should not be distorted. They should be copied honestly, even if the original contains an error or something that might be construed as your error by readers. To deal with that situation, you may use brackets and the Latin word *sic* (meaning "thus") to inform readers that the error appears in the original. Brackets can also be helpful in inserting your own comments or explanations into quotations:

Our contemporary writers, artists, and philosophers are not appreciably more effective than those of the golden age of Greece [about the fifth century B.C.], yet the average high-school student understands much more of nature than the greatest of Greek scientists.
—B. F. Skinner, *Science and Human Behavior*

Insertion   As a final point about quotations, we suggest that you weave them in gracefully instead of patching them together awkwardly. Here are some examples.

Patched: Sister Jeannine Gramick, SSND, in her article "The Myths of Homosexuality," makes a similar point. She says, "There are, undoubtedly, effeminate male homosexuals and masculine-type lesbians, but these constitute only a small minority of the gay population."[1]

Woven: In her article "The Myths of Homosexuality," Sister Jeannine Gramick, SSND, makes a similar point in stating that "there are, undoubtedly, effeminate homosexuals and masculine-type lesbians, but these constitute only a small minority of the gay population."[1]

And then there is the painful "tell 'em, quote, and tell 'em what you've quoted" technique:

Patched: Dr. Bettelheim points out a more serious adverse effect of television on children. "They lose the ability to learn from reality because life experiences are more complicated than the ones they see on screen, and there is no one who comes in at the end to explain it all."[2] This is another reason why Dr. Bettelheim is critical of television for children.

Woven: Dr. Bettelheim points out how television affects children more adversely by explaining that "they lose the ability to learn from reality because life experiences are more complicated than the ones they see on screen, and there is no one who comes in at the end to explain it to them."[2]

Our point is that quotations should be neatly worked into the fabric of the paper. A paper should not be a patchwork quilt of statements and quotations, but a carefully woven blanket.

435

STEP 7: DOCUMENTATION

The research paper requires documentation to allow writers to acknowledge their indebtedness to authors and to permit readers to verify information or learn more about the subject. This documentation may take the form of a numbered reference on the page where the source is referred to and a list of sources at the end of the paper. One problem with documentation is that no form is universal, even in a particular scholarly field, such as English, electrical engineering, or psychology.

What then should you do? The answer depends—as to some extent in all writing—on who your readers are. Documentation for history, marketing, and biology instructors will differ. You must follow the form they require, just as scholars and researchers follow whatever editors prescribe. For this course, we suggest you use the Modern Language Association form described in the following pages.

But your instructor in this or other courses may understandably prefer a different system. So be it. Follow that system either by requesting a style sheet from the instructor or by consulting a library source. It is not necessary to memorize numerous exasperating details. Open this book or some other model, and follow the prescribed form with meticulous care, noting precisely every punctuation mark, every abbreviation, every capitalization. Don't guess; don't be careless. Follow the form as if your paper depends on your handling documentation perfectly. And don't say we didn't warn you about being careful!

Endnotes

Until recently, research papers in fields other than the sciences contained footnotes. Readers could conveniently find information about a reference at the bottom of the page. But today many instructors and editors prefer these references to appear at the end of a paper on a page headed "Notes." This change is motivated by a desire to increase readability, as footnotes can be distracting to many readers not interested in them. Consequently, endnotes are in, footnotes generally out. But your instructor may prefer footnotes in your research paper.

In the future, you may find greater use of parenthetical documentation, which calls for some or all of the reference information to be inserted when the source is mentioned, as exemplified in the *MLA Handbook* (New York: Modern Language Association, 1977), pp. 91–92 and 94–96. Let us end this discussion with that example of parenthetical documentation and move on to endnote form.

Although an endnote may add a comment or an explanation, its most common function is to provide information about a source. If the reference is to a book, follow this basic form for its first citation.

Book

1. Author entry
   First name, middle name or initial, last name, comma.
2. Book entry
   Title of book underlined (to indicate italics in print), parenthesis, city of publication, colon, publisher, comma, year of publication, parenthesis, comma.
3. Page entry
   Abbreviation *p.* or *pp.,* number(s), period.

Here's how it looks:

> [1] Erich Fromm, *The Art of Loving* (New York: Harper & Row, 1956), p. 23.

Please note: at the beginning of an endnote is a raised number, which is keyed to the one in the text after the quotation or material from a source. Endnotes are numbered consecutively throughout the paper. Also, like a sentence, an endnote begins with a capital letter and ends with a period.

Because books come in an endless variety of forms, the list on page 438 provides numerous variations of the basic example. Please study these carefully. If that list does not contain a model, consult the *MLA Handbook,* your instructor, or as a last resort, write your note in the style of the closest example to it.

For the first reference to an article, the form is similar but the differences are important to note:

Article

1. Author entry (same)
   First name, middle name or initial, last name, comma.
2. Article-publication entry
   Quotation marks, title of the article, comma, quotation marks, title of the publication underlined (to indicate italics in print), comma, day, month (abbreviated if more than five letters), year, comma.
3. Page entry (same)
   The abbreviation *p.* or *pp.,* page number(s), period.

Here's an example:

> [1] Stuart Barr, "First Message from the Planet of the Apes," *New York,* 24 Feb. 1975, pp. 30–37.

This basic form is somewhat tricky because the date follows military usage instead of the regular month-day-year. And once again, like books, periodicals vary considerably, so you will probably have to consult the numerous examples in the list on page 439. .

Examples of Book Endnotes
(First reference)

Author—one

¹ Richard Lanham, *Style: An Anti-Textbook* (New Haven: Yale Univ. Press, 1974), p. 29.

    Comment: Subtitles, used as indicated after a colon, may be omitted in notes but not in the bibliography.

Author—two or more

² William Strunk, Jr. and E. B. White, *The Elements of Style,* 2nd ed. (New York: Norton, 1970), p. 63.

    Comment: List authors in order as printed on title page. For three, use *and* before last author (X, Y, and Z). For more than three use either *et al.* or *and others* (Robert Spiller et al.). Also, the publisher's name may be shortened (W. W. Norton & Co., Inc. to Norton).

Author—commission, government agency, committee

³ U.S. Commission on Civil Rights, *The Excluded Student,* Report III (Washington, D.C.: U.S. Government Printing Office, 1973), p. 54.

Author—unknown or anonymous

⁴ *The 1979 Buying Guide Issue of Consumer Reports* (Mt. Vernon, N.Y.: Consumer's Union, 1978), pp. 157–59.

    Comment: Because the location of Mt. Vernon might not be known, the state is noted.

Edition—after the first (see also note 2)

⁵ M. H. Abrams, *A Glossary of Literary Terms,* 3rd ed. (New York: Holt, Rinehart and Winston, 1971), p. 78.

Editor—one author

⁶ William Makepeace Thackeray, *Vanity Fair,* ed. Geoffrey and Kathleen Tillotson (Boston: Houghton Mifflin, 1963), pp. 34–36.

Editor—Collection of works by different authors

⁷ Jesse L. Jackson, "Give the People a Vision," in *The Reading Commitment,* ed. Michael E. Adelstein and Jean G. Pival (New York: Harcourt Brace Jovanovich, 1978), pp. 402–09.

Encyclopedia or other well-known reference work

⁸ "Holocaust," *The New Columbia Encyclopedia,* 1975 ed.

    Comment: If the author's name is given, it should appear first. For reference works not alphabetically arranged, write volume and page number.

Examples of Article Endnotes
(First reference)

Author unknown or anonymous

   [1] "Carter's Ailment," *Newsweek,* 1 Jan. 1979, p. 17.

Collection of articles

   [2] Art Buchwald, "Job Hunting," in *Short Essays,* ed. Gerald Levin (New York: Harcourt Brace Jovanovich, 1980), pp. 324–27.

   Comment: See also page 438, note 7.

Journal—scholarly (each issue paginated from page 1)

   [3] Carl F. Strauch, "Kings in the Back Row: Meaning Through Structure—A Reading of Salinger's *The Catcher in the Rye,*" *Wisconsin Studies in Contemporary Literature,* 2, No. 4 (1961), 5–30.

   Comment: This article appeared in volume 2, issue 4. Note that all the numbers are Arabic. Also note underlined (italicized) book title in title of the article.

Journal—scholarly (continuous pagination annually)

   [4] Timothy R. Donovan, "Writing Teachers and Why Write?" *College Composition and Communication,* 29 (1978), 397–98.

   Comment: When the title ends with a question mark, no comma follows the quotation marks.

Magazine—weekly

   [5] Roger Angell, "The Sporting Scene (Baseball)," *New Yorker,* 14 April 1975, pp. 90–95.

Magazine—monthly

   [6] Betsy Langman and Alexander Cockburn, "Sirhan's Gun," *Harper's,* Jan. 1975, pp. 16–27.

Newspaper

   [7] Bettye Lee Mastin, "Everything Is Simple—When Others Do It," *Lexington (Ky.) Herald-Leader,* 6 Jan. 1979, Sec. C, p. 3, cols. 2–3.

   Comment: Sec. = section; cols. = columns.

Review

   [8] Diane Johnson, "A Gift for Pen and Ink," rev. of *The Diary of Virginia Woolf,* Vol. II, ed. Anne Olivier Bell, *New York Times Book Review,* 31 Dec. 1978, p. 3.

But suppose your references are to neither books nor articles. If your source is a pamphlet, treat it like a book. Or if the source is not in print, perhaps these examples will be helpful:

Film

[1] Richard Donner, dir., *Superman,* with Marlon Brando and Christopher Reeve, Warner Bros., 1978.

> Comment: Title, distributor, and date must be. included. Other information about the length of film, director, producer, stars, screenwriter should appear if pertinent.

Interview

[2] Personal interview with Woody Allen, 4 July 1979.
[3] Telephone interview with Thomas Sawyer, Professor of English, College of Engineering, University of Michigan, 5 Jan. 1980.

Lecture

[4] William Jansen, Professor of English, "The Rationale For the Dirty Joke," Distinguished Professor Lecture, Arts and Sciences College, University of Kentucky, 17 April 1976.

Letter

[5] Letter received from Isaac Bashevis Singer, 15 Feb. 1978.

Television or radio program

[6] *The American Family: An Endangered Species?* hosted by Edwin Newman and Betty Rollin, NBC News Special, 2 Jan. 1979.

> Comment: Program title, network or station and city, and date must be provided. Other information should be furnished if pertinent.

All the examples of endnotes indicate the prescribed form for the first reference in the research paper. What about subsequent references?

You need only identify them briefly, usually with the author's last name and the relevant page number.

Lanham, p. 17.

If such a note would not be clear because you have previously referred to works by two authors named Lanham or to two works by the same author, simply add the necessary clarifying information:

Richard Lanham, p. 17.
Lanham, *Revising Prose,* p. 17.

The short author-page entry has replaced *ibid.,* which you may have learned about previously. Among others delighted at its demise are librarians, who will no longer have to respond to the perennial student question, "Where can I find a copy of *Ibid?*"

We'd like to end this section on endnotes by answering some questions that our students usually ask.

● Where do endnotes appear and how should they be typed?

See the sample research paper, page 461.

● If I mention the author's name and the title in my paper, should I include them again in the note?

Good question. Authors' names and sometimes book titles should be used whenever practical in the text. Therefore, you need not repeat the author's name in the note, but the title should be mentioned again.

● Where do I find the place and date of publication?

Usually this information appears on the title page or on the back of it. And, incidentally, if several cities are listed, select the first one.

● What if no date or publisher or publication place is printed?

Use the abbreviation "n.d." for no date, and "n.p." for both no publisher and no publication place. According to where you insert the abbreviation, its meaning will be clear (New York: n.p., 1980).

● My source contains several dates—copyrights, impressions, and printings. Which one should I use?

Use the latest copyright date.

● Where should I insert the raised numbers in my paper?

Numbers should appear at the end of an appropriate unit (phrase, sentence, or paragraph), not after an author's name. See the research paper examples on pages 452–60. Also, the number should be placed *after* all punctuation marks except the dash.

● Should I capitalize all words in a title? And should I use quotation marks or underlining for a short-story title?

For capitalization of titles, see page 511 in the Reference Guide. For writing of titles, see page 437.

● Can endnotes be used for comments and explanations?

Yes, if absolutely necessary. Usually all such remarks should be included in the paper because some readers may not turn to the endnotes.

● What if I have numerous references to a book, such as a novel?

In such instances, state at the end of the first note that "all further references to this work will appear in the text." And then put these references in parentheses at the end of the sentence, as we have done here (p. 125). Note that the period comes after the parentheses, even in quoted matter: We tend to forget that Henderson refers to himself as "probably mad" (p. 8).

● Is the form of a bibliography entry the same as the form of the endnote?

That's what we were just going to write about. Read on.

Bibliography

A bibliography is an alphabetized list of all works referred to in the paper. Some instructors may not require a bibliography for a short paper; others may want it to include not only the sources mentioned in the notes but other sources consulted. Do not try to impress your readers by padding the list. This is an old trick, and your instructor or other readers may themselves have resorted to it at some time. The best practice is to list only those books, articles, and other sources that have been of some significant help.

Study the following example to distinguish a bibliography entry from an endnote:

Bibliography entry

```
Holman, C. Hugh. The Immoderate Past: The Southern

    Writer and History. Athens: Univ. of Georgia

    Press, 1977.
```

Endnote

```
    ³C. Hugh Holman, The Immoderate Past (Athens: Univ.

of Georgia Press, 1977), p. 52.
```

Did you spot these differences?

1. Bibliography entry begins flush with left-hand margin and second line is indented like a paragraph. But the first line of an endnote is indented; second line is flush with the margin.
2. Bibliography entry is not numbered; endnote is numbered.

3. Bibliography entry uses author's last name first; endnote, first name first. (Easy to remember: bibliography is alphabetized.)
4. Bibliography entry uses periods to separate author, title, and publication data; endnote uses commas.
5. Bibliography entry lists title and subtitle; endnote may list only title.
6. Bibliography entry presents publication information in sentence form; endnote uses parentheses.
7. Bibliography entry does not list page(s) of a book; endnote does.

Like endnotes, bibliography entries come in all forms and fashions, as you can see in the list of examples below and on the following page.

You can realize now why the information on your bibliography cards must be complete and why we suggested that you need not worry about writing the entries in the required form at that time. And what we stated about endnotes applies here also: numerous other types of sources exist than are illustrated here. Consult your instructor, check a style sheet, or as a last resort, model your entry on the most similar one given here.

At first reading, all these conventions may seem incredibly complicated and complex. They are. But bear in mind that they have been designed to enable readers to obtain maximum information in minimum space and at the same time to avoid distracting other readers who are not curious about your sources. Just as baseball, backgammon, or bridge might have seemed impossible to understand when you first started to play but proved easier afterward, so with practice, documentation makes more sense and gets simpler. And what you should always realize is that you need not memorize or guess about documentation form. There is little excuse for errors except laziness or the unwillingness to look up the proper form.

Now it's time to look up and move on to the next step in writing the research paper.

Examples of Bibliographical Entries

Author—one

Lanham, Richard. *Style: An Anti-Textbook.* New Haven: Yale Univ. Press, 1974.

Author—two or more

Strunk, Jr., William, and E. B. White. *The Elements of Style.* New York: Norton, 1970.

Author—commission, Government Agency, Committee

U.S. Department of Housing and Urban Development. *Wise Home Buying.* Washington, D.C.: GPO, 1975.

Edition—after the first

Abrams, M. H. *A Glossary of Literary Terms.* 3rd. ed. New York: Holt,
Rinehart and Winston, 1971.

Editor—one author

Thackeray, William Makepeace. *Vanity Fair.* Ed. Geoffrey and Kathleen
Tillotson. Boston: Houghton Mifflin, 1963.

Editor—collection of works by different authors

Jackson, Jesse L. "Give the People a Vision." In *The Reading Commitment.* Ed. Michael E. Adelstein and Jean G. Pival. New York: Harcourt Brace Jovanovich, 1978, pp. 402–09.

> Comment: Give page numbers for short complete pieces in longer
> works.

Volumes—works or collections

McGiffert, Arthur Cushman. *A History of Christian Thought.* Vol. I. New
York: Charles Scribner's Sons, 1946.

Journal article—scholarly, each issue starting with page 1

Strauch, Carl F. "Kings in the Back Row: Meaning Through Structure—
A Reading of Salinger's *The Catcher in the Rye.*" *Wisconsin Studies in
Contemporary Literature,* 2, No. 4 (1961), 5–30.

Journal article—scholarly, paginated annually

Donovan, Timothy R. "Writing Teachers and Why Write?" *College
Composition and Communication,* 29 (1978), 397–98.

Magazine—weekly

Angell, Roger. "The Sporting Scene (Baseball)." *New Yorker,* 14 April
1975, pp. 90–95.

Magazine—monthly

Langman, Betsy and Alexander Cockburn. "Sirhan's Gun." *Harper's,* Jan.
1975, pp. 16–27.

Newspaper

Mastin, Bettye Lee. "Everything Is Simple—When Others Do It." *Lexington* (Ky.) *Herald-Leader,* 6 Jan. 1979, Sec C, p. 3, cols. 2–4.

Review

Johnson, Diane. "A Gift for Pen and Ink." Rev. of *The Diary of Virginia
Woolf, Vol II,* ed. Anne Olivier Bell. *New York Times Book Review,* 31
Dec. 1978, p. 3.

Article—author unidentified

"Carter's Ailment." *Newsweek,* 1 Jan. 1979, p. 17.

STEP 8: REVISION

After completing your first draft, revise it carefully, scrutinizing it closely for organizational, stylistic, and mechanical weaknesses. In addition, examine it with these questions in mind:

1. Could the introduction be more interesting and informative?
2. Do transitions enable the reader to move easily from one section of the paper to another and to see clearly the relationship between the sections?
3. Are the quotations smoothly woven into the text?
4. Can lengthy quotations be eliminated or shortened by using ellipses? Can they be clarified by inserting a few of your own words in brackets?
5. Are footnotes numbered properly? Is the reference information presented correctly?
6. Can the number and length of endnotes be reduced by shifting the names of authors and the titles of their works from endnotes to the text without creating awkwardness?
7. Does the paper end with a summary and, if appropriate, a call for action?

STEP 9: WRITING THE FINAL DRAFT

Four matters may be left for the final draft: the title, the title page, the final outline, and the bibliography. This is not to say that these may not be attended to earlier if you wish, just that they may be postponed.

The Title

Although a research paper requires a serious, scholarly investigation of a subject, it need not sport a deadly title. Everyone enjoys a touch of humor, as these titles of articles in professional journals indicate:

Sheila Shaw, "The Rape of Gulliver: Case Study of a Source," *PMLA,* 90 (Jan. 1975), 62–69.

Elizabeth Wooten, "English Up Against the Wall," *College English,* 36 (Dec. 1974), 466–70.

Or, if not amusing, the title should at least be interesting, even intriguing:

Garry Wills, *Inventing America: Jefferson's Declaration of Independence* (New York: Doubleday, 1978), pp. 89–98.

Marlys Harris, "Keeping a Working Marriage Working," *Money,* Jan. 1979, pp. 44–48.

The Title Page

In these days of conservation, with everyone trying to economize, it is natural that title pages, like free service station maps, should disappear. And so they have, as the first page of the research paper on page 452 will reveal. But we're old-fashioned enough to like them, and your instructor may be also, because they dress up a paper, giving it a touch of elegance. If you'd like to use one and know your instructor would not object, then follow one of these two forms:

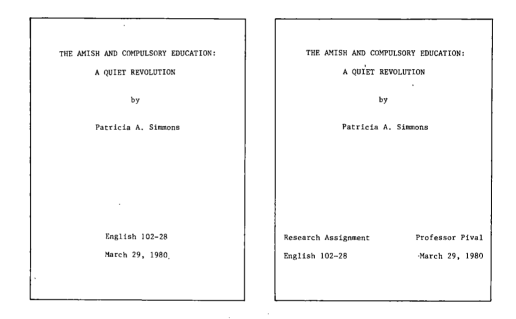

Notice that the title is capitalized (not underlined) and does not end with a period. Also, the title should be repeated at the top of the first manuscript page. Obviously, if you do not use a title page, follow the form in the sample research paper.

The Final Outline

Some instructors may request that you hand in a formal outline with your final paper. This outline consists mainly of a revision of your preliminary outline. Be sure, however, that any changes you have made between your preliminary investigation and your completed paper are incorporated into the formal outline. An illustration of the formal outline accompanies the student research paper reprinted at the end of this chapter.

STEP 10: PROOFREADING

You have put so much time and effort on your paper that you should proofread it carefully to avoid letting it be spoiled by careless mistakes. Plan to spend at least an hour checking for typing errors, searching for faulty endnotes and bibliographical entries, and trying to find the dozens of other things that can go wrong in a paper of this length. Patience in proofreading is a virtue. Practice it.

FINAL WORDS

We have treated this subject as completely as we think is necessary for most undergraduate research papers that you may write in English, economics, history, sociology, anthropology, political science, nursing, education, and other classes. But, as graduate or professional students, you may be required to follow some practices omitted or presented differently here.

The following student research paper should help you figure out how to deal with some typographical and other matters not covered specifically in this chapter. Refer to the paper as you write your first and final drafts. What we particularly like is that it is relatively free of quotations, not cluttered with them as so many student papers are. As this statement implies, you should know your subject so well, have digested all the information so thoroughly, and be so filled with ideas about it that you can write freely without relying constantly on numerous notes.

When you write endnotes and your bibliography, take care. A research paper, like a formal wedding ceremony, is steeped in tradition and protocol that must be followed to the letter. You may not like either, but you should show respect for both. Both are ceremonies of seriousness and importance that have evolved over the years. And despite the inconvenience imposed on the married couple and the writer, both ceremonies when completed bring joy, pleasure, and satisfaction.

The task of writing a research paper is formidable; the achievement fulfilling.

THE AMISH AND COMPULSORY EDUCATION: Title in capitals

A QUIET REVOLUTION

by

Patricia A. Simmons

English 102–28

March 29, 1980

448

The Amish and Compulsory Education

Thesis: The Supreme Court decision permitting Amish
children to be exempted after the eighth grade
from school attendance laws properly reaffirms
democratic respect for religious freedom.

    I. For years the Amish have been persecuted for
their beliefs about education.

        A. The attempt by law officers to force
students to attend public schools in
Olwein, Iowa is one example.

        B. The Amish have been fined, sentenced,
and jailed for refusing to comply with
the compulsory education law.

        C. The Wisconsin v. Yoder case resolved the
issue in 1972.

   II. The Amish culture explains the Amish resistance to public education.

        A. They believe that their simple farm life
belies the need for an education ade-
quate for a technological society.

        B. They believe that agricultural knowledge
best comes from tending a farm.

        C. They believe that public schools will
corrupt the values of their young people.

449

D. They believe that close adherence to
    Amish ways is necessary to get into
    Heaven.

III. The advantages gained by the Supreme Court
    decision outweigh the objections raised.

    A. John William Calhoun argued that no
        branch of government has the right to
        deny education to a group.

        1. The Amish do receive the equivalent
            of an eighth-grade education.

        2. Most Amish young people are not
            interested in leaving the community.

    B. The few Amish who leave to obtain a
        higher education are more highly moti-
        vated than the average college student,
        and, therefore, can succeed.

    C. Calhoun's argument that education is
        necessary to produce good citizens is
        belied by the exemplary social behavior
        of the Amish.

    D. Another objection is that the decision
        establishes a precedent for other groups.

        1. However, the ruling was limited to
            the Amish.

        2. Other groups must prove that they
            are providing an adequate education
            and that public education would

               undermine the religious values of

               the group.

      E. Castelli's concern about best protecting

           children within their family group is

           answered by the close community of the

           Amish.

IV. The decision protects the rights of a minority group to establish its own identity
and culture.

Student Research Paper

Patricia A. Simmons   Use this form
if no title page
English 102–28   is included

Professor Pival

March 29, 1979

The Amish and Compulsory Education: Title

A Quiet Revolution

It was almost like a scene out of a Dickens novel:
the truant officer explaining to the Amish children
that they had to leave on the bus for the town school,
the sheriff standing there with him, trying to smile at
the frightened youngsters. When the truant officer
finished, the sheriff turned around and walked to the
bus, expecting the children to file behind him. But
after someone yelled "Run!" in German, the children
dashed out the back door, and scattered into the woods.
Several days later, the truant officer and sheriff re—
turned with reinforcements, but soon retreated empty—
handed when confronted by begging fathers, weeping
mothers, and children who kept singing "Jesus Loves
Me," and refused to be pried from their desks.[1]

Summary from
source

This scene in Olwein, Iowa was not an isolated one. For years, the Amish in numerous states were arrested, jailed, sentenced, and fined for refusing to allow their children to attend state schools beyond the eighth grade. Joe Wittmer, a professor of education and former member of the Amish sect, has estimated that "literally hundreds of times, Amish fathers and mothers have gone to jail" and that some have left the country.[2] From their standpoint, the Amish maintained that the state education laws interfered with their First Amendment right to freedom of religion. School officials, on the other hand, declared that the state had the right to require children to attend school. In 1972, the issue was finally resolved in <u>Wisconsin</u> v. <u>Yoder</u>, in which the Supreme Court unanimously decided that the Amish children should be exempted from attending school after the eighth grade.

Woven quotation

To understand the Amish decision, it is necessary to know something about these people. Referred to by many as "the plain people" for their wearing of dark, unadorned clothes, driving of horse and buggy, use of windmills, and disregard for nearly all modern conveniences and inventions, the Amish represent a novelty to a government unaccustomed to a minority desiring self-sufficiency and isolation. Their preference for the simple life, close to nature, does not mean that the Amish are opposed to education. They have definite edu-

453

cation goals as stated by A. S. Kinsinger, chairman of
the Old Order Amish Steering Committee: "Our foremost
desire in education is to end with a respectful law-
abiding, and self-supporting citizen. . . . We are very
much in favor of a good, solid eighth grade education but in our own way. . . ."[3]

Ellipses used
to shorten
quotation

The "Amish way" is a decidedly different approach
to education. Modern techniques and supplies are of
little value in the Amish educational system. Amish education is, like Amish society in general, simple, and
to outsiders, rather old-fashioned.

To avoid sending their children to public schools
to be educated by others, the Amish built their own
schools in many communities. Usually they were one- or
two-room buildings, that for religious reasons had no
artificial light, visual aids such as films or records,
or modern sanitation facilities. The teachers were also
Amish, most with only an eighth grade traditional education. But regardless of whether their children attended
these schools, which were operated under state super-
vision, or regular public schools, the Amish did not
want their children to continue beyond the eighth grade.

Why did they object to further schooling? The
Amish contend that it is unnecessary because education
should prepare their children for life in the Amish
world. This life is in harmony with the soil and nature
because God is pleased when people care for plants and

animals. To the Amish, "nature is a garden, . . . man was made to be a caretaker (not an exploiter) in the garden, and . . . manual labor is good."[4] But children are educated in such areas as reading, writing, math, civics, religion, nature study, and German, which is used in relgious ceremonies but mainly taught at home. Education beyond the eighth grade, however, is deemed unnecessary since children in their teens should be working on the farm.

Ellipses within a sentence for stylistic purposes

In addition to believing that their children do not need this much formal education, the Amish worry that sending them to the traditional consolidated high school would corrupt their values. Parents fear that the public schools would expose their children to materialistic influences and would uphold the virtues of scientific and intellectual achievement, self-distinction, competition, worldly success, and socialization, with other values not admired by the Amish. Instead, they stress moral achievement, cooperative community welfare, wisdom, and good sense, and separation from other groups. In testifying before the Supreme Court, Hostetler affirmed the Amish's concern by stating that "the imposition of a high school's value system on Amish youth will psychologically alienate them and destroy their communities."[5]

Woven quotation

In addition to worrying about the adverse impact that a public high school would have on their children,

and to believing that an eighth grade education is sufficient, the Amish have a religious concern. William
Ball, attorney for the Amish, expressed it when explaining that the purpose of Amish education is to get to
heaven.[6] If parents should lose their children to another way of life, then according to Hostetler, the
parents would suffer for two reasons:

> (a) parents are held accountable for rearing
> their children in the fear of God; to fail in
> that is to leave a blemish on the church, and
> (b) to lose one's children to the world is to
> lose hope of their salvation and of spending
> eternity with them in heaven.[7]

Quotation of more than four lines indented; quotation marks not used.

In view of these beliefs, it is understandable why
the Amish were unwilling to comply with state compulsory attendance laws. And it is easy to realize why the
Supreme Court in a unanimous decision ruled that the
Amish children upon completing the eighth grade were
exempted from further schooling. The Court reached this
conclusion after pointing out that a state's interest
is by no means absolute and that Wisconsin had not
proved (1) that its attendance requirement did not violate religious freedom and (2) that there was a state
interest of sufficient magnitude to override First
Amendment protection interests.[8]

Despite this decision, some contrary views were expressed. In a strong dissenting article, John William Calhoun raised two issues.[9] First, he claimed that "no branch of government has the right to extinguish the lamp of knowledge" for children. To strengthen his argument, he referred to Stuart Chase's statement that "retreat to a simpler era may have had some merit 200 years ago when Rousseau was extolling . . . the virtues of Cro-Magnon man, but too much water has gone through the turbines."

> Note number appears at end of sentence.

This argument might be convincing if the Amish children had no schooling at all, were interested in becoming part of modern society, or were unable to cope with life. But they do receive instruction in the basic skills of reading, writing, arithmetic, and in other elementary subjects. And they are interested not in being assimilated into modern society but in working with their families and preserving the Amish way of life. This way of life, while not attractive to many, merits respect. As Joe Wittmer pointed out, the Amish are an exemplary people with a record of no murders, divorces, unemployment, or welfare cases.[10] In a positive sense, the Amish life-style with its emphasis on the virtues of love, peace, tranquility, nonviolence and nonpollution should be preserved and respected.

> Quotation unnecessary

But what of the children who want to leave Amish life to continue their education? The answer to this question can be found in the Hostetler and Huntington study, which mentions that the young people who decide to obtain a higher education are usually sufficiently well motivated and qualified to succeed.[11] The number of such individuals, although limited, is increasing as some young people decide to become teachers or nurses, professions useful to the more liberal elements of the Amish.

Calhoun raised another objection in discussing the importance of education to society in producing an educated electorate. He doubted that the Amish children could become good citizens unless they attend school beyond the eighth grade. But while education for citizenship is important, Calhoun offered no evidence to support the view that students receiving more than an eighth grade education are better citizens than the Amish children. In the absence of such evidence and in the presence of the facts that the Amish by virtue of their hard work, moral behavior, and lack of trouble to society have been excellent citizens, the conclusion is apparent that Amish children are good citizens.

Another objection to the Supreme Court decision is that a precedent has been established that will permit all sorts of religious groups to establish their own schools or be exempt from state laws.[12] It appears that the Court had this possibility in mind, however, when it declared that its ruling applied only to the Amish.

Quotation unnecessary

458

In other instances, the involved religious groups would at least have to offer proof that they are providing a sound education to their children and that abiding by state educational policies would seriously interfere with the teaching and practice of their religious values, attitudes, and beliefs.

A more basic objection is raised by Castelli, who approached the Amish decision from the viewpoint of what is best for the children. He asked, "How can we best protect the rights of children within their familial, religious, and political contexts?"[13] His article raises interesting theoretical considerations, suggesting that children should be broadly educated so that they can decide on a suitable life-style for themselves. But in practice, children do not exist in a vacuum; they are most affected by the homes they are raised in and the community they live in. In the case of the Amish children, forcing them to attend high school would cause frustration, anxiety, confusion, and alienation. Consequently, the rights of these children are best served by allowing them to work on their farms and be exempt from compulsory school attendance laws. To try to create some neutral learning experience that would protect them both from Amish and other influences to enable them to make a free choice is probably impossible. But if it were possible, it would raise questions about whether children in parochial schools

Note placement of question mark, quotation marks, and number.

should also be educated under such circumstances in order to make a free choice for themselves.

This review of the main objections and questions about the Supreme Court decision reveals that it was a sound one. In addition, it was significant because it meant not only a victory for the Amish but a triumph for religious freedom in the United States. It demonstrated that minorities need not be assimilated into the majority culture but may retain their own way of life and their identity. Furthermore, the state may not impose its rule when it violates the basic rights of people.

There is a place for the Amish in this country, which has much to learn from their simple, rural way of life and their high ethical standards. If they had been forced to send their children to school beyond the eighth grade, many Amish families would have left this country. This unfortunate occurrence would have meant that a freedom-seeking people had not, in two hundred years, found a home here. It is a testimonial to our belief in the principle of freedom of religion that the Amish have stayed. We are a better country for this decision and for having the Amish among us.

Notes

[1]John A. Hostetler and Gertrude Enders Huntington,
Children in Amish Society (New York: Holt, Rinehart and
Winston, 1971), pp. 97—98.

Two authors

[2]Joe Wittmer, "The Amish and the Supreme Court,"
Phi Delta Kappan, 54, No. 1 (1972), 52.

Journal that pages each issue separately

[3]Albert E. Holliday, "The Amish and Compulsory
Education," The Education Digest, 37, No. 9 (1972), 21.

[4]Hostetler and Huntington, p. 7.

[5]Stephen Arons, "The Plain People Persist," Saturday Review, 15 Jan. 1972, p. 53.

Weekly magazine

[6]Arons, p. 55.

[7]John A. Hostetler, Amish Society, 2nd ed. (Baltimore: Johns Hopkins, 1968), p. 206.

Second edition

[8]"Current Documents: Wisconsin v. Yoder, 1972,"
Current History, 63 (1972), 82.

No author

[9]"The State's Case," Saturday Review, 15 Jan.
1972, p. 58.

Author mentioned in paper

[10]"The Amish and the Supreme Court," p. 52.

[11]Children in Amish Society, p. 79.

[12]Holliday, p. 23, refers to this objection.

[13]Jim Castelli, "Catholics and the Amish," Commonweal, 16 June 1972, p. 332.

Parenthetical explanation placed in notes

461

Bibliography

Arons, Stephen. "The Plain People Persist," Saturday Re-
     view, 15 Jan. 1972, pp. 52–57.

Calhoun, John William. "The State's Case," Saturday Re-
     view, 15 Jan. 1972, p. 58.

Castelli, Jim. "Catholics and the Amish," Commonweal,
     16 June 1972, pp. 331–32.

"Current Documents: Wisconsin v. Yoder, 1972," Current
     History, 63 (1972), 82.

Hostetler, John A. Amish Society. 2nd ed. Baltimore:
     Johns Hopkins, 1968.

————————— and Gertrude Enders Huntington. Children in
     Amish Society: Socialization and Community Educa-
     tion. New York: Holt, Rinehart and Winston, 1971.

Wittmer, Joe. "The Amish and the Supreme Court," Phi
     Delta Kappan, 54, No. 1 (1972),50–52.

No pages for
books.

Ten-hyphen
dash used
instead of
repeating name
of previous
author.

Assignments

For Discussion

1   What errors can you find in the following endnotes? (Some may have more than one.)

¹ William Alexander, "The Holocaust, Vietnam, and the Contemporary Student," *College English,* (January 1978), pp. 548–52

² Langer, Lawrence, L. *The Holocaust and the Literary Imagination.* New Haven: Yale Univ. Press, 1975, p. 307.

³ Elie Wiesel, *Night,* (New York: Avon Books, 1958), pp. 37.

⁴ Robert Weltsch, "Wear the Yellow Badge with Pride," in *Out of the Whirlwind: A Reader of Holocaust Literature.* Ed. by Albert A. Friedlander (New York: Schocken Books, 1976), 119–23.

⁵ Elie Wiesel, *The Gates Of The Forest* (New York: Avon Books), p. 44.

⁶ Wiesel, p. 49.

⁷ William Alexander, "The Holocaust," P. 552.

⁸ Friedlander, p. 120.

⁹ Elie Wiesel, "Trivializing the Holocaust," *New York Times,* April 16, 1978, Sec. 5, p. 22, col. 1, p. 23. cols. 2–3.

2   What errors can you find in the following bibliography entries? (Some have more than one.)

Alter, Robert. *Rogue's Progress: Studies in the Picaresque Novel.* Cambridge: Harvard University Press, 1964, pp. 80–105.

Baker, Sheridan. "Henry Fielding and the Cliché", *Criticism,* 1 (Fall 1959), pp. 354–61.

Baker, Sheridan. "Henry Fielding's Comic Romances." *Papers of the Michigan Academy of Science, Arts, and Letters,* 45 (1960), 411–19.

Braudy, Leo. *Narrative Form in History and Fiction,* Princeton: Princeton University Press, 1970.

Morris Golden, *Fielding's Moral Psychology.* Boston: Univ. of Mass.Press, 1966

Preston, John. *The Reader's Role in Eighteenth-Century Fiction.* London, England: William Heinemann, 1970.

Work, James A. "Henry Fielding, Christian Censor." *The Age of Johnson: Essays Presented to Chauncey Brewster Tinker,* edited by Frederick W. Hilles. New Haven: Yale University Press, 1949.

3 Which of the following statements should be endnoted?

a Since its appearance in print in 1849, *Tom Jones* has been successful.

b Slippery Rock State College is located in Slippery Rock, Pa.

c An analysis of 40 prose nonfiction anthologies published between 1956 and 1960 revealed that of 2,529 selections, 10 percent were the same 45 essays, each of which had been published in at least four anthologies.

d Charles Darwin delayed writing *The Origin of Species* for twenty years because he could not explain how evolution was caused.

e Benjamin Franklin was a man of many roles: scientist, diplomat, author, journalist, publisher, inventor, humorist, and philanthropist.

4 Explain the use of brackets in the following:

a In January, 1604, he [King James I] ordered the principal clergymen of the Church of England to come to Hampton Court Palace to settle a dispute between the High Church and the Puritans.

b As a boy, the future English king, who would order thousands of men to wage war on the continent, wrote in his diary: "It seems silly for men to fight and be killed in a foriegn [*sic*] country, far away from their homes."

For Practice

1 Write endnotes for the following references in a paper about James Joyce's *A Portrait of the Artist as a Young Man*.

a From page 67 of Hugh Kenner's *Dublin's Joyce*. Published in 1956 by the Indiana University Press at Bloomington, Indiana.

b From J. Mitchell Morse's book *The Sympathetic Alien: Joyce and Catholicism*. Published by the New York University Press in New York, 1959, pages 34–37.

c From page 61 of *Joyce's* Portrait: *Criticisms and Critiques*, a collection of essays edited by Thomas E. Connolly in a book published by Appleton-Century-Crofts in New York, 1962. The reference is from an essay by Dorothy Van Ghent entitled *"On A Portrait of the Artist as a Young Man,"* which comes from her book, *The English Novel: Form and Function*, published by Holt, Rinehart and Winston in New York, 1953.

d From page 91 of the book referred to in endnote 1.

e From page 37 of J. Mitchell Morse's *ELH* article on "Augustine Theodicy and Joyce's Aesthetics," in volume 24, March 1957 issue of this scholarly journal.

f From pages 291–95 of Sidney Feshbach's article, "A Slow and Dark

Birth: A Study of the Organization of *A Portrait of the Artist as a Young Man*." This appeared in volume 4 of the 1967 issue of the *James Joyce Quarterly*.

g From page 82 of the book referred to in endnote 2.

h From page 97 of the same book.

i From page 299 of the article referred to in endnote 6.

2 Write a bibliography based on the following sources for a paper about the modern American novel.

a *Unequivocal Americanism* by Marcel D. Ezell, a Scarecrow Press book, published in Metuchen, New Jersey, in 1977. The subtitle of the book is *Right-Wing Novels in the Cold War Era.*

b Leslie Fiedler's book *The Return of the Vanishing American,* which was published in 1968 by Stein & Day (New York).

c Robert Alter's article "The New American Novel," in the November 1975 issue of Commentary magazine, pages 44–51.

d Alvin Greenberg's article "The Novel of Disintegration: Paradoxical Impossibility in Contemporary Fiction." It appeared in volume 8 in the Winter 1967 edition of the scholarly journal *Wisconsin Studies in Contemporary Literature,* pages 1–27.

e Leslie Fiedler's book *Waiting for the End,* published by Stein & Day in 1964.

f *Contemporary American Literature 1945–1972: An Introduction* by Ihab Hassan. This book was published by the Frederick Ungar Publishing Co., New York, 1973.

3 In a maximum of three sentences, write summary notes for each of the following passages:

a Let's examine the "need" for greatly increased energy supplies for the United States. . . .

According to the United Nations, Sweden's per-capita use of energy in 1972 was 49 percent that of the United States, West Germany's 46 percent, the United Kingdom's 46 percent and Japan's 28 percent. What about other nations that in the eyes of the world are thought to have a high quality of life? Beautiful, peaceful Denmark uses 48 percent as much energy per capita as we do, wine-soaked France (complete with its nuclear program) 38 percent, the notoriously well-off Swiss 31 percent, and New Zealand—which many people consider to have the highest quality of life on this planet—used only 25 percent as much energy per person as the United States. Western Europe as a whole uses 34 percent as much, the whole world 17 percent.

The case of Sweden is especially instructive. By the measure much beloved by the growthmaniacs, per-capita gross national product, this heavily industrialized nation in a cold climate has a standard of living slightly better than that of the United States. Yet it achieves this superiority while consuming about half as much energy per person as we do. Sweden, by the way, recently postponed 11 of 13 planned nuclear power plants.

Countries like Sweden are simply more clever than the United States in extracting benefit from less energy. Much of the "waste" heat from power plants in Sweden, for instance, is used to heat buildings. Homes and buildings are well insulated, automobiles small, and mass transit systems efficient.

Furthermore, the notion that vastly greater amounts of energy are required to maintain American prosperity has been dealt a lethal blow by the Ford Foundation's massive, detailed study of our energy options. It showed in a "zero energy growth" scenario that the United States could easily forgo nuclear power without serious economic dislocation.

—Paul R. Ehrlich, "Nuclear Power: Death Trip?"

b The drift of younger Americans, avowedly group-minded or not, is toward an ever more openly flaunted individualism. This means that human relationships of all kinds are being redefined on a more temporary basis than ever before. Communes, like ordinary marriages, tend to fold more rapidly than their 19th-century counterparts, as their members keep drifting away. Because of this individualism, the frequently voiced yearning for organic community turns out to be a deceptive illusion. The chances for maintaining such a community, on a sexual basis as on any other basis, were far greater 150 years ago than they are today, despite the earlier intolerance.

The signs are that, outside the marketplace, American culture is generally becoming more individualistic, not less. For self-absorbed Americans, the group is a vehicle to gain insight, liberation, or self-dramatization. It is not truly regarded as its own end.

Yet the self must be reined in, partially renounced in a spirit of sacrifice, if the group is to gain a steadfast life of its own rather than withering away with a sour, morning-after taste. Knowing this, the head nun of the highly successful Vendanta monastic community at La Crescenta, California, years ago said that manifestations of ego must be guarded against "as the zealous cat watches for the mouse." This group, founded by a Hindu swami in 1912, still quietly survives in an atmosphere not unlike the Shakers'.

The paradox that confronts those who would start communes today is that self-love, rather than self-vigilance, remains so much more attractive to most of us. As middle-class Americans, we are taught from birth that our individual destinies are supremely important, and we deal with others throughout our lives on this basis.

On the deepest level, it would seem almost unnatural to abandon such a titillatingly evolutionary conception of the self. Moreover, we now believe that we evolve by "letting it all hang out" in a continual mood of unrestrained self-acceptance.

The historical record of collective sexual ventures seems to teach us that, except in a context of religious or patriarchal authoritarianism, the sacrifices that individuals make will not be great enough to deflect them from the pervasive self-assertion that shows up time after time and tears down the undertaking. The recent hunger for community may be so great precisely because we are all being swept farther and farther away from its possible realization.

—Laurence Veysey

4 Write a paragraph assimilating the words and ideas of one of the following selections.

a By the time they reach adolescence, most girls, unconsciously or not, have learned enough about role definition to qualify for a master's degree. In general, the lesson has been that no matter what kind of career thoughts one may entertain, one must, first and foremost, be a wife and mother. A girl's mother is usually her first teacher. As Dr. Goode says, "A woman is not only taught by society to have a child; she is taught to have a child who will have a child." A woman who has hung her life on The Motherhood Myth will almost always reinforce her young married daughter's early training by pushing for grandchildren. Prospective grandmothers are not the only ones. Husbands, too, can be effective sellers. After all, they have The Fatherhood Myth to cope with. A married man is *supposed* to have children. Often, particularly among Latins, children are a sign of potency. They help him assure the world—and himself—that he is the big man he is supposed to be. Plus, children give him both immortality (whatever that means) and possibly the chance to become "more" in his lifetime through the accomplishments of his children, particularly his son. (Sometimes it's important, however, for the son to do better, but not *too* much better.)

Friends, too, can be counted on as myth-pushers. Naturally one wants to do what one's friends do. One study, by the way, found an absolute correlation between a woman's fertility and that of her three closest friends. The negative sell comes into play here, too. We have seen what the concept of non-mother means (cold, selfish, unwomanly, abnormal). In practice, particularly in the suburbs, it can mean, simply, exclusion—both from child-centered activities (that is, most activities) and child-centered conversations (that is, most conversations). It can also mean being the butt of a lot of unfunny jokes. ("Whaddya waiting for? An immaculate conception? Ha ha.") Worst of all, it can mean being an object of pity.

—Betty Rollin, "Motherhood: Who Needs It?"

b It is evident, then, from what has just been said about the complexity of the writing process and of the task of teaching writing that there can be no real short cut to writing skill. That is, there can be no quick and painless way to develop a well-stocked mind, a disciplined intelligence, and a discriminating taste in language and fluency in its use. None of these can be acquired without hard work over a period of years, and it is preposterous to claim or to expect that any single course in either school or college, no matter how well taught or how intensively studied, can assure them. They are to a considerable extent the result of increasing maturity and of the total educational process acting on an intelligent mind. They are of course not absolutes which one either has or does not have; but in their higher manifestations they lie forever beyond the reach of many people, even some of those who attend the most highly selective college.

All teachers of academic subjects can help students to fill their minds, to train and focus their intellectual powers, and to make their use of language more exact; but English teachers and English courses have the opportunity to be especially helpful in moving students toward the second and third of these goals. More than other teachers and courses, they concentrate directly on the *quality* of written expression as well as the thinking embodied in it, on the principles that lie behind it, and on disciplined practice in applying these principles in written composition. But no one should expect a particular device or method or kind of subject matter in the English course to transform what must always be a slow and difficult process into one that is quick, easy, and unfailingly successful. The habit of good writing, like the habit of ethical conduct, is of slow growth; it is an aspect of a person's general intellectual development and cannot be greatly hastened apart from that development.

—Albert R. Kitzhaber, from *Themes, Theories, and Therapy*

Reference
guide

Introduction

Throughout *The Writing Commitment,* we have stressed that writers have a number of options, depending on their purpose, their audience, and the occasion: they have choices of diction, of sentence and paragraph structure, and of ways to organize their material. In Chapters 3 and 8 we discussed the various dialects of spoken American English and the varieties of written English, pointing out that when writers broaden their audience, they shift to a form of written English that avoids regionalisms and uses conventions of vocabulary and syntactic structure common to all dialects. To avoid confusing or distracting their readers, they "take off" their comfortable, everyday language forms and "put on" a standard variety that is universally accepted and understood. In much the same way, you discard the cut-offs, jeans, and tennis shoes that you wear for relaxed, leisure-time activities, and dress in more conventional clothes when going about more formal daily routines.

This Reference Guide is designed to help you choose the most appropriate item of language usage for a particular writing occasion, distinguishing the ones most fitted for a casual, informal, situation and those suited for writing more formally to a general audience. It is not intended to dictate, but to serve as a guide. Approach it as you would a magazine like *Mademoiselle* or *Esquire* to research the current, widely accepted fashions. As you would use such magazines for clothing conventions, refer to this Reference Guide for quick solutions to problems arising while you are learning the language conventions of written English—conventions of grammar, usage, punctuation, spelling, and mechanics that will help you communicate clearly, effectively, and appropriately with the largest number of readers. For this reason, these conventions are an important part of your writing commitment.

Many conventions of grammar and usage are confusing because of the differences between spoken and written varieties, or between different varieties of written English. Throughout the grammar and usage sections, you will find options that reflect these different writing situations. Those most appropriate for informal, personal writing are marked *Casual;* those recommended for a broader audience are marked *General.* Unless indicated otherwise, the former are appropriate for all forms of personal writing— journal, autobiographical narrative, personal essay, and personal description—and the latter are appropriate for all writing, even the most specialized, formal varieties. It may be helpful to remember that most of the writing you will do in college and in the business or professional world will be in General English.

Throughout the Reference Guide, you will notice small marginal page numbers. These indicate the pages of text where an item is discussed more fully.

470

Grammar

In this section, we provide a quick review of grammatical terms and discuss special problems of usage involving parts of speech and the syntax of sentences.

The Parts of Speech

adjectives

Adjectives modify or describe nouns. They can also be recognized by the kinds of inflections they take and by the function slots they fill in a sentence. Adjectives can occur before or after nouns, or follow verbs such as *be, seem, appear, taste, smell, become.*

The *delightful* spring, *fresh* and *fragrant,* is *welcome.*
    adj   adj   adj   adj

Adjectives of one syllable and many of two syllables show comparison by adding *-er* or *-est:*

warm   lovely
warmer   lovelier
warmest   loveliest

while adjectives with three or more syllables use *more* or *most:*

beautiful   *more* beautiful   *most* beautiful

adjective comparison

Adjectives of one or two syllables add the comparative suffix *-er* for comparing two items and the superlative *-est* for comparing more than two. Multisyllabic adjectives substitute *more* or *most* for *-er* and *-est.*

Bob is the smar*ter* of the two. / Bob is *more* erudite than Tom.
Maria is the *happiest* of the three.
Maria is the *most* imaginative person in the class.

However, if special emphasis is desired or if the number being compared is indefinite, use the superlative *-est* or *most:*

Of the two, Bob is smart*est.* / May the *most* talented violinist win.

adverbs

Adverbs modify, qualify, or describe verbs, adjectives, other adverbs, or whole sentences.

1. verbs: He *easily* found her in the crowd.
2. adjectives: They were an *exceedingly* handsome pair.

3. adverbs: Mario sings *amazingly* well.

4. sentences: *Unfortunately,* we heard of the plans too late.

As sentence adverbials or adjuncts, single adverbs and adverbial phrases can indicate manner, time, or place.

We saw him *briefly   yesterday   at the bank.*
                        Manner   Time   Place

63–67   **adverbs: confusion with adjectives**

Although most adverbs in modern usage end in *-ly,* a number of adverbs have the same form as adjectives or have two adverb forms. These often present usage problems. (Note: Remember, not all *-ly* words are adverbs: *lovely, manly, womanly,* etc., are adjectives.)

General: That is a *fast* car. (adjective)
General: He runs *fast.* (adverb)
General: He is a *good* runner. (adjective)
General: He runs *well.* (adverb)
Casual: He runs *good.* (alternate adverb)

Some adverbs, like *slow,* present an even greater usage problem because they not only resemble an adjective in form, but have two acceptable adverb possibilities, one as an uninflected form, one with the *-ly* suffix.

General: He threw a *slow* ball. (adjective)
General: Drive *slow.* (adverb)   or   Drive *slowly.* (adverb)
General: He chewed the candy *slowly.* (adverb)
Casual, dialogue only: He chewed the candy *slow.* (adverb)

Although the *-ly* forms are preferred in General writing, make sure that you do not add *-ly* to adverbs that are normally uninflected; you will create hypercorrect monstrosities inappropriate in all varieties of written English. Here's an example:

Thusly, the war came to an end. (*Thus* is normally uninflected.)

67–68,   **conjunctions**
152–56
Conjunctions are "joiners"; they connect elements of a sentence or join several sentences together. Conjunctions are of two types: coordinate (*and, or, either . . . or*) and subordinate (*as, because, when, since*).

Gretchen *and* Peter are sister and brother. (*and* joins two elements)
Gretchen and Peter have the same parents *because* they are sister and brother. (*because* joins two sentences)

nouns

Nouns have traditionally been defined as "naming" words. Most nouns can show plurals (cats, *geese,* criteri*a*) or can add *'s* to show possession.

Such nouns are referred to as count nouns (*one* cat, *two* cats). Those that cannot be pluralized usually refer to a group or a substance, and are called mass nouns (*furniture, wheat, rice*). Many nouns such as *team* and *government* can be either mass or count. Nouns occur in sentences as subjects, objects of verbs, and objects of prepositions:

> The *corporation* sent *representatives* to other *countries.*
>   Subject   Object of verb   Object of preposition

Nouns can also be classified as common or proper, the latter referring to a particular person, place, or thing: *Margaret, Massachusetts, Senate.*

nouns: articles and verb agreement

Most usage problems involving nouns arise from two sources: subject-verb agreement and the kinds of determiners that can precede a noun. The choice depends largely on how the noun is classified. Here are some examples:

Singular count nouns take a singular verb:

> One girl *is*   One goose *is*   One deer *is*

Plural count nouns take a plural verb, even when no *s* is added to the noun:

> Two girls *are*   Three geese *are*   Four deer *are*

Articles with count nouns: The articles *a/an* can be used only with singular count nouns and carry the connotation of indefinite quality.

> *A* book is on the table. (any book)

The before a singular count noun makes it more definite:

> *The* book is on the table. (a particular book)

Verb agreement: In American English, most mass nouns take a singular verb.

> Glass *has* been used for windows for many years.
> Wheat *has* become a political issue.
> The government *needs* dedicated leaders.

prepositions

Prepositions, like conjunctions, are joining words. They join phrases to other elements in the sentence:

> The players *of* Michigan State beat the team *from* Penn *with* comparative ease. (each preposition is followed by a noun phrase)

Prepositions cannot, however, be used freely with every verb and every noun in every context. For instance, the noun *participation* can be followed by either *of* or *in;* but the prepositions can't be interchanged in these examples:

Participation in all sports is required. (but not *of*)
The participation of everyone here is required. (but not *in*)

When in doubt about the appropriate preposition to use with a verb or noun, consult your dictionary.

35–36, 52, 243–44, 259–62

pronouns

Pronouns substitute for nouns or noun phrases:

He (Sam) jogs every day. (*he* replaces the noun *Sam*)
She (The woman who jogs every day in the park) is a lawyer. (*she* substitutes for the noun phrase in parentheses)

Unlike nouns in modern English, pronouns show case functions; that is, they change form depending on their use in the language:

They told *them* of *their* plans.
subject   object   possessive

Most usage problems involving pronouns result from a confusion of case forms or from substituting the objective form of a personal pronoun for a demonstrative:

Casual, dialogue only: Them flowers smell good.
Casual, General: Those flowers smell good.

pronouns: agreement with antecedent

a. Pronouns should agree in number with the noun or pronoun they refer to:

Each pronoun should agree with *its* antecedent. (both *each pronoun* and *its* are singular)

b. Words with singular meaning followed by a plural noun present a particularly confusing usage situation:

General: Each of the boys *is* entitled to a turn at bat. (the verb is singular to agree with the subject *each,* not the plural *boys* that immediately precedes the verb)
Casual: Each of the boys *are* entitled to a turn at bat. (common in spoken and informal written English)

In most college writing, you would be wise to use the General usage; a good way to test is to remove the *of: each boy)*

c. A special problem arises with pronouns that are compounded with *one* or *body: everyone, somebody, everybody,* etc. In spoken English and in

Casual written English, plural pronouns are often used in referring to these problematical forms:

Casual: Did *anybody* leave *their* books in the classroom?
General: Did *anybody* leave *his* books in the classroom?

Traditionally, the singular masculine pronoun used in the General example has been the prescribed usage. However, in current English, *he, his,* and *him* usually connote masculine rather than the intended generic meaning of humankind in general. For this reason, many view them as discriminatory usages. However, many people still find the plural pronoun reference unacceptable; hence the usage becomes a problem. To solve it, many writers are turning to the stylistically awkward "his or her" or "he/she" combinations, or are recasting the sentence in the plural.

261–62

General: It is important that *everyone* accept *his or her* responsibility.
General: It is important that *all people* accept *their* responsibility.

pronouns: case after prepositions
In most forms of written English, pronouns acting as objects of prepositions should be in the objective case (*me, her, him, them, us, whom*). Usually, compound objects cause the most difficulty.

General, Casual: They gave the award to *Carl* (*him*) and *me*. (both are objective case)
Casual, dialogue only: They gave the award to *Carl* (*him*) and *I*. (*I* is in subjective case)

When in doubt about such constructions, test the second pronoun by removing the first; few people would say or write "They gave the award to *I*."

pronouns: *who/whom, whoever/whomever, whose/whosever*
a. In spoken and Casual written English, the objective forms *whom* and *whomever* have virtually disappeared, except after prepositions:

To *whom/whomever* it may concern.

But even in General written English, particularly in questions and relative clauses, often the formal *whom/whomever* is replaced by the subjective forms *who/whoever*.

Casual, General informal: Who did you write to about enrollment?
General formal: Whom did you write to about enrollment?
Casual, General informal: Bert asked Yvonne *who* she visited.
General formal: Bert asked Yvonne *whom* she visited.

To check when to use the objective form, reorder the sentence, as: You

475

wrote to *whom* about enrollment? She visited *whom?* In the first example, normal order reveals that the pronoun is the object of the preposition *to;* in the second, it is the object of the verb *visited.* In college writing, you would be wise to use the objective form in such situations. However, be careful to avoid such ungrammatical hypercorrections as:

Whom are you? (*Be* and other linking verbs take the subjective form.)

b.   *Whose* is the possessive form of *who* and functions like any other possessive:

Whose gloves are these? / I don't know *whose* (gloves) they are.

Caution: Don't confuse *whose* with *who's* (who is)!

c.   *Whosever,* the possessive form of *whoever,* although common in spoken English, is avoided in most writing because it can create awkward or ambiguous sentences.

Casual: Whosever gloves these are, they had better claim them.

477–78   verbs

Verbs have traditionally been defined as words that show action or state of being. However, recent language research indicates that verbs have many other functions, too complex to discuss here. Perhaps a better definition would be that verbs are words that can show present or past tense by some change in their form. Most verbs in modern English show past tense by adding *-d* or *-ed;* these are called regular verbs. Others are irregular and change form in other ways, as in *grow, grew; choose, chose. Transitive* verbs are followed by noun-phrase objects; *intransitive* verbs by adverbs; *linking* verbs link the subject with a noun phrase or adjective that refers directly to the subject.

Transitive verb: She *received* the package.
Intransitive verb: He *whistled* merrily.
Linking verb: She *seems* nice.

verb accord

Verb accord involves matching verb tenses throughout a sentence or paragraph. Usually, the main verbs are all present or all past, as these two versions of the same paragraph demonstrate:

Version A: All main verbs are *present.*

The other [girl] *does* stop just in time for Rosemary to get up before the tea *comes.* She *has* the table placed between them. She *plies* the poor little creature with everything, all the sandwiches, all the bread and butter, and every time her cup *is* empty she *fills* it with tea, cream, and sugar.

Version B: All main verbs are *past.*

The other [girl] *did* stop just in time for Rosemary to get up before tea *came.* She *had* the table placed between them. She *plied* the poor little creature with everything, all the sandwiches, all the bread and butter, and every time her cup *was* empty she *filled* it with tea, cream, and sugar.

—Katherine Mansfield, "A Cup of Tea"

verbs, irregular

Most verbs in English are regular; that is, *-d* or *-ed* is added to form both the past tense and the past participle form:

Present	Past	Past Participle
kick	kicked	kicked

But because many verbs in English are irregular, they create usage headaches. These problems are intensified by two factors: many irregular verbs are used frequently; and many have more than one acceptable past or past-participle form. Even though this makes irregular verbs seem chaotic, they do fall into certain patterns.

a. Past and past-participle forms are identical but differ from the present-tense form.

1. *-d* changes to *-t:*

Present	Past	Past Participle
send	sent	sent

2. *ee-* and *-ea-* spellings change to *-e-;* present-tense vowel sound rhymes with *beet;* past and past-participle vowel sound rhymes with *bet:*

Present	Past	Past Participle
breed	bred	bred
lead	led	led
leave	left	left

3. Some irregular verbs following this pattern also add *-t* to the past and past-participle forms:

Present	Past	Past Participle
creep	crept	crept
feel	felt	felt

4. *-ou-* spelling in past and past participle (pronunciation varies):

Present	Past	Past Participle
bring	brought	brought
bind	bound	bound
seek	sought	sought
think	thought	thought

5. Past and past-participle vowel spelling changes to *-u-:*

Present	Past	Past Participle
dig	dug	dug
slink	slunk	slunk

6. Miscellaneous:

Present	Past	Past Participle
make	made	made
mean	meant	meant
win	won	won

b. A second class of irregular verbs consists of those with three different forms, the past participle adding the suffix *-n* or *-en:*

Present	Past	Past Participle
blow	blew	blown
break	broke	broken
freeze	froze	frozen
give	gave	given

c. A third set of irregular verbs shows a vowel change (in both spelling and pronunciation) in the past and past-participle forms:

Present	Past	Past Participle
begin	began	begun
fly	flew	flown
see	saw	seen

d. Many verbs have more than one acceptable form. Some of the more common ones are:

Present	Past	Past Participle
beat	beat	beaten, beat
broadcast	broadcasted, broadcast	broadcasted, broadcast
dive	dived, dove	dived
forget	forgot	forgotten, forgot
get	got	got, gotten
hide	hid	hidden, hid
kneel	knelt, kneeled	knelt, kneeled
prove	proved	proven, proved
show	showed	shown, showed

When in doubt about other verbs, use your dictionary.

verb phrases

a. *Be.* Many American dialects omit the verb *be* as either a main verb or an auxiliary. Except in dialogue, these omissions are universally considered unacceptable in writing.

Casual, General: Jack *is* a good teacher. / They *are* going home.
Casual, dialogue only: Jack a good teacher. / They going home.

Some social dialects have two peculiar usages involving *be* to express variant degrees of continuing time. Both are acceptable in writing only in a journal or dialogue.

Casual, General: His mother *is* working. (now) / His mother *works.*
Casual, dialogue only: His mother working. / His mother *be* working. (His mother works every day.)

b. *Have* as an auxiliary verb. In both spoken English and in personal writing, we usually contract the forms of *have* (*have, has, had*) in verb phrases such as "I've never noticed that." This practice leads to two writing usage problems:

Deletion of *have* altogether:

Casual, dialogue only: I been there.

Substitution of *of* for *-ve:*

Casual, dialogue only: I should *of* known it. (for I should*'ve* known it)

c. Passive forms. Modern English has two ways to show passive:

The auxiliary *be* plus the past participle form of the verb:

She *was* seen by many people.

The auxiliary *get* plus the past participle (avoid in most writing situations):

Casual: They *got* disgusted and left.

verb phrases, contracted

The verb contractions common to spoken English—such as *we're going, we've seen her, he's a good friend, I'm not sure*—are all appropriate for Casual English and for General English when an informal tone is desired. Just remember that they require the apostrophe to indicate the omissions (*we + are = we're; a* is omitted and replaced by an apostrophe).

Sentence Structure

A sentence is a grammatical structure composed of a subject (S) and a predicate (P). The predicate consists of a tense-carrying verb (V) and usually a complement (C). The complement might be an object, an adjective, or an adverb. There are three types of sentences, in English: simple, compound, and complex.

63–65

479

65–67   **simple sentences**

A simple sentence consists of only one structure; sometimes it is called an *independent clause,* or *base clause.*

Examples: The cat slept. (SV)
Mimi bought a motorcycle. (SVC—the complement is an object)
I jog daily. (SVC—the complement is an adverb)

compound sentences

A compound sentence is formed by joining two or more simple sentences or independent clauses in any of several ways:

67   a.   SP $\left\{\begin{array}{l} and \\ but \\ for \\ or \\ nor \\ yet \\ ; \end{array}\right\}$ SP

Examples: Mimi bought a motorcycle, *but* Oscar bought roller skates.
Not one of them studied enough for the exam, *nor* did they do well on it.
(note the reordering of subject and verb in the second clause)
First she tried yoga *and* then karate. (repeated subject and verb "she tried" are deleted)

67   b. $\left\{\begin{array}{l} either \\ neither \\ both \\ not\ only \end{array}\right\}$ SP $\left\{\begin{array}{l} or \\ nor \\ and \\ but\ also \end{array}\right\}$ SP

Examples: *Either* you study tonight *or* you go unprepared to the exam in the morning.
Not only did they buy a new car, *but* they also bought a boat.

152–58   **complex sentences**

A complex sentence combines two or more simple sentences: an independent or base clause and one or more clauses dependent on the base clause for meaning. In the examples below, the joiners are italicized.

     Dependent   Independent
When the phone rang, I was in the bathtub.
     S   P   S P

Dependent   Independent
Before Hank went to college, he hitchhiked from Maine to California.   **70**
     S   P   S   P

Dependent   Independent
Malcolm, *who* used to be my best friend, is now my worst enemy.
    S   S   P   P

Dependent   Independent
The movie *that* I saw last Saturday was exciting.
    S   S   P   P

In the examples, the SP structures labeled as dependent clauses are logically incomplete without the independent clause. Used alone, they would be sentence fragments, as in:

Before Hank went to college.

Dependent clauses introduced by *that* can also serve as the complement of the verb in the independent or base clause.

            Independent   Dependent
Example: She hoped *that* they would become good friends.
            S   V   C

faulty parallelism
Faulty parallelism results from joining unlike structures when their   **149–50**
grammar or meaning indicates they should be identical in form. It is often caused by combining sentences whose subjects are not the same, as in:

Gary is not a good track man, and neither is his swimming.
    (*Gary* is the subject of the base clause; *his swimming* is the subject of the added clause)

A solution would be:

Gary is not a good track man, nor is *he* a good swimmer. (*he* refers to *Gary*)

Faulty parallelism can also result from using different grammatical structures in complex sentences to express coordinate ideas. Here's an example of faulty parallelism, followed by the effective, original version:

We used to root for the Indians against the cavalry, because we didn't think it was fair in the history books *that the cavalry's winning was a greaty victory, and when the Indians won it was a massacre.*

We used to root for the Indians against the cavalry, because we didn't think it was fair in the history books that *when the cavalry won it was a great victory, and when the Indians won it was a massacre.*
                                         —Dick Gregory

69–70   **fragments**

Fragments are incomplete sentences that commonly result from two main sources: 1) omitting one of the important grammatical sentence elements such as subject or verb, and 2) treating a dependent clause as a complete sentence (see *complex sentences* above). Common to Casual style, fragments are usually avoided in General English.

> *Fragment:* Being the only child in the family. (lacks subject and main verb)
> *Complete sentence:* He was the only child in the family.
> *Fragment:* Because he studied too hard. (dependent clause)
> *Complete sentence:* Because he studied too hard, he suffered from nervous exhaustion. (independent clause added)

502   **fused sentences**

Fused sentences occur when two sentences are run together without a joining conjunction or the appropriate punctuation.

> Ralph's trousers are torn he should get a new pair. (fused sentence resulting from lack of any punctuation between clauses)
> Ralph's trousers are torn, he should get a new pair. (fused sentence or comma splice; comma not appropriate)
> Ralph's trousers are torn; he should get a new pair. (sentence fault solved with semicolon)

68   **run-on sentences**

Run-on sentences are those suffering from over-coordination: too many joined by conjunctions such as *and, but,* or *so.* The term *run-on* is also frequently used as a synonym for *fused* sentences, or sentences joined without appropriate punctuation.

> *Fused sentence:* The Israelis and the Egyptians were having a hard time coming to an agreement *so* President Carter called a meeting at Camp David, *but* they still couldn't agree, *so* he made a personal trip to the two countries.
> *Revised:* The Israelis and the Egyptians were having a hard time coming to an agreement, so President Carter called a meeting at Camp David. *When* they still couldn't agree, he made a personal trip to the two countries. (divided into two sentences; *when* substituted for *but*)

52–53   **subject-verb agreement**

a.   A singular subject that can be replaced by *he, she,* or *it,* and that is followed by a present-tense verb, requires the *-s* form of the verb.

Al (he) *works* at the Med Center and Margaret (she) *runs* the lab there.

All other subjects take the plural form of the verb:

You *are* the only one here.
They *see* a fly on the ceiling.

b. A special problem in getting subjects and verbs to agree arises when a long noun modifier ending in a noun is inserted between the verb and the subject, and when this noun differs in number from the subject, as in: 473

The introductory essays, especially on the literary Indian stereotype, *is* superb. (singular *is* triggered by *stereotype*)

The introductory essays, especially on the literary Indian stereotype, *are* superb. (plural verb agrees with plural subject, *essays*)

c. Compound subjects can create subject-verb agreement problems. Subject nouns joined by *and* take the plural verb, even if individually they are singular: 476–77

Ken *and* Judy eat in the grill.

But when singular compound subjects are joined by *or, either . . . or,* or *neither . . . nor,* they require a singular verb, except in Casual English:

Casual: Either Mary *or* Elizabeth *are* planning to attend college.
General: Either Mary *or* Elizabeth *is* planning to attend college.

d. There *is/are.* Sentences beginning with the expletive *there* often present tricky agreement choices. It may help to realize that such sentences can be reordered; omitting *there* and changing to normal order will reveal the real subject-verb relationship: 478–79

There ___?___ some funny things going on in such sentences.
Normal order: Some funny *things are* going on in such sentences.

Usage

Listed here are those usage items that have two or more ways of expressing the same meaning. Some are common and appropriate in spoken English; others are appropriate in Casual written English; and still others are preferred when writing in General English. Because their usage is split, it is often difficult to determine the most appropriate for a particular writing situation. This list should help you decide. We include only the most troublesome usage items here; standard dictionaries or specialized American English usage dictionaries list many more. As in other parts of this reference guide, the label *Casual* indicates that the item is appropriate for personal writing; *General* for all other writing situations. When a usage is inappropriate for any written English, it will be so indicated in parentheses.

all together/altogether *All together* is used to describe all members of a group gathered together; *altogether* is an adverb meaning "wholly" or "completely."

At last, we're all together under one roof. (all members)
The scene he encountered at the top of the hill was *altogether* delightful. (wholly delightful)

allusion/illusion *Allusion* and *illusion* are often pronounced alike, which leads to confusion of the two words. *Allusion* refers to a casual reference to something; it should be followed by *to*. *Illusion* refers to a false or fanciful impression and should be followed by *of*.

Women resent *allusions* to feminine frailty.
Napoleon retained his *illusion* of power even after his banishment.

almost/most as adverbs In Casual English, there is very little resistance to the use of *most* in situations that would traditionally require *almost*. However written English does impose some restrictions.

Casual: Most everyone arrived late.
General: Almost everyone arrived late.
Inappropriate in written English: He is *most* the kindest person I know.

a lot of/lots of *A lot of* means the same as "many." It is frequently used with mass nouns or nouns having only a plural form. *Lots of* is a common variant in Casual spoken and written English.

General: A lot of sugar is grown in Cuba. (precedes a mass noun)
General: A lot of cattle become diseased every year. (*cattle* has only a plural form)
Casual: Lots of sugar is grown in Cuba.
Casual: Lots of cattle become diseased every year.

already/all ready These two, although frequently interchanged, are not synonymous. *Already* is an adverb meaning "prior to a specified time"; *all ready* means "completely prepared."

The signs of spring were *already* in evidence.
The expedition was *all ready* to set forth.
But not: The signs of spring were *all ready* in evidence.
                                    or
The expedition was *already* to set forth.

among/between *Among* is used with three or more items, never two; *between* in current usage is generally acceptable with any number of items.

General: The booty was divided *among* the twelve pirates.
Casual, General: Carolina and Maria divided the candy bar *between* themselves. (two people)
Casual, General: The director was unable to pick *between* the three people who tried out for the part. (three people)

However, some writers prefer the traditional distinction of retaining *between* for only two items; *among* for more than two. Also, many writers prefer *among* when a collective action or decision is involved:

General: The four men agreed *among* themselves on a course of action. (collective)

amount of/number of   *Amount of* is used with mass nouns and can be replaced with specific quantity words (*pounds, tons, gallons*) or *much.*
Number of occurs with count nouns and can be replaced by specific numbers (*ten, one hundred*) or words that imply number (*many, most*).

Casual, General: The United States exports a *large amount of* tobacco. (*tobacco* is a mass noun)
Casual, General: Income tax returns often require a *number of* forms (*forms,* with the *-s* plural, is a count noun)
Casual: Income tax returns often require a large *amount of* forms. (common in spoken English)

anywhere/anywheres   *Anywhere* is the generally used adverb form in written English. *Anywheres* is a variant common to spoken English and follows the pattern of adding *s* to similar adverb forms: *anyways, nowheres.*

Casual, General: We can't find one *anywhere.*
Casual, dialogue: We can't find one *anywheres.*

as (see also as . . . as and like)   Because *as* is an overworked word, functioning in many ways, it is often difficult to choose the right usage. One of its most common uses is as a conjunction, joining two sentence elements:

I weigh the same *as* you do.

As a conjunction, it can also replace *because, since,* and *while;* therefore you should take care to avoid ambiguity when using it in certain constructions, as in this example:

Ambiguous: Ivan didn't hear the doorbell *as* he was playing the stereo. (Does *as* mean *while* or *because?*)

As also functions as a preposition with the meaning of "in the capacity of":

He acted *as* an envoy from the President.

as . . . as *As . . . as* is now considered appropriate for comparison in all kinds of writing, even in negative comparisons that traditionally demanded *so . . . .as.*

> *Casual, General:* Ralph is not *as* proficient in math *as* Nina.

In *as . . . as* comparisons, a special problem arises when the second *as* is followed by a pronoun, and a predicate is implied but not stated. In most written English, the subjective case should be used.

> *General:* Nina is as well qualified as *he.* (*he* is the subject of the implied sentence "*he* is well qualified")
> *Casual:* Nina is as well qualified as *him.*

But if the pronoun functions as the object of the implied sentence, use the objective form to avoid ambiguity:

> My mother loves my sister as much as *me.* ("as much as mother loves me")
> My mother loves my sister as much as *I.* (ambiguous; could mean "as much as my mother loves *me*" or "as much as I love my sister")

When in doubt about such constructions, write out the implied sentence.

as follows The singular form of the verb, *follows,* is always used, even when several items are listed:

> *Casual, General:* Before we can review the case, we need more information, *as follows:* the amount contracted for, the payment received, and date of payment.

as/such as *As,* in spoken English, is commonly substituted for *such as:*

> *General:* They had many things in common, *such as* a love of music and an appreciation of nature.
> *Casual:* They had many things in common, *as* a love of music and an appreciation of nature.

as well as *As well as* usually introduces a nonrestrictive phrase (a parenthetical aside) and makes no change in the verb number in the main clause.

> *Casual, General:* The state university, *as well as* the private schools in the state, *has* an open admissions policy.

Although the subject of the example seems plural, grammatically it is singular; *university* is the subject.

awhile/a while Although these mean the same and are both acceptable in all forms of writing, they are not interchangeable in function. *Awhile* is an adverb similar to *anytime, anywhere; a while* is a noun phrase, analagous to *a time.*

Casual, General: I played tennis *awhile* on Sunday. (adverb)
Casual, General: I played tennis for *a while* on Sunday. (noun phrase, object of the preposition *for*)

being as/being that   Either is used as a replacement for *because* or *since* in some spoken dialects.

General: We gave up our fishing trip *because* it was raining.
Casual: We gave up our fishing trip, *being as* it was raining.

criterion/criteria   *Criterion* is the singular form:

A single *criterion* has been established.

Although *criteria* is frequently used as a singular form in spoken English, it should be treated only as a plural in written, General English. *Criterions* is also listed in recent dictionaries as an acceptable plural.

General: Several *criteria/criterions* have been established.
Casual: A *criteria* for an *A* paper is the use of accepted grammatical structures.

could of/would of/should of   These forms are often mistakenly substituted for the contracted *could have, would have, should have;* the punctuation of *could've* is a homonym to *could of.*

General: I would have done it.
Casual: I would've done it.
But not: I *would of* done it.

dangling modifier   Dangling modifiers are misplaced sentence constructions that create ambiguity or awkward sentence structure. They are distracting to your readers and impede clear communication. One common type is the introductory modifier that doesn't fit the subject:

Hugging his trophy, John's face lit up with a smile. (ambiguous; sounds as if John's face has arms)

data   *Data,* the Latin plural of *datum,* is now used interchangeably as a singular or plural form:

General: The data *are* conclusive. / The data *is* conclusive.

However, *datum* as a singular and *data* as a plural are preferred in scientific and technical writing. Whichever you choose, keep your data consistent.

different from/different than   Although these two forms are frequently interchanged in spoken English for all occasions, the following usage is recom-

479

164–66

mended for most levels of written English; use *different from* when a noun phrase follows; *different than* before a complete clause.

> *General:* The European cultural heritage is *different from* the American Indian's heritage. (*from* is a preposition followed by a noun phrase)
> *General:* Today's Indian culture is *different than* it was prior to the European invasion. (*than* is a conjunction followed by a complete SP clause)
> *Casual:* The European cultural heritage is *different than* the American Indian's heritage.

done   *Done* is the past-participle form of *do,* occurring in such constructions as:

> They have *done* the job. (after the auxiliary *have*)
> *Done* to perfection, the steak was served piping hot. (verbal phrase)

But replacing the auxiliary *have* with *done* or substituting *done* for the past tense *did* is considered unacceptable in most forms of written English.

> *Casual, General:* They have gone home.
> *Casual, dialogue only:* They *done* gone home.
> *Casual, General:* It was hard, but they *did* it.
> *Casual, dialogue only:* It was hard, but they *done* it.

except/accept   These two verbs are often confused. *Except* as a verb means to exclude or exempt:

> Juniors and seniors are *excepted* from obligatory dorm residence.

Accept is to receive something offered:

> He *accepted* the scholarship.

It might help to sort them out if you remember that *accept* has a higher frequency of use. Once you *accept* that fact, you can *except* most of the possibilities of *except.*

effect/affect   These are often confused when used as verbs. In relaxed speech, they sound alike, which adds to the confusion. *Effect* means to "bring something about":

> The doctors were able to *effect* a cure for his disease.

Affect means to "influence in some way":

> The disease *affected* him in peculiar ways.

Generally, however, *effect* is used as a noun; *affect* as a verb:

> The *effects* of marijuana have not yet *affected* the statistical evidence of lung cancer.

488

farther/further   In contemporary usage, *farther* is preferred to express greater distance in space:

> St. Louis is *farther* from New York than Cleveland is.
> I won't carry this piano any *farther*.

In careful English, *further* is restricted to a sense of greater advancement in time or degree:

> He is *further* along in graduate school than Mary is.
> I won't carry this argument any *further*.

However, the two have become so freely interchangeable that many usage experts look upon *further* as simply a variant of *farther*, so that "St. Louis is *further* from New York than Cleveland is" would be acceptable to most people even for written English. Adjust to the taste of your audience in making a choice.

fewer/less   *Fewer* is usually restricted to count nouns; *less* to mass nouns.

> *General:* Fewer birds are now found in the swamps of Florida.
> *General:* Less animosity toward the Establishment is apparent on campus today.
> *Casual:* Less birds are now found in the swamps of Florida.

first/firstly, second/secondly   The *-ly* forms of numbers are awkward and unnecessary. Like a diamond tiara at a high school prom, they are over-elegant.

former/latter   *Former*—the first-mentioned item; *latter*—the second-mentioned item. They should be used only when there can be no confusion about which item in the preceding context each refers to.

> When it came to apples and oranges, he preferred the *former*, but liked the *latter* also.

Because of a tendency to mispronounce *latter*, it is often misspelled as *ladder*. Also, avoid confusing it with *later*.

> *Later*, if you have a choice between walking in front of a truck or under a *ladder*, choose the *latter*.

get   *Get* is an overused verb in the language and certain usages are strictly idiomatic or colloquial. Other verbs, more specific in meaning, can do more for your writing style.   31–33

> *General:* Their political views really *anger* me.
> *Casual:* Their political views really *get* me.

had better/better In most writing situations, use the full form *had better*.

> *General:* We decided we *had better* do as he suggested.
> *Casual:* We decided we *better* do as he suggested.

had ought/hadn't ought *Had ought* and *hadn't ought* are common colloquialisms. In most writing situations, *ought to have* or *ought not to have* are preferred.

> *General:* You *ought not to have done* that.
> *Casual, dialogue particularly:* You hadn't ought to have done that.

hardly/barely/scarcely All three are weak negative adverbs meaning "not quite" or "just only." Addition of another negative is considered a double negative and is generally avoided in writing.

> *Casual, General:* Jim had *hardly* any appetite.
> *Casual, dialogue only:* Jim didn't have *hardly* any appetite.

in/within Both *in* and *within* as prepositions may convey the sense of "inside," but *within* is usually used when "inside" has the additional condition of limitation of space, substance, or time:

> I'll do it *within* the hour.
> He was trapped *within* the confines of the prison.
> They live *within* a mile's distance from each other.

indefinite pronouns: they/this The personal pronoun *they* and the demonstrative *this* are termed *indefinite* when they do not refer to a specific noun phrase, as in the gossiper's standby "They say that . . . ." The reader or listener cannot know who is responsible for the gossip tidbit. *This* commonly creates unclear reference when two or three items precede it, making it difficult to discern whether all or only one is included:

> College freshmen often fail to follow a regular study schedule; they may miss key class periods and even hand in assignments late. *This* can result in academic failure. (What does *this* clearly refer to?)

Avoid indefinites in writing, not because they are incorrect, but because they impede clear communication.

inside of/outside of/off of When these words are used as prepositions, the *of* is omitted in written General English, as in:

> *General: Inside* the building, people went about their business as usual.
> *Casual:* Inside of the building, people went about their business as usual.

When used as nouns, *inside* and *outside* require the preposition *of:*

> The *outside of* the building was painted a drab gray.

irregardless   A colloquial form of regardless; avoid in most writing.

> *General: Regardless* of the situation, you were wrong.
> *Casual, dialogue only: Irregardless* of the situation, you were wrong.

like/as/as though/as if   *Like,* when used as a preposition, ruffles no one's usage feathers:

> She *swims* like a fish. (preposition; universally accepted)

But when used as a conjunction replacing *as, as if,* or *as though, like* becomes controversial.

> *General:* He has never acted *as* he should.
> *Casual:* He has never acted *like* he should.
> *General:* The act *as if/as though* they were the only drivers on the road.
> *Casual:* They act *like* they were the only drivers on the road.

Because many people find the conjunctive *like* offensive, it is better to restrict it to personal writing and avoid it when writing to a wide audience. One word of caution, however: don't become so hyper-careful that you err in the other direction, substituting *as* for *like* as in:

> *As* my mother, my roommate always tells me when to get up. (replacing the preposition *like* with *as* creates ambiguity)

lose, loose   Although often confused, these are two separate items: *lose* is a verb meaning to misplace; *loose* is an adjective or adverb meaning free or unfastened.

> I *lose* at least three umbrellas every year.
> They were happy to set the deer *loose.*

negatives, multiple   Multiple negatives are generally unacceptable in all forms of written English except dialogue. Acceptable negatives are formed by negating only one element of the sentence—subject, verb, or object. One negative rules out the need for any others in the sentence, as these examples show:

> *No* crisis was ever quite like it. (one negative element attached to the subject makes the whole statement negative)
> Harry *did not/didn't* understand the question. (one negative element attached to the auxiliary verb)
> He had heard *no* sound in the house. (one negative element preceding the object noun)

45

The following examples of multiple negatives are generally inappropriate for written English.

Casual, dialogue only: Ain't nobody seen *nothin'*, or Nobody ain't seen *nothin'*. (negative added to subject, verb, and object of the verb)
Casual, dialogue only: He don't know *nothin'*. (negative added to auxiliary verb and to object of verb)

490 Double negatives resulting from negative adverbs such as *hardly* and *scarcely* used with *not* are avoided by most writers.

Casual, dialogue only: They didn't *hardly* see the car coming.
Casual, General: They *hardly* saw it. The *didn't* see it.

nowhere/nowheres *Nowheres* is a colloquial variant of *nowhere* and is generally avoided in written English.

General: Mary could find him *nowhere*.
Casual: Mary could find him *nowheres*.

Caution: Combining *not* with *nowhere* creates a double negative, appropriate only to dialogue: Mary could*n't* find him *nowhere*.

plus as a conjunction There are no usage restrictions involving *plus* as a preposition:

General: We invited all of Catherine's relatives to the wedding, *plus* Tom's family.

However, despite the fact that its use as a conjunction is becoming more widespread, substituting *plus* for *and* in a compound sentence is avoided in writing.

General: They spent a week on Oahu, *and* they took a tour to the other islands.
Casual: They spent a week on Oahu, *plus* they took a tour to the other islands.

possessives preceding nouns Writing problems stemming from possessive usage are of several kinds:

1. One arises from the tendency of some social dialects to omit the noun possessive -*s* altogether: "*John* old lady house on fire." This usage is almost universally frowned upon in written English, except when re-creating the spoken dialects that exhibit this usage.
2. Another problem involves substitution of the object form *him* for *his*. Again, this is only appropriate in written English when an attempt is made to re-create a dialect:

That's *him* baseball. (for "That's *his* baseball.")

possessives with -*ing* verbals (gerunds)   1. -*ing* verbals as subjects
When an -*ing* verbal is the subject of a sentence, the noun preceding it is in the possessive case, and needs an '*s*.

General: John's leaving was unfortunate.
Casual: John leaving was unfortunate.

2.   -*ing* verbals as the complement of the verb
When a gerund is the complement of the verb, the situation is more complex than when it is a subject. Some require the possessive case, some the objective case; in other situations, either case is acceptable.
a.   Requiring objective case:

She taught *him* skiing. but not She taught *his* skiing.
She taught *Mike* skiing. but not She taught *Mike's* skiing.

b.   Requiring possessive case:

John continued *his* shoveling (of) the snow. but not John continued *him* shoveling (of) the snow.

c.   Permitting either case:

We heard $\left\{ \begin{array}{l} \textit{Jim} \\ \textit{Jim's} \end{array} \right\}$ singing.

In situations such as this in which the -*ing* verbal is not modified, either case is acceptable. However, the possessive case is more appropriate in formal English. When modifiers are added, however, they can determine the case used, and they can be used as a test of which usage is appropriate.

We heard $\left\{ \begin{array}{l} \textit{Jim} \\ \textit{him} \end{array} \right\}$ singing loudly.

Loudly is an adverb; the -*ing* form is functioning as a verb, so the objective case is used; the noun or pronoun functions as the subject of the gerund.

We heard $\left\{ \begin{array}{l} \textit{his} \\ \textit{Jim's} \end{array} \right\}$ loud singing.

Loud is an adjective, indicating that *singing* is a verbal noun; the possessive case precedes it and can be paraphrased "the loud singing *of Jim.*"

proceed/precede   *Proceed* means "to go forward," in the sense of continued action; *precede* means "to go before":

The army *proceeded* to the enemy camps.
She *preceded* her husband down the aisle of the theater.

Caution: Watch the spelling—*precede,* not *preceed!*

real (as intensifier) *Real* is a popular substitute for *very* and *much* in spoken English; however, in writing, the latter two are preferred.

> *General:* The trees are *very* pretty this time of year.
> *Casual:* The trees are *real* pretty this time of year.

reason is because/reason is that In writing, *the reason is because* has been traditionally frowned upon as redundant, and *the reason is that* preferred. However, *the reason is because* in now widely used and accepted, even in scholarly writing. You need to realize, though, that some people still consider this usage unacceptable.

> *General:* The reason he didn't go *is because* his car broke down.
> *General:* The reason he didn't go *is that* his car broke down.

seems like/seems as if/seems as though/seems that/seems like that *Like* after verbs denoting sensation—*seem, look, feel, appear*—is as controversial as when used after other kinds of verbs (see *like/as*).

> *Casual, General:* He seems *like* an understanding person. (preposition *like*)
> *Casual:* It seems *like* he doesn't know what he's doing. (conjunction *like*; many writers avoid)
> *General:* It seems *as if/as* though he doesn't know what he's doing. (preferred by many to *like*)

In many dialect areas, after verbs such as *seem, feel,* and *appear, like* may be paired with *that* in some situations, but should be restricted to spoken English or personal writing.

> *General:* It seems *that* he doesn't know what he's doing.
> *Casual:* It seems *like that* he doesn't know what he's doing.

so/so that *So* is often overused in spoken English as an intensifier for emphasis, but generally this practice is avoided in writing.

> *General:* She looked *very* attractive in her new suit.
> *Casual:* She looked *so* attractive in her new suit.

So is just as vague and overused as a conjunction; in writing, generally, substitute *therefore, consequently,* or *thus,* for *so.*

So that is a handy joiner, but you should make sure that it carries the meaning of "in order that," rather than merely substituting for *so.*

> The farmer plowed the new field in the late fall *so that/in order that* he could plant an early crop.

somewhere/somewheres *Somewheres* is a colloquial variant of *somewhere,* following the same pattern as *nowhere/nowheres* of adding *-s.*

General: They were sure to find it *somewhere.*
Casual: They were sure to find it *somewheres.*

split infinitives   Infinitives (*to* + verb) are verbal forms that can function as nouns, filling sentence slots such as subject, object, or complement of an adjective.

To pass a red light is against the law. (subject)
John did not want *to leave.* (object)
It is good *to see* you. (complement of adjective)

Like other verbals, infinitives can be modified by adverbs. Although many people view as unacceptable the splitting of an infinitive by placing an adverb between *to* and the verb ("to *readily* see"), this construction frequently occurs in the works of our most influential writers. Split an infinitive if you wish the force of the adverbial applied directly to the verbal; otherwise, don't. However, you should avoid the awkwardness of inserting a long adverbial phrase between *to* and the verb.

Avoid: They wanted *to* with the utmost sincerity and friendship *wish* him success. (awkward and unclear)

squinting modifiers   In spoken English, many adverbs, particularly *only, even, hardly, nearly,* and *most,* often occur before the verb and create little ambiguity; intonation indicates the meaning. But in writing, it may not be clear whether they modify the verb or some other material in the sentence. To avoid reader confusion, make sure such adverbials immediately precede the word or structure they modify.

Ambiguous: He only anticipated a raise. (could mean that he merely *anticipated* or that he expected merely a *raise* and no other benefits)
Clear: He anticipated *only* a raise.
Ambiguous: The student who was running *frantically* yelled to the teacher. (*frantically* could modify either *running* or *yelled*)
Clear: The student who was frantically running yelled to the teacher.

subjunctive   In earlier English, special subjunctive verb forms were used to indicate hypothetical or contrary-to-fact conditions: for example, to signal the difference between "that *is* the case," and "if that *be* the case." The latter is now obsolete, along with other subjunctives. Modern usage is "if that *is* the case . . . ."

In contemporary usage, particularly in formal English, the subjunctive is retained in only two constructions: *if* clauses and *that* clauses when third-person verb forms are involved.

1.   In *if* clauses, only the verb *be* takes the subjunctive form, and then only in past tense.

General: If Liz *was* sure that she would be welcome, she would go.
General: If Liz *were* sure that she would be welcome, she would go. (Preferred by many over *was;* Specialized English would require *were.*)

2. In *that* clauses, in formal English, the subjunctive is used after verbs that carry a connotation of mandatory action: *demand, insist, request, command,* and so on. In less formal situations, a *to* + verb (*to meet*) or *should* + verb (*should meet*) can replace the subjunctive verb form.

> *General, formal:* The NCAA demands that an athletic dormitory *meet* certain standards. (The singular subject *dormitory* would be followed by the *-s* verb form in other contexts: The dormitory *meets* the standards.)
> *General:* The NCAA demands that an athletic dormitory *should meet* certain standards.

themselves/theirselves; himself/hisself The two reflexive pronouns *themselves* and *himself,* using the objective case, are often analogized in spoken English to others (*herself, yourself,* and *ourselves*) that use the possessive. This results in *theirselves* and *hisself,* forms that are usually considered nonstandard, even in spoken English.

> *Casual, General:* They had only *themselves* to blame for the situation.
> *Avoid:* They had only *theirselves* to blame for the situation.

through/thru *Thru* is a variant spelling, acceptable in personal writing.

> *General: Through* sheer determination, they succeeded in launching the boat.
> *Casual: Thru* sheer determination, they succeeded in launching the boat.

till/until *Till* is an acceptable variant of *until.* Avoid, however, *til, 'til, 'till,* and *untill.*

used to/use to *Use to* is a frequent misspelling of *used to* in statements like:

> He *used to* be the mayor of New York.

Pronunciation is the problem; we drop the final *d* sound in *used.* Remember that it is the same *used* as in: We *used* two sheets of paper.

while/although Because the conjunction *while* can be used either to indicate time (when, during) or as a replacement for *although,* there is danger of creating ambiguity:

> *While* the rest of the family eats at five, she eats alone. (Does *while* mean *when* or *although?*)

***-wise* as a suffix** The adverb-forming suffix *-wise* has become an overused device of spoken English in the last decade, resulting in such stylistic monstrosities as "religion-wise," "marriage-wise," "politics-wise," and so on. Generally avoid this device in writing, not because it is wrong, but because it jars the ear.

Politically speaking, the two-party system has stabilized the United States.
but not
Speaking *politics-wise*, the two-party system has stabilized the United States.

Grammar and Usage Exercises

1 The following student sentences contain verb usages that would be unacceptable in most written English. Identify the problems and revise to General English usage.

   a The easy turn consist of staying directly behind the boat all through the turn.
   b The only reasons I can think of for closing on Sunday is religious beliefs, to give one day free of commercialism or because of custom.
   c The inspector opened the door only to found himself coughing and gasping for air.
   d The city must also possessed a bakery because loaves of bread have been found with a baker's stamp.
   e Last year, I drop math altogether.
   f They was from a different school and really thought I was somebody.
   g What's you going to do?
   h The bed were made so careful that not even a single wrinkle was visible.
   i By the middle of the year my talent growed even more.
   j It would maked a stockyard smell like a bakery.
   k We sawed the monster movie at the drive-in.
   l We be using a new set of books in my high school.
   m I brung everything she told me to.
   n An infinite number of pants, shirts, socks, and shoes, along with the blankets from the unmaded bed, was scattered about the floor and made the room look as though a tornado had pass through it.
   o There was all kinds of problems involved in making the decision.

2 The following sentences taken from students' papers contain a number of noun and pronoun usages inappropriate for General English. Revise the sentences by using acceptable forms.

   a *Boomsville* warns us that unless we change ourselves we will continue to make our grandparents mistakes.

    b Anyone in business should be allowed to stay open by their choice.

    c The clothes were all hung neatly in the closet like tuxedo on a rack in a formal dress shop.

    d To have a best friend—a confidant with who you can share innermost thoughts—is something of great value to me.

    e One criteria that they used was the ACT or SAT score.

    f Less students are concerned with politics these days.

    g My father always made those sorghum molasses in the fall.

    h Because he wanted it done right, he always did it hisself.

    i My parents always sent money to my brother and I while we were in college.

    j Tobacco is the largest source of farm income in Kentucky, but cattle is becoming important, too.

    k I never found out whosever boots they were.

    l Each of his friends were happy to see him.

3 The following sentences contain usages that are generally acceptable except for writing in General English. Identify them, and substitute the more formal usage or the ones preferred by careful writers.

    a The further you travel down that road, the more desolate the country gets.

    b It looks like the river is going to overflow its banks.

    c We won't start 'til you get here.

    d The two cities had much in common, as an ocean bay and a large ship-building industry.

    e They sped thru the tunnel at break-neck speed.

    f He had all ready warned them many times.

    g The gait of trotting horses is different than that of pacers.

    h Grandfather was always a real expert fisherman.

    i This is the main problem that the United States faces.

    j You can't get enough pieces from that cake to feed this crowd, how ever you slice it.

    k Hardly hadn't the door closed behind him than a great uproar arose.

    l The reason for much of the failure in college is because students have not developed self-discipline.

    m After awhile, we all went for cokes.

4 The following sentences contain usages that involve some kind of confusion between two forms. Identify and revise.

    a The teacher preceded to lecture to the class.

    b She had the allusion that the sidewalks in America were made of gold.

    c The twin sisters talked similar.

    d The woman finally excepted her fate.

e   Congress was not able to affect a solution to the erosion problem in the west.
f   There wasn't a cloud in the sky anywheres.
g   Many of the villagers gathered altogether at the church.
h   Irregardless of the situation, students should try to learn something from every course.
i   With just an hour of cleaning, the room would of been presentable.
j   John chose to see the former movie; I chose the ladder.
k   It is very hard on students if they loose a parent while they are still in school.
l   They were trying to find out who's books were left in the library.
m   Jerry always parked his car within the garage.

5   The following sentences contain usages generally considered unacceptable for any kind of writing except dialogue. Revise the problems so that they would be acceptable for any writing situation.

a   You don't hardly ever see beauty like that in the eastern mountains.
b   He ain't gone nowheres.
c   When we came back, me and Russell played baseball.
d   I never tried to beat nobody out of nothing since I been in this world.
e   It seems like that he would know better.
f   John going to bed early inconvenienced us all.
g   She was always the most smartest girl in school.
h   You have to study intelligent to get the most out of school.
i   Every year for ten years, their football team got beaten by Madison High.

Punctuation

As we pointed out in Chapter 5, punctuation serves written English in many of the same ways that intonation serves the spoken: to show meaning and grammatical relationships, to signal the beginnings and endings of sentences and phrases, to indicate compound words, and so on. We pointed out also that punctuation conventions are often arbitrary, having no relationship to spoken English, but functioning as a feature of the dialect we call standard written English. Like universal traffic signals and signs, punctuation conventions, generally recognized and accepted, are beneficial to all of us. If each of us invented our own punctuation system, reading written English would be as confusing and chaotic as driving through a series of towns, each with its own approach to traffic problems. Thus, as frustrating and foolishly arbitrary as they sometimes seem, punctuation devices are important. Like careful structuring of sentences and selecting of words, choosing the appropriate punctuation device is an important aspect of your commitment as a writer to guide your readers through your written message.

apostrophe (')

a. With singular possessive nouns and compound pronouns

Janet's son   someone's car
the man's idea   nobody's business

Note that one test of the possessive is that an *of* phrase may be substituted: the son *of Janet.* Use the substitution test when in doubt about the relationships of time and value:

a dollar's worth (the worth *of* a *dollar*)
a month's vacation (a month *of vacation*)

b. With singular proper nouns ending in sibilants

One-syllable names ending in *s, z, sh, zh,* and *ch* add an apostrophe and -*s:* Strauss's waltzes. Two-syllable words add only the apostrophe. Janis' ruling.

c. With plural possessive nouns

1. Nouns with -*s* plural: Plurals such as *cats, dogs,* and *horses* add only the apostrophe (').

the cats' food   the dogs' barking   the horses' manes

2. Other plurals: Words with plural meaning, but which do not add -*s* to form the plural, need an apostrophe and the possessive -*s:*

men's attitudes   children's stories   the cattle's feed

d. With contractions (omitted letters)

can't   she'll   here's

Caution: Don't confuse *it's* (contraction of *it is*) with the possessive pronoun *its.* Possessive pronouns do not take '*s.*

It's a useless car because *its* tires are flat.
(it is)   (possessive)

e. Special use with plurals

Traditional usage demands that '*s* indicate the plural of numbers, letters used as words, and abbreviated names of organizations. However, this usage has now become optional in some cases:

with numbers: the 1970's or 1970s
with abbreviated names: PhD's or PhDs

500

But with letters the apostrophe is needed: the I's have it; your o's look like a's.

brackets ([ ])   Brackets are mainly used inside quotes for adding informa-   **435** tion in the form of a brief definition or explanation, or to indicate a misspelling or other error in the original:
Adding information:

"He [Chris] needed to be alone."
The Chinese Premier said, "We must stop Soviet hegemony [dominance]."

Indicating a misspelling:

"The elephants preceeded [sic] the giraffes."

Caution: Don't substitute parentheses for brackets.

comma (,)   The comma is the most common of all internal punctuation marks. Its work is manifold, from handling rather easy syntactical problems in simple sentences to the most complicated ones in complex sentences. Comma use, perhaps more than with other punctuation, is often arbitrary, having little to do with structure or intonation. For instance, a comma is sometimes used and sometimes not after introductory words like *finally*.

Finally they left me all alone.
Finally, no one knew his name or where he was buried.

There is sometimes a slight intonational relationship: in the first, there could be little pause after *finally*; in the second, the pause would be longer and more perceptible. However, don't rely on intonation alone to determine comma placement.

a.   Separating elements in a series   **167–68**

    1.   With compound subjects and predicates

Oats, peas, beans, and barley grow.

      In this example, a number of nouns make up the compound subject; the same punctuation is required for compound verbs:

He ran, danced, jogged, and sauntered his way through life.

      Although the comma is occasionally omitted before the *and* in a series, it is preferred in American usage to ensure clarity.

    2.   With adjectives in a series

      Adjectives in a series present more difficult problems than subjects and predicates. If modifiers before a noun occur in normal order, commas are not necessary, as in:

The ten most-informed professional women in the United States attended.

> The complete noun phrase, "the ten most-informed professional women," is a single group defined by the adjectives; therefore, no punctuation is needed. Also, the adjectives *ten, most-informed,* and *professional* cannot be shifted without creating awkwardness. However, in some noun phrases containing a number of adjectives, commas may be necessary, as the next example shows:

There was a loose, bulging, faded carpet on the floor.

> Here, because the adjectives *loose, bulging,* and *faded* are independent of one another, they can be arranged in different orders. Thus commas are required.

3. With phrases in a series

> The same rules that govern the separation of single-word items apply to phrases in sequence. The commas separate individual items from one another, keeping them in recognizable syntactic units:

I dressed as fast as I could, putting on *my best pair of jeans, a fresh shirt,* and *my newly polished hiking boots.*

482 b. With compound sentences

> When long sentences are joined by *and* or *or,* a comma helps readers to recognize the two sentence units. The comma is placed before the conjunction:

One of these terrors is a dud, and the job of the dedicated worrier is to find out which one it is.

> —Ralph Schoenstein

c. Comma splice

> Compound sentences are joined either by a conjunctions (*and, or*) or a semicolon (;):

Sixty years ago I knew everything; now I know nothing; education is a progressive discovery of our own ignorance.

> —Will Durant

> Although commas are sometimes used to separate short compound sentences in fiction or personal writing, this practice is considered a comma fault in most college writing.

152–53, 155 d. With complex sentences

> Commas with subordinate clauses
> Subordinate clauses are introduced by subordinating conjunctions (such as *while, since, because, that, although*) and by transitional adverbs

(such as *however, therefore, moreover, thus, then*). However, the two resulting clauses are not punctuated the same as these examples show:

Indian languages show a great variety of sounds, but this is not really surprising. (comma precedes the subordinating conjunction *but*)

Some charge that testing is harmful to students; however, it need not be. (the transitional adverb *however* is followed by a comma; a semicolon precedes it)

e. With nonrestrictive elements   168–69

The term *nonrestrictive* refers to any structure used to add information that is not specifically tied to the meaning of the sentence or that does not identify a noun phrase. The most frequently occurring nonrestrictives include: 1) appositives not essential to the meaning of the sentence, and 2) parenthetical structures that supply nonessential, additional information.

1. Appositives   168–69

An appositive that adds nonessential information to the sentence is set off by commas:

The dog, which bit Tommy last week, won a blue ribbon in the obedience trials yesterday. (the winning of the ribbon is not dependent on the information supplied by the appositive)

Some appositive clauses, however, are restrictive; that is, they supply essential information. These are not set off by commas.

The dog that bit Tommy last week has rabies. (here the appositive identifies a particular dog; no commas)

2. Parenthetical structures   167

Parenthetical information can serve as transitional material, as a written aside, or as further explanation:

Mr. Jones, on the other hand, could have driven his Ford. (transitional material not essential to the meaning of the sentence; set off by commas)
The situation, as any fool could plainly see, was hopeless. (an aside not central to the information in the sentence; set off by commas)

f. With reordered adjuncts   166–67

When sentence adjuncts are moved to the initial position in a sentence, they are usually set off by commas from the rest of the sentence.

Time: At nine o'clock in the morning, we saw him sauntering across the square.
Place: At the corner store, many spectators had gathered.
Manner: Mysteriously, the woman had vanished.

However, this punctuation rule may not always hold. Frequently, writers will not use the comma if the sentence is very short and close to a basic sentence, as in this example:

On the shore below me there was at first no sign of any living thing.

—Rachel Carson

In most instances, however, a good rule of thumb for reordered adjuncts is to use the comma if the adjunct precedes the subject. This eliminates the possibility of ambiguity.

g. With direct dialogue

1. Separating the dialogue line from a speaker tag.

"I'll only take forty for the lot," he said.

2. Setting off the speaker tag when it interrupts the dialogue.

"Thirty-five," I answered, "that's my limit."

Note that commas punctuating the dialogue line are inside the end quotation mark.

Colon (:)

a. With complex or compound sentences

A colon may replace a coordinating conjunction or a semicolon between two combined sentences, if the second amplifies or explains the first.

For her, the words were not "only words": they were horrifying things with their own terrible power. . . .

—Thomas H. Middleton

169 b. With elements in a series

A colon may replace a comma or dash to introduce a series, particularly when the series is material that amplifies or explains the sense of the sentence.

It is the prototype of man-made meteors that can be directed to atomize any spot on earth: Moscow, London, Tokyo, Rome, cities that can become a series of figures.

—Charles A. Lindbergh

437 c. With documentation

In citing the publication information about books in endnote and bibliographical entries, the colon separates the place of publication from the publishing house.

New York: Harcourt Brace Jovanovich, 1980.

d. With subtitles 438

When a book or article has a subtitle, it is separated from the title with a colon: "Walden: The Myth and the Mystery."

Dash (—)

The dash can replace any internal punctuation mark—comma, semicolon, 87–88 or colon. It is used freely in personal or informal General English, but it should not be overused. When typing your papers, use two unspaced hyphens for the dash.

a. With cumulative sentences 169

I spent my whole summer's salary on nothing—candy, cokes, pool, games of pinball, hamburgers from McDonald's.

b. With compound sentences

In very informal writing, the dash may replace a semicolon or comma between two short combined sentences:

That's how I spend every Sunday morning—I go through the whole newspaper.

c. With parenthetical information

The dash may replace a comma in setting off parenthetical information or appositives:

Providing such an upbringing for children is the easiest and most efficient way to bring up children who will be persons first—individuals able to use their full potentialities—and members of one sex or the other second.
—Margaret Mead

Exclamation mark (!)

An exclamation mark is used after interjections, such as *Oh!, At last!, Eureka!,* and at the end of strongly emphatic commands, as in: *Stop killing the whales!* But otherwise, it should be used sparingly.

Hyphen (-)

a. With compound adjectives

Adjectives compounded from a noun and a verbal form, such as *diesel-powered* truck, or from two or more nouns, such as *health-effects* research, often need hyphens to indicate their close grammatical relationship.

Diesel cars emit 30 to 70 times as many particulates as *catalyst-equipped gasoline-powered* cars.

b. With compound nouns

Two nouns not yet commonly regarded as a compound noun are hyphenated to indicate that they are to be understood as a grammatical unit. When in doubt about compound nouns, consult your dictionary.

At sunrise the local *dog-walkers* are out in force.

c. With numbers

Hyphens are used to join numbers or modifiers involving numbers: *twenty-one* cousins; *six-day* hike; *350-cubic-inch* area.

d. Dividing words into syllables

Ideally, you should plan the spacing in a line of writing or typing so that the last word is a complete unit. However, because this is not always possible, a word may have to be divided. You cannot arbitrarily decide where the division falls; the word should be divided so that it can be easily read. Here are some easy-to-remember rules for dividing words into syllables:

1. One-syllable words cannot be divided.
2. Words cannot be divided so that one letter stands at the end of a line: *e-. . . . lectric.*
3. Words of more than one syllable should be divided at a syllable break: *tre*-mendously or *tremen*-dously or *tremendous*-ly. If you're not sure about syllables, check a dictionary.
4. Words can frequently be divided by cutting off a prefix or a suffix: *in*-different; indiffer-*ent.* If the suffix requires the word to double a consonant, divide between the consonants: *run*-ning; *clan*-nish.

Parentheses ( )
a. With added information

When incidental information is added to a sentence, it is usually set off by parentheses.

Virtually all lobster pots (or "pots," as they were once invariably called) are alike.

—Gordon A. Reims

b. With endnotes and informal documentation

437

1. In endnotes that cite books as a reference, the publication information is enclosed in parentheses:

[1] Flannery O'Connor, *The Habit of Being* (New York: Farrar Straus Giroux, 1979), p. 177.

442

2. In informal documentation, the page number from which the cita-

tion was taken or the name of the author and the page number may be enclosed within parentheses before the period:

Hesse describes Demian as a spirit, his face "neither old nor young," but somehow ageless (p. 43) *or* (Hesse, p. 43).

Period (.)

a. As end punctuation   **84**

The period is used at the end of a declarative or imperative sentence:

A college degree is satisfying. (declarative sentence)
Hand your papers in on Tuesday. (imperative sentence)

b. With indirect questions   **84**

He asked *what I had been doing lately.* (Contrast with the direct question "What have you been doing lately?")

c. In ellipsis   **434–35**

When material is deleted in direct quotations, three periods usually indicate the omission:

In his Gettysburg Address, Abraham Lincoln ended with the hope that the country would be reborn and that the principles of democracy would not perish: " . . . government of the people, by the people, for the people. . . ."

Because the last ellipsis comes at the end of the sentence, the writer used the traditional option of three spaced periods plus the sentence period. Many contemporary writers prefer using only a period.

Question mark

a. The question mark is the end punctuation for all forms of interrogative   **84–86**
sentences.

Why don't you investigate it for yourself? (question form)
You call that a straight answer? (statement-form question)
You really meant that, didn't you? (tag question)

b. In direct dialogue with quotation marks   **88–89**

When a speaker tag follows the dialogue, the punctuation is as follows:

"How did you find that out?" my mother asked.

Quotation marks (")

a. With dialogue

Enclose direct dialogue in quotation marks: "You know that isn't so," he said. But in indirect dialogue, they are not needed: He said that it wasn't so.

401,
433–35

b. With quoted material

Quotation marks are necessary to enclose quoted sentences, phrases, or key words directly quoted from another source:

The senator said that the proposed limitation on health-cost reimbursement would be "catastrophic" for most families.

c. With words used as terms

Some marriage specialists estimate that anywhere from 40-60 percent of all marriages are at any given time "subclinical."

—Herbert A. Otto

d. With slang or regionalisms

On rare occasions, when you wish to use a word appropriate to your purpose, but which is perhaps too informal for the audience or tone of your paper, you may enclose it with quotation marks:

The farmers were forced to dump their souring milk during the trucking strike; they couldn't sell "blinky" milk.

e. For special emphasis

This new awareness is reflected in the charge of "cultural fascism" that is being leveled at traditional English classes, where "Standard English" is taught to blacks and their nonstandard "Black English" is frowned upon.

—Olivia Mellan

You should be careful, however, not to overuse this device. Used too often, quotation marks no longer signal special attention.

437

f. With titles

Quotation marks are used to enclose titles of articles, essays, short stories, short poems, chapters of books, songs, speeches, and unpublished works, such as dissertations.

Franklin Ducheneaux contended in his article "The American Indian: Beyond the Stereotypes" that the Indian still suffers from the conflicting stereotypes that society holds.

g. With quotations within quotations

When you include a quote from a work that has quoted material in it, enclose the original quoted material in single quotation marks:

"A student had written on the wall, 'Life's a bummer, but hang in there!' "

h. With other punctuation marks

1. Periods and commas go inside the quotation marks, as in the example in (*a*) and (*c*) above.

2. Colons and semicolons are placed outside the quotation marks:

You cited the quotation as coming from King's "I Have a Dream"; actually it came from "Letter from Birmingham Jail," an earlier statement of his position.

3. The dash, the question mark, and the exclamation mark are placed inside the quote if they are a part of the quote; outside, if applying to the whole sentence:

I enjoyed reading Ann Pincus' "Shape Up, Bionic Woman!" (exclamation point is part of the title.)

You won't believe this, but he expected me, in one night, to read Milton's "Areopagitica"! (exclamation mark belongs to the whole sentence.)

Semicolon (;)

a. With compound sentences

The most common use of the semicolon is to separate two (or more) complete sentences when they are combined without coordinating conjunctions. The semicolon replaces conjunctions such as *and, or, but, so.*

Liberty is not merely a privilege to be conferred; it is a habit to be acquired.
—Lloyd George

b. With parallel sentences

A semicolon is also used when two joined sentences have a parallel structure, but part of the second sentence is omitted:

Hate is dehumanizing; love, humanizing. (the second verb *is* is omitted)

c. With phrases in a series

167–68,
501,

Items in a series usually require commas. However, when the series is made up of long involved phrases, themselves punctuated with commas, semicolons are often used to avoid confusion:

The shelves in the room displayed an array of collected items: pieces of pottery, some valuable and some sentimental junk; well-worn books—novels, poetry, and drama; treasured rocks and driftwood, gathered on memorable outings.

Mechanics

Mechanics—capitalization, abbreviations, numbers—are exclusively features of written English, used to help readers sort out items that might be confusing, such as whether a title refers to a story or a book, or whether an item is used as a special term. Like punctuation devices, they offer a set of universally understood signals. And like punctuation, the conventions of mechanics are often arbitrary and confusing, and often their usages vary from one authority to another. This section should help you with the most common problems encountered in college writing. If you need information we have not provided, we remind you that all dictionaries include an extensive section on mechanical and editorial conventions.

Abbreviations

Unless you are writing informally to friends or trying to save space in some publication, avoid using abbreviations. They are generally accepted only in the following special situations:

a.   For common titles (*Mr., Ms., Mrs., Dr.*)

Mr. Darcy   *Ms.* Farmer   *Dr.* Taylor

b.   For family, academic, or religious designations after names

Howard Silk, *Jr.*   Thomas Swift, *Ph.D.*   Sister Treese, *O.S.M.*

c.   For dates (*A.D., B.C.*) and times (*a.m., p.m.*)

468 *B.C.*   10:47 *a.m.*

d.   For certain common Latin terms

etc.   from Latin *et cetera,* meaning *and so on.* Use only after a list of three or more items. Many writers prefer to substitute *and so forth* when referring to things, *and others* when referring to people. Note: never use *and et cetera.*

e.g.   from Latin *exempli gratia,* meaning *for example.* This abbreviation appears in formal writing, but is usually replaced by *for example* or *such as* in Casual and General English.

i. e.   from Latin *id est.* This abbreviation appears in formal writing, but may be replaced elsewhere by its English translation, *that is.*

e.   For certain businesses and organizations

IBM   NATO   CARE   UNICEF   F.B.I.

Because periods are increasingly omitted with these abbreviations, check the main or special section of your dictionary to find the correct form.

Except for these instances, do not abbreviate unless you are positive you should do so. In your papers, be certain to write the complete proper names of people, places, states, and countries (except D.C. and U.S.S.R.); measurement units (*feet, pounds*); time units (*hour, Thursday, February*); and book references (*page, chapter, volume*) except in documentation (pp. 72–74).

Capitals

a. With proper nouns

The names of specific people or places, days of the week, months, companies, historical events, races, languages, and countries are always capitalized.

Mary Jones; Cambridge, Massachusetts; Prudential Insurance Company; Tuesday; November; Caucasian; English; Russia

When common nouns are used in special ways, they too are capitalized: the Church (church as institution); a Black (but, a black man); North (region).

b. With titles

1. The first letter of the first and last words and all other main words in titles of books, articles, television programs, movies, newspapers, and magazines are capitalized. Articles, prepositions and conjunctions are not considered principal words.

The Tyranny of Words; "So You Want to Volunteer?"; *Murder on the Orient Express*

2. Titles are also capitalized when used with the name of the person:

Colonel William Brown; Professor Lopez; Aunt Mary; Mr. Klein

Numbers

The problem in writing numbers is to know whether to use words or figures. Practice varies: most writers prefer to spell out round or one-word numbers (sixty dollars, fifteen percent, thirty thousand students); otherwise, they use figures ($4.98, 24 percent, and 22,097 students). For large numbers they use a hybrid form: 24.5 million, $3.6 billion.

Only figures are used in the following situations:

a. Sentences, paragraphs, or papers with many numbers

The football manager packed 15 footballs, 87 pairs of shoes, 167 jerseys, 84 helmets, and 91 shoulder pads.

b. References to time or date

At 10:23 a.m. on the morning of May 12, 1980, he received his degree.

Note: When referring to whole hours, spell out the time: He awoke at four o'clock.

c. Addresses

You can write to her at 124 West 79th Street.

d. References to volumes, acts, scenes, pages

Anthony's famous speech in Act III, scene ii, appears on pages 552-54.

Note: Capital and lower-case Roman numerals are used for acts and scenes; Arabic numerals for pages.

e. Temperature

The temperature was −2 degrees but the wind-chill factor was −37.

f. Proper names

DC-7   Channel 12   Interstate 75   Louis XIV

Do not begin a sentence with a figure. Either spell out the number or recast the sentence.

Not: 127 passengers boarded the plane in Rome.
But: In Rome, 127 passengers boarded the plane.
or
One hundred twenty-seven passengers boarded the plane in Rome.

(see quotation marks, 437, 507–09)

Underlining (italics)

a. For titles

Underline titles of magazines or periodicals, books, plays, musical compositions, newspapers, long poems, pamphlets, films, radio and television shows, and names of ships and aircraft. In print, these would appear in *italics.*

Newsweek   *The Courier-Journal*   *Idylls of the King*   *Carmen*

Use quotation marks for other titles, such as magazine articles, short stories, short poems, film and play reviews, and chapter titles.

"Miss Brill"   "Save a Spot for Strawberries"   "Trees"

b. For words used as special terms

1. Terms to be defined:

Plagiarism can be defined as stealing.

2. Words used in unusual ways:

There are three *the's* in that sentence.

3. To show particular stress on a word:

You call *that* a proper meal? (be careful not to overuse this in most writing)

4. Foreign words not commonly used:

It was a time characterized by *Angst* and *Weltschmerz.*

Sample business letter

1883 College Drive
Lexington, KY 40506
February 1, 1980

Mr. David Kingman
2837 W. Logan Drive
Chicago, IL 60647

Dear Mr. Kingman:

If you have to write a business letter, here is a model to follow, although you should understand that its modified-block style is only one of several acceptable forms.

The heading in the upper right-hand corner consists of three lines, two for the address, one for the date. If you use printed stationery, only the date is necessary. In typing the heading, realize you are establishing the top and right-hand margins of your letter, which should be centered on the page to look like a picture in a white frame. The shorter the letter, the lower the heading and the wider the margins.

The inside address, four spaces below the heading, consists of the name, title, and complete address of the recipient. Like the heading, it should contain no abbreviations except those in the name of the company, common titles (Mr., Ms., Mrs., Dr.), and if you wish, the two-letter zip designations for state names. Also, no punctuation should ordinarily appear at the end of lines in either the heading or the inside address.

The salutation or greeting, typed two spaces below, is composed of the traditional "Dear" followed by the individual's name, if known. If not, you should refer to a person's title (Sales Manager, Account Executive) or select whichever of the following you believe most appropriate: "Dear Sir or Ms.," "Dear Sir," "Ladies and Gentlemen," or "Gentlemen." Whatever your decision, end with a colon, not a comma.

Beginning two spaces below the salutation, the body of the letter is made up of single-spaced paragraphs with two spaces between them. In a short letter, you may double-space within and triple-space between.

The complimentary close, placed two spaces beneath the last line of the letter and usually aligned with the heading, generally consists of "Sincerely," or the friendlier "Cordially," rather than the formal "Yours truly," or "Respectfully yours."

Your signature appears below, with your name typed several spaces beneath if it is not printed on the stationery.

Cordially,

Peter Rose

Peter Rose

Punctuation and Mechanics Exercises

1 Punctuate the following sentences with commas where necessary.

a She pulled in the driveway parked in the carport and entered the house which was dark.

b If a company wishes to increase customer traffic sales volume and turn over its merchandise it may lower prices.

c The seed-tree method of reproducing forests is a simple old concept and small land owners can use it with confidence.

d The realtor who offers flat-fee rates is usually not looked upon with favor by regular traditional brokers who operate on a six to seven pecent commission.

e It was a distinct contrast to the steel and wicker classic dining chairs the round glass top of the dining table which was neatly balanced on a sturdy rosewood cube as well as to the pale off-white Haitian cotton of the heavy upholstered pieces.

f The team however will probably not miss its huge high-scoring center too much because it has recruited a seven-foot high school star who was selected for the *Parade* All-American team.

g Having bought bonds for years through the convenient payroll savings plan he cashed them in upon retiring and spent the money on a trip to Williamsburg Virginia but he forgot to set aside some funds for taxes on the interest that he had earned on the bonds.

h *Sixty Minutes* the award-winning popular television program which is aired Sunday evenings is an excellent example of hard-hitting superb investigative reporting that appeals to people of all age groups income levels and educational backgrounds.

i A company may not admit it but the reason it sponsors institutional advertising which is relatively inexpensive on public television is not only to build good-will but to increase sales.

j On May 7 1945 at Rheims France the unconditional surrender of Germany was signed which ended the war in Europe and as a result the United States turned its attention to Japan which had lost most of its fleet at battles for the Philippines the Marianas islands Okinawa and Iwo Jima.

2 Punctuate the following sentences, paying particular attention to underlining and to the use of the colon, semicolon, dash, parentheses, quotation marks, and apostrophe.

a Students should receive grades for at least two reasons to reward them for their achievement and to evaluate their work in order to inform perspective employers, however, admission officials at graduate and professional schools are also interested in applicants grades.

b The first signs of spring kids playing outside at night, mocking birds singing at the top of their lungs, and onion grass sprouting everywhere were evident.

c   How can I be a spendthrift he asked when I don't have any money to spend and I am not thrifty.

d   The word imply means to hint or suggest the word infer means to conclude from facts or evidence.

e   He did not know which movie Star Wars or Gone with the Wind gave him his moneys worth at these advanced prices.

f   Peter Drucker, author of numerous books on modern organizational management, in a recent autobiography, Adventures of a Bystander, stated I am not an easy writer I usually make five or six drafts.

g   Many public figures have been afflicted with dyslexia, which is a serious reading impairment General Patton the World War II commander Woodrow Wilson the President, 1913-1921, and Nelson Rockefeller the Vice President, 1974-1976.

h   He questioned officials whether Chinese American trade would increase significantly in ten years time.

i   University officials will need to confront many problems decreasing enrollment, an over tenured faculty, and loss of federal revenues before the decades end.

j   The Chronicle of Higher Education contained a letter by Harvards President Derek C. Bok, which it explained in these words Mr. Bok said My statement is an attempt to explain this universitys reluctance to take an institutional stand on moral questions that arise in the outside world.

3   In the following sentences, correct any errors in the use of abbreviations, numbers, or capitals.

a   Among the notable books about world war two are Dwight D. Eisenhower's *Crusade In Europe* and Winston S. Churchill's *The 2nd World War,* which is published in 6 vols.

b   One college offers awards ranging from five hundred and fifty dollars to twelve hundred dollars to students who rank in the top fifteen percent of their high school class and who score twenty-six or above on the ACT or one thousand and one hundred or better on the SAT.

c   At Northern high school Mr. Johnson, my english and history teacher, was also a successful football coach, who had a record of 51 victories and 14 defeats.

d   Sen. Edward M. Kennedy, chairman of the senate judiciary committee, was faced with the task of considering nominees for the one hundred and fifty-three new Federal judgeships created by congress in 1978.

e   In the Fall of the year, if you drive North to the Lillian Annette

Rowe bird sanctuary—over 1,000 acres of islands, riverbed, wet meadowland, and farmland along the Platte river near Gibbon, Neb.—you will see the staging area for most of north America's migratory sandhill cranes.

f   Marie Curie, recipient of the nineteen eleven Nobel prize, was encouraged in her scientific work as a young girl by her Father, a Professor of Physics in Warsaw.

g   The Mako, a fast-swimming shark, highly prized as a game fish, may reach a length of 12 ft. and weigh 1,000 lbs., and can be found in the Atlantic ocean.

h   The new Doctor bought a mansion on Heritage St. on Tuesday, Oct. sixth, and moved in before six p.m. on Wednesday.

i   127 students signed up for professor Naomi Green's class in Ethics last Spring, a 10% increase in enrollment over her previous course at the Univ. of N. Carolina.

j   Although born in the east, he had lived for so many years in Ann Arbor, Mich, while studying for his m.a. and ph.d. degrees, that he considered himself a midwesterner.

Spelling

Background

Theoretically, English spelling should present no difficulties. Our writing system is alphabetic; if it were ideal, each letter would invariably represent a particular sound. Unfortunately, several historical developments have made our alphabetic system less than perfect. One influence was the introduction of the printing press in the fifteenth century. Thus, English spelling started to become conventionalized over 450 years ago, and since all languages undergo changes, especially in pronunciation, these conventions do not always reflect present-day pronunciation.

Since the fifteenth century there have been major changes in the pronunciation of English sounds, particularly the vowels. Many of these sound changes are not reflected in the spelling system; for instance, the spelling of *eye* (pronounced as *I* in modern English) is closer to the pronunciation it had when printing began in England: *eeyuh*. Some consonant spellings are also remnants from earlier pronunciations; the *gh* spelling in words like *right* represents a consonant sound no longer existent in the language; the initial *k* in *knife* or *know* was at one time pronounced.

A second contributor to modern spelling difficulties is our tendency to borrow words from other languages, retaining the original spellings. This trait has given us such spellings as the Greek *ps* in *psychology* and *pn* in *pneumonia,* and the French *eau* as in *bureau, beautiful.* The result of all these borrowings and changes in pronunciation is a spelling system that often seems chaotic. However, there is hope for baffled students. More than two-thirds of our words follow spelling patterns that can help you become a better speller if you learn them.

As with other conventions of the written language, there are good reasons for learning and applying these patterns. Our spelling system, imperfect as it seems, is recognizable throughout the United States and in other English-speaking countries. Also, it elevates no regional dialect over any other, but rather creates a leveled-off separate dialect. Last, and most important, many of the spelling conventions, although they seem unnecessary, prevent ambiguity: for instance, the spellings of the two words *pane* and *pain*, which are pronounced the same, but which for clarity, are spelled differently.

Tips for Improving Your Spelling

a. Make a list of all the words you misspell. Or better yet, write them correctly spelled on a small card and carry it in a pocket. During free moments, you can test yourself. Keep the cards in front of you as you write, and use the words often until you are sure you have mastered their spellings.

b. Try to analyze why you misspell certain words. Is the misspelling related to how the word is pronounced? Are you failing to note a general pattern in the spelling of several words that you consistently misspell? Are you unaware of the structure of the word, not realizing that some portions of it involve prefixes and suffixes that have fairly consistent spelling patterns? Making yourself aware of these weaknesses can help you not only master the misspelling of one word but of others like it.

c. When in doubt, look up the word in the dictionary. Because many weak spellers have trouble finding a word, we have provided a chart on page 520 to help you determine the possible initial spelling of a problem word.

d. Make yourself aware of the variant spellings of the weak vowel sound (*uh*) that often occurs as the middle syllable sound. Any of the vowel letters—*a, e, i, o,* or *u*—can have this sound. Be especially vigilant in checking the spelling of words like dis*a*ppoint, en*e*mies, defi*n*ite, hyp*o*crite, nat*u*rally.

e. You should also be aware that many words have more than one possible spelling, any of which may be acceptable; the word *judgment* for instance, may be spelled as it appears here or as *judgement;* the older plural of *scarf, scarves,* is rapidly being supplanted by *scarfs*. Again, the dictionary can help when you are uncertain.

517

f. You can master the spelling of certain repeatedly troublesome words by using mnemonic devices. By associating the correct spelling of the difficult part of a word with something you can remember, you will find these devices invaluable. For example, thousands of people have finally learned to spell *separate* by remembering that it's *a rat* (sep *a rat* e) of a word. Here are some other examples of mnemonic devices:

accommodations: Usually couples seek accommodations. Hence the two *a*'s, *c*'s, *o*'s, and *m*'s before the *-tion*.
address: An *ad* for the place you *dress* is an *ad + dress*.
grieve: Did Eve gri*eve?*
marriage: To *marry* someone for an *age* is a *marriage* (they *y* naturally changes to *i*).
similar: People look somewhat similar because they have two eyes (*i*'s).

We could go on and on. But have fun and games with your own trouble-makers. And the crazier or cornier the better, because you'll be more apt to remember them.

Spelling Patterns

a. Single-Syllable Words

Despite the irregularities in English spelling, there are many single-syllable words that have a one-to-one relationship between pronunciation and spelling. Poor spellers who make themselves aware of these patterns can drastically improve their skills in a short time. Not only do most of these single-syllable patterns occur with high frequency as complete words, but they appear again and again as syllables in longer words, although there may be a change in pronunciation. For example, *man* may occur as an individual word, patterning with words like *ran, scan,* and *stand*—all having the short *a* sound. As a syllable in a longer word, it may have the same pronunciation as in *manifest*, while in *manipulate* it is pronounced as if spelled *mun*. Despite this problem, however, making yourself aware that there are spelling patterns in English should help you to become a better speller.

1. Rhyming words are often spelled the same except for the initial consonant. The spelling pattern for these is fairly consistent. Here are some examples:

cat, rat, mat, sat, splat, fat, frat, slat (*-at* is the basic spelling pattern)
ale, pale, sale, bale, male, scale (*-ale* is the spelling pattern)

2. Words with the same vowel sound are frequently spelled the same, or may have two common spellings. Obviously, these often cause problems:

beet, meet, feet (*ee* is one spelling pattern for the vowel sound)

beat, meat, feat, pleat, bleat (*ea* is another common spelling pattern for this sound)

We can't deal with all the spelling patterns in the language here, but often if weak spellers become aware that patterns do exist, they begin to find them for themselves.

b. Prefixes and Suffixes

Because about 75 percent of the words in English are created by adding prefixes and suffixes to a base (*kind + un + ness = unkindness*), being aware of the spelling regularity of these word components can help solve spelling problems. Remember too that we have a limited number of these and we use them repeatedly.

1. Prefixes

With few exceptions, the spelling of prefixes is constant: *pro-, con-, re-, un-,* and so forth. There are several prefix pairs, however, that are close to being homonyms (words that sound the same but are spelled differently). The following are sometimes confused: *pre-* and *per-, anti-* and *ante-.* Knowing the meaning of these prefixes may help to un-confuse: *pre-* means "before, prior to," *per-* adds the connotation of "throughout" or "thoroughly" to a base. *Anti-* is against; while *ante-* means before.

2. Suffixes

Generally, suffixes also have regular spelling patterns: *-ive, -tion, -ness, -ing,* and so forth. However, the spelling of a base to which the suffix is added often needs adjustment. For example, when *-ive* is added to *act,* there is no problem: *active.* But when added to bases like *attend* or *intent,* the suffix *-tion* creates a spelling problem. To avoid an awkward sequence of consonants, the final consonant of the base is dropped: *attention, intention.* A similar situation occurs when several suffixes are added to a base. Adding *-ity* to *active* creates activ*ei*ty, a spelling monstrosity. To eliminate the confusing vowel situation, the unpronounced *e* on *-ive* is dropped. If we dropped the *i* in *-ity* there would be confusion as to whether the resulting *-ty* is a suffix or the end spelling of a base.

An Aid for Finding Words in a Dictionary

Using a dictionary to determine correct spelling is a problem for those who often can't guess the first few letters in the word. The following chart of the initial sounds with more than one common spelling should help. The omitted sounds have only one possible spelling; for example the sound *bee* is always spelled *b* when it is the first sound in the word. We do include sounds that have two consonants in the spelling.

INITIAL SOUNDS AND SPELLINGS

Initial Sounds (dictionary symbols*)	Initial Spellings (most common spelling first)	Examples
I. Consonants		
ch	ch	church
f	f, ph	feel, phone
g	g, gh, gu	give, ghost, guard
h	h, wh	hole, whole
j	j, g	jet, general
k	c, ch, k, qu	cat, character keep, quiet
l	l, ll	love, llama
r	r, rh	red, rhetoric
s	s, c, sc	sent, cent, scent
sh	sh, sch, ch	ship, schist, charlatan
t	t, th	time, thyme
th	th	thin
th	th	those
w	w, wh	wet, which (in some dialects)
z	z, x	zone, Xerox
II. Vowels		
ā	ai, a	aim, ate
e	e, a	ember, any
ē	e, ea, ei	eject, each, either
ī	i, ai, ey	idle, aisle, eye
ō	o, oa, oh	omen, oat, oh
oi	oi, oy	oil, oyster
ou	ou	out
yoo	u, you, yu	use, youth, yule
ə (as in but)	u, a, e	up, along, electric

* The pronunciation symbols are those in Webster's New World Dictionary, Second Edition.

Spelling Rules

a. Words ending in *-y*

To form the plural or third-person verb agreement, change the *y* to *i* and add *-es*: curr*y* to curr*ies*; carr*y* to carr*ies*. Possessive ending does not require the change: fair*y* to fair*y's* wing. Words ending in *-ey* require no change: journ*ey* to journ*eys*.

b. Words ending in *e*

(see suffixes, 519)

Drop the unpronounced final *e* when adding a suffix that begins with a vowel: *-ing, -ed, -en, -ish, -er, -est, -able*. Lov*e* to lov*ing*; lov*e* to lov*able*; pal*e* to pal*ish*. Because the vowel in the suffix signals the pronunciation of the preceding vowel, *e* is not needed.

c. Words ending in consonants

Double the final consonant when adding a suffix that begins with a vowel. This rule applies only to words having a single vowel preceding the final consonant: man, man*nish*; but not *clean*, clea*nning*. Again, pronunciation is the key; doubling the consonant of a word like ma*nn*ish avoids confusion with man*ish* (like a *mane*).

d. Words with *ie* and *ei*

A general rule is *i* before *e*, except after *c* or when sounded as *ā* as in n*ei*ghbor or w*ei*gh. This sentence contains most of the exceptions to the rule: Neither foreign financier seized either species of weird leisure.

Special Problems

a. Words ending in *-able, -ible*. Fewer words in English end in *-ible*, but when in doubt, check the dictionary.

b. Words ending in *-ant, -ance; -ent, -ence*. The vowels in the suffixes are all pronounced the same. You had better check these before handing in a paper.

c. Words ending in *-ar, -er,* and *-or* (all pronounced as in w*or*th).

d. Pluralizing words ending in *o:* sometimes *-s* is added as in hal*os*; for other words, *-es* as in her*oes*. For many of these words, either spelling is acceptable: fresc*os*, fresc*oes*; mang*os*, mang*oes*. When in doubt, check the dictionary.

e. Words ending in *-ous, -ious, -eous, -uous.* These syllables are pronounced so nearly alike that they frequently pose spelling problems. Pronouncing the word carefully can often reveal the differences. Try these words: riot*ous,* cur*ious,* right*eous,* ten*uous.* You should hear a "y" in curious; a *ch* in righteous; and "yu" in tenuous. These signal that the spelling is different from the *-ous* in riotous.

f. Words ending in *s, ch, sh, x.* In the plural, these words add *-es;* kiss, kiss*es;* church, church*es;* hash, hash*es;* hoax, hoax*es.* Pronounce them and you realize that the plural ending is pronounced as a separate syllable, thus requiring the vowel *e.*

g. Words ending in *-al* (legal); *-el* (cancel); *-il* (pencil); *-ol* (capitol); *-le* (rifle); *-ile* (facile). All are pronounced as m*ul*l

h. Homonyms. Many words in English sound the same but are spelled differently. They are easily confused and account for much misspelling. Here are some common ones:

bread, bred	piece, peace
break, brake	principle, principal
cite, sight, site	stationary, stationery
coarse, course	their, they're, there
passed, past	weather, whether
pen, pin (in some dialects)	which, witch
	your, you're

Then there are words that are confused or misspelled not because they are homonyms but because they sound similar:

accept, except	eminent, imminent
advice, advise	lose, loose
affect, effect	moral, morale
chose, choose	personal, personnel

100 Commonly Misspelled Words

Try to master the spelling of these words by having a friend dictate them to you. Analyze the words you misspell. Can you detect any patterns? If so, find the rule or way to master these and other words with the same spelling pattern. Also, keep practicing with other misspelled words until you have mastered them.

accommodate	courtesy	independent	privilege
ache	dangerous	interest	practice
acquaint	dealt	knowledge	psychology
across	decision	leisure	repetition
address	definite	librarian	racial
although	disappoint	license	recommend
analyze	divine	maintenance	receive
answer	disastrous	marriage	relevant
asked	embarrass	meant	restaurant
assist	equipped	missile	schedule
athlete	especially	misspelled	separate
beginning	excellent	muscle	similar
belief	familiar	niece	sincerely
believe	finally	ninety	sophomore
busing	foreign	obey	studying
business	fortune	occasion	succeed
category	friend	occurred	surprise
ceiling	gauge	odor	tendency
committee	government	optimistic	thought
conscious	grammar	origin	tragedy
consistent	guarantee	parallel	truly
convenient	handkerchief	perform	until
courageous	height	picnic	usually
criticize	hypocrite	picnicked	weight
curiosity	immediate	possess	writing

Spelling Exercises

1 A friend, a notoriously poor speller, has asked you to correct any misspellings in his paper, which follows:

Some scientific experiments indicate that the affect of television on people is too place them in an alpha state. This condition generally occurrs during some ocasion when people have the liesure to daydream, stair into space, or loose conscousness as they are beginning to fall asleep.

By studing a person's brain waves when television is turned on, scientists have gained knowledge of it's immediate affect. The patterns recieved on amplifiers and computors definately and consistantly indicate that television puts people into a non-thinking alpha state. A seperate study showed that a person was placed in this condition by three different commercials even though she beleived that one was booring, one relevent, and one irritating.

This result suprised scientists, who thought that she would be sincerly involved in the annoying or intresting program.

When scientists analized they're results, they concluded that television is not only an excellant and convient source of information and entertainmint, but that it ansers a nead for some people. Just as some individuals can rock for hours in a familar seting or can sit accross from a fire, so others can gaze at a television screen for a long wile without a brake and without criticising what they see. Of coarse, this explains why people have the tendancy to watch terrible preformances night after night. They do not care to gage the quality of television; they simply need to watch something.

Because these studys of televisions affects on the brain are still speculative, pschologists are continueing there work and are writting up there researsh.

2 Proofread the following student paper, correcting only careless spelling, punctuation, and similar mechanical errors.

When living in a dorm, you give up all your privacy. It seems you are not alone for one minute. There is either someone talking at you or looking at you. This makes life difficult and exasperating at times.

Everyone likes to have the opportunity to do some studing sit and day-dream undisturbed,or to have a private conversation with thier friends. The walls in the dorm, which are tissue-thin, conduct sound very well. This results in you're next store neighbor hearing all your most most valuable secrets. Besides accidental eavesdroping, there is the constant interruption of your thinking when someone plays there sterio or tv at full blast. Another difficulty is that guests always arrive at the most inconvient monent. At home they would call first. here they pop in whenever your a mess, at your worse.

Talking on the phone can also be a harrasing experience. There are no seperate lines, usually eight girls on a single one. And the same number on the other line. Providing you are lucky enough to get the person that you want to talk to to on the line, then the invasion of privacy begins. Every ten second one of the other fourteen people on the too lines tries to place a call, Or, someone sits near you, listenning, hopping you will hang up. You could go out of you mind?

That's not as bad as your date's being a topic of intrest and concern to all your dormitory friends. Take, for example, the "One O Clock Check-Up," which occurs on Friday and Saturdays nihgts when people return from their dats. Then the inspectors usally examine the new arrivals. They check for tale-tale signs such as drunken behavior, passion marks, overly red lips, wrinkled cloothing, messed hair, and and flushed faces. From this checklist they can detect what you did and what sort of time you had. You just cant keep anything a secret.

Usually the last stronghold of privacy is the bathroom, but in a dorm even this seems lost. The shower curtains do not insure privacy. they flap when the water is turned on, exposing all your fat and everything. Then there is the bathtub calamity. Every time you start you start daydreaming in a delicious, soothing, steeming tube of water, someone sticks her head in and tries to see if you are allmost done. Lying there, with faces peaking at your every few minites you want to scream.

Well, you finally realize that the privacy you had at home just isn't possible in the dorms. About all you can do is to expect the fact and enjoy invading the privacy of others. But then. if you get disparate, you can if you disire—go home again.